GEORGE WASHINGTON
A Biography

GEORGE WASHINGTON
A Biography

by Washington Irving

Illustrated

Abridged and edited with an introduction by
Charles Neider

DA CAPO PRESS

Library of Congress Cataloging in Publication Data

Irving, Washington, 1783–1859.
  George Washington: a biography / by Washington
Irving; abridged and edited with an introduction by
Charles Neider.—1st Da Capo Press ed.
     p.   cm.
  Originally published: New York: Doubleday, 1976.
  Abridged ed. of: The life of George Washington, 1856–
1859; originally published in 5 v.
  Includes index.
  ISBN 0-306-80593-6
  1. Washington, George 1732–1799. 2. Presidents—
United States—Biography. 3. Generals—United
States—Biography. 4. United States. Continental
Army— Biography. I. Neider, Charles, 1915— . II.
Irving, Washington, 1783–1859. Life of George Wash-
ington. III. Title.
E312.I734   1994
973.4′1′092—dc20
[B]   94-11170
                                                              CIP

First Da Capo Press edition 1994

This Da Capo Press paperback edition of *George Washington,
A Biography* is an unabridged republication of the edition
originally published in New York in 1976. It is reprinted
by arrangement with the author.

8   9   10

Published by Da Capo Press, Inc.
A member of the Perseus Books Group

Manufactured in the United States of America

To John Lowrance

CONTENTS

LIST OF ILLUSTRATIONS

INTRODUCTION

The present work affords a detailed view of the idealism and at times desperation of Washington and the founding fathers as they set in motion the experiment of the democratic process. Its particular relevance stems from two facts: the biography was written by one who has been styled, however romantically, as the "father of American literature," and concerns the person often referred to, however sentimentally and idolatrously, as "the father of his country."

Some observations about Washington are perhaps appropriate before a discussion of Irving's biography and the manner in which it was written and received. The composition of it was in itself a fascinating and heroic story. The observations are limited to those that particularly struck me during a review of Washington's life.

Being raised in Virginia, I was vividly aware of the figure of Washington in my early years. I knew well the famous marble statue of him by Houdon that stood inside the Capitol building in Richmond, and the equestrian statue in Capitol Square. I regarded him as the father of his country, primarily an American, but I also thought of him as a Virginian, product of a state that prided itself on being the "mother of presidents" (Jefferson, Madison, Monroe and Wilson came to mind) as well as one that was native to Patrick Henry and Light-Horse Harry Lee. I did not think of him then or later, before I undertook the present task, as a person with a powerful intellect, one who had a complex grasp of the issues of the day, nor as a man capable of having so large, so federal a view of the colonies. Although by his own admission this view came rather late to him, once he grasped it it was unshakable. He believed absolutely in the necessity of a federal union based on a federal system of laws. Otherwise, he was convinced, the great experiment in self-government was bound to fail.

When, in his retirement at Mount Vernon after the war, he saw many signs of national dissolution, he engaged in correspondence with leading statesmen, urging a constitutional convention, to which he was later sent by his state as a representative. He could be extremely obstinate about the dangers of fractionalism, sectionalism and secession, and this distinguished him from many Virginians of his class. There was a difference between Patrick Henry's impulsive, noble cry of "Give me liberty or give me death" and Washington's prolonged, patient, persistent belief, backed by practice, that the colonies had to be welded into a new nation, and that the only way they could avoid being gobbled up by the empires of Europe was through union, that in all respects there urgently had to be union.

One is impressed by his vast correspondence. His great health and stamina partly explain his astonishing ability to carry on a complicated correspondence from wherever he happened to be, and in the most trying circumstances. As a young man of sixteen or seventeen he was already noteworthy for his physical appearance. He was tall, lithe, powerful, graceful, a marvelous horseman, and was able to win the ungrudging admiration of both officers and soldiery. In all the various encampments and during the severe trials of the war he always found time not only to keep up an official correspondence both military and civilian but with friends and family as well. During the eight years of the war he rarely was ill. As far as physical courage was concerned, not even his worst enemies could cast doubt on it. He had a providential sense of his personal safety, as he had of the eventual triumph of the great cause he served. In the Braddock carnage he had a couple of horses shot from under him and his clothing was penetrated by bullets. Because he rode good horses and had a large, imposing physique he was an obvious target for marksmen, yet he never got hit, although there were times when, to the horror of his staff, he exposed himself to great danger in rallying forces at a turning point. Many of his letters are extremely complex in their understanding and statement, and not a few are surprisingly eloquent and possess a literary caliber for which one has not been prepared by his general reputation.

He is the man we think of as having great probity, determination and optimism. An Episcopalian, he was not a strict communicant and a Bible reader, but he believed that God was on the side of the colonies because they were oppressed and besieged, and that somehow or other they would come through. At the same time he never left anything undone in order to give God a helping hand. He was convinced that the Revolutionary War was not a conflict to be waged in the ordinary sense. From the American viewpoint it was one of the highest ideals, and men had to behave themselves accordingly. Therefore he would issue orders that card playing, gambling and drunkenness were not to be tolerated in the army.

He enjoyed excellent relations with legislatures, especially the Congress, having sat in one himself, the House of Burgesses of Virginia, and having noted the special interests, sensitivities and outlook of legislators. He made an extremely careful, almost wary distinction between civilian and military power and always meticulously respected the superiority of the civilian authority (the Congress) from which his power derived. He had a horror of the misuse of power either civilian or military, and especially of a military dictatorship.

His was far from being a simple mind. It was respected by minds such as those of Jefferson and Hamilton, members of his cabinet who, incidentally, because of their surfaced political differences caused him a good deal of anguish. If he was enigmatic as commander-in-chief and later as President, perhaps it was because he knew well how to relinquish claims to a personal life while he had the responsibility of the life of the new nation in his care. The cause's survival often hung by so fine a thread that at times he seemed close to being the country's one indispensable man, without whose temperate yet visionary guidance the experiment would not have succeeded.

His only travel away from what is now known as the continental United States was his trip to Barbados in company with his older half brother Lawrence, who was educated in England. Possibly there were beneficial effects in Washington's not having had an English education or a higher education in America. Lacking both, he was more inclined to be a man of action, closer to the soil, simpler in his manners and less removed from the "common" people. Despite his firmness he was usually a gentle, sensitive man, and it hurt him personally that his troops were often underfed, underclothed and underarmed, as in the famous instance of the winter at Valley Forge. But when it was necessary to have a man hanged, with justice and as an example to others, he ordered it done without a qualm. He had seen too many people die all around him to be softhearted about death, and had experienced death in his family while he was still very impressionable.

Some facts of his early life help to penetrate the façade which has stubbornly defied attempts to portray him in intimate depth. His mother, Mary Ball, was his father Augustine's second wife, and he, George, was her first-born child. Just before George was three, he was informed that his half sister Jane was dead. When he was eight and a half he learned that his sister Mildred was dead at a year and four months. When he was eleven, his father died. So George became, at an early age, familiar with the necessity of stoicism in dealing with death. He matured early, especially where business matters were concerned. It was a common practice of the time to have large families, which George saw exemplified by his father, who had ten children, six by Mary Ball. Yet George himself proved issueless, as far as is known. His wife, Martha Custis, had borne two children by her first marriage, so there was little doubt that she was fertile. Washington might have brooded about this lack in his life, yet there is no evidence that he did. On the contrary, the very lack may have engendered the feelings of paternalism that Irving notes so often in Washington's relations with his troops, officers, cabinet, and Martha's children and grandchildren. Irving, a bachelor, was himself childless (again as far as is known), and perhaps for this reason emphasized Washington's paternalism. It was psychologically appropriate to Washington's public image to style him in later life as "the father of his country."

George saw little of his land-dealing, prosperous father but he learned from him the trait of being acquisitive where land was concerned, which he emulated. He grew to dislike his mother because she was bossy and grasping, always wanting something from him. During the entire war, when he wrote thousands of letters to a great variety of people, he apparently never wrote once to her. But, though cool, he always behaved with meticulous filial loyalty toward her, as became an eighteenth-century gentleman, and generally gave her what she wanted although he kept his distance from her. Lawrence, fourteen years his senior, schooled in England, as we have noted, and possessing some experience in naval warfare, was the person George hero-worshipped. Lawrence died of tuberculosis when George was twenty. Perhaps George felt fatherless and, in a sense, at an early age motherless too, and, overshadowed by Lawrence, wanted very much to make his mark and therefore strove very hard to make good, and as an eager achiever was shy with girls and later with women. But he did have his adolescence, he wrote love-sighing poems, and possibly he was even more human as a young man than the evidence suggests. The available evidence is limited, for only thirty-five letters written by him before he was twenty-three have survived.

Despite the singularly unified image that he presented to his own time and to history, he was not without an interesting degree of ambiguity. Possessed of the reputation of a Virginia aristocrat, he was able to win not merely the loyalty but the affection of the so-called lower classes as well as of the officer class who served under him. He had a rare combination of virtues that made him acceptable as commander-in-chief to New England. He was of the landed gentry, wealthy through inheritance and marriage, and he refused financial compensation for his services to his country; consequently he could not be accused of trying to advance himself monetarily through the cause. To mercantile New Englanders he was "safe" in this respect. In addition he had a strict work ethic not typical of Southerners of his class, an ethic with perhaps puritan overtones that made him seem something more of a New Englander.

But despite his ambiguity, as an adult he was one of the least neurotic of American public figures. He did not have great depressions. He did not sin in the usual way of being mean or retaliatory. When his enemies under his command were vindictive, when they intrigued behind his back, hoping to have him deposed as commander-in-chief, he wrote strongly in his own defense, proving that he could be a formidable, even dangerous opponent, with many personal resources as well as those of numerous friends in Congress and out, but he did not seek to punish them. He was more interested in issues than in personalities, more in what was at stake nationally than in getting embroiled in the complexities of personal relationships. He had strict rules of social behavior that he had drawn up for himself when he was young, and he tended to follow them throughout his life. He did not waste energy brooding about maledictions, schemes against him. He rarely behaved in a petty manner. Sometimes in his letters he bemoans the terrible condition of the army, but he is selfless, humanitarian and patriotic in his complaints; he never says this is hopeless, there is insufficient support from the Congress, the people, and the mood of the day is too self-serving, parochial, greedy, I'm walking out. You expect him to crack somewhere under the pressure, to be more downcast, to break down in health. And you wonder how it was that he grew so fully in stature after he was chosen commander-in-chief, taking on a majestic character with an entirely national vision as against a sectional one.

Psychologically, he opened doors rather than closed them. Compared to the personages of our century and of the previous one, he seems much more of a piece, more whole. His self-discipline and self-mastery were legendary despite the fact that on rare occasions he could reveal a violent temper. He was above all a man with a cool head and innately modest without ever being self-deprecatory. Having mastered himself, he had respect for himself, and this showed in his demeanor and behavior.

Part of his growth and stature must be ascribed to the fact that, like others of the founding fathers, he possessed genius. Another part may have to do with the fact that he belonged to a much smaller and simpler society than ours. If you were of Washington's class you were "in," and you knew people at the seats of power or you even had a measure of power yourself, and this helped you to have a sense of responsibility for your own destiny and for that of others. Today we're many people, the average citizen feels remote from the decision-making processes, and a mood of helplessness rides the country. People feel not that they're making their lives happen but that they're being spied upon and manipulated and that they don't know what it's all about. Perhaps the times have become too complex, too intermeshed on a global scale, too out of joint for anyone to know what it's all about any longer. Still, the "ordinary" man of Washington's time may have felt the same way. He was called from his farm, he took up his musket and perhaps was killed, and few remembered him.

Is there something hidden? Are there unknown facts about Washington that might give us a better glimpse behind the façade? Regarding his supposed celibacy for long stretches of time, perhaps he had an iron will in that respect, too, or wasn't very sexual or tended to sublimate. You can never really put your finger on the man. In the case of Benedict Arnold, for example, there comes a point where you feel you can touch him. He had been a very brave man and had achieved significant feats in the Continental army in the northern areas, yet he was grossly mishandled by Congress when it came to promotion. Then he lived beyond his means, got badly into debt, and you can understand some of the pressures that caused him to become a traitor. True, it's difficult to understand why he turned so savagely on his own country and marauded the coast of Connecticut, his native state. But somehow you feel you can grasp him. In Washington's case, even though he left an enormous heritage of letters and speeches, it's as though he lived centuries more distant from us. One wonders how close even Martha got to the essential Washington. And yet how touchingly human he can seem at times, as when, having retired to Mount Vernon and there was a ball, and young people were dancing—he loved young people—he entered the ballroom. Suddenly everyone stopped dancing and a pall came over the room. Realizing it was due to his presence, he left, and felt chagrined that he could do that to young spirits. When the dancing resumed, he peeped through a crack in the doorway, enjoying what he saw.

Growing up in Richmond, Virginia, I was much aware of another famous military figure that the state had produced: Robert E. Lee, who symbolized secession. Historically, it was an interesting city to grow up in, being not far from Williamsburg, where first Lawrence and later George Washington had sat in the House of Burgesses, or from Yorktown, where Washington had led the Continental army that, with the indispensable aid of the French fleet, had won the war by bottling up and defeating Cornwallis. A city that Washington had known well, that Patrick Henry had given his "Give me liberty or give me death" speech in, that had hosted the trial of Aaron Burr and that later had been the capital of the Confederacy.

Irving, who wrote about Washington's fears of disunion and who published his *Life of George Washington* (the title of the original edition) just prior to the Civil War (the last volume appeared in the year before the conflict began), makes no mention anywhere in his biography of the coming strife. Was he too absorbed in trying to finish the work to note that Washington's greatest fears were on the verge of being realized, or did he subtly suggest the imminence of the tragedy by emphasizing Washington's anxiety about sectionalism and its disastrous end product, secession?

Before proceeding further, inasmuch as the facts of Irving's life are not as well known now as they once were, I shall present a brief biographical summary but I shall not feel obliged to mention all of his various publications. He was born April 3, 1783, in New York City, the youngest of eleven children, three of whom died in infancy. His parents had emigrated from Great Britain, where his father at one time had been an officer in the merchant marine. Washington Irving was raised on William Street in Manhattan.

The year of his birth was of some note in the history of the new republic. On February 14 the King's Proclamation, announcing the end of hostilities between Great Britain and the United States, was read in New York. On September 3 the formal peace treaty between the two nations was signed in Paris. On November 25 the last British troops were evacuated from New York by way of the Battery. On December 4 General George Washington said farewell to his officers in Fraunces Tavern in Manhattan, a gesture which symbolically ended the Revolution. The young Irving had reason to be proud of his native city, which was the first capital of the nation and which, on April 30, 1789, witnessed the inauguration of Washington as President at Federal Hall, the old city hall. According to Irving's official biographer, his nephew Pierre M. Irving, a young Scotch maidservant of the family, on seeing George Washington enter a shop, followed him inside with her charge, the young Irving, and said, "Please, your honor, here's a bairn was named after you," upon which Washington, touching the boy's head, gave him his blessing.

Although Irving's father often displayed the puritanical strictness of a Scotch Covenanter, his household was more literary and intellectual than that of many of his neighbors, and young Irving's artistic tendencies benefited by the influence. Irving received a fragmentary education in male seminaries in the city. Pierre M. Irving wrote in his biography, "His education was completed before he had attained his sixteenth year; at least from this period he assumed the direction of his own studies. His brothers, Peter and John, had been sent to Columbia College, and why he did not receive the same advantage he could never satisfactorily explain except that he was more alive to the drudgery than the advantage of a course of academic training. He never failed, however, to regret the omission in after life." Like many incipient writers before him, Irving was an addicted reader, and in the end his self-education adequately served his needs.

He was the first internationally prominent American author and was followed soon afterward in the distinction of international fame by James Fenimore Cooper and somewhat later by William Cullen Bryant. All three had a negligible formal education and all came from comfortable, what we would now call middle-class, homes. Irving's father was a successful merchant, Cooper's a lawyer, Bryant's a physician. Although only Irving was a native New Yorker, the literary careers of all three were connected with New York, whose largely mercantile society was proud of its international, intellectual and literary pursuits.

Between the ages of sixteen and eighteen Irving studied law in a Manhattan law office. In 1800 he made a voyage up the Hudson to visit two of his sisters, and in 1803 he traveled to Montreal. He had never had a robust constitution. When, early in 1804, his health seemed to be declining, his family decided to send him to Europe for the sea air, a change of scene and a rounding out of his education. He sailed from New York in May at the age of twenty-one. He visited France, mainland Italy, Sicily, Switzerland and London. He returned to New York early in 1806. In the fall he was admitted to the bar, but he was never seriously to practice law. In 1807 he attended the trial for treason of Aaron Burr in Richmond, Virginia. His father died October 25, 1807, when Washington Irving was twenty-four. In 1808 Irving began work on *Knickerbocker's History of New York*. Matilda Hoffman, whose death is supposed to have affected him for the rest of his life and to have contributed in some measure to his decision to remain a bachelor, died April 26, 1809, in her eighteenth and his twenty-seventh year. The *History of New York* was published in December.

In 1812, in a review of the recently issued works of Robert Treat Paine, a poet now long forgotten, Irving had some choice remarks to make about the condition of authorship in America.

"Unfitted for business, in a nation where every one is busy; devoted to literature, where literary leisure is confounded with idleness; the man of letters is almost an insulated being, with few to understand, less to value, and scarcely any to encourage his pursuits. It is not surprising, therefore, that our authors soon grow weary of a race which they have to run alone, and turn their attention to other callings of a more worldly and profitable nature. This is one of the reasons why the writers of this country so seldom attain to excellence. Before their genius is disciplined, and their taste refined, their talents are diverted into the ordinary channels of busy life, and occupied in what are considered its more useful purposes. In fact, the great demand for rough talent, as for common manual labor, in this country, prevents the appropriation of either mental or physical forces to elegant employments. The delicate mechanician may toil in penury, unless he devote himself to common manufactures, suitable to the ordinary consumption of the country; and the fine writer, if he depends upon his pen for a subsistence, will soon discover that he may starve on the very summit of Parnassus, while he sees herds of newspaper editors battening on the rank marshes of its borders."

One wonders if his visit to Europe helped give him the sharply focused perspective evident in the preceding statement, and if he didn't, while composing it, long for a return to the older continent, where, perhaps, he would not so soon grow weary of running the race alone. After him, Hawthorne and James would also complain eloquently of the burdens of authorship on native soil.

On May 25, 1815, by which time the war between Great Britain and France had ended, Irving embarked for England, where, in Liverpool, he worked in the declining family import-export business. It is doubtful that he had any intimation that he would stay in Europe so long and with such consequences for his career as a writer. During this visit he was to be absent from the United States for an unbroken seventeen years, a long stretch to be separated from family, friends, native roots and native idiom. As we shall see, he was to resist family pressure to come home. Perhaps he did so not only because of what he believed to be the necessities of his developing art but because, as the youngest sibling, he needed the opportunity to mature apart from his sometimes oversolicitous brothers and sisters.

His mother died April 9, 1817, just after he turned thirty-four. In August he visited Walter Scott, to whom he had a letter of introduction, at Abbotsford in Scotland. Scott, an enthusiastic admirer of the *History of New York*, excerpts of which he had read aloud to members of his family, was very cordial to him, and a few years later was to be instrumental in placing Irving's *Sketch Book* with John Murray, a prestigious London publisher. The romantic side of Irving revered Scott.

Early in 1818 the family business went bankrupt and Irving decided to try authorship as a means of earning his keep. During the summer he took up lodgings in London, where he worked on *The Sketch Book*. In October his brother William wrote him from Washington, saying he could get him a job in the Navy Department. Irving declined in favor of a possible literary career. On March 3, 1819, when he was almost thirty-six, he wrote a revealing letter to his brother Ebenezer, in which he gave his reasons for turning the job down.

"I find my declining the situation at Washington has given you chagrin. The fact is, that situation would have given me barely a genteel subsistence. It would have led to no higher situations, for I am quite unfitted for political life. My talents are merely literary, and all my habits of thinking, reading, etc., have been in a different direction from that required for the active politician. It is a mistake also to suppose I would fill an office there, and devote myself at the same time to literature. I require much leisure and a mind entirely abstracted from other cares and occupations, if I would write much or write well. I should therefore at Washington be completely out of my element, and instead of adding to my reputation, stand a chance of impairing that which I already possess. If I ever get any solid credit with the public, it must be in the quiet and assiduous operations of my pen, under the mere guidance of fancy or feeling.

"I have been for some time past nursing my mind up for literary operations, and collecting materials for the purpose. I shall be able, I trust, now to produce articles from time to time that will be sufficient for my present support, and form a stock of copyright property, that may be a little capital for me hereafter. To carry this into better effect it is important for me to remain a little longer in Europe, where there is so much food for observation, and objects of taste on which to meditate and improve. I feel myself completely committed in literary reputation by what I have already written; and I feel by no means satisfied to rest my reputation on my preceding writings. I have suffered several precious years of youth and lively imagination to pass by unimproved, and it behooves me to make the most of what is left. If I indeed have the means within me of establishing a legitimate literary reputation, this is the very period of life most auspicious for it, and I am resolved to devote a few years exclusively to the attempt. Should I succeed, besides the literary property I shall amass in copyright, I trust it will not be difficult to obtain some official situation of a moderate, unpretentious kind, in which I may make my bread. But as to reputation I can only look for it through the exertions of my pen. . . .

"In fact, I consider myself at present as making a literary experiment, in the course of which I only care to be kept in bread and cheese. Should it not succeed—should my writings not acquire critical applause, I am content to throw up the pen and take to any commonplace employment. But if they should succeed it would repay me for a world of care and privation to be placed among the established authors of my country, and to win the affections of my countrymen. . . .

"I have but one thing to add. I have now given you the leading motive of my actions—it may be a weak one, but it has full possession of me, and therefore the attainment of it is necessary to my comfort. I now wish to be left for a little while entirely to the bent of my own inclination, and not agitated by new plans for subsistence, or by entreaties to come home. My spirits are very unequal, and my mind depends upon them; and I am easily thrown into such a state of perplexity and such depression as to incapacitate me for any mental exertion. Do not, I beseech you, impute my lingering in Europe to any indifference to my own country or my friends. My greatest desire is to make myself worthy of the good will of my country, and my greatest anticipation of happiness is the return to my friends. I am living here in a retired and solitary way, and partaking in little of the gayety of life, but I am determined not to return home until I have sent some writings before me that shall, if they have merit, make me return to the smiles, rather than skulk back to the pity, of my friends."

Such a self-understanding statement is abundant proof that he was the first important American literary artist to come to grips with the allurements and traditions of Europe, the problems of European experiences and subjects, the pleasures and woes of expatriation, the need to obtain a long and cultured perspective on raw native materials, the artistic obligation to come to terms with the conflict between foreign interests and native debts. As such he was the first in a line that runs through Cooper, Hawthorne, Melville, James, Twain, T. S. Eliot, Ezra Pound, Hemingway and many others, and these have inevitably been influenced by the tradition he began. No discussion of the importance of expatriation in the production of works of American literature can be complete without beginning with his example. In order to help place him among the early prominent figures of American literature, we may note that in terms of the year of birth he was six years Cooper's senior, eleven Bryant's, twenty Emerson's, twenty-one Hawthorne's, twenty-four Longfellow's, twenty-six Poe's, thirty-four Thoreau's and thirty-six Melville's and Whitman's.

The same day Irving addressed a letter to his good friend Henry Brevoort in the United States.

"I feel great diffidence about this reappearance in literature. I am conscious of my imperfections, and my mind has been for a long time past so preyed upon and agitated by various cares and anxieties that I fear it has lost much of its cheerfulness and some of its activity.

"I have attempted no lofty theme, nor sought to look wise and learned, which appears to be very much the fashion among our American writers at present. I have preferred addressing myself to the feeling and fancy of the reader more than to his judgment. My writings, therefore, may appear light and trifling in our country of philosophers and politicians; but if they possess merit in the class of literature to which they belong, it is all to which I aspire in the work. I seek only to blow a flute accompaniment in the national concert, and leave others to play the fiddle and French horn."

He wrote Brevoort again July 10.

"It is a long time since I have heard from my brother William, and I am apt to attribute his silence to dissatisfaction at my not accepting the situation at Washington; a circumstance which I apprehend has disappointed others of my friends. In these matters, however, just weight should be given to a man's tastes and inclinations. The value of a situation is only as it contributes to a man's happiness, and I should have been perfectly out of my element and uncomfortable in Washington. The place could merely have supported me, and instead of rising, as my friends appeared to anticipate, I should have sunk even in my own opinion. My mode of life has unfortunately been such as to render me unfit for almost any useful purpose. I have not the kind of knowledge or the habits that are necessary for business or regular official duty. My acquirements, tastes, and habits are just such as to adapt me for the kind of literary exertions I contemplate. It is only in this way I have any chance of acquiring real reputation, and I am desirous of giving it a fair trial."

With the publication of *The Sketch Book* (1819-20), a collection of essays, sketches and tales, written in England, Irving became an English and to some extent a European celebrity. He was a sensitive, handsome, shy, sloe-eyed man of middle height, with a sensuous mouth; a fashionable and expensive dresser in London and Paris in the days of the first flush of his success; a man of polished manners, humorous, benign; to some of his European acquaintances a surprisingly cultivated transplant from the rawness of the new republic. He enjoyed the good life; was no ascetic; yet later, at forty-nine, he would be rugged and plastic enough to undertake and to endure without undue complaint a hard trip into what was then the Far West in his country. From 1820 on, he was to enjoy great popularity in his time and during four or five decades afterward, when various uniform editions of his collected works were successfully marketed, some lavishly illustrated and bound. Like Dickens he was a darling of illustrators.

Very early the standard litany about him, which still has some currency, took hold: that he was the first writer of his native land to make his living by authorship; the first American man of letters to win European fame; the father of the American short story; the creator, in *Knickerbocker's History of New York*, of the first great work of American humor. At times it even included the large statement that he was the father of American literature, thus perhaps affording him a closer affinity with the so-called father of his country than the possession of part of George Washington's name.

Two years after the publication of *The Sketch Book*, in a preface to *Bracebridge Hall* (1822), another collection of sketches, essays and tales, Irving wrote:

"It has been a matter of marvel, to my European readers, that a man from the wilds of America should express himself in tolerable English. I was looked upon as something new and strange in literature; as a kind of demi-savage, with a feather in his hand in-

stead of on his head; and there was a curiosity to hear what such a
being had to say about civilized society. . . . Having been born
and brought up in a new country, yet educated from infancy in
the literature of an old one, my mind was early filled with historical and poetical associations, connected with places, and manners,
and customs of Europe, but which could rarely be applied to those
of my own country. To a mind thus peculiarly prepared, the most
ordinary objects and scenes, on arriving in Europe, are full of
strange matter in interest—in novelty. . . . My only aim is to
paint characters and manners. I am no politician. The more I
have considered the study of politics, the more I have found it full
of perplexity; and I have contented myself, as I have in my
religion, with the faith in which I was brought up, regulating my
own conduct by its precepts, but leaving to abler heads the task of
making converts." Irving, it has been said, had "a distaste for democratic Jeffersonian policies." He was baptized a Presbyterian.

In the years between 1820 and 1824 he traveled on the Continent: Heidelberg, Munich, Salzburg, Vienna, Dresden, Prague,
Paris. In Paris he was involved unsuccessfully in trying to write or
doctor plays with John Howard Payne, author of "Home, Sweet
Home." Irving's *Tales of a Traveller* appeared in the summer and
fall of 1824. Its unexpected and distressingly poor, in places even
savage, reception determined Irving, despite his belief in its artistic merits—he was dependent now on authorship for his bread—
to move away from fiction to nonfiction. It may be said without
fear of exaggeration that the reception of *Tales of a Traveller*
brought about a turning point in his literary career. Whether a
stronger talent or character would have refused to accept the
largely mistaken verdict is idle to speculate. Irving had a gentle,
pliant nature and expensive tastes, and was only too familiar with
the garish, pendulating, garret life of one of his literary heroes,
Oliver Goldsmith, to wish to emulate it. His disappointment over
the fate of *Tales of a Traveller* spilled over into a letter he wrote
in Paris on December 7, 1824, to his young nephew, Pierre Paris
Irving (as distinguished from Pierre Munro; Pierre Paris became a
minister), who meant to embark on a career as a writer, in which
he stated:

"I hope none of those whose interests and happiness are dear to
me will be induced to follow my footsteps, and wander into the
seductive but treacherous paths of literature. There is no life more

precarious in its profits and fallacious in its enjoyments than that of an author. I speak from an experience which may be considered a favorable and prosperous one; and I would earnestly dissuade all those with whom my voice has any effect from trusting their fortunes to the pen. . . . Do not meddle much with works of the imagination. Your imagination needs no feeding; indeed it is a mental quality that always takes care of itself; and is too apt to interfere with the others. . . . If you think my path has been a flowery one, you are greatly mistaken; it has too often lain among thorns and brambles, and been darkened by care and despondency. Many and many a time have I regretted that at my early outset in life I had not been imperiously bound down to some regular and useful mode of life, and been thoroughly inured to habits of business; and I have a thousand times regretted with bitterness that ever I was led away by my imagination. Believe me, the man who earns his bread by the sweat of his brow, eats often a sweeter morsel, however coarse, than he who procures it by the labor of his brains."

In February 1826 Irving moved to Madrid to begin work on his life of Columbus. On April 4, 1827, at forty-four, he wrote from Madrid to his friend Brevoort:

"I am conscious that my long absence from home has subjected me to unfavorable representations, and has been used to my disadvantage. A man, however, must have firmness enough to pursue his plans when justified by his own conscience, without being diverted from them by the idle surmises and misconceptions of others. If my character and conduct are worth inquiring into, they will ultimately be understood and appreciated according to their merits; nor can anything I could say or do in contradiction place them an iota above or below their real standard. With the world, therefore, let these matters take their course; I shall not court it nor rail at it; but with cherished friends like yourself, my dear Brevoort, the present feeling is all-important to me. Do not let yourself be persuaded, therefore, that time or distance has estranged me in thought or feeling from my native country, my native place, or the friends of my youth. The fact is, that the longer I remain from home the greater charm it has in my eyes, and all the coloring that the imagination once gave to distant Europe now gathers about the scenes of my native country. I look forward to my return as to the only event of any very desirable kind that may yet be in store for me. I do not know whether it is the case with other wanderers, but with me, the various shifting scenes through which I have passed in Europe have pushed each other out of place successively and alternately faded away from my mind, while the scenes and friends of my youth alone remain fixed in my memory and my affections with their original strength and freshness."

From 1826 to 1829, enthralled by his work on Spanish subjects and materials, he traveled in Spain. In July 1829, on being appointed Secretary of Legation to London, he left Granada for Paris and London after a stay of two or three months in the Alhambra in Granada. In December of that year he resolved to write a life of Washington. In June 1831, at the age of forty-eight, he was awarded an LL.D by Oxford University. In September he retired from the Legation. In April 1832 he left Le Havre for New York, arriving on May 21 after an absence from the United States of seventeen years, as we have observed.

His native town, with its Dutch influence still palpable in architecture, speech, names and descendants, had contained some 23,000 inhabitants at the time of his birth and 33,000 when he was a boy of seven. It had grown to more than 60,000 by only a decade later, which was the turn of the politically fateful century, and had become the most populous city of the nation. When he had last embarked from it in the year of Waterloo the mother-country influence on it, although waning, was still strong; its population then had been 110,000. Since his departure the city had burgeoned for a variety of reasons, chief among them the opening of the Erie Canal in 1825, which linked it with the Great Lakes by means of the Hudson River and made it the country's greatest trade center, the chief port between the frontier, the eastern seaboard and the lands beyond the Atlantic. Now New York was an astonishing metropolis of 205,000 money-hungry, political-minded, ambitious, multilingual, freewheeling Americans with the usual and healthy proportion of recent immigrants. The degree of the city's change was an index of the extent the country at large had changed. Fortunately for Irving the change was not as severe as it would have been three years later, when the great fire of 1835 wiped out the business district and the last vestiges of old New Amsterdam.

A great public dinner was given in his honor by the city on May 30, shortly after which he went to Washington, Boston, the

White Mountains, and Tarrytown and Saratoga Springs, both in New York. In August he began a visit to the Oklahoma Territory, which resulted in A *Tour of the Prairies*. A companion, Henry Leavitt Ellsworth, described him in a letter as "rosy-faced and as plump as a partridge. Mr. Irving has a complexion a little darker than mine, which you know is not very light. His height is less than mine, but he is every way thicker set, and weighs I should suppose 20 lbs. more than I do." In 1835, at fifty-two, Irving bought the property that would later be called "Sunnyside," his estate near Tarrytown. In the same year he was nominated by Tammany Hall as mayor of New York, an honor he declined, as he also turned down the post of Secretary of the Navy, offered him by his friend, President Martin Van Buren. On June 27, 1838 his close brother Peter died. In 1840, at fifty-seven, he began to work fitfully on his life of Washington.

In February 1842 he was appointed minister to Spain. In April he left New York for Liverpool, visited London and Paris, and reached Madrid late in July. In the next four years, which were devoid of literary works, he made occasional forays from Madrid, going to Bordeaux, Paris, Barcelona, London, Birmingham. Early in September of 1846 he departed from London for Boston, reaching the United States after an absence of four and a half years. He returned to Sunnyside and soon resumed work on his biography of Washington. In July 1848, when he was sixty-five, he agreed to issue a revised, uniform edition of his works. In that year John Jacob Astor, at Irving's suggestion, founded the Astor Library, which became the basis of the great New York Public Library.

Mathew Brady's photograph of Irving shows a thick-set, thoughtful, perhaps dyspeptic, perhaps absent-minded man who has possibly experienced too much solitude; a man who does not much resemble his sensitive, handsome, winning early self; who could be taken for a mere man of business, overfed, underexercised, overworked and in retreat from himself as well as the world; a man aloof from his time and whom time has not handled gently in the physical sense; a person almost unattractive in his declining years and therefore so different in this respect from the elderly and photogenic Walt Whitman, who was also photographed by Brady.

Irving died November 28, 1859, shortly after the final volume of his five-volume life of Washington appeared. He was seventy-six, the same age as his father when he died.

It was natural that he should turn to the life of Washington as the subject of his final work. He had written biographies of Columbus, Goldsmith and Mahomet, all heroes in their way. He preferred heroes and epic materials. He had a romantic fondness for describing battles and a lot of experience in depicting them in his writings on Spain. And the biography of Washington, the American superhero, with its background of the Revolutionary War, gave him the chance to have a huge canvas. Furthermore, he had sentimental, private reasons. Washington was his namesake, and had patted him on the head when he was a boy in New York. Finally, what greater native subject could he, the formerly expatriated American, sensitive to the well-publicized charge that he had neglected his country in subject matter and by his prolonged absences, and eager to make amends, to put things right in his artist's overworked conscience, find than the Revolution? He could rightly feel that this would be the work for which he would chiefly be forgiven and remembered, his monumental, crowning, native opus.

But was old age a time to take on a monumental burden? As he proceeded with its research and composition, the effects of age weighed increasingly on him, and death sometimes felt like a frighteningly proximate companion, a spur to his claustrophobia, an incitement to his asthma, the thief of his mind's agility. The great, overbearing question was: Would his health, concentration and aggressive drive to shape, to control, to master, to complete hold up long enough to let him finish the work. Exhausted, he fought on a daily, weekly, monthly basis to cling to his waning strength and his now elusive mental clarity, obsessed by the task's incredible demands and by his prayerful hope he could satisfy them in time. It is doubtful that he regarded his current personal drama as having heroic overtones. He was a modest, gentle man and probably would have explained, if forced to the question, that he was merely driven in a mad need to satisfy the requirements of a posthumous self. But the fight was heroic nevertheless.

It began quietly, inconspicuously, long ago. In July 1825 the Scottish publisher Archibald Constable suggested to him that he write a biography of Washington. Replying on August 19, Irving

complained that it would be very difficult to deal with so well
known a subject in an original way and that the task "would
require a great deal of reading and research, and that too of a
troublesome and irksome kind among public documents and
state papers; for Washington's life was more important as a Statesman than as a General." Concluding, he added, "I feel myself incapable of executing my idea of the task. It is one that I dare not
attempt lightly. I stand in too great awe of it."

For a while he considered writing a history of the United States,
but in a letter of December 18, 1831, to his brother Peter he
stated, "I have abandoned the idea of the 'History of the United
States,' but have determined immediately to undertake a work in
lieu of it, which will be more universally popular; and which, if
tolerably executed, must be a valuable and lasting property. I
mean a life of Washington. I shall take my own time to execute
it, and will spare no pains. It must be my great and crowning
labor."

Years were to pass before he even began work on the project,
and two decades to elapse before he gave himself wholeheartedly
to it. In a letter from Madrid to his nephew Pierre M. Irving,
dated November 17, 1842, he writes, "I have, of late, been so
much occupied in diplomatic business, that I have not had time
to attend to the Life of Washington. Indeed, I have not done
much at it since I have been here, but I shall soon take it earnestly
in hand. I found it necessary to give up literary matters for a time,
and turn my thoughts entirely into the subjects connected with
my station." On December 21, in a letter to his brother Ebenezer,
he says that within the past week or two he was able to add a few
chapters "to my history."

Pierre writes in his biography, "Calling on Mr. Irving one morning [in March 1848] before breakfast at Mr. Astor's, I found him
engaged on his 'Life of Washington,' but somewhat out of patience at the want of feature in parts of the war. It was so barren
of interest—such a cursed sand flat; the two enemies, like two
drunken men, impotently striking at each other without hurting.
Sometimes, he said, he dragged along; at other times got a little
breeze, and went forward briskly; then adverting to the changes of
mood in his task, sometimes felt as if he could remove mountains;
at other times, the molehill was a mountain."

In the summer of 1850, after having interrupted the life of

Washington to do the *Life of Goldsmith* and *Mahomet and His Successors*, he was eager to begin anew on the biography of his namesake. Around this time he remarked to Pierre, "All I fear is to fail in health, and fail in completing this work at the same time. If I can only live to finish it, I would be willing to die the next moment. I think I can make it a most interesting book—can give interest and strength to many points, without any prostration of historic dignity. If I had only ten years more of life! I never felt more able to write. I might not conceive as I did in earlier days, when I had more romance of feeling, but I could execute with more rapidity and freedom."

In January 1853 he was in Washington, doing research at the State Department, living at the home of his friend John P. Kennedy, Secretary of State, and being heavily involved in social activities. On January 22 he visited Mount Vernon. On February 6 he wrote to Pierre, "I am making a longer sojourn in Washington than I had intended, but it takes time to make the necessary researches in the archives of state. . . . I cannot say that I find much that is new among the manuscripts of Washington, Sparks having published the most interesting; but it is important to get facts from the fountainhead, not at second hand through his publications." On February 25 he again visited Mount Vernon. He remained in the capital until after the inauguration of President Franklin Pierce, then returned to Sunnyside, from which he wrote on May 23 to Robert C. Winthrop:

"I doubt whether the world will ever get a more full and correct idea of Washington than is furnished by Sparks's collection of his letters, with the accompanying notes and illustrations, and the preliminary biography. I cannot join in the severe censures that have been passed upon Sparks for the verbal corrections and alterations he has permitted himself to make in some of Washington's letters. They have been spoken of too harshly. From the examination I have given to the correspondence of Washington, in the archives of the State Department, it appears to me that Sparks has executed his task of selection, arrangement, and copious illustration with great judgment and discrimination, and with consummate fidelity to the essential purposes of history. His intelligent and indefatigable labors in this and other fields of American history are of national and incalculable importance. Posterity will do justice to them and him."

In June he visited the Shenandoah Valley in Virginia, as well as other places connected with Washington's life. Meanwhile Pierre, at Sunnyside, read the *Life* in manuscript, the preliminary form of which was nearly completed to the beginning of Washington's presidency. Pierre wrote to Irving that he admired the work, to which Irving replied July 8, "I have just received your letter of the 6th, which I need not tell you has been most gratifying and inspiriting to me. I thank you for writing it; for I was looking most anxiously and dubiously for your verdict, after reading the narrative of the war, in which the interest, I feared, might suffer from diffusion, and from the difficulty of binding up a variety of enterprises and campaigns into one harmonious whole. I now feel my mind prodigiously relieved, and begin to think I have not labored in vain. . . . I feel that my working-days are over, and rejoice that I have arrived at a good stopping-place." Pierre comments in his biography, "At this period, he did not think of continuing the Life through the history of the administration, but proposed to make the inauguration of Washington his 'stopping-place.' Hence his premature felicitation that he had reached the end of his 'working-days.' He was yet to give a great deal of handling even to the part he deemed finished; but when he returned to Sunnyside, it was with the desire and intention of preparing the Life at once for the press—an intention frustrated by the condition of his health."

Somewhat later, Irving, brain-tired and finding it irksome "even to scrawl an ordinary letter," traveled to refresh himself, going to Saratoga, Buffalo, Ogdensburg, Niagara Falls. Later the same year, 1853, he visited Virginia again.

The reception of the work as it issued from the press in single volumes, printed in clean, large type with ample margins, greatly heartened the ailing, distracted author. Above all, the work's vividness and anecdotal qualities were praised, for a Washington of fits of temper and, to one's sense of relief, of a capacity for laughter to the point of tears, was seen to be emerging from the time-honored, enigmatic, superself-controlled figure with the chilling sobriquet of "father of his country." It has been suggested that Irving's biographical methods prefigured those of biographers in our own time in that his subject was made to seem less formidable and less actively sitting for his formal portrait. Irving had already had some experience in writing biography with warmer notes than those fashionable in his time. His life of Goldsmith was notable for its geniality. But after all, Irving, unlike previous biographers of Washington, was a literary genius who had a special feel for the living tissue and who knew how to be inspired by his own experiences, however remote, such as the one in which Washington touched him on the head, or his personal knowledge of the frontier derived from his tour of the Oklahoma Territory, the latter unquestionably vivifying his description of Washington's youthful frontier experiences. Also, Irving had not forgotten the example of Boswell, who had utilized anecdotes to marvelous effect in his portrayal of the incredible and unforgettable Johnson.

From newspapers and magazines he heard the sound of bravos, for example from the New York *Tribune*, the New York *Evening Post*, the *North American Review*, *Gentleman's Magazine*, *Putnam's Magazine* and the *Eclectic Review*. Such praise aided sales, and Irving was not a writer to ignore the financial side of his literary career. It also gave him renewed interest and strength to wrestle with the mind-wracking task that often seemed on the verge of overwhelming him, that seemed to have ripped the aged heart out of the lifelong bachelor and left him a mere, fragmentary, haunted shell, a pathetic creature dependent for his physical and mental survival on the endless, generous and wonderfully empathetic ministrations of nieces and nephews at Sunnyside. But of still greater importance to him, no doubt, was the praise of great contemporary historians. On May 30, 1855, George Bancroft wrote to him concerning the first volume, which had appeared early that year:

"Candor, good judgment that knows no bias, the felicity of selection, these are yours in common with the best historians. But, in addition, you have the peculiarity of writing from the heart, enchaining sympathy as well as commanding confidence; the happy magic that makes scenes, events, and personal anecdotes present themselves to you at your bidding, and fall into their natural places, and take color and warmth from your own nature. The style, too, is masterly, clear, easy, and graceful; picturesque without mannerism, and ornamented without losing simplicity. . . . You do everything rightly, as if by grace; and I am in no fear of offending your modesty, for I think you were elected and foreordained to excell your contemporaries."

In September, Irving remarked to Pierre, "I live only in the

Revolution. I have no other existence now—can think of nothing else. My desire is to give everything vividly, but to avoid all melo-dramatic effect. I wish the incidents to be brought out strongly, and speak for themselves; but no hubbub of language, no trickery of phrase, nothing wrought up." Pierre writes in his biography, "He had made great additions to the 'Life' since I had read it before. I spoke with admiration of his narrative of the battle of Princeton. 'It is very difficult,' said he, 'to give a clear account of a battle. Bancroft told me he was bothered about his battles, but Prescott likes them. I study it thoroughly, to seize the strong point, then dip my brush in the paint, and color up for that.'"

Volume two was issued December 1855. At the end of it there is a note of a correction in volume one, after which there is the following personal appeal from Irving: "The author takes this oc-casion to ask the indulgence of his numerous correspondents for any seeming remissness in answering their letters. Engrossed as he is by his literary task, he finds it utterly impossible to cope with the incessant claims of the post office."

On January 3, 1856, William H. Prescott wrote from Boston, "You have done with Washington just as I thought you would, and, instead of a cold, marble statue of a demigod, you have made him a being of flesh and blood, like ourselves—one with whom we can have sympathy. The general sentiment of the country has been too decidedly expressed for you to doubt for a moment that this is the portrait of him which is to hold a permanent place in the national gallery."

In a letter to H. T. Tuckerman written from Sunnyside January 8, 1856, Irving said, "You have discovered what I aimed at, 'the careful avoidance of rhetoric, the calm, patient, and faithful narra-tive of facts.' My great labor has been to arrange these facts in the most lucid order, and place them in the most favorable light, without exaggeration or embellishment, trusting to their own characteristic value for effect. Rhetoric does very well under the saddle, but is not to be trusted in harness, being apt to pull facts out of place and upset them. . . . I have availed myself of the license of biography to step down occasionally from the elevated walk of history, and relate familiar things in a familiar way; seek-ing to show the prevalent passions, and feelings, and humors of the day, and even to depict the heroes of Seventy-six as they really were—men in cocked hats, regimental coats, and breeches; and not classic warriors, in shining armor and flowing mantles, with brows bound with laurel, and truncheons in their hands. But enough of this. I have committed myself to the stream, and, right or wrong, must swim or sink. The latter I will not do, if I find the public sustain me."

In June 1856 Irving wrote a "Note to the Third Volume," which appeared as a sort of preface in July. "When the Author commenced the publication of this work, he informed his Publishers that he should probably complete it in three volumes. What he gave as a probability, they understood as a certainty, and worded their advertisements accordingly. His theme has unexpectedly expanded under his pen, and he now lays his third volume before the public, with his task yet unaccomplished. He hopes this may not cause unpleasant disappointment. To present a familiar and truthful picture of the Revolution and personages concerned in it, required much detail and copious citations, that the scenes might be placed in a proper light, and the characters introduced might speak for themselves, and have space in which to play their parts.

"The kindness with which the first two volumes have been received, has encouraged the author to pursue the plan he had adopted, and inspires the hope that the public good-will which has cheered him through so long a period of devious authorship, will continue with him to the approaching close of his career."

An insert at the back of the volume, smaller than page size, contains a Publishers' Advertisement calling attention to the author's "Note to the Third Volume," and a note addressed "To Correspondents," in which Irving writes, "The Author has again to crave indulgence on the part of his numerous correspondents for seeming remissness in not answering their letters. It is simply unavoidable, unless he gives up all other occupation. He would observe, also, that letters addressed to him at Tarrytown are liable to remain for some at the post-office uncalled for. His proper address is, Irvington, Westchester County, N.Y."

In the spring of 1857 Irving wrote some "Concluding Remarks" which appeared at the end of volume four, issued in May of that year.

"In the chapters here concluded, we have endeavored to narrate faithfully the career of Washington from childhood, through his early surveying expeditions in the wilderness, his diplomatic mis-

sion to the French posts on the frontier, his campaigns in the
French war, his arduous trials as commander-in-chief throughout
the Revolution, the noble simplicity of his life in retirement, until
we have shown him elevated to the presidential chair, by no effort
of his own, in a manner against his wishes, by the unanimous vote
of a grateful country.

"The plan of our work has necessarily carried us widely into the
campaigns of the Revolution, even where Washington was not
present in person; for his spirit pervaded and directed the whole,
and a general knowledge of the whole is necessary to appreciate
the sagacity, forecast, enduring fortitude, and comprehensive wisdom with which he conducted it. He himself has signified to one
who aspired to write his biography, that any memoirs of his life,
distinct and unconnected with the history of the war, would be
unsatisfactory. In treating of the Revolution, we have endeavored
to do justice to what we consider its most striking characteristic;
the greatness of the object and the scantiness of the means. We
have endeavored to keep in view the prevailing poverty of
resources, the scandalous neglects, the squalid miseries of all
kinds, with which its champions had to contend in their expeditions through trackless wildernesses, or thinly peopled regions; beneath scorching suns or inclement skies; their wintery marches to
be traced by bloody footprints on snow and ice; their desolate wintery encampments, rendered still more desolate by nakedness and
famine. It was in the patience and fortitude with which these ills
were sustained by a half-disciplined yeomanry, voluntary exiles
from their homes, destitute of all the 'pomp and circumstance' of
war to excite them, and animated solely by their patriotism, that
we read the noblest and most affecting characteristics of that great
struggle for human rights. They do wrong to its moral grandeur,
who seek by commonplace exaggeration, to give a melodramatic
effect and false glare to its military operations, and to place its
greatest triumphs in the conflicts of the field. Lafayette showed a
true sense of the nature of the struggle, when Napoleon, accustomed to effect ambitious purposes by hundreds of thousands of
troops, and tens of thousands of slain, sneered at the scanty
armies, of the American Revolution and its 'boasted allies.' 'Sire,'
was the admirable and comprehensive reply, 'it was the grandest
of causes won by skirmishes of sentinels and outposts.'

"In regard to the character and conduct of Washington, we

have endeavored to place his deeds in the clearest light, and left them to speak for themselves, generally avoiding comment or eulogium. We have quoted his own words and writings largely, to explain his feelings and motives, and give the true key to his policy; for never did man leave a more truthful mirror of his heart and mind, and a more thorough exponent of his conduct, than he has left in his copious correspondence. There his character is to be found in all its majestic simplicity, its massive grandeur, and quiet colossal strength. He was no hero of romance; there was nothing of romantic heroism in his nature. As a warrior, he was incapable of fear, but made no merit of defying danger. He fought for a cause, but not for personal renown. Gladly, when he had won the cause, he hung up his sword, never again to take it down. Glory, that blatant word, which haunts some military minds like the bray of the trumpet, formed no part of his aspirations. To act justly was his instinct, to promote the public weal his constant effort, to deserve the 'affections of good men' his ambition. With such qualifications for the pure exercise of sound judgment and comprehensive wisdom, he ascended the presidential chair.

"There for the present we leave him. So far our work is complete, comprehending the whole military life of Washington, and his agency in public affairs, up to the formation of our Constitution. How well we have executed it, we leave to the public to determine; hoping to find it, as heretofore, far more easily satisfied with the result of our labors than we are ourselves. Should the measure of health and good spirits, with which a kind Providence has blessed us beyond the usual term of literary labor, be still continued, we may go on, and in another volume give the presidential career and closing life of Washington. In the meantime, having found a resting-place in our task, we stay our hands, lay by our pen, and seek that relaxation and repose which gathering years require."

Bancroft wrote to Irving about volume four, calling it "the most vivid and the truest" portrait of Washington that had "ever been written." And Prescott wrote to him on August 7, 1857, "I have never before fully comprehended the character of Washington; nor did I know what capabilities it would afford to his biographer. Hitherto we have only seen him as a sort of marble Colossus, full of moral greatness, but without the touch of humanity that would give him interest. You have known how to give the marble flesh color, that brings it to the resemblance of life. This you have done throughout; but it is more especially observable in the first volume and in the last." By the "last" Prescott meant the fourth.

Troubled by weariness, insomnia, catarrh, shortness of breath and fear of night, Irving found it very difficult to work on volume five. Pierre writes that on September 18, 1858, "He gave me the first six chapters, some of which he had been taking to pieces and put together again. I read them, and recommended some rejections, to which he acceded. Told me he had got through the labor of constructing his fifth volume, but wanted to handle certain parts. Sometimes the way in which a thing should be done flashed upon him as he was going to bed, and he could not recall it the next morning. When in the mood, everything came easy; when *not*, the Devil himself could not make him write." In October, Irving, ill with "intermittent fever," was anxious about retaining his mental powers long enough to finish the task, and apprehensive that "the pitcher might have gone once too often to the well," as Pierre put it. Irving told his nephew, "I do not fear death, but I would like to go down with all sail set."

In January 1859, experiencing increasing shortness of breath, dreading to be alone in his bedroom at night, haunted by the notion he would not be able to sleep, feeling extremely nervous and anxious, Irving was muddling again, as he called it, with the final volume. In February he referred to his bedroom as his "haunted chamber" because it seemed to him that brooding phantoms perched, like Poe's raven, above the door. Once, when he entered the room with Pierre at about eleven in the evening, he begged Pierre not to leave but to "stick" by him, saying it was a great comfort to him to know that he was there with him. On March 15 he put the finishing touches on the last chapter of the biography. Next day, depressed, he had much difficulty breathing. On the seventeenth he asked Pierre if the final chapter had been set in type the previous night. "Yes," Pierre said. Irving remarked, "Well, I never got out a work in this style before, without looking at the proof-sheets. In better health, I could have given more effect to parts; but I was afraid to look at the proofs, lest I should get muddling." His health fluctuated in the spring. In April he wrote a moving "Author's Preface" for the fifth and final volume.

"The present volume completes a work to which the author had long looked forward as the crowning effort of his literary career.

"The idea of writing a life of Washington entered at an early day into his mind. It was especially pressed upon his attention nearly thirty years ago while he was in Europe, by a proposition of the late Mr. Archibald Constable, the eminent publisher of Edinburgh, and he resolved to undertake it as soon as he should return to the United States, and be within reach of the necessary documents. Various circumstances occurred to prevent him from carrying this resolution into prompt effect. It remained, however, a cherished purpose of his heart, which he has at length, though somewhat tardily, accomplished.

"The manuscript for the present volume was nearly ready for the press some months since, but the author, by applying himself too closely in his eagerness to finish it, brought on a nervous indisposition, which unfitted him for a time for the irksome but indispensable task of revision. In this he has been kindly assisted by his nephew, Pierre Munro Irving, who had previously aided him in the course of his necessary researches, and who now carefully collated the manuscript with the works, letters, and unedited documents from which the facts had been derived. He has likewise had the kindness to superintend the printing of the volume, and the correction of the proof sheets. Thus aided, the author is enabled to lay the volume before the public.

"How far this, the last labor of his pen, may meet with general acceptation is with him a matter of hope rather than of confidence. He is conscious of his own short-comings and of the splendid achievements of oratory of which the character of Washington has recently been made the theme. Grateful, however, for the kindly disposition which has greeted each successive volume, and with a profound sense of the indulgence he has experienced from the public through a long literary career, now extending through more than half a century, he resigns his last volume to its fate, with a feeling of satisfaction that he has at length reached the close of his task, and with the comforting assurance that it has been with him a labor of love, and as such has to a certain degree carried with it its own reward."

Pierre writes: "Those nights [in May], when I look back on them, seem a strange mingling; for, between the paroxysms of distress, he would seize on anything to divert his own thoughts, or to relieve what he feared must be the weariness of those who were watching with him. He would read or relate anything that interested him at the moment, and so endeavor to cheat the hours till day." One evening at the end of May, Irving said to Pierre, "I shall have to get you to mount guard again to-night. I am ashamed to ask it, but you cannot conceive what an abject coward this nervousness makes of me." Pierre assured him of his readiness to resume his post. At times Irving could still appear cheerful, playful; at others he was miserably depressed, and haunted by strange dreams.

On May 9, 1859, Bancroft wrote to him concerning volume five. "The narrative is beautifully told, in your own happy diction and style, felicitous always; never redundant; graceful and elegant. The throbbings of your heart are as marked and perceptible along the pages as in anything you ever wrote. But the charm is the loveliness that your portraiture sheds round the venerable patriot in his retirement. Much as I have read and studied about Washington, I was taken by the novelty that your ever fresh and warm manner has thrown about your sketch. . . . But I shall weary you; only I could not delay telling you how admirably you have, in my judgment, combined in this volume, grace of style, freshness, candor, and all the good qualities that make you the delight of your friends and the pride of the country."

At the end of June, Irving expressed the hope that his suffering would soon end. He said he had never wished to outlive a cheerful existence and that it puzzled him that he should be so miserable, for he had nothing really to worry him, no concerns about money or literary reputation. At times he had good days and seemed to Pierre like his old self. His life dragged on into November.

On the seventh of that month he was interviewed briefly at Sunnyside by Theodore Tilton, an editor of the *New York Independent*. Irving was muffled against the damp air with a Scotch shawl, "wrapped like a great loose scarf around his neck," in Tilton's description. He spoke hoarsely. Tilton asked him, "Now that you have laid aside your pen, which of your books do you look back upon with most pleasure?" Irving replied, "I scarcely look with full satisfaction upon any; for they do not seem what they might have been. I often wish that I could have twenty years more, to take them down from the shelf one by one, and write them over."

Tilton reported: "He spoke of his daily habits of writing, before he had made the resolution to write no more. His usual hours for literary work were from morning till noon. But, although he had generally found his mind most vigorous in the early part of the day, he had always been subject to moods and caprices, and could never tell, when he took up the pen, how many hours would pass before he would lay it down.

" 'But,' said he, 'these capricious periods of the heat and glow of composition have been the happiest hours of my life. I have never found, in anything outside of the four walls of my study, any enjoyment equal to sitting at my writing-desk, with a clean page, a new theme, and a mind wide awake.'

"His literary employments, he remarked, had always been more like entertainments than tasks. . . .

"He said that, whenever he had forced his mind unwillingly to work, the product was worthless, and he invariably threw it away, and began again; 'for,' as he observed, 'an essay or chapter that has been only *hammered out,* is seldom good for anything. An author's right time to work is when his mind is aglow—when his imagination is kindled. These are his precious moments. Let him wait until they come; but, when they have come, let him make the most of them.'

"I referred to his last and greatest work, the 'Life of Washington,' and asked if he felt, on finishing it, any such sensation as Gibbon is said to have experienced over the last sheet of the 'Decline and Fall.' He replied that the whole work had engrossed his mind to such a degree, that, before he was aware, he had written himself into feebleness of health; that he feared in the midst of his labor that it would break him down before he could end it; that when, at last, the final pages were written, he gave the manuscript to his nephew to be conducted through the press, and threw himself back upon his red-cushioned lounge with an indescribable feeling of relief. He added, that the great fatigue of mind, throughout the whole task, had resulted from the care and pains required in the construction and arrangement of materials, and not in the mere literary composition of the successive chapters."

On November 28 Irving watched a sunset and, in Pierre's words, "exclaimed again and again at the beauty of the prospect." He was depressed that evening but not nervous. He turned in at ten-thirty. His niece Sarah entered his bedroom and placed his medicines within easy reach.

"Well," Irving exclaimed, "I must arrange my pillows for

another weary night!" And then, as though to himself, he muttered, "If this could only end!" or "When will this end!"—Sarah was not sure which. He uttered a slight exclamation as if of pain, pressed his hand against his left side, repeated the exclamation, caught at the bed's footboard, and fell backward to the floor. The genial Irving, having given to his exhausting self-imposed task as much as he could manage to tear from himself after a long life, and having, by finishing the job despite painful impediments both mental and physical, shown that, like his great namesake he could live heroically, was dead.

The praise that he received near the end of his life was echoed after his death. In a memorial address on December 6, 1859, at the New York Historical Society, of which Irving had long been a member, Bancroft said of the *Life of George Washington:*

"No one has so painted the Father of his Country to the life; modestly disclaiming great extent of original research, he has yet added much that was not known before. But what distinguishes him is the grace and facility of his movement. He writes American history, as it were, by the aid of special endowments; he takes with him a candor that never fails; a clear, impartial judgment, and an unrivalled keenness of insight into character. He may err in minor details, but never in the general effect. No one has drawn so true, and touching, and vivid a picture of Washington in his retirement, as Irving, who published it while suffering from prostration of the nerves, a depression of spirits, and that attack of asthma which harassed him to the last."

And Charles Dudley Warner in his book *Washington Irving* (1881) wrote:

"Probably this work lost something in incisiveness and brilliancy by being postponed till the writer's old age. But whatever this loss, it is impossible for any biographer to be less pretentious in style, or less ambitious in proclamation. . . . But while he has given us a dignified portrait of Washington, it is as far as possible removed from that of the smile-less prig which has begun to weary even the popular fancy. The man he paints is flesh and blood, presented, I believe, with substantial faithfulness to his character; with a recognition of the defects of his education and the deliberation of his mental operations; with at least a hint of that want of breadth and culture and knowledge of the past, the possession of which characterized many of his great associates; and with no concealment that he had a dower of passions and a temper which only vigorous self-watchfulness kept under. But he portrays, with an admiration not too highly colored, the magnificent patience, the courage to bear misconstruction, the unfailing patriotism, the practical sagacity, the level balance of judgment combined with the wisest toleration, the dignity of mind, and the lofty moral nature which made him the great man of the epoch. Irving's grasp of this character; his lucid marshalling of the scattered, often wearisome and uninteresting details of our dragging, unpicturesque Revolutionary War; his just judgment of men; his even, almost judicial, moderation of tone; and his admirable proportion of space to events, render the discussion of style in reference to this work superfluous."

Although the biography entered a period of neglect partly paralleling the decline of Irving's reputation, modern estimates by authorities on the subject generally support the judgments of Irving's time. In his article on Washington in the *Dictionary of American Biography* (1936), J. C. Fitzpatrick wrote, "Washington Irving, *Life of George Washington* (5 vols., 1855–59) is satisfactory from most viewpoints, though its reliance on [Jared] Sparks lessens the confidence it would otherwise command." Fitzpatrick wrote, "The Sparks edition [of Washington's writings, in twelve volumes, issued 1834–37] suffers from unjustifiable textual alterations and unnoted omissions." However, as we have seen, these objections to Sparks were aired during Irving's lifetime and were dealt with by Irving.

Allan Nevins, in the fourteenth and fifteenth editions of the *Encyclopaedia Britannica*, in his article on Washington lists Irving's work "among good earlier biographies" (that is, earlier than Douglas Southall Freeman's definitive and modern one). In the sixth volume of Freeman's biography, Geneva B. Snelling noted (Freeman had died): "Biographies of Washington and the men around him are almost as numerous as the printed editions of their writings but for various reasons were of limited value in this [Freeman's] study. Those used extensively by Freeman are the biographies of Washington by Rupert Hughes (3 volumes), Washington Irving (5 volumes) and John Marshall (5 volumes)." One can hardly ask for a better modern recommendation of the Irving work than this.

Irving is a pleasure to read, and his literary gifts—of suspense, plasticity, sense of place, feeling for character, flow of narrative— are amply evident in the *Life*. Also, he has the great virtue of vividness. He *sees*, and possesses the literary ability to project his vision. But despite his hopes for the biography, it is unlikely that in its original form it will ever be considered his most artistic creation. Its chief defect is lack of economy, due especially to Washington's absence from many of its pages, indeed from whole chapters. Had Irving spared himself the labor of depicting events, personalities, scenes and battles remote from Washington's physical presence if not his intellectual interests, he no doubt would have written an even more vivid and human biography than he produced. Reading the original edition today, it is with a feeling of relief that one returns from these excursions, interesting though they may be, to the magnetic presence of Washington. Not surprisingly, Irving is at his best when writing about affairs in which Washington was directly involved, for Washington is the subject of subjects for him. Although he tried, as we have seen, in a note at the end of the fourth volume of the original edition, to justify the extent of his canvas, there is much to be said in favor of one tending to a sharper focus on Washington. This is a matter Freeman had to deal with. In a preface to volume three of his biography, he wrote:

"If the reader was not to be drowned in detail, a distinction manifestly had to be made between a Life of Washington and a History of the war in which his country was engaged. This requirement, which applies in varying degree to the writing of all military biography, is particularly severe in the case of Washington. Circumstances bring the hall of Congress very close to headquarters and often fuse the deliberations of that body with military planning. The nature and scope of Washington's administrative duties make it necessary to discuss questions of supply that would not be representative of their place in Washington's thought and labor if, in the most literal sense, they were not detailed, specific in background, and ipso facto, dull. To accept this unescapable reality and at the same time to keep this biography from becoming an encyclopedia of the American Revolution, these rules have been laid down: Military operations in which Washington had no direct part are described summarily, if at all —witness Montgomery's Canadian expedition and Gates's campaign against Burgoyne."

The *Life*'s great length has probably contributed to the decline in its popularity among readers at large. Who now reads this huge work, long out of print? At the time Irving wrote it there was much more leisure to read, and it was profitable to produce multivolume works, and authors could afford to be prolix. Today, a one-volume abridgment in which the focus is almost entirely on Washington is much more likely to be bought and read.

I have abridged the original text by somewhat more than 50 per cent. As examples, I have eliminated detailed examinations of the operations of Wolfe and Montcalm at Quebec, as well as the last stand of the French at Montreal; Benedict Arnold's military activities in the North, together with those of Ethan Allen and the Green Mountain Boys in the same region; and much military activity in the Carolinas and Georgia. I have also abridged sketches of characters whenever it seemed advisable to do so. Inasmuch as my edition is meant for the general reader, not the Irving or the Washington scholar, I have not indicated places of omission, reasoning that to do so would be distracting and pedantic. I have tried to keep my presence in the work to a minimum. My own text, strictly of a connective nature, is to be found in brackets. In the original edition Irving provided an often lengthy summary of each chapter not only in the table of contents but at the beginning of each chapter. It was a custom of his day that I have dispensed with as being cumbersome and expensively space-consuming.

The chapter divisions are almost always my own, and I have provided the chapter titles. Irving had a tendency to italicize lengthily when quoting letters and speeches. It was his way of stressing points that did not, in my opinion, need such obvious underlining. I have quietly reverted the italics to a roman text in a number of instances. I have changed the title of Irving's work for two reasons: to modernize it, and particularly to distinguish the present edition from the original one. Similarly, I titled the Clemens work *The Autobiography of Mark Twain* to avoid confusion between my edition and Albert B. Paine's earlier *Mark Twain's Autobiography*.

I have deleted thousands of commas from Irving's text, as I did from Mark Twain's when I edited the *Autobiography*. In the case of the *Autobiography* I worked in a tradition followed by Bernard DeVoto, editor of *Mark Twain in Eruption*. Irving modernized both the punctuation and spelling of his quotations from Wash-

ington. I have modernized Washington's punctuation more fully
than Irving to conform with present-day standards, but I have let
the spelling stand in Irving's version because it is sufficiently modern. In modernizing Irving and Washington's punctuation I have
had reassurance from the example of Freeman, who, in the first
volume of his work, wrote in defense of his position:

"What should be done about the punctuation and spelling of
Washington's letters and those of certain of his correspondents?
Faithful and scholarly editors to whom America has become indebted for many published collections of source material have
made it their rule in recent years to follow the original precisely.
This is as it should be; but when a quotation is made in a biography or other historical work, archaic spelling and punctuation
often turn the thought of the reader from what is said to the
manner in which it is said. Sometimes, even, spelling that does
not conform to modern usage may induce a vague ridicule of the
men who 'did not know how to spell.' In order that the reader
may not be brought to a halt by odd misspelling or by awkward
punctuation, the modern form of all words and the current usages
of punctuation have been employed in the present work with
these three exceptions: First, if the punctuation leaves the meaning in the least doubt, the original is reproduced or else the doubt
and the correction are mentioned in a footnote; second, in a few
instances where Washington's punctuation reflected his emotion,
it has been preserved; third, several letters presented such incredible examples of eighteenth-century phonetics that they have been
inserted as a *divertissement*."

I have also omitted many semicolons, which were stylish around
the time of the Civil War, sometimes changing them to commas,
at other times breaking up long, needlessly complicated sentences
into shorter ones. An examination of portions of Irving's manuscript indicates that, like Mark Twain, he did not punctuate as
heavily as the printed versions of his work often suggest. Also like
Clemens, occasionally in his correspondence he complains of the
heavy hands of printers in punctuating his work. Irving's
published text is so replete with commas and semicolons that at
times a modern reader has a feeling of stumbling. The punctuation is not consistent throughout the work. Occasionally it is so
light as almost to seem modern, at others it is bewilderingly thick.
Possibly the variations are due to the fact that several compositors

worked on the manuscript, and that Irving was unable to read proof on the biography. The effect of modernizing the punctuation is comparable to that of removing coats of discolored varnish from an old painting. The new punctuation lessens the distance between the modern reader and the intimacy of Irving's imagination and intelligence.

I have also eliminated some overly sentimental remarks as well as others that struck me as being too obviously idolatrous, but I have neither omitted nor abridged any that contained substantive matter. All abridgments of quoted letters, including letters by Washington, are Irving's, and all footnotes are also by him, unless otherwise indicated. The illustrations were selected from the first edition.

It is almost needless to add that Irving was our country's first great literary artist, and that a reading of his biography of Washington, either in the original version or in an abridged one, is a profoundly enriching experience. As I said in the introduction to his *Complete Tales*, published almost a year ago, his world is that of an extraordinarily gifted, romantic, strikingly humane, shy and often solitary writer who looked outside of himself for inspiration and materials. He deserves to be read anew. I trust the present edition will win him new admirers and stir the affection of old.

Princeton, New Jersey
February 1975

GEORGE WASHINGTON
A Biography

PREFACE

The following work was commenced several years ago but the prosecution of it has been repeatedly interrupted by other occupations, by a long absence in Europe and by occasional derangement of health. It is only within the last two or three years that I have been able to apply myself to it steadily. This is stated to account for the delay in its publication.

Though a biography, and of course admitting of familiar anecdote, excursive disgressions and a flexible texture of narrative, yet for the most part it is essentially historic. Washington in fact had very little private life but was eminently a public character. All his actions and concerns almost from boyhood were connected with the history of his country. In writing his biography, therefore, I am obliged to take glances over collateral history as seen from his point of view and influencing his plans, and to narrate distant transactions apparently disconnected with his concerns but eventually bearing upon the great drama in which he was the principal actor.

I have endeavored to execute my task with candor and fidelity, stating facts on what appeared to be good authority and avoiding as much as possible all false coloring and exaggeration. My work is founded on the correspondence of Washington, which in fact affords the amplest and surest groundwork for his biography. This I have consulted as it exists in manuscript in the archives of the Department of State, to which I have had full and frequent access. I have also made frequent use of *Washington's Writings* as published by Mr. Sparks, a careful collation of many of them with the originals having convinced me of the general correctness of the collection and of the safety with which it may be relied upon for historical purposes; and I am happy to bear this testimony to the essential accuracy of one whom I consider among the greatest benefactors to our national literature and to whose writings and researches I acknowledge myself largely indebted throughout my work.

W.I.

Sunnyside, 1855

Chapter 1

EARLY DAYS

The Washington family is of an ancient English stock, the genealogy of which has been traced up to the century immediately succeeding the Conquest. [John and Andrew Washington emigrated to Virginia,] which colony, from its allegiance to the exiled monarch and the Anglican Church, had become a favorite resort of the Cavaliers. The brothers arrived in Virginia in 1657 and purchased lands in Westmoreland County on the Northern Neck, between the Potomac and Rappahannock rivers. John married a Miss Anne Pope of the same county and took up his residence on Bridges Creek near where it falls into the Potomac. He became an extensive planter and, in process of time, a magistrate and member of the House of Burgesses. Having a spark of the old military fire of the family, we find him, as Colonel Washington, leading the Virginia forces in co-operation with those of Maryland against a band of Seneca Indians who were ravaging the settlements along the Potomac. In honor of his public services and private virtues the parish in which he resided was called after him and still bears the name of Washington. He lies buried in a vault on Bridges Creek, which for generations was the family place of sepulture.

The estate continued in the family. His grandson Augustine, the father of our Washington, was born there in 1694. He was twice married, first (April 20th, 1715) to Jane, daughter of Caleb Butler, Esq., of Westmoreland County, by whom he had four children, of whom only two, Lawrence and Augustine, survived the years of childhood. Their mother died November 24th, 1728 and was buried in the family vault.

On the 6th of March 1730 he married, in second nuptials, Mary, the daughter of Colonel Ball, a young and beautiful girl, said to be the belle of the Northern Neck. By her he had four sons, George, Samuel, John Augustine and Charles, and two daughters, Elizabeth or Betty as she was commonly called, and Mildred, who died in infancy.

George, the eldest, the subject of this biography, was born on the 22d of February 1732 in the homestead on Bridges Creek. This house commanded a view over many miles of the Potomac and the opposite shore of Maryland. It had probably been purchased with the property and was one of the primitive farmhouses of Virginia. The roof was steep and sloped down into low projecting eaves. It had four rooms on the ground floor and others in the attic and an immense chimney at each end. Not a vestige of it remains. Two or three decayed fig-trees, with shrubs and vines, linger about the place, and here and there a flower grown wild serves "to mark where a garden has been." Such at least was the case a few years since but these may have likewise passed away. A stone[1] marks the site of the house, and an inscription denotes its being the birthplace of Washington.

Not long after the birth of George his father removed to an estate in Stafford County, opposite Fredericksburg. The house was similar in style to the one at Bridges Creek and stood on a rising ground overlooking a meadow which bordered the Rappahannock. This was the home of George's boyhood. The meadow was his play-ground and the scene of his early athletic sports. But this home, like that in which he was born, has disappeared. The site is only to be traced by fragments of bricks, china and earthenware.

In those days the means of instruction in Virginia were limited and it was the custom among the wealthy planters to send their sons to England to complete their education. This was done by Augustine Washington with his eldest son Lawrence, then about fifteen years of age, and whom he no doubt considered the future head of the family. George was yet in early childhood. As his intellect dawned he received the rudiments of education in the best establishment for the purpose that the neighborhood afforded. It was what was called in popular parlance an "old field school-house," humble enough in its pretensions and kept by one of his father's tenants named Hobby, who moreover was sexton of the parish. The instruction doled out by him must have been the simplest kind, reading, writing and ciphering, perhaps, but George

[1] Placed there by George W. P. Custis, Esq.

had the benefit of mental and moral culture at home from an excellent father.

When George was about seven or eight years old his brother Lawrence returned from England, a well-educated and accomplished youth. There was a difference of fourteen years in their ages, which may have been one cause of the strong attachment which took place between them. Lawrence looked down with a protecting eye upon the boy whose dawning intelligence and perfect rectitude won his regard, while George looked up to his manly and cultivated brother as a model in mind and manners. We call particular attention to this brotherly interchange of affection, from the influence it had on all the future career of the subject of this memoir.

Lawrence Washington had something of the old military spirit of the family, and circumstances soon called it into action. Spanish depredations on British commerce had recently provoked reprisals. Admiral Vernon, commander-in-chief in the West Indies, had accordingly captured Porto Bello on the Isthmus of Darien. The Spaniards were preparing to revenge the blow. The French were fitting out ships to aid them. Troops were embarked in England for another campaign in the West Indies. A regiment of four battalions was to be raised in the colonies and sent to join them at Jamaica. There was a sudden outbreak of military ardor in the province. The sound of drum and fife was heard in the villages, with the parade of recruiting parties. Lawrence Washington, now twenty-two years of age, caught the infection. He obtained a captain's commission in the newly raised regiment and embarked with it for the West Indies in 1740. He served in the joint expeditions of Admiral Vernon and General Wentworth, in the land forces commanded by the latter, and acquired the friendship and confidence of both of those officers. He was present at the siege of Carthagena when it was bombarded by the fleet and when the troops attempted to escalade the citadel. It was an ineffectual attack. The ships could not get near enough to throw their shells into the town, and the scaling-ladders proved too short. That part of the attack, however, with which Lawrence was concerned distinguished itself by its bravery. The troops sustained unflinching a destructive fire for several hours and at length retired with honor, their small force having sustained a loss of about six hundred in killed and wounded.

We have here the secret of that martial spirit so often cited of George in his boyish days. He had seen his brother fitted out for the wars. He had heard by letter and otherwise of the warlike scenes in which he was mingling. All his amusements took a military turn. He made soldiers of his schoolmates. They had their mimic parades, reviews and sham fights. A boy named William Bustle was sometimes competitor but George was commander-in-chief of Hobby's school.

Lawrence Washington returned home in the autumn of 1742, the campaigns in the West Indies being ended and Admiral Vernon and General Wentworth being recalled to England. It was the intention of Lawrence to rejoin his regiment in that country and seek promotion in the army but circumstances completely altered his plans. He formed an attachment to Anne, the eldest daughter of the Honorable William Fairfax of Fairfax County. His addresses were well received and they became engaged. Their nuptials were delayed by the sudden and untimely death of his father, which took place on the 12th of April 1743 after a short but severe attack of gout in the stomach and when but forty-nine years of age. George had been absent from home on a visit during his father's illness and just returned in time to receive a parting look of affection.

Augustine Washington left large possessions, distributed by will among his children: to Lawrence the estate on the banks of the Potomac, with other real property and several shares in iron works; to Augustine, the second son by the first marriage, the old homestead and estate in Westmoreland. The children by the second marriage were severally well provided for, and George, when he became of age, was to have the house and lands on the Rappahannock.

In the month of July the marriage of Lawrence with Miss Fairfax took place. He now gave up all thoughts of foreign service and settled himself on his estate on the banks of the Potomac, to which he gave the name of Mount Vernon, in honor of the Admiral.

Augustine took up his abode at the homestead on Bridges Creek and married Anne, daughter and co-heiress of William Aylett, Esquire, of Westmoreland County.

George, now eleven years of age, and the other children of the second marriage had been left under the guardianship of their mother, to whom was intrusted the proceeds of all their property until they should severally come of age. She proved herself worthy of the trust. Endowed with plain, direct good sense, thorough conscientiousness and prompt decision, she governed her family strictly but kindly, exacting deference while she inspired affection. George, being her eldest son, was thought to be her favorite, yet she never gave him undue preference, and the implicit deference exacted from him in childhood continued to be habitually observed by him to the day of her death. He inherited from her a high temper and a spirit of command but her early precepts and example taught him to restrain and govern that temper and to square his conduct on the exact principles of equity and justice.

Having no longer the benefit of a father's instructions at home, and the scope of tuition of Hobby, the sexton, being too limited for the growing wants of his pupil, George was now sent to reside with Augustine Washington at Bridges Creek and enjoy the benefit of a superior school in that neighborhood, kept by a Mr. Williams. His education, however, was plain and practical. He never attempted the learned languages nor manifested any inclination for rhetoric or belles-lettres. His object, or the object of his friends, seems to have been confined to fitting him for ordinary business. His manuscript school-books still exist and are models of neatness and accuracy. One of them, it is true, a ciphering-book preserved in the library at Mount Vernon, has some school-boy attempts at calligraphy: nondescript birds executed with a flourish of the pen, or profiles of faces, probably intended for those of his schoolmates. The rest are all grave and business-like. Before he was thirteen years of age he had copied into a volume forms of all kinds of mercantile and legal papers, bills of exchange, notes of hand, deeds, bonds and the like. This early self-tuition gave him throughout life a lawyer's skill in drafting documents and a merchant's exactness in keeping accounts, so that all the concerns of his various estates, his dealings with his domestic stewards and foreign agents, his accounts with government and all his financial transactions are to this day to be seen posted up in books in his own handwriting, monuments of his method and unwearied accuracy.

He was a self-disciplinarian in physical as well as mental matters and practised himself in all kinds of athletic exercises, such as running, leaping, wrestling, pitching quoits and tossing bars. His frame even in infancy had been large and powerful and he now excelled most of his playmates in contests of agility and strength. Above all, his inherent probity and the principles of justice on which he regulated all his conduct even at this early period of life were soon appreciated by his schoolmates. As he had formerly been military chieftain, he was now legislator of the school, thus displaying in boyhood a type of the future man.

The attachment of Lawrence to [him] seems to have acquired additional strength and tenderness on their father's death. He now took a truly paternal interest in his concerns and had him as frequently as possible a guest at Mount Vernon. Lawrence had deservedly become a popular and leading personage in the country. He was a member of the House of Burgesses and Adjutant-General of the district, with the rank of major and a regular salary. A frequent sojourn with him brought George into familiar intercourse with the family of his father-in-law, the Hon. William Fairfax, who resided at a beautiful seat called Belvoir, a few miles below Mount Vernon and on the same woody ridge bordering the Potomac.

William Fairfax was a man of liberal education and intrinsic worth. He had seen much of the world and his mind had been enriched and ripened by varied and adventurous experience. Of an ancient English family in Yorkshire, he had entered the army at the age of twenty-one, had served with honor both in the East and West Indies, and officiated as Governor of New Providence after having aided in rescuing it from pirates. For some years past he had resided in Virginia to manage the immense landed estates of his cousin, Lord Fairfax, and lived at Belvoir in the style of an English country gentleman, surrounded by an intelligent and cultivated family of sons and daughters.

An intimacy with a family like this, in which the frankness and simplicity of rural and colonial life were united with European refinement, could not but have a beneficial effect in moulding the character and manners of a somewhat home-bred school-boy. It was probably his intercourse with them and his ambition to acquit himself well in their society that set him upon compiling a code of morals and manners which still exists in a manuscript in his own handwriting, entitled "Rules for Behavior in Company and Conversation." It is extremely minute and circumstantial. Some of the rules for personal deportment extend to such trivial matters and are so quaint and formal as almost to provoke a smile, but in the main a better manual of conduct could not be put into the hands of a youth. The whole code evinces that rigid propriety and self-control to which he subjected himself and by which he brought all the impulses of a somewhat ardent temper under conscientious government.

[He] continued his studies for nearly two years longer, devoting himself especially to mathematics and accomplishing himself in those branches calculated to fit him either for civil or military service. Among these one of the most important in the actual state of the country was land surveying. In this he schooled himself thoroughly, using the highest processes of the art, making surveys about the neighborhood and keeping regular field books, some of which we have examined, in which the boundaries and measurements of the fields surveyed were carefully entered and diagrams made with a neatness and exactness as if the whole related to important land transactions instead of being mere school exercises. Thus in his earliest days there was perseverance and completeness in all his undertakings. Nothing was left half done, or done in a hurried and slovenly manner. The habit of mind thus cultivated continued throughout life, so that however complicated his tasks and overwhelming his cares in the arduous and hazardous situations in which he was often placed, he found time to do everything and to do it well. He had acquired the magic of method, which of itself works wonders.

In one of these manuscript memorials of his practical studies and exercises we have come upon some documents singularly in contrast with all that we have just cited, and with his apparently unromantic character. In a word, there are evidences in his own handwriting that before he was fifteen years of age he had conceived a passion for some unknown beauty, so serious as to disturb his otherwise well-regulated mind and to make him really unhappy. Why this juvenile attachment was a source of unhappiness we have no positive means of ascertaining. Perhaps the object of it may have considered him a mere school-boy and treated him as such, or his own shyness may have been in his way, and his "rules for behavior and conversation" may as yet have sat awkwardly on him and rendered him formal and ungainly when he most sought to please. Even in later years he was apt to be silent and embarrassed in female society. "He was a very bashful young man," said an old lady whom he used to visit when they were both in their nonage. "I used often to wish that he would talk more."

Being a favorite of Sir William Fairfax, he was now an occasional inmate of Belvoir. Among the persons at present residing there was Thomas, Lord Fairfax, cousin of William Fairfax, and of whose immense landed property the latter was the agent. As this nobleman was one of Washington's earliest friends and in some degree the founder of his fortunes, his character and history are worthy of especial note.

Lord Fairfax was now nearly sixty years of age, upwards of six feet high, gaunt and raw-boned, near-sighted, with light gray eyes, sharp features and an aquiline nose. However ungainly his present appearance, he had figured to advantage in London life in his younger days. He had received his education at the University of Oxford, where he acquitted himself with credit. He afterwards held a commission, and remained for some time in a regiment of horse called the Blues. His title and connections, of course, gave him access to the best society, in which he acquired additional currency by contributing a paper or two to Addison's *Spectator*, then in great vogue.

He made a voyage to Virginia about the year 1739 to visit his vast estates there. These he inherited from his mother, Catharine, daughter of Thomas, Lord Culpepper, to whom they had been granted by Charles II. The original grant was for all the lands lying between the Rappahannock and Potomac rivers, meaning thereby, it is said, merely the territory on the Northern Neck east of the Blue Ridge. His lordship, however, discovering that the Potomac headed in the Alleghany Mountains, returned to England and claimed a correspondent definition of his grant. It was arranged by compromise, extending his domain into the Allegheny Mountains and comprising among other lands a great portion of the Shenandoah Valley.

Lord Fairfax had been delighted with his visit to Virginia. The amenity of the climate, the magnificence of the forest scenery, the abundance of game all pointed it out as a favored land. He was pleased too with the frank, cordial character of the Virginians and their independent mode of life, and returned to it with the resolution of taking up his abode there for the remainder of his days.

Another inmate of Belvoir at this time was George William Fairfax, about twenty-two years of age, the eldest son of the proprietor. He had been educated in England, and since his return had married a daughter of Colonel Carey, of Hampton on James River. He had recently brought home his bride and her sister to his father's house.

The merits of Washington were known and appreciated by the Fairfax family. Though not quite sixteen years of age, he no longer seemed a boy, nor was he treated as such. Tall, athletic and manly for his years, his early self-training and the code of conduct he had devised gave a gravity and decision to his conduct. His frankness and modesty inspired cordial regard. And the melancholy of which he speaks may have produced a softness in his manner calculated to win favor in ladies' eyes. According to his own account the female society by which he was surrounded had a soothing effect on that melancholy. The charms of Miss Carey, the sister of the bride, seem even to have caused a slight fluttering in his bosom, which, however, was constantly rebuked by the remembrance of his former passion—so at least we judge from letters to his youthful confidants, rough drafts of which are still to be seen in his tell-tale journal.

To one whom he addresses as his dear friend Robin he writes: "My residence is at present at his lordship's, where I might, was my heart disengaged, pass my time very pleasantly, as there's a very agreeable young lady lives in the same house (Col. George Fairfax's wife's sister); but as that's only adding fuel to fire it makes me the more uneasy, for by often and unavoidably being in company with her, revives my former passion for your Lowland Beauty; whereas was I to live more retired from young women I might in some measure alleviate my sorrows by burying that chaste and troublesome passion in the grave of oblivion," etc.

Similar avowals he makes to another of his young correspondents, whom he styles "Dear friend John," as also to a female confidant styled "Dear Sally," to whom he acknowledges that the company of the "very agreeable young lady, sister-in-law of Col. George Fairfax," in a great measure cheers his sorrow and dejectedness.

The object of this early passion is not positively known. Tradition states that the "lowland beauty" was a Miss Grimes of Westmoreland, afterwards Mrs. Lee and mother of General Henry Lee, who figured in revolutionary history as Light Horse Harry and was always a favorite with Washington.

Whatever may have been the soothing effect of the female society by which he was surrounded at Belvoir, the youth found a more effectual remedy for his love melancholy in the company of Lord Fairfax. His lordship was a stanch fox-hunter and kept horses and hounds in the English style. The hunting season had arrived. The neighborhood abounded with sport but fox-hunting in Virginia required bold and skilful horsemanship. He found Washington as bold as himself in the saddle and as eager to follow the hounds. He forthwith took him into peculiar favor, made him his hunting companion, and it was probably under the tuition of this hard-riding old nobleman that the youth imbibed that fondness for the chase for which he was afterwards remarked.

Their fox-hunting intercourse was attended with more important results. His lordship's possessions beyond the Blue Ridge had never been regularly settled nor surveyed. Lawless intruders—squatters as they were called—were planting themselves along the finest streams and in the richest valleys and virtually taking possession of the country. It was the anxious desire of Lord Fairfax to have these lands examined, surveyed and portioned out into lots preparatory to ejecting these interlopers or bringing them to reasonable terms. In Washington, notwithstanding his youth, he beheld one fit for the task, having noticed the exercises in surveying which he kept up while at Mount Vernon and the aptness and exactness with which every process was executed. He was well calculated too by his vigor and activity, his courage and hardihood, to cope with the wild country to be surveyed and with its still wilder inhabitants. The proposition had only to be offered to Washington to be eagerly accepted. It was the very kind of occupation for which he had been diligently training himself. All the preparations required by one of his simple habits were soon made, and in a very few days he was ready for his first expedition into the wilderness.

Chapter 2

EXPEDITIONS BEYOND THE BLUE RIDGE

It was in the month of March (1748) and just after he had completed his sixteenth year that Washington set out on horseback on this surveying expedition in company with George William Fairfax. Their route lay by Ashley's Gap, a pass through the Blue Ridge, that beautiful line of mountains which as yet almost formed the western frontier of inhabited Virginia. Winter still lingered on the tops of the mountains, whence melting snows sent down torrents which swelled the rivers and occasionally rendered them almost impassable. Spring, however, was softening in the lower parts of the landscape and smiling in the valleys.

They entered the great Valley of Virginia where it is about twenty-five miles wide, a lovely and temperate region diversified by gentle swells and slopes admirably adapted to cultivation. The Blue Ridge bounds it on one side, the North Mountain, a ridge of the Alleghenies, on the other, while through it flows that bright and abounding river which on account of its surpassing beauty was named by the Indians the Shenandoah—that is to say, "the daughter of the stars."

The first station of the travellers was at a kind of lodge in the wilderness, where the steward or land-bailiff of Lord Fairfax resided with such negroes as were required for farming purposes and which Washington terms "his lordship's quarters." It was situated not far from the Shenandoah and about twelve miles from the site of the present town of Winchester.

In a diary kept with his usual minuteness, Washington speaks with delight of the beauty of the trees and the richness of the land in the neighborhood and of his riding through a noble grove of sugar maples on the banks of the Shenandoah. And at the present day the magnificence of the forests which still exist in this favored region justifies his eulogium.

He looked around, however, with an eye to the profitable rather than the poetical. The gleam of poetry and romance inspired by his "lowland beauty" occurs no more. The real business of life has commenced with him. His diary affords no food for fancy. Everything is practical. The qualities of the soil, the relative value of sites and localities are faithfully recorded. In these his early habits of observation and his exercises in surveying had already made him a proficient.

His surveys commenced in the lower part of the valley some distance above the junction of the Shenandoah with the Potomac and extended for many miles along the former river. Here and there partial "clearings" had been made by squatters and hardy pioneers, and their rude husbandry had produced abundant crops of grain, hemp and tobacco. Civilization, however, had hardly yet entered the valley if we may judge from the note of a night's lodging at the house of one of the settlers, Captain Hite, near the site of the present town of Winchester. Here after supper most of the company stretched themselves in backwood style before the fire but Washington was shown into a bedroom. Fatigued with a hard day's work at surveying, he soon undressed, but instead of being nestled between sheets in a comfortable bed, as at the maternal home or at Mount Vernon, he found himself on a couch of matted straw, under a threadbare blanket, swarming with unwelcome bed-fellows. After tossing about for a few moments he was glad to put on his clothes again and rejoin his companions before the fire.

Such was his first experience of life in the wilderness. He soon, however, accustomed himself to "rough it" and adapt himself to fare of all kinds, though he generally preferred a bivouac before a fire in the open air to the accommodations of a woodman's cabin. Proceeding down the valley to the banks of the Potomac, they found that river so much swollen by the rain which had fallen among the Alleghenies as to be unfordable. To while away the time until it should subside, they made an excursion to examine certain warm springs in a valley among the mountains, since called the Berkeley Springs. There they camped out at night under the stars. The diary makes no complaint of their accommodations, and their camping-ground is now known as Bath, one of the favorite watering-places of Virgina. One of the warm springs was subsequently appropriated by Lord Fairfax to his own use and still bears his name.

After watching in vain for the river to subside, they procured a canoe on which they crossed to the Maryland side, swimming their horses. A weary day's ride of forty miles up the left side of the river in a continual rain and over what Washington pronounces the worst road ever trod by man or beast brought them to the house of a Colonel Cresap, opposite the south branch of the Potomac, where they put up for the night.

Here they were detained three or four days by inclement weather. On the second day they were surprised by the appearance of a war party of thirty Indians, bearing a scalp as a trophy. A little liquor procured the spectacle of a war dance. A large space was cleared and a fire made in the centre, round which the warriors took their seats. The principal orator made a speech reciting their recent exploits and rousing them to triumph. One of the warriors started up as if from sleep and began a series of movements, half grotesque, half tragical; the rest followed. For music one savage drummed on a deer-skin stretched over a pot half filled with water. Another rattled a gourd containing a few shot and decorated with a horse's tail. Their strange outcries and uncouth forms and garbs, seen by the glare of the fire, and their whoops and yells made them appear more like demons than human beings. All this savage gambol was no novelty to Washington's companions, experienced in frontier life. But to the youth fresh from school it was a strange spectacle, which he sat contemplating with deep interest and carefully noted down in his journal. It will be found that he soon made himself acquainted with the savage character and became expert at dealing with these inhabitants of the wilderness.

From this encampment the party proceeded to the mouth of Patterson's Creek, where they recrossed the river in a canoe, swimming their horses as before. More than two weeks were now passed by them in the wild mountainous regions of Frederick County and about the south branch of the Potomac, surveying lands and laying out lots, camping out the greater part of the time and subsisting on wild turkeys and other game. Each one was his own cook. Forked sticks served for spits, and chips of wood for dishes. The weather was unsettled. At one time their tent was blown down. At another they were driven out of it by smoke. Now they were drenched with rain and now the straw on which Washington was sleeping caught fire and he was awakened by a companion just in time to escape a scorching.

Having completed his surveys, he set forth from the south

branch of the Potomac on his return homeward, crossed the mountains to the great Cacapehon, traversed the Shenandoah Valley, passed through the Blue Ridge and on the 12th of April found himself once more at Mount Vernon. For his services he received, according to his note-book, a doubloon per day when actively employed and sometimes six pistoles.[1]

The manner in which he had acquitted himself in this arduous expedition and his accounts of the country surveyed gave great satisfaction to Lord Fairfax, who shortly afterwards moved across the Blue Ridge and took up his residence at the place heretofore noted as his "quarters." Here he laid out a manor, containing ten thousand acres of arable grazing lands, vast meadows and noble forests, and projected a spacious manor house, giving to the place the name of Greenway Court.

It was probably through the influence of Lord Fairfax that Washington received the appointment of public surveyor. This conferred authority on his surveys and entitled them to be recorded in the county offices, and so invariably correct have these surveys been found that to this day wherever any of them stand on record they receive implicit credit.

For three years he continued in his occupation, which proved extremely profitable from the vast extent of country to be surveyed and the very limited number of public surveyors. It made him acquainted also with the country, the nature of the soil in various parts and the value of localities, all which proved advantageous to him in his purchases in after years. Many of the finest parts of the Shenandoah Valley are yet owned by members of the Washington family.

While thus employed for months at a time surveying the lands beyond the Blue Ridge, he was often an inmate of Greenway Court. The projected manor house was never even commenced. On a green knoll overshadowed by trees was a long stone building one story in height, with dormer windows, two wooden belfries, chimneys studded with swallow and martin coops and a roof sloping down in the old Virginia fashion into low projecting eaves that formed a verandah the whole length of the house. It was probably the house originally occupied by his steward or land agent, but was now devoted to hospitable purposes and the reception of guests. As to his lordship, it was one of his many eccen-

---

[1] A pistole is $3.60.

tricities that he never slept in the main edifice but lodged apart in a wooden house not much above twelve feet square. In a small building was his office, where quit-rents were given, deeds drawn and business transacted with his tenants.

About the knoll were out-houses for his numerous servants, black and white, with stables for saddle-horses and hunters and kennels for his hounds; for his lordship retained his keen hunting propensities and the neighborhood abounded in game. Indians, half-breeds and leathern-clad woodsmen loitered about the place and partook of the abundance of the kitchen. His lordship's table was plentiful but plain and served in the English fashion.

Here Washington had full opportunity, in the proper seasons, of indulging his fondness for field sports and once more accompanying his lordship in the chase. The conversation of Lord Fairfax, too, was full of interest and instruction to an inexperienced youth, from his cultivated talents, his literary taste, and his past intercourse with the best society of Europe and its most distinguished authors. He had brought books, too, with him into the wilderness and from Washington's diary we find that during his sojourn here he was diligently reading the history of England and the essays of the *Spectator*.

Such was Greenway Court in these its palmy days. We visited it recently and found it tottering to its fall, mouldering in the midst of a magnificent country where nature still flourishes in full luxuriance and beauty.

Three or four years were thus passed by Washington, the greater part of the time beyond the Blue Ridge, but occasionally with his brother Lawrence at Mount Vernon. His rugged and toilsome expeditions in the mountains among rude scenes and rough people inured him to hardships and made him apt at expedients, while his intercourse with his cultivated brother and with the various members of the Fairfax family had a happy effect in toning up his mind and manners and counteracting the careless and self-indulgent habitudes of the wilderness.

During the time of Washington's surveying campaigns among the mountains a grand colonizing scheme had been set on foot, destined to enlist him in hardy enterprises and in some degree to shape the course of his future fortunes.

The treaty of peace concluded at Aix-la-Chapelle, which had put an end to the general war of Europe, had left undefined the boundaries between the British and French possessions in America; a singular remissness, considering that they had long been a subject in dispute and a cause of frequent conflicts in the colonies. Immense regions were still claimed by both nations and each was now eager to forestall the other by getting possession of them and strengthening its claim by occupancy.

The most desirable of these regions lay west of the Allegheny Mountains, extending from the lakes to the Ohio and embracing the valley of that river and its tributary streams—an immense territory, possessing a salubrious climate, fertile soil, fine hunting and fishing grounds and facilities by lakes and rivers for a vast internal commerce.

The French claimed all this country quite to the Allegheny Mountains by the right of discovery. In 1673 Padre Marquette with his companion, Joliet of Quebec, both subjects of the crown of France, had passed down the Mississippi in a canoe to the Arkansas, thereby, according to an alleged maxim in the law of nations, establishing the right of their sovereign not merely to the river so discovered and its adjacent lands but to all the country drained by its tributary streams, of which the Ohio was one; a claim the ramifications of which might be spread like the meshes of a web over half the continent.

To this illimitable claim the English opposed a right derived at second hand from a traditionary Indian conquest. A treaty, they said, had been made at Lancaster in 1741 between commissioners from Pennsylvania, Maryland and Virginia, and the Iroquois, or Six Nations, whereby the latter, for four hundred pounds, gave up all right and title to the land west of the Allegheny Mountains, even to the Mississippi, which land, *according to their traditions*, had been conquered by their forefathers.

It is undoubtedly true that such a treaty was made and such a pretended transfer of title did take place (under the influence of spirituous liquors) but it is equally true that the Indians in question did not at the time possess an acre of the land conveyed and that the tribes actually in possession scoffed at their pretensions and claimed the country as their own from time immemorial.

Such were the shadowy foundations of claims which the two nations were determined to maintain to the uttermost and which ripened into a series of wars ending in a loss to England of a great part of her American possessions and to France of the whole.

As yet in the region in question there was not a single white settlement. Mixed Iroquois tribes of Delawares, Shawnees and Mingoes had migrated into it early in the century from the French settlements in Canada and taken up their abodes about the Ohio and its branches. The French pretended to hold them under their protection, but their allegiance, if ever acknowledged, had been sapped of late years by the influx of fur traders from Pennsylvania. These were often rough, lawless men, half Indians in dress and habits, prone to brawls and sometimes deadly in their feuds. They were generally in the employ of some trader, who, at the head of his retainers and a string of pack-horses, would make his way over mountains and through forests to the banks of the Ohio, establish his head-quarters in some Indian town and disperse his followers to traffic among the hamlets, hunting-camps and wigwams, exchanging blankets, gaudy-colored cloth, trinketry, powder, shot and rum for valuable furs and peltry. In this way a lucrative trade with these western tribes was springing up and becoming monopolized by the Pennsylvanians.

To secure a participation in this. trade and to gain a foothold in this desirable region became now the wish of some of the most intelligent and enterprising men of Virginia and Maryland, among whom were Lawrence and Augustine Washington. With these views they projected a scheme in connection with John Hanbury, a wealthy London merchant, to obtain a grant of land from the British government for the purpose of forming settlements or colonies beyond the Alleghenies. Government readily countenanced a scheme by which French encroachments might be forestalled and prompt and quiet possession secured of the great Ohio Valley. An association was accordingly chartered in 1749 by the name of "the Ohio Company" and five hundred thousand acres of land was granted to it west of the Alleghenies between the Monongahela and Kanawha rivers, though part of the land might be taken up north of the Ohio should it be deemed expedient. The Company were to pay no quit-rent for ten years but they were to select two fifths of their lands immediately, to settle one hundred families upon them within seven years, to build a fort at their own expense and maintain a sufficient garrison in it for defense against the Indians.

Mr. Thomas Lee, president of the council of Virginia, took the lead in the concerns of the company at the outset and by many has been considered its founder. On his death, which soon took place, Lawrence Washington had the chief management.

[Both the English and the French soon set into motion schemes to possess the disputed territory.]

An old Delaware sachem propounded a somewhat puzzling question. "The French," said he, "claim all the land on one side of the Ohio, the English claim all the land on the other side— now where does the Indians' land lie?"

Poor savages! Between their "fathers," the French, and their "brothers," the English, they were in a fair way of being most lovingly shared out of the whole country.

The French prepared for hostile contingencies. They launched an armed vessel of unusual size on Lake Ontario, fortified their trading house at Niagara, strengthened their outposts and advanced others on the upper waters of the Ohio. A stir of warlike preparation was likewise to be observed among the British colonies. It was evident that the adverse claims to the disputed territories, if pushed home, could only be settled by the stern arbitrament of the sword.

In Virginia especially the war spirit was manifest. The province was divided into military districts, each having an adjutant-general with the rank of major and the pay of one hundred and fifty pounds a year, whose duty was to attend to the organization and equipment of the militia.

Such an appointment was sought by Lawrence Washington for his brother George. It shows what must have been the maturity of mind of the latter and the confidence inspired by his judicious conduct and aptness for business, that the post should not only be sought for him but readily obtained, though he was yet but nineteen years of age. He proved himself worthy of the appointment.

He now set about preparing himself with his usual method and assiduity for his new duties. Virginia had among its floating population some military relics of the late Spanish war. Among these was a certain Adjutant Muse, a Westmoreland volunteer who had served with Lawrence Washington in the campaigns in the West Indies and had been with him in the attack on Carthagena. He now undertook to instruct his brother George in the art of war, lent him treatises on military tactics, put him through the manual exercise and gave him some idea of evolutions in the field. Another of Lawrence's campaigning comrades was Jacob Van

Braam, a Dutchman by birth, a soldier of fortune of the Dalgetty order, who had been in the British army but was now out of service and, professing to be a complete master of fence, recruited his slender purse in this time of military excitement by giving the Virginian youth lessons in the sword exercise.

Under the instructions of these veterans, Mount Vernon, from being a quiet rural retreat where Washington three years previously had indited love ditties to his "lowland beauty," was suddenly transformed into a school of arms as he practised the manual exercise with Adjutant Muse or took lessons on the broadsword from Van Braam.

His martial studies, however, were interrupted for a time by the critical state of his brother's health. The constitution of Lawrence had always been delicate and he had been obliged repeatedly to travel for a change of air. There were now pulmonary symptoms of a threatening nature, and by advice of his physicians he determined to pass a winter in the West Indies, taking with him his favorite brother George as a companion.

[Lawrence lived for a while in Barbados, where George caught small-pox, which slightly but permanently marked his face. Then Lawrence tried Bermuda. George meanwhile returned to Virginia. Lawrence died at Mount Vernon July 26, 1752, at the age of thirty-four. He] left a wife and an infant daughter to inherit his ample estates. In case his daughter should die without issue, the estate of Mount Vernon and other lands specified in his will were to be enjoyed by her mother during her lifetime, and at her death to be inherited by his brother George. The latter was appointed one of the executors of the will. But such was the implicit confidence reposed in his judgment and integrity that, although he was but twenty years of age, the management of the affairs of the deceased was soon devolved upon him almost entirely. It is needless to say that they were managed with consummate skill and scrupulous fidelity.

Chapter 3

WASHINGTON IN THE OHIO COUNTRY

The meeting of the Ohio tribes, Delawares, Shawnees and Mingoes, to form a treaty of alliance with Virginia took place at Logstown at the appointed time. The chiefs of the Six Nations declined to attend. "It is not our custom," said they proudly, "to meet to treat of affairs in the woods and weeds. If the Governor of Virginia wants to speak with us and deliver us a present from our father (the king), we will meet him at Albany, where we expect the Governor of New York will be present."[1]

At Logstown, Colonel Fry and two other commissioners from Virginia concluded a treaty with the tribes above named, by which the latter engaged not to molest any English settlers south of the Ohio. Tanacharisson, the half-king, now advised that his brothers of Virginia should build a strong house at the fork of the Monongahela to resist the designs of the French. Mr. [Christopher] Gist was accordingly instructed to lay out a town and build a fort at Chartier's Creek on the east side of the Ohio a little below the site of the present city of Pittsburg. He commenced a settlement also in a valley just beyond Laurel Hill not far from the Youghiogheny and prevailed on eleven families to join him. The Ohio Company about the same time established a trading post, well stocked with English goods, at Wills' Creek (now the town of Cumberland).

The Ohio tribes were greatly incensed at the aggressions of the French, who were erecting posts within their territories, and sent deputations to remonstrate, but without effect. The half-king, as chief of the western tribes, repaired to the French post on Lake Erie, where he made his complaint in person. [But he] returned wounded at heart both by the language and the haughty manner of the French commandant. He saw the ruin impending over his

[1] Letter of Col. Johnson to Gov. Clinton, *Doc. Hist. N.Y.*, ii. 624.

race but looked with hope and trust to the English as the power least disposed to wrong the red man.

French influence was successful in other quarters. Some of the Indians who had been friendly to the English showed signs of alienation. Others menaced hostilities. There were reports that the French were ascending the Mississippi from Louisiana. France, it was said, intended to connect Louisiana and Canada by a chain of military posts and hem the English within the Allegheny Mountains.

The Ohio Company complained loudly to the Lieutenant-governor of Virginia, the Hon. Robert Dinwiddie, of the hostile conduct of the French and their Indian allies. They found in Dinwiddie a ready listener. He was a stockholder in the Company. [He] looked round for a person fitted to fulfil a mission which required physical strength and moral energy, a courage to cope with savages and a sagacity to negotiate with white men. Washington was pointed out as possessed of those requisites. It is true he was not yet twenty-two years of age, but public confidence in his judgment and abilities had been manifested a second time by renewing his appointment of adjutant-general and assigning him the northern division. He was acquainted too with the matters in litigation, having been in the bosom councils of his deceased brother. His woodland experience fitted him for an expedition through the wilderness, and his great discretion and self-command for a negotiation with wily commanders and fickle savages. He was accordingly chosen for the expedition.

By his letter of instruction he was directed to repair to Logstown and hold communication with Tanacharisson, Monaca-toocha, alias Scarooyadi, the next in command, and the other sachems of the mixed tribes friendly to the English, inform them of the purport of his errand and request an escort to the headquarters of the French commander. To that commander he was to deliver his credentials and the letter of Governor Dinwiddie and demand an answer in the name of His Britannic Majesty, but not to wait for it beyond a week. On receiving it he was to request a sufficient escort to protect him on his return.

He was moreover to acquaint himself with the numbers and force of the French stationed on the Ohio and in its vicinity, their capability of being reinforced from Canada, the forts they had erected, where situated, how garrisoned, the object of their advancing into those parts and how they were likely to be supported.

Washington set off from Williamsburg on the 30th of October (1753), the very day on which he received his credentials. At Fredericksburg he engaged his old "master of fence," Jacob Van Braam, to accompany him as interpreter, though it would appear from subsequent circumstances that the veteran swordsman was but indifferently versed either in French or English.

Having provided himself at Alexandria with necessaries for the journey, he proceeded to Winchester, then on the frontier, where he procured horses, tents and other travelling equipments and then pushed on by a road newly opened to Wills' Creek (town of Cumberland), where he arrived on the 14th of November.

Here he met with Mr. Gist, the intrepid pioneer, who had explored the Ohio in the employ of the company and whom he engaged to accompany and pilot him in the present expedition. He secured the services also of one John Davidson as Indian interpreter and of four frontiersmen, two of whom were Indian traders. With this little band he set forth on the 15th of November through a wild country rendered almost impassable by recent storms of rain and snow.

[He visited Shingiss, the king or chief sachem of the Delawares,] at his village to invite him to the council at Logstown. He was one of the greatest warriors of his tribe and subsequently took up the hatchet at various times against the English though now he seemed favorably disposed and readily accepted the invitation.

They arrived at Logstown after sunset on the 24th of November. The half-king was absent at his hunting lodge on Beaver Creek, about fifteen miles distant, but Washington had runners sent out to invite him and all the other chiefs to a grand talk on the following day.

In the morning four French deserters came into the village. They had deserted from a company of one hundred men sent up from New Orleans with eight canoes laden with provisions. Washington drew from them an account of the French force at New Orleans and of the forts along the Mississippi and at the mouth of the Wabash by which they kept up a communication with the lakes, all which he carefully noted down. The deserters were on their way to Philadelphia, conducted by a Pennsylvania trader.

About three o'clock the half-king arrived. Washington had a private conversation with him in his tent, through Davidson, the interpreter. He found him intelligent, patriotic and proudly tenacious of his territorial rights. [The half-king] stated that the French had built two forts, differing in size but on the same model, a plan of which he gave, of his own drawing. The largest was on Lake Erie, the other on French Creek, fifteen miles apart, with a wagon road between them. The nearest and levelest way to them was now impassable, lying through large and miry savannas. They would have therefore to go by Venango and it would take five or six sleeps (or days) of good travelling to reach the nearest fort.

On the following morning at nine o'clock the chiefs assembled in the council-house, where Washington, according to his instructions, informed them that he was sent by their brother, the Governor of Virginia, to deliver to the French commandant a letter of great importance both to their brothers the English and to themselves; and that he was to ask their advice and assistance, and some of their young men to accompany and provide for him on the way, and be his safeguard against the "French Indians" who had taken up the hatchet. He concluded by presenting the indispensable document in Indian diplomacy, a string of wampum.

The chiefs, according to etiquette, sat for some moments silent after he had concluded, as if ruminating on what had been said or to give him time for further remark.

The half-king then rose and spoke in behalf of the tribes, assuring him that they considered the English and themselves brothers and one people and that they intended to return the French the "speech-belts" or wampums which the latter had sent them. This in Indian diplomacy is a renunciation of all friendly relations. An escort would be furnished to Washington composed of Mingoes, Shannoahs and Delawares in token of the love and loyalty of those several tribes, but three days would be required to prepare for the journey.

The chiefs determined that but three of their number should accompany the mission, as a greater number might awaken the suspicions of the French. Accordingly, on the 30th of November Washington set out for the French post, having his usual party augmented by an Indian hunter and being accompanied by the half-king, an old Shannoah sachem named Jeskakake, and another chief called sometimes Belt of Wampum, from being the keeper of the speech-belts, but generally bearing the sounding appellation of White Thunder.

[Washington reached Venango on December 4. Here some French officers got his Indian companions drunk and thereby delayed him until the 7th, after which he proceeded to the French fort about fifteen miles south of Lake Erie and delivered Governor Dinwiddie's letter to the commandant. He then returned by hard stages to Williamsburg.]

The prudence, sagacity, resolution, firmness and self-devotion manifested by him throughout; his admirable tact and self-possession in treating with fickle savages and crafty white men; the soldier's eye with which he had noticed the commanding and defensible points of the country and everything that would bear upon military operations; and the hardihood with which he had acquitted himself during a wintry tramp through the wilderness through constant storms of rain and snow, often sleeping on the ground, without a tent, in the open air and in danger from treacherous foes—all pointed him out not merely to the governor but to the public at large as one eminently fitted, notwithstanding his youth, for important trusts involving civil as well as military duties. It is an expedition that may be considered the foundation of his fortunes. From that moment he was the rising hope of Virginia.

The information given by [him] of what he had observed on the frontier convinced Governor Dinwiddie and his council that the French were preparing to descend the Ohio in the spring and take military possession of the country. Washington's journal was printed and widely promulgated throughout the colonies and England, and awakened the nation to a sense of the impending danger and the necessity of prompt measures to anticipate the French movements.

Captain [William] Trent was despatched to the frontier, commissioned to raise a company of one hundred men, march with all speed to the Fork of the Ohio and finish as soon as possible the fort commenced there by the Ohio Company. Washington was empowered to raise a company of like force at Alexandria, to procure and forward munitions and supplies for the projected fort at the Fork and ultimately to have command of both companies. When on the frontier he was to take counsel of George Croghan and Andrew Mountour, the interpreter, in all matters relating to the Indians, they being esteemed perfect oracles in that department.

Governor Dinwiddie in the meantime called upon the governors of the other provinces to make common cause against the foe. He endeavored also to effect alliances with the Indian tribes of the south, the Catawbas and Cherokees, by way of counterbalancing the Chippewas and Ottawas, who were devoted to the French.

The colonies, however, felt as yet too much like isolated territories. The spirit of union was wanting. Some pleaded a want of military funds, some questioned the justice of the cause, some declined taking any hostile step that might involve them in a war unless they should have direct orders from the crown.

Dinwiddie convened the House of Burgesses to devise measures for the public security. Here his high idea of prerogative and of gubernatorial dignity met with a grievous countercheck from the dawning spirit of independence. High as were the powers vested in the colonial government of Virginia, of which, though but Lieutenant-governor, he had the actual control, they were counterbalanced by the power inherent in the people, growing out of their situation and circumstances and acting through their representatives.

There was no turbulent factious opposition to government in Virginia, no "fierce democracy," the rank growth of crowded cities and a fermenting populace, but there was the independence of men living apart in patriarchal style on their own rural domains, surrounded by their families, dependants and slaves, among whom their will was law—and there was the individuality in character and action of men prone to nurture peculiar notions and habits of thinking in the thoughtful solitariness of country life.

When Dinwiddie propounded his scheme of operations on the Ohio, some of the burgesses had the hardihood to doubt the claims of the king to the disputed territory, a doubt which the governor reprobated as savoring strongly of a most disloyal French spirit. He fired, as he says, at the thought "that an English legislature should presume to doubt the right of His Majesty to the interior parts of this continent, the back part of his dominions!"

Others demurred to any grant of means for military purposes which might be construed into an act of hostility. To meet this scruple it was suggested that the grant might be made for the purpose of encouraging and protecting all settlers on the waters of the Mississippi. And under this specious plea ten thousand pounds were grudgingly voted, but even this moderate sum was not put at the absolute disposition of the governor. A committee was appointed with whom he was to confer as to its appropriation.

This precaution Dinwiddie considered an insulting invasion of the right he possessed as governor to control the purse as well as the sword, and he complained bitterly of the Assembly as deeply tinctured with a republican way of thinking and disposed to encroach on the prerogative of the crown, "which he feared would render them more and more difficult to be *brought to order.*"

Ways and means being provided, Governor Dinwiddie augmented the number of troops to be enlisted to three hundred, divided into six companies. The command of the whole, as before, was offered to Washington, but he shrank from it as a charge too great for his youth and inexperience. It was given therefore to Colonel Joshua Fry, an English gentleman of worth and education, and Washington was made second in command, with the rank of lieutenant-colonel.

The recruiting at first went on slowly. Those who offered to enlist, says Washington, were for the most part loose, idle persons without house or home, some without shoes or stockings, some shirtless and many without coat or waistcoat.

He was young in the recruiting service or he would have known that such is generally the stuff of which armies are made. In this country especially it has always been difficult to enlist the active yeomanry by holding out merely the pay of a soldier. The means of subsistence are too easily obtained by the industrious for them to give up home and personal independence for a mere daily support. Some may be tempted by a love of adventure, but in general they require some prospect of ultimate advantage that may "better their condition."

Governor Dinwiddie became sensible of this and resorted to an expedient rising out of the natural resources of the country, which has since been frequently adopted and always with efficacy. He proclaimed a bounty of two hundred thousand acres of land on the Ohio River, to be divided among the officers and soldiers who should engage in this expedition, one thousand to be laid off contiguous to the fort on the Fork for the use of the garrison. This was a tempting bait to the sons of farmers, who readily enlisted in the hope of having at the end of a short campaign a snug farm of their own in this land of promise.

It was a more difficult matter to get officers than soldiers. Very few of those appointed made their appearance. One of the captains had been promoted. Two declined. Washington found himself left almost alone to manage a number of self-willed, undisciplined recruits. Happily he had with him, in the rank of lieutenant, that soldier of fortune, Jacob Van Braam, his old "master of fence" and traveling interpreter.

In his emergency he forthwith nominated him captain and wrote to the governor to confirm the appointment, representing him as the oldest lieutenant and an experienced officer.

On the 2d of April Washington set off from Alexandria for the new fort at the Fork of the Ohio. He had but two companies with him, amounting to about one hundred and fifty men. The remainder of the regiment was to follow under Colonel Fry with the artillery, which was to be conveyed up to the Potomac. While on the march he was joined by a detachment under Captain Adam Stephen, an officer destined to serve with him at distant periods of his military career.

At Winchester he found it impossible to obtain conveyances by gentle means and was obliged reluctantly to avail himself of the militia law of Virginia and impress horses and wagons for their service, giving the owners orders on government for their ap- praised value. Even then, out of a great number impressed, he obtained but ten after waiting a week. These too were grudgingly furnished by farmers with their worst horses, so that in steep and difficult passes they were incompetent to the draught and the sol- diers had continually to put their shoulders to the wheels.

Thus slenderly fitted out, Washington and his little force made their way toilfully across the mountains, having to prepare the roads as they went for the transportation of the cannon, which were to follow on with the other division under Colonel Fry. They cheered themselves with the thoughts that this hard work would cease when they should arrive at the company's trading-post and storehouse at Wills' Creek, where Captain Trent was to have pack-horses in readiness, with which they might make the rest of the way by light stages. Before arriving there they were startled by a rumor that Trent and all his men had been captured by the French. With regard to Trent the news soon proved to be false, for they found him at Wills' Creek on the 20th of April. With regard to his men there was still an uncertainty. He had recently left them at the Fork of the Ohio, busily at work on the fort under the command of his lieutenant, Frazier, late Indian trader and gunsmith but now a provincial officer. If the men had been captured it must have been since the captain's departure. Washington was eager to press forward and ascertain the truth but it was impossible. Trent, inefficient as usual, had failed to provide pack-horses. It was necessary to send to Winchester, sixty miles distant, for baggage wagons and await their arrival. All uncertainty as to the fate of the men, however, was brought to a close by their arrival on the 25th, conducted by an ensign and bringing with them their working implements. The French might well boast that they had again been too quick for the English. Captain Contrecœur, an alert officer, had embarked about a thousand men with field-pieces in a fleet of sixty bateaux and three hundred canoes, dropped down the river from Venango and suddenly made his appearance before the fort, on which the men were working and which was not half completed. Landing, drawing up his men and planting his artillery, he summoned the fort to surrender, allowing one hour for a written reply.

What was to be done! The whole garrison did not exceed fifty men. Captain Trent was absent at Wills' Creek. Frazier, his lieutenant, was at his own residence at Turtle Creek, ten miles distant. There was no officer to reply but a young ensign of the name of Ward. In his perplexity he turned for council to Tanacharisson, the half-king, who was present in the fort. The chief advised the ensign to plead insufficiency of rank and powers and crave delay until the arrival of his superior officer. The ensign repaired to the French camp to offer this excuse in person and was accompanied by the half-king. They were courteously received but Contrecœur was inflexible. There must be instant surrender or he would take forcible possession. All that the ensign could obtain was permission to depart with his men, taking with them their working tools. The capitulation ended. Contrecœur with true French gayety invited the ensign to sup with him, treated him with the utmost politeness and wished him a pleasant journey as he set off the next morning with his men laden with their working tools.

Such was the ensign's story. He was accompanied by two Indian warriors, sent by the half-king to ascertain where the detachment was, what was its strength and when it might be expected at the Ohio. They bore a speech from that sachem to Washington, and another with a belt of wampum for the Governor of Virginia. In these he plighted his steadfast faith to the English and claimed assistance from his brothers of Virginia and Pennsylvania.

One of these warriors Washington forwarded on with the speech and wampum to Governor Dinwiddie. The other he prevailed on to return to the half-king, bearing a speech from him addressed to the "sachems, warriors of the Six United Nations, Shannoahs and Delawares, our friends and brethren." In this he informed them that he was on the advance with a part of the army to clear the road for a greater force coming with guns, ammunition and provisions; and he invited the half-king and another sachem to meet him on the road as soon as possible to hold a council.

In fact, his situation was arduous in the extreme. Regarding the conduct of the French in the recent occurrence an overt act of war, he found himself thrown with a handful of raw recruits far on a hostile frontier in the midst of a wilderness with an enemy at hand greatly superior in number and discipline, provided with artillery and all the munitions of war and within reach of constant supplies and reinforcements. Beside the French that had come from Venango, he had received credible accounts of another party ascending the Ohio and of six hundred Chippewas and Ottawas marching down Scioto Creek to join the hostile camp. Still, notwithstanding the accumulating danger, it would not do to fall back nor show signs of apprehension. His Indian allies in such case might desert him. The soldiery too might grow restless and dissatisfied. He was already annoyed by Captain Trent's men, who, having enlisted as volunteers, considered themselves exempt from the rigor of martial law, and by their example of loose and refractory conduct threatened to destroy the subordination of his own troops.

In this dilemma he called a council of war, in which it was determined to proceed to the Ohio Company store-house at the mouth of Redstone Creek, fortify themselves there and wait for reinforcements. Here they might keep up a vigilant watch upon the enemy and get notice of any hostile movement in time for defense or retreat; and should they be reinforced sufficiently to enable them to attack the fort, they could easily drop down the river with their artillery.

With these alternatives in view Washington detached sixty men in advance to make a road, and at the same time wrote to

Governor Dinwiddie for mortars and grenadoes and cannon of heavy metal.

On the 29th of April [he] set out from Wills' Creek at the head of one hundred and sixty men. He soon overtook those sent in advance to work the road. They had made but little progress. It was a difficult task to break a road through the wilderness sufficient for the artillery coming on with Colonel Fry's division. All hands were now set to work, but with all their labor they could not accomplish more than four miles a day. They were toiling through Savage Mountain and that dreary forest region beyond it, since bearing the sinister name of "The Shades of Death." On the 9th of May they were not further than twenty miles from Wills' Creek at a place called the Little Meadows.

Every day came gloomy accounts from the Ohio, brought chiefly by traders who, with pack-horses bearing their effects, were retreating to the more settled parts of the country. Some exaggerated the number of the French as if strongly reinforced. All represented them as diligently at work constructing a fort. By their account Washington perceived the French had chosen the very place which he had noted in his journal as best fitted for the purpose.

One of the traders gave information concerning La Force, the French emissary who had beset Washington when on his mission to the frontier and acted, as he thought, the part of a spy. He had been at Gist's new settlement beyond Laurel Hill and was prowling about the country with four soldiers at his heels on a pretended hunt after deserters. Washington suspected him to be on a reconnoitering expedition.

It was reported moreover that the French were lavishing presents on the Indians about the lower part of the river to draw them to their standard. Among all these flying reports and alarms Washington was gratified to learn that the half-king was on his way to meet him at the head of fifty warriors.

After infinite toil through swamps and forests and over rugged mountains, the detachment arrived at the Youghiogheny River, where they were detained some days constructing a bridge to cross it. The Indians assured Washington he would never be able to open a wagon-road across the mountains to Redstone Creek. He embarked therefore in a canoe with a lieutenant, three soldiers and an Indian guide to try whether it was possible to descend the river. They had not descended above ten miles before the Indian refused to go further. Washington soon ascertained the reason. "Indians," said he, "expect presents—nothing can be done without them. The French take this method. If you want one or more to conduct a party, to discover the country, to hunt, or for any particular purpose, they must be bought. Their friendship is not so warm as to prompt them to these services gratis." The Indian guide in the present instance was propitiated by the promise of one of Washington's ruffled shirts and watch-coat.

The river was bordered by mountains and obstructed by rocks and rapids. Indians might thread such a labyrinth in their light canoes but it would never admit the transportation of troops and military stores. Washington kept on for thirty miles until he came to a place where the river fell nearly forty feet in the space of fifty yards. There he ceased to explore and returned to camp, resolving to continue forward by land.

On the 23d Indian scouts brought word that the French were not above eight hundred strong and that about half their number had been detached at night on a secret expedition. Close upon this report came a message from the half-king addressed "to the first of His Majesty's officers whom it may concern."

"It is reported," said he, "that the French army is coming to meet Major Washington. Be on your guard against them, my brethren, for they intend to strike the first English they shall see. They have been on their march two days. I know not their number. The half-king and the rest of the chiefs will be with you in five days to hold a council."

In the evening Washington was told that the French were crossing the ford of the Youghiogheny about eighteen miles distant. He now hastened to take a position in a place called the Great Meadows, where he caused the bushes to be cleared away, made an intrenchment and prepared what he termed "a charming field for an encounter."

A party of scouts were mounted on wagon horses and sent out to reconnoiter. They returned without having seen an enemy. A sensitiveness prevailed in the camp. They were surrounded by forests, threatened by unseen foes and hourly in danger of surprise. There was an alarm about two o'clock in the night. The sentries fired upon what they took to be prowling foes. The troops sprang to arms and remained on the alert until daybreak. Not an enemy was to be seen. The roll was called. Six men were missing, who had deserted.

On the 25th Mr. Gist arrived from his place about fifteen miles distant. La Force had been there at noon on the previous day with a detachment of fifty men, and Gist had since come upon their track within five miles of the camp. Washington considered La Force a bold, enterprising man, subtle and dangerous, one to be particularly guarded against. He detached seventy-five men in pursuit of him and his prowling band.

About nine o'clock at night came an Indian messenger from the half-king, who was encamped with several of his people about six miles off. The chief had seen tracks of two Frenchmen and was convinced their whole body must be in ambush near by.

Washington considered this the force which had been hovering about him for several days and determined to forestall their hostile designs. Leaving a guard with the baggage and ammunition, he set out before ten o'clock with forty men to join his Indian ally. They groped their way in single file by footpaths through the woods in a heavy rain and murky darkness, tripping occasionally and stumbling over each other, sometimes losing the track for fifteen or twenty minutes, so that it was near sunrise when they reached the camp of the half-king.

That chieftain received the youthful commander with great demonstrations of friendship and engaged to go hand in hand with him against the lurking enemy. He set out accordingly, accompanied by a few of his warriors and his associate sachem Scarooyadi or Monacatoocha, and conducted Washington to the tracks which he had discovered. Upon these he put two of his Indians. They followed them up like hounds and brought back word that they had traced them to a low bottom surrounded by rocks and trees, where the French were encamped, having built a few cabins for shelter from the rain.

A plan was now concerted to come upon them by surprise, Washington with his men on the right, the half-king with his men on the left; all as silently as possible. Washington was the first upon the ground. As he advanced from among the rocks and trees at the head of his men, the French caught sight of him and ran to their arms. A sharp firing instantly took place and was kept up on both sides for about fifteen minutes. Washington and his party were most exposed and received all the enemy's fire. The balls whistled around him. One man was killed close by him and three others wounded. The French at length, having lost several of their number, gave way and ran. They were soon overtaken. Twenty-one were captured and but one escaped, a Canadian, who carried the tidings of the affair to the fort on the Ohio. The Indians would have massacred the prisoners had not Washington prevented them. Ten of the French had fallen in the skirmish and one been wounded. Washington's loss was the one killed and three wounded which we have mentioned. He had been in the hottest fire, and, having for the first time heard balls whistle about him, considered his escape miraculous. Jumonville, the French leader, had been shot through the head at the first fire. He was a young officer of merit and his fate was made the subject of lamentation in prose and verse—chiefly through political motives.

Of the twenty-one prisoners the two most important were an officer of some consequence named Drouillon, and the subtle and redoubtable La Force. As Washington considered the latter an arch mischief-maker, he was rejoiced to have him in his power. La Force and his companion would fain have assumed the sacred characters of ambassadors, pretending they were coming with a summons to him to depart from the territories belonging to the crown of France.

Unluckily for their pretensions a letter of instructions, found on Jumonville, betrayed their real errand, which was to inform themselves of the roads, rivers and other features of the country as far as the Potomac, to send back from time to time by fleet messengers all the information they could collect and to give word of the day on which they intended to serve the summons. The prisoners were conducted to the camp at the Great Meadows and sent on the following day (29th) under a strong escort to Governor Dinwiddie, then at Winchester.

Chapter 4

DEFEAT AT FORT NECESSITY

The situation of Washington was now extremely perilous. Contrecœur, it was said, had nearly a thousand men with him at the fort, besides Indian allies; and reinforcements were on the way to join him. The messengers sent by Jumonville previous to the late affair must have apprised him of the weakness of the encampment on the Great Meadows. Washington hastened to strengthen it. He wrote by express also to Colonel Fry, who lay ill at Wills' Creek, urging instant reinforcements but declaring his resolution to "fight with very unequal numbers rather than give up one inch of what he had gained."

The half-king was full of fight. He sent the scalps of the Frenchmen slain in the late skirmish, accompanied by black wampum and hatchets, to all his allies, summoning them to take up arms and join him at Redstone Creek, "for their brothers, the English, had now begun in earnest." It is said he would even have sent the scalps of the prisoners had not Washington interfered.[1] He went off for his home, promising to send down the river for all the Mingoes and Shawnees and to be back at the camp on the 30th with thirty or forty warriors, accompanied by their wives and children. To assist him in the transportation of his people and their effects thirty men were detached and twenty horses.

"I shall expect every hour to be attacked," writes Washington to Governor Dinwiddie on the 29th, "and by unequal numbers, which I must withstand, if there are five to one, for I fear the consequence will be that we shall lose the Indians if we suffer ourselves to be driven back. Your honor may depend I will not be surprised, let them come at what hour they will, and this is as much as I can promise. But my best endeavors shall not be want-

[1] Letter from Virginia. *London Mag.*, 1754.

ing to effect more. I doubt not, if you hear I am beaten, but you will hear at the same time that we have done our duty in fighting as long as there is a shadow of hope."

Scarcity began to prevail in the camp. Contracts had been made with George Croghan for flour, of which he had large quantities at his frontier establishment, for he was now trading with the army as well as with the Indians. None, however, made its appearance. There was mismanagement in the commissariat. At one time the troops were six days without flour and even then had only a casual supply from an Ohio trader. In this time of scarcity the half-king, his fellow-sachem Scarooyadi and thirty or forty warriors arrived, bringing with them their wives and children—so many more hungry mouths to be supplied. Washington wrote urgently to Croghan to send forward all the flour he could furnish.

News came of the death of Colonel Fry at Wills' Creek and that he was to be succeeded in command of the expedition by Colonel James Innes of North Carolina, who was actually at Winchester with three hundred and fifty North Carolina troops. Washington, who felt the increasing responsibilities and difficulties of his situation, rejoiced at the prospect of being under the command of an experienced officer who had served in company with his brother Lawrence at the siege of Carthagena. The colonel, however, never came to the camp, nor did the North Carolina troops render any service in the campaign, the fortunes of which might otherwise have been very different.

By the death of Fry the command of the regiment devolved on Washington. Finding a blank major's commission among Fry's papers, he gave it to Captain Adam Stephen, who had conducted himself with spirit. As there would necessarily be other changes, he wrote to Governor Dinwiddie in behalf of Jacob Van Braam. "He has acted as captain ever since we left Alexandria. He is an experienced officer and worthy of the command he has enjoyed."

The palisaded fort was now completed and was named Fort Necessity from the pinching famine that had prevailed during its construction. The scanty force in camp was augmented to three hundred by the arrival from Wills' Creek of the men who had been under Colonel Fry. With them came the surgeon of the regiment, Dr. James Craik, a Scotchman by birth and one destined to become a faithful and confidential friend of Washington for the remainder of his life.

A letter from Governor Dinwiddie announced, however, that Captain Mackay would soon arrive with an independent company of one hundred men from South Carolina.

The title of independent company had a sound ominous of trouble. Troops of the kind, raised in the colonies under direction of the governors, were paid by the Crown, and the officers had king's commissions. Such, doubtless, had Captain Mackay. "I should have been particularly obliged," writes Washington to Governor Dinwiddie, "if you had declared whether he was under my command or independent of it. I hope he will have more sense than to insist upon any unreasonable distinction because he and his officers have commissions from His Majesty. Let him consider, though we are greatly inferior in respect to advantages of profit, yet we have the same spirit to serve our gracious king as they have and are as ready and willing to sacrifice our lives for our country's good. And here once more and for the last time, I must say that it will be a circumstance which will act upon some officers of this regiment above all measure to be obliged to serve upon such different terms, when their lives, their fortunes and their operations are equally and, I dare say, as effectually exposed as those of others who are happy enough to have the king's commission."

On the 9th arrived Washington's early instructor in military tactics, Adjutant Muse, recently appointed a major in the regiment. He was accompanied by Montour, the Indian interpreter, now a provincial captain, and brought with him nine swivels and a small supply of powder and ball. Fifty or sixty horses were forthwith sent to Wills' Creek to bring on further supplies, and Mr. Gist was urged to hasten forward the artillery.

Major Muse was likewise the bearer of a belt of wampum and a speech from Governor Dinwiddie to the half-king, with medals for the chiefs and goods for presents among the friendly Indians, a measure which had been suggested by Washington. They were distributed with that grand ceremonial so dear to the red man. The chiefs assembled, painted and decorated in all their savage finery. Washington wore a medal sent him by the governor for such occasions. The wampum and speech having been delivered, he advanced and with all due solemnity decorated the chiefs and warriors with the medals, which they were to wear in remembrance of their father the King of England.

Among the warriors thus decorated was a son of Queen

Aliquippa, the savage princess whose good graces Washington had secured in the preceding year by the present of an old watch-coat and whose friendship was important, her town being at no great distance from the French fort. She had requested that her son might be admitted into the war councils of the camp and receive an English name. The name of Fairfax was accordingly given to him, in the customary Indian form. The half-king, being desirous of like distinction, received the name of Dinwiddie. The sachems returned the compliment in kind by giving Washington the name of Connotaucarius, the meaning of which is not explained.

William Fairfax, Washington's paternal adviser, had recently counselled him, by letter, to have public prayers in his camp, especially when there were Indian families there. This was accordingly done at the encampment in the Great Meadows, and it certainly was not one of the least striking pictures presented in this wild campaign—the youthful commander presiding with calm seriousness over a motley assemblage of half-equipped soldiery, leathern-clad hunters and woodsmen, and painted savages with their wives and children, and uniting them all in solemn devotion by his own example and demeanor.

On the 10th there was agitation in the camp. Scouts hurried in with word, as Washington understood them, that a party of ninety Frenchmen were approaching. He instantly ordered out a hundred and fifty of his best men, put himself at their head and, leaving Major Muse with the rest to man the fort and mount the swivels, sallied forth "in the full hope," as he afterwards wrote to Governor Dinwiddie, "of procuring him another present of French prisoners."

It was another effervescence of his youthful military ardor and doomed to disappointment. The report of the scouts had either been exaggerated or misunderstood. The ninety Frenchmen in military array dwindled down into nine French deserters.

According to their account, the fort at the Fork was completed, and named Duquesne in honor of the Governor of Canada. It was proof against all attack excepting with bombs on the land side. The garrison did not exceed five hundred, but two hundred more were hourly expected, and nine hundred in the course of a fortnight.

Washington's suspicions with respect to La Force's party were justified by the report of these deserters. They had been sent out as spies and were to show the summons if discovered or overpowered. The French commander, they added, had been blamed for sending out so small a party.

On the same day Captain Mackay arrived with his independent company of South Carolinians. The cross-purposes which Washington had apprehended soon manifested themselves. The captain was civil and well disposed but full of formalities and points of etiquette. Holding a commission direct from the king, he could not bring himself to acknowledge a provincial officer as his superior. He encamped separately, kept separate guards, would not agree that Washington should assign any rallying place for his men in case of alarm, and objected to receive from him the parole and countersign, though necessary for their common safety.

Washington conducted himself with circumspection, avoiding everything that might call up a question of command and reasoning calmly whenever such question occurred. But he urged the governor by letter to prescribe their relative rank and authority. "He thinks you have not a power to give commissions that will command him. If so, I can very confidently say that his absence would tend to the public advantage."

On the 11th of June, Washington resumed the laborious march for Redstone Creek. As Captain Mackay could not oblige his men to work on the road unless they were allowed a shilling sterling a day, and as Washington did not choose to pay this nor to suffer them to march at their ease while his own faithful soldiers were laboriously employed, he left the captain and his independent company as a guard at Fort Necessity and undertook to complete the military road with his own men.

Accordingly, he and his Virginia troops toiled forward through the narrow defiles of the mountains, working on the road as they went. Scouts were sent out in all directions to prevent surprise. While on the march he was continually beset by sachems with their tedious ceremonials and speeches, all to very little purpose. Some of these chiefs were secretly in the French interest. Few rendered any real assistance and all expected presents.

At Gist's establishment, about thirteen miles from Fort Necessity, Washington received certain intelligence that ample reinforcements had arrived at Fort Duquesne and a large force would instantly be detached against him. Coming to a halt, he began to throw up intrenchments, calling in two foraging parties and sending word to Captain Mackay to join him with all speed. The captain and his company arrived in the evening, the foraging parties the next morning. A council of war was held, in which the idea of awaiting the enemy at this place was unanimously abandoned.

A rapid and toilsome retreat ensued. There was a deficiency of horses. Washington gave up his own to aid in transporting the military munitions, leaving his baggage to be brought on by soldiers, whom he paid liberally. The other officers followed his example. The weather was sultry, the roads were rough, provisions were scanty and the men dispirited by hunger. The Virginian soldiers took turns to drag the swivels but felt almost insulted by the conduct of the South Carolinians, who, piquing themselves upon their assumed privileges as "king's soldiers," sauntered along at their ease, refusing to act as pioneers or participate in the extra labors incident to a hurried retreat.

On the 1st of July they reached the Great Meadows. Here the Virginians, exhausted by fatigue, hunger and vexation, declared they would carry the baggage and drag the swivels no further. Contrary to his original intentions, therefore, Washington determined to halt here for the present and fortify, sending off expresses to hasten supplies and reinforcements from Wills' Creek, where he had reason to believe that two independent companies from New York were by this time arrived.

The retreat to the Great Meadows had not been in the least too precipitate. Captain de Villiers, a brother-in-law of Jumonville, had actually sallied forth from Fort Duquesne at the head of upwards of five hundred French and several hundred Indians, eager to avenge the death of his relative. Arriving about dawn of day at Gist's plantation, he surrounded the works which Washington had hastily thrown up there and fired into them. Finding them deserted, he concluded that those of whom he came in search had made good their retreat to the settlements and it was too late to pursue them. He was on the point of returning to Fort Duquesne when a deserter arrived, who gave word that Washington had come to a halt in the Great Meadows, where his troops were in a starving condition. For his own part, he added, hearing that the French were coming, he had deserted to them to escape starvation.

De Villiers ordered the fellow into confinement, to be rewarded if his words proved true, otherwise to be hanged. He then pushed forward for the Great Meadows.[2]

In the meantime Washington had exerted himself to enlarge

2 Hazard's *Register of Pennsylvania*, vol. iv., p. 22.

and strengthen Fort Necessity, nothing of which had been done by Captain Mackay and his men while encamped there. The fort was about a hundred feet square, protected by trenches and palisades. It stood on the margin of a small stream, nearly in the centre of the Great Meadows, which is a grassy plain, perfectly level, surrounded by wooded hills of a moderate height and at that place about two hundred and fifty yards wide. Washington asked no assistance from the South Carolina troops but set to work with his Virginians, animating them by word and example, sharing in the labor of felling trees, hewing off the branches and rolling up the trunks to form a breastwork.

At this critical juncture he was deserted by his Indian allies. They were disheartened at the scanty preparations for defense against a superior force, and offended at being subjected to military command. The half-king thought he had not been sufficiently consulted and that his advice had not been sufficiently followed. Such at least were some of the reasons which he subsequently gave for abandoning the youthful commander on the approach of danger. The true reason was a desire to put his wife and children in a place of safety. Most of his warriors followed his example. Very few, and those probably who had no families at risk, remained in the camp.

Early in the morning of the 3d, while Washington and his men were working on the fort, a sentinel came in wounded and bleeding, having been fired upon. Scouts brought word shortly afterwards that the French were in force about four miles off. Washington drew up his men on level ground outside of the works to await their attack. About 11 o'clock there was a firing of musketry from among trees on rising ground but so distant as to do no harm. Suspecting this to be a strategem designed to draw his men into the woods, he ordered them to keep quiet and refrain from firing until the foe should show themselves and draw near.

The firing was kept up but still under cover. He now fell back with his men into the trenches, ordering them to fire whenever they could get sight of an enemy. In this way there was skirmishing throughout the day, the French and Indians advancing as near as the covert of the woods would permit, which in the nearest place was sixty yards, but never into open sight. In the meanwhile the rain fell in torrents, the harassed and jaded troops were half drowned in their trenches, and many of their muskets were rendered unfit for use.

About eight at night the French requested a parley. Washington hesitated. It might be a stratagem to gain admittance for a spy into the fort. The request was repeated, with the addition that an officer might be sent to treat with them under their parole for his safety. Unfortunately the Chevalier de Peyrouney, engineer of the regiment and the only one who could speak French correctly, was wounded and disabled. Washington had to send, therefore, his ancient swordsman and interpreter, Jacob Van Braam. The captain returned twice with separate terms, in which the garrison was required to surrender. Both were rejected. He returned a third time, with written articles of capitulation. They were in French. As no implements for writing were at hand, Van Braam undertook to translate them by word of mouth. A candle was brought and held close to the paper while he read. The rain fell in torrents. It was difficult to keep the light from being extinguished. The captain rendered the capitulation article by article in mongrel English while Washington and his officers stood listening, endeavoring to disentangle the meaning. One article stipulated that on surrendering the fort they should leave all their military stores, munitions and artillery in possession of the French. This was objected to and was readily modified.

The main articles, as Washington and his officers understood them, were that they should be allowed to return to the settlements without molestation from French or Indians; that they should march out of the fort with the honors of war, drums beating and colors flying, and with all their effects and military stores excepting the artillery, which should be destroyed; that they should be allowed to deposit their effects in some secret place and leave a guard to protect them until they could send horses to bring them away—their horses having been nearly all killed or lost during the action; that they should give their word of honor not to attempt any buildings or improvements on the lands of His Most Christian Majesty for the space of a year; that the prisoners taken in the skirmish of Jumonville should be restored, and until their delivery Captain Van Braam and Captain Stobo should remain with the French as hostages.[3]

The next morning, accordingly, Washington and his men

[3] Horace Walpole, in a flippant notice of this capitulation, says: "The French have tied up the hands of an excellent *fanfaron*, a Major Washington, whom they took and engaged not to serve for one year." (*Correspondence*, vol. iii., p. 73.) Walpole, at this early date, seems to have considered Washington a perfect fire-eater.

marched out of their forlorn fortress with the honors of war, bearing with them their regimental colors but leaving behind a large flag too cumbrous to be transported. Scarcely had they begun their march, however, when, in defiance of the terms of capitulation, they were beset by a large body of Indians, allies to the French, who began plundering the baggage and committing other irregularities. Seeing that the French did not or could not prevent them and that all the baggage which could not be transported on the shoulders of his troops would fall into the hands of these savages, Washington ordered it to be destroyed, as well as the artillery, gunpowder and other military stores. All this detained him until ten o'clock, when he set out on his melancholy march. He had not proceeded above a mile when two or three of the wounded men were reported to be missing. He immediately detached a few men back in quest of them and continued on until three miles from Fort Necessity, where he encamped for the night and was rejoined by the stragglers.

In this affair, out of the Virginia regiment, consisting of three hundred and five men, officers included, twelve had been killed and forty-three wounded. The number killed and wounded in Captain Mackay's company is not known. The loss of the French and Indians is supposed to have been much greater.

In the following day's march the troops seemed jaded and disheartened. They were encumbered and delayed by the wounded. Provisions were scanty, and they had seventy weary miles to accomplish before they could meet with supplies. Washington, however, encouraged them by his own steadfast and cheerful demeanor and by sharing all their toils and privations and at length conducted them in safety to Wills' Creek, where they found ample provisions in the military magazines. Leaving them here to recover their strength, he proceeded with Captain Mackay to Williamsburg to make his military report to the governor.

A copy of the capitulation was subsequently laid before the Virginia House of Burgesses, with explanations. Notwithstanding the unfortunate result of the campaign, the conduct of Washington and his officers was properly appreciated and they received a vote of thanks for their bravery, and gallant defense of their country. Three hundred pistoles (nearly eleven hundred dollars) also were voted to be distributed among the privates who had been in action.

Early in August Washington rejoined his regiment, which had arrived at Alexandria by the way of Winchester. Letters from Governor Dinwiddie urged him to recruit it to the former number of three hundred men and join Colonel Innes at Wills' Creek, where that officer was stationed with Mackay's independent company of South Carolinians and two independent companies from New York, and had been employed in erecting a work to serve as a frontier post and rallying point, which work received the name of Fort Cumberland in honor of the Duke of Cumberland, captain-general of the British army.

In the meantime the French, elated by their recent triumph and thinking no danger at hand, relaxed their vigilance at Fort Duquesne. Stobo, who was a kind of prisoner at large there, found means to send a letter secretly by an Indian, dated July 28th and directed to the commander of the English troops. It was accompanied by a plan of the fort. "There are two hundred men here," writes he, "and two hundred expected. The rest have gone off in detachments to the amount of one thousand, besides Indians. None lodge in the fort but Contrecœur and the guard, consisting of forty men and five officers. The rest lodge in bark cabins around the fort. The Indians have access day and night and come and go when they please. If one hundred trusty Shawnees, Mingoes and Delawares were picked out they might surprise the fort, lodging themselves under the palisades by day, and at night secure the guard with their tomahawks, shut the sally-gate, and the fort is ours."

One part of Stobo's letter breathes a loyal and generous spirit of self-devotion. Alluding to the danger in which he and Van Braam, his fellow-hostage, might be involved, he says: "Consider the good of the expedition without regard to us. When we engaged to serve the country it was expected we were to do it with our lives. For my part, I would die a hundred deaths to have the pleasure of possessing this fort but one day. They are so vain of their success at the Meadows it is worse than death to hear them. Haste to strike."[4]

The Indian messenger carried the letter to Aughquick and delivered it into the hands of George Croghan. The Indian chiefs who were with him insisted upon his opening it. He did so, but on finding the tenor of it transmitted it to the Governor of Pennsyl-

[4] Hazard's *Register of Penn.*, iv., 329.

vania. The secret information communicated by Stobo may have been the cause of a project suddenly conceived by Governor Dinwiddie of a detachment which, by a forced march across the mountains, might descend upon the French and take Fort Duquesne at a single blow; or, failing that, might build a rival fort in its vicinity. He accordingly wrote to Washington to march forthwith for Wills' Creek with such companies as were complete, leaving orders with the officers to follow as soon as they should have enlisted men sufficient to make up their companies. "The season of the year," added he, "calls for despatch. I depend upon your usual diligence and spirit to encourage your people to be active on this occasion."

The ignorance of Dinwiddie in military affairs and his want of forecast led him perpetually into blunders. Washington saw the rashness of an attempt to dispossess the French with a force so inferior that it could be harassed and driven from place to place at their pleasure. Before the troops could be collected and munitions of war provided, the season would be too far advanced. There would be no forage for the horses, the streams would be swollen and unfordable, the mountains rendered impassable by snow and frost and slippery roads. The men, too, unused to campaigning on the frontier, would not bé able to endure a winter in the wilderness with no better shelter than a tent, especially in their present condition, destitute of almost everything. Such are a few of the cogent reasons urged by Washington in a letter to his friend William Fairfax, then in the House of Burgesses, which no doubt was shown to Governor Dinwiddie and probably had an effect in causing the rash project to be abandoned.

The governor, in truth, was sorely perplexed about this time by contradictions and cross-purposes both in military and civil affairs. A body of three hundred and fifty North Carolinian troops had been enlisted at high pay and were to form the chief reinforcement of Colonel Innes at Wills' Creek. By the time they reached Winchester, however, the provincial military chest was exhausted and future pay seemed uncertain, whereupon they refused to serve any longer, disbanded themselves tumultuously and set off for their homes without taking leave.

The governor found the House of Burgesses equally unmanageable. His demands for supplies were resisted on what he considered presumptuous pretexts, or granted sparingly under mortifying restrictions. His high Tory notions were outraged by such republican conduct. "There appears to me," said he, "an infatuation in all the assemblies in this part of the world." In a letter to the Board of Trade he declared that the only way effectually to check the progress of the French would be an act of parliament requiring the colonies to contribute to the common cause independently of assemblies; and in another, to the Secretary of State, he urged the policy of compelling the colonies to their duty to the king by a general poll-tax of two and sixpence a head. The worthy governor would have made a fitting counsellor for the Stuart dynasty. Subsequent events have shown how little his policy was suited to compete with the dawning republicanism of America.

In the month of October the House of Burgesses made a grant of twenty thousand pounds for the public service. And ten thousand more were sent out from England, beside a supply of fire-arms. The governor now applied himself to military matters with renewed spirit, increased the actual force to ten companies and, as there had been difficulties among the different kinds of troops with regard to precedence, he reduced them all to independent companies so that there would be no officer in a Virginia regiment above the rank of captain.

This shrewd measure, upon which Dinwiddie secretly prided himself as calculated to put an end to the difficulties in question, immediately drove Washington out of the service; considering it derogatory to his character to accept a lower commission than that under which his conduct had gained him a vote of thanks from the Legislature.

Governor Sharpe of Maryland, appointed by the king commander-in-chief of all the forces engaged against the French, sought to secure his valuable services and authorized Colonel Fitzhugh, whom he had placed in temporary command of the army, to write to him to that effect. The reply of Washington (15th November) is full of dignity and spirit and shows how deeply he felt his military degradation.

"You make mention," says he, "of my continuing in the service and retaining my colonel's commission. This idea has filled me with surprise, for if you think me capable of holding a commission that has neither rank nor emolument annexed to it you must maintain a very contemptible opinion of my weakness and believe me more empty than the commission itself." After intimating a suspicion that the project of reducing the regiment into independent companies and thereby throwing out the higher officers was "generated and hatched at Wills' Creek"—in other words was an expedient of Governor Dinwiddie instead of being a peremptory order from England—he adds: "Ingenuous treatment and plain dealing I at least expected. It is to be hoped the project will answer. It shall meet with my acquiescence in everything except personal services. I herewith inclose Governor Sharpe's letter, which I beg you will return to him with my acknowledgments for the favor he intended me. Assure him, sir, as you truly may, of my reluctance to quit the service and the pleasure I should have received in attending his fortunes. Inform him also that it was to obey the call of honor and the advice of my friends that I declined it, and not to gratify any desire I had to leave the military line. My feelings are strongly bent to arms."

Even had Washington hesitated to take this step, it would have been forced upon him by a further regulation of government in the course of the ensuing winter, settling the rank of officers of His Majesty's forces when joined of serving with the provincial forces in North America, "which directed that all such as were commissioned by the king or by his general commander-in-chief in North America should take rank of all officers commissioned by the governors of the respective provinces. And further, that the general and field officers of the provincial troops should have no rank when serving with the general and field officers commissioned by the crown, but that all captains and other inferior officers of the royal troops should take rank over provincial officers of the same grade, having older commissions."

These regulations, originating in that supercilious assumption of superiority which sometimes overruns and degrades true British pride, would have been spurned by Washington as insulting to the character and conduct of his high-minded brethren of the colonies. How much did this open disparagement of colonial honor and understanding contribute to wean from England the affection of her American subjects and prepare the way for their ultimate assertion of independence.

Chapter 5

WASHINGTON ON GENERAL BRADDOCK'S STAFF

Having resigned his commission and disengaged himself from public affairs, Washington's first care was to visit his mother, inquire into the state of domestic concerns and attend to the welfare of his brothers and sisters. In these matters he was ever his mother's adjunct and counsellor, discharging faithfully the duties of an eldest son, who should consider himself a second father to the family.

He now took up his abode at Mount Vernon and prepared to engage in those agricultural pursuits for which, even in his youthful days, he had as keen a relish as for the profession of arms. Scarcely had he entered upon his rural occupations, however, when the service of his country once more called him to the field.

The disastrous affair at the Great Meadows and the other acts of French hostility on the Ohio had roused the attention of the British ministry. The British government now prepared for military operations in America, none of them professedly aggressive, but rather to resist and counteract aggressions. A plan of campaign was devised for 1755, having four objects.

To eject the French from lands which they held unjustly in the province of Nova Scotia.

To dislodge them from a fortress which they had erected at Crown Point on Lake Champlain within what was claimed as British territory.

To dispossess them of the fort which they had constructed at Niagara between Lake Ontario and Lake Erie.

To drive them from the frontiers of Pennsylvania and Virginia and recover the valley of the Ohio.

The Duke of Cumberland, captain-general of the British army, had the organization of this campaign, and through his patronage

Major-general Edward Braddock was intrusted with the execution of it, being appointed generalissimo of all the forces in the colonies.

Braddock was a veteran in service and had been upwards of forty years in the Guards, that school of exact discipline and technical punctilio. Cumberland, who held a commission in the Guards and was bigoted to its routine, may have considered Braddock fitted, by his skill and preciseness as a tactician, for a command in a new country, inexperienced in military science, to bring its raw levies into order and to settle those questions of rank and etiquette apt to arise where regular and provincial troops are to act together.

The result proved the error of such an opinion. Braddock was a brave and experienced officer but his experience was that of routine and rendered him pragmatical and obstinate, impatient of novel expedients "not laid down in the books" but dictated by emergencies in a "new country," and his military precision, which would have been brilliant on parade, was a constant obstacle to alert action in the wilderness.[1]

Braddock was to lead in person the grand enterprise of the campaign, that destined for the frontiers of Virginia and Pennsylvania. It was the enterprise in which Washington became enlisted and, therefore, claims our especial attention.

Prior to the arrival of Braddock came out from England Lieutenant-colonel Sir John St. Clair, deputy quartermaster-general, eager to make himself acquainted with the field of operations. He

[1] Horace Walpole in his letters relates some anecdotes of Braddock which give a familiar picture of him in the fashionable life in which he had mingled in London and are of value as letting us into the private character of a man whose name has become proverbial in American history. "Braddock," says Walpole, "is a very Iroquois in disposition. He had a sister who, having gamed away all her little fortune at Bath, hanged herself with a truly English deliberation, leaving a note on the table with these lines: 'To die is landing on some silent shore,' etc. When Braddock was told of it, he only said: 'Poor Fanny! I always thought she would play till she would be forced to tuck herself up.' "

Braddock himself had been somewhat of a spendthrift. He was touchy also and punctilious. "He once had a duel," says Walpole, "with Colonel Glumley, Lady Bath's brother, who had been his great friend. As they were going to engage, Glumley, who had good humor and wit (Braddock had the latter), said: 'Braddock, you are a poor dog! here, take my purse. If you kill me you will be forced to run away and then you will not have a shilling to support you.' Braddock refused the purse, insisted on the duel, was disarmed and would not even ask for his life."

made a tour of inspection in company with Governor Sharpe of Maryland and appears to have been dismayed at sight of the impracticable wilderness, the region of Washington's campaign. From Fort Cumberland he wrote in February to Governor Morris of Pennsylvania to have the road cut or repaired toward the head of the river Youghiogheny and another opened from Philadelphia for the transportation of supplies. "No general," writes he, "will advance with an army without having a communication open to the provinces in his rear both for the security of retreat and to facilitate the transport of provisions, the supplying of which must greatly depend on your province."[2]

Unfortunately the Governor of Pennsylvania had no money at his command and was obliged for expenses to apply to his Assembly, "a set of men," writes he, "quite unacquainted with every kind of military service and exceedingly unwilling to part with money on any terms." However, by dint of exertions he procured the appointment of commissioners to explore the country and survey and lay out the roads required. At the head of the commission was George Croghan, the Indian trader. Times had gone hard with Croghan. The French had seized great quantities of his goods. The Indians with whom he traded had failed to pay their debts and he had become a bankrupt. Being an efficient agent on the frontier and among the Indians, he still enjoyed the patronage of the Pennsylvania government.

When Sir John St. Clair had finished his tour of inspection he descended Wills' Creek and the Potomac for two hundred miles in a canoe to Alexandria and repaired to Virginia to meet General Braddock. The latter had landed on the 20th of February at Hampton in Virginia and proceeded to Williamsburg to consult with Governor Dinwiddie. Shortly afterwards he was joined there by Commodore Keppel, whose squadron of two ships of war and several transports had anchored in the Chesapeake. On board of these ships were two prime regiments of about five hundred men each, one commanded by Sir Peter Halket, the other by Colonel Dunbar, together with a train of artillery and the necessary munitions of war. The regiments were to be augmented to seven hundred men each by men selected by Sir John St. Clair from Virginia companies recently raised.

Alexandria was fixed upon as the place where the troops should

[2] *Colonial Records*, vi., 300.

disembark and encamp. The ships were accordingly ordered up to that place and the levies directed to repair thither.

The plan of the campaign included the use of Indian allies. Governor Dinwiddie had already sent Christopher Gist, the pioneer, Washington's guide in 1753, to engage the Cherokees and Catawbas, the bravest of the Southern tribes, who he had no doubt would take up the hatchet for the English, peace being first concluded, through the mediation of his government, between them and the Six Nations. And he gave Braddock reason to expect at least four hundred Indians to join him at Fort Cumberland. He laid before him also contracts that he had made for cattle and promises that the Assembly of Pennsylvania had made of flour. These, with other supplies and a thousand barrels of beef on board of the transports, would furnish six months' provisions for four thousand men.

General Braddock apprehended difficulty in procuring wagons and horses sufficient to attend him in his march. Sir John St. Clair in the course of his tour of inspection had met with two Dutch settlers at the foot of the Blue Ridge who engaged to furnish two hundred wagons and fifteen hundred carrying horses, to be at Fort Cumberland early in May.

Governor Sharpe was to furnish above a hundred wagons for the transportation of stores on the Maryland side of the Potomac.

Keppel furnished four cannons from his ships for the attack on Fort Duquesne and thirty picked seamen to assist in dragging them over the mountains; for "soldiers," said he, "cannot be as well acquainted with the nature of purchases and making use of tackles as seamen." They were to aid also in passing the troops and artillery on floats or in boats across the rivers and were under the command of a midshipman and lieutenant.[3]

"Everything," writes Captain Robert Orme, one of the general's aides-de-camp, "seemed to promise so far the greatest success. The transports were all arrived safe and the men in health. Provisions, Indians, carriages and horses were already provided; at least were to be esteemed so, considering the authorities on which they were promised to the general."

Trusting to these arrangements, Braddock proceeded to Alexandria. The troops had all been disembarked before his arrival, and the Virginia levies selected by Sir John St. Clair to join the regiments of regulars, were arrived. There were beside two companies of hatchet men, or carpenters, six of rangers and one troop of light horse. The levies having been clothed, were ordered to march immediately for Winchester, to be armed, and the general gave them in charge of an ensign of the 44th, "to make them as like soldiers as possible."[4] The light horse were retained by the general as his escort and body-guard.

The din and stir of warlike preparation disturbed the quiet of Mount Vernon. Washington looked down from his rural retreat upon the ships of war and transports as they passed up the Potomac with the array of arms gleaming along their decks. The booming of cannon echoed among his groves. Alexandria was but a few miles distant. Occasionally he mounted his horse and rode to that place. It was like a garrisoned town, teeming with troops and resounding with the drum and fife. A brilliant campaign was about to open under the auspices of an experienced general and with all the means and appurtenances of European warfare. How different from the starveling expeditions he had hitherto been doomed to conduct! What an opportunity to efface the memory of his recent disaster! All his thoughts of rural life were put to flight. The military part of his character was again in the ascendant. His great desire was to join the expedition as a volunteer.

It was reported to General Braddock. The latter was apprised by Governor Dinwiddie and others of Washington's personal merits, his knowledge of the country and his experience in frontier service. The consequence was a letter from Captain Orme, written by the general's order, inviting Washington to join his staff. The letter concluded with frank and cordial expressions of esteem on the part of Orme, which were warmly reciprocated and laid the foundation of a soldierlike friendship between them.

A volunteer situation on the staff of General Braddock offered no emolument nor command and would be attended with considerable expense beside a sacrifice of his private interests, having no person in whom he had confidence to take charge of his affairs in his absence. Still he did not hesitate a moment to accept the invitation. In the position offered to him all the questions of military rank which had hitherto annoyed him would be obviated. He could indulge his passion for arms without any sacrifice of dignity, and he looked forward with high anticipation to an opportunity of acquiring military experience in a corps well organized and

[4] Orme's *Journal*.

thoroughly disciplined, and in the family of a commander of acknowledged skill as a tactician.

His arrival [at the headquarters of General Braddock at Alexandria] was hailed by his young associates, Captains Orme and Morris, the general's aides-de-camp, who at once received him into frank companionship, and a cordial intimacy commenced between them that continued throughout the campaign.

He experienced a courteous reception from the general, who expressed in flattering terms the impression he had received of his merits. Washington soon appreciated the character of the general. He found him stately and somewhat haughty, exact in matters of military etiquette and discipline, positive in giving an opinion and obstinate in maintaining it, but of an honorable and generous though somewhat irritable nature.

There were at that time four governors beside Dinwiddie assembled at Alexandria at Braddock's request to concert a plan of military operations—Governor Shirley of Massachusetts, Lieutenant-Governor Delancey of New York, Lieutenant-Governor Sharpe of Maryland, Lieutenant-Governor Morris of Pennsylvania. Washington was presented to them in a manner that showed how well his merits were already appreciated. Shirley seems particularly to have struck him as the model of a gentleman and statesman. He was originally a lawyer and had risen not more by his talents than by his implicit devotion to the crown. His son William was military secretary to Braddock.

A grand council was held on the 14th of April, composed of General Braddock, Commodore Keppel and the governors, at which the general's commission was read, as were his instructions from the king, relating to a common fund to be established by the several colonies toward defraying the expenses of the campaign.

The governors were prepared to answer on this head, letters to the same purport having been addressed to them by Sir Thomas Robinson, one of the king's secretaries of state, in the preceding month of October. They informed Braddock that they had applied to their respective Assemblies for the establishment of such a fund, but in vain, and gave it as their unanimous opinion that such a fund could never be established in the colonies without the aid of Parliament. They had found it impracticable, also, to obtain from their respective governments the proportions expected from them by the crown toward military expenses in

America, and suggested that ministers should find out some mode of compelling them to do it and that in the meantime the general should make use of his credit upon government for current expenses, lest the expedition should come to a stand.[5]

In discussing the campaign, the governors were of opinion that New York should be made the centre of operations, as it afforded easy access by water to the heart of the French possessions in Canada. Braddock, however, did not feel at liberty to depart from his instructions, which specified the recent establishments of the French on the Ohio as the objects of his expedition.

The business of the Congress being finished, General Braddock would have set out for Fredericktown in Maryland, but few wagons or teams had yet come to remove the artillery. Washington had looked with wonder and dismay at the huge paraphernalia of war and the world of superfluities to be transported across the mountains, recollecting the difficulties he had experienced in getting over them with his nine swivels and scanty supplies. "If our march is to be regulated by the slow movements of the train," said he, "it will be tedious, very tedious indeed."

His predictions excited a sarcastic smile in Braddock as betraying the limited notions of a young provincial officer little acquainted with the march of armies.

Braddock set out from Alexandria on the 20th of April. Washington remained behind a few days to arrange his affairs, and then rejoined him at Fredericktown in Maryland where, on the 10th of May, he was proclaimed one of the general's aides-de-camp. The troubles of Braddock had already commenced. The Virginian contractors failed to fulfil their engagements. Of all the immense means of transportation so confidently promised, but fifteen wagons and a hundred draught-horses had arrived and there was no prospect of more. There was equal disappointment in provisions both as to quantity and quality, and he had to send round the country to buy cattle for the subsistence of the troops.

Braddock, attended by his staff and his guard of light horse, set off for Wills' Creek by the way of Winchester, the road along the north side of the Potomac not being yet made. "This gave him," writes Washington, "a good opportunity to see the absurdity of the route and of damning it very heartily."[6]

[5] *Colonial Records*, vol. vi., p. 366.
[6] Draft of a letter, among Washington's papers, addressed to Major John Carlyle.

Three of Washington's horses were knocked up before they reached Winchester, and he had to purchase others. This was a severe drain of his campaigning purse. Fortunately he was in the neighborhood of Greenway Court and was enabled to replenish it by a loan from his old friend Lord Fairfax.

The discomforts of the rough road were increased with the general by his travelling with some degree of state in a chariot which he had purchased of Governor Sharpe. In this he dashed by Dunbar's division of the troops, which he overtook near Wills' Creek, his bodyguard of light horse galloping on each side of his chariot, and his staff accompanying him, the drums beating the Grenadiers' March as he passed. In this style too he arrived at Fort Cumberland, amid a thundering salute of seventeen guns.[7]

By this time the general discovered that he was not in a region fitted for such display, and his travelling chariot was abandoned at Fort Cumberland, otherwise it would soon have become a wreck among the mountains beyond.

By the 19th of May the forces were assembled at Fort Cumberland: the two royal regiments, originally one thousand strong, now increased to fourteen hundred by men chosen from the Maryland and Virginia levies; two provincial companies of carpenters or pioneers, thirty men each, with subalterns and captains; a company of guides composed of a captain, two aids and ten men; the troop of Virginia light horse, commanded by Captain Stewart; the detachment of thirty sailors with their officers; and the remnants of two independent companies from New York, one of which was commanded by Captain Horatio Gates, of whom we shall have to speak much hereafter in the course of this biography.

Another person in camp of subsequent notoriety and who became a warm friend of Washington was Dr. Hugh Mercer, a Scotchman about thirty-three years of age. About ten years previously he had served as assistant surgeon in the forces of Charles Edward and followed his standard to the disastrous field of Culloden. After the defeat of the "chevalier," Mercer had escaped by the way of Inverness to America and taken up his residence in Virginia. He was now with the Virginia troops, rallying under the standard of the House of Hanover in an expedition led by a general who had aided to drive the chevalier from Scotland.

Another young Scotchman in the camp was Dr. James Craik,

<hr>

[7] *Journal of the Seamen's Detachment.*

who had become strongly attached to Washington, being about the same age and having been with him in the affair of the Great Meadows, serving as surgeon in the Virginia regiment, to which he still belonged.

At Fort Cumberland, Washington had an opportunity of seeing a force encamped according to the plan approved of by the council of war, and military tactics enforced with all the precision of a martinet.

There was great detention at the fort, caused by the want of forage and supplies, the road not having been finished from Philadelphia. Mr. Richard Peters, the secretary of Governor Morris, was in camp to attend to the matter. He had to bear the brunt of Braddock's complaints. The general declared he would not stir from Wills' Creek until he had the governor's assurance that the road would be opened in time. Mr. Peters requested guards to protect the men, while at work, from attacks by the Indians. Braddock swore he would not furnish guards for the wood-cutters—"Let Pennsylvania do it!" He scoffed at the talk about danger from Indians. Peters endeavored to make him sensible of the peril which threatened him in this respect. Should an army of them, led by French officers, beset him in his march he would not be able, with all his strength and military skill, to reach Fort Duquesne without a body of rangers, as well on foot as horseback. The general, however, "despised his observations."[8] Still, guards had ultimately to be provided or the work on the road would have been abandoned.

Braddock in fact was completely chagrined and disappointed about the Indians. The Cherokees and Catawbas, whom Dinwiddie had given him reason to expect in such numbers, never arrived.

During the halt of the troops at Wills' Creek, Washington had been sent to Williamsburg to bring on four thousand pounds for the military chest. He returned after a fortnight's absence, escorted from Winchester by eight men, "which eight men," writes he, "were two days assembling but I believe would not have been more than as many seconds dispersing if I had been attacked."

He found the general out of all patience and temper at the delays and disappointments in regard to horses, wagons and forage, making no allowances for the difficulties incident to a new

[8] *Colonial Records*, vi., p. 396.

country and to the novel and great demands upon its scanty and scattered resources. He accused the army contractors of want of faith, honor and honesty, and in his moments of passion, which were many, extended the stigma to the whole country. This stung the patriotic sensibility of Washington and overcame his usual self-command, and the proud and passionate commander was occasionally surprised by a well-merited rebuke from his aide-de-camp. "We have frequent disputes on this head," writes Washington, "which are maintained with warmth on both sides, especially on his, as he is incapable of arguing without it or of giving up any point he asserts, be it ever so incompatible with reason or common sense."

The same pertinacity was maintained with respect to the Indians. George Croghan informed Washington that the sachems considered themselves treated with slight, in never being consulted in war matters; that he himself had repeatedly offered the services of the warriors under his command as scouts and outguards, but his offers had been rejected. Washington ventured to interfere and to urge their importance for such purposes, especially now when they were approaching the stronghold of the enemy. As usual, the general remained bigoted in his belief of the all-sufficiency of well-disciplined troops.

Either from disgust thus caused, or from being actually dismissed, the warriors began to disappear from the camp. It is said that Colonel Innes, who was to remain in command at Fort Cumberland, advised the dismissal of all but a few to serve as guides. Certain it is, before Braddock recommenced his march none remained to accompany him but Scarooyadi and eight of his warriors.

Seeing the general's impatience at the nonarrival of conveyances, Washington again represented to him the difficulties he would encounter in attempting to traverse the mountains with such a train of wheel-carriages, assuring him it would be the most arduous part of the campaign, and recommended from his own experience the substitution as much as possible of pack-horses. Braddock, however, had not been sufficiently harassed by frontier campaigning to depart from his European modes or to be swayed in his military operations by so green a counsellor.

Chapter 6

DEFEAT AND DEATH OF BRADDOCK

On the 10th of June, Braddock set off from Fort Cumberland with his aides-de-camp and others of his staff, and his body-guard of light horse. Sir Peter Halket, with his brigade, had marched three days previously, and a detachment of six hundred men under the command of Colonel Chapman and the supervision of Sir John St. Clair had been employed upwards of ten days in cutting down trees, removing rocks and opening a road.

The march over the mountain proved, as Washington had foretold, a "tremendous undertaking." It was with difficulty the heavily laden wagons could be dragged up the steep and rugged roads, newly made or imperfectly repaired. Often they extended for three or four miles in a straggling and broken line, with the soldiers so dispersed in guarding them that an attack on any side would have thrown the whole in confusion. It was the dreary region of the great Savage Mountain and the "Shades of Death" that was again made to echo with the din of arms.

What outraged Washington's notions of the abstemious frugality suitable to campaigning in the "backwoods" was the great number of horses and wagons required by the officers for the transportation of their baggage, camp equipage and a thousand articles of artificial necessity. Simple himself in his tastes and habits and manfully indifferent to personal indulgences, he almost doubted whether such sybarites in the camp could be efficient in the field.

By the time the advanced corps had struggled over two mountains and through the intervening forest and reached (16th June) the Little Meadows, where Sir John St. Clair had made a temporary camp, General Braddock had become aware of the difference between campaigning in a new country or on the old, well-beaten battle-grounds of Europe. He now of his own accord turned to Washington for advice though it must have been a sore trial to his pride to seek it of so young a man, but he had by this time sufficient proof of his sagacity and his knowledge of the frontier.

Thus unexpectedly called on, Washington gave his counsel with becoming modesty but with his accustomed clearness. There was just now an opportunity to strike an effective blow at Fort Duquesne, but it might be lost by delay. The garrison, according to credible reports, was weak. Large reinforcements and supplies which were on their way would be detained by the drought, which rendered the river by which they must come low and unnavigable. The blow must be struck before they could arrive. He advised the general, therefore, to divide his forces, leave one part to come on with the stores and baggage and all the cumbrous appurtenances of an army, and to throw himself in the advance with the other part, composed of his choicest troops, lightened of everything superfluous that might impede a rapid march.

His advice was adopted. Twelve hundred men selected out of all the companies and furnished with ten field-pieces were to form the first division, their provisions and other necessaries to be carried on pack-horses. The second division, with all the stores, munitions and heavy baggage, was to be brought on by Colonel Dunbar.

The least practicable part of the arrangement was with regard to the officers of the advance. Washington had urged a retrenchment of their baggage and camp equipage, that as many of their horses as possible might be used as pack-horses. Here was the difficulty. Brought up, many of them, in fashionable and luxurious life or the loitering indulgence of country quarters, they were so encumbered with what they considered indispensable necessaries that out of two hundred and twelve horses generally appropriated to their use, not more than a dozen could be spared by them for the public service. Washington, in his own case, acted up to the advice he had given. He retained no more clothing and effects with him than would about half fill a portmanteau, and gave up his best steed as a pack-horse, which he never heard of afterwards.[1]

On the 19th of June, Braddock's first division set out with less than thirty carriages, including those that transported ammunition for the artillery, all strongly horsed. The Indians marched

[1] Letter to J. Augustine Washington. Sparks, ii., 81.

with the advanced party. In the course of the day, Scarooyadi and his son being at a small distance from the line of march, were surrounded and taken by some French and Indians. His son escaped and brought intelligence to his warriors. They hastened to rescue or revenge him but found him tied to a tree. The French had been disposed to shoot him but their savage allies declared they would abandon them should they do so, having some tie of friendship or kindred with the chieftain, who thus rejoined the troops unharmed.

Washington was disappointed in his anticipations of rapid march. The general, though he had adopted his advice in the main, could not carry it out in detail. His military education was in the way. Bigoted to the regular and elaborate tactics of Europe, he could not stoop to make-shift expedients of a new country where every difficulty is encountered and mastered in a rough-and-ready style. "I found," said Washington, "that instead of pushing on with vigor, without regarding a little rough road, they were halting to level every molehill and to erect bridges over every brook, by which means we were four days in getting twelve miles."

For several days Washington had suffered from fever accompanied by intense headache, and his illness increased in violence to such a degree that he was unable to ride and had to be conveyed for a part of the time in a covered wagon. His illness continued without intermission until the 23d, "when I was relieved," says he, "by the general's absolutely ordering the physician to give me Dr. James' powders, one of the most excellent medicines in the world. It gave me immediate relief and removed my fever and other complaints in four days' time."

He was still unable to bear the jolting of the wagon but it needed another interposition of the kindly-intended authority of General Braddock to bring him to a halt at the great crossings of the Youghiogheny. There the general assigned him a guard, provided him with necessaries and requested him to remain under care of his physician, Dr. Craik, until the arrival of Colonel Dunbar's detachment, which was two days' march in the rear, giving him his word of honor that he should at all events he enabled to rejoin the main division before it reached the French fort.[2]

This kind solicitude on the part of Braddock shows the real estimation in which he was held by that officer. Doctor Craik

[2] Letter to John Augustine Washington. Sparks, ii., 80.

backed the general's orders by declaring that should Washington persevere in his attempts to go on in the condition he then was, his life would be in danger. Orme also joined his entreaties and promised, if he would remain, he would keep him informed by letter of every occurrence of moment.

Notwithstanding all kind assurances of Braddock and his aide-de-camp Orme, it was with gloomy feelings that Washington saw the troops depart, fearful he might not be able to rejoin them in time for the attack upon the fort, which, he assured his brother aide-de-camp, he would not miss for five hundred pounds.

Leaving Washington at the Youghiogheny, we will follow the march of Braddock. In the course of the first day (June 24th), he came to a deserted Indian camp. Judging from the number of wigwams, there must have been about one hundred and seventy warriors. Some of the trees about it had been stripped, and painted with threats and bravadoes and scurrilous taunts written on them in the French language, showing that there were white men with the savages.

The next morning at daybreak three men venturing beyond the sentinels were shot and scalped. Parties were immediately sent out to scour the woods and drive in the stray horses.

The day's march passed by the Great Meadows and Fort Necessity, the scene of Washington's capitulation. Several Indians were seen hovering in the woods, and the light horse and Indian allies were sent out to surround them but did not succeed. In crossing a mountain beyond the Great Meadows, the carriages had to be lowered with the assistance of the sailors by means of tackle. The camp for the night was about two miles beyond Fort Necessity. Several French and Indians endeavored to reconnoiter it but were fired upon by the advanced sentinels.

The following day (26th) there was a laborious march of but four miles owing to the difficulties of the road. The evening halt was at another deserted Indian camp, strongly posted on a high rock, with a steep and narrow ascent. It had a spring in the middle and stood at the termination of the Indian path to the Monongahela. By this pass the party had come which attacked Washington the year before in the Great Meadows. The Indians and French, too, who were hovering about the army, had just left this camp. The fires they had left were yet burning. The French had inscribed their names on some of the trees with insulting bravadoes and the Indians had designated in triumph the scalps they had taken two days previously. A party was sent out with guides to follow their tracks and fall on them in the night, but again without success. In fact, it was the Indian boast that throughout this march of Braddock they saw him every day from the mountains and expected to be able to shoot down his soldiers "like pigeons."

The march continued to be toilful and difficult. On one day it did not exceed two miles, having cut a passage over a mountain. In cleaning their guns the men were ordered to draw the charge instead of firing it off. No fire was to be lighted in front of the pickets. At night the men were to take their arms into the tents with them.

Further on the precautions became still greater. On the advanced pickets the men were in two divisions, relieving each other every two hours. Half remained on guard with fixed bayonets, the other half lay down by their arms. The picket sentinels were doubled.

On the 4th of July they encamped at Thicketty Run. The country was less mountainous and rocky, and the woods, consisting chiefly of white pine, were more open. The general now supposed himself to be within thirty miles of Fort Duquesne. Ever since his halt at the deserted camp on the rock beyond the Great Meadows, he had endeavored to prevail upon the Croghan Indians to scout in the direction of the fort and bring him intelligence, but never could succeed. They had probably been deterred by the number of French and Indian tracks and by the recent capture of Scarooyadi. This day, however, two consented to reconnoiter, and shortly after their departure Christopher Gist, the resolute pioneer who acted as guide to the general, likewise set off as a scout.

The Indians returned on the 6th. They had been close to Fort Duquesne. There were no additional works there. They saw a few boats under the fort and one with a white flag coming down the Ohio, but there were few men to be seen and few tracks of any. They came upon an unfortunate officer, shooting within half a mile of the fort, and brought a scalp as a trophy of his fate. None of the passes between the camp and fort were occupied. They believed there were few men abroad reconnoitering.

Gist returned soon after them. His account corroborated theirs but he had seen a smoke in a valley between the camp and the fort, made probably by some scouting party. He had intended to prowl about the fort at night but had been discovered and pursued by two Indians, and narrowly escaped with his life.

On the same day, during the march, three or four loitering in the rear of the grenadiers were killed and scalped. Several of the grenadiers set off to take revenge. They came upon a party of Indians, who held up boughs and grounded their arms, the concerted sign of amity. Not perceiving or understanding it, the grenadiers fired upon them and one fell. It proved to be the son of Scarooyadi. Aware too late of their error, the grenadiers brought the body to the camp. The conduct of Braddock was admirable on the occasion. He sent for the father and the other Indians and condoled with them on the lamentable occurrence, making them the customary presents of expiation. But what was more to the point, he caused the youth to be buried with the honors of war. At his request the officers attended the funeral and a volley was fired over the grave.

These soldierlike tributes of respect to the deceased and sympathy with the survivors soothed the feelings and gratified the pride of the father and attached him more firmly to the service. We are glad to record an anecdote so contrary to the general contempt for the Indians with which Braddock stands charged. It speaks well for the real kindness of his heart.

We will now return to Washington in his sick encampment on the banks of the Youghiogheny, where he was left repining at the departure of the troops without him. To add to his annoyances, his servant, John Alton, a faithful Welshman, was taken ill with the same malady, and was unable to render him any services. Letters from his fellow aides-de-camp showed him the kind solicitude that was felt concerning him. At the general's desire Captain Morris wrote to him, informing him of their intended halts.

"It is the desire of every individual in the family," adds he, "and the general's positive commands to you not to stir but by the advice of the person [Dr. Craik] under whose care you are, till you are better, which we all hope will be very soon."

Orme, too, according to promise, kept him informed of the incidents of the march, the frequent night alarms and occasional scalping parties. The night alarms Washington considered mere feints designed to harass the men and retard the march. The enemy, he was sure, had not sufficient force for a serious attack. And he was glad to learn from Orme that the men were in high spirits and confident of success.

He now considered himself sufficiently recovered to rejoin the troops, and his only anxiety was that he should not be able to do it in time for the great blow. He was rejoiced therefore on the 3d of July by the arrival of an advanced party of one hundred men convoying provisions. Being still too weak to mount his horse, he set off with the escort in a covered wagon, and after a most fatiguing journey over mountain and through forest reached Braddock's camp on the 8th of July. It was on the east side of the Monongahela, about two miles from the river, in the neighborhood of the town of Queen Aliquippa and about fifteen miles from Fort Duquesne.

In consequence of adhering to technical rules and military forms, General Braddock had consumed a month in marching little more than a hundred miles. The tardiness of his progress was regarded with surprise and impatience even in Europe, where his patron, the Duke of Brunswick, was watching the events of the campaign he had planned. "The Duke," writes Horace Walpole, "is much dissatisfied at the slowness of General Braddock, who does not march as if he was at all impatient to be scalped." The insinuation of the satirical wit was unmerited. Braddock was a stranger to fear, but in his movements he was fettered by system.

Washington was warmly received on his arrival, especially by his fellow aides-de-camp, Morris and Orme. He was just in time, for the attack upon Fort Duquesne was to be made on the following day. The neighboring country had been reconnoitered to determine upon a plan of attack. The fort stood on the same side of the Monongahela with the camp but there was a narrow pass between them of about two miles, with the river on the left and a very high mountain on the right, and in its present state quite impassable for carriages. The route determined on was to cross the Monongahela by a ford immediately opposite to the camp, proceed along the west bank of the river for about five miles, then recross by another ford to the eastern side and push on to the fort. The river at these fords was shallow and the banks were not steep.

According to the plan of arrangement Lieutenant-Colonel Gage, with the advance, was to cross the river before daybreak, march to the second ford and, recrossing there, take post to secure the passage of the main force. The advance was to be composed of two companies of grenadiers, one hundred and sixty infantry, the independent company of Captain Horatio Gates, and two six-pounders.

Washington, who had already seen enough of regular troops to doubt their infallibility in wild bush-fighting, and who knew the dangerous nature of the ground they were to traverse, ventured to suggest that on the following day the Virginia rangers, being accustomed to the country and to Indian warfare, might be thrown in the advance. The proposition drew an angry reply from the general, indignant very probably that a young provincial officer should presume to school a veteran like himself.

Early next morning (July 9th) before daylight Colonel Gage crossed with the advance. He was followed at some distance by Sir John St. Clair, quartermaster-general, with a working party of two hundred and fifty men to make roads for the artillery and baggage. They had with them their wagons of tools and two six-pounders. A party of about thirty savages rushed out of the woods as Colonel Gage advanced but were put to flight before they had done any harm.

By sunrise the main body turned out in full uniform. At the beating of "the general" their arms, which had been cleaned the night before, were charged with fresh cartridges. The officers were perfectly equipped. All looked as if arrayed for a *fête* rather than a battle. Washington, who was still weak and unwell, mounted his horse and joined the staff of the general, who was scrutinizing everything with the eye of a martinet. As it was supposed the enemy would be on the watch for the crossing of the troops, it had been agreed that they should do it in the greatest order, with bayonets fixed, colors flying and drums and fifes beating and playing.[3] They accordingly made a gallant appearance as they forded the Monongahela and wound along its banks and through the open forests, gleaming and glittering in morning sunshine and stepping buoyantly to the "Grenadiers' March."

Washington, with his keen and youthful relish for military affairs, was delighted with their perfect order and equipment, so different from the rough bush-fighters to which he had been accustomed. Roused to new life, he forgot his recent ailments and broke forth in expressions of enjoyment and admiration as he rode

[3] Orme's *Journal.*

in company with his fellow aides-de-camp, Orme and Morris. Often in after life he used to speak of the effect upon him of the first sight of a well-disciplined European army marching in high confidence and bright array on the eve of a battle.

About noon they reached the second ford. Gage, with the advance, was on the opposite side of the Monongahela, posted according to orders, but the river bank had not been sufficiently sloped. The artillery and baggage drew up along the beach and halted until one, when the second crossing took place, drums beating, fifes playing and colors flying as before. When all had passed there was again a halt close by a small stream called Frazier's Run until the general arranged the order of march.

First went the advance under Gage, preceded by the engineers and guides and six light horsemen.

Then, Sir John St. Clair and the working party, with their wagons and the two six-pounders. On each side were thrown out four flanking parties.

Then, at some distance, the general was to follow with the main body. The artillery and baggage were preceded and flanked by light horse and squads of infantry, while the Virginian and other provincial troops were to form the rear-guard.

The ground before them was level until about half a mile from the river, where a rising ground, covered with long grass, low bushes and scattered trees, sloped gently up to a range of hills. The whole country, generally speaking, was a forest, with no clear opening but the road, which was about twelve feet wide and flanked by two ravines, concealed by trees and thickets.

Had Braddock been schooled in the warfare of the woods or had he adopted the suggestions of Washington, which he rejected so impatiently, he would have thrown out Indian scouts or Virginian rangers in the advance and on the flanks to beat up the woods and ravines. But, as has been sarcastically observed, he suffered his troops to march forward through the centre of the plain with merely their usual guides and flanking parties, "as if in a review in St. James's Park."

It was now near two o'clock. The advanced party and the working party had crossed the plain and were ascending the rising ground. Braddock was about to follow with the main body and had given the word to march when he heard an excessively quick and heavy firing in front. Washington, who was with the general, surmised that the evil he had apprehended had come to pass. For want of scouting parties ahead, the advance parties were suddenly and warmly attacked. Braddock ordered Lieutenant-Colonel Burton to hasten to their assistance with the vanguard of the main body, eight hundred strong. The residue, four hundred, were halted, and posted to protect the artillery and baggage.

The firing continued with fearful yelling. There was a terrible uproar. By the general's orders an aide-de-camp spurred forward to bring him an account of the nature of the attack. Without waiting for his return the general himself, finding the turmoil increase, moved forward, leaving Sir Peter Halket with the command of the baggage.[4]

The van of the advance had indeed been taken by surprise. It was composed of two companies of pioneers to cut the road and two flank companies of grenadiers to protect them. Suddenly the engineer who preceded them to mark out the road gave the alarm, "French and Indians!" A body of them was approaching rapidly, cheered on by a Frenchman in gayly fringed hunting-shirt, whose gorget showed him to be an officer. There was sharp firing on both sides at first. Several of the enemy fell, among them their leader, but a murderous fire broke out from among trees and a ravine on the right, and the woods resounded with unearthly whoops and yellings. The Indian rifle was at work, levelled by unseen hands. Most of the grenadiers and many of the pioneers were shot down. The survivors were driven in on the advance.

Gage ordered his men to fix bayonets and form in order of battle. They did so in hurry and trepidation. He would have scaled a hill on the right whence there was the severest firing. Not a platoon would quit the line of march. They were more dismayed by the yells than by the rifles of the unseen savages. The latter extended themselves along the hill and in the ravines but their whereabouts was only known by their demoniac cries and the puffs of smoke from their rifles. The soldiers fired wherever they saw the smoke. Their officers tried in vain to restrain them until they should see their foe. All orders were unheeded. In their fright they shot at random, killing some of their own flanking parties and of the vanguard as they came running in. The covert fire grew more intense. In a short time most of the officers and many of the men of the advance were killed or wounded. Colonel Gage him-

[4] Orme's *Journal*

self received a wound. The advance fell back in dismay upon Sir John St. Clair's corps, which was equally dismayed. The cannon belonging to it were deserted.

Colonel Burton had come up with the reinforcement and was forming his men to face the rising ground on the right, when both of the advanced detachments fell back upon him, and all now was confusion.

By this time the general was upon the ground. He tried to rally the men. "They would fight," they said, "if they could see their enemy, but it was useless to fire at trees and bushes, and they could not stand to be shot down by an invisible foe."

The colors were advanced in different places to separate the men of the two regiments. The general ordered the officers to form the men, tell them off into small divisions and advance with them. But the soldiers could not be prevailed upon either by threats or entreaties. The Virginia troops, accustomed to the Indian mode of fighting, scattered themselves and took post behind trees, whence they could pick off the lurking foe. In this way they in some degree protected the regulars. Washington advised General Braddock to adopt the same plan with the regulars but he persisted in forming them into platoons, consequently they were cut down from behind logs and trees as fast as they could advance. Several attempted to take to the trees without orders but the general stormed at them, called them cowards and even struck them with the flat of his sword. Several of the Virginians who had taken post and were doing good service in this manner were slain by the fire of the regulars, directed wherever a smoke appeared among the trees.

The officers behaved with consummate bravery, and Washington beheld with admiration those who, in camp or on the march, had appeared to him to have an almost effeminate regard for personal ease and convenience now exposing themselves to imminent death with a courage that kindled with the thickening horrors. In the vain hope of inspiriting the men to drive off the enemy from the flanks and regain the cannon, they would dash forward singly or in groups. They were invariably shot down, for the Indians aimed from their coverts at every one on horseback or who appeared to have command.

Some were killed by random shot of their own men, who, crowded in masses, fired with affrighted rapidity but without aim. Soldiers in the front ranks were killed by those in the rear. Between friend and foe the slaughter of the officers was terrible. All this while the woods resounded with the unearthly yellings of the savages; and now and then one of them, hideously painted and ruffling with feathered crest, would rush forth to scalp an officer who had fallen or seize a horse galloping wildly without a rider.

Throughout this disastrous day Washington distinguished himself by his courage and presence of mind. His brother aides, Orme and Morris, were wounded and disabled early in the action and the whole duty of carrying the orders of the general devolved on him. His danger was imminent and incessant. He was in every part of the field, a conspicuous mark for the murderous rifle. Two horses were shot under him. Four bullets passed through his coat. His escape without a wound was almost miraculous. Dr. Craik, who was on the field attending to the wounded, watched him with anxiety as he rode about in the most exposed manner, and used to say that he expected every moment to see him fall. At one time he was sent to the main body to bring the artillery into action. All there was likewise in confusion, for the Indians had extended themselves along the ravine so as to flank the reserve and carry slaughter into the ranks. Sir Peter Halket had been shot down at the head of his regiment. The men who should have served the guns were paralyzed. Had they raked the ravines with grape-shot the day might have been saved. In his ardor Washington sprang from his horse, wheeled and pointed a brass field-piece with his own hand and directed an effective discharge into the woods, but neither his efforts nor example were of avail. The men could not be kept to the guns.

Braddock still remained in the centre of the field in the desperate hope of retrieving the fortunes of the day. The Virginia rangers, who had been most efficient in covering his position, were nearly all killed or wounded. His secretary, Shirley, had fallen by his side. Many of his officers had been slain within his sight, and many of his guard of Virginia light horse. Five horses had been killed under him. Still he kept his ground, vainly endeavoring to check the flight of his men, or at least to effect their retreat in good order. At length a bullet passed through his right arm and lodged itself in his lungs. He fell from his horse but was caught by Captain Stewart of the Virginia guards, who, with the assistance of another American and a servant, placed him in a tumbril. It was with much difficulty they got him out of the field—in his despair he desired to be left there.[5]

The rout now became complete. Baggage, stores, artillery, everything was abandoned. The wagoners took each a horse out of his team and fled. The officers were swept off with the men in this headlong flight. It was rendered more precipitate by the shouts and yells of the savages, numbers of whom rushed forth from their coverts and pursued the fugitives to the river side, killing several as they dashed across in tumultuous confusion. Fortunately for the latter, the victors gave up the pursuit in their eagerness to collect the spoil.

The shattered army continued its flight after it had crossed the Monongahela, a wretched wreck of the brilliant little force that had recently gleamed along its banks, confident of victory. Out of eighty-six officers, twenty-six had been killed and thirty-six wounded. The number of rank and file killed and wounded was upwards of seven hundred. The Virginia corps had suffered the most. One company had been almost annihilated. Another, beside those killed and wounded in the ranks, had lost all its officers, even to the corporal.

About a hundred men were brought to a halt about a quarter of a mile from the ford of the river. Here was Braddock with his wounded aides-de-camp and some of his officers, Dr. Craik dressing his wounds and Washington attending him with faithful assiduity. Braddock was still able to give orders and had a faint hope of being able to keep possession of the ground until reinforced. Most of the men were stationed in a very advantageous spot about two hundred yards from the road, and Lieutenant-Colonel Burton posted out small parties and sentinels. Before an hour had elapsed most of the men had stolen off. Being thus deserted, Braddock and his officers continued their retreat. He would have mounted his horse but was unable and had to be carried by soldiers. Orme and Morris were placed on litters borne by horses. They were subsequently joined by Colonel Gage with eighty men whom he had rallied.

Washington, in the meantime, notwithstanding his weak state, being found most efficient in frontier service, was sent to Colonel Dunbar's camp, forty miles distant, with orders for him to hurry

[5] *Journal of the Seamen's Detachment.*

forward provisions, hospital stores and wagons for the wounded under the escort of two grenadier companies. It was a hard and a melancholy ride throughout the night and the following day. The tidings of the defeat preceded him, borne by the wagoners who had mounted their horses, on Braddock's fall, and fled from the field of battle. They had arrived, haggard, at Dunbar's camp at midday, the Indian yells still ringing in their ears. "All was lost!" they cried. "Braddock was killed! They had seen wounded officers borne off from the field in bloody sheets! The troops were all cut to pieces!" A panic fell upon the camp. The drums beat to arms. Many of the soldiers, wagoners and attendants took to flight. But most of them were forced back by the sentinels.

Washington arrived at the camp in the evening and found the agitation still prevailing. The orders which he brought were executed during the night and he was in the saddle early in the morning accompanying the convoy of supplies. At Gist's plantation, about thirteen miles off, he met Gage and his scanty force escorting Braddock and his wounded officers. Captain Stewart and a sad remnant of the Virginia light horse still accompanied the general as his guard. The captain had been unremitting in his attentions to him during the retreat. There was a halt of one day at Dunbar's camp for the repose and relief of the wounded. On the 13th they resumed their melancholy march, and that night reached the Great Meadows.

The proud spirit of Braddock was broken by his defeat. He remained silent the first evening after the battle, only ejaculating at night, "Who would have thought it!" He was equally silent the following day, yet hope still seemed to linger in his breast, from another ejaculation, "We shall better know how to deal with them another time!"

He died on the night of the 13th at the Great Meadows, the place of Washington's discomfiture in the previous year. His obsequies were performed before break of day. The chaplain having been wounded, Washington read the funeral service. All was done in sadness and without parade so as not to attract the attention of lurking savages who might discover and outrage his grave. It is doubtful even whether a volley was fired over it, that last military honor which he had recently paid to the remains of an Indian warrior. The place of his sepulture, however, is still known and pointed out.

Reproach spared him not, even when in his grave. The failure of the expedition was attributed both in England and America to his obstinacy, his technical pedantry and his military conceit. He had been continually warned to be on his guard against ambush and surprise but without avail. Had he taken the advice urged on him by Washington and others, to employ scouting parties of Indians and rangers, he would never have been so signally surprised and defeated.

Still his dauntless conduct on the field of battle shows him to have been a man of fearless spirit, and he was universally allowed to be an accomplished disciplinarian. His melancholy end, too, disarms censure of its asperity. Whatever may have been his faults and errors, he in a manner expiated them by the hardest lot that can befall a brave soldier ambitious of renown—an unhonored grave in a strange land, a memory clouded by misfortune, and a name forever coupled with defeat.

Note

In narrating the expedition of Braddock we have frequently cited the journals of Captain Orme and of the *Seamen's Detachment*. They were procured in England by the Hon. Joseph R. Ingersoll while Minister at the Court of St. James, and recently published by the Historical Society of Pennsylvania, ably edited and illustrated with an admirable Introductory Memoir by Winthrop Sargent, Esq., member of that Society.

Chapter 7

MEASURES FOR PUBLIC SAFETY

The obsequies of the unfortunate Braddock being finished, the escort continued its retreat with the sick and wounded. Washington, assisted by Dr. Craik, watched with assiduity over his comrades, Orme and Morris. As the horses which bore their litters were nearly knocked up, he despatched messengers to the commander of Fort Cumberland requesting that others might be sent on and that comfortable quarters might be prepared for the reception of those officers.

On the 17th the sad cavalcade reached the fort and were relieved from the incessant apprehension of pursuit. Here, too, flying reports had preceded them, brought by fugitives from the battle, who, with the disposition usual in such cases to exaggerate, had represented the whole army as massacred. Fearing these reports might reach home and affect his family, Washington wrote to his mother and his brother, John Augustine, apprising them of his safety. "The Virginia troops," says he in a letter to his mother, "showed a good deal of bravery, and were nearly all killed. . . . The dastardly behavior of those they called regulars exposed all others, that were ordered to do their duty, to almost certain death, and, at last, in despite of all the efforts of the officers to the contrary, they ran as sheep pursued by dogs and it was impossible to rally them."

To his brother he writes: "As I have heard, since my arrival at this place, a circumstantial account of my death and dying speech, I take this early opportunity of contradicting the first and of assuring you that I have not composed the latter. But, by the all-powerful dispensations of Providence, I have been protected beyond all human probability or expectation, for I had four bullets through my coat and two horses shot under me, yet escaped unhurt though death was levelling my companions on every side of me!

"We have been most scandalously beaten by a trifling body of men, but fatigue and want of time prevent me from giving you any of the details until I have the happiness of seeing you at Mount Vernon, which I now most earnestly wish for, since we are driven in thus far. A feeble state of health obliges me to halt here for two or three days to recover a little strength, that I may thereby be enabled to proceed homeward with more ease."

Dunbar arrived shortly afterward with the remainder of the army. No one seems to have shared more largely in the panic of the vulgar than that officer. From the moment he received tidings of the defeat, his camp became a scene of confusion. All the ammunition, stores and artillery were destroyed to prevent, it was said, their falling into the hands of the enemy; but, as it was afterwards alleged, to relieve the terror-stricken commander from all incumbrances and furnish him with more horses in his flight toward the settlements.[1]

At Cumberland his forces amounted to fifteen hundred effective men, enough for a brave stand to protect the frontier and recover some of the lost honor, but he merely paused to leave the sick and wounded under care of two Virginia and Maryland companies and some of the train, and then continued his hasty march, or rather flight, through the country, not thinking himself safe, as was sneeringly intimated, until he arrived in Philadelphia, where the inhabitants could protect him.

The true reason why the enemy did not pursue the retreating army was not known until some time afterwards, and added to the disgrace of the defeat. They were not the main force of the French but a mere detachment of 72 regulars, 146 Canadians and 637 Indians, 855 in all, led by Captain de Beaujeu. De Contrecœur, the commander of Fort Duquesne, had received information through his scouts that the English, three thousand strong, were within six leagues of his fort. Despairing of making an effectual defense against such a superior force, he was balancing in his mind whether to abandon his fort without awaiting their arrival or to capitulate on honorable terms. In this dilemma Beaujeu prevailed on him to let him sally forth with a detachment to form an ambush and give check to the enemy. De Beaujeau was to have taken post at the river and disputed the passage at the ford. For that purpose he was hurrying forward when discovered by the pio-

[1] Franklin's *Autobiography*.

neers of Gage's advance party. He was a gallant officer and fell at the beginning of the fight. The whole number of killed and wounded of French and Indians did not exceed seventy.

Such was the scanty force which the imagination of the panic-stricken army had magnified into a great host and from which they had fled in breathless terror, abandoning the whole frontier. No one could be more surprised than the French commander himself when the ambuscading party returned in triumph with a long train of pack-horses laden with booty; the savages uncouthly clad in the garments of the slain, grenadier caps, officers' gold-laced coats and glittering epaulettes; flourishing swords and sabres or firing off muskets and uttering fiendlike yells of victory. But when De Contrecœur was informed of the utter rout and destruction of the much dreaded British army, his joy was complete. He ordered the guns of the fort to be fired in triumph, and sent out troops in pursuit of the fugitives.

The affair of Braddock remains a memorable event in American history and has been characterized as "the most extraordinary victory ever obtained, and the furthest flight ever made." It struck a fatal blow to the deference for British prowess, which once amounted almost to bigotry throughout the provinces. "This whole transaction," observes Franklin in his Autobiography, "gave us the first suspicion that our exalted ideas of the prowess of British regular troops had not been well founded."

Washington arrived at Mount Vernon on the 26th of July, still in feeble condition from his long illness. His campaigning thus far had trenched upon his private fortune and impaired one of the best of constitutions.

In a letter to his brother Augustine, then a member of Assembly at Williamsburg, he casts up the result of his frontier experience. "I was employed," he writes, "to go a journey in the winter, when I believe few or none would have undertaken it, and what did I get by it?—my expenses borne! I was then appointed, with trifling pay, to conduct a handful of men to the Ohio. What did I get by that? Why, after putting myself to a considerable expense in equipping and providing necessaries for the campaign, I went out, was soundly beaten and lost all! Came in, and had my commission taken from me, or, in other words, my command reduced under pretense of an order from home (England). I then went out a volunteer with General Braddock and lost all my horses and many other things. But this being a voluntary act, I ought not to have mentioned it, nor should I have done it, were it not to show that I have been on the losing order ever since I entered the service, which is now nearly two years."

What a striking lesson is furnished by this brief summary! How little was he aware of the vast advantages he was acquiring in this school of bitter experience! "In the hand of Heaven he stood," to be shaped and trained for its great purpose, and every trial and vicissitude of his early life but fitted him to cope with one or other of the varied and multifarious duties of his future destiny.

But though under the saddening influence of debility and defeat he might count the cost of his campaigning, the martial spirit still burned within him. His connection with the army, it is true, had ceased at the death of Braddock, but his military duties continued as adjutant-general of the northern division of the province, and he immediately issued orders for the county lieutenants to hold the militia in readiness for parade and exercise, foreseeing that in the present defenseless state of the frontier there would be need of their services.

Tidings of the rout and retreat of the army had circulated far and near and spread consternation throughout the country. Immediate incursions both of French and Indians were apprehended, and volunteer companies began to form for the purpose of marching across the mountains to the scene of danger. It was intimated to Washington that his services would again be wanted on the frontier. He declared instantly that he was ready to serve his country to the extent of his powers but never on the same terms as heretofore.

On the 4th of August, Governor Dinwiddie convened the Assembly to devise measures for the public safety. The sense of danger had quickened the slow patriotism of the burgesses. They no longer held back supplies. Forty thousand pounds were promptly voted, and orders issued for the raising of a regiment of one thousand men.

Washington's friends urged him to present himself at Williamsburg as a candidate for the command. They were confident of his success, notwithstanding that strong interest was making for the governor's favorite, Colonel Innes.

With mingled modesty and pride, Washington declined to be a

solicitor. The only terms, he said, on which he would accept a command were a certainty as to rank and emoluments, a right to appoint his field-officers, and the supply of a sufficient military chest. But to solicit the command and, at the same time, to make stipulations, would be a little incongruous and carry with it the face of self-sufficiency. "If," added he, "the command should be offered to me, the case will then be altered, as I should be at liberty to make such objections as reason and my small experience have pointed out."

While this was in agitation he received letters from his mother, again imploring him not to risk himself in these frontier wars. His answer was characteristic, blending the filial deference with which he was accustomed from childhood to treat her, with a calm patriotism of the Roman stamp:

"Honored Madam, If it is in my power to avoid going to the Ohio again, I shall. But if the command is pressed upon me by the general voice of the country and offered upon such terms as cannot be objected against, it would reflect dishonor on me to refuse it. And that, I am sure, must and ought to give you greater uneasiness than my going in an honorable command. Upon no other terms will I accept it. At present I have no proposals made to me, nor have I any advice of such intention except from private hands."

· On the very day that this letter was despatched (Aug. 14th), he received intelligence of his appointment to the command on the terms specified in his letters to his friends. His commission nominated him commander-in-chief of all the forces raised or to be raised in the colony. The Assembly also voted three hundred pounds to him and proportionate sums to the other officers and to the privates of the Virginia companies in consideration of their gallant conduct and their losses in the late battle.

The officers next in command under him were Lieutenant-Colonel Adam Stephen and Major Andrew Lewis. The former, it will be recollected, had been with him in the unfortunate affair at the Great Meadows. His advance in rank shows that his conduct had been meritorious.

The appointment of Washington to his present station was the more gratifying and honorable from being a popular one, made in deference to public sentiment, to which Governor Dinwiddie was obliged to sacrifice his strong inclination in favor of Colonel

Innes. It is thought that the governor never afterwards regarded Washington with a friendly eye. His conduct towards him subsequently was on various occasions cold and ungracious.[2]

It is worthy of note that the early popularity of Washington was not the result of brilliant achievements nor signal success. On the contrary, it rose among trials and reverses, and may almost be said to have been the fruit of defeats. It remains an honorable testimony of Virginian intelligence that the sterling, enduring but undazzling qualities of Washington were thus early discerned and appreciated, though only heralded by misfortunes. The admirable manner in which he had conducted himself under these misfortunes and the sagacity and practical wisdom he had displayed on all occasions were universally acknowledged, and it was observed that, had his modest counsels been adopted by the unfortunate Braddock, a totally different result might have attended the late campaign.

Mortifying experience had convinced Washington of the inefficiency of the militia laws, and he now set about effecting a reformation. Through his great and persevering efforts an act was passed in the Virginia Legislature giving prompt operation to courts-martial, punishing insubordination, mutiny and desertion with adequate severity, strengthening the authority of a commander so as to enable him to enforce order and discipline among officers as well as privates and to avail himself, in time of emergency and for the common safety, of the means and services of individuals.

This being effected, he proceeded to fill up his companies and to enforce this newly defined authority within his camp. All gaming, drinking, quarrelling, swearing and similar excesses were prohibited under severe penalities.

In disciplining his men, they were instructed not merely in ordinary and regular tactics but in all the strategy of Indian warfare, and what is called "bush-fighting," a knowledge indispensable in the wild wars of the wilderness. Stockaded forts, too, were constructed at various points as places of refuge and defense in exposed neighborhoods. Under shelter of these, the inhabitants began to return to their deserted homes. A shorter and better road, also, was opened by him between Winchester and Cumberland for the transmission of reinforcements and supplies.

[2] Sparks, *Writings of Washington*, vol. ii., p. 61, note.

His exertions, however, were impeded by one of those questions of precedence which had so often annoyed him, arising from the difference between crown and provincial commissions. Maryland having by a scanty appropriation raised a small militia force, stationed Captain Dagworthy with a company of thirty men at Fort Cumberland, which stood within the boundaries of that province. Dagworthy had served in Canada in the preceding war and had received a king's commission. This he had since commuted for half-pay and, of course, had virtually parted with its privileges. He was nothing more, therefore, than a Maryland provincial captain at the head of thirty men. He now, however, assumed to act under his royal commission and refused to obey the orders of any officer, however high his rank, who merely held his commission from a governor. Nay, when Governor, or rather Colonel Innes, who commanded at the fort, was called away to North Carolina by his private affairs, the captain took upon himself the command and insisted upon it as his right.

Parties instantly arose and quarrels ensued among the inferior officers. Grave questions were agitated between the governors of Maryland and Virginia as to the fort itself, the former claiming it as within his province, the latter insisting that, as it had been built according to orders sent by the king, it was the king's fort and could not be subject to the authority of Maryland.

Washington refrained from mingling in this dispute but intimated that if the commander-in-chief of the forces of Virginia must yield precedence to a Maryland captain of thirty men he should have to resign his commission, as he had been compelled to do before, by a question of military rank.

So difficult was it, however, to settle these disputes of precedence, especially where the claims of two governors came in collision, that it was determined to refer the matter to Major-General Shirley, who had succeeded Braddock in the general command of the colonies. For this purpose Washington was to go to Boston, obtain a decision from Shirley of the point in dispute, and a general regulation by which these difficulties could be prevented in future. It was thought also that in a conference with the commander-in-chief he might inform himself of the military measures in contemplation.

Accordingly, on the 4th of February (1756), leaving Colonel Adam Stephen in command of the troops, Washington set out on his mission, accompanied by his aide-de-camp, Captain George Mercer of Virginia, and Captain Stewart of the Virginia light horse, the officer who had taken care of General Braddock in his last moments.

In those days the conveniences of travelling, even between our main cities, were few and the roads execrable. The party therefore travelled in Virginia style, on horseback, attended by their black servants in livery.[3] In this way they accomplished a journey of five hundred miles in the depth of winter, stopping for some days at Philadelphia and New York. Those cities were then comparatively small, and the arrival of a party of young Southern officers attracted attention. The late disastrous battle was still the theme of every tongue, and the honorable way in which these young officers had acquitted themselves in it made them objects of universal interest. Washington's fame especially had gone before him, having been spread by the officers who had served with him and by the public honors decreed him by the Virginia Legislature. "Your name," wrote his former fellow-campaigner, Gist, in a letter dated in the preceding autumn, "is more talked of in Philadelphia than that of any other person in the army, and everybody seems willing to venture under your command."

With these prepossessions in his favor, when we consider Washington's noble person and demeanor, his consummate horsemanship, the admirable horses he was accustomed to ride, and the aristocratical style of his equipments, we may imagine the

[3] We have hitherto treated of Washington in his campaigns in the wilderness, frugal and scanty in his equipments, often, very probably, in little better than hunter's garb. His present excursion through some of the Atlantic cities presents him in a different aspect. His recent intercourse with young British officers had probably elevated his notions as to style in dress and appearance. At least we are inclined to suspect so from the following aristocratical order for clothes sent shortly before the time in question to his correspondent in London.

"2 complete livery suits for servants; with a spare cloak, all other necessary trimmings for two suits more. I would have you choose the livery by our arms, only as the field of the arms is white, I think the clothes had better not be quite so, but nearly like the inclosed. The trimmings and facings of scarlet, and a scarlet waistcoat. If livery lace is not quite disused, I should be glad to have the cloaks laced. I like that fashion best, and two silver-laced hats for the above servants.

"1 set of horse furniture, with livery lace, with the Washington crest on the housings, &c. The cloak to be of the same piece and color of the clothes.

"3 gold and scarlet sword-knots. 3 silver and blue do. 1 fashionable gold-laced hat."

effect produced by himself and his little cavalcade as they clattered through the streets of Philadelphia and New York and Boston. It is needless to say their sojourn in each city was a continual *fête*.

The mission to General Shirley was entirely successful as to the question of rank. A written order from the commander-in-chief determined that Dagworthy was entitled to the rank of a provincial captain only and, of course, must on all occasions give precedence to Colonel Washington, as a provincial field-officer. The latter was disappointed, however, in the hope of getting himself and his officers put upon the regular establishment with commissions from the king, and had to remain subjected to mortifying questions of rank and etiquette when serving in company with regular troops.

From General Shirley he learnt that the main objects of the ensuing campaign would be the reduction of Fort Niagara so as to cut off the communication between Canada and Louisiana; the capture of Ticonderoga and Crown Point, as a measure of safety for New York; the besieging of Fort Duquesne; and the menacing of Quebec by a body of troops which were to advance by the Kennebec River.

The official career of General Shirley was drawing to a close. Though a man of good parts, he had always until recently acted in a civil capacity and proved incompetent to conduct military operations. He was recalled to England and was to be superseded by General Abercrombie, who was coming out with two regiments.

The general command in America, however, was to be held by the Earl of Loudoun, who was invested with powers almost equal to those of a viceroy, being placed above all the colonial governors. These might claim to be civil and military representatives of their sovereign within their respective colonies but even there were bound to defer and yield precedence to this their official superior. This was part of a plan devised long ago but now first brought into operation, by which the ministry hoped to unite the colonies under military rule and oblige the assemblies, magistrates and people to furnish quarters and provide a general fund subject to the control of this military dictator.

Beside his general command, the Earl of Loudoun was to be governor of Virginia and colonel of a royal American regiment of four battalions, to be raised in the colonies but furnished with officers who, like himself, had seen foreign service. The campaign would open on his arrival, which, it was expected, would be early in the spring, and brilliant results were anticipated.

Washington remained ten days in Boston, attending with great interest the meetings of the Massachusetts Legislature, in which the plan of military operations was ably discussed, and receiving the most hospitable attentions from the polite and intelligent society of the place, after which he returned to New York.

Tradition gives very different motives from those of business for his two sojourns in the latter city. He found there an early friend and schoolmate, Beverley Robinson, son of John Robinson, Speaker of the Virginia House of Burgesses. He was living happily and prosperously with a young and wealthy bride, having married one of the nieces and heiresses of Mr. Adolphus Phillipse, a rich landholder whose manor-house is still to be seen on the banks of the Hudson. At the house of Mr. Beverley Robinson, where Washington was an honored guest, he met Miss Mary Phillipse, sister of and co-heiress with Mrs. Robinson, a young lady whose personal attractions are said to have rivalled her reputed wealth.

We have already given an instance of Washington's early sensibility to female charms. A life, however, of constant activity and care passed for the most part in the wilderness and on the frontier, far from the female society, had left little mood or leisure for the indulgence of the tender sentiment; but made him more sensible, in the present brief interval of gay and social life, to the attractions of an elegant woman brought up in the polite circle of New York.

That he was an open admirer of Miss Phillipse is an historical fact. That he sought her hand but was refused is traditional and not very probable. His military rank, his early laurels and distinguished presence were all calculated to win favor in female eyes. But his sojourn in New York was brief. He may have been diffident in urging his suit with a lady accustomed to the homage of society and surrounded by admirers. The most probable version of the story is that he was called away by his public duties before he had made sufficient approaches in his siege of the lady's heart to warrant a summons to surrender. In the latter part of March we find him at Williamsburg attending the opening of the Legislature of Virginia, eager to promote measures for the protection of the frontier and the capture of Fort Duquesne, the leading object of his ambition. Maryland and Pennsylvania were erecting forts for the defense of their own borders but showed no disposition to co-operate with Virginia in the field, and artillery, artillerymen and engineers were wanting for an attack on fortified places. Washington urged therefore an augmentation of the provincial forces and various improvements in the militia laws.

While thus engaged he received a letter from a friend and confidant in New York, warning him to hasten back to that city before it was too late, as Captain Morris, who had been his fellow aide-de-camp under Braddock, was laying close siege to Miss Phillipse. Sterner alarms, however, summoned him in another direction. Expresses from Winchester brought word that the French had made another sortie from Fort Duquesne, accompanied by a band of savages, and were spreading terror and desolation through the country. In this moment of exigency all softer claims were forgotten. Washington repaired in all haste to his post at Winchester, and Captain Morris was left to urge his suit unrivalled and carry off the prize.

Chapter 8

DEPARTURE OF DINWIDDIE

Report had not exaggerated the troubles of the frontier. It was marauded by merciless bands of savages, led in some instances by Frenchmen. Travellers were murdered, farm-houses burnt down, families butchered, and even stockaded forts or houses of refuge attacked in open day. The marauders had crossed the mountains and penetrated the valley of the Shenandoah, and several persons had fallen beneath the tomahawk in the neighborhood of Winchester.

Washington, on his arrival at Winchester, found the inhabitants in great dismay. He resolved immediately to organize a force composed partly of troops from Fort Cumberland, partly of militia from Winchester and its vicinity, to put himself at its head and "scour the woods and suspected places in all the mountains and valleys of this part of the frontier, in quest of the Indians and their more cruel associates."

He accordingly despatched an express to Fort Cumberland with orders for a detachment from the garrison. "But how," said he, "are men to be raised at Winchester, since orders are no longer regarded in the county?"

Lord Fairfax and other militia officers with whom he consulted advised that each captain should call a private muster of his men and read before them an address or "exhortation" as it was called, being an appeal to their patriotism and fears and a summons to assemble on the 15th of April to enroll themselves for the projected mountain foray.

This measure was adopted, the private musterings occurred, the exhortation was read, the time and place of assemblage appointed. But when the day of enrollment arrived not more than fifteen men appeared upon the ground. In the meantime the express returned with sad accounts from Fort Cumberland. No troops could be furnished from that quarter. The garrison was scarcely strong enough for self-defense, having sent out detachments in different directions. The express had narrowly escaped with his life, having been fired upon repeatedly, his horse shot under him and his clothes riddled with bullets. The roads, he said, were infested by savages. None but hunters, who knew how to thread the forests at night, could travel with safety.

Horrors accumulated at Winchester. Every hour brought its tale of terror, true or false, of houses burnt, families massacred or beleaguered and famishing in stockaded forts. The danger approached. A scouting party had been attacked in the Warm Spring Mountain, about twenty miles distant, by a large body of French and Indians, mostly on horseback. The captain of the scouting party and several of his men had been slain and the rest put to flight.

An attack on Winchester was apprehended and the terrors of the people rose to agony. They now turned to Washington as their main hope. The women surrounded him, holding up their children and imploring him with tears and cries to save them from the savages. The youthful commander looked round on the supplicant crowd with a countenance beaming with pity and a heart wrung with anguish. A letter to Governor Dinwiddie shows the conflict of his feelings. "I am too little acquainted with pathetic language to attempt a description of these people's distresses. But what can I do? I see their situation, I know their danger and participate their sufferings, without having it in my power to give them further relief than uncertain promises. . . . The supplicating tears of the women and moving petitions of the men melt me into such deadly sorrow that I solemnly declare, if I know my own mind, I could offer myself a willing sacrifice to the butchering enemy, provided that would contribute to the people's ease."

The unstudied eloquence of this letter drew from the governor an instant order for a militia force from the upper counties to his assistance. But the Virginia newspapers, in descanting on the frontier troubles, threw discredit on the army and its officers and attached blame to its commander. Stung to the quick by this injustice, Washington publicly declared that nothing but the imminent danger of the times prevented him from instantly resigning a command from which he could never reap either

honor or benefit. His sensitiveness called forth strong letters from
his friends assuring him of the high sense entertained at the seat
of government and elsewhere of his merits and services. "Your
good health and fortune are the toast of every table," wrote his
early friend, Colonel Fairfax, at that time a member of the governor's council. "Your endeavors in the service and defense of your
country must redound to your honor."

"Our hopes, dear George," wrote Mr. Robinson, the speaker of
the House of Burgesses, "are all fixed on you for bringing our
affairs to a happy issue. Consider what fatal consequences to your
country your resigning the command at this time may be,
especially as there is no doubt most of the officers will follow your
example."

In fact, the situation and services of the youthful commander,
shut up in a frontier town, destitute of forces, surrounded by savage foes, gallantly though despairingly devoting himself to the
safety of a suffering people, were properly understood throughout
the country and excited a glow of enthusiasm in his favor. The
Legislature too began at length to act, but timidly and
inefficiently. "The country knows her danger," writes one of the
members, "but such is her parsimony that she is willing to wait for
the rains to wet the powder and the rats to eat the bowstrings of
the enemy rather than attempt to drive them from her frontiers."

The measure of relief voted by the Assembly was an additional
appropriation of twenty thousand pounds and an increase of the
provincial force to fifteen hundred men. With this it was
proposed to erect and garrison a chain of frontier forts extending
through the ranges of the Allegheny Mountains from the Potomac to the borders of North Carolina, a distance of between
three and four hundred miles. This was one of the inconsiderate
projects devised by Governor Dinwiddie.

Washington in letters to the governor and to the speaker of the
House of Burgesses urged the impolicy of such a plan, with their
actual force and means. The forts, he observed, ought to be within
fifteen or eighteen miles of each other, that their spies might be
able to keep watch over the intervening country, otherwise the Indians would pass between them unperceived, effect their ravages
and escape to the mountains, swamps and ravines before the
troops from the forts could be assembled to pursue them. They
ought each to be garrisoned with eighty or a hundred men so as to

afford detachments of sufficient strength without leaving the garrison too weak, for the Indians are the most stealthy and patient of spies and lurkers, will lie in wait for days together about small forts of the kind and, if they find, by some chance prisoner, that the garrison is actually weak, will first surprise and cut off its scouting parties and then attack the fort itself. It was evident, therefore, observed he, that to garrison properly such a line of forts would require at least two thousand men. And even then a line of such extent might be broken through at one end before the other end could yield assistance. Feint attacks also might be made at one point while the real attack was made at another, quite distant, and the country be overrun before its widely-posted defenders could be alarmed and concentrated. Then must be taken into consideration the immense cost of building so many forts, and the constant and consuming expense of supplies and transportation.

His idea of a defensive plan was to build a strong fort at Winchester, the central point, where all the main roads met, of a wide range of scattered settlements, where tidings could soonest be collected from every quarter and whence reinforcements and supplies could most readily be forwarded. It was to be a grand deposit of military stores, a residence for commanding officers, a place of refuge for the women and children in time of alarm, when the men had suddenly to take the field. In a word, it was to be the citadel of the frontier.

Besides this, he would have three or four large fortresses erected at convenient distances upon the frontiers, with powerful garrisons so as to be able to throw out in constant succession strong scouting parties to range the country. Fort Cumberland he condemned as being out of the province and out of the track of Indian incursions, insomuch that it seldom received an alarm until all the mischief had been effected.

His representations with respect to military laws and regulations were equally cogent. In the late act of the Assembly for raising a regiment it was provided that in cases of emergency, if recruits should not offer in sufficient number the militia might be drafted to supply the deficiencies, but only to serve until December and not to be marched out of the province. In this case, said he, before they have entered upon service or got the least smattering of duty they will claim a discharge. If they are pursuing an enemy who has committed the most unheard-of-cruelties, he has only to step across the Potomac and he is safe. Then, as to the limits of service, they might just as easily have been enlisted for seventeen months as seven. They would then have been seasoned as well as disciplined. "For we find by experience," says he, "that our poor ragged soldiers would kill the most active militia in five days' marching."

Then, as to punishments. Death, it was true, had been decreed for mutiny and desertion, but there was no punishment for cowardice, for holding correspondence with the enemy, for quitting or sleeping on one's post—all capital offenses according to the military codes of Europe. Neither were there provisions for quartering or billeting soldiers or impressing wagons and other conveyances in times of exigency. To crown all, no court-martial could sit out of Virginia; a most embarrassing regulation when troops were fifty or a hundred miles beyond the frontier. He earnestly suggested amendments on all these points, as well as with regard to the soldiers' pay, which was less than that of the regular troops, or the troops of most of the other provinces.

All these suggestions, showing at this youthful age that forethought and circumspection which distinguished him throughout life, were repeatedly and eloquently urged upon Governor Dinwiddie, with very little effect. The plan of a frontier line of twenty-three forts was persisted in. Fort Cumberland was pertinaciously kept up at a great and useless expense of men and money, and the militia laws remained lax and inefficient. It was decreed, however, that the great central fort at Winchester recommended by Washington should be erected.

Throughout the summer of 1756 Washington exerted himself diligently in carrying out measures determined upon for frontier security. The fortress at Winchester was commenced, and the work urged forward as expeditiously as the delays and perplexities incident to a badly organized service would permit. It received the name of Fort Loudoun in honor of the commander-in-chief, whose arrival in Virginia was hopefully anticipated.

As to the sites of the frontier posts, they were decided upon by Washington and his officers after frequent and long consultations. Parties were sent out to work on them, and men recruited, and militia drafted to garrison them. Washington visited occasionally such as were in progress and near at hand. It was a service of some peril, for the mountains and forests were still infested by prowling savages, especially in the neighborhood of these new forts. At one time when he was reconnoitering a wild part of the country, attended merely by a servant and a guide, two men were murdered by the Indians in a solitary defile shortly after he had passed through it.

In the autumn he made a tour of inspection along the whole line, accompanied by his friend, Captain Hugh Mercer, who had recovered from his recent wounds. This tour furnished repeated proofs of the inefficiency of the militia system. In one place he attempted to raise a force with which to scour a region infested by roving bands of savages. After waiting several days, but five men answered to his summons. In another place, where three companies had been ordered to the relief of a fort attacked by the Indians, all that could be mustered were a captain, a lieutenant and seven or eight men.

When the militia were drafted, and appeared under arms, the case was not much better. It was now late in the autumn. Their term of service, by the act of the legislature, expired in December. Half of the time therefore was lost in marching out and home. Their waste of provisions was enormous. To be put on allowance, like other soldiers, they considered an indignity. They would sooner starve than carry a few days' provisions on their backs. On the march, when breakfast was wanted, they would knock down the first beeves they met with and, after regaling themselves, march on till dinner, when they would take the same method; and so for supper, to the great oppression of the people. For the want of proper military laws, they were obstinate, self-willed and perverse. Every individual had his own crude notion of things and would undertake to direct. If his advice were neglected he would think himself slighted, abused and injured and, to redress himself, would depart for his home.

The garrisons were weak for want of men but more so from indolence and irregularity. Not one was in a posture of defense. Few but might be surprised with the greatest ease. At one fort the Indians rushed from their lurking-place, pounced upon several children playing under the walls and bore them off before they were discovered. Another fort was surprised and many of the people massacred in the same manner. In the course of his tour, as he and his party approached a fort, he heard a quick firing for several minutes. Concluding that it was attacked, they hastened to its relief but found the garrison were merely amusing themselves firing at a mark or for wagers. In this way they would waste their ammunition as freely as they did their provisions. In the meantime the inhabitants of the country were in a wretched situation, feeling the little dependence to be put on militia, who were slow in coming to their assistance, indifferent about their preservation, unwilling to continue, and regardless of everything but of their own ease. In short, they were so apprehensive of approaching ruin that the whole back country was in a general motion towards the southern colonies.

From the Catawba he was escorted along a range of forts by a colonel and about thirty men, chiefly officers. "With this small company of irregulars," says he, "with whom order, regularity, circumspection and vigilance were matters of derision and contempt, we set out and, by the protection of Providence, reached Augusta Court-House in seven days without meeting the enemy, otherwise, we must have fallen a sacrifice through the indiscretion of these whooping, hallooing, *gentlemen* soldiers!"

How lively a picture does this give of the militia system at all times when not subjected to strict military law.

What rendered this year's service peculiarly irksome and embarrassing to Washington was the nature of his correspondence with Governor Dinwiddie. That gentleman, either from the natural hurry and confusion of his mind or from a real disposition to perplex, was extremely ambiguous and unsatisfactory in most of his orders and replies. "So much am I kept in the dark," says Washington in one of his letters, "that I do not know whether to prepare for the offensive or defensive. What would be absolutely necessary for the one would be quite useless for the other." And again: "The orders I receive are full of ambiguity. I am left like a wanderer in the wilderness, to proceed at hazard. I am answerable for consequences and blamed without the privilege of defense."

In nothing was this disposition to perplex more apparent than in the governor's replies respecting Fort Cumberland. Washington had repeatedly urged the abandonment of this fort as a place of frontier deposit, being within the bounds of another province and out of the track of Indian incursion, so that often the alarm would not reach there until after the mischief had been effected. He applied at length for particular and positive directions from the governor on this head. "The following," says he, "is an exact copy of his answer: 'Fort Cumberland is a *king's* fort and built chiefly at the charge of the colony, therefore properly under our direction until a new governor is appointed.' Now, whether I am to understand this aye or no to the plain simple question asked, Is the fort to be continued or not? I know not. But in all important matters I am directed in this ambiguous and uncertain way."

Governor Dinwiddie subsequently made himself explicit on this point. Taking offense at some of Washington's comments on the military affairs of the frontier, he made the stand of a self-willed and obstinate man in the case of Fort Cumberland and represented it to Lord Loudoun, as to draw from his lordship an order that it should be kept up, and an implied censure of the conduct of Washington in slighting a post of such paramount importance. "I cannot agree with Colonel Washington," writes his lordship, "in not drawing in the posts from the stockade forts in order to defend that advanced one, and I should imagine much more of the frontier will be exposed by retiring your advanced posts near Winchester, where I understand he is retired, for, from your letter, I take it for granted he has before this executed his plan without waiting for any advice. If he leaves any of the great quantity of stores behind it will be very unfortunate, and he ought to consider that it must lie at his own door."

Thus powerfully supported, Dinwiddie went so far as to order that the garrisons should be withdrawn from the stockades and small frontier forts and most of the troops from Winchester, to strengthen Fort Cumberland, which was now to become headquarters; thus weakening the most important points and places to concentrate a force where it was not wanted and would be out of the way in most cases of alarm. By these meddlesome moves, made by Governor Dinwiddie from a distance, without knowing anything of the game, all previous arrangements were reversed, everything was thrown into confusion, and enormous losses and expenses were incurred.

"Whence it arises or why, I am truly ignorant," writes Washington to Mr. Speaker Robinson, "but my strongest representations of matters relative to the frontiers are disregarded as idle and frivolous, my propositions and measures as partial and selfish and all my sincerest endeavors for the service of my country are perverted to the worst purposes. My orders are dark and uncertain, to-day approved, to-morrow disapproved."

Whence all this contradiction and embarrassment arose has since been explained and with apparent reason. Governor Dinwiddie had never recovered from the pique caused by the popular elevation of Washington to the command in preference to his favorite, Colonel Innes. His irritation was kept alive by a little Scottish faction who were desirous of disgusting Washington with the service, so as to induce him to resign and make way for his rival. They might have carried their point during the panic at Winchester had not [Washington's] patriotism and his sympathy with the public distress been more powerful than his self-love. He determined, he said, to bear up under these embarrassments in the hope of better regulations when Lord Loudoun should arrive, to whom he looked for the future fate of Virginia.

Circumstances had led Washington to think that Lord Loudoun "had received impressions to his prejudice by false representations of facts," and that a wrong idea prevailed at headquarters respecting the state of military affairs in Virginia. He was anxious therefore for an opportunity of placing all these matters in a proper light; and, understanding that there was to be a meeting in Philadelphia in the month of March between Lord Loudoun and the southern governors to consult about measures of defense for their respective provinces, he wrote to Governor Dinwiddie for permission to attend it.

"I cannot conceive," writes Dinwiddie in reply, "what service you can be of in going there, as the plan concerted will in course be communicated to you and the other officers. However, as you seem so earnest to go, I now give you leave."

This ungracious reply seemed to warrant the suspicions entertained by some of Washington's friends that it was the busy pen of Governor Dinwiddie which had given the "false representation of facts" to Lord Loudoun. About a month, therefore, before the time of the meeting, Washington addressed a long letter to his lordship explanatory of military affairs in the quarter where he had commanded. In this he set forth the various defects in the militia laws of Virginia, the errors in its system of defense and the inevitable confusion which had thence resulted.

Adverting to his own conduct: "The orders I receive," said he, "are full of ambiguity. I am left like a wanderer in the wilderness to proceed at hazard. I am answerable for consequences and blamed without the privilege of defense. . . . It is not to be wondered at if, under such peculiar circumstances, I should be sick of a service which promises so little of a soldier's reward.

"I have long been satisfied of the impossibility of continuing in this service without loss of honor. Indeed, I was fully convinced of it before I accepted the command the second time, seeing the cloudy prospect before me. And I did for this reason reject the offer until I was ashamed any longer to refuse, not caring to expose my character to public censure. The solicitations of the country overcame my objections and induced me to accept it. Another reason has of late operated to continue me in the service until now and that is the dawn of hope that arose when I heard your lordship was destined by His Majesty for the important command of his armies in America, and appointed to the government of his dominion of Virginia. Hence it was that I drew my hopes and fondly pronounced your lordship our patron. Although I have not the honor to be known to your lordship, yet your name was familiar to my ear on account of the important services rendered to His Majesty in other parts of the world."

The manner in which Washington was received by Lord Loudoun on arriving in Philadelphia showed him at once that his long, explanatory letter had produced the desired effect and that his character and conduct were justly appreciated. During his sojourn in Philadelphia he was frequently consulted on points of frontier service, and his advice was generally adopted.

The year wore away on [Washington's] part in the harassing service of defending a wide frontier with an insufficient and badly organized force, and the vexations he experienced were heightened by continual misunderstandings with Governor Dinwiddie. From the ungracious tenor of several of that gentleman's letters and from private information, he was led to believe that some secret enemy had been making false representations of his motives and conduct and prejudicing the governor against him. He vindicated himself warmly from the alleged aspersions, proudly appealing to the whole course of his public career in proof of their falsity. "It is uncertain," said he, "in what light my services may have appeared to your honor. But this I know, and it is the highest consolation I am capable of feeling, that no man has endeavored to discharge the trust reposed in him with greater honesty and more zeal for the country's interest than I have done. And if there is any person living who can say with justice that I have offered any intentional wrong to the public, I will cheerfully submit to the most ignominious punishment that an injured people ought to inflict. On the other hand, it is hard to have my character arraigned and my actions condemned without a hearing."

His magnanimous appeal had but little effect. Dinwiddie was evidently actuated by the petty pique of a narrow and illiberal mind impatient of contradiction even when in error. He took advantage of his official station to vent his spleen and gratify his petulance in a variety of ways incompatible with the courtesy of a gentleman. It may excite a grave smile at the present day to find Washington charged by this very small-minded man with looseness in his way of writing to him, with remissness in his duty towards him, and even with impertinence in the able and eloquent representations which he felt compelled to make of diastrous mismanagement in military affairs; and still more, to find his reasonable request, after a long course of severe duty, for a temporary leave of absence to attend to his private concerns, peremptorily refused, and that with as little courtesy as though he were a mere subaltern seeking to absent himself on a party of pleasure.

The multiplied vexations which Washington had latterly experienced from this man had preyed upon his spirits and contributed, with his incessant toils and anxieties, to undermine his health. For some time he struggled with repeated attacks of dysentery and fever, and continued in the exercise of his duties, but the increased violence of his malady and the urgent advice of his friend Dr. Craik, the army surgeon, induced him to relinquish his post towards the end of the year and retire to Mount Vernon.

The administration of Dinwiddie, however, was now at an end. He set sail for England in January 1758, very little regretted excepting by his immediate hangers-on, and leaving a character overshadowed by the imputation of avarice and extortion in the exaction of illegal fees and of downright delinquency in regard to large sums transmitted to him by government to be paid over to the province in indemnification of its extra expenses, for the disposition of which sums he failed to render an account.

He was evidently a sordid, narrow-minded and somewhat arrogant man, bustling rather than active, prone to meddle with matters of which he was profoundly ignorant, and absurdly unwilling to have his ignorance enlightened.

Chapter 9

CAPITULATION OF THE FRENCH

For several months Washington was afflicted by returns of his malady accompanied by symptoms indicative, as he thought, of a decline. "My constitution," writes he to his friend Colonel Stanwix, "is much impaired and nothing can retrieve it but the greatest care and the most circumspect course of life. This being the case, as I have now no prospect left of preferment in the military way, and despair of rendering that immediate service which my country may require from the person commanding its troops, I have thoughts of quitting my command and retiring from all public business, leaving my post to be filled by some other person more capable of the task and who may perhaps have his endeavors crowned with better success than mine have been."

A gradual improvement in his health and a change in his prospects encouraged him to continue in what really was his favorite career, and at the beginning of April he was again in command at Fort Loudoun. Mr. Francis Fauquier had been appointed successor to Dinwiddie and, until he should arrive, Mr. John Blair, president of the council, had, from his office, charge of the government. In the latter Washington had a friend who appreciated his character and services and was disposed to carry out his plans.

The general aspect of affairs, also, was more animating. Under the able and intrepid administration of William Pitt, who had control of the British cabinet, an effort was made to retrieve the disgraces of the late American campaign and to carry on the war with greater vigor. The instructions for a common fund were discontinued. There was no more talk of taxation by parliament. Lord Loudoun, from whom so much had been anticipated, had disappointed by his inactivity, and been relieved from a command in which he had attempted much and done so little. His friends alleged that his inactivity was owing to a want of unanimity and co-operation in the colonial governments, which paralyzed all his well-meant efforts. Franklin, it is probable, probed the matter with his usual sagacity when he characterized him as a man "entirely made up of indecision."—"Like St. George on the signs, he was always on horseback but never rode on."

On the return of his lordship to England, the general command in America devolved on Major-General Abercrombie, and the forces were divided into three detached bodies. One, under Major-General Amherst, was to operate in the north with the fleet under Boscawen for the reduction of Louisburg and the island of Cape Breton. Another, under Abercrombie himself, was to proceed against Ticonderoga and Crown Point on Lake Champlain. And the third, under Brigadier-General Forbes, who had the charge of the middle and southern colonies, was to undertake the reduction of Fort Duquesne. The colonial troops were to be supplied, like the regulars, with arms, ammunition, tents and provisions at the expense of government, but clothed and paid by the colonies, for which the king would recommend to Parliament a proper compensation. The provincial officers appointed by the governors, and of no higher rank than colonel, were to be equal in command when united in service with those who held direct from the king, according to the date of their commissions. By these wise provisions of Mr. Pitt, a fertile cause of heartburnings and dissensions was removed.

It was with the greatest satisfaction Washington saw his favorite measure at last adopted, the reduction of Fort Duquesne, and he resolved to continue in the service until that object was accomplished. In a letter to Stanwix, who was now a bridgadier-general, he modestly requested to be mentioned in favorable terms to General Forbes, "not," said he, "as a person who would depend upon him for further recommendation to military preferment (for I have long conquered all such inclinations and shall serve this campaign merely for the purpose of affording my best endeavors to bring matters to a conclusion), but as a person who would gladly be distinguished in some measure from the *common run* of provincial officers, as I understand there will be a motley herd of us." He had the satisfaction subsequently of enjoying the fullest confidence of General Forbes, who knew too well the sound judgment and practical ability evinced by him in the unfortunate campaign of Braddock not to be desirous of availing himself of his counsels.

Washington still was commander-in-chief of the Virginia troops, now augmented by an act of the Assembly to two regiments of one thousand men each, one led by himself, the other by Colonel Byrd, the whole destined to make a part of the army of General Forbes in the expedition against Fort Duquesne.

Of the animation which he felt at the prospect of serving in this long-desired campaign and revisiting with an effective force the scene of past disasters, we have a proof in a short letter written during the excitement of the moment to Major Francis Halket, his former companion in arms:

"My Dear Halket, Are we to have you once more among us? And shall we revisit together a hapless spot that proved so fatal to many of our former brave companions? Yes, and I rejoice at it, hoping it will now be in our power to testify a just abhorrence of the cruel butcheries exercised on our friends in the unfortunate day of General Braddock's defeat. And, moreover, to show our enemies that we can practice all that lenity of which they only boast without affording any adequate proof."

[But] operations went on slowly in the expedition against Fort Duquesne. Brigadier-General Forbes, who was commander-in-chief, was detained at Philadelphia by those delays and cross-purposes incident to military affairs in a new country. Colonel Bouquet, who was to command the advanced division, took his station with a corps of regulars at Raystown in the centre of Pennsylvania. There slowly assembled troops from various parts. Three thousand Pennsylvanians, twelve hundred and fifty South Carolinians and a few hundred men from elsewhere.

Washington in the meantime gathered together his scattered regiments at Winchester, some from a distance of two hundred miles, and diligently disciplined his recruits. He had two Virginia regiments under him, amounting when complete to about nineteen hundred men. Seven hundred Indian warriors also came lagging into his camp, lured by the prospect of a successful campaign.

The president of the council had given Washington a discretionary power in the present juncture to order out militia for the purpose of garrisoning the fort in the absence of the regular troops. Washington exercised the power with extreme reluctance.

He considered it, he said, an affair of too important and delicate a nature for him to manage, and apprehended the discontent it might occasion. In fact, his sympathies were always with the husbandmen and the laborers of the soil, and he deplored the evils imposed upon them by arbitrary drafts for military service, a scruple not often indulged by youthful commanders.

The force thus assembling was in want of arms, tents, field-equipage and almost every requisite. Washington had made repeated representations by letter of the destitute state of the Virginia troops but without avail. He was now ordered by Sir John St. Clair, the quartermaster-general of the forces, under General Forbes, to repair to Williamsburg and lay the state of the case before the council. He set off promptly on horseback, attended by Bishop, the well-trained military servant who had served the late General Braddock. It proved an eventful journey, though not in a military point of view. In crossing a ferry of the Pamunkey, a branch of York River, he fell in company with a Mr. Chamberlayne, who lived in the neighborhood and who, in the spirit of Virginian hospitality, claimed him as a guest. It was with difficulty Washington could be prevailed on to halt for dinner, so impatient was he to arrive at Williamsburg and accomplish his mission.

Among the guests at Mr. Chamberlayne's was a young and blooming widow, Mrs. Martha Custis, daughter of Mr. John Dandridge, both patrician names in the province. Her husband, Daniel Parke Custis, had been dead about three years, leaving her with two young children and a large fortune. She is represented as being rather below the middle size but extremely well shaped, with an agreeable countenance, dark hazel eyes and hair, and those frank, engaging manners so captivating in Southern women. We are not informed whether Washington had met with her before; probably not during her widowhood, as during that time he had been almost continually on the frontier. We have shown that with all his gravity and reserve he was quickly susceptible to female charms, and they may have had a greater effect upon him when thus casually encountered in fleeting moments snatched from the cares and perplexities and rude scenes of frontier warfare. At any rate, his heart appears to have been taken by surprise.

The dinner, which in those days was an earlier meal than at present, seemed all too short. The afternoon passed away like a dream. Bishop was punctual to the orders he had received on halting. The horses pawed at the door, but for once Washington loitered in the path of duty. The horses were countermanded and it was not until the next morning that he was again in the saddle, spurring for Williamsburg. Happily the White House, the residence of Mrs. Custis, was in New Kent County, at no great distance from that city, so that he had opportunities of visiting her in the intervals of business. His time for courtship, however, was brief. Military duties called him back almost immediately to Winchester. But he feared, should he leave the matter in suspense, some more enterprising rival might supplant him during his absence, as in the case of Miss Phillipse at New York. He improved therefore his brief opportunity to the utmost. The blooming widow had many suitors but Washington was graced with that renown so ennobling in the eyes of woman. In a word, before they separated, they had mutually plighted their faith, and the marriage was to take place as soon as the campaign against Fort Duquesne was at an end.

Before returning to Winchester, Washington was obliged to hold conferences with Sir John St. Clair and Colonel Bouquet at an intermediate rendezvous to give them information respecting the frontiers and arrange about the marching of his troops. His constant word to them was forward! forward! For the precious time for action was slipping away, and he feared their Indian allies, so important to their security while on the march, might with their usual fickleness lose patience and return home.

On arriving at Winchester he found his troops restless and discontented from prolonged inaction, the inhabitants impatient of the burdens imposed on them and of the disturbances of an idle camp, while the Indians, as he apprehended, had deserted outright. It was a great relief therefore when he received orders from the commander-in-chief to repair to Fort Cumberland. He arrived there on the 2d of July and proceeded to open a road between that post and head-quarters at Raystown, thirty miles distant, where Colonel Bouquet was stationed.

His troops were scantily supplied with regimental clothing. The weather was oppressively warm. He now conceived the idea of equipping them in the light Indian hunting garb, and even of adopting it himself. Two companies were accordingly equipped in this style and sent under the command of Major Lewis to head-quarters. "It is an unbecoming dress, I own, for an officer," writes

Washington, "but convenience rather than show, I think, should be consulted. The reduction of bat-horses alone would be sufficient to recommend it, for nothing is more certain than that less baggage would be required."

The experiment was successful. "The dress takes very well here," writes Colonel Bouquet, "and, thank God, we see nothing but shirts and blankets. . . . Their dress should be one pattern for this expedition." Such was probably the origin of the American rifle dress, afterwards so much worn in warfare, and modelled on the Indian costume.

The army was now annoyed by scouting parties of Indians hovering about the neighborhood. Expresses passing between the posts were fired upon. A wagoner was shot down. Washington sent out counter-parties of Cherokees. Colonel Bouquet required that each party should be accompanied by an officer and a number of white men. Washington complied with the order, though he considered them an encumbrance rather than an advantage. "Small parties of Indians," said he, "will more effectually harass the enemy by keeping them under continual alarms than any parties of white men can do. For small parties of the latter are not equal to the task, not being so dexterous at skulking as Indians. And large parties will be discovered by their spies early enough to have a superior force opposed to them." With all his efforts, however, he was never able fully to make the officers of the regular army appreciate the importance of Indian allies in these campaigns in the wilderness.

On the other hand he earnestly discountenanced a proposition of Colonel Bouquet to make an irruption into the enemy's country with a strong party of regulars. Such a detachment, he observed, could not be sent without a cumbersome train of supplies, which would discover it to the enemy, who must at that time be collecting his whole force at Fort Duquesne. The enterprise therefore would be likely to terminate in a miscarriage if not in the destruction of the party. We shall see that his opinion was oracular.

As Washington intended to retire from military life at the close of this campaign, he had proposed himself to the electors of Frederick County as their representative in the House of Burgesses. The election was coming on at Winchester. His friends pressed him to attend it, and Colonel Bouquet gave him leave of absence, but he declined to absent himself from his post for the promotion of his political interests. There were three competitors in the field, yet so high was the public opinion of his merit that, though Winchester had been his headquarters for two or three years past and he had occasionally enforced martial law with a rigorous hand, he was elected by a large majority. The election was carried on somewhat in the English style. There was much eating and drinking at the expense of the candidate. Washington appeared on the hustings by proxy and his representative was chaired about the town with enthusiastic applause and huzzaing for Colonel Washington.

On the 21st of July arrived tidings of the brilliant success of that part of the scheme of the year's campaign conducted by General Amherst and Admiral Boscawen, who had reduced the strong town of Louisburg and gained possession of the Island of Cape Breton. This intelligence increased Washington's impatience at the delay of the expedition with which he was connected. He wished to rival these successes by a brilliant blow in the South. Perhaps a desire for personal distinction in the eyes of the lady of his choice may have been at the bottom of this impatience, for we are told that he kept up a constant correspondence with her throughout the campaign.

Understanding that the commander-in-chief had some thoughts of throwing a body of light troops in the advance, he wrote to Colonel Bouquet, earnestly soliciting his influence to have himself and his Virginia regiment included in the detachment. "If any argument is needed to obtain this favor," said he, "I hope without vanity I may be allowed to say that from long intimacy with these woods and frequent scouting in them, my men are at least as well acquainted with all the passes and difficulties as any troops that will be employed."

He soon learnt to his surprise, however, that the road to which his men were accustomed and which had been worked by Braddock's troops in his campaign was not to be taken in the present expedition, but a new one opened through the heart of Pennsylvania, from Raystown to Fort Duquesne, on the track generally taken by the northern traders. He instantly commenced long and repeated remonstrances on the subject, representing that Braddock's road from recent examination only needed partial repairs, and showing by clear calculation that an army could reach Fort

Duquesne by that route in thirty-four days, so that the whole campaign might be effected by the middle of October; whereas the extreme labor of opening a new road across mountains, swamps and through a densely wooded country would detain them so late that the season would be over before they could reach the scene of action. His representations were of no avail. The officers of the regular service had received a fearful idea of Braddock's road from his own despatches, wherein he had described it as lying "across mountains and rocks of an excessive height, vastly steep, and divided by torrents and rivers," whereas the Pennsylvania traders, who were anxious for the opening of the new road through their province, described the country through which it would pass as less difficult and its streams less subject to inundation. Above all, it was a direct line and fifty miles nearer. This route, therefore, to the great regret of Washington and the indignation of the Virginia Assembly, was definitely adopted, and sixteen hundred men were immediately thrown in the advance from Raystown to work upon it.

The first of September found Washington still encamped at Fort Cumberland, his troops sickly and dispirited, and the brilliant expedition which he had anticipated dwindling down into a tedious operation of road-making. In the meantime his scouts brought him word that the whole force at Fort Duquesne on the 13th of August, Indians included, did not exceed eight hundred men. Had an early campaign been pressed forward as he recommended, the place by this time would have been captured. At length, in the month of September, he received orders from General Forbes to join him with his troops at Raystown, where he had just arrived, having been detained by severe illness. He was received by the general with the highest marks of respect. On all occasions, both in private and at councils of war, that commander treated his opinions with the greatest deference. He moreover adopted a plan drawn out by Washington for the march of the army, and an order of battle which still exists, furnishing a proof of his skill in frontier warfare.

It was now the middle of September, yet the great body of men engaged in opening the new military road, after incredible toil had not advanced above forty-five miles, to a place called Loyal Hannan, a little beyond Laurel Hill. Colonel Bouquet, who commanded the division of nearly two thousand men sent forward to open this road, had halted at Loyal Hannan to establish a military post and deposit.

He was upwards of fifty miles from Fort Duquesne and was tempted to adopt the measure, so strongly discountenanced by Washington, of sending a party on a foray into the enemy's country. He accordingly detached Major Grant with eight hundred picked men, some of them Highlanders, others, in Indian garb, the part of Washington's Virginian regiment sent forward by him from Cumberland under command of Major Lewis.

The instructions given to Major Grant were merely to reconnoiter the country in the neighborhood of Fort Duquesne and ascertain the strength and position of the enemy. He conducted the enterprise with the foolhardiness of a man eager for personal notoriety. His whole object seems to have been by open bravado to provoke an action. The enemy were apprised through their scouts of his approach but suffered him to advance unmolested. Arriving at night in the neighborhood of the fort, he posted his men on a hill and sent out a party of observation, who set fire to a log-house near the walls and returned to the encampment. As if this were not sufficient to put the enemy on the alert, he ordered the reveille to be beaten in the morning in several places. Then, posting Major Lewis with his provincial troops at a distance in the rear to protect the baggage, he marshalled his regulars in battle array and sent an engineer with a covering party to take a plan of the works in full view of the garrison.

Not a gun was fired by the fort. The silence which was maintained was mistaken for fear and increased the arrogance and blind security of the British commander. At length, when he was thrown off his guard, there was a sudden sally of the garrison and an attack on the flanks by Indians hid in ambush. A scene now occurred similar to that at the defeat of Braddock. The British officers marshalled their men according to European tactics, and the Highlanders for some time stood their ground bravely, but the destructive fire and horrid yells of the Indians soon produced panic and confusion. Major Lewis at the first noise of the attack left Captain Bullitt with fifty Virginians to guard the baggage, and hastened with the main part of his men to the scene of action. The contest was kept up for some time but the confusion was irretrievable. The Indians sallied from their concealment and attacked with the tomahawk and scalping-knife. Lewis fought hand to hand with an Indian brave, whom he laid dead at his feet, but was surrounded by others and only saved his life by surrendering himself to a French officer. Major Grant surrendered himself in like manner. The whole detachment was put to the rout with dreadful carnage.

Captain Bullitt rallied several of the fugitives and prepared to make a forlorn stand as the only chance where the enemy was overwhelming and merciless. Despatching the most valuable baggage with the strongest horses, he made a barricade with the baggage wagons, behind which he posted his men, giving them orders how they were to act. All this was the thought and the work almost of a moment, for the savages, having finished the havoc and plunder of the field of battle, were hastening in pursuit of the fugitives. Bullitt suffered them to come near, when, on a concerted signal, a destructive fire was opened from behind the baggage wagons. They were checked for a time but were again pressing forward in greater numbers when Bullitt and his men held out the signal of capitulation and advanced as if to surrender. When within eight yards of the enemy they suddenly levelled their arms, poured a most effective volley and then charged with the bayonet. The Indians fled in dismay and Bullitt took advantage of this check to retreat with all speed, collecting the wounded and the scattered fugitives as he advanced. The routed detachment came back in fragments to Colonel Bouquet's camp at Loyal Hannan, with the loss of twenty-one officers and two hundred and seventy-three privates killed and taken. The Highlanders and the Virginians were those that fought the best and suffered the most in this bloody battle. Washington's regiment lost six officers and sixty-two privates.

If Washington could have taken any pride in seeing his presages of misfortune verified he might have been gratified by the result of this rash "irruption into the enemy's country," which was exactly what he had predicted. In his letters to Governor Fauquier, however, he bears lightly on the error of Col. Bouquet. "From all accounts I can collect," says he, "it appears very clear that this was a very ill-concerted or a very ill-executed plan, perhaps both, but it seems to be generally acknowledged that Major Grant exceeded his orders and that no disposition was made for engaging."

Washington, who was at Raystown when the disastrous news arrived, was publicly complimented by General Forbes on the gallant conduct of his Virginian troops, and Bullitt's behavior was "a matter of great admiration." The latter was soon after rewarded with a major's commission.

As a further mark of the high opinion now entertained of provincial troops for frontier service, Washington was given the command of a division, partly composed of his own men, to keep in the advance of the main body, clear the roads, throw out scouting parties and repel Indian attacks.

It was the 5th of November before the whole army assembled at Loyal Hannan. Winter was now at hand and upwards of fifty miles of wilderness were yet to be traversed by a road not yet formed, before they could reach Fort Duquesne. Again, Washington's predictions seemed likely to be verified and the expedition to be defeated by delay, for in a council of war it was determined to be impracticable to advance further with the army that season. Three prisoners, however, who were brought in gave such an account of the weak state of the garrison at Fort Duquesne, its want of provisions and the defection of the Indians, that it was determined to push forward. The march was accordingly resumed but without tents or baggage and with only a light train of artillery.

Washington still kept the advance. After leaving Loyal Hannan, the road presented traces of the late defeat of Grant, being strewed with human bones, the sad relics of fugitives cut down by the Indians, or of wounded soldiers who had died on the retreat. They lay mouldering in various stages of decay, mingled with the bones of horses and of oxen. As they approached Fort Duquesne these mementoes of former disasters became more frequent and the bones of those massacred in the defeat of Braddock still lay scattered about the battlefield, whitening in the sun.

At length the army arrived in sight of Fort Duquesne, advancing with great precaution and expecting a vigorous defense. But that formidable fortress, the terror and scourge of the frontier and the object of such warlike enterprise, fell without a blow. The recent successes of the English forces in Canada, particularly the capture and destruction of Fort Frontenac, had left the garrison without hope of reinforcements and supplies. The whole force at the time did not exceed five hundred men and the provisions were nearly exhausted. The commander therefore waited only until the English army was within one day's march, when he embarked his troops at night in bateaux, blew up his magazines, set fire to the fort and retreated down the Ohio by the light of the flames. On the 25th of November, Washington, with the advanced guard, marched in and planted the British flag on the yet smoking ruins.

One of the first offices of the army was to collect and bury in one common tomb the bones of their fellow-soldiers who had fallen in the battles of Braddock and Grant. In this pious duty it is said every one joined, from the general down to the private soldier, and some veterans assisted, with heavy hearts and frequent ejaculations of poignant feeling, who had been present in the scenes of defeat and carnage.

The ruins of the fortress were now put in a defensible state and garrisoned by two hundred men from Washington's regiment. The name was changed to that of Fort Pitt in honor of the illustrious British minister whose measures had given vigor and effect to this year's campaign. It has since been modified into Pittsburg and designates one of the most busy and populous cities of the interior.

The reduction of Fort Duquesne terminated, as Washington had foreseen, the troubles and dangers of the southern frontier. The French domination of the Ohio was at an end. The Indians, as usual, paid homage to the conquering power, and a treaty of peace was concluded with all the tribes between the Ohio and the lakes.

With this campaign ended for the present the military career of Washington. His great object was attained, the restoration of quiet and security to his native province; and, having abandoned all hope of attaining rank in the regular army, and his health being much impaired, he gave up his commission at the close of the year and retired from the service, followed by the applause of his fellow-soldiers and the gratitude and admiration of all his countrymen.

His marriage with Mrs. Custis took place shortly after his return. It was celebrated on the 6th of January 1759 at the White House, the residence of the bride, in the good old hospitable style of Virginia amid a joyous assemblage of relatives and friends.

Before following Washington into the retirement of domestic life, we think it proper to notice the events which closed the great struggle between England and France for empire in America. In that struggle he had first become practised in arms and schooled in the ways of the world, and its results will be found connected with the history of his later years. [The conflict between England

and France for control of America ended in the capitulation of the French, who ceded not only Montreal but all of Canada.]

A French statesman and diplomatist consoled himself by the persuasion that it would be a fatal triumph to England. It would remove the only check by which her colonies were kept in awe. "They will no longer need her protection," said he. "She will call on them to contribute toward supporting the burdens they have helped to bring on her, and they will answer by striking off all dependence."[1]

[1] Count de Vergennes, French ambassador at Constantinople.

Chapter 10

INCREASING DISCONTENT IN THE
COLONIES

For three months after his marriage Washington resided with his bride at the "White House." During his sojourn there he repaired to Williamsburg to take his seat in the House of Burgesses. By a vote of the House it had been determined to greet his installation by a signal testimonal of respect. Accordingly, as soon as he took his seat, Mr. Robinson, the Speaker, in eloquent language dictated by the warmth of private friendship returned thanks on behalf of the colony for the distinguished military services he had rendered to his country.

Washington rose to reply, blushed, stammered, trembled and could not utter a word. "Sit down, Mr. Washington," said the Speaker with a smile. "Your modesty equals your valor, and that surpasses the power of any language I possess."

Such was Washington's first launch into civil life, in which he was to be distinguished by the same judgment, devotion, courage and magnanimity exhibited in his military career. He attended the House frequently during the remainder of the session, after which he conducted his bride to his favorite abode of Mount Vernon.

Mr. Custis, the first husband of Mrs. Washington, had left large landed property and forty-five thousand pounds sterling in money. One third fell to his widow in her own right. Two thirds were inherited equally by her two children, a boy of six and a girl of four years of age. By a decree of the General Court, Washington was intrusted with the care of the property inherited by the children, a sacred and delicate trust which he discharged in the most faithful and judicious manner, becoming more like a parent than a mere guardian to them.

A style of living prevailed among the opulent Virginian families in those days that has long since faded away. The houses were spacious, commodious, liberal in all their appointments and fitted to cope with the free-handed, open-hearted hospitality of the owners. Nothing was more common than to see handsome services of plate, elegant equipages and superb carriage horses, all imported from England.

The Virginians have always been noted for their love of horses, a manly passion which in those days of opulence they indulged without regard to expense. The rich planters vied with each other in their studs, importing the best English stocks. Mention is made of one of the Randolphs of Tuckahoe, who built a stable for his favorite dapple-gray horse, Shakespeare, with a recess for the bed of the negro groom, who always slept beside him at night.

Washington by his marriage had added above one hundred thousand dollars to his already considerable fortune and was enabled to live in ample and dignified style. His intimacy with the Fairfaxes and his intercourse with British officers of rank had perhaps had their influence on his mode of living. He had his chariot and four, with black postilions in livery, for the use of Mrs. Washington and her lady visitors. As for himself, he always appeared on horseback. His stable was well filled and admirably regulated. His stud was thoroughbred and in excellent order. His household books contain registers of the names, ages and marks of his various horses, such as Ajax, Blueskin, Valiant, Magnolia (an Arab), etc.; also his dogs, chiefly fox-hounds, Vulcan, Singer, Ringwood, Sweetlips, Forester, Music, Rockwood, Truelove, etc.[1]

A large Virginia estate in those days was a little empire. The mansion-house was the seat of government, with its numerous dependencies, such as kitchens, smoke-houses, workshops and stables. In this mansion the planter ruled supreme. His steward or overseer was his prime minister and executive officer. He had his

[1] In one of his letter-books we find orders on his London agent for riding equipments. For example:

1 man's riding-saddle, hogskin seat, large plated stirrups and everything complete. Double-reined bridle and Pelham bit, plated.

A very neat and fashionable Newmarket saddle-cloth.

A large and best portmanteau, saddle, bridle and pillion.

Cloak-bag surcingle; checked saddle-cloth, holsters, etc.

A riding-frock of a handsome drab-colored broadcloth, with plain double gilt buttons.

A riding waistcoat of superfine scarlet cloth and gold lace, with buttons like those of the coat.

A blue surtout coat.

A neat switch whip, silver cap.

Black velvet cap for servant.

legion of house negroes for domestic service and his host of field negroes for the culture of tobacco, Indian corn and other crops, and for other out-of-door labor. Their quarter formed a kind of hamlet apart composed of various huts, with little gardens and poultry yards, all well stocked, and swarms of little negroes gambolling in the sunshine. Then there were large wooden edifices for curing tobacco, the staple and most profitable production, and mills for grinding wheat and Indian corn, of which large fields were cultivated for the supply of the family and the maintenance of the negroes.

Among the slaves were artificers of all kinds, tailors, shoemakers, carpenters, smiths, wheelwrights and so forth, so that a plantation produced everything within itself for ordinary use. As to articles of fashion and elegance, luxuries and expensive clothing, they were imported from London, for the planters on the main rivers, especially the Potomac, carried on an immediate trade with England. Their tobacco was put up by their own negroes, bore their own marks, was shipped on board of vessels which came up the river for the purpose and consigned to some agent in Liverpool or Bristol with whom the planter kept an account.

The Virginia planters were prone to leave the care of their estates too much to their overseers and to think personal labor a degradation. Washington carried into his rural affairs the same method, activity and circumspection that had distinguished him in military life. He kept his own accounts, posted up his books and balanced them with mercantile exactness. We have examined them as well as his diaries recording his daily occupations, and his letter-books containing entries of shipments of tobacco, and correspondence with his London agents. They are monuments of his business habits.

The products of his estate also became so noted for the faithfulness as to quality and quantity with which they were put up, that it is said any barrel of flour that bore the brand of George Washington, Mount Vernon, was exempted from the customary inspection in the West Indian ports.[2]

He was an early riser, often before daybreak in the winter when the nights were long. On such occasions he lit his own fire and wrote or read by candle-light. He breakfasted at seven in summer, at eight in winter. Two small cups of tea and three or four cakes

[2] Speech of the Hon. Robert C. Winthrop, on laying the corner-stone of Washington's Monument.

of Indian meal (called hoe-cakes) formed his frugal repast. Immediately after breakfast he mounted his horse and visited those parts of the estate where any work was going on, seeing to everything with his own eyes and often aiding with his own hands.

Dinner was served at two o'clock. He ate heartily but was no epicure, nor critical about his food. His beverage was small beer or cider and two glasses of old Madeira. He took tea, of which he was very fond, early in the evening and retired for the night about nine o'clock.

If confined to the house by bad weather, he took that occasion to arrange his papers, post up his accounts or write letters, passing part of the time in reading, and occasionally reading aloud to the family.

He treated his negroes with kindness, attended to their comforts, was particularly careful of them in sickness, but never tolerated idleness and exacted a faithful performance of all their allotted tasks. He had a quick eye at calculating each man's capabilities. An entry in his diary gives a curious instance of this. Four of his negroes, employed as carpenters, were hewing and shaping timber. It appeared to him, in noticing the amount of work accomplished between two succeeding mornings, that they loitered at their labor. Sitting down quietly, he timed their operations, how long it took them to get their cross-cut saw and other implements ready, how long to clear away the branches from the trunk of a fallen tree, how long to hew and saw it, what time was expended in considering and consulting and after all, how much work was effected during the time he looked on. From this he made his computation how much they could execute in the course of a day, working entirely at their ease.

At another time we find him working for a part of two days with Peter, his smith, to make a plough on a new invention of his own. This, after two or three failures, he accomplished. Then, with less than his usual judgment, he put his two chariot horses to the plough and ran a great risk of spoiling them in giving his new invention a trial over ground thickly swarded.

Anon, during a thunderstorm, a frightened negro alarms the house with word that the mill is giving way, upon which there is a general turn-out of all the forces, with Washington at their head, wheeling and shovelling gravel during a pelting rain to check the rushing water.

Washington delighted in the chase. In the hunting season, when he rode out early in the morning to visit distant parts of the estate where work was going on, he often took some of the dogs with him for the chance of starting a fox, which he occasionally did, though he was not always successful in killing him. He was a bold rider and an admirable horseman though he never claimed the merit of being an accomplished fox-hunter. In the height of the season, however, he would be out with the fox-hounds two or three times a week, accompanied by his guests at Mount Vernon and the gentlemen of the neighborhood, especially the Fairfaxes of Belvoir, of which estate his friend George William Fairfax was now the proprietor. On such occasions there would be a hunting dinner at one or other of those establishments, at which convivial repasts Washington is said to have enjoyed himself with unwonted hilarity.

Occasionally he and Mrs. Washington would pay a visit to Annapolis, at that time the seat of government of Maryland, and partake of the gayeties which prevailed during the session of the legislature. The society of these seats of provincial government was always polite and fashionable and more exclusive than in these republican days, being in a manner the outposts of the English aristocracy, where all places of dignity or profit were secured for younger sons and poor but proud relatives. During the session of the legislature, dinners and balls abounded and there were occasional attempts at theatricals. The latter was an amusement for which Washington always had a relish though he never had an opportunity of gratifying it effectually. Neither was he disinclined to mingle in the dance, and we remember to have heard venerable ladies, who had been belles in his day, pride themselves on having had him for a partner, though, they added, he was apt to be a ceremonious and grave one.[3]

In this round of rural occupation, rural amusements and social

---

[3] We have had an amusing picture of Annapolis, as it was at this period, furnished to us some years since by an octogenarian who had resided there in his boyhood. "In those parts of the country," said he, "where the roads were too rough for carriages the ladies used to ride on ponies, followed by black servants on horseback." In this way his mother, then advanced in life, used to travel in a scarlet cloth riding-habit which she had procured from England. "Nay, in this way, on emergencies," he added, "the young ladies from the country used to come to the balls at Annapolis, riding with their hoops arranged 'fore and aft' like lateen sails, and after dancing all night would ride home again in the morning."

intercourse, Washington passed several tranquil years, the halcyon season of his life. His already established reputation drew many visitors to Mount Vernon. Some of his early companions in arms were his occasional guests, and his friendships and connections linked him with some of the most prominent and worthy people of the country, who were sure to be received with cordial but simple and unpretending hospitality. His marriage was unblessed with children, but those of Mrs. Washington experienced from him parental care and affection, and the formation of their minds and manners was one of the dearest objects of his attention. His domestic concerns and social enjoyments, however, were not permitted to interfere with public duties. He was active by nature and eminently a man of business by habit. As judge of the county court and member of the House of Burgesses he had numerous calls upon his time and thoughts and was often drawn from home, for whatever trust he undertook he was sure to fulfil with scrupulous exactness.

Public events were now taking a tendency which, without any political aspiration or forethought of his own, was destined gradually to bear him away from his quiet home and individual pursuits and launch him upon a grander and wider sphere of action than any in which he had hitherto been engaged.

The recent war of Great Britain for dominion in America, though crowned with success, had engendered a progeny of discontents in her colonies. Washington was among the first to perceive its bitter fruits. British merchants had complained loudly of losses sustained by the depreciation of the colonial paper issued during the late war in times of emergency, and had addressed a memorial on the subject to the Board of Trade. Scarce was peace concluded when an order from the board declared that no paper issued by colonial assemblies should thenceforward be a legal tender in the payment of debts. Washington deprecated this "stir of the merchants" as peculiarly ill-timed and expressed an apprehension that the orders in question "would set the whole country in flames."

We do not profess in this personal memoir to enter into a wide scope of general history but shall content ourselves with a glance at the circumstances and events which gradually kindled the conflagration thus apprehended by the anxious mind of Washington.

Whatever might be the natural affection of the colonies for the mother country—and there are abundant evidences to prove that it was deep-rooted and strong—it had never been properly reciprocated. They yearned to be considered as children. They were treated by her as changelings. Burke testifies that her policy towards them from the beginning had been purely commercial and her commercial policy wholly restrictive. "It was the system of a monopoly."

Her navigation laws had shut their ports against foreign vessels, obliged them to export their productions only to countries belonging to the British crown, to import European goods solely from England and in English ships, and had subjected the trade between the colonies to duties. All manufactures, too, in the colonies that might interfere with those of the mother country had been either totally prohibited or subjected to intolerable restraints.

The acts of Parliament imposing these prohibitions and restrictions had at various times produced sore discontent and opposition on the part of the colonies, especially among those of New England. The interests of these last were chiefly commercial and among them the republican spirit predominated. They had sprung into existence during that part of the reign of James I when disputes ran high about kingly prerogatives and popular privilege.

The Pilgrims, as they styled themselves, who founded Plymouth Colony in 1620, had been incensed while in England by what they stigmatized as the oppressions of the monarchy and the Established Church. They had sought the wilds of America for the indulgence of freedom of opinion and had brought with them the spirit of independence and self-government. Those who followed them in the reign of Charles I were imbued with the same spirit and gave a lasting character to the people of New England.

Other colonies, having been formed under other circumstances, might be inclined toward a monarchical government and disposed to acquiesce in its exactions, but the republican spirit was ever alive in New England, watching over "natural and chartered rights" and prompt to defend them against any infringement. Its example and instigation had gradually an effect on the other colonies. A general impatience was evinced from time to time of parliamentary interference in colonial affairs and a disposition in the various provincial legislatures to think and act for themselves in matters of civil and religious as well as commercial polity.

There was nothing, however, to which the jealous sensibilities of the colonies were more alive than to any attempt of the mother country to draw a revenue from them by taxation. From the earliest period of their existence they had maintained the principle that they could only be taxed by a legislature in which they were represented. Sir Robert Walpole, when at the head of the British Government, was aware of their jealous sensibility on this point and cautious of provoking it. When American taxation was suggested, "it must be a bolder man than himself," he replied, "and one less friendly to commerce, who should venture on such an expedient." For his part, he would encourage the trade of the colonies to the utmost. One half of the profits would be sure to come into the royal exchequer through the increased demand for British manufactures. "This," said he sagaciously, "is taxing them more agreeably to their own constitution and laws."

Subsequent ministers adopted a widely different policy. During the progress of the French war, various projects were discussed in England with regard to the colonies, which were to be carried into effect on the return of peace. The open avowal of some of these plans and vague rumors of others more than ever irritated the jealous feelings of the colonists and put the dragon spirit of New England on the alert.

In 1760 there was an attempt in Boston to collect duties on foreign sugar and molasses imported into the colonies. Writs of assistance were applied for by the custom-house officers, authorizing them to break open ships, stores and private dwellings in quest of all articles that had paid no duty, and to call the assistance of others in the discharge of their odious task. The merchants opposed the execution of the writ on constitutional grounds. The question was argued in court, where James Otis spoke so eloquently in vindication of American rights that all his hearers went away ready to take arms against writs of assistance. "Then and there," says John Adams, who was present, "was the first scene of opposition to the arbitrary claims of Great Britain. Then and there American Independence was born."

Another ministerial measure was to instruct the provincial governors to commission judges, not as theretofore "during good behavior," but "during the king's pleasure." New York was the first to resent this blow at the independence of the judiciary. The lawyers appealed to the public through the press against an act which subjected the halls of justice to the prerogative. Their appeals were felt beyond the bounds of the province and awakened a general spirit of resistance.

Thus matters stood at the conclusion of the war. One of the first measures of ministers on the return of peace was to enjoin on all naval officers stationed on the coasts of the American colonies the performance under oath of the duties of the custom-house officers for the suppression of smuggling. This fell ruinously upon a clandestine trade which had long been connived at between the English and Spanish colonies, profitable to both but especially to the former and beneficial to the mother country, opening a market to her manufactures.

"Men-of-war," says Burke, "were for the first time armed with the regular commissions of custom-house officers, invested the coasts and gave the collection of revenue the air of hostile contribution. . . . They fell so indiscriminately on all sorts of contraband or supposed contraband that some of the most valuable branches of trade were driven violently from our ports, which caused an universal consternation throughout the colonies."[4]

As a measure of retaliation, the colonists resolved not to purchase British fabrics but to clothe themselves as much as possible in home manufactures. The demand for British goods in Boston alone was diminished upwards of £10,000 sterling in the course of a year.

In 1764 George Grenville, now at the head of government, ventured upon the policy from which Walpole had so wisely abstained. Early in March the eventful question was debated "whether they had a right to tax America." It was decided in the affirmative. Next followed a resolution declaring it proper to charge certain stamp duties in the colonies and plantations, but no immediate step was taken to carry it into effect. Mr. Grenville, however, gave notice to the American agents in London that he should introduce such a measure on the ensuing session of Parliament. In the meantime Parliament perpetuated certain duties on sugar and molasses—heretofore subjects of complaint and opposition—now reduced and modified so as to discourage smuggling and thereby to render them more productive. Duties also were imposed on other articles of foreign produce or manufacture imported into the colonies. To reconcile the latter to these impositions it was stated that the revenue thus raised was to be

[4] Burke on the State of the Nation.

appropriated to their protection and security, in other words to the support of a standing army intended to be quartered upon them.

We have briefly stated but a part of what Burke terms an "infinite variety of paper chains," extending through no less than twenty-nine acts of Parliament, from 1660 to 1764, by which the colonies had been held in thraldom.

The New Englanders were the first to take the field against the project of taxation. They denounced it as a violation of their rights as freemen; of their chartered rights, by which they were to tax themselves for their support and their defense; of their rights as British subjects, who ought not to be taxed but by themselves or their representatives. They sent petitions and remonstrances on the subject to the king, the lords and the commons, in which they were seconded by New York and Virginia. Franklin appeared in London at the head of agents from Pennsylvania, Connecticut and South Carolina to deprecate in person measures so fraught with mischief. The most eloquent arguments were used by British orators and statesmen to dissuade Grenville from enforcing them. He was warned of the sturdy independence of the colonists and the spirit of resistance he might provoke. All was in vain. Grenville, "great in daring and little in views," says Horace Walpole, "was charmed to have an untrodden field before him of calculation and experiment." In March 1765 the act was passed according to which all instruments in writing were to be executed on stamped paper to be purchased from the agents of the British government. What was more, all offenses against the act could be tried in any royal, marine or admiralty court throughout the colonies, however distant from the place where the offense had been committed, thus interfering with that most inestimable right, a trial by jury.

It was an ominous sign that the first burst of opposition to this act should take place in Virginia. That colony had hitherto been slow to accord with the republican spirit of New England. Founded at an earlier period of the reign of James I, before kingly prerogative and ecclesiastical supremacy had been made matters of doubt and fierce dispute, it had grown up in loyal attachment to king, church and constitution; was aristocratical in its tastes and habits and had been remarked above all the other colonies for its sympathies with the mother country. Moreover, it had not so many pecuniary interests involved in these questions as had the people of New England, being an agricultural rather than a commercial province. But the Virginians are of a quick and generous spirit, readily aroused on all points of honorable pride, and they resented the stamp act as an outrage on their rights.

Washington occupied his seat in the House of Burgesses when on the 29th of May the stamp act became a subject of discussion. We have seen no previous opinions of his on the subject. His correspondence hitherto had not turned on political or speculative themes, being engrossed by either military or agricultural matters and evincing little anticipation of the vortex of public duties into which he was about to be drawn. All his previous conduct and writings show a loyal devotion to the crown, with a patriotic attachment to his country. It is probable that on the present occasion that latent patriotism received its first electric shock.

Among the burgesses sat Patrick Henry, a young lawyer who had recently distinguished himself by pleading against the exercise of the royal prerogative in church matters and who was now for the first time a member of the House. Rising in his place, he introduced his celebrated resolutions declaring that the General Assembly of Virginia had the exclusive right and power to lay taxes and impositions upon the inhabitants and that whoever maintained the contrary should be deemed an enemy to the colony.

The Speaker, Mr. Robinson, objected to the resolutions as inflammatory. Henry vindicated them as justified by the nature of the case, went into an able and constitutional discussion of colonial rights and an eloquent exposition of the manner in which they had been assailed; wound up by one of those daring flights of declamation for which he was remarkable, and startled the House by a warning flash from history: "Cæsar had his Brutus, Charles his Cromwell and George the Third—('Treason! treason!' resounded from the neighborhood of the Chair)—may profit by their examples," added Henry. "Sir, if this be treason (bowing to the Speaker), make the most of it!"

These resolutions were modified to accommodate them to the scruples of the Speaker and some of the members but their spirit was retained. The Lieutenant-Governor (Fauquier), startled by this patriotic outbreak, dissolved the Assembly and issued writs for a new election but the clarion had sounded. "The resolves of the Assembly of Virginia," says a correspondent of the ministry, "gave the signal for a general outcry over the continent. The movers and supporters of them were applauded as the protectors and asserters of American liberty."[5]

[5] Letter to Secretary Conway, New York, Sept. 23. *Parliamentary Register.*

Chapter 11

SPIRITED MEASURES IN BOSTON

Washington returned to Mount Vernon full of anxious thoughts inspired by the political events of the day and the legislative scene which he witnessed. His recent letters had spoken of the state of peaceful tranquillity in which he was living. Those now written from his rural home show that he fully participated in the popular feeling and that while he had a presentiment of an arduous struggle, his patriotic mind was revolving means of coping with it. Such is the tenor of a letter written to his wife's uncle, Francis Dandridge, then in London.

"The stamp act," said he, "engrosses the conversation of the speculative part of the colonists, who look upon this unconstitutional method of taxation as a direful attack upon their liberties and loudly exclaim against the violation. What may be the result of this and of some other (I think I may add ill-judged) measures, I will not undertake to determine; but this I may venture to affirm, that the advantage accruing to the mother country will fall greatly short of the expectation of the ministry; for certain it is that our whole substance already in a manner flows to Great Britain and that whatsoever contributes to lessen our importations must be hurtful to her manufactures. The eyes of our people already begin to be opened, and they will perceive that many luxuries for which we lavish our substance in Great Britain can well be dispensed with. This, consequently, will introduce frugality and be a necessary incitement to industry. . . . As to the stamp act, regarded in a single view, one of the first bad consequences attending it is that our courts of judicature must inevitably be shut up, for it is impossible or next to impossible under our present circumstances that the act of Parliament can be complied with, were we ever so willing to enforce its execution. And not to say (which alone would be sufficient) that we have not money enough to pay for the stamps, there are many other cogent reasons which prove that it would be ineffectual."

A letter of the same date to his agents in London, of ample length and minute in its details, shows that, while deeply interested in the course of public affairs, his practical mind was enabled thoroughly and ably to manage the financial concerns of his estate and of the estate of Mrs. Washington's son, John Parke Custis, towards whom he acted the part of a faithful and affectionate guardian. In those days, Virginia planters were still in direct and frequent correspondence with their London factors, and Washington's letters respecting his shipments of tobacco and the returns required in various articles for household and personal use are perfect models for a man of business. And this may be remarked throughout his whole career: that no pressure of events nor multiplicity of cares prevented a clear, steadfast, under-current of attention to domestic affairs and the interest and well-being of all dependent upon him.

In the meantime, from his quiet abode at Mount Vernon he seemed to hear the patriotic voice of Patrick Henry, which had startled the House of Burgesses, echoing throughout the land and rousing one legislative body after another to follow the example of that of Virginia. At the instigation of the General Court or Assembly of Massachusetts, a Congress was held in New York in October, composed of delegates from Massachusetts, Rhode Island, Connecticut, New York, New Jersey, Pennsylvania, Delaware, Maryland and South Carolina. In this they denounced the acts of Parliament imposing taxes on them without their consent, and extending the jurisdiction of the courts of admiralty, as violations of their rights and liberties as natural-born subjects of Great Britain, and prepared an address to the king and a petition to both Houses of Parliament, praying for redress. Similar petitions were forwarded to England by the colonies not represented in the Congress.

The very preparations for enforcing the stamp act called forth popular tumults in various places. In Boston the stamp distributer was hanged in effigy, his windows were broken, a house intended for a stamp office was pulled down, and the effigy burnt in a bonfire made of the fragments. The lieutenant-governor, chief-justice and sheriff, attempting to allay the tumult, were pelted. The stamp officer thought himself happy to be hanged in effigy, and the next day publicly renounced the perilous office.

Various were the proceedings in other places, all manifesting public scorn and defiance of the act. In Virginia, Mr. George Mercer had been appointed distributer of stamps but on his arrival at Williamsburg publicly declined officiating. It was a fresh triumph to the popular cause. The bells were rung for joy, the town was illuminated and Mercer was hailed with acclamations of the people.[1]

The 1st of November, the day when the act was to go into operation, was ushered in with portentous solemnities. There was great tolling of bells and burning of effigies in the New England colonies. At Boston the ships displayed their colors but half-mast high. Many shops were shut, funeral knells resounded from the steeples, and there was a grand *auto-da-fé* in which the promoters of the act were paraded and suffered martyrdom in effigy.

At New York the printed act was carried about the streets on a pole, surmounted by a death's head with a scroll bearing the inscription: "The folly of England and ruin of America." Colden, the lieutenant-governor, who acquired considerable odium by recommending to government the taxation of the colonies, the institution of hereditary Assemblies and other Tory measures, seeing that a popular storm was rising, retired into the fort, taking with him the stamp papers, and garrisoned it with marines from a ship of war. The mob broke into his stable, drew out his chariot, put his effigy into it, paraded it through the streets to the common (now the Park), where they hung it on a gallows. In the evening it was taken down, put again into the chariot, with the devil for a companion, and escorted back by torchlight to the Bowling Green, where the whole pageant, chariot and all, was burnt under the very guns of the fort.

These are specimens of the marks of popular reprobation with which the stamp act was universally nullified. No one would venture to carry it into execution. In fact no stamped paper was to be seen; all had been either destroyed or concealed. All transactions which required stamps to give them validity were suspended or were executed by private compact. The courts of justice were closed, until at length some conducted their business without stamps. Union was becoming the watchword. The merchants of

[1] Holmes's *Annals*, vol. ii., p. 138.

New York, Philadelphia, Boston and such other colonies as had ventured publicly to oppose the stamp act agreed to import no more British manufactures after the 1st of January unless it should be repealed. So passed away the year 1765.

As yet Washington took no prominent part in the public agitation. Indeed, he was never disposed to put himself forward on popular occasions; his innate modesty forbade it. It was others, who knew his worth, that called him forth; but when once he engaged in any public measure, he devoted himself to it with conscientiousness and persevering zeal. At present he remained a quiet but vigilant observer of events from his eagle nest at Mount Vernon. He had some few intimates in his neighborhood who accorded with him in sentiment. One of the ablest and most efficient of these was Mr. George Mason, with whom he had occasional conversations on the state of affairs. His friends the Fairfaxes, though liberal in feelings and opinions, were too strong in their devotion to the crown not to regard with an uneasy eye the tendency of the popular bias. From one motive or other, the earnest attention of all the inmates and visitors at Mount Vernon was turned to England, watching the movements of the ministry.

The dismissal of Mr. Grenville from the cabinet gave a temporary change to public affairs. Perhaps nothing had a greater effect in favor of the colonies than an examination of Dr. Franklin before the House of Commons on the subject of the stamp act.

"What," he was asked, "was the temper of America towards Great Britain before the year 1763?"

"The best in the world. They submitted willingly to the government of the crown and paid, in all their courts, obedience to the acts of Parliament. Numerous as the people are in the several old provinces, they cost you nothing in forts, citadels, garrisons or armies to keep them in subjection. They were governed by this country at the expense only of a little pen and ink and paper. They were led by a thread. They had not only a respect but an affection for Great Britain, for its laws, its customs and manners, and even a fondness for its fashions, that greatly increased the commerce. Natives of Great Britain were always treated with particular regard. To be an Old-England man was of itself a character of some respect and gave a kind of rank among us."

"And what is their temper now?"

"Oh! Very much altered."

"If the act is not repealed, what do you think will be the consequences?"

"A total loss of the respect and affection the people of America bear to this country, and of all the commerce that depends on that respect and affection."

"Do you think the people of America would submit to pay the stamp duty if it was moderated?"

"No, never, unless compelled by force of arms."[2]

The act was repealed on the 18th of March 1766 to the great joy of the sincere friends of both countries and to no one more than to Washington. In one of his letters he observes: "Had the Parliament of Great Britain resolved upon enforcing it, the consequences, I conceive, would have been more direful than is generally apprehended, both to the mother country and her colonies. All, therefore, who were instrumental in procuring the repeal are entitled to the thanks of every British subject, and have mine cordially."[3]

Still there was a fatal clause in the repeal, which declared that the king, with the consent of Parliament, had power and authority to make laws and statutes of sufficient force and validity to "bind the colonies and people of America in all cases whatsoever."

As the people of America were contending for principles, not mere pecuniary interests, this reserved power of the crown and Parliament left the dispute still open and chilled the feeling of gratitude which the repeal might otherwise have inspired. Further aliment for public discontent was furnished by other acts of Parliament. One imposed duties on glass, pasteboard, white and red lead, painters' colors and tea, the duties to be collected on the arrival of the articles in the colonies. Another empowered naval officers to enforce the acts of trade and navigation. Another wounded to the quick the pride and sensibilities of New York. The mutiny act had recently been extended to America with an additional clause, requiring the provincial assemblies to provide the troops sent out with quarters, and to furnish them with fire, beds, candles and other necessaries at the expense of the colonies. The Governor and Assembly of New York refused to comply with this requisition as to stationary forces, insisting that it applied only to troops on a march. An act of Parliament now suspended

[2] *Parliamentary Register,* 1766.
[3] Sparks, *Writings of Washington,* ii., 345, note.

the powers of the Governor and Assembly until they should comply. Chatham attributed this opposition of the colonists to the mutiny act to "their jealousy of being somehow or other taxed internally by the Parliament. The act," said he, "asserting the right of Parliament has certainly spread a most unfortunate jealousy and diffidence of government here throughout America, and makes them jealous of the least distinction between this country and that, lest the same principle may be extended to taxing them."[4]

Boston continued to be the focus of what the ministerialists term sedition. The General Court of Massachusetts, not content with petitioning the king for relief against the recent measures of Parliament, especially those imposing taxes as a means of revenue, drew up a circular calling on the other colonial legislatures to join with them in suitable efforts to obtain redress. In the ensuing session Governor Sir Francis Bernard called upon them to rescind the resolution on which the circular was founded. They refused to comply and the General Court was consequently dissolved. The governors of other colonies required of their legislatures an assurance that they would not reply to the Massachusetts circular. These legislatures likewise refused compliance and were dissolved. All this added to the growing excitement.

Memorials were addressed to the lords, spiritual and temporal, and remonstrances to the House of Commons, against taxation for revenue, as destructive to the liberties of the colonists; and against the act suspending the legislative power of the province of New York as menacing the welfare of the colonies in general.

Nothing, however, produced a more powerful effect upon the public sensibilities throughout the country than certain military demonstrations at Boston. In consequence of repeated collisions between the people of that place and the commissioners of customs, two regiments were held in readiness at Halifax to embark for Boston in the ships of Commodore Hood whenever Governor Bernard or the general should give the word. "Had this force been landed in Boston six months ago," writes the commodore, "I am perfectly persuaded no address or remonstrances would have been sent from the other colonies and that all would have been tolerably quiet and orderly at this time throughout America."[5]

[4] Chatham's *Correspondence*, vol. iii., pp. 186–192.
[5] *Grenville Papers*, vol. iv., p. 362.

Tidings reached Boston that these troops were embarked and that they were coming to overawe the people. What was to be done? The General Court had been dissolved, and the governor refused to convene it without the royal command. A convention, therefore, from various towns met at Boston on the 22d of September to devise measures for the public safety but disclaiming all pretensions to legislative powers. While the convention was yet in session (September 28th), the two regiments arrived with seven armed vessels. "I am very confident," writes Commodore Hood from Halifax, "the spirited measures now pursuing will soon effect order in America."

On the contrary, these "spirited measures" added fuel to the fire they were intended to quench. It was resolved in a town meeting that the king had no right to send troops thither without the consent of the Assembly, that Great Britain had broken the original compact and that therefore the king's officers had no longer any business there.[6]

The "selectmen" accordingly refused to find quarters for the soldiers in the town. The council refused to find barracks for them lest it should be construed into a compliance with the disputed clause of the mutiny act. Some of the troops, therefore, which had tents were encamped on the common. Others, by the governor's orders, were quartered in the state-house, and others in Faneuil Hall, to the great indignation of the public, who were grievously scandalized at seeing field-pieces planted in front of the state-house, sentinels stationed at the doors, challenging every one who passed and, above all, at having the sacred quiet of the Sabbath disturbed by drum and fife and other military music.

Throughout these public agitations Washington endeavored to preserve his equanimity. Removed from the heated throngs of cities, his diary denotes a cheerful and healthful life at Mount Vernon, devoted to those rural occupations in which he delighted and varied occasionally by his favorite field sports. Sometimes he is duck-shooting on the Potomac. Repeatedly we find note of his being out at sunrise with the hounds in company with old Lord Fairfax, Bryan Fairfax and others and ending the day's sport by a dinner at Mount Vernon or Belvoir.

Still he was too true a patriot not to sympathize in the struggle for colonial rights which now agitated the whole country, and we

6 Whately to Grenville. *Gren. Papers*, vol. iv., p. 389.

find him gradually carried more and more into the current of political affairs.

A letter written on the 5th of April 1769 to his friend, George Mason, shows the important stand he was disposed to take. In the previous year the merchants and traders of Boston, Salem, Connecticut and New York had agreed to suspend for a time the importation of all articles subject to taxation. Similar resolutions had recently been adopted by the merchants of Philadelphia. Washington's letter is emphatic in support of the measure.

"At a time," writes he, "when our lordly masters in Great Britain will be satisfied with nothing less than the deprivation of American freedom, it seems highly necessary that something should be done to avert the stroke and maintain the liberty which we have derived from our ancestors. But the manner of doing it, to answer the purpose effectually, is the point in question. That no man should scruple or hesitate a moment in defense of so valuable a blessing is clearly my opinion; yet arms should be the last resource—the *dernier ressort*. We have already, it is said, proved the inefficiency of addresses to the throne and remonstrances to Parliament. How far their attention to our rights and interests is to be awakened or alarmed by starving their trade and manufactures remains to be tried.

"The northern colonies, it appears, are endeavoring to adopt this scheme. In my opinion it is a good one and must be attended with salutary effects, provided it can be carried pretty generally into execution. . . . That there will be a difficulty attending it everywhere from clashing interests and selfish, designing men ever attentive to their own gain and watchful of every turn that can assist their lucrative views cannot be denied, and in the tobacco colonies, where the trade is so diffused and in a manner wholly conducted by factors for their principals at home, these difficulties are certainly enhanced, but I think not insurmountably increased if the gentlemen in their several counties will be at some pains to explain matters to the people and stimulate them to cordial agreements to purchase none but certain enumerated articles out of any of the stores, after a definite period, and neither import nor purchase any themselves. . . . I can see but one class of people, the merchants excepted, who will not or ought not, to wish well to the scheme—namely, they who live genteelly and hospitably on clear estates. Such as these, were they not to consider the valuable object in view and the good of others, might think it hard to be curtailed in their living and enjoyments."

This was precisely the class to which Washington belonged but he was ready and willing to make the sacrifices required. "I think the scheme a good one," added he, "and that it ought to be tried here with such alterations as our circumstances render absolutely necessary."

Mason, in his reply, concurred with him in opinion.

"Our all is at stake," said he, "and the little conveniences and comforts of life, when set in competition with our liberty, ought to be rejected, not with reluctance but with pleasure. Yet it is plain that in the tobacco colonies we cannot at present confine our importations within such narrow bounds as the northern colonies. A plan of this kind, to be practicable, must be adapted to our circumstances; for, if not steadily executed, it had better have remained unattempted. We may retrench all manner of superfluities, finery of all descriptions, and confine ourselves to linens, woollens, etc., not exceeding a certain price. It is amazing how much this practice, if adopted in all the colonies, would lessen the American imports and distress the various trades and manufactures of Great Britain. This would awaken their attention. They would see, they would feel the oppressions we groan under, and exert themselves to procure us redress. This, once obtained, we should no longer discontinue our importations, confining ourselves still not to import any article that should hereafter be taxed by act of Parliament for raising a revenue in America; for, however singular I may be in the opinion, I am thoroughly convinced that, justice and harmony happily restored, it is not the interest of these colonies to refuse British manufactures. Our supplying our mother country with gross materials and taking her manufactures in return is the true chain of connection between us. These are the bands which, if not broken by oppression, must long hold us together by maintaining a constant reciprocation of interests."

The latter part of the above quotation shows the spirit which actuated Washington and the friends of his confidence. As yet there was no thought nor desire of alienation from the mother country but only a fixed determination to be placed on an equality of rights and privileges with her other children.

A single word in the passage cited from Washington's letter evinces the chord which still vibrated in the American bosom: he incidentally speaks of England as *home*. It was the familiar term with which she was usually indicated by those of English decent; and the writer of these pages remembers when the endearing phrase still lingered on Anglo-American lips even after the Revolution. How easy would it have been before that era for the mother country to have rallied back the affections of her colonial children by a proper attention to their complaints! They asked for nothing but what they were entitled to and what she had taught them to prize as their dearest inheritance. The spirit of liberty which they manifested had been derived from her own precept and example.

The result of the correspondence between Washington and Mason was the draft by the latter of a plan of association, the members of which were to pledge themselves not to import or use any articles of British merchandise or manufacture subject to duty. This paper Washington was to submit to the consideration of the House of Burgesses at the approaching session in the month of May.

The Legislature of Virginia opened on this occasion with a brilliant pageant. While military force was arrayed to overawe the republican Puritans of the east, it was thought to dazzle the aristocratical descendants of the cavaliers by the reflex of regal splendor. Lord Botetourt, one of the king's lords of the bed-chamber, had recently come out as governor of the province. Junius described him as "a cringing, bowing, fawning, sword-bearing courtier." Horace Walpole predicted that he would turn the heads of the Virginians in one way or another. "If his graces do not captivate them he will enrage them to fury; for I take all his *douceur* to be enamelled on iron."[7] The words of political satirists and court wits, however, are always to be taken with great distrust. However his lordship may have bowed in presence of royalty, he elsewhere conducted himself with dignity and won general favor by his endearing manners. He certainly showed promptness of spirit in his reply to the king on being informed of his appointment. "When will you be ready to go?" asked George III. "To-night, sir."

He had come out, however, with a wrong idea of the Americans. They had been represented to him as factious, immoral and prone to sedition; but vain and luxurious and easily captivated by parade and splendor. The latter foibles were aimed at in his appointment and fitting out. It was supposed that his titled rank

[7] *Grenville Papers*, iv., note to p. 330.

would have its effect. Then to prepare him for occasions of ceremony, a coach of state was presented to him by the king. He was allowed, moreover, the quantity of plate usually given to ambassadors, whereupon the joke was circulated that he was going "plenipo to the Cherokees."[8]

His opening of the session was in the style of the royal opening of Parliament. He proceeded in due parade from his dwelling to the capitol in his state coach, drawn by six milk-white horses. Having delivered his speech according to royal form, he returned home with the same pomp and circumstance.

The time had gone by, however, for such display to have the anticipated effect. The Virginian legislators penetrated the intention of this pompous ceremonial and regarded it with a deprecating smile. Sterner matters occupied their thoughts. They had come prepared to battle for their rights, and their proceedings soon showed Lord Botetourt how much he had mistaken them. Spirited resolutions were passed denouncing the recent act of Parliament imposing taxes, the power to do which, on the inhabitants of this colony, "was legally and constitutionally vested in the House of Burgesses, with consent of the council and of the king, or of his governor for the time being." Copies of these resolutions were ordered to be forwarded by the speaker to the legislatures of the other colonies, with a request for their concurrence.

Other proceedings of the burgesses showed their sympathy with their fellow-patriots of New England. A joint address of both Houses of Parliament had recently been made to the king, assuring him of their support in any further measures for the due execution of the laws in Massachusetts and beseeching him that all persons charged with treason or misprision of treason committed within that colony since the 30th of December 1767, might be sent to Great Britain for trial.

As Massachusetts had no General Assembly at this time, having been dissolved by government, the Legislature of Virginia generously took up the cause. An address to the king was resolved on, stating that all trials for treason or misprision of treason or for any crime whatever committed by any person residing in a colony ought to be in and before His Majesty's courts within said colony, and beseeching the king to avert from his loyal subjects those dangers and miseries which would ensue from seizing and carrying

---

[8] Whately to Geo. Grenville. *Grenville Papers.*

beyond sea any person residing in America suspected of any crime whatever, thereby depriving them of the inestimable privilege of being tried by a jury from the vicinage, as well as the liberty of producing witnesses on such trial.

Disdaining any further application to Parliament, the House ordered the speaker to transmit this address to the colonies' agent in England, with directions to cause it to be presented to the king and afterwards to be printed and published in the English papers.

Lord Botetourt was astonished and dismayed when he heard of these high-toned proceedings. Repairing to the capitol next day at noon, he summoned the speaker and members to the council chamber and addressed them in the following words:

"Mr. Speaker, and gentlemen of the House of Burgesses, I have learned of your resolves and augur ill of their effects. You have made it my duty to dissolve you, and you are dissolved accordingly."

The spirit conjured up by the late decrees of Parliament was not so easily allayed. The burgesses adjourned to a private house. Peyton Randolph, their late speaker, was elected moderator. Washington now brought forward a draft of the articles of the association concerted between him and George Mason. They formed the groundwork of an instrument signed by all present, pledging themselves neither to import nor use any goods, merchandise or manufactures taxed by Parliament to raise a revenue in America. This instrument was sent throughout the country for signature, and the scheme of non-importation, hitherto confined to a few northern colonies, was soon universally adopted. For his own part, Washington adhered to it rigorously throughout the year. The articles proscribed by it were never to be seen in his house, and his agent in London was enjoined to ship nothing for him while subject to taxation.

The popular ferment in Virginia was gradually allayed by the amiable and conciliatory conduct of Lord Botetourt. His lordship soon became aware of the erroneous notions with which he had entered upon office. His semiroyal equipage and state were laid aside. He examined into public grievances, became a strenuous advocate for the repeal of taxes and, authorized by his despatches from the ministry, assured the public that such repeal would speedily take place. His assurance was received with implicit faith, and for a while Virginia was quieted.

Chapter 12

MATTERS AT A CRISIS

"The worst is past and the spirit of sedition broken," writes Hood to Grenville early in the spring of 1769.[1] When the commodore wrote this his ships were in the harbor and troops occupied the town and he flattered himself that at length turbulent Boston was quelled. But it only awaited its time to be seditious according to rule. There was always an irresistible "method in its madness."

In the month of May the General Court, hitherto prorogued, met according to charter. A committee immediately waited on the governor, stating it was impossible to do business with dignity and freedom while the town was invested by sea and land and a military guard was stationed at the state-house, with cannon pointed at the door; and they requested the governor, as His Majesty's representative, to have such forces removed out of the port and gates of the city during the session of the Assembly.

The governor replied that he had no authority over either the ships or the troops. The court persisted in refusing to transact business while so circumstanced, and the governor was obliged to transfer the session to Cambridge. There he addressed a message to that body in July, requiring funds for the payment of the troops, and quarters for their accommodation. The Assembly, after ample discussion of past grievances, resolved that the establishment of a standing army in the colony in a time of peace was an invasion of natural rights, that a standing army was not known as a part of the British constitution and that the sending an armed force to aid the civil authority was unprecedented and highly dangerous to the people.

After waiting some days without receiving an answer to his message, the governor sent to know whether the Assembly would or

[1] *Grenville Papers*, vol. iii.

would not make provision for the troops. In their reply they followed the example of the Legislature of New York in commenting on the mutiny or billeting act, and ended by declining to furnish funds for the purposes specified, "being incompatible with their own honor and interest and their duty to their constituents." They were in consequence again prorogued, to meet in Boston on the 10th of January.

So stood affairs in Massachusetts. In the meantime the non-importation associations, being generally observed throughout the colonies, produced the effect on British commerce which Washington had anticipated, and Parliament was incessantly importuned by petitions from British merchants imploring its intervention to save them from ruin.

Early in 1770 an important change took place in the British cabinet. The Duke of Grafton suddenly resigned, and the reins of government passed into the hands of Lord North. He was a man of limited capacity but a favorite of the king and subservient to his narrow colonial policy. His administration, so eventful to America, commenced with an error. In the month of March an act was passed revoking all the duties laid in 1767, *excepting that on tea.* This single tax was continued, as he observed, "to maintain the parliamentary right of taxation," the very right which was the grand object of contest. In this, however, he was in fact yielding against his better judgment to the tenacity of the king.

He endeavored to reconcile the opposition, and perhaps himself, to the measure by plausible reasoning. An impost of threepence on the pound could never, he alleged, be opposed by the colonists unless they were determined to rebel against Great Britain. Besides, a duty on that article, payable in England and amounting to nearly one shilling on the pound, was taken off on its exportation to America so that the inhabitants of the colonies saved ninepence on the pound.

Here was the stumbling-block at the threshold of Lord North's administration. In vain the members of the opposition urged that this single exception, while it would produce no revenue, would keep alive the whole cause of contention; that so long as a single external duty was enforced, the colonies would consider their rights invaded and would remain unappeased. Lord North was not to be convinced, or rather he knew the royal will was inflexible, and he complied with its behests. "The properest time to exert our

right to taxation," said he, "is when the right is refused. To tem-
porize is to yield. And the authority of the mother country, if it is
now unsupported, will be relinquished forever: a total repeal cannot be thought of till America is prostrate at our feet."[2]

On the very day in which this ominous bill was passed in Parliament a sinister occurrence took place in Boston. Some of the
young men of the place insulted the military while under arms.
The latter resented it. The young men, after a scuffle, were put to
flight and pursued. The alarm bells rang. A mob assembled. The
custom-house was threatened. The troops in protecting it were assailed with clubs and stones and obliged to use their fire-arms,
before the tumult could be quelled. Four of the populace were
killed and several wounded. The troops were now removed from
the town, which remained in the highest state of exasperation.
And this untoward occurrence received the opprobrious and somewhat extravagant name of "the Boston massacre."

The colonists as a matter of convenience resumed the consumption of those articles on which the duties had been repealed but
continued on principle the rigorous disuse of tea, excepting such as
had been smuggled in. New England was particularly earnest in
the matter. Many of the inhabitants, in the spirit of their Puritan
progenitors, made a covenant to drink no more of the forbidden
beverage until the duty on tea should be repealed.

In Virginia the public discontents, which had been allayed by
the conciliatory conduct of Lord Botetourt and by his assurances,
made on the strength of letters received from the ministry, that
the grievances complained of would be speedily redressed, now
broke out with more violence than ever. The Virginians spurned
the mock-remedy which left the real cause of complaint un-
touched. His lordship also felt deeply wounded by the disin-
genuousness of ministers which led him into such a predicament,
and wrote home demanding his discharge. Before it arrived, an attack of bilious fever, acting upon a delicate and sensitive frame en-
feebled by anxiety and chagrin, laid him in his grave. He left
behind him a name endeared to the Virginians by his amiable
manners, his liberal patronage of the arts and, above all, by his
zealous intercession for their rights. Washington himself testifies
that he was inclined "to render every just and reasonable service to
the people whom he governed." A statue to his memory was

2 Holmes's *Amer. Annals*, vol. ii., p. 173.

decreed by the House of Burgesses, to be erected in the area of the capitol. It is still to be seen, though in a mutilated condition, in Williamsburg, the old seat of government, and a county in Virginia continues to bear his honored name.

The discontents of Virginia were irritated anew under his successor, the Earl of Dunmore. This nobleman had for a short time held the government of New York. When appointed to that of Virginia, he lingered for several months at his former post. In the meantime he sent his military secretary, Captain Foy, to attend to the despatch of business until his arrival, awarding to him a salary and fees to be paid by the colony.

The pride of the Virginians was piqued at his lingering at New York, as if he preferred its gayety and luxury to the comparative quiet and simplicity of Williamsburg. Their pride was still more piqued on his arrival by what they considered haughtiness on his part. The spirit of the "Ancient Dominion" was roused and his lordship experienced opposition at his very outset.

The first measure of the Assembly, at its opening, was to demand by what right he had awarded a salary and fees to his secretary without consulting it, and to question whether it was authorized by the crown.

His lordship had the good policy to rescind the unauthorized act, and in so doing mitigated the ire of the Assembly, but he lost no time in proroguing a body which, from various symptoms, appeared to be too independent and disposed to be untractable.

He continued to prorogue it from time to time, seeking in the interim to conciliate the Virginians and soothe their irritated pride. At length, after repeated prorogations, he was compelled by circumstances to convene it on the 1st of March 1773.

Washington was prompt in his attendance on the occasion and foremost among the patriotic members who eagerly availed themselves of this long wished-for opportunity to legislate upon the general affairs of the colonies. One of their most important measures was the appointment of a committee of eleven persons, "whose business it should be to obtain the most clear and authentic intelligence of all such acts and resolutions of the British Parliament, or proceedings of administration, as may relate to or affect the British colonies, and to maintain with their sister colonies a correspondence and communication."

The plan thus proposed by their "noble, patriotic sister colony of Virginia,"[3] was promptly adopted by the people of Massachusetts and soon met with general concurrence. These corresponding committees, in effect, became the executive power of the patriot party, producing the happiest concert of design and action throughout the colonies.

The general covenant against the use of taxed tea had operated disastrously against the interests of the East India Company and produced an immense accumulation of the proscribed article in their warehouses. To remedy this, Lord North brought in a bill (1773) by which the company were allowed to export their teas from England to any part whatever, without paying export duty. This, by enabling them to offer their teas at a low price in the colonies would, he supposed, tempt the Americans to purchase large quantities, thus relieving the company and at the same time benefiting the revenue by the impost duty. Confiding in the wisdom of this policy, the company disgorged their warehouses, freighted several ships with tea and sent them to various parts of the colonies. This brought matters to a crisis. One sentiment, one determination, pervaded the whole continent. Taxation was to receive its definite blow. Whoever submitted to it was an enemy to his country. From New York and Philadelphia the ships were sent back unladen to London. In Charleston the tea was unloaded and stored away in cellars and other places, where it perished. At Boston the action was still more decisive. The ships anchored in the harbor. Some small parcels of tea were brought on shore but the sale of them was prohibited. The captains of the ships, seeing the desperate state of the case, would have made sail back for England but they could not obtain the consent of the consignees, a clearance at the custom-house or a passport from the governor to clear the fort. It was evident the tea was to be forced upon the people of Boston and the principle of taxation established.

To settle the matter completely and prove that on a point of principle they were not to be trifled with, a number of inhabitants, disguised as Indians, boarded the ships in the night (18th December), broke open all the chests of tea and emptied the contents into the sea. This was no rash and intemperate proceeding of a mob but the well-considered though resolute act of sober, respectable citizens, men of reflection but determination. The whole was done calmly and in perfect order, after which the actors in the

[3] Boston Town Records.

scene dispersed without tumult and returned quietly to their homes.

The general opposition of the colonies to the principle of taxation had given great annoyance to government, but this individual act concentrated all its wrath upon Boston. A bill was forthwith passed in Parliament (commonly called the Boston Port bill), by which all lading and unlading of goods, wares and merchandise were to cease in that town and harbor on and after the 4th of June, and the officers of the customs to be transferred to Salem.

Another law, passed soon after, altered the charter of the province, decreeing that all counsellors, judges and magistrates should be appointed by the crown and hold office during the royal pleasure.

This was followed by a third, intended for the suppression of riots, and providing that any person indicted for murder or other capital offense committed in aiding the magistracy, might be sent by the governor to some other colony or to Great Britain for trial.

Such was the bolt of Parliamentary wrath fulminated against the devoted town of Boston. Before it fell there was a session in May of the Virginia House of Burgesses. The social position of Lord Dunmore had been strengthened in the province by the arrival of his lady and a numerous family of sons and daughters. The old Virginia aristocracy had vied with each other in hospitable attentions to the family. A court circle had sprung up. Regulations had been drawn up by a herald and published officially, determining the rank and precedence of civil and military officers and their wives. The aristocracy of the Ancient Dominion was furbishing up its former splendor. Carriages and four rolled into the streets of Williamsburg with horses handsomely caparisoned, bringing the wealthy planters and their families to the seat of government.

Washington arrived in Williamsburg on the 16th and dined with the governor on the day of his arrival, having a distinguished position in the court circle and being still on terms of intimacy with his lordship. The House of Burgesses was opened in form, and one of its first measures was an address of congratulation to the governor on the arrival of his lady. It was followed up by an agreement among the members to give her ladyship a splendid ball on the 27th of the month.

All things were going on smoothly and smilingly, when a letter, received through the corresponding committee, brought intelligence of the vindictive measure of Parliament by which the port of Boston was to be closed on the approaching 1st of June.

The letter was read in the House of Burgesses and produced a general burst of indignation. All other business was thrown aside and this became the sole subject of discussion. A protest against this and other recent acts of Parliament was entered upon the journal of the House, and a resolution was adopted on the 24th of May setting apart the 1st of June as a day of fasting, prayer and humiliation, in which the divine interposition was to be implored to avert the heavy calamity threatening destruction to their rights, and all the evils of civil war, and to give the people one heart and one mind in firmly opposing every injury to American liberties.

On the following morning, while the Burgesses were engaged in animated debate, they were summoned to attend Lord Dunmore in the council chamber, where he made them the following laconic speech: "Mr. Speaker and Gentlemen of the House of Burgesses: I have in my hand a paper, published by order of your House, conceived in such terms as reflect highly upon His Majesty and the Parliament of Great Britain, which makes it necessary for me to dissolve you, and you are dissolved accordingly."

As on a former occasion the Assembly, though dissolved, was not dispersed. The members adjourned to the long room of the old Raleigh tavern and passed resolutions denouncing the Boston Port bill as a most dangerous attempt to destroy the constitutional liberty and rights of all North America; recommending their countrymen to desist from the use not merely of tea but of all kinds of East Indian commodities; pronouncing an attack on one of the colonies, to enforce arbitrary taxes, an attack on all; and ordering the committee of correspondence to communicate with the other corresponding committees on the expediency of appointing deputies from the several colonies of British America to meet annually in General Congress at such place as might be deemed expedient, to deliberate on such measures as the united interests of the colonies might require.

This was the first recommendation of a General Congress by any public assembly, though it had been previously proposed in town meetings at New York and Boston. A resolution to the same effect was passed in the Assembly of Massachusetts before it was aware of the proceedings of the Virginia Legislature. The measure recommended met with prompt and general concurrence throughout the colonies, and the fifth day of September next ensuing was fixed upon for the first Congress, which was to be held at Philadelphia.

Notwithstanding Lord Dunmore's abrupt dissolution of the House of Burgesses, the members still continued on courteous terms with him, and the ball which they had decreed early in the session in honor of Lady Dunmore was celebrated on the 27th with unwavering gallantry.

As to Washington, widely as he differed from Lord Dunmore on important points of policy, his intimacy with him remained uninterrupted. By memorandums in his diary it appears that he dined and passed the evening at his lordship's on the 25th, the very day of the meeting at the Raleigh tavern; that he rode out with him to his farm and breakfasted there with him on the 26th, and on the evening of the 27th attended the ball given to her ladyship. Such was the well-bred decorum that seemed to quiet the turbulence of popular excitement without checking the full and firm expression of popular opinion.

On the 29th, two days after the ball, letters arrived from Boston giving the proceedings of a town-meeting, recommending that a general league should be formed throughout the colonies suspending all trade with Great Britain. But twenty-five members of the late House of Burgesses, including Washington, were at that time remaining in Williamsburg. They held a meeting on the following day, at which Peyton Randolph presided as moderator. After some discussion it was determined to issue a printed circular bearing their signatures and calling a meeting of all the members of the late House of Burgesses on the 1st of August to take into consideration this measure of a general league. The circular recommended them also to collect in the meantime the sense of their respective counties.

Washington was still at Williamsburg on the 1st of June, the day when the Port bill was to be enforced at Boston. It was ushered in by the tolling of bells and observed by all true patriots as a day of fasting and humiliation. Washington notes in his diary that he fasted rigidly and attended the services appointed in the church. Still his friendly intercourse with the Dunmore family was continued during the remainder of his sojourn in Williamsburg, where he was detained by business until the 20th, when he set out on his return to Mount Vernon.

In the meantime the Boston Port bill had been carried into effect. On the 1st of June the harbor of Boston was closed at noon and all business ceased. The two other Parliamentary acts altering the charter of Massachusetts were to be enforced. No public meeting, excepting the annual town meetings in March and May, were to be held without permission of the governor.

General Thomas Gage had recently been appointed to the military command of Massachusetts and the carrying out of these offensive acts. He was the same officer who as lieutenant-colonel had led the advance guard on the field of Braddock's defeat. Fortune had since gone well with him. Rising in the service, he had been governor of Montreal, and had succeeded Amherst in the command of the British forces on this continent. He was linked to the country also by domestic ties, having married into one of the most respectable families of New Jersey. In the various situations in which he had hitherto been placed he had won esteem and rendered himself popular.

[But his attempts to enforce the recent acts of Parliament were resented.] At the suggestion of the Assembly a paper was circulated through the province by the committee of correspondence, entitled "a solemn league and convenant," the subscribers to which bound themselves to break off all intercourse with Great Britain from the 1st of August until the colony should be restored to the enjoyment of its chartered rights, and to renounce all dealings with those who should refuse to enter into this compact.

The very title of league and covenant had an ominous sound and startled General Gage. He issued a proclamation denouncing it as illegal and traitorous. Furthermore, he encamped a force of infantry and artillery on Boston Common, as if prepared to enact the lion. An alarm spread through the adjacent country. "Boston is to be blockaded! Boston is to be reduced to obedience by force or famine!" The spirit of the yeomanry was aroused. They sent in word to the inhabitants promising to come to their aid if necessary and urging them to stand fast to the faith. Affairs were coming to a crisis. It was predicted that the new acts of Parliament would bring on "a most important and decisive trial."

Shortly after Washington's return to Mount Vernon in the latter part of June, he presided as a moderator at a meeting of the inhabitants of Fairfax County, wherein, after the recent acts of Parliament had been discussed, a committee was appointed, with himself as chairman, to draw up resolutions expressive of the sentiments of the present meeting and to report the same at a general meeting of the county, to be held in the courthouse on the 18th of July.

The course that public measures were taking shocked the loyal feelings of Washington's valued friend, Bryan Fairfax, of Tarlston Hall, a younger brother of George William, who was absent in England. He was a man of liberal sentiments but attached to the ancient rule; and, in a letter to Washington, advised a petition to the throne, which would give Parliament an opportunity to repeal the offensive acts.

"I would heartily join you in your political sentiments," writes Washington in reply, "as far as relates to a humble and dutiful petition to the throne, provided there was the most distant hope of success. But have we not tried this already? Have we not addressed the lords and remonstrated to the commons? And to what end? Does it not appear as clear as the sun in its meridian brightness that there is a regular, systematic plan to fix the right and practice of taxation upon us? . . . Is not the attack upon the liberty and property of the people of Boston, before restitution of the loss to the India Company was demanded, a plain and self-evident proof of what they are aiming at? Do not the subsequent bills for depriving the Massachusetts Bay of its charter and for transporting offenders to other colonies or to Great Britain for trial, where it is impossible, from the nature of things, that justice can be obtained, convince us that the administration is determined to stick at nothing to carry its point? Ought we not, then, to put our virtue and fortitude to the severest tests?"

The committee met according to appointment, with Washington as chairman. The resolutions framed at the meeting insisted as usual on the right of self-government and the principle that taxation and representation were in their nature inseparable. That the various acts of Parliament—for raising revenue, taking away trials by jury, ordering that persons might be tried in a different country than that in which the cause of accusation originated, closing the port of Boston, abrogating the charter of Massachusetts Bay, etc., etc.—were all part of a premeditated design and system to introduce arbitrary government into the colonies. That the sudden and repeated dissolutions of Assemblies whenever they presumed to examine the illegality of ministerial mandates, or deliberated on the violated rights of their constituents, were part of the same system and calculated and intended to drive the people of the colonies to a state of desperation and to dissolve the compact by which their ancestors bound themselves and their posterity to remain dependent on the British crown. The resolutions, furthermore, recommended the most perfect union and co-operation among the colonies, solemn covenants with respect to non-importation and non-intercourse, and a renunciation of all dealings with any colony, town or province that should refuse to agree to the plan adopted by the General Congress.

They also recommended a dutiful petition and remonstrance from the Congress to the king, asserting their constitutional rights and privileges, lamenting the necessity of entering into measures that might be displeasing, declaring their attachment to his person, family and government and their desire to continue in dependence upon Great Britain, beseeching him not to reduce his faithful subjects of America to desperation, and to reflect that from our sovereign there can be but one appeal.

These resolutions are the more worthy of note as expressive of the opinions and feelings of Washington at this eventful time, if not being entirely dictated by him. The last sentence is of awful import, suggesting the possibility of being driven to an appeal to arms.

The resolutions reported by the committee were adopted, and Washington was chosen a delegate to represent the county at the General Convention of the province, [which was] to be held in Williamsburg on the 1st of August.

Washington appeared on behalf of Fairfax County and presented the resolutions already cited, as the sense of his constituents. He is said by one who was present to have spoken in support of them in a strain of uncommon eloquence, which shows how his latent ardor had been excited on the occasion, as eloquence was not in general among his attributes. It is evident, however, that he was roused to an unusual pitch of enthusiasm, for he is said to have declared that he was ready to raise one thousand men, subsist them at his own expense and march at their head to the relief of Boston.[4]

[4] See information given to the elder Adams by Mr. Lynch of South Carolina.—*Adams's Diary.*

The Convention was six days in session. Resolutions in the same spirit with those passed in Fairfax County were adopted, and Peyton Randolph, Richard Henry Lee, George Washington, Patrick Henry, Richard Bland, Benjamin Harrison and Edmund Pendleton were appointed delegates to represent the people of Virginia in the Congress.

Washington had formed a correct opinion of General Gage. From the time of taking command at Boston, [Gage] had been perplexed how to manage its inhabitants. Had they been hot-headed, impulsive and prone to paroxysm, his task would have been comparatively easy, but it was the cool, shrewd common sense by which all their movements were regulated that confounded him.

High-handed measures had failed of the anticipated effect. Their harbor had been thronged with ships, their town with troops. The port bill had put an end to commerce. Wharves were deserted, warehouses closed, streets grass-grown and silent. The rich were growing poor, and the poor were without employ, yet the spirit of the people was unbroken. There was no uproar, however, no riots. Everything was awfully systematic and according to rule. Town meetings were held in which public rights and public measures were eloquently discussed by John Adams, Josiah Quincy and other eminent men. Over these meetings Samuel Adams presided as moderator, a man clear in judgment, calm in conduct, inflexible in resolution, deeply grounded in civil and political history, and infallible on all points of constitutional law.

Alarmed at the powerful influence of these assemblages, government issued an act prohibiting them after the 1st of August. The act was evaded by convoking the meetings before that day, and *keeping them alive* indefinitely. Gage was at a loss how to act. It would not do to disperse these assemblages by force of arms, for the people who composed them mingled the soldier with the polemic, and, like their prototypes, the Covenanters of yore, if prone to argue, were as ready to fight. So the meetings continued to be held pertinaciously. Faneuil Hall was at times unable to hold them, and they swarmed from that revolutionary hive into old South Church. The liberty-tree became a rallying place for any popular movement, and a flag hoisted on it was saluted by all processions as the emblem of the popular cause.

Opposition to the new plan of government assumed a more violent aspect at the extremity of the province and was abetted by Connecticut. "It is very high," writes Gage (August 27th), "in Berkshire County and makes way rapidly to the rest. At Worcester they threaten resistance, purchase arms, provide powder, cast balls and threaten to attack any troops who may oppose them. I apprehend I shall soon have to march a body of troops into that township."

The time appointed for the meeting of the General Congress at Philadelphia was now at hand. Delegates had already gone on from Massachusetts. "It is not possible to guess," writes Gage, "what a body composed of such heterogeneous matter will determine, but the members from hence, I am assured, will promote the most haughty and insolent resolves, for their plan has ever been, by threats and high-sounding sedition, to terrify and intimidate."

Chapter 13

THE FIRST CONGRESS

When the time approached for the meeting of the General
Congress, Washington was joined at Mount Vernon by Patrick
Henry and Edmund Pendleton and they performed the journey
together on horseback. Henry was then in the youthful vigor and
elasticity of his bounding genius, ardent, acute, fanciful, eloquent;
Pendleton, schooled in public life, a veteran in council, with native force of intellect and habits of deep reflection; Washington,
in the meridian of his days, mature in wisdom, comprehensive in
mind, sagacious in foresight. Such were the apostles of liberty
repairing on their august pilgrimage to Philadelphia from all parts
of the land to lay the foundations of a mighty empire. Well may
we say of that eventful period, "There were giants in those days."

Congress assembled on Monday the 5th of September in a large
room in Carpenter's hall. There were fifty-one delegates, representing all the colonies excepting Georgia.

The meeting has been described as "awfully solemn." The most
eminent men of the various colonies were now for the first time
brought together. They were known to each other by fame but
were, personally, strangers. The object which had called them
together was of incalculable magnitude. The liberties of no less
than three millions of people, with that of all their posterity, were
staked on the wisdom and energy of their councils.[1]

"It is such an assembly," writes John Adams, who was present,
"as never before came together on a sudden in any part of the
world. Here are fortunes, abilities, learning, eloquence, acuteness
equal to any I ever met with in my life. Here is a diversity of
religions, educations, manners, interests, such as it would seem
impossible to unite in one plan of conduct."

There being an inequality in the number of delegates from the

1 Wirt's *Life of Patrick Henry*, p. 224.

different colonies, a question arose as to the mode of voting, whether by colonies, by the poll or by interests.

Patrick Henry scouted the idea of sectional distinctions or individual interests. "All America," said he, "is thrown into one mass. Where are your landmarks—your boundaries of colonies? They are all thrown down. The distinctions between Virginians, Pennsylvanians, New Yorkers and New Englanders are no more. I am not a Virginian, but an American."[2]

After some debate it was determined that each colony should have but one vote, whatever might be the number of its delegates. The deliberations of the House were to be with closed doors, and nothing but the resolves promulgated, unless by order of the majority.

To give proper dignity and solemnity to the proceedings of the House, it was moved on the following day that each morning the session should be opened by prayer. To this it was demurred, that as the delegates were of different sects they might not consent to join in the same form of worship.

Upon this, Mr. Samuel Adams arose and said: "He would willingly join in prayer with any gentleman of piety and virtue, whatever might be his cloth, provided he was a friend of his country"; and he moved that the Reverend Mr. Duché of Philadelphia, who answered to that description, might be invited to officiate as chaplain. This was one step towards unanimity of feeling, Mr. Adams being a strong Congregationalist and Mr. Duché an eminent Episcopalian clergyman. The motion was carried into effect, the invitation was given and accepted.

In the course of the day a rumor reached Philadelphia that Boston had been cannonaded by the British. It produced a strong sensation, and when Congress met on the following morning (7th) the effect was visible in every countenance. The delegates from the east were greeted with a warmer grasp of the hand by their associates from the south.

The rumored attack rendered the service of the day deeply affecting to all present. They were one political family, actuated by one feeling and sympathizing with the weal and woe of each individual member. The rumor proved to be erroneous but it had produced a most beneficial effect in calling forth and quickening the spirit of union so vitally important in that assemblage.

Owing to closed doors and the want of reporters, no record

2 J. Adams's *Diary*.

exists of the discussions and speeches made in the first Congress. Mr. Wirt, speaking from tradition, informs us that a long and deep silence followed the organization of that august body, the members looking round upon each other, individually reluctant to open a business so fearfully momentous. This "deep and deathlike silence" was beginning to become painfully embarrassing, when Patrick Henry arose. He faltered at first, as was his habit, but his exordium was impressive, and as he launched forth into a recital of colonial wrongs he kindled with his subject until he poured forth one of those eloquent appeals which had so often shaken the House of Burgesses and gained him the fame of being the greatest orator of Virginia. He sat down, according to Mr. Wirt, amidst murmurs of astonishment and applause and was now admitted on every hand to be the first orator of America. He was followed by Richard Henry Lee, who, according to the same writer, charmed the House with a different kind of eloquence, chaste and classical, contrasting, in its cultivated graces, with the wild and grand effusions of Henry.

"The superior powers of these great men, however," adds he, "were manifested only in debate and while general grievances were the topic. When called down from the heights of declamation to that severer test of intellectual excellence, the details of business, they found themselves in a body of cool-headed, reflecting and most able men, by whom they were, in their turn, completely thrown into the shade."[3]

The first public measure of Congress was a resolution declaratory of their feelings with regard to the recent acts of Parliament violating the rights of the people of Massachusetts, and of their determination to combine in resisting any force that might attempt to carry those acts into execution.

A committee of two from each province reported a series of resolutions which were adopted by Congress as a "declaration of colonial rights."

In this were enumerated their natural rights to the enjoyment of life, liberty and property, and their rights as British subjects. Among the latter was participation in legislative councils. This they could not exercise through representatives in Parliament. They claimed, therefore, the power of legislating in the provincial Assemblies, consenting, however, to such acts of Parliament as

[3] Wirt's *Life of Patrick Henry.*

might be essential to the regulation of trade, but excluding all taxation, internal or external, for raising revenue in America.

The common law of England was claimed as a birthright, including the right of trial by a jury of the vicinage; of holding public meetings to consider grievances; and of petitioning the king. The benefits of all such statutes as existed at the time of the colonization were likewise claimed, together with the immunities and privileges granted by royal charters or secured by provincial laws.

The maintenance of a standing army in any colony in time of peace, without the consent of its legislature, was pronounced contrary to law. The exercise of its legislative power in the colonies by a council appointed during pleasure by the crown was declared to be unconstitutional and destructive to the freedom of American legislation.

Then followed a specification of the acts of Parliament, passed during the reign of George III, infringing and violating these rights. These were: the sugar act, the stamp act, the two acts for quartering troops, the tea act, the act suspending the New York Legislature, the two acts for the trial in Great Britain of offenses committed in America, the Boston port bill, the act for regulating the government of Massachusetts, and the Quebec act.

"To these grievous acts and measures," it was added, "Americans cannot submit; but in hopes their fellow-subjects in Great Britain will, on a revision of them, restore us to that state in which both countries found happiness and prosperity, we have, for the present, only resolved to pursue the following peaceable measures:

"1st. To enter into a non-importation, non-consumption and non-exportation agreement or association.

"2d. To prepare an address to the people of Great Britain and a memorial to the inhabitants of British America.

"3d. To prepare a loyal address to His Majesty."

The above-mentioned association was accordingly formed and committees were to be appointed in every county, city and town to maintain it vigilantly and strictly.

Masterly state papers were issued by Congress in conformity to the resolutions; namely, a petition to the king, drafted by Mr. Dickinson of Philadelphia; an address to the people of Canada by the same hand, inviting them to join the league of the colonies; another to the people of Great Britain, drafted by John Jay of

New York; and a memorial to the inhabitants of the British colonies, by Richard Henry Lee of Virginia.[4]

The Congress remained in session fifty-one days. Every subject, according to Adams, was discussed "with a moderation, an acuteness and a minuteness equal to that of Queen Elizabeth's privy council."[5] The papers issued by it have deservedly been pronounced masterpieces of practical talent and political wisdom. Chatham, when speaking on the subject in the House of Lords, could not restrain his enthusiasm.

"When your lordships," said he, "look at the papers transmitted to us from America; when you consider their decency, firmness and wisdom, you cannot but respect their cause and wish to make it your own. For myself, I must declare and avow that in the master states of the world I know not the people or senate who, in such a complication of difficult circumstances, can stand in preference to the delegates of America assembled in General Congress at Philadelphia."

From the secrecy that enveloped its discussions, we are ignorant of the part taken by Washington in the debates. The similarity of the resolutions, however, in spirit and substance to those of the Fairfax County meeting, in which he presided, and the coincidence of the measures adopted with those therein recommended, show that he had a powerful agency in the whole proceedings of this eventful assembly. Patrick Henry, being asked on his return home whom he considered the greatest man in Congress, replied: "If you speak of eloquence, Mr. Rutledge of South Carolina is by far the greatest orator, but if you speak of solid information and sound judgment, Colonel Washington is unquestionably the greatest man on that floor."

How thoroughly and zealously [Washington] participated in the feelings which actuated Congress in this memorable session may be gathered from his correspondence with a friend enlisted in the royal cause. This was Captain Robert Mackenzie, who had formerly served under him in his Virginia regiment during the French war but now held a commission in the regular army and was stationed among the British troops at Boston.

Mackenzie, in a letter, had spoken with loyal abhorrence of the state of affairs in the "unhappy province" of Massachusetts, and

---

[4] See *Correspondence and Diary of J. Adams*, vols. ii. and ix.
[5] Letter to William Tudor, 26th of Sept., 1774.

the fixed aim of its inhabitants at "total independence." "The rebellious and numerous meetings of men at arms," said he, "their scandalous and ungenerous attacks upon the best characters in the province, obliging them to save themselves by flight, and their repeated but feeble threats to dispossess the troops, have furnished sufficient reasons to General Gage to put the town in a formidable state of defense, about which we are now fully employed, and which will be shortly accomplished to their great mortification."

"Permit me," writes Washington in reply, "with the freedom of a friend (for you know I always esteemed you), to express my sorrow that fortune should place you in a service that must fix curses to the latest posterity upon the contrivers and, if success (which, by the by, is impossible) accompanies it, execrations upon all those who have been instrumental in the execution. . . . When you condemn the conduct of the Massachusetts people you reason from effects, not causes, otherwise you would not wonder at a people who are every day receiving fresh proofs of a systematic assertion of an arbitrary power, deeply planned to overturn the laws and constitution of their country and to violate the most essential and valuable rights of mankind, being irritated, and with difficulty restrained from acts of the greatest violence and intemperance.

"For my own part, I view things in a very different point of light from the one in which you seem to consider them, and though you are led to believe, by venal men, that the people of Massachusetts are rebellious, setting up for independency and what not, give me leave, my good friend, to tell you that you are abused, grossly abused. . . . I think I can announce it as a fact that it is not the wish or interest of that government or any other upon this continent, separately or collectively, to set up for independence; but this you may at the same time rely on, that none of them will ever submit to the loss of their valuable rights and privileges, which are essential to the happiness of every free state and without which life, liberty and property are rendered totally insecure.

"These, sir, being certain consequences which must naturally result from the late acts of Parliament relative to America in general and the government of Massachusetts in particular, is it to be wondered at that men who wish to avert the impending blow should attempt to oppose its progress or prepare for their defense if it cannot be averted? Surely I may be allowed to answer in the negative; and give me leave to add, as my opinion, that more

blood will be spilled on this occasion, if the ministry are determined to push matters to extremity, than history has ever yet
furnished instances of in the annals of North America; and such a
vital wound will be given to the peace of this great country as time
itself cannot cure, or eradicate the remembrance of."

In concluding, he repeats his views with respect to independence: "I am well satisfied that no such thing is desired by any
thinking man in all North America; on the contrary, that it is the
ardent wish of the warmest advocates for liberty that peace and
tranquillity, upon constitutional grounds, may be restored and the
horrors of civil discord prevented."[6]

This letter we have considered especially worthy of citation,
from its being so full and explicit a declaration of Washington's
sentiments and opinions at this critical juncture. His views on the
question of independence are particularly noteworthy, from his
being at this time in daily and confidential communication with
the leaders of the popular movement, and among them with the
delegates from Boston. It is evident that the filial feeling still
throbbed toward the mother country, and a complete separation
from her had not yet entered into the alternatives of her colonial
children.

On the breaking up of Congress, Washington hastened back to
Mount Vernon, where his presence was more than usually important to the happiness of Mrs. Washington, from the loneliness
caused by the recent death of her daughter and the absence of her
son. The cheerfulness of the neighborhood had been diminished
of late by the departure of George William Fairfax for England to
take possession of estates which had devolved to him in that king-
dom. His estate of Belvoir, so closely allied to that of Mount Vernon by family ties and reciprocal hospitality, was left in charge of
a steward or overseer. Through some accident the house took fire
and was burnt to the ground. It was never rebuilt. The course of
political events which swept Washington from his quiet home
into the current of public and military life prevented William
Fairfax, who was a royalist though a liberal one, from returning to
his once happy abode, and the hospitable intercommunion of
Mount Vernon and Belvoir was at an end forever.

The rumor of the cannonading of Boston, which had thrown
such a gloom over the religious ceremonial at the opening of

6 Sparks, *Washington's Writings*, vol. ii., p. 899.

Congress, had been caused by measures of Governor Gage. The public mind in Boston and its vicinity had been rendered excessively jealous and sensitive by the landing and encamping of artillery upon the Common, and Welsh Fusiliers on Fort Hill, and by the planting of four large field-pieces on Boston Neck, the only entrance to the town by land. The country people were arming and disciplining themselves in every direction and collecting and depositing arms and ammunition in places where they would be at hand in case of emergency. Gage, on the other hand, issued orders that the munitions of war in all the public magazines should be brought to Boston. One of these magazines was the arsenal in the northwest part of Charlestown, between Medford and Cambridge. Two companies of the king's troops passed silently in boats up Mystic River in the night, took possession of a large quantity of gunpowder deposited there and conveyed it to Castle Williams. Intelligence of this sacking of the arsenal flew with lightning speed through the neighborhood. In the morning several thousands of patriots were assembled at Cambridge, weapon in hand, and were with difficulty prevented from marching upon Boston to compel a restitution of the powder. In the confusion and agitation, a rumor stole out into the country that Boston was to be attacked; followed by another that the ships were cannonading the town and the soldiers shooting down the inhabitants. The whole country was forthwith in arms. Numerous bodies of the Connecticut people had made some marches before the report was contradicted.[7]

To guard against any irruption from the country, Gage encamped the 59th regiment on Boston Neck and employed the soldiers in intrenching and fortifying it.

In the meantime the belligerent feelings of the inhabitants were encouraged by learning how the rumor of their being cannonaded had been received in the General Congress and by assurances from all parts that the cause of Boston would be made the common cause of America. "It is surprising," writes General Gage, "that so many of the other provinces interest themselves so much in this. They have some warm friends in New York, and I learn that the people of Charleston, South Carolina, are as mad as they are here."[8]

[7] Holmes's *Annals*, ii., 191. Letter of Gage to Lord Dartmouth.
[8] Gage to Dartmouth, Sept. 20.

The commissions were arrived for those civil officers appointed by the crown under the new modifications of the charter. Many, however, were afraid to accept of them. Those who did soon resigned, finding it impossible to withstand the odium of the people. The civil government throughout the province became obstructed in all its operations. It was enough for a man to be supposed of the governmental party to incur the popular ill-will.

Among other portentous signs, war-hawks began to appear above the horizon. Mrs. Cushing, wife to a member of Congress, writes to her husband: "Two of the greatest military characters of the day are visiting this distressed town. General Charles Lee, who has served in Poland, and Colonel Israel Putnam, whose bravery and character need no description."

Gage, on the 1st of September, before this popular agitation, had issued writs for an election of an Assembly to meet at Salem in October. Seeing, however, the irritated state of the public mind, he now countermanded the same by proclamation. The people, disregarding the countermand, carried the election, and ninety of the new members thus elected met at the appointed time. They waited a whole day for the governor to attend, administer the oaths and open the session, but as he did not make his appearance they voted themselves a provincial Congress and chose for president of it John Hancock, a man of great wealth, popular, and of somewhat showy talents and ardent patriotism, and eminent from his social position.

This self-constituted body adjourned to Concord, about twenty miles from Boston, quietly assumed supreme authority and issued a remonstrance to the governor, virtually calling him to account for his military operations in fortifying Boston Neck and collecting warlike stores about him, thereby alarming the fears of the whole province and menacing the lives and property of the Bostonians.

General Gage, overlooking the irregularity of its organization, entered into explanations with the Assembly but failed to give satisfaction. As winter approached, he found his situation more and more critical. Boston was the only place in Massachusetts that now contained British forces, and it had become the refuge of all the "tories" of the province; that is to say, of all those devoted to the British government. There was animosity between them and the principal inhabitants, among whom revolutionary principles prevailed. The town itself, almost insulated by nature and surrounded by a hostile country, was like a place besieged.

The provincial Congress conducted its affairs with the order and system so formidable to General Gage. Having adopted a plan for organizing the militia, it had nominated general officers, two of whom, Artemas Ward and Seth Pomeroy, had accepted.

The executive powers were vested in a committee of safety. This was to determine when the services of the militia were necessary; was to call them forth; to nominate their officers to the Congress; to commission them; and direct the operations of the army. Another committee was appointed to furnish supplies to the forces when called out—hence, named the Committee of Supplies.

Under such auspices the militia went on arming and disciplining itself in every direction. They associated themselves in large bodies and engaged verbally or by writing to assemble in arms at the shortest notice for the common defense, subject to the orders of the committee of safety.

Arrangements had been made for keeping up an active correspondence between different parts of the country and spreading an alarm in case of any threatening danger. Under the direction of the committees just mentioned, large quantities of military stores had been collected and deposited at Concord and at Worcester.

This semi-belligerent state of affairs in Massachusetts produced a general restlessness throughout the land. The weak-hearted apprehended coming troubles, the resolute prepared to brave them. Military measures, hitherto confined to New England, extended to the middle and southern provinces, and the roll of the drum resounded through the villages.

Virginia was among the first to buckle on its armor. It had long been a custom among its inhabitants to form themselves into independent companies, equipped at their own expense, having their own peculiar uniform and electing their own officers, though holding themselves subject to militia law. They had hitherto been self-disciplined but now they continually resorted to Washington for instruction and advice, considering him the highest authority on military affairs. He was frequently called from home therefore in the course of the winter and spring to different parts of the country to review independent companies, all of which were anxious to put themselves under his command as field-officer.

Mount Vernon therefore again assumed a military tone as in former days, when he took his first lessons there in the art of war. He had his old campaigning associates with him occasionally, Dr. Craik and Captain Hugh Mercer, to talk of past scenes and discuss the possibility of future service. Mercer was already bestirring himself in disciplining the militia about Fredericksburg, where he resided.

Two occasional and important guests at Mount Vernon in this momentous crisis were General Charles Lee and Major Horatio Gates. To Washington the visits of these gentlemen were extremely welcome at this juncture, from their military knowledge and experience, especially as much of it had been acquired in America in the same kind of warfare if not the very same campaigns in which he himself had mingled. Both were interested in the popular cause. Lee was full of plans for the organization and disciplining of the militia, and occasionally accompanied Washington in his attendance on provincial reviews. He was subsequently very efficient at Annapolis in promoting and superintending the organization of the Maryland militia.

It is doubtful whether the visits of Lee were as interesting to Mrs. Washington as to the general. He was whimsical, eccentric and at times almost rude; negligent also, and slovenly in person and attire; for though he had occasionally associated with kings and princes, he had also campaigned with Mohawks and Cossacks and seems to have relished their "good-breeding." What was still more annoying in a well-regulated mansion, he was always followed by a legion of dogs, which shared his affections with his horses and took their seats by him when at table. "I must have some object to embrace," said he misanthropically. "When I can be convinced that men are as worthy objects as dogs, I shall transfer my benevolence and become as staunch a philanthropist as the canting Addison affected to be."[9]

In his passion for horses and dogs Washington to a certain degree could sympathize with him, and had noble specimens of both in his stable and kennel, which Lee doubtless inspected with a learned eye. During the season in question, Washington, according to his diary, was occasionally in the saddle at an early hour following the fox-hounds. It was the last time for many a year that he

[9] Lee to Adams, *Life and Works of Adams*, ii., 414.

was to gallop about his beloved hunting-grounds of Mount Vernon and Belvoir.

In the month of March the second Virginia convention was held at Richmond. Washington attended as delegate from Fairfax County. In this assembly Patrick Henry with his usual ardor and eloquence advocated measures for embodying, arming and disciplining a militia force, and providing for the defense of the colony. "It is useless," said he, "to address further petitions to government or to await the effect of those already addressed to the throne. The time for supplication is past. The time for action is at hand. We must fight, Mr. Speaker," exclaimed he, emphatically. "I repeat it, sir, we must fight! An appeal to arms and to the God of Hosts is all that is left to us!"

Washington joined him in the conviction and was one of a committee that reported a plan for carrying those measures into effect. He was not an impulsive man to raise the battle-cry, but the executive man to marshal the troops into the field and carry on the war.

His brother, John Augustine, was raising and disciplining an independent company. Washington offered to accept the command of it should occasion require it to be drawn out. He did the same with respect to an independent company at Richmond. "It is my full intention, if needful," writes he to his brother, "to devote my life and fortune to the cause."[10]

[10] Letter to John Augustine. Sparks, iv., 405.

Chapter 14

WASHINGTON MADE COMMANDER-IN-CHIEF

At length the bolt, so long suspended, fell! The troops at Boston had been augmented to about four thousand men. Goaded on by the instigations of the tories and alarmed by the energetic measures of the whigs, General Gage now resolved to deal the latter a crippling blow. This was to surprise and destroy their magazines of military stores at Concord, about twenty miles from Boston. It was to be effected on the night of the 18th of April by a force detached for that purpose.

Preparations were made with great secrecy. Boats for the transportation of the troops were launched, and moored under the sterns of the men-of-war. Grenadiers and light infantry were relieved from duty and held in readiness. On the 18th, officers were stationed on the roads leading from Boston to prevent any intelligence of the expedition getting into the country. At night orders were issued by General Gage that no person should leave the town. About ten o'clock, from eight to nine hundred men, grenadiers, light infantry and marines, commanded by Lieutenant-Colonel Smith, embarked in the boats at the foot of Boston Common and crossed to Lechmere Point in Cambridge, whence they were to march silently and without beat of drum to the place of destination.

The measures of General Gage had not been shrouded in all the secrecy he imagined. Mystery often defeats itself by the suspicions it awakens. Dr. Joseph Warren, one of the committee of safety, had observed the preparatory disposition of the boats and troops and surmised some sinister intention. He sent notice of these movements to John Hancock and Samuel Adams, both members of the provincial Congress but at that time privately sojourning with a friend at Lexington. A design on the magazine at Concord was suspected and the committee of safety ordered that the cannon collected there should be secreted and part of the stores removed.

On the night of the 18th, Dr. Warren sent off two messengers by different routes to give the alarm that the king's troops were actually sallying forth. The messengers got to Boston just before the order of General Gage went into effect to prevent any one from leaving the town. About the same time a lantern was hung out of an upper window of the north church, in the direction of Charlestown. This was a preconcerted signal to the patriots of that place, who instantly despatched swift messengers to rouse the country.

In the meantime Colonel Smith set out on his nocturnal march from Lechmere Point by an unfrequented path across the marshes, where at times the troops had to wade through water. He had proceeded but a few miles when alarm guns, booming through the night air, and the clang of village bells, showed that the news of his approach was travelling before him and the people were rising. He now sent back to General Gage for a reinforcement, while Major Pitcairn was detached with six companies to press forward and secure the bridges at Concord.

Pitcairn advanced rapidly, capturing every one he met or overtook. Within a mile and a half of Lexington, however, a horseman was too quick on the spur for him and, galloping to the village, gave the alarm that the redcoats were coming. Drums were beaten, guns fired. By the time that Pitcairn entered the village, about seventy or eighty of the yeomanry, in military array, were mustered on the green near the church. It was a part of the "constitutional army," pledged to resist by force any open hostility of British troops. Besides these, there were a number of lookers-on, armed and unarmed.

The sound of drum and the array of men in arms indicated a hostile determination. Pitcairn halted his men within a short distance of the church and ordered them to prime and load. They then advanced at double quick time. The major, riding forward, waved his sword and ordered the rebels, as he termed them, to disperse. Other of the officers echoed his words as they advanced: "Disperse, ye villains! Lay down your arms, ye rebels, and disperse!" The orders were disregarded. A scene of confusion ensued, with firing on both sides. Which party commenced it has been a matter of dispute. Pitcairn always maintained that, finding the militia would not disperse, he turned to order his men to draw out and surround them, when he saw a flash in the pan from a gun of a countryman behind a wall, and almost instantly the report of two or three muskets. These he supposed to be from the Americans, as his horse was wounded, as was also a soldier close by him. His troops rushed on and a promiscuous fire took place, though, as he declared, he made repeated signals with his sword for his men to forbear.

The firing of the Americans was irregular and without much effect. That of the British was more fatal. Eight of the patriots were killed and ten wounded, and the whole put to flight. The victors formed on the common, fired a volley and gave three cheers for one of the most inglorious and disastrous triumphs ever achieved by British arms.

Colonel Smith soon arrived with the residue of the detachment, and they all marched on towards Concord, about six miles distant.

The alarm had reached that place in the dead hour of the preceding night. The church bell roused the inhabitants. They gathered together in anxious consultation. The militia and minute men seized their arms and repaired to the parade ground, near the church. Here they were subsequently joined by armed yeomanry from Lincoln and elsewhere. Exertions were now made to remove and conceal the military stores. A scout who had been sent out for intelligence brought word that the British had fired upon the people at Lexington and were advancing upon Concord. There was great excitement and indignation. Part of the militia marched down the Lexington road to meet them, but returned, reporting their force to be three times that of the Americans. The whole of the militia now retired to an eminence about a mile from the centre of the town and formed themselves into two battalions.

About seven o'clock, the British came in sight, advancing with quick step, their arms glittering in the morning sun. They entered in two divisions by different roads. Concord is traversed by a river of the same name, having two bridges, the north and the south. The grenadiers and light infantry took post in the centre of the town, while strong parties of light troops were detached to secure the bridges and destroy the military stores. Two hours were expended in the work of destruction without much success, so much of the stores having been removed or concealed. During all this time the yeomanry from the neighboring towns were hurrying in with such weapons as were at hand and joining the militia on the height, until the little cloud of war gathering there numbered about four hundred and fifty.

About ten o'clock a body of three hundred undertook to dislodge the British from the north bridge. As they approached, the latter fired upon them, killing two and wounding a third. The patriots returned the fire with spirit and effect. The British retreated to the main body, the Americans pursuing them across the bridge.

By this time all the military stores which could be found had been destroyed. Colonel Smith, therefore, made preparations for a retreat. The scattered troops were collected, the dead were buried and conveyances procured for the wounded. About noon he commenced his retrograde march for Boston. It was high time. His troops were jaded by the night march and the morning's toils and skirmishings.

The country was thoroughly alarmed. The yeomanry were hurrying from every quarter to the scene of action. As the British began their retreat, the Americans began the work of sore and galling retaliation. Along the open road the former were harassed incessantly by rustic marksmen who took deliberate aim from behind trees or over stone fences. Where the road passed through woods the British found themselves between two fires, dealt by unseen foes, the minute men having posted themselves on each side among the bushes. It was in vain they threw out flankers and endeavored to dislodge their assailants. Each pause gave time for other pursuers to come within reach and open attacks from different quarters. For several miles they urged their way along woody defiles, or roads skirted with fences and stone walls, the retreat growing more and more disastrous. Some were shot down, some gave out through mere exhaustion. The rest hurried on without stopping to aid the fatigued or wounded. Before reaching Lexington, Colonel Smith received a severe wound in the leg, and the situation of the retreating troops was becoming extremely critical when, about two o'clock, they were met by Lord Percy with a brigade of one thousand men and two field-pieces. His lordship had been detached from Boston about nine o'clock by General Gage in compliance with Colonel Smith's urgent call for a reinforcement, and had marched gayly through Roxbury to the tune of "Yankee Doodle" in derision of the "rebels." He now found the latter a more formidable foe than he had anticipated. Opening his brigade to the right and left, he received the retreating troops into a hollow square, where, fainting and exhausted, they threw themselves on the ground to rest. His lordship showed no disposition to advance upon their assailants but contented himself with keeping them at bay with his field-pieces, which opened a vigorous fire from an eminence.

Hitherto the provincials, being hasty levies without a leader, had acted from individual impulse, without much concert, but now General Heath was upon the ground. He was one of those authorized to take command when the minute men should be called out. That class of combatants promptly obeyed his orders, and he was efficacious in rallying them and bringing them into military order, when checked and scattered by the fire of the field-pieces.

Dr. Warren, also, arrived on horseback, having spurred from Boston on receiving news of the skirmishing. In the subsequent part of the day he was one of the most active and efficient men in the field. His presence, like that of General Heath, regulated the infuriated ardor of the militia and brought it into system.

Lord Percy, having allowed the troops a short interval for repose and refreshment, continued the retreat toward Boston. As soon as he got under march, the galling assault by the pursuing yeomanry was recommenced in flank and rear. The British soldiery, irritated in turn, acted as if in an enemy's country. Houses and shops were burnt down in Lexington, private dwellings along the road were plundered and their inhabitants maltreated. In one instance, an unoffending invalid was wantonly slain in his own house. All this increased the exasperation of the yeomanry. There was occasional sharp skirmishing, with bloodshed on both sides, but in general a dogged pursuit, where the retreating troops were galled at every step. Their march became more and more impeded by the number of their wounded. Lord Percy narrowly escaped death from a musket-ball, which struck off a button of his waistcoat. One of his officers remained behind wounded in West Cambridge. His ammunition was failing as he approached Charlestown. The provincials pressed upon him in rear, others were advancing from Roxbury, Dorchester and Milton. Colonel Pickering, with the Essex militia, seven hundred strong, was at hand. There was danger of being intercepted in the retreat to Charlestown. The field-pieces were again brought into play to check the ardor of the pursuit but they were no longer objects of terror. The sharpest firing of the provincials was near Prospect Hill as the harassed enemy hurried along the Charlestown road, eager to reach the Neck and get under cover of their ships. The pursuit terminated a little after sunset at Charlestown Common, where General Heath brought the minute men to a halt. Within half an hour more a powerful body of men from Marblehead and Salem came up to join in the chase. "If the retreat," writes Washington, "had not been as precipitate as it was—and God knows it could not well have been more so—the ministerial troops must have surrendered or been totally cut off."

The distant firing from the mainland had reached the British at Boston. The troops which in the morning had marched through Roxbury to the tune of "Yankee Doodle" might have been seen at sunset hounded along the old Cambridge road to Charleston Neck by mere armed yeomanry. Gage was astounded at the catastrophe. It was but a short time previous that one of his officers, in writing to friends in England, scoffed at the idea of the Americans taking up arms. "Whenever it comes to blows," said he, "he that can run the fastest will think himself well off, believe me. Any two regiments here ought to be decimated if they did not beat in the field the whole force of the Massachusetts province." How frequently throughout this Revolution had the English to pay the penalty of thus undervaluing the spirit they were provoking!

In this memorable affair the British loss was seventy-three killed, one hundred and seventy-four wounded and twenty-six missing. Among the slain were eighteen officers. The loss of the Americans was forty-nine killed, thirty-nine wounded and five missing. This was the first blood shed in the revolutionary struggle, a mere drop in amount but a deluge in its effects, rending the colonies forever from the mother country.

The cry of blood from the field of Lexington went through the land. None felt the appeal more than the old soldiers of the French war. It roused John Stark of New Hampshire, a trapper and hunter in his youth, a veteran in Indian warfare, a campaigner under Abercrombie and Amherst, now the military oracle of a rustic neighborhood. Within ten minutes after receiving the alarm he was spurring towards the sea-coast, and on the way stirring up the volunteers of the Massachusetts borders to assemble forthwith at Bedford in the vicinity of Boston.

Equally alert was his old comrade in frontier exploits, Colonel Israel Putnam. A man on horseback, with a drum, passed through his neighborhood in Connecticut, proclaiming British violence at Lexington. Putnam was in the field ploughing, assisted by his son. In an instant the team was unyoked, the plough left in the furrow, the lad sent home to give word of his father's departure, and Putnam, on horseback, in his working garb, urging with all speed to the camp. Such was the spirit aroused throughout the country. The sturdy yeomanry from all parts were hastening toward Boston with such weapons as were at hand, and happy was he who could command a rusty fowling-piece and a powder-horn.

The news reached Virginia at a critical moment. Lord Dunmore, obeying a general order issued by the ministry to all the provincial governors, had seized upon the military munitions of the province. Here was a similar measure to that of Gage. The cry went forth that the subjugation of the colonies was to be attempted. All Virginia was in combustion. The standard of liberty was reared in every county. There was a general cry to arms. Washington was looked to from various quarters to take command. His old comrade in arms, Hugh Mercer, was about marching down to Williamsburg at the head of a body of resolute men, seven hundred strong, entitled "The friends of constitutional liberty and America," whom he had organized and drilled in Fredericksburg, and nothing but a timely concession of Lord Dunmore with respect to some powder which he had seized, prevented his being beset in his palace.

Before Hugh Mercer and the Friends of Liberty disbanded themselves they exchanged a mutual pledge to reassemble at a moment's warning whenever called on to defend the liberty and rights of this or any other sister colony.

Washington was at Mount Vernon, preparing to set out for Philadelphia as a delegate to the second Congress, when he received tidings of the affair at Lexington. Bryan Fairfax and Major Horatio Gates were his guests at the time. They all regarded the event as decisive in its consequences but they regarded it with different feelings. The worthy and gentle-spirited Fairfax deplored it deeply. He foresaw that it must break up all his pleasant relations in life, arraying his dearest friends against the government to which, notwithstanding the errors of its policy, he was loyally attached and resolved to adhere.

Gates, on the contrary, viewed it with the eye of a soldier and a place-hunter, hitherto disappointed in both capacities. This event promised to open a new avenue to importance and command and he determined to enter upon it.

Washington's feelings were of a mingled nature. They may be gathered from a letter to his friend and neighbor, George William Fairfax, then in England, in which he lays the blame of this "deplorable affair" on the ministry and their military agents and concludes with the following words, in which the yearnings of the patriot give affecting solemnity to the implied resolve of the soldier: "Unhappy it is to reflect that a brother's sword has been sheathed in a brother's breast and that the once happy and peaceful plains of America are to be either drenched with blood or inhabited by slaves. Sad alternative! But can a virtuous man hesitate in his choice?"

The second General Congress assembled at Philadelphia on the 10th of May. Peyton Randolph was again elected as president, but being obliged to return and occupy his place as Speaker of the Virginia Assembly, John Hancock of Massachusetts was elevated to the chair.

A lingering feeling of attachment to the mother country, struggling with the growing spirit of self-government, was manifested in the proceedings of this remarkable body. Many of those most active in vindicating colonial rights, and Washington among the number, still indulged the hope of an eventual reconciliation, while few entertained or at least avowed the idea of complete independence.

A second "humble and dutiful" petition to the king was moved but met with strong opposition. John Adams condemned it as an imbecile measure calculated to embarrass the proceedings of Congress. He was for prompt and vigorous action. Other members concurred with him. Indeed, the measure itself seemed but a mere form intended to reconcile the half-scrupulous, for subsequently, when it was carried, Congress in face of it went on to assume and exercise the powers of a sovereign authority. A federal union was formed, leaving to each colony the right of regulating its internal affairs according to its own individual constitution but vesting in Congress the power of making peace or war, of entering into treaties and alliances, of regulating general commerce; in a word, of legislating on all such matters as regarded the security and welfare of the whole community.

The executive power was to be vested in a council of twelve

chosen by Congress from among its own members, and to hold office for a limited time. Such colonies as had not sent delegates to Congress might yet become members of the confederacy by agreeing to its conditions. Georgia, which had hitherto hesitated, soon joined the league, which thus extended from Nova Scotia to Florida.

Congress lost no time in exercising their federated powers. In virtue of them, they ordered the enlistment of troops, the construction of forts in various parts of the colonies, the provision of arms, ammunition and military stores, while to defray the expenses of these and other measures, avowedly of self-defense, they authorized the emission of notes to the amount of three millions of dollars, bearing the inscription of "The United Colonies," the faith of the confederacy being pledged for their redemption.

A retaliating decree was passed, prohibiting all supplies of provisions to the British fisheries; and another, declaring the province of Massachusetts Bay absolved from its compact with the crown by the violation of its charter and recommending it to form an internal government for itself.

The public sense of Washington's military talents and experience was evinced in his being chairman of all the committees appointed for military affairs. Most of the rules and regulations for the army, and the measures for defense, were devised by him.

The situation of the New England army actually besieging Boston became an early and absorbing consideration. It was without munitions of war, without arms, clothing or pay; in fact, without legislative countenance or encouragement. Unless sanctioned and assisted by Congress, there was danger of its dissolution. If dissolved, how could another be collected? If dissolved, what would there be to prevent the British from sallying out of Boston and spreading desolation throughout the country?

All this was the subject of much discussion out of doors. The disposition to uphold the army was general. But the difficult question was, who should be commander-in-chief? Adams in his diary gives us glimpses of the conflict of opinions and interests within doors. There was a southern party, he said, which could not brook the idea of a New England army, commanded by a New England general.

"Whether this jealousy was sincere," writes he, "or whether it was mere pride and a haughty ambition of furnishing a southern general to command the northern army, I cannot say, but the intention was very visible to me that Colonel Washington was their object, and so many of our stanchest men were in the plan that we could carry nothing without conceding to it. There was another embarrassment which was never publicly known and which was carefully concealed by those who knew it: the Massachusetts and other New England delegates were divided. Mr. Hancock and Mr. Cushing hung back. Mr. Paine did not come forward, and even Mr. Samuel Adams was irresolute. Mr. Hancock himself had an ambition to be appointed commander-in-chief. Whether he thought an election a compliment due to him and intended to have the honor of declining it or whether he would have accepted it, I know not. To the compliment he had some pretensions: for, at that time, his exertions, sacrifices and general merits in the cause of his country had been incomparably greater than those of Colonel Washington. But the delicacy of his health, and his entire want of experience in actual service, though an excellent militia officer, were decisive objections to him in my mind."

The opinion evidently inclined in favor of Washington, yet it was promoted by no clique of partisans or admirers. More than one of the Virginia delegates, says Adams, were cool on the subject of this appointment and, particularly, Mr. Pendleton was clear and full against it. It is scarcely necessary to add that Washington in this, as in every other situation in life, made no step in advance to clutch the impending honor.

Adams in his diary claims the credit of bringing the members of Congress to a decision. Rising in his place one day and stating briefly but earnestly the exigencies of the case, he moved that Congress should adopt the army at Cambridge and appoint a general. Though this was not the time to nominate the person, "yet," adds he, "as I had reason to believe this was a point of some difficulty, I had no hesitation to declare that I had but one gentleman in my mind for that important command, and that was a gentleman from Virginia who was among us and very well known to all of us; a gentleman whose skill and experience as an officer, whose independent fortune, great talents and excellent universal character would command the approbation of all America and unite the cordial exertions of all the colonies better than any other person in the Union. Mr. Washington, who happened to sit near the door, as soon as he heard me allude to him, from his usual modesty darted into the library-room. Mr. Hancock, who was our president, which gave me an opportunity to observe his countenance, while I was speaking on the state of the colonies, the army at Cambridge and the enemy heard me with visible pleasure, but when I came to describe Washington for the commander, I never remarked a more sudden and striking change of countenance. Mortification and resentment were expressed as forcibly as his face could exhibit them.

"When the subject came under debate, several delegates opposed the appointment of Washington, not from personal affections but because the army were all from New England and had a general of their own, General Artemas Ward, with whom they appeared well satisfied and under whose command they had proved themselves able to imprison the British army in Boston, which was all that was to be expected or desired."

The subject was postponed to a future day. In the interim, pains were taken out of doors to obtain a unanimity, and the voices were in general so clearly in favor of Washington that the dissentient members were persuaded to withdraw their opposition.

On the 15th of June the army was regularly adopted by Congress and the pay of the commander-in-chief fixed at five hundred dollars a month. Many still clung to the idea that in all these proceedings they were merely opposing the measures of the ministry and not the authority of the crown, and thus the army before Boston was designated as the Continental Army in contradistinction to that under General Gage, which was called the Ministerial Army.

In this stage of the business Mr. Johnson of Maryland rose and nominated Washington for the station of commander-in-chief. The election was by ballot and was unanimous. It was formally announced to him by the president on the following day when he had taken his seat in Congress. Rising in his place, he briefly expressed his high and grateful sense of the honor conferred on him, and his sincere devotion to the cause. "But," added he, "lest some unlucky event should happen unfavorable to my reputation, I beg it may be remembered by every gentleman in the room, that I this day declare, with the utmost sincerity, I do not think myself equal to the command I am honored with. As to pay, I beg leave to assure the Congress that, as no pecuniary consideration could have tempted me to accept this arduous employment at the expense of my domestic ease and happiness, I do not wish to make any profit of it. I will keep an exact account of my expenses. Those, I doubt not, they will discharge, and that is all I desire."

"There is something charming to me in the conduct of Washington," writes Adams to a friend, "a gentleman of one of the first fortunes upon the continent, leaving his delicious retirement, his family and friends, sacrificing his ease and hazarding all in the cause of his country. His views are noble and disinterested. He declared, when he accepted the mighty trust, that he would lay before us an exact account of his expenses and not accept a shilling of pay."

Four major-generals were to be appointed. Among those specified were General Charles Lee and General Ward. Mr. Mifflin of Philadelphia, who was Lee's especial friend and admirer, urged that he should be second in command. "General Lee," said he, "would serve cheerfully under Washington, but considering his rank, character, and experience, could not be expected to serve under any other. He must be *aut secundus, aut nullus.*"

Adams on the other hand as strenuously objected that it would be a great deal to expect that General Ward, who was actually in command of the army of Boston, should serve under any man; but under a stranger he ought not to serve. General Ward accordingly was elected the second in command and Lee the third. The other two major-generals were Philip Schuyler of New York and Israel Putnam of Connecticut. Eight brigadier-generals were likewise appointed: Seth Pomeroy, Richard Montgomery, David Wooster, William Heath, Joseph Spencer, John Thomas, John Sullivan and Nathaniel Greene.

Notwithstanding Mr. Mifflin's objections to having Lee ranked under Ward as being beneath his dignity and merits, he himself made no scruple to acquiesce, though judging from his supercilious character and from circumstances in his subsequent conduct, he no doubt considered himself vastly superior to the provincial officers placed over him.

At Washington's express request, his old friend, Major Horatio Gates, then absent at his estate in Virginia, was appointed adjutant-general, with the rank of brigadier.

Adams, according to his own account, was extremely loth to admit Lee or Gates into the American service, although he considered them officers of great experience and confessed abilities. He apprehended difficulties, he said, from the "natural prejudices and virtuous attachment of our countrymen to their own officers." "But," adds he, "considering the earnest desire of General Washington to have the assistance of those officers, the extreme attachment of many of our best friends in the southern colonies to them, the reputation they would give to our arms in Europe, and especially with the ministerial generals and army in Boston, as well as the real American merit of both, I could not withhold my vote from either."

The reader will possibly call these circumstances to mind when, on a future page, he finds how Lee and Gates requited the friendship to which chiefly they owed their appointments.

In this momentous change in his condition, which suddenly altered all his course of life and called him immediately to the camp, Washington's thoughts recurred to Mount Vernon and its rural delights, so dear to his heart, whence he was to be again exiled. His chief concern, however, was on account of the distress it might cause to his wife. His letter to her on the subject is written in a tone of manly tenderness.

"You may believe me," writes he, "when I assure you in the most solemn manner that, so far from seeking this appointment, I have used every endeavor in my power to avoid it, not only from my unwillingness to part with you and the family but from a consciousness of its being a trust too great for my capacity; and I should enjoy more real happiness in one month with you at home than I have the most distant prospect of finding abroad, if my stay were to be seven times seven years. But as it has been a kind of destiny that has thrown me upon this service, I shall hope that my undertaking it is designed to answer some good purpose. . . .

"I shall rely confidently on that Providence which has hitherfore preserved and been bountiful to me, not doubting but that I shall return safe to you in the fall. I shall feel no pain from the toil or danger of the campaign. My unhappiness will flow from the uneasiness I know you will feel from being left alone. I therefore beg that you will summon your whole fortitude and pass your time as agreeably as possible. Nothing will give me so much sincere satisfaction as to hear this and to hear it from your own pen."

And to his favorite brother, John Augustine, he writes: "I am now to bid adieu to you and to every kind of domestic ease for a while. I am embarked on a wide ocean, boundless in its prospect, and in which, perhaps, no safe harbor is to be found. I have been called upon by the unanimous voice of the colonies to take the command of the continental army, an honor I neither sought after, nor desired, as I am thoroughly convinced that it requires great abilities and much more experience than I am master of."

On the 20th of June he received his commission from the President of Congress. The following day was fixed upon for his departure for the army. He reviewed previously, at the request of their officers, several militia companies of horse and foot. Every one was anxious to see the new commander, and rarely has the public *beau ideal* of a commander been so fully answered. He was now in the vigor of his days, forty-three years of age, stately in person, noble in his demeanor, calm and dignified in his deportment. As he sat his horse with manly grace his military presence delighted every eye, and wherever he went the air rang with acclamations.

Chapter 15

THE PATRIOT ARMY

While Congress had been deliberating on the adoption of the army and the nomination of a commander-in-chief, events had been thickening and drawing to a crisis in the excited region about Boston. The provincial troops which blockaded the town prevented supplies by land. The neighboring country refused to furnish them by water. Fresh provisions and vegetables were no longer to be procured, and Boston began to experience the privations of a besieged city.

On the 25th of May arrived ships of war and transports from England, bringing large reinforcements under Generals Howe, Burgoyne and Henry Clinton, commanders of high reputation.

As the ships entered the harbor and the "rebel camp" was pointed out—ten thousand yeomanry beleaguering a town garrisoned by five thousand regulars—Burgoyne could not restrain a burst of surprise and scorn. "What!" cried he, "ten thousand peasants keep five thousand king's troops shut up! Well, let us get in and we'll soon find elbow-room."

Inspirited by these reinforcements, General Gage determined to take the field. Previously, however, in conformity to instructions from Lord Dartmouth, the head of the war department, he issued a proclamation (12th June) putting the province under martial law, threatening to treat as rebels and traitors all malcontents who should continue under arms, together with their aiders and abettors, but offering pardon to all who should lay down their arms and return to their allegiance. From this proffered amnesty, however, John Hancock and Samuel Adams were especially excepted, their offenses being pronounced too "flagitious not to meet with condign punishment."

This proclamation only served to put the patriots on the alert against such measures as might be expected to follow and of which their friends in Boston stood ready to apprise them. The besieging force in the meantime was daily augmented by recruits and volunteers and now amounted to about fifteen thousand men distributed at various points. Its character and organization were peculiar. As has well been observed, it could not be called a national army, for as yet there was no nation to own it. It was not under the authority of the Continental Congress, the act of that body recognizing it not having as yet been passed and the authority of that body itself not having been acknowledged. It was in fact a fortuitous assemblage of four distinct bodies of troops belonging to different provinces and each having a leader of its own election. About ten thousand belonged to Massachusetts and were under the command of General Artemas Ward, whose head-quarters were at Cambridge. Another body of troops, under Colonel John Stark, already mentioned, came from New Hampshire. Rhode Island furnished a third, under the command of General Nathaniel Greene. A fourth was from Connecticut, under the veteran Putnam.

These bodies of troops, being from different colonies, were independent of each other and had their several commanders. Those from New Hampshire were instructed to obey General Ward as commander-in-chief; with the rest it was a voluntary act, rendered in consideration of his being military chief of Massachusetts, the province which, as allies, they came to defend. There was in fact but little organization in the army. Nothing kept it together and gave it unity of action but a common feeling of exasperated patriotism.

The troops knew but little of military discipline. Almost all were familiar with the use of fire-arms in hunting and fowling. Many had served in frontier campaigns against the French and in "bush-fighting" with the Indians but none were acquainted with regular service or the discipline of European armies. There was a regiment of artillery, partly organized by Colonel Gridley, a skilful engineer, and furnished with nine field-pieces, but the greater part of the troops were without military dress or accoutrements. Most of them were hasty levies of yeomanry, some of whom had seized their rifles and fowling-pieces and turned out in their working-clothes and homespun country garbs. It was an army of volunteers, subordinate through inclination and respect to officers of their own choice, and depending for sustenance on supplies sent from their several towns.

Such was the army spread over an extent of ten or twelve miles and keeping watch upon the town of Boston, containing at that time a population of seventeen thousand souls and garrisoned with more than ten thousand British troops, disciplined and experienced in the wars of Europe.

Both parties panted for action, the British through impatience of their humiliating position and an eagerness to chastise what they considered the presumption of their besiegers, the provincials through enthusiasm in their cause, a thirst for enterprise and exploit and, it must be added, an unconsciousness of their own military deficiencies.

[The provincials fortified Bunker's Hill overlooking the town but did so tardily and inadequately. The British stormed the hill three times at great cost, finally dislodging the Americans, who retreated to Cambridge. The battle of Bunker's Hill] was one of the most momentous conflicts in our Revolutionary history. It was the first regular battle between the British and the Americans, and most eventful in its consequences. The former had gained the ground for which they contended; but, if a victory, it was more disastrous and humiliating to them than an ordinary defeat. They had ridiculed and despised their enemy, representing them as dastardly and inefficient, yet here their best troops, led on by experienced officers, had repeatedly been repulsed by an inferior force of that enemy—mere yeomanry—from works thrown up in a single night, and had suffered a loss rarely paralleled in battle with the most veteran soldiery; for, according to their own returns, their killed and wounded, out of a detachment of two thousand men, amounted to one thousand and fifty-four, and a large proportion of them officers. The loss of the Americans did not exceed four hundred and fifty.

To the latter this defeat, if defeat it might be called, had the effect of a triumph. It gave them confidence in themselves and consequence in the eyes of their enemies. They had proved to themselves and to others that they could measure weapons with the disciplined soldiers of Europe and inflict the most harm in the conflict.

[Washington set out on horseback from Philadelphia for Boston] on the 21st of June, having for military companions of his journey

Major-Generals Lee and Schuyler and being accompanied for a distance by several private friends. As an escort he had a "gentleman troop" of Philadelphia commanded by Captain Markoe. The whole formed a brilliant cavalcade.

They had scarcely proceeded twenty miles when they were met by a courier spurring with all speed, bearing despatches from the army to Congress, communicating tidings of the battle of Bunker's Hill. Washington eagerly inquired particulars. Above all, how acted the militia? When told that they stood their ground bravely, sustained the enemy's fire, reserved their own until at close quarters and then delivered it with deadly effect, it seemed as if a weight of doubt and solicitude was lifted from his heart. "The liberties of the country are safe!" exclaimed he.

The news of the battle of Bunker's Hill had startled the whole country; and this clattering cavalcade escorting the commander-in-chief to the army was the gaze and wonder of every town and village.

The journey may be said to have been a continual council of war between Washington and the two generals. Even the contrast in character of the two latter made them regard questions from different points of view—Schuyler a warm-hearted patriot with everything staked on the cause; Lee, a soldier of fortune, indifferent to the ties of home and country, drawing his sword without enthusiasm, more through resentment against a government which had disappointed him than zeal for liberty or for colonial rights.

One of the most frequent subjects of conversation was the province of New York. Its power and position rendered it the great link of the confederacy. What measures were necessary for its defense and most calculated to secure its adherence to the cause? A lingering attachment to the crown, kept up by the influence of British merchants and military and civil functionaries in royal pay, had rendered it slow in coming into the colonial compact and it was only on the contemptuous dismissal of their statement of grievances, unheard, that its people had thrown off their allegiance, as much in sorrow as in anger.

No person was better fitted to give an account of the interior of New York than General Schuyler; and the hawk-eyed Lee during a recent sojourn had made its capital somewhat of a study; but there was much yet for both of them to learn.

The population of New York was more varied in its elements

than that of almost any other of the provinces and had to be cautiously studied. The New Yorkers were of a mixed origin and stamped with the peculiarities of their respective ancestors. The descendants of the old Dutch and Huguenot families, the earliest settlers, were still among the soundest and best of the population. They inherited the love of liberty, civil and religious, of their forefathers and were those who stood foremost in the present struggle for popular rights. Such were the Jays, the Bensons, the Beekmans, the Hoffmans, the Van Homes, the Roosevelts, the Duyckinks, the Pintards, the Yateses and others whose names figure in the patriotic documents of the day. Some of them doubtless cherished a remembrance of the time when their forefathers were lords of the land, and felt an innate propensity to join in resistance to the government by which their supremacy had been overturned. A great proportion of the more modern families, dating from the downfall of the Dutch government in 1664, were English and Scotch, and among these were many loyal adherents to the crown. Then there was a mixture of the whole, produced by the intermarriages of upwards of a century, which partook of every shade of character and sentiment. The operations of foreign commerce and the regular communications with the mother country through packets and ships of war kept these elements in constant action and contributed to produce that mercurial temperament, that fondness for excitement and proneness to pleasure, which distinguished them from their neighbors on either side—the austere Puritans of New England and the quiet "Friends" of Pennsylvania.

There was a power, too, of a formidable kind within the interior of the province, which was an object of much solicitude. This was the "Johnson Family." Sir John Johnson and his sons-in-law, Colonel Guy Johnson and Colonel Claus, lived in a degree of rude feudal style in stone mansions capable of defense, situated on the Mohawk River and in its vicinity. They had many Scottish Highlanders for tenants; and among their adherents were violent men such as the Butlers of Tryon County, and Brant, the Mohawk sachem, since famous in Indian warfare.

They had recently gone about with armed retainers, overawing and breaking up patriotic assemblages, and it was known they could at any time bring a force of warriors in the field.

Recent accounts stated that Sir John was fortifying the old family hall at Johnstown with swivels and had a hundred and fifty Roman Catholic Highlanders quartered in and about it, all armed and ready to obey his orders.

Colonel Guy Johnson, however, was the most active and zealous of the family. Pretending to apprehend a design on the part of the New England people to surprise and carry him off, he fortified his stone mansion on the Mohawk, called Guy's Park, and assembled there a part of his militia regiment and other of his adherents, to the number of five hundred. He held a great Indian council there, likewise, in which the chiefs of the Six Nations recalled the friendship and good deeds of the late Sir William Johnson and avowed their determination to stand by and defend every branch of his family.

As yet it was uncertain whether Colonel Guy really intended to take an open part in the appeal to arms. Should he do so, he would carry with him a great force of the native tribes and might almost domineer over the frontier.

Tryon, the governor of New York, was at present absent in England, having been called home by the ministry to give an account of the affairs of the province and to receive instructions for its management. He was a tory in heart and had been a zealous opponent of all colonial movements, and his talents and address gave him great influence over an important part of the community. Should he return with hostile instructions and should he and the Johnsons co-operate, the one controlling the bay and harbor of New York and the waters of the Hudson by means of ships and land forces, the others overrunning the valley of the Mohawk and the regions beyond Albany with savage hordes, this great central province might be wrested from the confederacy and all intercourse broken off between the eastern and southern colonies.

All these circumstances and considerations, many of which came under discussion in the course of this military journey, rendered the command of New York a post of especial trust and importance and determined Washington to confide it to General Schuyler. He was peculiarly fitted for it by his military talents, his intimate knowledge of the province and its concerns, especially what related to the upper parts of it, and his experience in Indian affairs.

At Newark in the Jerseys, Washington was met on the 25th by a committee of the provincial Congress sent to conduct him to the city. The Congress was in a perplexity. It had in a manner usurped and exercised the powers of Governor Tryon during his absence, while at the same time it professed allegiance to the crown which had appointed him. He was now in the harbor, just arrived from England, and hourly expected to land. Washington too was approaching. How were these double claims to ceremonious respect, happening at the same time, to be managed?

In this dilemma a regiment of militia was turned out and the colonel instructed to pay military honors to whichever of the distinguished functionaries should first arrive. Washington was earlier than the governor by several hours and received those honors. Peter Van Burgh Livingston, president of the New York Congress, next delivered a congratulatory address, the latter part of which evinces the cautious reserve with which, in those revolutionary times, military power was intrusted to an individual:

"Confiding in you, sir, and in the worthy generals immediately under your command, we have the most flattering hopes of success in the glorious struggle for American liberty, and the fullest assurances that whenever this important contest shall be decided by that fondest wish of each American soul, an accommodation with our mother country, you will cheerfully resign the important deposit commited into your hands and reassume the character of our worthiest citizen."

The following was Washington's reply in behalf of himself and his generals to this part of the address:

"As to the fatal but necessary operations of war, when we assumed the soldier we did not lay aside the citizen, and we shall most sincerely rejoice with you in that happy hour when the establishment of American liberty on the most firm and solid foundations shall enable us to return to our private stations in the bosom of a free, peaceful and happy country."

The landing of Governor Tryon took place about eight o'clock in the evening. The military honors were repeated. He was received with great respect by the mayor and common council, and transports of loyalty by those devoted to the crown. It was unknown what instructions he had received from the ministry but it was rumored that a large force would soon arrive from England, subject to his directions. At this very moment a ship of war, the *Asia*, lay anchored opposite the city, its grim batteries bearing upon it, greatly to the disquiet of the faint-hearted among its inhabitants.

In this situation of affairs Washington was happy to leave such an efficient person as General Schuyler in command of the place. According to his instructions, the latter was to make returns once a month, and oftener should circumstances require it, to Washington as commander-in-chief, and to the Continental Congress, of the forces under him, and the state of his supplies, and to send the earliest advices of all events of importance. He was to keep a wary eye on Colonel Guy Johnson and to counteract any prejudicial influence he might exercise over the Indians. With respect to Governor Tryon, Washington hinted at a bold and decided line of conduct. "If forcible measures are judged necessary respecting the person of the governor, I should have no difficulty in ordering them, if the Continental Congress were not sitting; but as that is the case, and the seizing of a governor quite a new thing, I must refer you to that body for direction."

Had Congress thought proper to direct such a measure, Schulyer certainly would have been the man to execute it.

At New York, Washington had learned all the details of the battle of Bunker's Hill. They quickened his impatience to arrive at the camp. He departed therefore on the 26th, accompanied by General Lee and escorted as far as Kingsbridge, the termination of New York Island, by Markoe's Philadelphia light horse and several companies of militia.

In the meantime the provincial Congress of Massachusetts, then in session at Watertown, had made arrangements for the expected arrival of Washington. According to a resolve of that body, the president's house in Cambridge, excepting one room reserved by the president for his own use, was to be taken, cleared, prepared and furnished for the reception of the Commander-in-chief and General Lee. The Congress had likewise sent on a deputation which met Washington at Springfield, on the frontiers of the province, and provided escorts and accommodations for him along the road. Thus honorably attended from town to town and escorted by volunteer companies and cavalcades of gentlemen, he arrived at Watertown on the 2d of July, where he was greeted by Congress with a congratulatory address, in which however was frankly stated the undisciplined state of the army he was summoned to command. An address of cordial welcome was likewise made to General Lee.

The ceremony over, Washington was again in the saddle and, escorted by a troop of light horse and a cavalcade of citizens, proceeded to the head-quarters provided for him at Cambridge, three miles distant. As he entered the confines of the camp the shouts of the multitude and the thundering of artillery gave note to the enemy beleaguered in Boston of his arrival.

His military reputation had preceded him and excited great expectations. They were not disappointed. His personal appearance, notwithstanding the dust of travel, was calculated to captivate the public eye. As he rode through the camp amidst a throng of officers, he was the admiration of the soldiery and of a curious throng collected from the surrounding country. "I have been much gratified this day with a view of General Washington," writes a contemporary chronicler. "His excellency was on horseback, in company with several military gentlemen. It was not difficult to distinguish him from all others. He is tall and well-proportioned, and his personal appearance truly noble and majestic."[1]

With Washington, modest at all times, there was no false excitement on the present occasion, nothing to call forth emotions of self-glorification. The honors and congratulations with which he was received, the acclamations of the public, the cheerings of the army, only told him how much was expected from him; and when he looked round upon the raw and rustic levies he was to command, "a mixed multitude of people, under very little discipline, order or government," scattered in rough encampments about hill and dale, beleaguering a city garrisoned by veteran troops, with ships of war anchored about its harbor and strong outposts guarding it, he felt the awful responsibility of his situation and the complicated and stupendous task before him. He spoke of it, however, not despondingly nor boastfully and with defiance but with that solemn and sedate resolution and that hopeful reliance on Supreme Goodness which belonged to his magnanimous nature. The cause of his country, he observed, had called him to an active and dangerous duty, but he trusted that Divine Providence, which wisely orders the affairs of men, would enable him to discharge it with fidelity and success.[2]

On the 3d of July, the morning after his arrival at Cambridge, Washington took formal command of the army. It was drawn up on the common about half a mile from head-quarters. A multitude

---

[1] Thacher. *Military Journal.*
[2] Letter to Governor Trumbull. Sparks, iii., 31.

had assembled there, for as yet miltary spectacles were novelties, and the camp was full of visitors, men, women and children from all parts of the country who had relatives among the yeoman soldiery.

An ancient elm is still pointed out, under which Washington, as he arrived from head-quarters accompanied by General Lee and a numerous suite, wheeled his horse and drew his sword as commander-in-chief of the armies. Accompanied by this veteran campaigner [Lee], on whose military judgment he had great reliance, Washington visited the different American posts and rode to the heights commanding views over Boston and its environs, being anxious to make himself acquainted with the strength and relative positions of both armies. And here we will give a few particulars concerning the distinguished commanders with whom he was brought immediately in competition.

Congress, speaking of them reproachfully, observed, "Three of England's most experienced generals are sent to wage war with their fellow-subjects." The first here alluded to was the Honorable William Howe, next in command to Gage. He was a man of a fine presence, six feet high, well proportioned and of graceful deportment. He is said to have been not unlike Washington in appearance, though wanting his energy and activity. He lacked also his air of authority, but affability of manners and a generous disposition made him popular with both officers and soldiers.

There was a sentiment in his favor even among Americans at the time when he arrived at Boston. It was remembered that he was brother to the gallant and generous youth, Lord Howe, who fell in the flower of his days on the banks of Lake George and whose untimely death had been lamented throughout the colonies. It was remembered that the general himself had won reputation in the same campaign, commanding the light infantry under Wolfe on the famous Plains of Abraham. A mournful feeling had therefore gone through the country when General Howe was cited as one of the British commanders who had most distinguished themselves in the bloody battle of Bunker's Hill. Congress spoke of it with generous sensibility in their address to the people of Ireland. "America is amazed," said they, "to find the name of Howe on the catalogue of her enemies—she loved his brother!"

General Henry Clinton, the next in command, was grandson of the Earl of Lincoln and son of George Clinton, who had been governor of the province of New York for ten years, from 1743. The general had seen service on the continent in the Seven Years' War. He was of short stature and inclined to corpulency, with a full face and prominent nose. His manners were reserved, and altogether he was in strong contrast with Howe and by no means so popular.

Burgoyne, the other British general of note, was natural son of Lord Bingley and had entered the army at an early age. While yet a subaltern he had made a runaway match with a daughter of the Earl of Derby, who threatened never to admit the offenders to his presence. In 1758 Burgoyne was a lieutenant-colonel of light dragoons. In 1761 he was sent with a force to aid the Portuguese against the Spaniards, joined the army commanded by the Count de la Lippe and signalized himself by surprising and capturing the town of Alcantara. He had since been elected to Parliament for the borough of Middlesex, and displayed considerable parliamentary talents. In 1772 he was made a major-general. His taste, wit and intelligence and his aptness at devising and promoting elegant amusements made him for a time leader in the gay world, though Junius accuses him of unfair practices at the gaming table. His reputation for talents and services had gradually mollified the heart of his father-in-law, the Earl of Derby. In 1774 he gave celebrity to the marriage of a son of the Earl with Lady Betty Hamilton by producing an elegant dramatic trifle, entitled *The Maid of the Oaks*, afterwards performed at Drury Lane and honored with a biting sarcasm by Horace Walpole. "There is a new puppet show at Drury Lane," writes the wit, "as fine as the scenes can make it and as dull as the author could not help making it."[3]

It is but justice to Burgoyne's memory to add that in after years he produced a dramatic work, *The Heiress*, which extorted even Walpole's approbation, who pronounced it the genteelest comedy in the English language.

Such were the three British commanders at Boston, who were considered especially formidable; and they had with them eleven thousand veteran troops, well appointed and well disciplined.

In visiting the different posts, Washington halted for a time at Prospect Hill, which, as its name denotes, commanded a wide view over Boston and the surrounding country. Here Putnam had taken his position after the battle of Bunker's Hill, fortifying himself

[3] Walpole to the Hon. W. S. Conway.

with works which he deemed impregnable, and here the veteran was enabled to point out to the commander-in-chief and to Lee the main features of the belligerent region which lay spread out like a map before them.

Bunker's Hill was but a mile distant to the east, the British standard floating as if in triumph on its summit. The main force under General Howe was intrenching itself strongly about half a mile beyond the place on the recent battle. Scarlet uniforms gleamed about the hill, tents and marquees whitened its sides. All up there was bright, brilliant and triumphant. At the base of the hill lay Charlestown in ashes, "nothing to be seen of that fine town but chimneys and rubbish."

Howe's sentries extended a hundred and fifty yards beyond the neck or isthmus over which the Americans retreated after the battle. Three floating batteries in Mystic River commanded this isthmus, and a twenty-gun ship was anchored between the peninsula and Boston.

General Gage, the commander-in-chief, still had his headquarters in the town but there were few troops there besides Burgoyne's light horse. A large force, however, was intrenched south of the town on the neck leading to Roxbury, the only entrance to Boston by land.

The American troops were irregularly distributed in a kind of semicircle eight or nine miles in extent, the left resting on Winter Hill, the most northern post, the right extending on the south to Roxbury and Dorchester Neck.

Washington reconnoitered the British posts from various points of view. Everything about them was in admirable order. The works appeared to be constructed with military science, the troops to be in a high state of discipline. The American camp, on the contrary, disappointed him. He had expected to find eighteen or twenty thousand men under arms. There were not much more than fourteen thousand. He had expected to find some degree of system and discipline, whereas all were raw militia. He had expected to find works scientifically constructed, and proofs of knowledge and skill in engineering, whereas what he saw of the latter was very imperfect and confined to the mere manual exercise of cannon. There was abundant evidence of aptness at trenching and throwing up rough defenses, and in that way General Thomas had fortified Roxbury Neck and Putnam had strengthened Prospect Hill. But the semicircular line which linked the extreme posts was formed of rudely-constructed works far too extensive for the troops which were at hand to man them.

Within this attenuated semicircle the British forces lay concentrated and compact, and, having command of the water, might suddenly bring their main strength to bear upon some weak point, force it and sever the American camp.

In fact, when we consider the scanty, ill-conditioned and irregular force which had thus stretched itself out to beleaguer a town and harbor defended by ships and floating batteries and garrisoned by eleven thousand strongly posted veterans, we are at a loss whether to attribute its hazardous position to ignorance or to that daring self-confidence which at times in our military history has snatched success in defiance of scientific rules. It was revenge for the slaughter at Lexington, which, we are told, first prompted the investment of Boston. "The universal voice," says a contemporary, "is, starve them out. Drive them from the town and let His Majesty's ships be their own place of refuge."

In riding throughout the camp, Washington observed that nine thousand of the troops belonged to Massachusetts; the rest were from other provinces. They were encamped in separate bodies, each with its own regulations and officers of its own appointment. Some had tents, others were in barracks, and others sheltered themselves as best they might. Many were sadly in want of clothing and all, said Washington, were strongly imbued with the spirit of insubordination, which they mistook for independence.

A chaplain of one of the regiments[4] has left on record a graphic sketch of this primitive army of the Revolution. "It is very diverting," writes he, "to walk among the camps. They are as different in their forms as the owners are in their dress, and every tent is a portraiture of the temper and taste of the persons who encamp in it. Some are made of boards and some are made of sail-cloth; some are partly of one, and partly of the other. Again others are made of stone and turf, brick and brush. Some are thrown up in a hurry, others curiously wrought with wreaths and withes."

[Brigadier-General Nathaniel Greene] made a soldier-like address to Washington, welcoming him to the camp. His appearance and manner were calculated to make a favorable impression. He was about thirty-nine years of age, nearly six feet high, well built and

---

[4] The Rev. William Emerson.

vigorous, with an open, animated, intelligent countenance and a frank, manly demeanor. He may be said to have stepped at once into the confidence of the commander-in-chief, which he never forfeited, but became one of his most attached, faithful and efficient coadjutors throughout the war.

Having taken his survey of the army, Washington wrote to the President of Congress, representing its various deficiencies and, among other things, urging the appointment of a commissary-general, a quartermaster-general, a commissary of musters and a commissary of artillery. Above all things, he requested a supply of money as soon as possible. "I find myself already much embarrassed for want of a military chest."

In one of his recommendations we have an instance of frontier expediency learnt in his early campaigns. Speaking of the ragged condition of the army and the difficulty of procuring the requisite kind of clothing, he advises that a number of hunting shirts, not less then ten thousand, should be provided, as being the cheapest and quickest mode of supplying this necessity. "I know nothing in a speculative view more trivial," observes he, "yet which, if put in practice, would have a happier tendency to unite the men and abolish those provincial distinctions that lead to jealousy and dissatisfaction."

Among the troops most destitute were those belonging to Massachusetts, which formed the larger part of the army. Washington made a noble apology for them. "This unhappy and devoted province," said he, "has been so long in a state of anarchy, and the yoke has been laid so heavily on it, that great allowances are to be made for troops raised under such circumstances. The deficiency of numbers, discipline and stores can only lead to this conclusion: that their spirit has exceeded their strength."

This apology was the more generous coming from a Southerner, for there was a disposition among the Southern officers to regard the Eastern troops disparagingly. But Washington already felt as commander-in-chief, who looked with an equal eye on all; or rather as a true patriot, who was above all sectional prejudices.

Chapter 16

STRENGTHENING THE DEFENSES

The Congress of Massachusetts manifested considerate liberality with respect to head-quarters. According to their minutes, a committee was charged to procure a steward, a housekeeper and two or three women cooks, Washington no doubt having brought with him none but the black servants who had accompanied him to Philadelphia and who were but little fitted for New England housekeeping. His wishes were to be consulted in regard to the supply of his table. This his station as commander-in-chief required should be kept up in ample and hospitable style. Every day a number of his officers dined with him. As he was in the neighborhood of the seat of the Provincial Government, he would occasionally have members of Congress and other functionaries at his board. Though social, however, he was not convivial in his habits. He received his guests with courtesy but his mind and time were too much occupied by grave and anxious concerns to permit him the genial indulgence of the table. His own diet was extremely simple, sometimes nothing but baked apples or berries, with cream and milk. He would retire early from the board, leaving an aide-de-camp or one of his officers to take his place.

The member of Washington's [official] family most deserving of mention at present was his secretary, Mr. Joseph Reed. With this gentleman he had formed an intimacy in the course of his visits to Philadelphia to attend the sessions of the Continental Congress. Mr. Reed was an accomplished man, had studied law in America and at the Temple in London and had gained a high reputation at the Philadelphia bar. In the dawning of the Revolution he had embraced the popular cause and carried on a correspondence with the Earl of Dartmouth, endeavoring to enlighten that minister on the subject of colonial affairs. He had since been highly instrumental in rousing the Philadelphians to co-operate with the patriots of Boston. A sympathy of views and feelings had attached him to Washington and induced him to accompany him to the camp. He had no definite purpose when he left home, and his friends in Philadelphia were surprised, on receiving a letter from him written from Cambridge, to find that he had accepted the post of secretary to the commander-in-chief.

They expostulated with him by letter. That a man in the thirty-fifth year of his age, with a lucrative profession, a young wife and growing family and a happy home, should suddenly abandon all to join the hazardous fortunes of a revolutionary camp appeared to them the height of infatuation. They remonstrated on the peril of the step.

"I have no inclination," replied Reed, "to be hanged for half treason. When a subject draws his sword against his prince he must cut his way through if he means to sit down in safety. I have taken too active a part in what may be called the civil part of opposition to renounce without disgrace the public cause when it seems to lead to danger, and have a most sovereign contempt for the man who can plan measures he has not the spirit to execute."

Washington has occasionally been represented as cold and reserved, yet his intercourse with Mr. Reed is a proof to the contrary. His friendship towards him was frank and cordial and the confidence he reposed in him full and implicit. Reed in fact became in a little time the intimate companion of his thoughts, his bosom counsellor. He felt the need of such a friend in the present exigency, placed as he was in a new and untried situation and having to act with persons hitherto unknown to him.

In military affairs, it is true, he had a shrewd counsellor in General Lee, but Lee was a wayward character, a cosmopolite, without attachment to country, somewhat splenetic, and prone to follow the bent of his whims and humors, which often clashed with propriety and sound policy. Reed, on the contrary, though less informed on military matters, had a strong common sense unclouded by passion or prejudice, and a pure patriotism, which regarded everything as it bore upon the welfare of his country.

Washington's confidence in Lee had always to be measured and guarded in matters of civil policy.

The arrival of Gates in camp was heartily welcomed by the commander-in-chief, who had received a letter from that officer gratefully acknowledging his friendly influence in procuring him the appointment of adjutant-general. Washington may have promised himself much cordial co-operation from him, recollecting the warm friendship professed by him when he visited at Mount Vernon, and they talked together over their early companionship in arms; but of that kind of friendship there was no further manifestation. Gates was certainly of great service, from his practical knowledge and military experience at this juncture when the whole army had in a manner to be organized, but from the familiar intimacy of Washington he gradually estranged himself. A contemporary has accounted for this by alleging that he was secretly chagrined at not having received the appointment of major-general, to which he considered himself well fitted by his military knowledge and experience and which he thought Washington might have obtained for him had he used his influence with Congress. We shall have to advert to this estrangement of Gates on subsequent occasions.

The hazardous position of the army from the great extent and weakness of its lines was what most pressed on the immediate attention of Washington, and he summoned a council of war to take the matter into consideration. In this it was urged that to abandon the line of works after the great labor and expense of their construction would be dispiriting to the troops and encouraging to the enemy, while it would expose a wide extent of the surrounding country to maraud and ravage. Besides, no safer position presented itself on which to fall back. This being generally admitted, it was determined to hold on to the works and defend them as long as possible and in the meantime to augment the army to at least twenty thousand men.

Washington now hastened to improve the defenses of the camp, strengthen the weak parts of the line and throw up additional works round the main forts. No one seconded him more effectually in this matter than General Putnam. No works were thrown up with equal rapidity to those under his superintendence. "You seem, general," said Washington, "to have the faculty of infusing your own spirit into all the workmen you employ." And it was the fact.

The observing chaplain already cited gazed with wonder at the rapid effects soon produced by the labors of an army. "It is surprising," writes he, "how much work has been done. The lines are extended almost from Cambridge to Mystic River. Very soon it will be mortally impossible for the enemy to get between the works except in one place, which is supposed to be left purposely unfortified to entice the enemy out of their fortresses. Who would have thought, twelve months past, that all Cambridge and Charlestown would be covered over with American camps and cut up into forts and intrenchments, and all the lands, fields, orchards, laid common—horses and cattle feeding on the choicest mowing land, whole fields of corn eaten down to the ground, and large parks of well-regulated forest trees cut down for firewood and other public uses."

Beside the main dispositions above mentioned, about seven hundred men were distributed in the small towns and villages along the coast to prevent depredations by water, and horses were kept ready saddled at various points of the widely extended lines to convey to head-quarters intelligence of any special movement of the enemy.

The army was distributed by Washington into three grand divisions. One, forming the right wing, was stationed on the heights of Roxbury. It was commanded by Major-General Ward, who had under him Brigadier-Generals Spencer and Thomas. Another, forming the left wing, under Major-General Lee, having with him Brigadier-Generals Sullivan and Greene, was stationed on Winter and Prospect Hills; while the centre, under Major-General Putnam and Brigadier-General Heath, was stationed at Cambridge. With Putnam was encamped his favorite officer, Knowlton, who had been promoted by Congress to the rank of major for his gallantry at Bunker's Hill.

At Washington's recommendation, Joseph Trumbull, the eldest son of the governor, received on the 24th of July the appointment of commissary-general of the continental army. He had already officiated with talent in that capacity in the Connecticut militia. "There is a great overturning in the camp as to order and regularity," writes the military chaplain. "New lords, new laws. The Generals Washington and Lee are upon the lines every day. New orders from his excellency are read to the respective regiments every morning after prayers. The strictest government is taking place, and great distinction is made between officers and soldiers. Every one is made to know his place and keep it, or be tied up and receive thirty or forty lashes according to his crime. Thousands are at work every day from four till eleven o'clock in the morning."

While all his forces were required for the investment of Boston,

Washington was importuned by the Legislature of Massachusetts and the governor of Connecticut to detach troops for the protection of different points of the seacoast, where depredations by armed vessels were apprehended. The case of New London was specified by Governor Trumbull, where Captain Wallace of the *Rose* frigate, with two other ships of war, had entered the harbor, landed men, spiked the cannon and gone off threatening future visits.

Washington referred to his instructions and consulted with his general officers and such members of the Continental Congress as happened to be in the camp before he replied to these requests; he then respectfully declined compliance.

In his reply to the General Assembly of Massachusetts he stated frankly and explicitly the policy and system on which the war was to be conducted and according to which he was to act as commander-in-chief.

"It has been debated in Congress and settled," writes he, "that the militia or other internal strength of each province is to be applied for defense against those small and particular depredations which were to be expected and to which they were supposed to be competent. This will appear the more proper when it is considered that every town, and indeed every part of our seacoast, which is exposed to these depredations would have an equal claim upon this army.

"It is the misfortune of our situation which exposes us to these ravages and against which, in my judgment, no such temporary relief could possibly secure us. The great advantage the enemy have of transporting troops by being masters of the sea will enable them to harass us by diversions of this kind; and should we be tempted to pursue them upon every alarm, the army must either be so weakened as to expose it to destruction, or a great part of the coast be still left unprotected. Nor, indeed, does it appear to me that such a pursuit would be attended with the least effect. The first notice of such an excursion would be its actual execution, and long before any troops could reach the scene of action the enemy would have an opportunity to accomplish their purpose and retire. It would give me great pleasure to have it in my power to extend protection and safety to every individual, but the wisdom of the General Court will anticipate me on the necessity of conducting our operations on a general and impartial scale, so as to exclude any just cause of complaint and jealousy."

His reply to the governor of Connecticut was to the same effect. "I am by no means insensible to the situation of the people on the coast. I wish I could extend protection to all, but the numerous detachments necessary to remedy the evil would amount to a dissolution of the army, or make the most important operations of the campaign depend upon the piratical expeditions of two or three men-of-war and transports."

His refusal to grant the required detachments gave much dissatisfaction in some quarters until sanctioned and enforced by the Continental Congress. All at length saw and acquiesced in the justice and wisdom of his decision. It was in fact a vital question, involving the whole character and fortune of the war, and it was acknowledged that he met it with a forecast and determination befitting a commander-in-chief.

The great object of Washington at present was to force the enemy to come out of Boston and try a decisive action. His lines had for some time cut off all communication of the town with the country and he had caused the live stock within a considerable distance of the place to be driven back from the coast out of reach of the men-of-war's boats. Fresh provisions and vegetables were consequently growing more and more scarce and extravagantly dear, and sickness began to prevail. "I have done and shall do everything in my power to distress them," writes he to his brother, John Augustine. "The transports have all arrived and their whole reinforcement is landed, so that I see no reason why they should not, if they ever attempt it, come boldly out and put the matter to issue at once."

"We are in the strangest state in the world," writes a lady from Boston, "surrounded on all sides. The whole country is in arms and intrenched. We are deprived of fresh provisions, subject to continual alarms and cannonadings, the provincials being very audacious and advancing to our lines since the arrival of Generals Washington and Lee to command them."

At this critical juncture, when Washington was pressing the siege and endeavoring to provoke a general action, a startling fact came to light: the whole amount of powder in the camp would not furnish more than nine cartridges to a man![1]

A gross error had been made by the committee of supplies when Washington, on taking command, had required a return of the ammunition. They had returned the whole amount of powder

[1] Letter to the President of Congress, Aug. 4.

collected by the province, upwards of three hundred barrels, without stating what had been expended. The blunder was detected on an order being issued for a new supply of cartridges. It was found that there were but thirty-two barrels of powder in store.

This was an astounding discovery. Washington instantly despatched letters and expresses to Rhode Island, the Jerseys, Ticonderoga and elsewhere, urging immediate supplies of powder and lead, no quantity, however small, to be considered beneath notice.

Day after day elapsed without the arrival of any supplies, for in these irregular times the munitions of war were not readily procured. It seemed hardly possible that the matter could be kept concealed from the enemy. Their works on Bunker's Hill commanded a full view of those of the Americans on Winter and Prospect Hills. Each camp could see what was passing in the other. The sentries were almost near enough to converse. There was furtive intercourse occasionally between the men. In this critical state the American camp remained for a fortnight, the anxious commander incessantly apprehending an attack. At length a partial supply from the Jerseys put an end to this imminent risk. Washington's secretary, Reed, who had been the confidant of his troubles and anxieties, gives a vivid expression of his feelings on the arrival of this relief. "I can hardly look back without shuddering at our situation before this increase of our stock. *Stock* did I say? It was next to nothing. Almost the whole powder of the army was in the cartridge-boxes."[2]

It is thought that, considering the clandestine intercourse carried on between the two camps, intelligence of this deficiency of ammunition on the part of the besiegers must have been conveyed to the British commander but that the bold face with which the Americans continued to maintain their position made him discredit it.

Notwithstanding the supply from the Jerseys, there was not more powder in camp than would serve the artillery for one day of general action. None, therefore, was allowed to be wasted. The troops were even obliged to bear in silence an occasional cannonading. "Our poverty in ammunition," writes Washington, "prevents our making a suitable return."

[2] Reed to Thomas Bradford. *Life and Correspondence*, vol. i., p. 118.

A correspondence of [an important] character took place between Washington and General Gage. It was one intended to put the hostile services on a proper footing. A strong disposition had been manifested among the British officers to regard those engaged in the patriot cause as malefactors, outlawed from the courtesies of chivalric warfare. Washington was determined to have a full understanding on this point. He was peculiarly sensitive with regard to Gage. They had been companions in arms in their early days, but Gage might now effect to look down upon him as the chief of a rebel army. Washington took an early opportunity to let him know that he claimed to be the commander of a legitimate force engaged in a legitimate cause, and that both himself and his army were to be treated on a footing of perfect equality. The correspondence arose from the treatment of several American officers.

"I understand," writes Washington to Gage, "that the officers engaged in the cause of liberty and their country, who by the fortune of war have fallen into your hands, have been thrown indiscriminately into a common jail appropriated to felons, that no consideration has been had for those of the most respectable rank when languishing with wounds and sickness, and that some have been amputated in this unworthy situation. Let your opinion, sir, of the principles which actuate them be what it may, they suppose that they act from the noblest of all principles, love of freedom and their country. But political principles, I conceive, are foreign to this point. The obligations arising from the rights of humanity and claims of rank are universally binding and extensive, except in case of retaliation. These I should have hoped would have dictated a more tender treatment of those individuals whom chance or war had put in your power. Nor can I forbear suggesting its fatal tendency to widen that unhappy breach which you and those ministers under whom you act have repeatedly declared your wish to see forever closed. My duty now makes it necessary to apprise you that for the future I shall regulate all my conduct towards those gentlemen who are or may be in our possession exactly by the rule you shall observe towards those of ours now in your custody.

"If severity and hardships mark the line of your conduct, painful as it may be to me, your prisoners will feel its effects. But if kindness and humanity are shown to us, I shall with pleasure consider those in our hands only as unfortunate, and they shall receive from me that treatment to which the unfortunate are ever entitled."

The following are the essential parts of a letter from General Gage in reply:

"Sir,—To the glory of civilized nations, humanity and war have been compatible, and humanity to the subdued has become almost a general system. Britons, ever pre-eminent in mercy, have outgone common examples and overlooked the criminal in the captive. Upon these principles your prisoners, whose lives by the law of the land are destined to the cord, have hitherto been treated with care and kindness, and more comfortably lodged than the king's troops in the hospitals; indiscriminately, it is true, for I acknowledge no rank that is not derived from the king.

"My intelligence from your army would justify severe recriminations. I understand there are of the king's faithful subjects, taken some time since by the rebels, laboring like negro slaves to gain their daily subsistence, or reduced to the wretched alternative to perish by famine or take arms against their king and country. Those who have made the treatment of the prisoners in my hands, or of your other friends in Boston, a pretense for such measures, found barbarity upon falsehood.

"I would willingly hope, sir, that the sentiments of liberality which I have always believed you to possess will be exerted to correct these misdoings. Be temperate in political disquisition; give free operation to truth, and punish those who deceive and misrepresent; and not only the effects, but the cause of this unhappy conflict will be removed. Should those, under whose usurped authority you act, control such a disposition and dare to call severity retaliation; to God, who knows all hearts, be the appeal of the dreadful consequences," etc.

There were expressions in the foregoing letter well calculated to rouse indignant feelings in the most temperate bosom. Had Washington been as readily moved to transports of passion as some are pleased to represent him, the *rebel* and the *cord* might readily have stung him to fury, but with him anger was checked in its impulses by higher energies and reined in to give a grander effect to the dictates of his judgment. The following was his noble and dignified reply to General Gage:

"I addressed you, sir, on the 11th instant in terms which gave the fairest scope for that humanity and politeness which were supposed to form a part of your character. I remonstrated with you on the unworthy treatment shown to the officers and citizens of America, whom the fortune of war, chance or a mistaken confidence had thrown into your hands. Whether British or American mercy, fortitude, and patience are most pre-eminent; whether our virtuous citizens, whom the hand of tyranny has forced into arms to defend their wives, their children and their property, or the merciless instruments of lawless domination, avarice and revenge, best deserve the appellation of rebels and the punishment of that cord which your affected clemency has forborne to inflict; whether the authority under which I act is usurped, or founded upon the genuine principles of liberty, were altogether foreign to the subject. I purposely avoided all political disquisition, nor shall I now avail myself of those advantages which the sacred cause of my country, of liberty and of human nature give me over you. Much less shall I stoop to retort and invective. But the intelligence you say you have received from our army requires a reply. I have taken time, sir, to make a strict inquiry and find it has not the least foundation in truth. Not only your officers and soldiers have been treated with the tenderness due to fellow-citizens and brethren, but even those execrable parricides, whose counsels and aid have deluged their country with blood, have been protected from the fury of a justly enraged people. Far from compelling or permitting their assistance, I am embarrassed with the numbers who crowd to our camp, animated with the purest principles of virtue and love to their country. . . .

"You affect, sir, to despise all rank not derived from the same source with your own. I cannot conceive one more honorable than that which flows from the uncorrupted choice of a brave and free people, the purest source and original fountain of all power. Far from making it a plea for cruelty, a mind of true magnanimity and enlarged ideas would comprehend and respect it.

"What may have been the ministerial views which have precipitated the present crisis, Lexington, Concord and Charlestown can best declare. May that God to whom you, too, appeal, judge between America and you. Under his providence, those who influence the councils of America, and all the other inhabitants of the united colonies, at the hazard of their lives are determined to hand down to posterity those just and invaluable privileges which they received from their ancestors.

"I shall now, sir, close my correspondence with you, perhaps forever. If your officers, our prisoners, receive a treatment from me different from that which I wished to show them, they and you will remember the occasion of it."

We have given these letters of Washington almost entire, for they contain his manifesto as commander-in-chief of the armies of the Revolution, setting forth the opinions and motives by which he was governed and the principles on which hostilities on his part would be conducted. It was planting with the pen that standard which was to be maintained by the sword.

The siege of Boston had been kept up for several weeks without any remarkable occurrence. The British remained within their lines, diligently strengthening them. The besiegers, having received further supplies of ammunition, were growing impatient of a state of inactivity. Towards the latter part of August there were rumors from Boston that the enemy were preparing for a sortie. Washington was resolved to provoke it by a kind of challenge. He accordingly detached fourteen hundred men to seize at night upon a height within musket-shot of the enemy's line on Charlestown Neck, presuming that the latter would sally forth on the following day to dispute possession of it and thus be drawn into a general battle. The task was executed with silence and celerity, and by daybreak the hill presented to the astonished foe the aspect of a fortified post.

The challenge was not accepted. The British opened a heavy cannonade from Bunker's Hill but kept within their works. The Americans, scant of ammunition, could only reply with a single nine-pounder. This, however, sank one of the floating batteries which guarded the Neck. They went on to complete and strengthen this advanced post, exposed to daily cannonade and bombardment, which, however, did but little injury. They continued to answer from time to time with a single gun, reserving their ammunition for a general action. "We are just in the situation of a man with little money in his pocket," writes Secretary Reed. "He will do twenty mean things to prevent his breaking in upon his little stock. We are obliged to bear with the rascals on Bunker's Hill, when a few shot now and then in return would keep our men attentive to their business and give the enemy alarms."[3]

The evident unwillingness of the latter to come forth was

perplexing. "Unless the ministerial troops in Boston are waiting for reinforcements," writes Washington, "I cannot devise what they are staying there for, nor why, as they affect to despise the Americans, they do not come forth and put an end to the contest at once."

Perhaps they persuaded themselves that his army, composed of crude, half-disciplined levies from different and distant quarters, would gradually fall asunder and disperse or that its means of subsistence would be exhausted. He had his own fears on the subject and looked forward with doubt and anxiety to a winter's campaign; the heavy expense that would be incurred in providing barracks, fuel and warm clothing; the difficulty there would be of keeping together through the rigorous season troops unaccustomed to military hardships, and none of whose terms of enlistment extended beyond the first of January; the supplies of ammunition, too, that would be required for protracted operations, the stock of powder on hand, notwithstanding the most careful husbandry, being fearfully small. Revolving these circumstances in his mind, he rode thoughtfully about the commanding points in the vicinity of Boston, considering how he might strike a decisive blow that would put an end to the murmuring inactivity of the army and relieve the country from the consuming expense of maintaining it. The result was a letter to the major and brigadier-generals, summoning them to a council of war to be held at the distance of three days and giving them previous intimation of its purpose. It was to know whether in their judgment a successful attack might not be made upon the troops at Boston by means of boats, in co-operation with an attempt upon their lines at Roxbury. "The success of such an enterprise," adds he, "depends, I well know, upon the All-wise Disposer of events, and it is not within the reach of human wisdom to foretell the issue, but if the prospect is fair the undertaking is justifiable."

He proceeded to state the considerations already cited which appeared to justify it. The council having thus had time for previous deliberation met on the 11th of September. It was composed of Major-Generals Ward, Lee and Putnam, and Bragadier-Generals Thomas, Heath, Sullivan, Spencer and Greene. They unanimously pronounced the suggested attempt inexpedient, at least for the present.

On the 15th of October a Committee from Congress arrived in

camp, sent to hold a conference with Washington, and with delegates from the governments of Connecticut, Rhode Island, Massachusetts and New Hampshire, on the subject of a new organization of the army. The committee consisted of Benjamin Franklin, Thomas Lynch of Carolina and Colonel Harrison of Virginia. It was just twenty years since Washington had met Franklin in Braddock's camp, aiding that unwary general by his sagacious counsels and prompt expedients. Franklin was regarded with especial deference in the camp at Cambridge. Greene, who had never met with him before, listened to him as to an oracle.

Washington was president of the board of conference and Mr. Joseph Reed secretary. The committee brought an intimation from Congress that an attack upon Boston was much desired, if practicable.

Washington called a council of war of his generals on the subject. They were unanimously of the opinion that an attack would not be prudent at present.

Another question now arose. An attack upon the British forces in Boston, whenever it should take place, might require a bombardment. Washington inquired of the delegates how far it might be pushed to the destruction of houses and property. They considered it a question of too much importance to be decided by them and said it must be referred to Congress. But though they declined taking upon themselves the responsiblity, the majority of them were strongly in favor of it and expressed themselves so when the matter was discussed informally in camp. Two of the committee, Lynch and Harrison, as well as Judge Wales, delegate from Connecticut, when the possible effects of a bombardment were suggested at a dinner table, declared that they would be willing to see Boston in flames. Lee, who was present, observed that it was impossible to burn it unless they sent in men with bundles of straw to do it. "It could not be done with carcasses and red-hot shot. Isle Royal," he added, "in the river St. Lawrence, had been fired at for a long time in 1760 with a fine train of artillery, hotshot and carcasses, without effect."[4]

The board of conference was repeatedly in session for three or four days. The report of its deliberations rendered by the committee produced a resolution of Congress that a new army of twenty-

[4] *Life of Dr. Belknap*, p. 96. The doctor was present at the above cited conversation.

two thousand two hundred and seventy-two men and officers should be formed, to be recruited as much as possible from the troops actually in service. Unfortunately the term for which they were to be enlisted was to be but for one year. It formed a precedent which became a recurring cause of embarrassment throughout the war.

Washington's secretary, Mr. Reed, had after the close of the conference signified to him his intention to return to Philadelphia, where his private concerns required his presence. His departure was deeply regretted. His fluent pen had been of great assistance to Washington in the despatch of his multifarious correspondence, and his judicious counsels and cordial sympathies had been still more appreciated by the commander-in-chief amid the multiplied difficulties of his situation. On the departure of Mr. Reed, his place as secretary was temporarily supplied by Mr. Robert Harrison of Maryland and subsequently by Colonel Mifflin. Neither, however, attained to the affectionate confidence reposed in their predecessor.

We shall have occasion to quote the correspondence kept up between Washington and Reed during the absence of the latter. The letters of the former are peculiarly interesting as giving views of what was passing not merely around him but in the recesses of his own heart. No greater proof need be given of the rectitude of that heart than the clearness and fulness with which, in these truthful documents, every thought and feeling is laid open.

Chapter 17

MRS. WASHINGTON IN CAMP

The measures which General Howe had adopted after taking command in Boston rejoiced the royalists, seeming to justify their anticipations. He proceeded to strengthen the works on Bunker's Hill and Boston Neck and to clear away houses and throw up redoubts on eminences within the town. The patriot inhabitants were shocked by the desecration of the Old South Church, which for more than a hundred years had been a favorite place of worship, where some of the most eminent divines had officiated. The pulpit and pews were now removed, the floor was covered with earth, and the sacred edifice was converted into a riding-school for Burgoyne's light dragoons. To excuse its desecration, it was spoken of scoffingly as a "meeting-house, where sedition had often been preached."

The North Church, another "meeting-house," was entirely demolished and was used for fuel. "Thus," says the chronicler of the day, "thus are our houses, devoted to religious worship, profaned and destroyed by the subjects of His Royal Majesty."[1]

About the last of October Howe issued three proclamations. The first forbade all persons to leave Boston without his permission under pain of military execution. The second forbade any one so permitted to take with him more than five pounds sterling, under pain of forfeiting all the money found upon his person and being subject to fine and imprisonment. The third called upon the inhabitants to arm themselves for the preservation of order within the town, they to be commanded by officers of his appointment.

Washington had recently been incensed by the conflagration of Falmouth. The conduct of Governor Dunmore, who had proclaimed martial law in Virginia and threatened ruin to the pa-

[1] Thacher's *Military Journal*, p. 50.

triots, had added to this provocation. The measures of General Howe seemed of the same harsh character, and he determined to retaliate.

"Would it not be prudent," writes he to Governor Trumbull of Connecticut, "to seize those tories who have been, are and we know will be active against us? Why should persons who are preying upon the vitals of their country be suffered to stalk at large whilst we know they will do us every mischief in their power?"

In this spirit he ordered General Sullivan, who was fortifying Portsmouth, "to seize upon such persons as held commissions under the crown and were acting as open and avowed enemies to their country and hold them as hostages for the security of the town." Still he was moderate in his retaliation and stopped short of private individuals. "For the present," said he, "I shall avoid giving the like order with regard to the *tories* of Portsmouth but the day is not far off when they will meet with this or a worse fate if there is not a considerable reformation in their conduct."[2]

The season was fast approaching when the bay between the camp and Boston would be frozen over and military operations might be conducted upon the ice. General Howe, if reinforced, would then very probably "endeavor to relieve himself from the disgraceful confinement in which the ministerial troops had been all summer." Washington felt the necessity, therefore, of guarding the camps wherever they were most assailable and of throwing up batteries for the purpose. He had been embarrassed throughout the siege by the want of artillery and ordnance stores but never more so than at the present moment. In this juncture Mr. Henry Knox stepped forward and offered to proceed to the frontier forts on Champlain in quest of a supply.

Knox was one of those providential characters which spring up in emergencies, as if they were formed by and for the occasion. A thriving bookseller in Boston, he had thrown up business to take up arms for the liberties of his country. He was one of the patriots who had fought on Bunker's Hill, since when he had aided in planning the defenses of the camp before Boston. The aptness and talent here displayed by him as an artillerist had recently induced Washington to recommend him to Congress for the command of the regiment of artillery in place of the veteran Gridley, who was considered by all the officers of the camp too old for active

[2] Letter to William Palfrey. Sparks, iii., 158.

employment. Congress had not yet acted on that recommendation. In the meantime Washington availed himself of the offered services of Knox in the present instance. He was accordingly instructed to examine into the state of the artillery in camp and take an account of the cannon, mortars, shells, lead and ammunition that were wanting. He was then to hasten to New York, procure and forward all that could be had there, and thence proceed to the head-quarters of General Schuyler, who was requested by letter to aid him in obtaining what further supplies of the kind were wanting from the forts of Ticonderoga, Crown Point, St. John's and even Quebec, should it be in the hands of the Americans. Knox set off on his errand with promptness and alacrity and shortly afterwards the commission of colonel of the regiment of artillery which Washington had advised was forwarded to him by Congress.

The re-enlistment of troops actually in service was now attempted and proved a fruitful source of perplexity. In a letter to the President of Congress, Washington observes that half of the officers of the rank of captain were inclined to retire and it was probable their example would influence their men. Of those who were disposed to remain, the officers of one colony were unwilling to mix in the same regiment with those of another. Many sent in their names to serve in expectation of promotion. Others stood aloof to see what advantages they could make for themselves. While those who had declined sent in their names again to serve.[8] The difficulties were greater, if possible, with the soldiers than with the officers. They would not enlist unless they knew their colonel, lieutenant-colonel and captain, Connecticut men being unwilling to serve under officers from Massachusetts, and Massachusetts men under officers from Rhode Island, so that it was necessary to appoint the officers first.

Twenty days later he again writes to the President of Congress: "I am sorry to be necessitated to mention to you the egregious want of public spirit which prevails here. Instead of pressing to be engaged in the cause of their country, which I vainly flattered myself would be the case, I find we are most likely to be deserted in a most critical time. . . . Our situation is truly alarming, and of this General Howe is well apprised. No doubt when he is reinforced he will avail himself of the information."

[8] Washington to the President of Congress, Nov. 8.

In a letter to Reed he disburdened his heart more completely. "Such dearth of public spirit and such want of virtue; such stock-jobbing and fertility in all the low arts to obtain advantage of one kind or another in this great change of military arrangement I never saw before and I pray God's mercy that I may never be witness to again. What will be the end of these manœuvres is beyond my scan. I tremble at the prospect. We have been till this time (Nov. 28th) enlisting about three thousand five hundred men. To engage these I have been obliged to allow furloughs as far as fifty men to a regiment, and the officers I am persuaded indulge many more. The Connecticut troops will not be prevailed upon to stay longer than their term, saving those who have enlisted for the next campaign and are mostly on furlough; and such a mercenary spirit pervades the whole that I should not be surprised at any disaster that may happen. . . . Could I have foreseen what I have experienced and am likely to experience, no consideration upon earth should have induced me to accept this command."

No one drew closer to Washington in this time of his troubles and perplexities than General Greene. He had a real veneration for his character and thought himself "happy in an opportunity to serve under so good a general." He grieved at Washington's annoyances but attributed them in part to his being somewhat of a stranger in New England. "He has not had time," writes he, "to make himself acquainted with the genius of this people. They are naturally as brave and spirited as the peasantry of any other country but you cannot expect veterans of a raw militia from only a few months' service. The common people are exceedingly avaricious. The genius of the people is commercial, from their long intercourse of trade. The sentiment of honor, the true characteristic of a soldier, has not yet got the better of interest. His Excellency has been taught to believe the people here a superior race of mortals; and finding them of the same temper and dispositions, passions and prejudices, virtues and vices of the common people of other governments, they sank in his esteem."[4]

The forming even of the skeleton of an army under the new regulations had been a work of infinite difficulty. To fill it up was still more difficult. The first burst of revolutionary zeal had passed away. Enthusiasm had been chilled by the inaction and monotony of a long encampment, an encampment, moreover, destitute of

[4] Greene to Dep. Gov. Ward. *Am. Archives*, 4th Series, iii., 1145.

those comforts which, in experienced warfare, are provided by a well-regulated commissariat. The troops had suffered privations of every kind, want of food, clothing, provisions. They looked forward with dismay to the rigors of winter and longed for their rustic homes and their family firesides.

Apprehending that some of them would incline to go home when the time of their enlistment expired, Washington summoned the general officers to headquarters, and invited a delegation of the General Court to be present, to adopt measures for the defense and support of the lines. The result of their deliberations was an order that three thousand of the minute men and militia of Massachusetts and two thousand from New Hampshire should be at Cambridge by the 10th of December to relieve the Connecticut regiments and supply the deficiency that would be caused by their departure and by the absence of others on furlough.

With this arrangement the Connecticut troops were made acquainted and, as the time of most of them would not be out before the 10th, they were ordered to remain in camp until relieved. Their officers assured Washington that he need apprehend no defection on the part of their men; they would not leave the lines. The officers themselves were probably mistaken in their opinion of their men, for on the 1st of December many of the latter, some of whom belonged to Putnam's regiment, resolved to go home immediately. Efforts were made to prevent them but in vain. Several carried off with them their arms and ammunition. Washington sent a list of their names to Governor Trumbull. "I submit it to your judgment," writes he, "whether an example should not be made of these men who have deserted the cause of their country at this critical juncture when the enemy are receiving reinforcements?"

We anticipate the reply of Governor Trumbull, received several days subsequently. "The late extraordinary and reprehensible conduct of some of the troops of this colony," writes he, "impresses me, and the minds of many of our people, with great surprise and indignation, since the treatment they met with and the order and request made to them were so reasonable, and apparently necessary for the defense of our common cause, and safety of our rights and privileges, for which they freely engaged."

We will here add that the homeward-bound warriors seem to have run the gauntlet along the road, for their conduct on quitting the army drew upon them such indignation that they could hardly get anything to eat on their journey, and when they arrived at home they met with such a reception (to the credit of the Connecticut women be it recorded), that many were soon disposed to return again to the camp.[5]

On the very day after the departure homeward of these troops and while it was feared their example would be contagious, a long, lumbering train of wagons laden with ordnance and military stores and decorated with flags came wheeling into the camp, escorted by continental troops and country militia. They were part of the cargo of a large brigantine laden with munitions of war, captured and sent in to Cape Ann by the schooner *Lee*, Captain Manly, one of the cruisers sent out by Washington. "Such universal joy ran through the whole camp," writes an officer, "as if each one grasped a victory in his own hands."

Besides the ordnance captured, there were two thousand stand of arms, one hundred thousand flints, thirty thousand round shot and thirty-two tons of musket-balls.

"Surely nothing," writes Washington, "ever came more apropos."

It was indeed a cheering incident and was eagerly turned to account. Among the ordnance was a huge brass mortar of a new construction, weighing near three thousand pounds. It was considered a glorious trophy and there was a resolve to christen it. Mifflin, Washington's secretary, suggested the name. The mortar was fixed in a bed. Old Putnam mounted it, dashed on it a bottle of rum and gave it the name of "Congress." The shouts which rent the air were heard in Boston. When the meaning of them was explained to the British they observed that "should their expected reinforcements arrive in time, the rebels would pay dear in the spring for all their petty triumphs."

[Soon] Washington was earnestly occupied preparing works for the bombardment of Boston, should that measure be resolved upon by Congress. General Putnam, in the preceding month, had taken possession in the night of Cobble Hill without molestation from the enemy, though a commanding eminence, and in two days had constructed a work which, from its strength, was named Putnam's impregnable fortress.

[5] See Letter of Gen. Greene to Samuel Ward. *Am. Archives*, 4th Series, vol. iv.

He was now engaged on another work on Lechmere Point, to be connected with the works at Cobble Hill by a bridge thrown across Willis's Creek, and a covered way. Lechmere Point is immediately opposite the west part of Boston and the *Scarborough* ship-of-war was anchored near it. Putnam availed himself of a dark and foggy day (Dec. 17th) to commence operations, and broke ground with four hundred men at ten o'clock in the morning on a hill at the Point. "The mist," says a contemporary account, "was so great as to prevent the enemy from discovering what he was about until near twelve o'clock, when it cleared up and opened to their view our whole party at the Point, and another at the causeway throwing a bridge over the creek. The *Scarborough*, anchored off the Point, poured in a broadside. The enemy from Boston threw shells. The garrison at Cobble Hill returned fire. Our men were obliged to decamp from the Point but the work was resumed by the brave old general at night."

On the next morning a cannonade from Cobble Hill obliged the *Scarborough* to weigh anchor and drop down below the ferry, and General Heath was detached with a party of men to carry on the work which Putnam had commenced. The enemy resumed their fire. Sentinels were placed to give notice of a shot or shell. The men would crouch down or dodge it and continue on with their work. The fire ceased in the afternoon, and Washington visited the hill accompanied by several officers and inspected the progress of the work. It was to consist of two redoubts, on one of which was to be a mortar battery. There was as yet a deficiency of ordnance but the prize mortar was to be mounted which Putnam had recently christened, "The Congress." From the spirit with which the work was carried on, Washington trusted that it would soon be completed, "and then," said he, "if we have powder to sport with, and Congress gives the word, Boston can be bombarded from this point."

For several days the labor at the works was continued, the redoubts were thrown up and a covered way was constructed leading down to the bridge. All this was done notwithstanding the continual fire of the enemy.

Putnam anticipated great effects from this work and especially from his grand mortar, "The Congress." Shells there were in abundance for a bombardment. The only thing wanting was a supply of powder. One of the officers, writing of the unusual mildness of the

winter, observes: "Everything thaws here except old Put. He is
still as hard as ever, crying out for powder—powder—powder. Ye
gods, give us powder."

Amid the various concerns of the war and the multiplied
perplexities of the camp, the thoughts of Washington continually
reverted to his home on the banks of the Potomac. A constant correspondence was kept up between him and his agent, Mr. Lund
Washington, who had charge of his varied estates. The general
gave clear and minute directions as to their management, and the
agent rendered as clear and minute returns of everything that had
been done in consequence.

According to recent accounts, Mount Vernon had been considered in danger. Lord Dunmore was exercising martial law in the
Ancient Dominion, and it was feared that the favorite abode of
the "rebel commander-in-chief" would be marked out for hostility
and that the enemy might land from their ships in the Potomac
and lay it waste. Washington's brother, John Augustine, had entreated Mrs. Washington to leave it. The people of Loudoun had
advised her to seek refuge beyond the Blue Ridge and had offered
to send a guard to escort her. She had declined the offer, not considering herself in danger. Lund Washington was equally free
from apprehensions on the subject. "Lord Dunmore," writes he,
"will hardly himself venture up this river, nor do I believe he will
send on that errand. You may depend I will be watchful, and
upon the least alarm persuade her to move."

Though alive to everything concerning Mount Vernon, Washington agreed with them in deeming it in no present danger of
molestation by the enemy. Still he felt for the loneliness of Mrs.
Washington's situation, heightened as it must be by anxiety on his
own account. On taking command of the army, he had held out a
prospect to her that he would rejoin her at home in the autumn.
There was now a probability of his being detained before Boston
all winter. He wrote to her therefore by express in November, inviting her to join him at the camp. He at the same time wrote to
Lund Washington, engaging his continued services as an agent.
This person, though bearing the same name, and probably of the
same stock, does not appear to have been in any near degree of
relationship. Washington's letter to him gives a picture of his
domestic policy.

"I will engage for the year coming, and the year following, if these troubles and my absence continue, that your wages shall be standing and certain at the highest amount that any one year's crop has produced you yet. I do not offer this as any temptation to induce you to go on more cheerfully in prosecuting those schemes of mine. I should do injustice to you were I not to acknowledge that your conduct has ever appeared to me above everything sordid; but I offer it in consideration of the great charge you have upon your hands and my entire dependence upon your fidelity and industry.

"It is the greatest, indeed it is the only comfortable reflection I enjoy on this score, that my business is in the hands of a person concerning whose integrity I have not a doubt, and on whose care I can rely. Were it not for this I should feel very unhappy on account of the situation of my affairs. But I am persuaded you will do for me as you would for yourself."

The following were his directions concerning Mount Vernon:

"Let the hospitality of the house with respect to the poor be kept up. Let no one go hungry away. If any of this kind of people should be in want of corn, supply their necessaries, provided it does not encourage them to idleness. And I have no objection to your giving my money in charity to the amount of forty or fifty pounds a year, when you think it well bestowed. What I mean by having no objection is, that it is my desire it should be done. You are to consider that neither myself nor wife is now in the way to do those good offices."

Mrs. Washington came on with her own carriage and horses, accompanied by her son, Mr. Custis, and his wife. She travelled by very easy stages, partly on account of the badness of the roads, partly out of regard to the horses, of which Washington was always very careful and which were generally remarkable for beauty and excellence. Escorts and guards of honor attended her from place to place, and she was detained some time at Philadelphia by the devoted attention of the inhabitants.

Her arrival at Cambridge was a glad event in the army. Incidental mention is made of the equipage in which she appeared there. A chariot and four, with black postilions in scarlet and white liveries. It has been suggested that this was an English style of equipage, derived from the Fairfaxes, but in truth it was a style still prevalent at that day in Virginia.

It would appear that dinner invitations to headquarters were becoming matters of pride and solicitude. "I am much obliged to you," writes Washington to Reed, "for the hints respecting the jealousies which you say are gone abroad. I cannot charge myself with incivility, or what in my opinion is tantamount, ceremonious civility to gentlemen of this colony; but if such my conduct appears, I will endeavor at a reformation; as I can assure you, my dear Reed, that I wish to walk in such a line as will give most general satisfaction. You know that it was my wish at first to invite a certain number to dinner, but unintentionally we somehow or other missed of it. If this has given rise to the jealousy, I can only say that I am very sorry for it. At the same time I add that it was rather owing to inattention or, more properly, too much attention to other matters, which caused me to neglect it."

And in another letter:

"My constant attention to the great and perplexing objects which continually arise to my view absorbs all lesser considerations and, indeed, scarcely allows me to reflect that there is such a body as the General Court of this colony, but when I am reminded of it by a committee. Nor can I, upon recollection, discover in what instance I have been inattentive to, or slighted them. They could not surely conceive that there was a propriety in unbosoming the secrets of the army to them; that it was necessary to ask their opinion in throwing up an intrenchment or forming a battalion. It must be, therefore, what I before hinted to you, and how to remedy it I hardly know, as I am acquainted with few of the members, never go out of my own lines, nor see any of them in them."

The presence of Mrs. Washington soon relieved the general from this kind of perplexity. She presided at headquarters with mingled dignity and affability. We have an anecdote or two of the internal affairs of headquarters, furnished by the descendant of one who was an occasional inmate there.

Washington had prayers morning and evening and was regular in his attendance at the church in which he was a communicant. On one occasion, for want of a clergyman, the Episcopal service was read by Colonel William Palfrey, one of Washington's aides-de-camp, who substituted a prayer of his own composition in place of the one formerly offered up for the king.

Not long after her arrival in camp, Mrs. Washington claimed to keep Twelfth-night in due style, as the anniversary of her wedding.

"The general," says the same informant, "was somewhat thoughtful and said he was afraid he must refuse it." His objections were overcome and Twelfth-night and the wedding anniversary were duly celebrated.

There seems to have been more conviviality at the quarters of some of the other generals. Their time and minds were less intensely engrossed by anxious cares, having only their individual departments to attend to. Adjutant-General Mifflin's house appears to have been a gay one. "He was a man of education, ready apprehension and brilliancy," says Graydon; "had spent some time in Europe, particularly in France, and was very easy of access, with the manners of genteel life, though occasionally evolving those of the Quaker."[6]

Mrs. [John] Adams gives an account of an evening party at his house. "I was very politely entertained and noticed by the generals," writes she, "more especially General Lee, who was very urgent for me to tarry in town and dine with him and the ladies present at Hobgoblin Hall, but I excused myself. The general was determined that I should not only be acquainted with him but with his companions too and therefore placed a chair before me, into which he ordered Mr. Spada (his dog) to mount and present his paw to me for a better acquaintance. I could not do otherwise than accept it."[7]

John Adams, likewise, gives us a picture of festivities at headquarters, where he was a visitant on the recess of Congress.

"I dined at Colonel Mifflin's with the general (Washington) and lady, and a vast collection of other company, among whom were six or seven sachems and warriors of the French Caughnawaga Indians, with their wives and children. A savage feast they made of it, yet were very polite in the Indian style. I was introduced to them by the general as one of the grand council at Philadelphia, which made them prick up their ears. They came and shook hands with me."[8]

While giving these familiar scenes and occurrences at the camp, we are tempted to subjoin one furnished from the manuscript memoir of an eye-witness. A large party of Virginia riflemen who

[6] Graydon's *Memoirs*, p. 154.
[7] *Letters of Mr. Adams*, vol. i., p. 85.
[8] *Adams's Letters*, vol. ii., p. 80. Adams adds that they made him "low bows and scrapes," a kind of homage never paid by an Indian warrior.

had recently arrived in camp were strolling about Cambridge and
viewing the collegiate buildings, now turned into barracks. Their
half Indian equipments and fringed and ruffled hunting garbs
provoked the merriment of some troops from Marblehead, chiefly
fishermen and sailors, who thought nothing equal to the round
jacket and trowsers. A bantering ensued between them. There was
snow upon the ground, and snow-balls began to fly when jokes
were wanting. The parties waxed warm with the contest. They
closed and came to blows. Both sides were reinforced and in a little while at least a thousand were at fisticuffs and there was a
tumult in the camp worthy of the days of Homer. "At this juncture," writes our informant, "Washington made his appearance,
whether by accident or design, I never knew. I saw none of his
aides with him; his black servant just behind him mounted. He
threw the bridle of his own horse into his servant's hands, sprang
from his seat, rushed into the thickest of the mêlée, seized two tall
brawny riflemen by the throat, keeping them at arm's-length, talking to and shaking them."

As they were from his own province, he may have felt peculiarly
responsible for their good conduct. They were engaged, too, in one
of those sectional brawls which were his especial abhorrence. His
reprimand must, therefore, have been a vehement one. He was
commanding in his serenest moments but irresistible in his bursts
of indignation. On the present occasion, we are told, his appearance and strong-handed rebuke put an instant end to the tumult.
The combatants dispersed in all directions, and in less than three
minutes none remained on the ground but the two he had
collared.

The veteran who records this exercise of military authority
seems at a loss which most to admire, the simplicity of the process
or the vigor with which it was administered. "Here," writes he,
"bloodshed, imprisonments, trials by court-martial, revengeful feelings between the different corps of the army, were happily
prevented by the physical and mental energies of a single person,
and the only damage resulting from the fierce encounter was a few
torn hunting frocks and round jackets."[9]

[9] From memoranda written at an advanced age by the late Hon. Israel
Trask, who, when but ten years old, was in the camp at Cambridge with his
father, who was a lieutenant.

Chapter 18

CRITICAL STATE OF THE ARMY

In the month of December a vessel had been captured bearing supplies from Lord Dunmore to the army at Boston. A letter on board from his lordship to General Howe invited him to transfer the war to the southern colonies or, at all events, to send reinforcements thither, intimating at the same time his plan of proclaiming liberty to indentured servants, negroes and others appertaining to rebels, and inviting them to join His Majesty's troops. In a word, to inflict upon Virginia the horrors of a servile war.

"If this man is not crushed before spring," writes Washington, "he will become the most formidable enemy America has. His strength will increase as a snowball. . . . Motives of resentment actuate his conduct to a degree equal to the destruction of the colony."

General Lee took the occasion to set forth his own system of policy, which was particularly rigid wherever men in authority and tories were concerned. It was the old grudge against ministers and their adherents set on edge.

"Had my opinion been thought worthy of attention," would he say, "Lord Dunmore would have been disarmed of his teeth and claws." He would have seized Tryon too "and all his tories at New York" and, having struck the stroke, would have applied to Congress for approbation.

"I propose the following measures," would he add: "To seize every governor, government man, placeman, tory and enemy to liberty on the continent, to confiscate their estates, or at least lay them under heavy contributions for the public. Their persons should be secured in some of the interior towns as hostages for the treatment of those of our party whom the fortune of war shall throw into their hands. They should be allowed a reasonable pension out of their fortunes for their maintenance."[1]

Such was the policy advocated by Lee in his letters and conversation and he soon had an opportunity of carrying it partly into operation. Rhode Island had for some time past been domineered over by Captain Wallace of the royal navy, who had stationed himself at Newport with an armed vessel and obliged the place to furnish him with supplies. Latterly he had landed in Conanicut Island, opposite to Newport, with a number of sailors and marines, plundered and burnt houses and driven off cattle for the supply of the army. In his exactions and maraudings he was said to have received countenance from the tory part of the inhabitants. It was now reported that a naval armament was coming from Boston against the island. In this emergency the governor (Cooke) wrote to Washington, requesting military aid and an efficient officer to put the island in a state of defense, suggesting the name of General Lee for the purpose.

Lee undertook the task with alacrity. "I sincerely wish," said Washington, "he may be able to do it with effect, as that place, in its present state, is an asylum for such as are disaffected to American liberty."

Lee set out for Rhode Island with his guard and a party of riflemen, and at Providence was joined by the cadet company of that place and a number of minute men. Preceded by these, he entered the town of Newport on Christmas day in military style. While there, he summoned before him a number of persons who had supplied the enemy, some according to a convention originally made between Wallace and the authorities, others, as it was suspected, through tory feelings. All were obliged by Lee to take a test oath of his own devising, by which they "religiously swore that they would neither directly nor indirectly assist the wicked instruments of ministerial tyranny and villainy commonly called the king's troops and navy, by furnishing them with provisions and refreshments." They swore, moreover, to "denounce all traitors before the public authority, and to take arms in defense of American liberty whenever required by Congress or the provincial authority." Two custom-house officers and another person who refused to take the oath were put under guard and sent to Providence. Having laid out works and given directions for fortifica-

[1] Lee to Rich. Henry Lee. *Am. Archives*, 4th Series, iv., 248.

tions, Lee returned to camp after an absence of ten days. Some of his proceedings were considered too highhanded and were disapproved by Congress. Lee made light of legislative censures. "One must not be trammelled by laws in war-time," said he. "In a revolution all means are legal."

Washington approved of his measures. "I have seen General Lee since his expedition," writes he, "and hope Rhode Island will derive some advantage from it. I am told that Captain Wallace's ships have been supplied for some time by the town of Newport on certain conditions stipulated between him and the committee. . . . I know not what pernicious consequences may result from a precedent of this sort. Other places, circumstanced as Newport is, may follow the example and by that means their whole fleet and army will be furnished with what it highly concerns us to keep from them. . . . Vigorous regulations and such as at another time would appear extraordinary are now become absolutely necessary for preserving our country against the strides of tyranny making against it."[2]

December had been throughout a month of severe trial to Washington, during which he saw his army dropping away piecemeal before his eyes. Homeward every face was turned as soon as the term of enlistment was at an end. Scarce could the disbanding troops be kept a few days in camp until militia could be procured to supply their place. Washington made repeated and animated appeals to their patriotism. They were almost unheeded. He caused popular and patriotic songs to be sung about the camp. They passed by like the idle wind. Home! home! home! throbbed in every heart. "The desire of retiring into a chimney-corner," says Washington reproachfully, "seized the troops as soon as their terms expired."

Can we wonder at it? They were for the most part yeomanry, unused to military restraint and suffering all the hardships of a starveling camp almost within sight of the smoke of their own firesides.

Greene throughout this trying month was continually by Washington's side. His letters, expressing the same cares and apprehensions and occasionally in the same language with those of the commander-in-chief, show how completely he was in his councils. He could well sympathize with him in his solicitudes. Some of his

2 Washington to Gov. Cooke. Sparks, iii., 227.

own Rhode Island troops were with Arnold in his Canada expedition. Others, encamped on Prospect Hill and whose order and discipline had been his pride, were evincing the prevalent disposition to disband. "They seem to be so sick of this way of life, and so homesick," writes he, "that I fear the greater part of the best troops from our colony will soon go home." To provide against such a contingency, he strengthened his encampment, so that, "if the soldiery should not engage as cheerfully as he expected, he might defend it with a less number."[3]

Still he was buoyant and cheerful, frequently on his white horse about Prospect Hill, haranguing his men and endeavoring to keep them in good humor. "This is no time for disgusting the soldiery," would he say, "when their aid is so essential to the preservation of the rights of human nature and the liberties of America."

He wore the same cheery aspect to the commander-in-chief, or rather he partook of his own hopeful spirit. "I expect," would he say, "the army, notwithstanding all the difficulties we meet with, will be full in about six weeks."

It was this loyalty in time of trouble, this buoyancy under depression, this thorough patriotism, which won for him the entire confidence of Washington.

The thirty-first of December arrived, the crisis of the army, for with that month expired the last of the old terms of enlistment. "We never have been so weak," writes Greene, "as we shall be tomorrow when we dismiss the old troops." On this day Washington received cheering intelligence from Canada. A junction had taken place a month previously between Arnold and Montgomery at Point aux Trembles. They were about two thousand strong and were making preparations for attacking Quebec. Carleton was said to have with him but about twelve hundred men, the majority of whom were sailors. It was thought that the French would give up Quebec if they could get the same conditions that were granted to the inhabitants of Montreal.[4]

Thus the year closed upon Washington with a ray of light from Canada while all was doubt around him.

On the following morning (January 1st, 1776), his army did not amount to ten thousand men and was composed of but half-filled regiments. Even in raising this inadequate force it had been neces-

[3] Greene to Henry Ward.
[4] Letter of Washington to the President of Congress, Dec. 31.

sary to indulge many of the men with furloughs, that they might visit their families and friends. The expedients resorted to in equipping the army show the prevailing lack of arms. Those soldiers who retired from service were obliged to leave their weapons for their successors, receiving their appraised value. Those who enlisted were required to bring a gun, or were charged a dollar for the use of one during the campaign. He who brought a blanket was allowed two dollars. It was impossible to furnish uniforms. The troops, therefore, presented a motley appearance in garments of divers cuts and colors, the price of each man's garb being deducted from his pay.

The detachments of militia from the neighboring provinces which replaced the disbanding troops remained but for brief periods, so that, in despite of every effort, the lines were often but feebly manned and might easily have been forced.

The anxiety of Washington in this critical state of the army may be judged from his correspondence with Reed.

"It is easier to conceive than to describe the situation of my mind for some time past, and my feelings under our present circumstances," writes he on the 4th of January. "Search the volumes of history through and I much question whether a case similar to ours is to be found, namely, to maintain a post against the power of the British troops for six months together, without powder, and then to have one army disbanded and another raised within the same distance (musket shot) of a reinforced enemy. What may be the issue of the last manœuvre, time only can unfold. I wish this month were well over our head. . . . We are now left with a good deal less than half-raised regiments and about five thousand militia who only stand engaged to the middle of this month, when, according to custom, they will depart, let the necessity of their stay be ever so urgent. Thus, for more than two months past, I have scarcely emerged from one difficulty before I have been plunged in another. How it will end, God, in his great goodness, will direct. I am thankful for his protection to this time. We are told that we shall soon get the army completed but I have been told so many things which have never come to pass that I distrust everything."

In a subsequent letter to Mr. Reed he reverts to the subject and pours forth his feelings with confiding frankness. What can be more touching than the picture he draws of himself and his lonely vigils about his sleeping camp?

"The reflection on my situation and that of this army produces many an unhappy hour when all around me are wrapped in sleep. Few people know the predicament we are in on a thousand accounts. Fewer still will believe, if any disaster happens to these lines, from what cause it flows. I have often thought how much happier I should have been if, instead of accepting the command under such circumstances, I had taken my musket on my shoulder and entered the ranks; or, if I could have justified the measure to posterity and my own conscience, had retired to the back country and lived in a wigwam. If I shall be able to rise superior to these and many other difficulties which might be enumerated, I shall most religiously believe that the finger of Providence is in it to blind the eyes of our enemies, for surely if we get well through this month it must be for want of their knowing the disadvantages which we labor under."

Recurring to the project of an attack upon Boston, which he had reluctantly abandoned in deference to the adverse opinions of a council of war, "Could I have foreseen the difficulties which have come upon us; could I have known that such a backwardness would have been discovered among the old soldiers to the service, all the generals upon earth should not have convinced me of the propriety of delaying an attack upon Boston till this time. When it can now be attempted I will not undertake to say, but thus much I will answer for, that no opportunity can present itself earlier than my wishes."

In the midst of his discouragements Washington received letters from Knox showing the spirit and energy with which he was executing his mission in quest of cannon and ordnance stores. He had struggled manfully and successfully with all kinds of difficulties from the advanced season, and head winds, in getting them from Ticonderoga to the head of Lake George. "Three days ago," writes he on the 17th of December, "it was very uncertain whether we could get them over until next spring, but now, please God, they shall go. I have made forty-two exceedingly strong sleds and have provided eighty yoke of oxen to drag them as far as Springfield, where I shall get fresh cattle to take them to camp."

It was thus that hardships and emergencies were bringing out the merits of the self-made soldiers of the Revolution and showing their commander-in-chief on whom he might rely.

Early in the month of January there was a great stir of preparation in Boston harbor. A fleet of transports were taking in supplies and making arrangements for the embarkation of troops. Bomb-ketches and flat-bottomed boats were getting ready for sea, as were two sloops-of-war which were to convey the armament. Its destination was kept secret but was confidently surmised by Washington.

In the preceding month of October, a letter had been laid before Congress, written by some person in London of high credibility and revealing a secret plan of operations said to have been sent out by ministers to the commanders in Boston. The following is the purport: Possession was to be gained of New York and Albany through the assistance of Governor Tryon, on whose influence with the tory part of the population much reliance was placed. These cities were to be very strongly garrisoned. All who did not join the king's forces were to be declared rebels. The Hudson River and the East River or Sound were to be commanded by a number of small men-of-war and cutters stationed in different parts so as wholly to cut off all communication by water between New York and the provinces to the northward of it; and between New York and Albany, except for the king's service; and to prevent, also, all communication between the city of New York and the provinces of New Jersey, Pennsylvania and those to the southward of them.

"By these means," said the letter, "the administration and their friends fancy they shall soon either starve out or retake the garrisons of Crown Point and Ticonderoga and open and maintain a safe intercourse and correspondence between Quebec, Albany and New York; and thereby offer the fairest opportunity to their soldiery and the Canadians, in conjunction with the Indians to be procured by Guy Johnson, to make continual irruptions into New Hampshire, Massachusetts and Connecticut and so distract and divide the provincial forces as to render it easy for the British army at Boston to defeat them, break the spirits of the Massachusetts people, depopulate their country and compel an absolute subjection to Great Britain."[5]

It was added that a lord, high in the American department, had been very particular in his inquiries about the Hudson River; what sized vessels could get to Albany; and whether, if batteries were erected in the Highlands, they would not control the navigation of the river and prevent vessels from going up and down.

[5] Am. Archives, 4th Series, iii., 1281.

This information had already excited solicitude respecting the Hudson and led to measures for its protection. It was now surmised that the expedition preparing to sail from Boston and which was to be conducted by Sir Henry Clinton might be destined to seize upon New York. How was the apprehended blow to be parried? General Lee, who was just returned from his energetic visit to Rhode Island, offered his advice and services in the matter. In a letter to Washington he urged him to act at once and on his own responsibility, without awaiting the tardy and doubtful sanction of Congress, for which, in military matters, Lee had but small regard.

Washington, while he approved of Lee's military suggestions, was cautious in exercising the extraordinary powers so recently vested in him, and fearful of transcending them. John Adams was at that time in the vicinity of the camp and he asked his opinion as to the practicability and expediency of the plan and whether it "might not be regarded as beyond his line."

Adams, resolute of spirit, thought the enterprise might easily be accomplished by the friends of liberty in New York in connection with the Connecticut people, "who are very ready," said he, "upon such occasions."

As to the expediency, he urged the vast importance, in the progress of this war, of the city and province of New York and the Hudson River, being the *nexus* of the northern and southern colonies, a kind of key to the whole continent, as it is a passage to Canada, to the Great Lakes and to all the Indian nations. No effort to secure it ought to be omitted.

That it was within the limits of Washington's command, he considered perfectly clear, he being "vested with full power and authority to act as he should think for the good and welfare of the service."

If there was a body of people on Long Island armed to oppose the American system of defense and furnishing supplies to the British army and navy, they were invading American liberty as much as those besieged in Boston.

If, in the city of New York a body of tories were waiting only for a force to protect them, to declare themselves on the side of the enemy, it was high time that city was secured.[6]

Thus fortified, as it were, by congressional sanction through one of its most important members, who pronounced New York as

6 Adams to Washington, *Corr. of Rev.*, i., 113.

much within his command as Massachusetts, he gave Lee authority to carry out his plans. He was to raise volunteers in Connecticut; march at their head to New York; call in military aid from New Jersey; put the city and the posts on the Hudson in a posture of security against surprise; disarm all persons on Long Island and elsewhere inimical to the views of Congress, or secure them in some other manner if necessary; and seize upon all medicines, shirts and blankets and send them on for the use of the American army.

Lee departed on his mission on the 8th of January. On the 16th he was at New Haven, railing at the indecision of Congress. They had ordered the enlistment of troops for the security of New York. A Connecticut regiment under Colonel Waterbury had been raised, equipped and on the point of embarking for Oyster Bay, Long Island, to attack the tories, who were to be attacked on the other side by Lord Stirling, "when suddenly," says Lee, "Colonel Waterbury received an order to disband his regiment, and the tories are to remain unmolested till they are joined by the king's assassins."

Trumbull, the governor of Connecticut, however, "like a man of sense and spirit," had ordered the regiment to be reassembled, and Lee trusted it would soon be ready to march with him. "I shall send immediately," said he, "an express to the Congress, informing them of my situation and, at the same time, conjuring them not to suffer the accursed Provincial Congress of New York to defeat measures so absolutely necessary to salvation."

Lee's letter to the President of Congress showed that the instructions dictated by the moderate and considerate spirit of Washington were not strong enough on some points to suit his stern military notions. The scheme simply of disarming the tories seemed to him totally ineffectual. It would only embitter their minds and add virus to their venom. They could and would always be supplied with fresh arms by the enemy. That of seizing the most dangerous would, from its vagueness, be attended with some bad consequences and could answer no good one. "The plan of explaining to these deluded people the justice of the American cause is certainly generous and humane," observed he, "but I am afraid will be fruitless. They are so riveted in their opinions that I am persuaded, should an angel descend from heaven with his golden trumpet and ring in their ears that their conduct was criminal, he would be disregarded."

Lee's notion of the policy proper in the present case was, to disarm the disaffected of all classes, supplying our own troops with the arms thus seized; to appraise their estates and oblige them to deposit at least one half the value with the Continental Congress as a security for good behavior; to administer the strongest oath that could be devised, that they would act offensively and defensively in support of the common rights; and finally, to transfer all such as should prove refractory to some place in the interior, where they would not be dangerous.

The people of New York, at all times very excitable, were thrown into a panic on hearing that Lee was in Connecticut, on his way to take military possession of the city. They apprehended his appearance there would provoke an attack from the ships in the harbor. Some, who thought the war about to be brought to their own doors, packed up their effects and made off into the country with their wives and children. Others beleaguered the committee of safety with entreaties against the deprecated protection of General Lee. The committee, through Pierre Van Cortlandt, their chairman, addressed a letter to Lee, inquiring into the motives of his coming with an army to New York, and stating the incapacity of the city to act hostilely against the ships of war in port, from deficiency of powder and a want of military works. For these and other reasons, they urged the impropriety of provoking hostilities for the present, and the necessity of "saving appearances" with the ships of war till at least the month of March, when they hoped to be able to face their enemies with some countenance.

"We, therefore," continued the letter, "ardently wish to remain in peace for a little time, and doubt not we have assigned sufficient reasons for avoiding at present a dilemma in which the entrance of a large body of troops into the city will almost certainly involve us. Should you have such an entrance in design, we beg at least the troops may halt on the western confines of Connecticut till we have been honored by you with such an explanation on this important subject as you may conceive your duty may permit you to enter upon with us, the grounds of which, you may easily see, ought to be kept an entire secret."

Lee, in reply, dated Stamford, January 23d, disclaimed all intention of commencing actual hostilities against the men-of-war in the harbor, his instructions from the commander-in-chief being solely to prevent the enemy from taking post in the city or lodging themselves on Long Island. Some subordinate purposes were like-wise to be executed, which were much more proper to be com-municated by word of mouth than by writing. In compliance with the wishes of the committee, he promised to carry with him into the town just troops enough to secure it against any present designs of the enemy, leaving his main force on the western border of Connecticut. "I give you my word," added he, "that no active service is proposed, as you seem to apprehend. If the ships of war are quiet, I shall be quiet. But I declare solemnly that if they make a pretext of my presence to fire on the town, the first house set on flames by their guns shall be the funeral pile of some of their best friends."

In a letter to Washington, written on the following day, he says of his recruiting success in Connecticut: "I find the people throughout this province more alive and zealous than my most sanguine expectations. I believe I might have collected two thousand volunteers. I take only four companies with me, and Waterbury's regiment. . . . These Connecticutians are, if possi-ble, more eager to go out of their country than they are to return home, when they have been absent for any considerable time."

Speaking of the people of New York and the letter from their Provincial Congress, which he incloses: "The whigs," says he, "I mean the stout ones, are, it is said, very desirous that a body of troops should march and be stationed in the city—the timid ones are averse merely from the spirit of procrastination, which is the characteristic of timidity. The letter from the Provincial Congress, you will observe, breathes the very essence of this spirit. It is woefully hysterical."

By the by, the threat contained in Lee's reply about a "funeral pile," coming from a soldier of his mettle, was not calculated to soothe the hysterical feelings of the committee of safety.

Chapter 19

THE AMERICANS ENTER BOSTON

The recent reverses in Canada had heightened the solicitude of Washington about the province of New York. That province was the central link in the confederacy but he feared it might prove a brittle one. [He] charged Lee, in his instructions, to keep a stern eye upon the tories, who were active in New York. "You can seize upon the persons of the principals," said he. "They must be so notoriously known that there will be little danger of committing mistakes." Lee acted up to the letter of these instructions and weeded out with a vigorous hand some of the rankest of the growth. This gave great offense to the peace-loving citizens, who insisted that he was arrogating a power vested solely in the civil authority.

[Lee] now proceeded with his plan of defenses. In the midst of his schemes he received orders from Congress to the command in Canada vacant by the death of Montgomery. He bewailed the defenseless condition of the city, the Continental Congress, as he said, not having as yet taken the least step for its security. "The instant I leave it," said he, "I conclude the Provincial Congress and the inhabitants in general will relapse into their former hysterics. The men-of-war and Mr. Tryon will return to their old station at the wharves, and the first regiments who arrive from England will take quiet possession of the town and Long Island."

The siege of Boston continued through the winter without any striking incident to enliven its monotony. The British remained within their works, leaving the beleaguering army slowly to augment its forces. The country was dissatisfied with the inaction of the latter. Even Congress was anxious for some successful blow that might revive popular enthusiasm. Washington shared this anxiety, and had repeatedly in councils of war suggested an attack upon the town but had found a majority of his general officers opposed to it. He had hoped some favorable opportunity would present when, the harbor being frozen, the troops might approach the town upon the ice. The winter, however, though severe at first, proved a mild one and the bay continued open.

The British officers, like all soldiers by profession, endeavored to while away the time by every amusement within their reach, but in truth the condition of the besieged town was daily becoming more and more distressing. The inhabitants were without flour, pulse or vegetables. The troops were nearly as destitute. There was a lack of fuel, too, as well as food. The small-pox broke out and it was necessary to inoculate the army. Men, women and children either left the city voluntarily or were sent out of it, yet the distress increased. Several houses were broken open and plundered. Others were demolished by the soldiery for fuel. General Howe resorted to the sternest measures to put a stop to these excesses. The provost was ordered to go the rounds with the hangman and hang up the first man he should detect in the fact, without waiting for further proof for trial. Offenders were punished with four hundred, six hundred and even one thousand lashes. The wife of a private soldier, convicted of receiving stolen goods, was sentenced to one hundred lashes on her bare back at the cart's tail in different parts of the town, and an imprisonment of three months.

Meanwhile Washington was incessantly goaded by the impatient murmurs of the public, as we may judge by his letters to Mr. Reed.

"I know the integrity of my own heart," writes he on the 10th of February, "but to declare it, unless to a friend, may be an argument of vanity. I know the unhappy predicament I stand in. I know that much is expected of me. I know that without men, without arms, without ammunition, without anything fit for the accommodation of a soldier, little is to be done. And, what is mortifying, I know that I cannot stand justified to the world without exposing my own weakness and injuring the cause by declaring my wants; which I am determined not to do further than unavoidable necessity brings every man acquainted with them.

"My own situation is so irksome to me at times that if I did not consult the public good more than my own tranquillity I should long ere this have put everything on the cast of a die. So far from my having an army of twenty thousand men well armed, I have been here with less than one half that number, including sick, furloughed and on command, and those neither armed nor clothed as they should be. In short, my situation has been such that I have been obliged to use art to conceal it from my own officers."

How precious are those letters! And how fortunate that the absence of Mr. Reed from camp should have procured for us such confidential outpourings of Washington's heart at this time of its great trial.

He still adhered to his opinion in favor of an attempt upon the town. He was aware that it would be attended with considerable loss but believed it would be successful if the men should behave well. Within a few days after the date of this letter the bay became sufficiently frozen for the transportation of troops.

"This," writes he to Reed, "I thought, knowing the ice would not last, a favorable opportunity to make an assault upon the troops in town. I proposed it in council, but behold, though we had been waiting all the year for this favorable event, the enterprise was thought too dangerous. Perhaps it was. Perhaps the irksomeness of my situation led me to undertake more than could be warranted by prudence. I did not think so and I am sure yet that the enterprise, if it had been undertaken with resolution, must have succeeded; without it, any would fail."

His proposition was too bold for the field-officers assembled in council (Feb. 16th), who objected that there was not force nor arms and ammunition sufficient in camp for such an attempt. Washington acquiesced in the decision, it being almost unanimous, yet he felt the irksomeness of his situation.

"To have the eyes of the whole continent," said he, "fixed with anxious expectation of hearing of some great event, and to be restrained in every military operation for want of the necessary means of carrying it on, is not very pleasing, especially as the means used to conceal my weakness from the enemy conceal it also from our friends and add to their wonder."

In the council of war above mentioned, a cannonade and bombardment were considered advisable as soon as there should be a sufficiency of powder. In the meantime preparations might be made for taking possession of Dorchester Heights and Noddle's Island.

At length the camp was rejoiced by the arrival of Colonel Knox with his long train of sledges drawn by oxen, bringing more than fifty cannon, mortars and howitzers, besides supplies of lead and flints. The zeal and perseverance which he had displayed in his wintry expedition across frozen lakes and snowy wastes, and the intelligence with which he had fulfilled his instructions, won him the entire confidence of Washington. His conduct in this enterprise was but an earnest of that energy and ability which he displayed throughout the war.

Further ammunition being received from the royal arsenal at New York and other quarters, and a reinforcement of ten regiments of militia, Washington no longer met with opposition to his warlike measures. Lechmere Point, which Putnam had fortified, was immediately to be supplied with mortars and heavy cannon so as to command Boston on the north, and Dorchester Heights on the south of the town were forthwith to be taken possession of. "If anything," said Washington, "will induce the enemy to hazard an engagement it will be our attempting to fortify those heights, as, in that event taking place, we shall be able to command a great part of the town and almost the whole harbor." Their possession, moreover, would enable him to push his works to Nook's Hill and other points opposite Boston, whence a cannonade and bombardment must drive the enemy from the city.

The council of Massachusetts at his request ordered the militia of the towns contiguous to Dorchester and Roxbury to hold themselves in readiness to repair to the lines at those places with arms, ammunition and accoutrements on receiving a preconcerted signal.

Washington felt painfully aware how much depended upon the success of this attempt. There was a cloud of gloom and distrust lowering upon the public mind. Danger threatened on the north and on the south. Montgomery had fallen before the walls of Quebec. The army in Canada was shattered. Tryon and the tories were plotting mischief in New York. Dunmore was harassing the lower part of Virginia, and Clinton and his fleet were prowling along the coast on a secret errand of mischief.

In the general plan it was concerted that should the enemy detach a large force to dislodge our men from Dorchester Heights, as had been done in the affair of Bunker's Hill, an attack upon the opposite side of the town should forthwith be made by General Putnam. For this purpose he was to have four thousand picked men in readiness in two divisions under Generals Sullivan and

Greene. At a concerted signal from Roxbury they were to embark in boats near the mouth of the Charles River, cross under cover of the fire of three floating batteries, land in two places in Boston, secure its strong posts, force the gates and works at the Neck and let in the Roxbury troops.

The evening of Monday the 4th of March was fixed upon for the occupation of Dorchester Heights. The ground was frozen too hard to be easily intrenched. Fascines, therefore, and gabions and bundles of screwed hay were collected during the two preceding nights, with which to form breastworks and redoubts. During these two busy nights the enemy's batteries were cannonaded and bombarded from opposite points to occupy their attention and prevent their noticing these preparations. They replied with spirit, and the incessant roar of artillery thus kept up covered completely the rumbling of wagons and ordnance.

The detachment under General Thomas set out on its cautious and secret march from the lines of Roxbury and Dorchester. Everything was conducted as regularly and quietly as possible. A covering party of eight hundred men preceded the carts with the intrenching tools. Then came General Thomas with the working party, twelve hundred strong, followed by a train of three hundred wagons laden with fascines, gabions and hay screwed into bundles of seven or eight hundred-weight. A great number of such bundles were ranged in a line along Dorchester Neck on the side next the enemy to protect the troops, while passing, from being raked by the fire of the enemy. Fortunately, although the moon, as Washington writes, was shining in its full lustre, the flash and roar of cannonry from opposite points and the bursting of bombshells high in the air so engaged and diverted the attention of the enemy that the detachment reached the heights about eight o'clock without being heard or perceived. The covering party then divided. One half proceeded to the point nearest Boston, the other to the one nearest to Castle Williams. The working party commenced to fortify under the directions of Gridley, the veteran engineer, who had planned the works on Bunker's Hill. It was severe labor, for the earth was frozen eighteen inches deep, but the men worked with more than their usual spirit, for the eye of the commander-in-chief was upon them. Though not called there by his duties, Washington could not be absent from this eventful operation.

The labors of the night were carried on by the Americans with

their usual activity and address. When a relief party arrived at four
o'clock in the morning, two forts were in sufficient forwardness to
furnish protection against small-arms and grapeshot. And such use
was made of the fascines and bundles of screwed hay that at dawn
a formidable-looking fortress frowned along the height. We have
the testimony of a British officer, already quoted, for the fact.
"This morning at daybreak we discovered two redoubts on Dorchester Point and two smaller ones on their flanks. They were all
raised during the last night, with an expedition equal to that of the
genii belonging to Aladdin's wonderful lamp. From these hills
they command the whole town, so that we must drive them from
their post or desert the place."

Howe gazed at the mushroom fortress with astonishment as it
loomed indistinctly but grandly through a morning fog. "The
rebels," exclaimed he, "have done more work in one night than
my whole army would have done in one month."

Washington had watched with intense anxiety the effect of the
revelation at daybreak. "When the enemy first discovered our
works in the morning," writes he, "they seemed to be in great confusion and, from their movements, to intend an attack."

General Thomas was reinforced with two thousand men. Old
Putnam stood ready to make a descent upon the north side of the
town with his four thousand picked men as soon as the heights on
the south should be assailed.

As Washington rode about the heights he reminded the troops
that it was the 5th of March, the anniversary of the Boston massacre, and called on them to revenge the slaughter of their brethren.
They answered him with shouts. "Our officers and men," writes
he, "appeared impatient for the appeal. The event, I think, must
have been fortunate; nothing less than success and victory on our
side."

Howe in the meantime was perplexed between his pride and the
hazards of his position. In his letters to the ministry he had
scouted the idea of "being in danger from the rebels." He had
"hoped they would attack him." Apparently they were about to
fulfil his hopes and with formidable advantages of position. He
must dislodge them from Dorchester Heights or evacuate Boston.
The latter was an alterative too mortifying to be readily adopted.
He resolved on an attack but it was to be a night one.

In the evening the British began to move. Lord Percy was to

lead the attack. Twenty-five hundred men were embarked in transports which were to convey them to the rendezvous at Castle Williams. A violent storm set in from the east. The transports could not reach their place of destination. The men-of-war could not cover and support them. A furious surf beat on the shore where the boats would have to land. The attack was consequently postponed until the following day.

That day was equally unpropitious. The storm continued, with torrents of rain. The attack was again postponed. In the meantime the Americans went on strengthening their works. By the time the storm subsided, General Howe deemed them too strong to be easily carried. The attempt, therefore, was relinquished altogether.

What was to be done? The shells thrown from the heights into the town proved that it was no longer tenable. The fleet was equally exposed. Admiral Shuldham, the successor to Graves, assured Howe that if the Americans maintained possession of the heights his ships could not remain in the harbor. It was determined therefore in a council of war to evacuate the place as soon as possible. But now came on a humiliating perplexity. The troops, in embarking, would be exposed to a destructive fire. How was this to be prevented? General Howe's pride would not suffer him to make capitulations. He endeavored to work on the fears of the Bostonians by hinting that if his troops were molested while embarking he might be obliged to cover their retreat by setting fire to the town.

The hint had its effect. Several of the principal inhabitants communicated with him through the medium of General Robertson. The result of the negotiation was that a paper was concocted and signed by several of the "selectmen" of Boston, stating the fears they had entertained of the destruction of the place, but that those fears had been quieted by General Howe's declaration that it should remain uninjured provided his troops were unmolested while embarking. The selectmen therefore begged "some assurance that so dreadful a calamity might not be brought on by any measures from without."

This paper was sent out from Boston on the evening of the 8th with a flag of truce, which bore it to the American lines at Roxbury. There it was received by Colonel Learned and carried by him to headquarters. Washington consulted with such of the general officers as he could immediately assemble. The paper was not addressed to him nor to any one else. It was not authenticated by the signature of General Howe, nor was there any other act obliging that commander to fulfil the promise asserted to have been made by him. It was deemed proper therefore that Washington should give no answer to the paper but that Colonel Learned should signify, in a letter, his having laid it before the commander-in-chief and the reasons assigned for not answering it.

With this uncompromising letter the flag returned to Boston. The Americans suspended their fire but continued to fortify their positions. On the night of the 9th a detachment was sent to plant a battery on Nook's Hill, an eminence at Dorchester which lies nearest to Boston Neck. A fire kindled behind the hill revealed the project. It provoked a cannonade from the British, which was returned with interest from Cobble Hill, Lechmere Point, Cambridge and Roxbury. The roar of cannonry and bursting of bomb-shells prevailed from half after eight at night until six in the morning. It was another night of terror to the people of Boston. But the Americans had to desist for the present from the attempt to fortify Nook's Hill. Among the accidents of the bombardment was the bursting of Putnam's vaunted mortar, "The Congress."

Daily preparations were now made by the enemy for departure. By proclamation, the inhabitants were ordered to deliver up all linen and woollen goods and all other goods that, in possession of the rebels, would aid them in carrying on the war. Crean Bush, a New York tory, was authorized to take possession of such goods and put them on board of two of the transports. Under cover of his commission, he and his myrmidons broke open stores and stripped them of their contents. Marauding gangs from the fleet and army followed their example and extended their depredations to private houses. On the 14th, Howe in a general order declared that the first soldier caught plundering should be hanged on the spot. Still, on the 16th houses were broken open, goods destroyed and furniture defaced by the troops. Some of the furniture, it is true, belonged to the officers and was destroyed because they could neither sell it nor carry it away.

For some days the embarkation of the troops was delayed by adverse winds. Washington, who was imperfectly informed of affairs in Boston, feared that the movements there might be a feint. Determined to bring things to a crisis, he detached a force to Nook's Hill on Saturday the sixteenth, which threw up a breastwork in the night regardless of the cannonading of the enemy. This commanded Boston Neck and the south part of the town, and a deserter brought a false report to the British that a general assault was intended.

The embarkation, so long delayed, began with hurry and confusion at four o'clock in the morning. The harbor of Boston soon presented a striking and tumultuous scene. There were seventy-eight ships and transports casting loose for sea, and eleven or twelve thousand men, soldiers, sailors and refugees hurrying to embark, many, especially of the latter, with their families and personal effects. The refugees in fact labored under greater disadvantages than the king's troops, being obliged to man their own vessels, as sufficient seaman could not be spared from the king's transports.

Speaking of those "who had taken upon themselves the style and title of government men" in Boston and acted an unfriendly part in this great contest, Washington observes: "By all accounts there never existed a more miserable set of beings than these wretched creatures now are. Taught to believe that the power of Great Britain was superior to all opposition and that foreign aid, if not, was at hand, they were even higher and more insulting in their opposition than the Regulars. When the order issued therefore for embarking the troops in Boston no electric shock, no sudden clap of thunder, in a word the last trump could not have struck them with greater consternation. They were at their wits' ends and, conscious of their black ingratitude, chose to commit themselves in the manner I have above described: to the mercy of the waves at a tempestuous season rather than meet their offended countrymen."[1]

While this tumultuous embarkation was going on, the Americans looked on in silence from their batteries on Dorchester Heights without firing a shot. "It was lucky for the inhabitants now left in Boston that they did not," writes a British officer, "for I am informed everything was prepared to set the town in a blaze had they fired one cannon."[2]

At an early hour of the morning the troops stationed at Cambridge and Roxbury had paraded, and several regiments under Putnam had embarked in boats and dropped down Charles

[1] Letter to John A. Washington, *Am. Archives*, 4th Series, v., 560.
[2] Frothingham, *Siege of Boston*, p. 310.

River to Sewall's Point to watch the movements of the enemy by land and water. About nine o'clock a large body of troops was seen marching down Bunker's Hill, while boats full of soldiers were putting off for the shipping. Two scouts were sent from the camp to reconnoiter. The works appeared still to be occupied, for sentries were posted about them with shouldered muskets. Observing them to be motionless, the scouts made nearer scrutiny and discovered them to be mere effigies set up to delay the advance of the Americans. Pushing on, they found the works deserted and gave signal of the fact, whereupon a detachment was sent from the camp to take possession.

Part of Putnam's troops were now sent back to Cambridge. A part were ordered forward to occupy Boston. General Ward, too, with five hundred men made his way from Roxbury across the Neck, about which the enemy had scattered caltrops or crow's feet[3] to impede invasion. The gates were unbarred and thrown open and the Americans entered in triumph with drums beating and colors flying.

By ten o'clock the enemy were all embarked and under way. Putnam had taken command of the city and occupied the important points, and the flag of thirteen stripes, the standard of the Union, floated above all the forts.

On the following day Washington himself entered the town, where he was joyfully welcomed. He beheld around him sad traces of the devastation caused by the bombardment, though not to the extent that he had apprehended. There were evidences also of the haste with which the British had retreated—five pieces of ordnance with their trunnions knocked off, others hastily spiked, others thrown off the wharf.

"General Howe's retreat," writes Wasington, "was precipitate beyond anything I could have conceived. The destruction of the stores at Dunbar's camp after Braddock's defeat was but a faint image of what may be seen at Boston: artillery carts cut to pieces in one place, gun carriages in another; shells broke here, shots buried there; and everything carrying with it the face of disorder and confusion, as also of distress."[4]

To add to the mortification of General Howe, he received, we are told, while sailing out of the harbor, despatches from the

[3] Iron balls with four sharp points to wound the feet of men or horses.
[4] Lee's *Memoirs*, p. 162.

ministry approving the resolutions he had so strenuously expressed of maintaining his post until he should receive reinforcements.

As the small-pox prevailed in some parts of the town, precautions were taken by Washington for its purification, and the main body of the army did not march in until the 20th. "The joy manifested in the countenances of the inhabitants," says an observer, "was overcast by the melancholy gloom caused by ten tedious months of siege." But when on the 22d the people from the country crowded into the town, "it was truly interesting," writes the same observer, "to witness the tender interviews and fond embraces of those who had been long separated under circumstances so peculiarly distressing."[5]

Notwithstanding the haste with which the British army was embarked, the fleet lingered for some days in Nantasket Road. Apprehensive that the enemy, now that their forces were collected in one body, might attempt by some blow to retrieve their late disgrace, Washington hastily threw up works on Fort Hill, which commanded the harbor, and demolished those which protected the town from the neighboring country. The fleet at length disappeared entirely from the coast, and the deliverance of Boston was assured.

The eminent services of Washington throughout this arduous siege, his admirable management, by which "in the course of a few months an undisciplined band of husbandmen became soldiers and were enabled to invest for nearly a year and finally to expel a brave army of veterans commanded by the most experienced generals," drew forth the enthusiastic applause of the nation. No higher illustration of this great achievement need be given than the summary of it contained in the speech of a British statesman, the Duke of Manchester, in the House of Lords.

"The army of Britain, equipped with every possible essential of war; a chosen army, with chosen officers, backed by the power of a mighty fleet, sent to correct revolted subjects; sent to chastise a resisting city; sent to assert Britain's authority, has for many tedious months been imprisoned within that town by the provincial army, who, their watchful guards, permitted them no inlet to the country; who braved all their efforts and defied all their skill and ability in war could ever attempt. One way, indeed, of escape was left. The fleet is yet respected. To the fleet the army has

[5] Thacher's *Mil. Journal*, p. 50.

recourse. And British generals whose name never met with a blot of dishonor are forced to quit that town which was the first object of the war, the immediate cause of hostilities, the place of arms which has cost this nation more than a million to defend."

We close this eventful chapter of Washington's history with the honor decreed to him by the highest authority of his country. On motion of John Adams, who had first moved his nomination as commander-in-chief, a unanimous vote of thanks to him was passed in Congress, and it was ordered that a gold medal be struck, commemorating the evacuation of Boston, bearing the effigy of Washington as its deliverer.

Chapter 20

DECLARATION OF INDEPENDENCE

The British fleet bearing the army from Boston had disappeared from the coast. "Whither they are bound and where they next will pitch their tents," writes Washington, "I know not." He conjectured their destination to be New York and made his arrangements accordingly but he was mistaken. General Howe had steered for Halifax, there to await the arrival of strong reinforcements from England and the fleet of his brother, Admiral Lord Howe, who was to be commander-in-chief of the naval forces on the North American station.

It was presumed the enemy in the ensuing campaign would direct their operations against the Middle and Southern colonies. Congress divided those colonies into two departments. One, comprehending New York, New Jersey, Pennsylvania, Delaware and Maryland, was to be under the command of a major-general and two brigadier-generals, the other, comprising Virginia, the Carolinas and Georgia, to be under the command of a major-general and four brigadiers.

In this new arrangement the orders destining General Lee to Canada were superseded and he was appointed to the command of the Southern department, where he was to keep watch upon the movements of Sir Henry Clinton. On Lee's departure for the South, Brigadier-General Lord Stirling remained in temporary command at New York. Washington, however, presuming that the British fleet had steered for that port with the force which had evacuated Boston, hastened detachments thither under Generals Heath and Sullivan and wrote for three thousand additional men to be furnished by Connecticut. The command of the whole he gave to General Putnam, who was ordered to fortify the city and the passes of the Hudson, according to the plans of General Lee.

In the meantime Washington delayed to come on himself until he should have pushed forward the main body of his army by divisions.

Lee's anticipations that laxity and confusion would prevail after his departure were not realized. The veteran Putnam, on taking command, put the city under rigorous military rule. The soldiers were to retire to their barracks and quarters at the beating of the tattoo and remain there until the reveille in the morning. The inhabitants were subjected to the same rule. None would be permitted to pass a sentry without the countersign, which would be furnished to them on applying to any of the brigade majors. All communication between the "ministerial fleet" and shore was stopped. The ships were no longer to be furnished with provisions. Any person taken in the act of holding communication with them would be considered an enemy and treated accordingly.

Washington came on by the way of Providence, Norwich and New London, expediting the embarkation of troops from these posts, and arrived at New York on the 13th of April. Many of the works which Lee had commenced were by this time finished. Others were in progress. It was apprehended the principal operations of the enemy would be on Long Island, the high grounds of which in the neighborhood of Brooklyn commanded the city. Washington saw that an able and efficient officer was needed at that place. Greene was accordingly stationed there with a division of the army. He immediately proceeded to complete the fortifications of that important post and to make himself acquainted with the topography and defensive points of the surrounding country.

The aggregate force distributed at several extensive posts in New York and its environs and on Long Island, Staten Island and elsewhere amounted to little more than ten thousand men. Some of those were on the sick list, others absent on command or on furlough. There were but about eight thousand available and fit for duty. These, too, were without pay, those recently enlisted without arms, and no one could say where arms were to be procured.

Washington saw the inadequacy of the force to the purposes required and was full of solicitude about the security of a place, the central point of the Confederacy and the grand deposit of ordnance and military stores. He was aware too of the disaffection to the cause among many of the inhabitants, and apprehensive of treachery. The process of fortifying the place had induced the ships of war to fall down into the outer bay within the Hook, upwards of twenty miles from the city, but Governor Tryon was still on board of one of them, keeping up an active correspondence with the tories on Staten and Long Islands and in other parts of the neighborhood.

Washington took an early occasion to address an urgent letter to the committee of safety, pointing out the dangerous and even treasonable nature of this correspondence. He had more weight and influence with that body than had been possessed by General Lee, and procured the passage of a resolution prohibiting, under severe penalties, all intercourse with the king's ships.

Headquarters at this time was a scene of incessant toil on the part of the commander-in-chief, his secretaries and aides-de-camp. "I give in to no kind of amusements myself," writes he, "and consequently those about me can have none, but are confined from morning until evening, hearing and answering applications and letters." The presence of Mrs. Washington was a solace in the midst of these stern military cares and diffused a feminine grace and decorum and a cheerful spirit over the domestic arrangements of headquarters, where everything was conducted with simplicity and dignity. The wives of some of the other generals and officers rallied around Mrs. Washington but social intercourse was generally at an end. "We all live here," writes a lady of New York, "like nuns shut up in a nunnery. No society with the town, for there are none there to visit; neither can we go in or out after a certain hour without the countersign."

In addition to his cares about the security of New York, Washington had to provide for the perilous exigencies of the army in Canada. Since his arrival in the city, four regiments of troops, a company of riflemen and another of artificers had been detached under the command of Brigadier-General Thompson, and a further corps of six regiments under Brigadier-General Sullivan, with orders to join General Thomas as soon as possible.

Washington at that time was not aware of the extraordinary expedients England had recently resorted to against the next campaign. The Duke of Brunswick, the Landgrave of Hesse Cassel and the Hereditary Prince of Cassel, Count of Hanau, had been subsidized to furnish troops to assist in the subjugation of her colonies. Four thousand three hundred Brunswick troops and nearly thirteen thousand Hessians had entered the British service. Besides the subsidy exacted by the German princes, they were to be paid seven pounds four shillings and four pence sterling for every soldier furnished by them and as much more for every one slain.

Of this notable arrangement Washington, as we observed, was not yet aware. "The designs of the enemy," writes he, "are too much behind the curtain for me to form any accurate opinion of their plan of operations for the summer's campaign. We are left to wander therefore in the field of conjecture."[1]

Within a few days afterwards he had vague accounts of "Hessians and Hanoverian troops coming over." But it was not until the 17th of May, when he received letters from General Schuyler inclosing others from the commanders in Canada, that he knew in what direction some of these bolts of war were launched.

[He was summoned by Congress to Philadelphia for conferences. Accompanied by Mrs. Washington, he] departed from New York on the 21st of May, and they were invited by Mr. Hancock, the President of Congress, to be his guests during their sojourn at Philadelphia.

Lee, when he heard of Washington's visit there, argued good effects from it. "I am extremely glad, dear general," writes he, "that you are in Philadelphia, for their councils sometimes lack a little of military electricity."

Washington, in his conferences with Congress, appears to have furnished this electricity. He roundly expressed his conviction that no accommodation could be effected with Great Britain on acceptable terms. Ministerialists had declared in Parliament that, the sword being drawn, the most coercive measures would be persevered in until there was complete submission. The recent subsidizing of foreign troops was a part of this policy and indicated unsparing hostility. A protracted war, therefore, was inevitable but it would be impossible to carry it on successfully with the scanty force actually embodied, and with transient enlistments of militia.

In consequence of his representations, resolutions were passed in Congress that soldiers should be enlisted for three years, with a bounty of ten dollars for each recruit; that the army at New York should be reinforced until the 1st of December with thirteen thousand eight hundred militia; that gondolas and fire-rafts should

[1] Letter to the President of Congress, 5th May.

be built to prevent the men-of-war and enemy's ships from coming into New York Bay or the Narrows; and that a flying camp of ten thousand militia, furnished by Pennsylvania, Delaware and Maryland, and likewise engaged until the 1st of December, should be stationed in the Jerseys for the defense of the Middle colonies. Washington was moreover empowered, in case of emergency, to call on the neighboring colonies for temporary aid with their militia.

Another important result of his conferences with Congress was the establishment of a war office. Military affairs had hitherto been referred in Congress to committees casually appointed and had consequently been subject to great irregularity and neglect. Henceforth a permanent committee, entitled "the Board of War and Ordnance," was to take cognizance of them. The first board was composed of five members: John Adams, Colonel Benjamin Harrison, Roger Sherman, James Wilson and Edward Rutledge; with Richard Peters as secretary. It went into operation on the 12th of June.

The prevalence of the small-pox had frequently rendered Washington uneasy on Mrs. Washington's account during her visits to the army. He was relieved therefore by her submitting to inoculation during their sojourn in Philadelphia, and having a very favorable time.

He was gratified also by procuring the appointment of his late secretary, Joseph Reed, to the post of adjutant-general, vacated by the promotion of General Gates, thus placing him once more by his side.

Despatches from Canada continued to be disastrous. [In the meanwhile] preparations were made for the protection of the Hudson, and the works about Brooklyn on Long Island were carried on with great activity under the superintendence of General Greene. In a word, the utmost exertions were made at every point to put the city, its environs and the Hudson River in a state of defense before the arrival of another hostile armament.

The great aim of the British at present was to get possession of New York and the Hudson and make them the basis of military operations. This they hoped to effect on the arrival of a powerful armament hourly expected, and designed for operations on the seaboard.

At this critical juncture there was an alarm of a conspiracy among the tories in the city and on Long Island, suddenly to take up arms and co-operate with the British troops on their arrival. The wildest reports were in circulation concerning it. Some of the tories were to break down King's Bridge, others were to blow up the magazines, spike the guns and massacre all the field-officers. Washington was to be killed or delivered up to the enemy. Some of his own body-guard were said to be in the plot.

Several publicans of the city were pointed out as having aided or abetted the plot. One was landlord of the "Highlander," at the corner of Beaver Street and Broadway. Another dispensed liquor under the sign of "Robin Hood." Another, named Lowry, described as a "fat man in a blue coat," kept tavern in a low house opposite the Oswego market. Another, James Houlding, kept a beer-house in Tryon Row, opposite the gates of the upper barracks. It would seem as if a network of corruption and treachery had been woven throughout the city by means of these liquor dealers. One of the most noted, however, was Corbie, whose tavern was said to be "to the southeast of General Washington's house, to the westward of Bayard's Woods and north of Lispenard's Meadows," from which it would appear that at that time the general was quartered at what was formerly called Richmond Hill, a mansion surrounded by trees, at a short distance from the city, in rather an isolated situation.

A committee of the New York Congress, of which John Jay was chairman, traced the plot up to Governor Tryon, who, from his safe retreat on shipboard, acted through agents on shore. The most important of these was David Matthews, the tory mayor of the city. He was accused of disbursing money to enlist men, purchase arms and corrupt the soldiery.

Washington was authorized and requested by the committee to cause the mayor to be apprehended and all his papers secured. Matthews was at that time residing at Flatbush on Long Island, at no great distance from General Greene's encampment. Washington transmitted the warrant of the committee to the general on the 21st, with directions that it should "be executed with precision, and exactly by one o'clock of the ensuing morning, by a careful officer."

Precisely at the hour of one, a detachment from Greene's brigade surrounded the house of the mayor and secured his person, but no papers were found, though diligent search was made.

Numerous other arrests took place, and among the number, some of Washington's body-guard. A great dismay fell upon the tories. Some of those on Long Island who had proceeded to arm themselves, finding the plot discovered, sought refuge in woods and morasses. Washington directed that those arrested who belonged to the army should be tried by a court-martial, and the rest handed over to the secular power.

According to statements made before the committee, five guineas bounty was offered by Governor Tryon to each man who should enter the king's service, with ·a promise of two hundred acres of land for himself, one hundred for his wife and fifty for each child. The men thus recruited were set to act on shore in co-operation with the king's troops when they came.

Corbie's tavern, near Washington's quarters, was a kind of rendezvous of the conspirators. There one Gilbert Forbes, a gunsmith, "a short, thick man with a white coat," enlisted men, gave them money and "swore them on the book to secrecy." From this house a correspondence was kept up with Governor Tryon on shipboard through a "mulatto-colored negro dressed in blue clothes." At this tavern it was supposed Washington's body-guards were tampered with. Thomas Hickey, one of the guards, a dark-complexioned man, five feet six inches high and well set, was said not only to be enlisted but to have aided in corrupting his comrades, among others Greene the drummer and Johnson the fifer.

It was further testified before the committee that one Sergeant Graham, an old soldier, formerly of the royal artillery, had been employed by Governor Tryon to prowl round and survey the grounds and works about the city and on Long Island, and that, on information thus procured, a plan of operations had been concerted. On the arrival of the fleet, a man-of-war should cannonade the battery at Red Hook. While that was doing, a detachment of the army should land below with cannon, and by a circuitous march surprise and storm the works on Long Island. The shipping then, with the remainder of the army, were to divide, one part to run up the Hudson, the other up the East River. Troops were to land above New York, secure the pass at King's Bridge and cut off all communication between city and country.[2]

Much of the evidence given was of a dubious kind. It was cer-

[2] *Am. Archives,* 5th Series, vi., 1177.

tain that persons had secretly been enlisted and sworn to hostile operations but Washington did not think that any regular plan had been digested by the conspirators. "The matter," writes he, "I am in hopes, by a timely discovery, will be suppressed."[8]

According to the mayor's own admission before the committee, he had been cognizant of attempts to enlist tories and corrupt Washington's guards, though he declared he had discountenanced them. He had on one occasion also, at the request of Governor Tryon, paid money for him to Gilbert Forbes, the gunsmith, for rifles and round-bored guns which he had already furnished, and for others which he was to make. He had done so, however (according to his account), with great reluctance and after much hesitation and delay, warning the gunsmith that he would be hanged if found out. The mayor, with a number of others, were detained in prison to await a trial.

Thomas Hickey, the individual of Washington's guard, was tried before a court-martial. He was an Irishman and had been a deserter from the British army. The court-martial found him guilty of mutiny and sedition and treacherous correspondence with the enemy and sentenced him to be hanged.

The sentence was approved by Washington and was carried promptly into effect in the most solemn and impressive manner to serve as a warning and example in this time of treachery and danger. On the morning of the 28th, all the officers and men off duty belonging to the brigades of Heath, Spencer, Stirling and Scott assembled under arms at their respective parades at ten o'clock and marched thence to the ground. Twenty men from each brigade, with bayonets fixed, guarded the prisoner to the place of execution, which was a field near the Bowery Lane. There he was hanged in the presence, we are told, of nearly twenty thousand persons.

While the city was still brooding over this doleful spectacle, four ships-of-war, portentous visitants, appeared off the Hook, stood quietly in at the Narrows and dropped anchor in the bay.

In his orderly book Washington expressed a hope that the unhappy fate of Thomas Hickey, executed that day for mutiny, sedition and treachery, would be a warning to every soldier in the line to avoid the crimes for which he suffered.

On the 29th of June an express from the lookout on Staten

[8] Washington to the President of Congress, June 28.

Island announced that forty sail were in sight. They were in fact ships from Halifax, bringing between nine and ten thousand of the troops recently expelled from Boston together with six transports filled with Highland troops, which had joined the fleet at sea. At sight of this formidable armament standing into the harbor, Washington instantly sent notice of its arrival to Colonel James Clinton, who had command of the posts in the Highlands, and urged all possible preparations to give the enemy a warm reception should they push their frigates up the river.

According to general orders issued from headquarters on the following day (June 30th), the officers and men not on duty were to march from their respective regimental parades to their alarm posts at least once every day, that they might become well acquainted with them. They were to go by routes least exposed to a fire from the shipping, and all the officers, from the highest to the lowest, were to make themselves well acquainted with the grounds. Upon a signal of the enemy's approach or upon any alarm, all fatigue parties were immediately to repair to their respective corps with their arms, ammunition and accoutrements, ready for instant action.

It was ascertained that the ramifications of the conspiracy lately detected extended up the Hudson. Many of the disaffected in the upper counties were enlisted in it. The committee of safety at Cornwall in Orange County sent word to Colonel James Clinton, Fort Constitution, of the mischief that was brewing. James Haff, a tory, had confessed before them that he was one of a number who were to join the British troops as soon as they should arrive. It was expected the latter would push up the river and land at Verplanck's Point, whereupon the guns at the forts in the Highlands were to be spiked by soldiers of their own garrisons and the tories throughout the country were to be up in arms.[4]

Clinton received letters, also, from a meeting of committees in the precincts of Newburg, apprising him that persons dangerous to the cause were lurking in that neighborhood and requesting him to detach twenty-five men under a certain lieutenant acquainted with the woods "to aid in getting some of these rascals apprehended and secured."

While city and country were thus agitated by apprehensions of

[4] Extracts from minutes of the committee. Am. Archives, 4th Series, vi., 1112.

danger, internal and external, other arrivals swelled the number of ships in the bay of New York to one hundred and thirty men-of-war and transports. They made no movement to ascend the Hudson but anchored off Staten Island, where they landed their troops, and the hill-sides were soon whitened with their tents.

In the frigate *Greyhound*, one of the four ships which first arrived, came General Howe. He had preceded the fleet in order to confer with Governor Tryon and inform himself of the state of affairs. In a letter to his government he writes: "I met with Governor Tryon on board of a ship at the Hook, and many gentlemen, fast friends of government, attending him, from whom I have the fullest information of the state of the rebels. . . . We passed the Narrows with three ships-of-war and the first division of transports, landed the grenadiers and light infantry, as the ships came up, on this island, to the great joy of a most loyal people, long suffering on that account under the oppression of the rebels stationed among them, who precipitately fled on the approach of the shipping. . . . There is great reason to expect a numerous body of the inhabitants to join the army from the province of York, the Jerseys and Connecticut, who, in this time of universal oppression, only wait for opportunities to give proofs of their loyalty and zeal."

Washington beheld the gathering storm with an anxious eye, aware that General Howe only awaited the arrival of his brother the admiral to commence hostile operations. He wrote to the President of Congress, urging a call on the Massachusetts government for its quota of continental troops, and the formation of a flying camp of ten thousand men to be stationed in the Jerseys as a central force, ready to act in any direction as circumstances might require.

On the 2d of July he issued a general order calling upon the troops to prepare for a momentous conflict which was to decide their liberties and fortunes. Those who should signalize themselves by acts of bravery would be noticed and rewarded. Those who proved craven would be exposed and punished. No favor would be shown to such as refused or neglected to do their duty at so important a crisis.

About this time we have the first appearance in the military ranks of the Revolution of one destined to take an active and distinguished part in public affairs and to leave the impress of his genius on the institutions of the country.

As General Greene one day, on his way to Washington's headquarters, was passing through a field—then on the outskirts of the city, now in the heart of its busiest quarter and known as "the Park"—he paused to notice a provincial company of artillery and was struck with its able performances and with the tact and talent of its commander. He was a mere youth, apparently about twenty years of age, small in person and stature but remarkable for his alert and manly bearing. It was Alexander Hamilton.

Greene was an able tactician, and quick to appreciate any display of military science. A little conversation sufficed to convince him that the youth before him had a mind of no ordinary grasp and quickness. He invited him to his quarters and from that time cultivated his friendship. Further acquaintance heightened the general's opinion of his extraordinary merits, and he took an early occasion to introduce him to the commander-in-chief, by whom we shall soon find him properly appreciated.

While danger was gathering round New York, and its inhabitants were in mute suspense and fearful anticipations, the General Congress at Philadelphia was discussing, with closed doors, what John Adams pronounced "the greatest question ever debated in America and as great as ever was or will be debated among men." The result was a resolution passed unanimously on the 2d of July, "that these United Colonies are, and of right ought to be, free and independent States."

"The 2d of July," adds the same patriot statesman, "will be the most memorable epoch in the history of America. I am apt to believe that it will be celebrated by succeeding generations as the great anniversary festival. It ought to be commemorated as the day of deliverance, by solemn acts of devotion to Almighty God. It ought to be solemnized with pomp and parade, with shows, games, sports, guns, bells, bonfires and illuminations from one end of this continent to the other, from this time forth for evermore."

The glorious event has indeed given rise to an annual jubilee but not on the day designated by Adams. The 4th of July is the day of national rejoicing, for on that day the "Declaration of Independence," that solemn and sublime document, was adopted. Tradition gives a dramatic effect to its announcement. It was known to be under discussion but the closed doors of Congress excluded the populace. They awaited in throngs an appointed signal. In the steeple of the state-house was a bell, imported twenty-three years previously from London by the Provincial Assembly of Pennsylvania. It bore the portentous text from Scripture: "Proclaim liberty throughout all the land, unto all the inhabitants thereof." A joyous peal from that bell gave notice that the bill had been passed. It was the knell of British domination.

No one felt the importance of the event more deeply than John Adams, for no one had been more active in producing it. We quote his words written at the moment. "When I look back to the year 1761 and recollect the argument concerning writs of assistance in the superior court, which I have hitherto considered as the commencement of the controversy between Great Britain and America, and run through the whole period from that time to this and recollect the series of political events, the chain of causes and effects, I am surprised at the suddenness as well as the greatness of this Revolution. Great Britain has been filled with folly, America with wisdom."

His only regret was that the declaration of independence had not been made sooner. "Had it been made seven months ago," said he, "we should have mastered Quebec and been in possession of Canada, and might before this hour have formed alliances with foreign states. Many gentlemen in high stations and of great influence have been duped by the ministerial bubble of commissioners to treat, and have been slow and languid in promoting measures for the reduction of that province."

Washington hailed the declaration with joy. It is true, it was but a formal recognition of a state of things which had long existed, but it put an end to all those temporizing hopes of reconciliation which had clogged the military action of the country.

On the 9th of July he caused it to be read at six o'clock in the evening at the head of each brigade of the army. "The general hopes," said he in his orders, "that this important event will serve as a fresh incentive to every officer and soldier to act with fidelity and courage, as knowing that now the peace and safety of his country depend, under God, solely on the success of our arms, and that he is now in the service of a state possessed of sufficient power to reward his merit and advance him to the highest honors of a free country."

The excitable populace of New York were not content with the ringing of bells to proclaim their joy. There was a leaden statue of George III in the Bowling Green in front of the fort. Since kingly rule is at an end, why retain its effigy? On the same evening, therefore, the statue was pulled down amid the shouts of the multitude and broken up to be run into bullets "to be used in the cause of independence."

Some of the soldiery having been implicated in this popular effervescence, Washington censured it in general orders as having much the appearance of a riot and a want of discipline, and the army was forbidden to indulge in any irregularities of the kind. It was his constant effort to inspire his countrymen in arms with his own elevated idea of the cause in which they were engaged and to make them feel that it was no ordinary warfare admitting of vulgar passions and perturbations. "The general hopes and trusts," said he, "that every officer and man will endeavor so to live and act as becomes a Christian soldier, defending the dearest rights and liberties of his country."[5]

[5] Orderly book, July 9th. Sparks, iii., 456.

Chapter 21

NEW YORK ENDANGERED

The exultation of the patriots of New York caused by the Declaration of Independence was soon overclouded. On the 12th of July several ships stood in from sea and joined the naval force below. Every nautical movement was now a matter of speculation and alarm, and all the spy-glasses in the city were incessantly reconnoitering the bay.

While the vigilant Clinton was preparing to defend the passes of the Highlands, danger was growing more imminent at the mouth of the Hudson.

New York has always been a city prone to agitations. That into which it was thrown on the afternoon of the 12th of July by the broadsides of the *Phœnix* and the *Rose* was almost immediately followed by another. On the same evening there was a great booming of cannon, with clouds of smoke, from the shipping at anchor at Staten Island. Every spy-glass was again in requisition. The British fleet were saluting a ship-of-the-line, just arrived from sea. She advanced grandly, every man-of-war thundering a salute as she passed. At her foretop masthead she bore St. George's flag. "It is the admiral's ship!" cried the nautical men on the look-out at the Battery. "It is the admiral's ship!" was echoed from mouth to mouth, and the word soon flew through the city, "Lord Howe is come!"

We have heretofore shown the tenacity with which Washington, in his correspondence with Generals Gage and Howe, exacted the consideration and deference due to him as commander-in-chief of the American armies. He did this not from official pride and punctilio but as the guardian of American rights and dignities. A further step of the kind was yet to be taken. The British officers, considering the Americans in arms rebels without valid commissions, were in the habit of denying them all military title. Washington's general officers had urged him not to submit to this tacit indignity but to reject all letters directed to him without a specification of his official rank.

An occasion now presented itself for the adjustment of this matter. Within a day or two an officer of the British navy, Lieutenant Brown, came with a flag from Lord Howe, seeking a conference with Washington. Colonel Reed, the adjutant-general, embarked in a barge and met him half way between Governor's and Staten Islands. The lieutenant informed him that he was the bearer of a letter from Lord Howe to *Mr.* Washington. Colonel Reed replied that he knew no such person in the American army. The lieutenant produced and offered the letter. It was addressed to George Washington, Esquire. He was informed that it could not be received with such a direction. The lieutenant expressed much concern. The letter, he said, was of a civil rather than a military nature—Lord Howe regretted he had not arrived sooner—he had great powers—it was much to be wished the letter could be received.

While the lieutenant was embarrassed and agitated, Reed maintained his coolness, politely declining to receive the letter as inconsistent with his duty. They parted, but after the lieutenant had been rowed some little distance his barge was put about and Reed waited to hear what further he had to say. It was to ask by what title *General*—but catching himself, *Mr.* Washington, chose to be addressed.

Reed replied that the general's station in the army was well known and they could not be at a loss as to the proper mode of addressing him, especially as this matter had been discussed in the preceding summer, of which, he presumed, the admiral could not be ignorant. The lieutenant again expressed his disappointment and regret, and their interview closed.

On the 19th an aide-de-camp of general Howe came with a flag and requested to know, as there appeared to be an obstacle to a correspondence between the two generals, whether Colonel Patterson, the British adjutant-general, could be admitted to an interview with General Washington. Colonel Reed, who met the flag, consented in the name of the general and pledged his honor for the safety of the adjutant-general during the interview, which was fixed for the following morning.

At the appointed time, Colonel Reed and Colonel Webb, one of Washington's aides, met the flag in the harbor, took Colonel Patterson into their barge and escorted him to town, passing in front of the grand battery. The customary precaution of blindfolding was dispensed with and there was a lively and sociable conversation the whole way. Washington received the adjutant-general at headquarters with much form and ceremony, in full military array, with his officers and guards about him.

Colonel Patterson, addressing him by the title of *your excellency*, endeavored to explain the address of the letter as consistent with propriety and founded on a similar address in the previous summer to General Howe. That General Howe did not mean to derogate from the rank or respect of General Washington, but conceived such an address consistent with what had been used by ambassadors or plenipotentiaries where difficulties of rank had arisen. He then produced but did not offer a letter addressed to George Washington, Esquire, etc. etc., hoping that the *et ceteras*, which implied everything, would remove all impediments.

Washington replied that it was true the *et ceteras* implied everything, but they also implied anything. His letter alluded to, of the previous summer, was in reply to one addressed in like manner. A letter, he added, addressed to a person acting in a public character should have some inscriptions to designate it from a mere private letter, and he should absolutely decline any letter addressed to himself as a private person when it related to his public station.

Colonel Patterson, finding the letter would not be received, endeavored, as far as he could recollect, to communicate the scope of it in the course of a somewhat desultory conversation. What he chiefly dwelt upon was that Lord Howe and his brother had been specially nominated commissioners for the promotion of peace, which was esteemed a mark of favor and regard to America; that they had great powers and would derive the highest pleasure from effecting an accommodation; and he concluded by adding that he wished his visit to be considered as making the first advance toward that desirable object.

Washington replied that, by what had appeared (alluding no doubt to Lord Howe's circular), their powers, it would seem, were only to grant pardons. Now those who had committed no fault needed no pardon, and such was the case with the Americans, who were only defending what they considered their indisputable rights.

Colonel Patterson avoided a discussion of this matter, which, he observed, would open a very wide field. So here the conference, which had been conducted on both sides with great courtesy, terminated. The colonel took his leave, excusing himself from partaking of a collation, having made a late breakfast, and was again conducted to his boat. He expressed himself highly sensible of the courtesy of his treatment in having the usual ceremony of blindfolding dispensed with.

Washington received the applause of Congress and of the public for sustaining the dignity of his station. His conduct in this particular was recommended as a model to all American officers in corresponding with the enemy. And Lord Howe informed his government that thenceforward it would be politic to change the superscription of his letters.

In the meantime the irruption of the *Phœnix* and the *Rose* into the waters of the Hudson had roused a belligerent spirit along its borders. The lower part of that noble river is commanded on the eastern side by the bold woody heights of Manhattan Island and Westchester County, and on the western side by the rocky cliffs of the Palisades. Beyond those cliffs the river expands into a succession of what may almost be termed lakes: first the Tappan Sea, then Haverstraw Bay, then the Bay of Peekskill; separated from each other by long stretching points or high beetling promontories but affording ample sea-room and safe anchorage. Then come the redoubtable Highlands, that strait, fifteen miles in length, where the river bends its course, narrow and deep, between rocky, forest-clad mountains.

"He who has command of that grand defile," said an old navigator, "may at any time throttle the Hudson."

The New York Convention, aware of the impending danger, despatched military envoys to stir up the yeomanry along the river and order out militia. Powder and ball were sent to Tarrytown, before which the hostile ships were anchored, and yeoman troops were stationed there and along the neighboring shores of the Tappan Sea. In a little while the militia of Dutchess County and Cortlandt's Manor were hastening, rudely armed, to protect the public stores at Peekskill and mount guard at the entrance of the Highlands.

No one showed more zeal in this time of alarm than Colonel Pierre Van Cortlandt, of an old colonial family, which held its manorial residence at the mouth of the Croton. With his regiment he kept a dragon watch along the eastern shore of the Tappan Sea and Haverstraw Bay, while equal vigilance was maintained night and day along the western shore, from Nyack quite up to the Dunderberg, by Colonel Hay and his regiment of Haverstraw. Sheep and cattle were driven inland out of the reach of maraud. Sentinels were posted to keep a lookout from heights and headlands and give the alarm should any boats approach the shore, and rustic marksmen were ready to assemble in a moment and give them a warm reception.

The ships of war which caused this alarm and turmoil lay quietly anchored in the broad expanses of the Tappan Sea and Haverstraw Bay, shifting their ground occasionally and keeping out of musket shot of the shore, apparently sleeping in the summer sunshine with awnings stretched above their decks while their boats were out taking soundings quite up to the Highlands, evidently preparing for further operations. At night, too, their barges were heard rowing up and down the river on mysterious errands. Perriaugers, also, paid them furtive visits occasionally; it was surmised, with communications and supplies from tories on shore.

While the ships were anchored in Haverstraw Bay, one of the tenders stood into the Bay of Peekskill and beat up within long shot of Fort Montgomery, where General George Clinton was ensconced with six hundred of the militia of Orange and Ulster counties. As the tender approached, a thirty-two pounder was brought to range upon her. The ball passed through her quarter, whereupon she put about and ran round the point of the Dunderberg, where the boat landed, plundered a solitary house at the foot of the mountain and left it in flames. The marauders, on their way back to the ships, were severely galled by rustic marksmen from a neighboring promontory.

The ships, now acquainted with the channel, moved up within six miles of Fort Montgomery. General Clinton apprehended they might mean to take advantage of a dark night and slip by him in the deep shadows of the mountains. The shores were high and bold, the river was deep, the navigation of course safe and easy. Once above the Highlands, they might ravage the country beyond and destroy certain vessels of war which were being constructed at Poughkeepsie.

To prevent this, he stationed a guard at night on the farthest point in view, about two miles and a half below the fort, prepared to kindle a blazing fire should the ships appear in sight. Large piles of dry brushwood mixed with combustibles were prepared at various places up and down the shore opposite to the fort, and men stationed to set fire to them as soon as a signal should be given from the lower point. The fort, therefore, while it remained in darkness would have a fair chance with its batteries as the ships passed between it and these conflagrations.

A private committee sent up by the New York Convention had a conference with the general to devise further means of obstructing the passage of ships up the river. Fire rafts were to be brought from Poughkeepsie and kept at hand ready for action. These were to be lashed two together with chains between old sloops filled with combustibles, and sent down with a strong wind and tide to drive upon the ships. An iron chain also was to be stretched obliquely across the river from Fort Montgomery to the foot of Anthony's Nose, thus, as it were, chaining up the gate of the Highlands.

For a protection below the Highlands, it was proposed to station whale-boats about the coves and promontories of Tappan Sea and Haverstraw Bay to reconnoiter the enemy, cruise about at night, carry intelligence from post to post, seize any craft that might bring the ships supplies and cut off their boats when attempting to land. Galleys also were prepared, with nine-pounders mounted at the bows.

Letters from General Lee gave Washington intelligence of the fate of Sir Henry Clinton's expedition to the South, that expedition which had been the subject of so much surmise and perplexity. Sir Henry in his cruise along the coast had been repeatedly foiled by Lee, first when he looked in at New York, next when he paused at Norfolk in Virginia, and lastly when he made a bold attempt at Charleston in South Carolina. For scarce did his ships appear off the bar of the harbor than the omnipresent Lee was marching his troops into the city.

[Clinton failed in his attempt to take Charleston.]

"For God's sake, my dear general," writes Lee to Washington, "urge the Congress to furnish me with a thousand cavalry. With a thousand cavalry I could insure the safety of these Southern provinces, and without cavalry I can answer for nothing. From want of this species of troops we had infallibly lost this capital, but the dilatoriness and stupidity of the enemy saved us."

The tidings of this signal repulse of the enemy came most opportunely to Washington when he was apprehending an attack
upon New York.

During the latter part of July and the early part of August, ships
of war with their tenders continued to arrive, and Scotch
Highlanders, Hessians and other troops to be landed on Staten
Island. At the beginning of August the squadron with Sir Henry
Clinton, recently repulsed at Charleston, anchored in the bay.
"His coming," writes Colonel Reed, "was as unexpected as if he
had dropped from the clouds." He was accompanied by Lord
Cornwallis and brought three thousand troops.

The force of the enemy collected in the neighborhood of New
York was about thirty thousand men. That of the Americans a little more than seventeen thousand but was subsequently increased
to twenty thousand, for the most part raw and undisciplined. One
fourth were on the sick-list with bilious and putrid fevers and dysentery. Others were absent on furlough or command. The rest had
to be distributed over posts and stations fifteen miles apart.

[Washington] kept the most watchful eye upon the movements
of the enemy. Beside their great superiority in point of numbers as
well as discipline to his own crude and scanty legions, they possessed a vast advantage in their fleet. "They would not be half the
enemy they are," observed Colonel Reed, "if they were once separated from their ships." Every arrival and departure of these,
therefore, was a subject of speculation and conjecture. Aaron Burr,
at that time in New York, aide-de-camp to General Putnam,
speaks, in a letter to an uncle, of thirty transports which, under
convoy of three frigates, had put to sea on the 7th of August with
the intention of sailing round Long Island and coming through
the Sound and thus investing the city by the North and East
Rivers. "They are then to land on both sides of the island," writes
he, "join their forces and draw a line across, which will hem us in
and totally cut off all communication, after which they will have
their own fun." He adds: "They hold us in the utmost contempt.
Talk of forcing all our lines without firing a gun. The bayonet is
their pride. They have forgot Bunker's Hill."[1]

In this emergency Washington wrote to General Mercer for
2,000 men from the flying camp. Colonel Smallwood's battalion
was immediately furnished as a part of them. The Convention of

[1] *Am. Archives*, 5th Series, i., 887.

the State ordered out hasty levies of country militia to form temporary camps on the shore of the Sound and on that of the Hudson above King's Bridge, to annoy the enemy should they attempt to land from their ships on either of these waters. Others were sent to reinforce the posts on Long Island. As King's County on Long Island was noted for being a stronghold of the disaffected, the Convention ordered that, should any of the militia of that county refuse to serve, they should be disarmed and secured and their possessions laid waste.

Many of the yeoman of the country thus hastily summoned from the plough were destitute of arms, in lieu of which they were ordered to bring with them a shovel, spade, or pickaxe or a scythe straightened and fastened to a pole.

This rustic array may have provoked the thoughtless sneers of city scoffers such as those cited by Graydon but it was in truth one of the glorious features of the Revolution to be thus aided in its emergencies by "hasty levies of husbandmen."

By the authority of the New York Convention, Washington had appointed General George Clinton to the command of the levies on both sides of the Hudson. He now ordered him to hasten down with them to the fort just erected on the north side of King's Bridge, leaving two hundred men under the command of a brave and alert officer to throw up works at the pass of Anthony's Nose, where the main road to Albany crosses that mountain. Troops of horse also were to be posted by him along the river to watch the motions of the enemy.

Washington now made the last solemn preparations for the impending conflict. All suspected persons whose presence might promote the plans of the enemy were removed to a distance. All papers respecting affairs of state were put up in a large case, to be delivered to Congress. As to his domestic arrangements, Mrs. Washington had some time previously gone to Philadelphia with the intention of returning to Virginia, as there was no prospect of her being with him any part of the summer, which threatened to be one of turmoil and danger. The other ladies, wives of general officers who used to grace and enliven headquarters, had all been sent out of the way of the storm which was lowering over this devoted city.

Accounts of deserters and other intelligence informed Washington on the 17th that a great many of the enemy's troops had gone on board of the transports, that three days' provisions had been cooked and other steps taken, indicating an intention of leaving Staten Island. Putnam, also, came up from below with word that at least one fourth of the fleet had sailed. There were many conjectures at headquarters as to whither they were bound or whether they had not merely shifted their station. Everything indicated, however, that affairs were tending to a crisis.

The "hysterical alarms" of the peaceful inhabitants of New York, which had provoked the soldierlike impatience and satirical sneers of Lee, inspired different sentiments in the benevolent heart of Washington and produced the following letter to the New York Convention:

"When I consider that the city of New York will in all human probability very soon be the scene of a bloody conflict, I cannot but view the great numbers of women, children and infirm persons remaining in it with the most melancholy concern. When the men-of-war (the *Phœnix* and *Rose*) passed up the river, the shrieks and cries of these poor creatures, running every way with their children, were truly distressing, and I fear they will have an unhappy effect upon the ears and minds of our young and inexperienced soldiery. Can no method be devised for their removal?"

How vividly does this call to mind the compassionate sensibility of his younger days when commanding at Winchester in Virginia in time of public peril, and melted to "deadly sorrow" by the "supplicating tears of the women and moving petitions of the men." As then, he listened to the prompt suggestions of his own heart and, without awaiting the action of the Convention, issued a proclamation advising the inhabitants to remove, and requiring the officers and soldiery to aid the helpless and the indigent. The Convention soon responded to his appeal and appointed a committee to effect these purposes in the most humane and expeditious manner.

Chapter 22

THE BATTLE OF LONG ISLAND

Reports from different quarters gave Washington reason to apprehend that the design of the enemy might be to land part of their force on Long Island and endeavor to get possession of the heights of Brooklyn, which overlooked New York, while another part should land above the city, as General Heath suggested. Thus, various disconnected points distant from each other, and a great extent of intervening country, had to be defended by raw troops against a superior force well disciplined and possessed of every facility for operating by land and water.

General Greene with a considerable force was stationed at Brooklyn. He had acquainted himself with all the localities of the island from Hell Gate to the Narrows and made his plan of defense accordingly. His troops were diligently occupied in works which he laid out about a mile beyond the village of Brooklyn and facing the interior of the island, whence a land attack might be attempted.

Brooklyn was immediately opposite to New York. The Sound, commonly called the East River, in that place about three-quarters of a mile in width, swept its rapid tides between them. The village stood on a kind of peninsula formed by the deep inlets of Wallabout Bay on the north and Gowanus Cove on the south. A line of intrenchments and strong redoubts extended across the neck of the peninsula from the bay to a swamp and creek emptying into the cove. To protect the rear of the works from the enemy's ships, a battery was erected at Red Hook, the southwest corner of the peninsula, and a fort on Governor's Island, nearly opposite.

About two miles and a half in front of the line of intrenchments and redoubts, a range of hills, densely wooded, extended from southwest to northeast, forming a natural barrier across the island. It was traversed by three roads. One, on the left of the works, stretched eastwardly to Bedford and then by a pass through the Bedford Hills to the village of Jamaica. Another, central and direct, led through the woody heights to Flatbush. A third, on the right of the lines, passed by Gowanus Cove to the Narrows and Gravesend Bay.

The occupation of this range of hills and the protection of its passes had been designed by General Greene, but unfortunately in the midst of his arduous toils he was taken down by a raging fever which confined him to his bed, and General Sullivan, just returned from Lake Champlain, had the temporary command.

Washington saw that to prevent the enemy from landing on Long Island would be impossible, its great extent affording so many places favorable for that purpose, and the American works being at that part opposite to New York. "However," writes he to the President of Congress, "we shall attempt to harass them as much as possible, which is all that we can do."

On the 21st came a letter written in all haste by Brigadier-General William Livingston of New Jersey. Movements of the enemy on Staten Island had been seen from his camp. He had sent over a spy at midnight, who brought back the following intelligence. Twenty thousand men had embarked to make an attack on Long Island and up the Hudson. Fifteen thousand remained on Staten Island to attack Bergen Point, Elizabethtown Point and Amboy. The spy declared that he had heard orders read and the conversation of the generals. "They appear very determined," added he, "and will put all to the sword!"

Washington sent a copy of the letter to the New York Convention. On the following morning (August 22d) the enemy appeared to be carrying their plans into execution. The reports of cannon and musketry were heard from Long Island, and columns of smoke were descried rising above the groves and orchards at a distance. The city as usual was alarmed and had reason to be so, for word soon came that several thousand men, with artillery and light-horse, were landed at Gravesend and that Colonel Hand, stationed there with the Pennsylvania rifle regiment, had retreated to the lines, setting fire to stacks of wheat and other articles to keep them from falling into the enemy's hands.

Washington apprehended an attempt of the foe by a forced

march to surprise the lines at Brooklyn. He immediately sent over a reinforcement of six battalions. It was all that he could spare, as with the next tide the ships might bring up the residue of the army and attack the city. Five battalions more, however, were ordered to be ready as a reinforcement if required. "Be cool but determined," was the exhortation given to the departing troops. "Do not fire at a distance, but wait the commands of your officers. It is the general's express orders that if any man attempt to skulk, lie down, or retreat without orders, he be instantly shot down for an example."

In justice to the poor fellows, most of whom were going for the first time on a service of life and death, Washington observes that "they went off in high spirits" and that the whole capable of duty evinced the same cheerfulness.[1]

Nine thousand of the enemy had landed with forty pieces of cannon. Sir Henry Clinton had the chief command and led the first division. His associate officers were the Earls of Cornwallis and Percy, General Grant and General Sir William Erskine. As their boats approached the shore Colonel Hand, stationed, as has been said, in the neighborhood with his rifle regiment, retreated to the chain of wooded hills and took post on a height commanding the central road leading from Flatbush. The enemy having landed without opposition, Lord Cornwallis was detached with the reserve to Flatbush, while the rest of the army extended itself from the ferry at the Narrows through Utrecht and Gravesend to the village of Flatland.

Lord Cornwallis, with two battalions of light-infantry, Colonel Donop's corps of Hessians and six field-pieces, advanced rapidly to seize upon the central pass through the hills. He found Hand and his riflemen ready to make a vigorous defense. This brought him to a halt, having been ordered not to risk an attack should the pass be occupied. He took post for the night, therefore, in the village of Flatbush.

It was evidently the aim of the enemy to force the lines at Brooklyn and get possession of the heights. Should they succeed, New York would be at their mercy. The panic and distress of the inhabitants went on increasing. Most of those who could afford it had already removed to the country.

On the 24th [Washington] crossed over to Brooklyn to inspect

[1] Washington to the President of Congress.

the lines and reconnoiter the neighborhood. In this visit he felt sensibly the want of General Greene's presence, to explain his plans and point out the localities.

The American advanced posts were in the wooded hills. Colonel Hand with his riflemen kept watch over the central road, and a strong redoubt had been thrown up in front of the pass to check any advance of the enemy from Flatbush. Another road leading from Flatbush to Bedford, by which the enemy might get round to the left of the works at Brooklyn, was guarded by two regiments, one under Colonel Williams, posted on the north side of the ridge, the other by a Pennsylvania rifle regiment under Colonel Miles, posted on the south side. The enemy were stretched along the country beyond the chain of hills.

As yet, nothing had taken place but skirmishing and irregular firing between the outposts. It was with deep concern Washington noticed a prevalent disorder and confusion in the camp. There was a want of system among the officers and co-operation among the troops, each corps seeming to act independently of the rest. Few of the men had any military experience except, perchance, in bush-fighting with the Indians. Unaccustomed to discipline and the restraint of camps, they sallied forth whenever they pleased, singly or in squads, prowling about and firing upon the enemy like hunters after game.

Much of this was no doubt owing to the protracted illness of General Greene.

On returning to the city, therefore, Washington gave the command on Long Island to General Putnam, warning him however in his letter of instructions to summon the officers together and enjoin them to put a stop to the irregularities which he had observed among the troops. Lines of defense were to be formed round the encampment, and works on the most advantageous ground. Guards were to be stationed on the lines with a brigadier of the day constantly at hand to see that orders were executed. Field-officers were to go the rounds and report the situation of the guards, and no one was to pass beyond the lines without a special permit in writing. At the same time, partisan and scouting parties, under proper officers and with regular license, might sally forth to harass the enemy and prevent their carrying off the horses and cattle of the country people.

Especial attention was called to the wooded hills between the works and the enemy's camp. The passes through them were to be secured by abatis and defended by the best troops, who should at all hazards prevent the approach of the enemy. The militia, being the least tutored and experienced, might man the interior works.

Putnam crossed with alacrity to his post. "He was made happy," writes Colonel Reed, "by obtaining leave to go over. The brave old man was quite miserable at being kept here."

In the meantime the enemy were augmenting their forces on the island. Two brigades of Hessians, under Lieutenant-General De Heister, were transferred from the camp on Staten Island on the 25th. This movement did not escape the vigilant eye of Washington. By the aid of his telescope he had noticed that from time to time tents were struck on Staten Island and portions of the encampment broken up, while ship after ship weighed anchor and dropped down to the Narrows.

He now concluded that the enemy were about to make a push with their main force for the possession of Brooklyn Heights. He accordingly sent over additional reinforcements, and among them Colonel John Haslet's well equipped and well disciplined Delaware regiment, which was joined to Lord Stirling's brigade, chiefly composed of Southern troops and stationed outside of the lines. These were troops which Washington regarded with peculiar satisfaction on account of their soldier-like appearance and discipline.

On the 29th he crossed over to Brooklyn, accompanied by Reed, the adjutant-general. There was much movement among the enemy's troops, and their number was evidently augmented. In fact, General De Heister had reached Flatbush with his Hessians and taken command of the centre, whereupon Sir Henry Clinton, with the right wing, drew off to Flatlands in a diagonal line to the right of De Heister, while the left wing, commanded by General Grant, extended to the place of landing on Gravesend Bay.

Washington remained all day, aiding General Putnam with his counsels, who, new to the command, had not been able to make himself well acquainted with the fortified posts beyond the lines. In the evening Washington returned to the city, full of anxious thought. A general attack was evidently at hand. Where would it be made? How would his inexperienced troops stand the encounter? What would be the defense of the city if assailed by the ships? It was a night of intense solicitude, and well might it be, for during that night a plan was carried into effect fraught with disaster to the Americans.

The plan to which we allude was concerted by General Howe,

the commander-in-chief. Sir Henry Clinton, with the vanguard, composed of the choicest troops, was by a circuitous march in the night to throw himself into the road leading from Jamaica to Bedford, seize upon a pass through the Bedford Hills, within three miles of that village, and thus turn the left of the American advanced posts. It was preparatory to this nocturnal march that Sir Henry during the day had fallen back with his troops from Flatbush to Flatlands and caused that stir and movement which had attracted the notice of Washington.

To divert the attention of the Americans from this stealthy march on their left, General Grant was to menace their right flank toward Gravesend before daybreak, and General De Heister to cannonade their centre, where Colonel Hand was stationed. Neither, however, was to press an attack until the guns of Sir Henry Clinton should give notice that he had effected his purpose and turned the left flank of the Americans. Then the latter were to be assailed at all points with the utmost vigor.

About nine o'clock in the evening of the 26th, Sir Henry Clinton began his march from Flatlands with the vanguard, composed of light infantry. Lord Percy followed with the grenadiers, artillery and light dragoons, forming the centre. Lord Cornwallis brought up the rear-guard with the heavy ordnance. General Howe accompanied this division.

It was a silent march, without beat of drum or sound of trumpet, under guidance of a Long Island tory along by-roads traversing a swamp by a narrow causeway, and so across the country to the Jamaica road. About two hours before daybreak they arrived within half a mile of the pass through the Bedford Hills and halted to prepare for an attack. At this juncture they captured an American patrol and learnt to their surprise that the Bedford pass was unoccupied. In fact, the whole road beyond Bedford leading to Jamaica was left unguarded excepting by some light volunteer troops. Colonels Williams and Miles, who were stationed to the left of Colonel Hand, among the wooded hills, had been instructed to send out parties occasionally to patrol the road, but no troops had been stationed at the Bedford pass. The road and pass may not have been included in General Greene's plan of defense or may have been thought too far out of the way to need special precaution. The neglect of them, however, proved fatal.

Sir Henry Clinton immediately detached a battalion of light-infantry to secure the pass and, advancing with his corps at the first break of day, possessed himself of the heights. He was now within three miles of Bedford and his march had been undiscovered. Having passed the heights, therefore, he halted his division for the soldiers to take some refreshment preparatory to the morning's hostilities.

There we will leave them while we note how the other divisions performed their part of the plan.

About midnight General Grant moved from Gravesend Bay with the left wing, composed of two brigades and a regiment of regulars, a battalion of New York loyalists and ten field-pieces. He proceeded along the road leading past the Narrows and Gowanus Cove toward the right of the American works. A picket guard of Pennsylvanian and New York militia, under Colonel Atlee, retired before him fighting to a position on the skirts of the wooded hills.

In the meantime scouts had brought in word to the American lines that the enemy were approaching in force upon the right. General Putnam ordered Lord Stirling to hasten with the two regiments nearest at hand and hold them in check. These were Haslet's Delaware and Smallwood's Maryland regiments, the latter the *macaronis*, in scarlet and buff, who had outshone in camp their yeoman fellow-soldiers in homespun. They turned out with great alacrity, and Stirling pushed forward with them on the road toward the Narrows. By the time he had passed Gowanus Cove, daylight began to appear. Here, on a rising ground, he met Colonel Atlee with his Pennsylvania provincials and learned that the enemy were near. Indeed, their front began to appear in the uncertain twilight. Stirling ordered Atlee to place himself in ambush in an orchard on the left of the road and await their coming up while he formed the Delaware and Maryland regiments along a ridge from the road up to a piece of woods on the top of the hill.

Atlee gave the enemy two or three volleys as they approached, and then retreated and formed in the wood on Lord Stirling's left. By this time his lordship was reinforced by Kichline's riflemen, part of whom he placed along a hedge at the foot of the hill, and part in front of the wood. General Grant threw his light troops in the advance and posted them in an orchard and behind hedges extending in front of the Americans and about one hundred and fifty yards distant.

It was now broad daylight. A rattling fire commenced between the British light troops and the American riflemen which continued for about two hours, when the former retired to their main body. In the meantime Stirling's position had been strengthened by the arrival of Captain Carpenter with two field-pieces. These were placed on the side of the hill so as to command the road and the approach for some hundred yards. General Grant likewise brought up his artillery within three hundred yards and formed his brigade on opposite hills, about six hundred yards distant. There was occasional cannonading on both sides, but neither party sought a general action.

Lord Stirling's object was merely to hold the enemy in check; and the instructions of General Grant, as we have shown, were not to press an attack until aware that Sir Henry Clinton was on the left flank of the Americans.

During this time De Heister had commenced his part of the plan by opening a cannonade, from his camp at Flatbush, upon the redoubt at the pass of the wooded hills where Hand and his riflemen were stationed. On hearing this General Sullivan, who was within the lines, rode forth to Colonel Hand's post to reconnoiter. De Heister, however, according to the plan of operations, did not advance from Flatbush but kept up a brisk fire from his artillery on the redoubt in front of the pass, which replied as briskly. At the same time a cannonade from a British ship upon the battery at Red Hook contributed to distract the attention of the Americans.

In the meantime terror reigned in New York. The volleying of musketry and the booming of cannon at early dawn had told of the fighting that had commenced. As the morning advanced and platoon firing and the occasional discharge of a field-piece were heard in different directions, the terror increased. Washington was still in doubt whether this was but a part of a general attack, in which the city was to be included. Five ships-of-the-line were endeavoring to beat up the bay. Were they to cannonade the city or to land troops above it? Fortunately a strong head-wind baffled all their efforts, but one vessel of inferior force got up far enough to open the fire already mentioned upon the fort at Red Hook.

Seeing no likelihood of an immediate attack upon the city, Washington hastened over to Brooklyn in his barge and galloped up to the works. He arrived there in time to witness the catastrophe for which all the movements of the enemy had been concerted.

The thundering of artillery in the direction of Bedford had given notice that Sir Henry had turned the left of the Americans. De Heister immediately ordered Colonel Count Donop to advance with his Hessian regiment and storm the redoubt while he followed with his whole division. Sullivan did not remain to defend the redoubt. Sir Henry's cannon had apprised him of the fatal truth, that his flank was turned and he in danger of being surrounded. He ordered a retreat to the lines but it was already too late. Scarce had he descended from the height and emerged into the plain when he was met by the British light-infantry and dragoons, and driven back into the woods. By this time De Heister and his Hessians had come up and now commenced a scene of confusion, consternation and slaughter, in which the troops under Williams and Miles were involved. Hemmed in and entrapped between the British and Hessians and driven from one to the other, the Americans fought for a time bravely, or rather desperately. Some were cut down and trampled by the cavalry, others bayoneted without mercy by the Hessians. Some rallied in groups and made a brief stand with their rifles from rocks or behind trees. The whole pass was a scene of carnage, resounding with the clash of arms, the tramp of horses, the volleying of fire-arms and the cries of the combatants, with now and then the dreary braying of the trumpet. We give the words of one who mingled in the fight and whom we have heard speak with horror of the sanguinary fury with which the Hessians plied the bayonet. At length some of the Americans, by a desperate effort, cut their way through the host of foes and effected a retreat to the lines, fighting as they went. Others took refuge among the woods and fastnesses of the hills but a great part were either killed or taken prisoners. Among the latter was General Sullivan.

Washington, as we have observed, arrived in time to witness this catastrophe but was unable to prevent it. He had heard the din of the battle in the woods and seen the smoke rising from among the trees, but a deep column of the enemy was descending from the hills on the left, his choicest troops were all in action and he had none but militia to man the works. His solicitude was now awakened for the safety of Lord Stirling and his corps, who had been all the morning exchanging cannonades with General Grant. The forbearance of the latter in not advancing, though so superior in force, had been misinterpreted by the Americans. According to Colonel Haslet's statement, the Delawares and Marylanders, drawn up on the side of the hill, "stood upwards of four hours with a firm and determined countenance, in close array, their colors flying, the enemy's artillery playing on them all the while, not daring to advance and attack them though six times their number and nearly surrounding them."[2]

Washington saw the danger to which these brave fellows were exposed, though they could not. Stationed on a hill within the lines, he commanded with his telescope a view of the whole field and saw the enemy's reserve under Cornwallis marching down by a cross road to get in the rear and thus place them between two fires. With breathless anxiety he watched the result.

The sound of Sir Henry Clinton's cannon apprised Stirling that the enemy was between him and the lines. General Grant, too, aware that the time had come for earnest action, was closing up and had already taken Colonel Atlee prisoner. His lordship now thought to effect a circuitous retreat to the lines by crossing the creek which empties into Gowanus Cove near what was called the Yellow Mills. There was a bridge and milldam, and the creek might be forded at low water, but no time was to be lost, for the tide was rising.

Leaving part of his men to keep face towards General Grant, Stirling advanced with the rest to pass the creek but was suddenly checked by the appearance of Cornwallis and his grenadiers.

Washington and some of his officers on the hill, who watched every movement, had supposed that Stirling and his troops, finding the case desperate, would surrender in a body without firing. On the contrary his lordship boldly attacked Cornwallis with half of Smallwood's battalion while the rest of his troops retreated across the creek. Washington wrung his hands in agony at the sight. "Good God!" cried he, "what brave fellows I must this day lose!"[3]

It was indeed a desperate fight, and now Smallwood's *macaronis* showed their game spirit. They were repeatedly broken, but as often rallied and renewed the fight. "We were on the point of driving Lord Cornwallis from his station," writes Lord Stirling, "but large reinforcements, arriving, rendered it impossible to do more than provide for safety."

"Being thus surrounded, and no probability of a reinforcement,"

2 Atlee to Colonel Rodney. Sparks, iv., 516.
8 Letter from an American officer. Am. Archives, 5th Series, ii., 108.

writes a Maryland officer, "his lordship ordered me to retreat with the remaining part of our men and force our way to our camp. We soon fell in with a party of the enemy, who clubbed their firelocks and waved their hats to us as if they meant to surrender as prisoners. But on our advancing within sixty yards, they presented their pieces and fired, which we returned with so much warmth that they soon quitted their post and retired to a large body that was lying in ambuscade."[4]

The enemy rallied and returned to the combat with additional force. Only five companies of Smallwood's battalion were now in action. There was a warm and close engagement for nearly ten minutes. The struggle became desperate on the part of the Americans. Broken and disordered, they rallied in a piece of woods and made a second attack. They were again overpowered with numbers. Some were surrounded and bayoneted in a field of Indian corn. Others joined their comrades who were retreating across a marsh. Lord Stirling had encouraged and animated his young soldiers by his voice and example, but when all was lost he sought out General De Heister and surrendered himself as his prisoner.

More than two hundred and fifty brave fellows, most of them of Smallwood's regiment, perished in this deadly struggle, within sight of the lines of Brooklyn. That part of the Delaware troops who had first crossed the creek and swamp made good their retreat to the lines with a trifling loss and entered the camp covered with mud and drenched with water but bringing with them twenty-three prisoners, and their standard tattered by grape-shot.

The enemy now concentrated their forces within a few hundred yards of the redoubts. The grenadiers were within musket shot. Washington expected they would storm the works, and prepared for a desperate defense. The discharge of a cannon and volleys of musketry from the part of the lines nearest to them seemed to bring them to a pause.

It was, in truth, the forbearance of the British commander that prevented a bloody conflict. His troops, heated with action and flushed with success, were eager to storm the works but he was unwilling to risk the loss of life that must attend an assault, when the object might be attained at a cheaper rate by regular approaches. Checking the ardor of his men, therefore, though with some difficulty, he drew them off to a hollow way in front of the lines

[4] Letter from a Marylander. *Am. Archives*, 5th Series, i., 1232.

but out of reach of the musketry and encamped there for the night.[5]

The loss of the Americans in this disastrous battle has been variously stated but is thought, in killed, wounded and prisoners, to have been nearly two thousand; a large number, considering that not above five thousand were engaged. The enemy acknowledged a loss of 380 killed and wounded.[6]

The success of the enemy was attributed in some measure to the doubt in which Washington was kept as to the nature of the intended attack, and at what point it would chiefly be made. This obliged him to keep a great part of his forces in New York and to distribute those at Brooklyn over a wide extent of country and at widely distant places. In fact, he knew not the superior number of the enemy encamped on Long Island, a majority of them having been furtively landed in the night some days after the debarkation of the first division.

Much of the day's disaster has been attributed also to a confusion in the command caused by the illness of General Greene. Putnam, who had supplied his place in the emergency after the enemy had landed, had not time to make himself acquainted with the post and the surrounding country. Sullivan, though in his letters he professes to have considered himself subordinate to General Putnam within the lines, seems still to have exercised somewhat of an independent command and to have acted at his own discretion, while Lord Stirling was said to have command of all the troops outside of the works.

The fatal error, however, and one probably arising from all these causes consisted in leaving the passes through the wooded hills too weakly fortified and guarded, and especially in neglecting the eastern road, by which Sir Henry Clinton got in the rear of the advanced troops, cut them off from the lines and subjected them to a cross fire of his own men and De Heister's Hessians.

This able and fatal scheme of the enemy might have been thwarted had the army been provided with a few troops of light horse to serve as videttes. With these to scour the roads and bring intelligence, the night march of Sir Henry Clinton, so decisive of the fortunes of the day, could hardly have failed to be discovered and reported. The Connecticut horsemen, therefore, ridiculed by

[5] General Howe to Lord G. Germaine. *Remembrancer*, iii., 347.
[6] Howe states the prisoners at 1,094 and computes the whole American loss at 3,300.

the Southerners for their homely equipments, sneered at as useless and dismissed for standing on their dignity and privileges as troopers, might, if retained, have saved the army from being surprised and severed, its advanced guards routed and those very Southern troops cut up, captured and almost annihilated.

The night after the battle was a weary yet almost sleepless one to the Americans. Fatigued, dispirited, many of them sick and wounded, yet they were for the most part without tent or other shelter. To Washington it was a night of anxious vigil. Everything boded a close and deadly conflict. The enemy had pitched a number of tents about a mile distant. Their sentries were but a quarter of a mile off and close to the American sentries. At four o'clock in the morning Washington went the round of the works to see that all was right and to speak words of encouragement. The morning broke lowering and dreary. Large encampments were gradually descried. To appearance, the enemy were twenty thousand strong. As the day advanced, their ordnance began to play upon the works. They were proceeding to intrench themselves but were driven into their tents by a drenching rain.

Early in the morning General Mifflin arrived in camp with part of the troops which had been stationed at Fort Washington and King's Bridge. He brought with him Shee's prime Philadelphia regiment and Magaw's Pennsylvania regiment, both well disciplined and officered, and accustomed to act together. They were so much reduced in number, however, by sickness that they did not amount in the whole to more than eight hundred men. With Mifflin came also Colonel Glover's Massachusetts regiment, composed chiefly of Marblehead fishermen and sailors, hardy, adroit and weather-proof, trimly clad in blue jackets and trousers. The detachment numbered in the whole about thirteen hundred men, all fresh and full of spirits. Every eye brightened as they marched briskly along the line with alert step and cheery aspect. They were posted at the left extremity of the intrenchments towards the Wallabout.

There were skirmishes throughout the day between the riflemen on the advanced posts and the British "irregulars" which at times were quite severe, but no decided attack was attempted. The main body of the enemy kept within their tents until the latter part of the day, when they began to break ground at about five hundred yards' distance from the works, as if preparing to carry them by regular approaches.

On the 29th there was a dense fog over the island, that wrapped everything in mystery. In the course of the morning General Mifflin, with Adjutant-General Reed and Colonel Grayson of Virginia, one of Washington's aides-de-camp, rode to the western outposts in the neighborhood of Red Hook. While they were there a light breeze lifted the fog from a part of the New York Bay and revealed the British ships at their anchorage opposite Staten Island. There appeared to be an unusual bustle among them. Boats were passing to and from the admiral's ship, as if seeking or carrying orders. Some movement was apparently in agitation. The idea occurred to the reconnoitering party that the fleet was preparing, should the wind hold and the fog clear away, to come up the bay at the turn of the tide, silence the feeble batteries at Red Hook and the city, and anchor in the East River. In that case the army on Long Island would be completely surrounded and entrapped.

Alarmed at this perilous probability, they spurred back to headquarters to urge the immediate withdrawal of the army. As this might not be acceptable advice, Reed, emboldened by his intimacy with the commander-in-chief, undertook to give it. Washington instantly summoned a council of war. The difficulty was already apparent of guarding such extensive works with troops fatigued and dispirited and exposed to the inclemencies of the weather. Other dangers now presented themselves. Their communication with New York might be cut off by the fleet from below. Other ships had passed round Long Island and were at Flushing Bay on the Sound. These might land troops on the east side of Harlem River and make themselves masters of King's Bridge, that key of Manhattan Island. Taking all these things into consideration, it was resolved to cross with the troops to the city that very night.

Never did retreat require greater secrecy and circumspection. Nine thousand men, with all the munitions of war, were to be withdrawn from before a victorious army encamped so near that every stroke of spade and pickaxe from their trenches could be heard. The retreating troops moreover were to be embarked and conveyed across a strait three-quarters of a mile wide, swept by rapid tides. The least alarm of their movement would bring the enemy upon them and produce a terrible scene of confusion and carnage at the place of embarkation.

Washington made the preparatory arrangements with great alertness yet profound secrecy. Verbal orders were sent to Colonel Hughes, who acted as quartermaster-general, to impress all water craft, large and small, from Spyt den Duivel on the Hudson round to Hell Gate on the Sound, and have them on the east side of the city by evening. The order was issued at noon and so promptly executed that, although some of the vessels had to be brought a distance of fifteen miles, they were all at Brooklyn at eight o'clock in the evening, and put under the management of Colonel Glover's amphibious Marblehead regiment.

To prepare the army for a general movement without betraying the object, orders were issued for the troops to hold themselves in readiness for a night attack upon the enemy. The orders caused surprise, for the poor fellows were exhausted and their arms rendered nearly useless by the rain. All, however, prepared to obey but several made nuncupative wills, as is customary among soldiers on the eve of sudden and deadly peril.

According to Washington's plan of retreat to keep the enemy from discovering the withdrawal of the Americans until their main body should have embarked in the boats and pushed off from the shore, General Mifflin was to remain at the lines with his Pennsylvania troops and the gallant remains of Haslet, Smallwood and Hand's regiments, with guards posted and sentinels alert, as if nothing extraordinary was taking place. When the main embarkation was effected they were themselves to move off quietly, march briskly to the ferry and embark. In case of any alarm that might disconcert the arrangements, Brooklyn church was to be the rallying place, whither all should repair so as unitedly to resist any attack.

It was late in the evening when the troops began to retire from the breastworks. As one regiment quietly withdrew from their station on guard, the troops on the right and left moved up and filled the vacancy. There was a stifled murmur in the camp, unavoidable in a movement of the kind, but it gradually died away in the direction of the river as the main body moved on in silence and order. The youthful Hamilton, whose military merits had won the favor of General Greene and who had lost his baggage and a field-piece in the battle, brought up the rear of the retreating party. In the dead of the night and in the midst of this hushed and anxious movement, a cannon went off with a tremendous roar. "The effect," says an American who was present, "was at once alarming and sublime. If the explosion was within our lines the gun was probably discharged in the act of spiking it and could have been no less a matter of speculation to the enemy than to ourselves."[7]

"What with the greatness of the stake, the darkness of the night, the uncertainty of the design and the extreme hazard of the issue," adds the same writer, "it would be difficult to conceive a more deeply solemn and interesting scene."

The meaning of this midnight gun was never ascertained. Fortunately, though it startled the Americans it failed to rouse the British camp.

In the meantime the embarkation went on with all possible despatch under the vigilant eye of Washington, who stationed himself at the ferry, superintending every movement. In his anxiety for despatch he sent back Colonel Scammel, one of his aides-de-camp, to hasten forward all the troops that were on the march. Scammel blundered in executing his errand and gave the order to Mifflin likewise. The general instantly called in his pickets and sentinels and set off for the ferry.

By this time the tide had turned. There was a strong wind from the northeast. The boats with oars were insufficient to convey the troops. Those with sails could not make headway against wind and tide. There was some confusion at the ferry, and in the midst of it General Mifflin came down with the whole covering party, adding to the embarrassment and uproar.

"Good God! General Mifflin!" cried Washington. "I am afraid you have ruined us by so unseasonably withdrawing the troops from the lines."

"I did so by your order," replied Mifflin with some warmth.

"It cannot be!" exclaimed Washington.

"By G—, I did!" was the blunt rejoinder. "Did Scammel act as aide-de-camp for the day or did he not?"

"He did."

"Then," said Mifflin, "I had orders through him."

"It is a dreadful mistake," rejoined Washington, "and unless the troops can regain the lines before their absence is discovered by the enemy, the most disastrous consequences are to be apprehended."

Mifflin led back his men to the lines, which had been com-

[7] Graydon's *Memoirs*, edited by I. S. Littell, p. 167.

pletely deserted for three-quarters of an hour. Fortunately, the dense fog had prevented the enemy from discovering that they were unoccupied. The men resumed their former posts and remained at them until called off to cross the ferry. "Whoever has seen troops in a similar situation," writes General Heath, "or duly contemplates the human heart in such trials, will know how to appreciate the conduct of these brave men on this occasion."

The fog which prevailed all this time seemed almost providential. While it hung over Long Island and concealed the movements of the Americans, the atmosphere was clear on the New York side of the river. The adverse wind, too, died away, the river become so smooth that the row-boats could be laden almost to the gunwale, and a favoring breeze sprang up for the sail-boats. The whole embarkation of troops, artillery, ammunition, provisions, cattle, horses and carts was happily effected, and by daybreak the greater part had safely reached the city, thanks to the aid of Glover's Marblehead men. Scarce anything was abandoned to the enemy excepting a few heavy pieces of artillery. At a proper time, Mifflin with his covering party left the lines and effected a silent retreat to the ferry. Washington, though repeatedly entreated, refused to enter a boat until all the troops were embarked, and crossed the river with the last.

This extraordinary retreat, which, in its silence and celerity equalled the midnight fortifying of Bunker's Hill, was one of the most signal achievements of the war and redounded greatly to the reputation of Washington, who, we are told, for forty-eight hours preceding the safe extricating of his army from their perilous situation, scarce closed his eyes and was the greater part of the time on horseback. Many, however, who considered the variety of risks and dangers which surrounded the camp and the apparently fortuitous circumstances which averted them all, were disposed to attribute the safe retreat of the patriot army to a peculiar Providence.

Chapter 23

EVACUATION OF NEW YORK

The enemy had now possession of Long Island. British and Hessian troops garrisoned the works at Brooklyn or were distributed at Bushwick, Newton, Hell Gate and Flushing. Admiral Howe came up with the main body of the fleet and anchored close to Governor's Island, within cannon shot of the city.

"Our situation is truly distressing," writes Washington to the President of Congress on the 2d of September. "The check our detachment sustained on the 27th ultimo has dispirited too great a proportion of our troops and filled their minds with apprehension and despair. The militia, instead of calling forth their utmost efforts to a brave and manly opposition in order to repair our losses, are dismayed, intractable and impatient to return. Great numbers of them have gone off, in some instances almost by whole regiments, by half ones and by companies at a time. . . . With the deepest concern, I am obliged to confess my want of confidence in the generality of the troops. . . . Our number of men at present fit for duty is under twenty thousand. I have ordered General Mercer to send the men intended for the flying camp to this place, about a thousand in number, and to try with the militia, if practicable, to make a diversion upon Staten Island. Till of late, I had no doubt in my own mind of defending this place; nor should I have yet if the men would do their duty, but this I despair of.

"If we should be obliged to abandon the town, ought it to stand as winter quarters for the enemy? They would derive great conveniences from it on the one hand, and much property would be destroyed on the other. It is an important question but will admit of but little time for deliberation. At present I dare say the enemy mean to preserve it if they can. If Congress therefore should resolve upon the destruction of it, the resolution should be a profound secret, as the knowledge will make a capital change in their plans."

Colonel Reed, writing on the same day to his wife, says, "I have only time to say I am alive and well; as to spirits, but middling. . . . My country will I trust yet be free, whatever may be our fate who are cooped up or in danger of so being on this tongue of land where we ought never to have been."[1]

As the city might speedily be attacked, Washington caused all the sick and wounded to be conveyed to Orangetown in the Jerseys, and such military stores and baggage as were not immediately needed to be removed as fast as conveyances could be procured to a post partially fortified at Dobbs Ferry, on the eastern bank of the Hudson about twenty-two miles above the city.

The "shameful and scandalous desertions," as Washington termed them, continued. In a few days the Connecticut militia dwindled down from six to less than two thousand. "The impulse for going home was so irresistible," writes he, "that it answered no purpose to oppose it. Though I would not discharge them, I have been obliged to acquiesce."

Still his considerate mind was tolerant of their defection. "Men," said he, "accustomed to unbounded freedom cannot brook the restraint which is indispensably necessary to the good order and government of an army." And again, "Men just dragged from the tender scenes of domestic life, unaccustomed to the din of arms, totally unacquainted with every kind of military skill (which is followed by a want of confidence in themselves when opposed to troops regularly trained, superior in knowledge and superior in arms), are timid and ready to fly from their own shadows. Besides, the sudden change in their manner of living brings on an unconquerable desire to return to their homes."

Nor was this ill-timed yearning for home confined to the yeomanry of Connecticut, who might well look back to their humble farms, where they had left the plough standing in the furrow and where everything might go to ruin and their family to want in their absence. Some of the gentlemen volunteers from beyond the Delaware, who had made themselves merry at the expense of the rustic soldiery of New England, were likewise among the first to feel the homeward impulse. "When I look around," said Reed, the adjutant-general, "and see how few of the numbers who talked

[1] Force's *Am. Archives*, 5th Series, ii., 123.

so loudly of death and honor are around me, I am lost in wonder and surprise. Some of our Philadelphia gentlemen who came over on visits, upon the first cannon went off in a most violent hurry. Your noisy sons of liberty are, I find, the quietest on the field."[2]

Present experience induced Washington to reiterate the opinion he had repeatedly expressed to Congress, that little reliance was to be placed on militia enlisted for short periods. The only means of protecting the national liberties from great hazard if not utter loss was, he said, an army enlisted for the war.

Since the retreat from Brooklyn, Washington had narrowly watched the movements of the enemy to discover their further plans. Their whole force, excepting about four thousand men, had been transferred from Staten to Long Island. A great part was encamped on the peninsula between Newtown Inlet and Flushing Bay. A battery had been thrown up near the extremity of the peninsula to check an American battery at Horen's Hook opposite and to command the mouth of Harlem River. Troops were subsequently stationed on the islands about Hell Gate.

"It is evident," writes Washington, "the enemy mean to inclose us on the island of New York by taking post in our rear while the shipping secures the front, and thus, by cutting off our communication with the country, oblige us to fight them on their own terms or surrender at discretion, or by a brilliant stroke endeavor to cut this army in pieces and secure the collection of arms and stores which, they well know, we shall not be able soon to replace."[3]

The question was, how could their plans be most successfully opposed? On every side he saw a choice of difficulties. Every measure was to be formed with some apprehension that all the troops would not do their duty. History, experience, the opinions of able friends in Europe, the fears of the enemy, even the declarations of Congress all concurred in demonstrating that the war on the American side should be defensive, a war of posts, that on all occasions a general action should be avoided and nothing put at risk unnecessarily. "With these views," said Washington, "and being fully persuaded that it would be presumption to draw out our young troops into open ground against their superiors both in

2 *Life of Reed*, i., 231.
8 Letter to the President of Congress.

number and discipline, I have never spared the spade and pickaxe."

In a council of war held on the 7th of September the question was discussed whether the city should be defended or evacuated. All admitted that it would not be tenable should it be cannonaded and bombarded. Several of the council, among whom was General Putnam, were for a total and immediate removal from the city, urging that one part of the army might be cut off before the other could support it, the extremities being at least sixteen miles apart, and the whole, when collected, being inferior to the enemy. By removing, they would deprive the enemy of the advantage of their ships, they would keep them at bay, put nothing at hazard, keep the army together to be recruited another year, and preserve the unspent stores and the heavy artillery. Washington himself inclined to this opinion. Others, however, were unwilling to abandon a place which had been fortified with great cost and labor and seemed defensible, and which, by some, had been considered the key to the northern country. It might dispirit the troops and enfeeble the cause. General Mercer, who was prevented by illness from attending the council, communicated his opinion by letter. "We should keep New York if possible," said he, "as the acquiring of it will give eclat to the arms of Great Britain, afford the soldiers good quarters and furnish a safe harbor for the fleet."

General Greene, also, being still unwell, conveyed his opinion in a letter to Washington, dated September 5th. He advised that the army should abandon both city and island and post itself at King's Bridge and along the Westchester shore; that there was no object to be obtained by holding any position below King's Bridge. The enemy might throw troops on Manhattan Island from their camps on Long Island and their ships on the Hudson, and form an intrenched line across it between the city and the middle division of the army, and support the two flanks of the line by their shipping. In such case it would be necessary to fight them on disadvantageous terms or submit.

The city and island, he observed, were objects not to be put in competition with the general interests of America. Two thirds of the city and suburbs belonged to tories. There was no great reason therefore to run any considerable risk in its defense. The honor and interest of America required a general and speedy retreat. But as the enemy, once in possession, could never be dislodged without a superior naval force; as the place would furnish them with excellent winter quarters and barrack room and an abundant market, he advised to burn both city and suburbs before retreating.[4]

Well might the poor, harassed citizens feel hysterical, threatened as they were by sea and land, and their very defenders debating the policy of burning their houses over their heads. Fortunately for them, Congress had expressly forbidden that any harm should be done to New York, trusting, that though the enemy might occupy it for a time, it would ultimately be regained.

After much discussion a middle course was adopted. Putnam, with five thousand men, was to be stationed in the city. Heath, with nine thousand, was to keep guard on the upper part of the island and oppose any attempt of the enemy to land. His troops, among whom were Magaw's, Shee's, Hand's and Miles's Pennsylvania battalions and Haslet's Delaware regiment, were posted about King's Bridge and its vicinity.

The third division, composed principally of militia, was under the command of Generals Greene and Spencer, the former of whom, however, was still unwell. It was stationed about the centre of the island, chiefly along Turtle Bay and Kip's Bay, where strong works had been thrown up to guard against any landing of troops from the ships or from the encampments on Long Island. It was also to hold itself ready to support either of the other divisions. Washington himself had his headquarters at a short distance from the city. A resolution of Congress, passed the 10th of September, left the occupation or abandonment of the city entirely at Washington's discretion. Nearly the whole of his officers, too, in a second council of war retracted their former opinion and determined that the removal of his army was not only prudent but absolutely necessary. Three members of the council, however, Generals Spencer, Heath and George Clinton, tenaciously held to the former decision.

Convinced of the propriety of evacuation, Washington prepared for it by ordering the removal of all stores excepting such as were indispensable for the subsistence of the troops while they remained. A letter from a Rhode Island officer on a visit to New York gives an idea of its agitations. "On the 13th of September, just after dinner, three frigates and a forty-gun ship sailed up the

East River with a gentle breeze toward Hell Gate and kept up an incessant fire, assisted by the cannon at Governor's Island. The batteries of the city returned the ships the like salutation. Three men agape, idle spectators, had the misfortune of being killed by one cannon ball. One shot struck within six feet of General Washington as he was on horseback riding into the fort."[5]

On the 14th, Washington's baggage was removed to King's Bridge, whither headquarters were to be transferred the same evening, it being clear that the enemy were preparing to encompass him on the island. "It is now a trial of skill whether they will or not," writes Colonel Reed, "and every night we lie down with the most anxious fears for the fate of to-morrow."[6]

About sunset of the same day six more ships, two of them men-of-war, passed up the Sound and joined those above. Within half an hour came expresses spurring to headquarters, one from Mifflin at King's Bridge, the other from Colonel Sargent at Horen's Hook. Three or four thousand of the enemy were crossing at Hell Gate to the islands at the mouth of Harlem River, where numbers were already encamped. An immediate landing at Harlem, or Morrisania, was apprehended. Washington was instantly in the saddle, spurring to Harlem Heights. The night, however, passed away quietly.

In the morning the enemy commenced operations. Three ships of war stood up the Hudson, "causing a most tremendous firing, assisted by the cannons of Governor's Island, which firing was returned from the city as well as the scarcity of heavy cannon would allow."[7] The ships anchored opposite Bloomingdale, a few miles above the city, and put a stop to the removal by water of stores and provisions to Dobbs Ferry. About eleven o'clock the ships in the East River commenced a heavy cannonade upon the breastworks between Turtle Bay and the city. At the same time two divisions of the troops encamped on Long Island, one British, under Sir Henry Clinton, the other Hessian, under Colonel Donop, emerged in boats from the deep, woody recesses of Newton Inlet, and under cover of the fire from the ships began to land at two points between Turtle and Kip's Bays. The breastworks were manned by militia who had recently served at Brooklyn. Dis-

[5] Col. Babcock to Gov. Cooke. Am. Archives, 5th Series, ii., 443.
[6] Reed to Mrs. Reed.
[7] Letter of Col. Babcock to Gov. Cooke.

heartened by their late defeat, they fled at the first advance of the enemy. Two brigades of Putnam's Connecticut troops (Parsons' and Fellows') which had been sent that morning to support them, caught the panic and, regardless of the commands and entreaties of their officers, joined in the general scamper.

At this moment Washington, who had mounted his horse at the first sound of the cannonade, came galloping to the scene of confusion. Riding in among the fugitives, he endeavored to rally and restore them to order. All in vain. At the first appearance of sixty or seventy red-coats, they broke again without firing a shot and fled in headlong terror. Losing all self-command at the sight of such dastardly conduct, he dashed his hat upon the ground in a transport of rage. "Are these the men," exclaimed he, "with whom I am to defend America!" In a paroxysm of passion and despair he snapped his pistols at some of them, threatened others with his sword and was so heedless of his own danger that he might have fallen into the hands of the enemy, who were not eighty yards distant, had not an aide-de-camp seized the bridle of his horse and absolutely hurried him away.

It was one of the rare moments of his life when the vehement element of his nature was stirred up from its deep recesses. He soon recovered his self-possession and took measures against the general peril. The enemy might land another force about Hell Gate, seize upon Harlem Heights, the strong central portion of the island, cut off all retreat of the lower divisions and effectually sever his army. In all haste therefore he sent off an express to the forces encamped above, directing them to secure that position immediately, while another express to Putnam ordered an immediate retreat from the city to those heights.

It was indeed a perilous moment. Had the enemy followed up their advantage and seized upon the heights before thus occupied, or had they extended themselves across the island and from the place where they had effected a landing, the result might have been most disastrous to the Americans. Fortunately they contented themselves for the present with sending a strong detachment down the road along the East River leading to the city, while the main body, British and Hessians, rested on their arms.

The fortified camp where the main body of the army was now assembled was upon that neck of land several miles long, and for the most part not above a mile wide, which forms the upper part of Manhattan or New York Island. It forms a chain of rocky heights and is separated from the mainland by Harlem River, a narrow strait extending from Hell Gate, on the Sound, to Spyt den Duivel, a creek or inlet of the Hudson. Fort Washington occupied the crest of one of the rocky heights above mentioned, overlooking the Hudson, and about two miles north of it was King's Bridge, crossing Spyt den Duivel Creek and forming at that time the only pass from Manhattan Island to the mainland.

About a mile and a half south of the fort a double row of lines extended across the neck from Harlem River to the Hudson. They faced south towards New York, were about a quarter of a mile apart and were defended by batteries.

There were strong advanced posts, about two miles south of the outer line, one on the left of Harlem, commanded by General Spencer, the other on the right at what was called McGowan's Pass, commanded by General Putnam. About a mile and a half beyond these posts the British lines extended across the island from Horen's Hook to the Hudson, being a continuous encampment two miles in length, with both flanks covered by shipping. An open plain intervened between the hostile camps.

Washington had established his headquarters about a quarter of a mile within the inner line at a country-seat the owners of which were absent.

In the dead of the night on the 20th of September a great light was beheld by the picket guards, looming up from behind the hills in the direction of the city. It continued throughout the night and was at times so strong that the heavens in that direction appeared to them, they said, as if in flames. At daybreak huge columns of smoke were still rising. It was evident there had been a great conflagration in New York.

In the course of the morning Captain Montresor, aide-de-camp to General Howe, came out with a flag, bearing a letter to Washington on the subject of an exchange of prisoners. According to Montresor's account a great part of the city had been burnt down, and as the night was extremely windy, the whole might have been so but for the exertions of the officers and men of the British army. He implied it to be the act of American incendiaries, several of whom, he informed Colonel Reed, had been caught in the fact and instantly shot. General Howe in his private correspondence makes the same assertion and says they were detected and killed on the spot by the enraged troops in garrison.

Enraged troops, with weapons in their hands, are not apt in a time of confusion and alarm to be correct judges of fact or dispensers of justice. The act was always disclaimed by the Americans and it is certain their commanders knew nothing about it. We have shown that the destruction of the city was at one time discussed in a council of war as a measure of policy but never adopted and was expressly forbidden by Congress.

The enemy were now bringing up their heavy cannon preparatory to an attack upon the American camp by the troops and by the ships. What was the state of Washington's army? The terms of engagement of many of his men would soon be at an end, most of them would terminate with the year, nor did Congress hold out offers to encourage re-enlistments. "We are now, as it were, upon the eve of another dissolution of the army," writes he, "and unless some speedy and effectual measures are adopted by Congress our cause will be lost." Under these gloomy apprehensions he borrowed, as he said, "a few moments from the hours allotted to sleep" and on the night of the 24th of September penned an admirable letter to the President of Congress, setting forth the total inefficiency of the existing military system, the total insubordination, waste, confusion and discontent produced by it among the men, and the harassing cares and vexations to which it subjected the commanders. Nor did he content himself with complaining, but, in his full, clear and sagacious manner pointed out the remedies. To the achievements of his indefatigable pen we may trace the most fortunate turns in the current of our revolutionary affairs. In the present instance his representations, illustrated by sad experience, produced at length a reorganization of the army and the establishment of it on a permanent footing. It was decreed that eighty-eight battalions should be furnished in quotas by the different States according to their abilities. The pay of the officers was raised. The troops which engaged to serve throughout the war were to receive a bounty of twenty dollars and one hundred acres of land, besides a yearly suit of clothes while in service. Those who enlisted for but three years received no bounty in land. The bounty to officers was on a higher ratio. The States were to send commissioners to the army to arrange with the commander-in-chief as to the appointment of officers in their quotas, but as they might occasionally be slow in complying with this regulation, Washington was empowered to fill up all vacancies.

All this was a great relief to his mind. He was gratified also by effecting, after a long correspondence with the British commander, an exchange of prisoners, in which those captured in Canada were included. Among those restored to the service were Lord Stirling and Captain Daniel Morgan. The latter, in reward of his good conduct in the expedition with [Benedict] Arnold and of "his intrepid behavior in the assault upon Quebec, where the brave Montgomery fell," was recommended to Congress by Washington for the command of a rifle regiment about to be raised. We shall see how eminently he proved himself worthy of this recommendation.

Nothing perplexed Washington at this juncture more than the conduct of the enemy. He beheld before him a hostile army, armed and equipped at all points, superior in numbers, thoroughly disciplined, flushed with success and abounding in the means of pushing a vigorous campaign, yet suffering day after day to elapse unimproved. What could be the reason of this supineness on the part of Sir William Howe? He must know the depressed and disorganized state of the American camp, the absolute chaos that reigned there. Did he meditate an irruption into the Jerseys? A movement towards Philadelphia? Did he intend to detach a part of his forces for a winter's campaign against the South?

In this uncertainty Washington wrote to General Mercer, of the flying camp, to keep a vigilant watch from the Jersey shore on the movements of the enemy by sea and land and to station videttes on the Neversink Heights to give immediate intelligence should any of the British fleet put to sea. At the same time he himself practised unceasing vigilance, visiting the different parts of his camp on horseback. Occasionally he crossed over to Fort Constitution on the Jersey shore, of which General Greene had charge, and, accompanied by him, extended his reconnoiterings down to Paulus Hook to observe what was going on in the city and among the enemy's ships. Greene had recently been promoted to the rank of major-general and now had command of all the troops in the Jerseys. He had liberty to shift his quarters to Baskingridge or Bergen, as circumstances might require, but was enjoined to keep up a communication with the main army, east of the Hudson, so as to secure a retreat in case of necessity.

[Washington and his staff decided to abandon New York, but Fort Washington in Manhattan would, in accordance with the wish of Congress, be held as long as possible. Meanwhile General Lee, "the military idol of the day" as a consequence of his successes in the South, joined Washington. The latter moved his headquarters to White Plains,] where he stationed himself in a fortified camp.

While he was thus incessantly in action, General, now Sir William, Howe (having recently, in reward for his services, been made a knight companion of the Bath), remained for six days passive in his camp on Throg's Point awaiting the arrival of supplies and reinforcements instead of pushing across to the Hudson and throwing himself between Washington's army and the upper country. His inaction lost him a golden opportunity. By the time his supplies arrived the Americans had broken up the causeway leading to the mainland and taken positions too strong to be easily forced.

[After several engagements with the Americans the British force disappeared from White Plains.]

Chapter 24

SURRENDER OF FORT WASHINGTON

Various were the speculations at headquarters on the sudden movement of the enemy. Washington writes to General William Livingston (now governor of the Jerseys): "They have gone towards the North River and King's Bridge. Some suppose they are going into winter quarters and will sit down in New York without doing more than investing Fort Washington. I cannot subscribe wholly to this opinion myself. That they will invest Fort Washington is a matter of which there can be no doubt and I think there is a strong probability that General Howe will detach a part of his force to make an incursion into the Jerseys, provided he is going to New York. He must attempt something on account of his reputation, for what has he done, as yet, with his great army?"

In the same letter he expressed his determination, as soon as it should appear that the present manœuvre was a real retreat and not a feint, to throw over a body of troops into the Jerseys to assist in checking Howe's progress. He moreover recommended to the governor to have the militia of that State put on the best possible footing and a part of them held in readiness to take the place of the State levies, whose term of service would soon expire. He advised also that the inhabitants contiguous to the water should be prepared to remove their stock, grain, effects and carriages on the earliest notice.

In a letter of the same date he charged General Greene, should Howe invest Fort Washington with part of his force, to give the garrison all possible assistance.

On the following day (Nov. 8th) his aide-de-camp, Colonel Tilghman, writes to General Greene from headquarters: "The enemy are at Dobbs Ferry with a great number of boats, ready to go into Jersey, or proceed up the river."

Greene doubted any intention of the enemy to cross the river. It might only be a feint to mislead. Still, as a precaution, he had ordered troops up from the flying camp and was posting them opposite Dobbs Ferry and at other passes where a landing might be attempted, the whole being under the command of General Mercer.

Affairs at Fort Washington soon settled the question of the enemy's intentions with regard to it. Lord Percy took his station with a body of troops before the lines to the south. Knyphausen advanced on the north. The Americans had previously abandoned Fort Independence, burnt its barracks and removed the stores and cannon. Crossing King's Bridge, Knyphausen took a position between it and Fort Washington. The approach to the fort on this side was exceedingly steep and rocky, as indeed were all its approaches excepting that on the south, where the country was more open and the ascent gradual. The fort could not hold within its walls above one thousand men. The rest of the troops were distributed about the lines and outworks. While the fort was thus menaced, the chevaux-de-frise had again proved inefficient. On the night of the 5th a frigate and two transports, bound up to Dobbs Ferry with supplies for Howe's army, had broken through, though, according to Greene's account, not without being considerably shattered by the batteries.

Informed of these facts, Washington wrote to Greene on the 8th: "If we cannot prevent vessels from passing up the river, and the enemy are possessed of all the surrounding country, what valuable purpose can it answer to hold a post from which the expected benefit cannot be had? I am therefore inclined to think that it will not be prudent to hazard the men and stores at Mount Washington. But, as you are on the spot, I leave it to you to give such orders as to evacuating Mount Washington as you may judge best, and so far revoking the orders given to Colonel Magaw to defend it to the last."

Accounts had been received at headquarters of a considerable movement on the preceding evening (Nov. 7th) among the enemy's boats at Dobbs Ferry, with the intention, it was said, of penetrating the Jerseys and falling down upon Fort Lee. Washington therefore in the same letter directed Greene to have all the stores not necessary to the defense removed immediately and to destroy all the stock, the hay and grain, in the neighborhood, which the owners refused to remove. "Experience has shown," adds he, "that a contrary conduct is not of the least advantage to the poor inhabitants, from whom all their effects of every kind are taken without distinction and without the least satisfaction."

Greene, in reply (Nov. 9th), adhered with tenacity to the policy of maintaining Fort Washington. "The enemy," said he, "must invest it with double the number of men required for its defense. They must keep troops at King's Bridge to cut off all communication with the country, and in considerable force for fear of an attack." He did not consider the fort in immediate danger. Colonel Magaw thought it would take the enemy until the end of December to carry it. In the meantime the garrison could at any time be brought off and even the stores removed should matters grow desperate. If the enemy should not find it an object of importance they would not trouble themselves about it. If they should, it would be a proof that they felt an injury from its being maintained. The giving it up would open for them a free communication with the country by the way of King's Bridge.[1]

It is doubtful when or where Washington received this letter, as he left the camp at Northcastle at eleven o'clock of the following morning. There being still considerable uncertainty as to the intentions of the enemy, all his arrangements were made accordingly. All the troops belonging to the States west of the Hudson were to be stationed in the Jerseys, under command of General Putnam. Lord Stirling had already been sent forward with the Maryland and Virginia troops to Peekskill, to cross the river at King's Ferry. Another division, composed of Connecticut and Massachusetts troops under General Heath, was to co-operate with the brigade of New York militia under General George Clinton in securing the Highland posts on both sides of the river.

The troops which would remain at Northcastle after the departure of Heath and his division were to be commanded by Lee. Washington's letter of instructions to that general is characterized by his own modesty and his deference for Lee's superior military experience. He suggests rather than orders, yet his letter is sufficiently explicit.

"A little time now," writes he, "must manifest the enemy's designs and point out to you the measures proper to be pursued by that part of the army under your command. I shall give no direc-

[1] *Am. Archives*, 5th Series, iii., 618.

tions therefore on this head, having the most entire confidence in your judgment and military exertions. One thing, however, I will suggest, namely that the appearance of embarking troops for the Jerseys may be intended as a feint to weaken us and render the post we now hold more vulnerable, or the enemy may find that troops are assembled with more expedition and in greater numbers than they expected on the Jersey shore to oppose them; and, as it is possible from one or other of these motives that they may yet pay the party under your command a visit, it will be unnecessary, I am persuaded, to recommend to you the propriety of putting this post, if you stay at it, into a proper posture of defense and guarding against surprises. But I would recommend it to your consideration whether, under the suggestion above, your retiring to Croton Bridge and some strong post still more easterly (covering the passes through the Highlands), may not be more advisable than to run the hazard of an attack with unequal numbers. At any rate, I think all your baggage and stores except such as are necessary for immediate use ought to be to the northward of Croton River. . . . You will consider the post at Croton's (or Pine's) Bridge as under your immediate care. . . . If the enemy should remove the whole or the greater part of their force to the west side of Hudson's River, I have no doubt of your following with all possible despatch, leaving the militia and invalids to cover the frontiers of Connecticut in case of need."

We have been minute in stating these matters, from their bearing on subsequent operations.

On the 10th of November Washington left the camp at Northcastle at 11 o'clock and arrived at Peekskill at sunset, whither General Heath with his division had preceded him by a few hours. Lord Stirling was there likewise, having effected the transportation of the Maryland and Virginia troops across the river and landed them at the ferry south of Stony Point, though a better landing was subsequently found north of the point. His lordship had thrown out a scouting party in the advance, and a hundred men to take possession of a gap in the mountain, through which a road passed toward the Jerseys.

Washington was now at the entrance of the Highlands, that grand defile of the Hudson, the object of so much precaution and solicitude. On the following morning, accompanied by Generals Heath, Stirling, James and George Clinton, Mifflin and others, he made a military visit in boats to the Highland posts. Fort Montgomery was in a considerable state of forwardness, and a work in the vicinity was projected to co-operate with it. Fort Constitution commanded a sudden bend of the river but Lord Stirling in his report of inspection had intimated that the fort itself was commanded by West Point opposite. A glance of the eye, without going on shore, was sufficient to convince Washington of the fact. A fortress subsequently erected on that point has been considered the Key of the Highlands.

On the morning of the 12th, at an early hour, Washington rode out with General Heath to reconnoiter the east side of the Hudson at the gorge of the Highlands. Henry Wisnor, in a report to the New York Convention, had mentioned a hill to the north of Peekskill, so situated, with the road winding along the side of it, that ten men on the top, by rolling down stones, might prevent ten thousand from passing. "I believe," said he, "nothing more need be done than to keep great quantities of stones at the different places where the troops must pass, if they attempt penetrating the mountains."

Near Robinson's Bridge, in this vicinity, about two miles from Peekskill, Washington chose a place where troops should be stationed to cover the south entrance into the mountains, and here afterwards was established an important military depot called Continental Village.

On the same day (12th) he wrote to General Lee, inclosing a copy of resolutions just received from Congress respecting levies for the new army, showing the importance of immediately beginning the recruiting service. If no commissioners arrived from Rhode Island, he was to appoint the officers recommended to that State by General Greene. "I cannot conclude," adds he, "without reminding you of the military and other stores about your encampment and at Northcastle, and to press the removal of them above Croton Bridge or such other places of security as you may think proper. General Howe, having sent no part of his force to Jersey yet, makes the measure more necessary as he may turn his views another way and attempt their destruction."

It was evidently Washington's desire that Lee should post himself as soon as possible beyond the Croton, where he would be safe from surprise and at hand to throw his troops promptly across the Hudson should the Jerseys be invaded.

Having made all these surveys and arrangements, Washington placed Heath in the general command of the Highlands, with written instructions to fortify the passes with all possible despatch, and directions how the troops were to be distributed on both sides of the river. And here we take occasion to give some personal notice of this trusty officer.

Heath was now in the fortieth year of his age. Like many of the noted officers of the Revolution, he had been brought up in rural life, on an hereditary farm near Boston; yet, according to his own account, though passionately fond of agricultural pursuits, he had also, almost from childhood, a great relish for military affairs and had studied every treatise on the subject in the English language, so that he considered himself "fully acquainted with the *theory* of war, in all its branches and duties, from the private soldier to the commander-in-chief."

He describes himself to be of a middling stature, light complexion, very corpulent and bald-headed, so that the French officers who served in America compared him in person to the Marquis of Granby.[2]

Such was the officer intrusted with the command of the Highland passes and encamped at Peekskill, their portal. We shall find him faithful to his trust, scrupulous in obeying the letter of his instructions, but sturdy and punctilious in resisting any undue assumption of authority.

On the morning of the 12th of November, Washington crossed the Hudson to the ferry below Stony Point with the residue of the troops destined for the Jerseys. Far below were to be descried the *Phœnix*, the *Roebuck* and the *Tartar* at anchor in the broad waters of Haverstraw Bay and the Tappan Sea, guarding the lower ferries. The army, thus shut out from the nearer passes, was slowly winding its way by a circuitous route through the gap in the mountains, which Lord Stirling had secured. Leaving the troops which had just landed to pursue the same route to the Hackensack, Washington, accompanied by Colonel Reed, struck a direct course for Fort Lee, being anxious about affairs at Fort Washington. He arrived there on the following day and found, to his disappointment, that General Greene had taken no measures for the evacuation of that fortress but on the contrary had reinforced it with a part of Colonel Durkee's regiment and the regiment of Col-

[2] Heath's *Memoirs.*

onel Rawlings, so that its garrison now numbered upwards of two thousand men. A great part, however, were militia. Washington's orders for its evacuation had in fact been discretionary, leaving the execution of them to Greene's judgment, "as being on the spot." The latter had differed in opinion as to the policy of such a measure, and Colonel Magaw, who had charge of the fortress, was likewise confident it might be maintained.

Colonel Reed was of opposite counsels, but then he was personally interested in the safety of the garrison. It was composed almost entirely of Pennsylvania troops under Magaw and Lambert Cadwalader, excepting a small detachment of Maryland riflemen commanded by Otho H. Williams. They were his friends and neighbors, the remnant of the brave men who had suffered so severely under Atlee and Smallwood.[3] The fort was now invested on all sides but one, and the troops under Howe which had been encamped at Dobbs Ferry were said to be moving down toward it. Reed's solicitude was not shared by the garrison itself. Colonel Magaw, its brave commander, still thought it was in no immediate danger.

Washington was much perplexed. The main object of Howe was still a matter of doubt with him. He could not think that Sir William was moving his whole force upon that fortress, to invest which a part would be sufficient. He suspected an ulterior object, probably a Southern expedition, as he was told a large number of ships were taking in wood and water at New York. He resolved therefore to continue a few days in this neighborhood, during which he trusted the designs of the enemy would be more apparent. In the meantime he would distribute troops at Brunswick, Amboy, Elizabethtown and Fort Lee so as to be ready at these various points to check any incursions into the Jerseys.

In a letter to the President of Congress he urged for an increase of ordnance and field-artillery. The rough, hilly country east of the Hudson, and the strongholds and fastnesses of which the Americans had possessed themselves, had prevented the enemy from profiting by the superiority of their artillery. But this would not be the case should the scene of action change to an open campaign country like the Jerseys.

Washington was mistaken in his conjecture as to Sir William Howe's design. The capture of Fort Washington was at present

8 W. B. Reed's *Life of Reed*, i., 252.

his main object, and he was encamped on Fordham Heights, not far from King's Bridge, until preliminary steps should be taken. In the night of the 14th thirty flat-bottomed boats stole quietly up the Hudson, passed the American forts undiscovered and made their way through Spyt den Duivel Creek into Harlem River. The means were thus provided for crossing that river and landing before unprotected parts of the American works.

On the 15th General Howe sent in a summons to surrender, with a threat of extremities should he have to carry the place by assault. Magaw in his reply intimated a doubt that General Howe would execute a threat "so unworthy of himself and the British nation; but give me leave," added he, "to assure his Excellency that, actuated by the most glorious cause that mankind ever fought in, I am determined to defend this post to the very last extremity."

Apprised by the colonel of his peril, General Greene sent over reinforcements, with an exhortation to him to persist in his defense, and despatched an express to Washington, who was at Hackensack, where the troops which had crossed from Peekskill were encamped. It was nightfall when Washington arrived at Fort Lee. Greene and Putnam were over at the besieged fortress. He threw himself into a boat and had partly crossed the river when he met those generals returning. They informed him of the garrison's having been reinforced and assured him that it was in high spirits and capable of making a good defense. It was with difficulty, however, they could prevail on him to return with them to the Jersey shore, for he was excessively excited.

Early the next morning (16th), Magaw made his dispositions for the expected attack. His forces, with the recent addition, amounted to nearly three thousand men. As the fort could not contain above a third of that number, most of them were stationed about the outworks.

Colonel Lambert Cadwalader, with eight hundred Pennsylvanians, was posted in the outer lines about two miles and a half south of fort, the side menaced by Lord Percy with sixteen hundred men. Colonel Rawlings of Maryland, with a body of troops, many of them riflemen, was stationed by a three-gun battery on a rocky, precipitous hill north of the fort and between it and Spyt den Duivel Creek. Colonel Baxter, of Bucks County, Pennsylvania, with his regiment of militia was posted east of the fort on rough, woody heights bordering the Harlem River, to watch the motions of the enemy, who had thrown up redoubts on high and commanding ground on the opposite side of the river, apparently to cover the crossing and landing of troops.

Sir William Howe had planned four simultaneous attacks, one on the north by Knyphausen, who was encamped on the York side of King's Bridge within cannon shot of Fort Washington but separated from it by high and rough hills covered with almost impenetrable woods. He was to advance in two columns formed by detachments made from the Hessians of his corps: the brigade of Rahl and the regiment of Waldeckers. The second attack was to be by two battalions of light infantry and two battalions of guards, under Brigadier-General Mathew, who was to cross Harlem River in flat-boats under cover of the redoubts above mentioned and to land on the right of the fort. This attack was to be supported by the first and second grenadiers and a regiment of light infantry under command of Lord Cornwallis. The third attack, intended as a feint to distract the attention of the Americans, was to be by Colonel Sterling with the forty-second regiment, who was to drop down the Harlem River in bateaux to the left of the American lines, facing New York. The fourth attack was to be on the south by Lord Percy with the English and Hessian toops under his command, on the right flank of the American intrenchments.[4]

About noon a heavy cannonade thundering along the rocky hills and sharp volleys of musketry proclaimed that the action was commenced. Knyphausen's division was pushing on from the north in two columns, as had been arranged. The right was led by Colonel Rahl, the left by himself. Rahl essayed to mount a steep, broken height called Cock Hill, which rises from Spyt den Duivel Creek and was covered with woods. Knyphausen undertook a hill rising from the King's Bridge road but soon found himself entangled in a woody defile difficult to penetrate, and where his Hessians were exposed to the fire of the three-gun battery and Rawlings' riflemen.

While this was going on at the north of the fort, General Mathew with his light infantry and guards crossed the Harlem River in the flat-boats, under cover of a heavy fire from the redoubts.

He made good his landing, after being severely handled by Baxter and his men, from behind rocks and trees and the breastworks thrown up on the steep river bank. A short contest ensued.

[4] Sir William Howe to Lord George Germaine.

Baxter, while bravely encouraging his men, was killed by a British officer. His troops, overpowered by numbers, retreated to the fort. General Mathew now pushed on with his guards and light infantry to cut off Cadwalader. That officer had gallantly defended the lines against the attack of Lord Percy until informed that Colonel Sterling was dropping down Harlem River in bateaux to flank the lines and take him in the rear. He sent off a detachment to oppose his landing. They did it manfully. About ninety of Sterling's men were killed or wounded in their boats, but he persevered, landed and forced his way up a steep height, which was well defended, gained the summit, forced a redoubt and took nearly two hundred prisoners. Thus doubly assailed, Cadwalader was obliged to retreat to the fort. He was closely pursued by Percy with his English troops and Hessians, but turned repeatedly on his pursuers. Thus he fought his way to the fort, with the loss of several killed and more taken prisoners, but marking his track by the number of Hessians slain.

The defense on the north side of the fort was equally obstinate and unsuccessful. Rawlings, with his Maryland riflemen and the aid of the three-gun battery, had for some time kept the left column of Hessians and Waldeckers under Knyphausen at bay. At length Colonel Rahl with the right column of the division, having forced his way directly up the north side of the steep hill at Spyt den Duivel Creek, came upon Rawlings' men, whose rifles from frequent discharges had become foul and almost useless, drove them from their strong post and followed them until within a hundred yards of the fort, where he was joined by Knyphausen, who had slowly made his way through dense forest and over felled trees. Here they took post behind a large stone house and sent in a flag with a second summons to surrender.

Washington, surrounded by several of his officers, had been an anxious spectator of the battle from the opposite side of the Hudson. Much of it was hidden from him by intervening hills and forest, but the roar of cannonry from the valley of Harlem River, the sharp and incessant reports of rifles and the smoke rising above the tree tops told him of the spirit with which the assault was received at various points and gave him for a time a hope that the defense might be successful. The action about the lines to the south lay open to him and could be distinctly seen through a telescope, and nothing encouraged him more than the gallant style in which Cadwalader with an inferior force maintained his position. When he saw him, however, assailed in flank, the line broken and his troops, overpowered by numbers, retreating to the fort, he gave up the game as lost. The worst sight of all was to behold his men cut down and bayoneted by the Hessians while begging quarter. It is said so completely to have overcome him that he wept "with the tenderness of a child."

Seeing the flag go into the fort from Knyphausen's division and surmising it to be a summons to surrender, he wrote a note to Magaw, telling him that if he could hold out until evening and the place could not be maintained, he would endeavor to bring off the garrison in the night. Captain Gooch, of Boston, a brave and daring man, offered to be the bearer of the note. "He ran down to the river, jumped into a small boat, pushed over the river, landed under the bank, ran up to the fort and delivered the message; came out, ran and jumped over the broken ground, dodging the Hessians, some of whom struck at him with their pieces and others attempted to thrust him with their bayonets; escaping through them, he got to his boat and returned to Fort Lee."[5]

Washington's message arrived too late. "The fort was so crowded by the garrison and the troops which had retreated into it that it was difficult to move about. The enemy, too, were in possession of the little redoubts around and could have poured in showers of shells and ricochet balls that would have made dreadful slaughter." It was no longer possible for Magaw to get his troops to man the lines. He was compelled therefore to yield himself and his garrison prisoners of war. The only terms granted them were that the men should retain their baggage and the officers their swords.

The sight of the American flag hauled down and the British flag waving in its place told Washington of the surrender. His instant care was for the safety of the upper country now that the lower defenses of the Hudson were at an end. Before he knew anything about the terms of capitulation he wrote to General Lee, informing him of the surrender and calling his attention to the passes of the Highlands and those which lay east of the river, begging him to have such measures adopted for their defense as his judgment should suggest to be necessary. "I do not mean," added he, "to advise abandoning your present post, contrary to your own opinion;

[5] Heath's *Memoirs*, p. 86.

but only to mention my own ideas of the importance of those passes, and that you cannot give too much attention to their security, by having works erected on the most advantageous places for that purpose."

Lee, in reply, objected to removing from his actual encampment at Northcastle. "It would give us," said he, "the air of being frightened. It would expose a fine, fertile country to their ravages. And I must add that we are as secure as we could be in any position whatever." After stating that he should deposit his stores, etc., in a place fully as safe and more central than Peekskill, he adds: "As to ourselves, light as we are, several retreats present themselves. In short, if we keep a good look-out we are in no danger. But I must entreat your Excellency to enjoin the officers posted at Fort Lee to give us the quickest intelligence if they observe any embarkation on the North River." As to the affair of Fort Washington, all that Lee observed on the subject was: "O general, why would you be over-persuaded by men of inferior judgment to your own? It was a cursed affair."

Lee's allusion to men of inferior judgment was principally aimed at Greene, whose influence with the commander-in-chief seems to have excited a jealousy of other officers of rank. So Colonel Tilghman, Washington's aide-de-camp, writes on the 17th to Robert R. Livingston of New York, "We were in a fair way of finishing the campaign with credit to ourselves and, I think, to the disgrace of Mr. Howe, and, had the general followed his own opinion, the garrison would have been withdrawn immediately upon the enemy's falling down from Dobbs Ferry. But General Greene was positive that our forces might at any time be drawn off under the guns of Fort Lee. Fatal experience has evinced the contrary."[6]

Washington's own comments on the reduction of the fort, made in a letter to his brother Augustine, are worthy of special note.

"This is a most unfortunate affair and has given me great mortification, as we have lost not only two thousand men[7] that were there but a good deal of artillery and some of the best arms we had. And what adds to my mortification is that this post, after

6 *Am. Archives*, 5th Series, iii., 780.

7 The number of prisoners, as returned by Sir William Howe, was 2,818, of whom 2,607 were privates. They were marched off to New York at midnight.

the last ships went past it, was held contrary to my wishes and opinion, as I conceived it to be a hazardous one; but it having been determined on by a full council of general officers, and a resolution of Congress having been received, strongly expressive of their desire that the channel of the river which we had been laboring to stop for a long time at that place, might be obstructed if possible; and knowing that this could not be done unless there were batteries to protect the obstructions, I did not care to give an absolute order for withdrawing the garrison till I could get round and see the situation of things; and then it became too late, as the place was invested. Upon the passing of the last ships, I had given it as my opinion to General Greene, under whose care it was, that it would be best to evacuate the place; but, as the order was discretionary and his opinion differed from mine, it was unhappily delayed too long, to my great grief."

The correspondence of Washington with his brother is full of gloomy anticipations.

"In ten days from this date there will not be above two thousand men, if that number, of the fixed established regiments on this side of Hudson River to oppose Howe's whole army, and very little more on the other to secure the eastern colonies and the important passes leading through the Highlands to Albany and the country about the lakes. In short, it is impossible for me in the compass of a letter to give you any idea of our situation, of my difficulties and of the constant perplexities I meet with, derived from the unhappy policy of short enlistments, and delaying them too long. Last fall or winter, before the army which was then to be raised was set about, I represented in clear and explicit terms the evils which would arise from short enlistments, the expense which must attend the raising an army every year and the futility of such an army when raised. And if I had spoken with a prophetic spirit I could not have foretold the evils with more accuracy than I did. All the year since, I have been pressing Congress to delay no time in engaging men upon such terms as would insure success, telling them that the longer it was delayed the more difficult it would prove. But the measure was not commenced until it was too late to be effected. . . . I am wearied almost to death with the retrograde motion of things, and I solemnly protest that a pecuniary reward of twenty thousand pounds a year would not induce me to undergo what I do and, after all, perhaps to lose my character, as it is impossible under such a variety of distressing circumstances to conduct matters agreeably to public expectations."

Chapter 25

WASHINGTON RETREATS ACROSS THE DELAWARE

With the capture of Fort Washington, the project of obstructing the navigation of the Hudson at that point was at an end. Fort Lee consequently became useless and Washington ordered all the ammunition and stores to be removed preparatory to its abandonment. This was effected with the whole of the ammunition and a part of the stores, and every exertion was making to hurry off the remainder, when early in the morning of the 20th, intelligence was brought that the enemy, with two hundred boats, had crossed the river and landed a few miles above. General Greene immediately ordered the garrison under arms, sent out troops to hold the enemy in check and sent off an express to Washington at Hackensack.

The enemy had crossed the Hudson on a very rainy night, in two divisions, one diagonally upward from King's Bridge, landing on the west side about eight o'clock. The other marched up the east bank three or four miles and then crossed to the opposite shore. The whole corps, six thousand strong and under the command of Lord Cornwallis, were landed with their cannon by ten o'clock at a place called Closter Dock, five or six miles above Fort Lee and under that line of lofty and perpendicular cliffs known as the Palisades.

Washington arrived at the fort in three-quarters of an hour. Being told that the enemy were extending themselves across the country, he at once saw that they intended to form a line from the Hudson to the Hackensack and hem the whole garrison in between the two rivers. Nothing would save it but a prompt retreat to secure the bridge over the Hackensack. No time was to be lost. The troops sent out to check the enemy were recalled. The retreat commenced in all haste. There was a want of horses and wagons.

A great quantity of baggage, stores and provisions therefore was abandoned. So was all the artillery excepting two twelve-pounders. Even the tents were left standing, and campkettles on the fire. With all their speed they did not reach the Hackensack River before the vanguard of the enemy was close upon them. Expecting a brush, the greater part hurried over the bridge, others crossed at the ferry, and some higher up. The enemy, however, did not dispute the passage of the river. But Cornwallis stated in his despatches that, had not the Americans been apprised of his approach, he would have surrounded them at the fort. Some of his troops that night occupied the tents they had abandoned.

From Hackensack, Colonel Grayson, one of Washington's aides-de-camp, wrote instantly, by his orders, to General Lee, informing him that the enemy had crossed into the Jerseys and, as was reported, in great numbers. "His Excellency," adds Grayson, "thinks it would be advisable in you to remove the troops under your command on this side of the North River and there wait for further commands."

Washington himself wrote to Lee on the following day (Nov. 21st). "I am of opinion," said he, "and the gentlemen about me concur in it, that the public interest requires your coming over to this side of the Hudson with the continental troops. . . . The enemy is evidently changing the seat of war to this side of the North River, and the inhabitants of this country will expect the continental army to give them what support they can, and failing in that, they will cease to depend upon or support a force from which no protection is to be derived. It is therefore of the utmost importance that at least an appearance of force should be made, to keep this province in connection with the others."

In this moment of hurry and agitation, Colonel Reed, also, Washington's *fidus Achates*, wrote to Lee, but in a tone and spirit that may surprise the reader, knowing the devotion he had hitherto manifested for the commander-in-chief. After expressing the common wish that Lee should be at the principal scene of action, he adds: "I do not mean to flatter or praise you at the expense of any other, but I do think it is entirely owing to you that this army, and the liberties of America, so far as they are dependent on it, are not entirely cut off. You have decision, a quality often wanting in minds otherwise valuable, and I ascribe to this our escape from York Island, King's Bridge and the Plains. And I have no doubt, had you been here, the garrison of Mount Washington would now have composed a part of this army. And from all these circumstances, I confess, I do ardently wish to see you removed from a place where there will be so little call for your judgment and experience, to the place where they are likely to be so necessary. Nor am I singular in my opinion. Every gentleman of the family, the officers and soldiers generally, have a confidence in you. The enemy constantly inquire where you are and seem to be less confident when you are present."

Then alluding to the late affair at Fort Washington, he continues: "General Washington's own judgment, seconded by representations from us, would, I believe, have saved the men, and their arms; but, unluckily, General Greene's judgment was contrary. This kept the general's mind in a state of suspense till the stroke was struck. O general! An indecisive mind is one of the greatest misfortunes that can befall an army. How often have I lamented it this campaign. All circumstances considered, we are in a very awful and alarming situation, one that requires the utmost wisdom and firmness of mind. As soon as the season will admit, I think yourself and some others should go to Congress and form the plan of the new army. . . . I must conclude with my clear and explicit opinion that your presence is of the last importance."[1]

Well might Washington apprehend that his character and conduct, in the perplexities in which he was placed, would be liable to be misunderstood by the public, when the friend of his bosom could so misjudge him.

Reed had evidently been dazzled by the daring spirit and unscrupulous policy of Lee, who, in carrying out his measures, heeded but little the counsels of others or even the orders of government. Washington's respect for both, and the caution with which he hesitated in adopting measures in opposition to them, was stamped by the bold soldier and his admirers as indecision.

At Hackensack the army did not exceed three thousand men, and they were dispirited by ill-success and the loss of tents and baggage. They were without intrenching tools in a flat country where there were no natural fastnesses. Washington resolved therefore to avoid any attack from the enemy, though by so doing he must leave a fine and fertile region open to their ravages, or a plentiful storehouse from which they would draw voluntary

[1] *Memoirs of Reed*, i., 255.

supplies. A second move was necessary, again to avoid the danger of being inclosed between two rivers. Leaving three regiments therefore to guard the passes of the Hackensack and serve as covering parties, he again decamped, and threw himself on the west bank of the Passaic in the neighborhood of Newark.

His army, small as it was, would soon be less. The term of enlistment of those under General Mercer, from the flying camp, was nearly expired and it was not probable that, disheartened as they were by defeats and losses, exposed to inclement weather and unaccustomed to military hardships, they would longer forego the comforts of their homes to drag out the residue of a ruinous campaign.

In addition too to the superiority of the force that was following him, the rivers gave the enemy facilities, by means of their shipping, to throw troops in his rear. In this extremity he cast about in every direction for assistance. Colonel Reed, on whom he relied as on a second self, was despatched to Burlington with a letter to Governor William Livingston, describing his hazardous situation and entreating him to call out a portion of the New Jersey militia; and General Mifflin was sent to Philadelphia to implore immediate aid from Congress and the local authorities.

His main reliance for prompt assistance, however, was upon Lee. On the 24th came a letter from that general, addressed to Colonel Reed. Washington opened it, as he was accustomed to do, in the absence of that officer, with letters addressed to him on the business of the army. Lee was at his old encampment at Northcastle. He had no means, he said, of crossing at Dobbs Ferry, and the round by King's Ferry would be so great that he could not get there in time to answer any purpose. "I have therefore," added he, "ordered General Heath, who is close to the only ferry which can be passed, to detach two thousand men to apprise his Excellency and await his further orders, a mode which I flatter myself will answer better what I conceive to be the spirit of the orders than should I move the corps from hence. Withdrawing our troops from hence would be attended with some very serious consequences, which at present would be tedious to enumerate. As to myself," adds he, "I hope to set out tomorrow."

A letter of the same date (Nov. 23d), from Lee to James Bowdoin, president of the Massachusetts council, may throw some light on his motives for delaying to obey the orders of the commander-in-chief.

"Before the unfortunate affair at Fort Washington it was my opinion that the two armies—that on the east and that on the west side of the North River—must rest each on its own bottom; that the idea of detaching and reinforcing from one side to the other on every motion of the enemy was chimerical; but to harbor such a thought in our present circumstances is absolute insanity. In this invasion, should the enemy alter the present direction of their operations and attempt to open the passage of the Highlands or enter New England, I should never entertain the thought of being succoured by the western army. I know it is impossible. We must therefore depend upon ourselves. To Connecticut and Massachusetts I shall look for assistance. . . . I hope the cursed job of Fort Washington will occasion no dejection. The place itself was of no value. For my own part, I am persuaded that if we only act with common sense, spirit and decision, the day must be our own."

In another letter to Bowdoin, dated on the following day and inclosing an extract from Washington's letter of Nov. 21st, he writes:

"Indecision bids fair for tumbling down the goodly fabric of American freedom and with it the rights of mankind. 'T was indecision of Congress prevented our having a noble army and on an excellent footing. 'T was indecision in our military councils which cost us the garrison of Fort Washington, the consequence of which must be fatal unless remedied in time by a contrary spirit. Inclosed I send you an extract of a letter from the general, on which you will make your comments, and I have no doubt you will concur with me in the necessity of raising immediately an army to save us from perdition. Affairs appear in so important a crisis that I think the resolves of the Congress must no longer too nicely weigh with us. We must save the community in spite of the ordinances of the Legislature. There are times when we must commit treason against the laws of the State, for the salvation of the State. The present crisis demands this brave, virtuous kind of treason." He urges President Bowdoin, therefore, to waive all formalities and not only complete the regiments prescribed to the province but to add four companies to each regiment. "We must not only have a force sufficient to cover your province, and all these fertile districts, from the insults and irruptions of the tyrant's troops, but sufficient to drive 'em out of all their quarters in the Jerseys, or all is lost. . . . In the meantime, send up a formidable body of militia to supply the place of the continental troops, which I am ordered to convey over the river. Let your people be well supplied with blankets and warm clothes, as I am determined, by the help of God, to unnest 'em even in the dead of winter."[2]

It is evident Lee considered Washington's star to be on the decline and his own in the ascendant. The "affair of Fort Washington" and the "indecision of the commander-in-chief" were apparently his watchwords.

On the following day (24th) he writes to Washington from Northcastle on the subject of removing troops across the Hudson.

"I have received your orders and shall endeavor to put them in execution, but question whether I shall be able to carry with me any considerable number, not so much from a want of zeal in the men as from their wretched condition with respect to shoes, stockings and blankets, which the present bad weather renders more intolerable. I sent Heath orders to transport two thousand men across the river, apprise the general and wait for further orders; but that great man (as I might have expected) intrenched himself within the letter of his instructions and refused to part with a single file, though I undertook to replace them with a part of my own." He concludes by showing that, so far from hurrying to the support of his commander-in-chief, he was meditating a side blow of his own devising. "I should march this day with Glover's brigade, but have just received intelligence that Rogers' corps, a part of the light horse and another brigade lie in so exposed a situation as to present us the fairest opportunity of carrying them off. If we succeed it will have a great effect and amply compensate for two days' delay."

Scarce had Lee sent this letter when he received one from Washington, informing him that he had mistaken his views in regard to the troops required to cross the Hudson. It was his (Lee's) division that he wanted to have over. The force under Heath must remain to guard the posts and passes through the Highlands, the importance of which was so infinitely great that there should not be the least possible risk of losing them. In the same letter Washington, who presumed Lee was by this time at Peekskill, advised him to take every precaution to come by a safe route, and by all means to keep between the enemy and the mountains, as he understood they were taking measures to intercept his march.

Lee's reply was still from Northcastle. He explained that his idea of detaching troops from Heath's division was merely for expedition's sake, intending to replace them from his own. The want of carriages and other causes had delayed him. From the force of the enemy remaining in Westchester County, he did not conceive the number of them in the Jerseys to be near so great as Washington was taught to believe. He had been making a sweep of the country to clear it of the tories. Part of his army had now moved on, and he would set out on the following day. He concluded with the assurance, "I shall take care to obey your Excellency's orders in regard to my march as exactly as possible."

On the same day he vents his spleen in a tart letter to Heath. "I perceive," writes he, "that you have formed an idea that should General Washington remove to the Straits of Magellan, the instructions he left with you upon a particular occasion have, to all intents and purposes, invested you with a command separate from and independent of any other superiors. . . . That General Heath is by no means to consider himself obliged to obey the second in command." He concluded by informing him that, as the commander-in-chief was now separated from them, he (Lee) commanded, of course, on this side of the water, and for the future would and must be obeyed.

Before receiving this letter, Heath, doubtful whether Washington might not be pressed and desirous of having his troops across the Hudson, had sent off an express to him for explicit instructions on that point and, in the meantime, had kept them ready for a move.

General George Clinton, who was with him and had the safety of the Hudson at heart, was in an agony of solicitude. "We have been under marching orders these three days past," writes he, "and only wait the directions of General Washington. Should they be to move, all's over with the river this season and, I fear, forever. General Lee, four or five days ago, had orders to move with his division across the river. Instead of so doing, he ordered General Heath to march his men through, and he would replace them with so many of his. General Heath could not do this consistent with his instructions, but put his men under marching orders to wait his Excellency's orders."

The return of the express sent to Washington relieved Clinton's anxiety about the Highlands; reiterating the original order, that the division under Heath should remain for the protection of the passes.

Washington was still at Newark when, on the 27th, he received Lee's letter of the 24th, speaking of his scheme of capturing Rogers the partisan. Under other circumstances it might have been a sufficient excuse for his delay, but higher interests were at stake. He immediately wrote to Lee as follows: "My former letters were so full and explicit as to the necessity of your marching as early as possible, that it is unnecessary to add more on that head. I confess I expected you would have been sooner in motion. The force here, when joined by yours, will not be adequate to any great opposition. At present it is weak, and it has been more owing to the badness of the weather that the enemy's progress has been checked, than any resistance we could make. They are now pushing this way—part of 'em have passed the Passaic. Their plan is not entirely unfolded, but I shall not be surprised if Philadelphia should turn out the object of their movement."

The situation of the little army was daily becoming more perilous. In a council of war several of the members urged a move to Morristown to form a junction with the troops expected from the Northern army. Washington, however, still cherished the idea of making a stand at Brunswick on the Raritan, or, at all events, of disputing the passage of the Delaware, and in this intrepid resolution he was warmly seconded by Greene.

Breaking up his camp once more, therefore, he continued his retreat towards New Brunswick, but so close was Cornwallis upon him that his advance entered one end of Newark just as the American rear-guard had left the other.

From Brunswick, Washington wrote on the 29th to William Livingston, governor of the Jerseys, requesting him to have all boats and river craft for seventy miles along the Delaware removed to the western bank out of the reach of the enemy and put under guard. He was disappointed in his hope of making a stand on the banks of the Raritan. All the force he could muster at Brunswick, including the New Jersey militia, did not exceed four thousand men. Colonel Reed had failed in procuring aid from the New Jersey legislature. That body, shifting from place to place, was on the eve of dissolution. The term of the Maryland and New Jersey troops in the flying camp had expired. General Mercer endeavored to detain them, representing the disgrace of turning their back upon the cause when the enemy was at hand. His remonstrances were fruitless. As to the Pennsylvania levies, they deserted in such numbers that guards were stationed on the roads and ferries to intercept them.

At this moment of care and perplexity a letter, forwarded by express, arrived at headquarters. It was from General Lee, dated from his camp at Northcastle, to Colonel Reed, and was in reply to the letter written by that officer from Hackensack on the 21st, which we have already laid before the reader. Supposing that it related to official business, Washington opened it and read as follows:

"My Dear Reed, I received your most obliging, flattering letter; lament with you that fatal indecision of mind which in war is a much greater disqualification than stupidity or even want of personal courage. Accident may put a decisive blunderer in the right, but eternal defeat and miscarriage must attend the man of the best parts if cursed with indecision. The general recommends in so pressing a manner as almost to amount to an order, to bring over the continental troops under my command, which recommendation or order throws me into the greatest dilemma from several considerations." After stating these considerations, he adds: "My reason for not having marched already is that we have just received intelligence that Rogers' corps, the light horse, part of the Highlanders, and another brigade lie in so exposed a situation as to give the fairest opportunity of being carried. I should have attempted it last night but the rain was too violent, and when our pieces are wet, you know our troops are *hors de combat*. This night I hope will be better. . . . I only wait myself for this business of Rogers and company being over. I shall then fly to you, for, to confess a truth, I really think our chief will do better with me than without me."

A glance over this letter sufficed to show Washington that, at this dark moment, when he most needed support and sympathy, his character and military conduct were the subject of disparaging comments between the friend in whom he had so implicitly confided and a sarcastic and apparently self-constituted rival. Whatever may have been his feelings of wounded pride and outraged friendship, he restrained them, and inclosed the letter to Reed with the following chilling note:

"Dear Sir, The inclosed was put into my hands by an express from White Plains. Having no idea of its being a private letter, much less suspecting the tendency of the correspondence, I opened it, as I have done all other letters to you from the same place, and Peekskill, upon the business of your office, as I conceived and found them to be. This, as it is the truth, must be my excuse for seeing the contents of a letter which neither inclination nor intention would have prompted me to," etc.

The very calmness and coldness of this note must have had a greater effect upon Reed than could have been produced by the most vehement reproaches. In subsequent communications he endeavored to explain away the offensive paragraphs in Lee's letter, dclaring there was nothing in his own inconsistent with the respect and affection he had ever borne for Washington's person and character.

Fortunately for Reed, Washington never saw that letter. There were passages in it beyond the reach of softening explanation. As it was, the purport of it as reflected in Lee's reply had given him a sufficient shock. His magnanimous nature, however, was incapable of harboring long resentments, especially in matters relating solely to himself. His personal respect for Colonel Reed continued. He invariably manifested a high sense of his merits and consulted him, as before, on military affairs, but his hitherto affectionate confidence in him as a sympathizing friend had received an incurable wound. His letters, before so frequent and such perfect outpourings of heart and mind, became few and far between and confined to matters of business.

It must have been consoling to Washington at this moment of bitterness to receive the following letter (dated Nov. 27th) from William Livingston, the intelligent and patriotic governor of New Jersey. It showed that while many misjudged him and friends seemed falling from his side, others appreciated him truly and the ordeal he was undergoing.

"I can easily form some idea of the difficulties under which you labor," writes Livingston, "particularly of one for which the public can make no allowance, because your prudence and fidelity to the cause will not suffer you to reveal it to the public; an instance of magnanimity, superior, perhaps, to any that can be shown in battle. But depend upon it, my dear sir, the impartial world will do you ample justice before long. May God support you under the fatigue, both of body and mind, to which you must be constantly exposed."

Washington lingered at Brunswick until the 1st of December in the vain hope of being reinforced. The enemy in the meantime advanced through the country, impressing wagons and horses and collecting cattle and sheep, as if for a distant march. At length their vanguard appeared on the opposite side of the Raritan. Washington immediately broke down the end of the bridge next the village and after nightfall resumed his retreat. In the meantime, as the river was fordable, Captain Alexander Hamilton planted his field-pieces on high, commanding ground and opened a spirited fire to check any attempt of the enemy to cross.

At Princeton, Washington left twelve hundred men in two brigades under Lord Stirling and General Adam Stephen to cover the country and watch the motions of the enemy. Stephen was the same officer that had served as a colonel under Washington in the French war as second in command of the Virginia troops, and had charge of Fort Cumberland. In consideration of his courage and military capacity he had in 1764 been intrusted with the protection of the frontier. He had recently brought a detachment of Virginia troops to the army and received from Congress in September the commission of brigadier-general.

The harassed army reached Trenton on the 2d of December. Washington immediately proceeded to remove his baggage and stores across the Delaware. In his letters from this place to the President of Congress, he gives his reasons for his continued retreat.

"Nothing but necessity obliged me to retire before the enemy and leave so much of the Jerseys unprotected. Sorry am I to observe that the frequent calls upon the militia of this State, the want of exertion in the principal gentlemen of the country, and a fatal supineness and insensibility of danger till it is too late to prevent an evil that was not only foreseen but foretold, have been the causes of our late disgraces.

"If the militia of this State had stepped forth in season (and timely notice they had), we might have prevented the enemy's

crossing the Hackensack. We might with equal possibility of success have made a stand at Brunswick on the Raritan. But as both
these rivers were fordable in a variety of places, being knee deep
only, it required many men to guard the passes, and these we had
not."

In excuse for the people of New Jersey, it may be observed that
they inhabited an open, agricultural country, where the sound of
war had never been heard. Many of them looked upon the Revolution as rebellion. Others thought it a ruined enterprise. The armies
engaged in it had been defeated and broken up. They beheld the
commander-in-chief retreating through their country with a handful of men, weary, wayworn, dispirited, without tents, without
clothing, many of them barefooted, exposed to wintry weather,
and driven from post to post by a well-clad, well-fed, triumphant
force tricked out in all the glittering bravery of war. Could it be
wondered at that peaceful husbandmen, seeing their quiet fields
thus suddenly overrun by adverse hosts and their very hearthstones
threatened with outrage should, instead of flying to arms, seek for
the safety of their wives and little ones and the protection of their
humble means from the desolation which too often marks the
course even of friendly armies?

Lord Howe and his brother sought to profit by this dismay and
despondency. A proclamation dated 30th of November commanded all persons in arms against His Majesty's government to
disband and return home, and all Congresses to desist from
treasonable acts; offering a free pardon to all who should comply
within fifty days.

Many who had been prominent in the cause hastened to take
advantage of this proclamation. Those who had most property to
lose were the first to submit. The middle ranks remained generally
steadfast in this time of trial.[3]

The following extract of a letter from a field-officer in New
York, dated December 2d, to his friend in London, gives the British view of affairs.

"The rebels continue flying before our army. Lord Cornwallis
took the fort opposite Brunswick, plunged into Raritan River and
seized the town. Mr. Washington had orders from the Congress to
rally and defend that post but he sent them word he could not. He
was seen retreating with two brigades to Trenton, where they talk

[3] Gordon's *Hist. Am. War*, ii., p. 129.

of resisting, but such a panic has seized the rebels that no part of the Jerseys will hold them, and I doubt whether Philadelphia itself will stop their career. The Congress have lost their authority. . . . They are in such consternation that they know not what to do. The two Adamses are in New England, Franklin gone to France. Lynch has lost his senses. Rutledge has gone home disgusted. Dana is persecuting at Albany. And Jay's in the country playing as bad a part. So that the fools have lost the assistance of the knaves. However, should they embrace the inclosed proclamation they may yet escape the halter. . . . Honest David Matthew, the mayor, has made his escape from them and arrived here this day."[4]

In this dark day of peril to the cause and to himself Washington remained firm and undaunted. In casting about for some stronghold where he might make a desperate stand for the liberties of his country, his thoughts reverted to the mountain regions of his early campaigns. General Mercer was at hand, who had shared his perils among these mountains, and his presence may have contributed to bring them to his mind. "What think you," said Washington, "if we should retreat to the back parts of Pennsylvania, would the Pennsylvanians support us?"

"If the lower counties give up, the back counties will do the same," was the discouraging reply.

"We must then retire to Augusta County in Virginia," said Washington. "Numbers will repair to us for safety and we will try a predatory war. If overpowered, we must cross the Alleghanies."

Such was the indomitable spirit, rising under difficulties and buoyant in the darkest moment, that kept our tempest-tossed cause from foundering.

[4] *Am. Archives*, 5th Series, iii., 1037.

Chapter 26

CAPTURE OF GENERAL LEE

Notwithstanding the repeated and pressing orders and entreaties of the commander-in-chief, Lee did not reach Peekskill until the 30th of November. In a letter of that date to Washington, who had complained of his delay, he simply alleged difficulties, which he would explain *when both had leisure*. His scheme to entrap Rogers, the renegade, had failed. The old Indian hunter had been too much on the alert. He boasted, however, to have rendered more service by his delay than he would have done had he moved sooner. His forces were thereby augmented, so that he expected to enter the Jerseys with four thousand firm and willing men, who would make *a very important diversion*.

"The day after to-morrow," added he, "we shall pass the river, when I should be glad to receive your instructions, but I could wish you would bind me as little as possible, not from any opinion, I do assure you, of my own parts, but from a persuasion that detached generals cannot have too great latitude unless they are very incompetent indeed."

Lee had calculated upon meeting no further difficulty in obtaining men from Heath. He rode to that general's quarters in the evening and was invited by him to alight and take tea. On entering the house, Lee took Heath aside and, alluding to his former refusal to supply troops as being inconsistent with the orders of the commander-in-chief, "In point of *law*," said he, "you are right, but in point of policy I think you are wrong. I am going into the Jerseys for the salvation of America. I wish to take with me a larger force than I now have, and request you to order two thousand of your men to march with me."

Heath answered that he could not spare that number. He was then asked to order one thousand, to which he replied that the business might be as well brought to a point at once—that not a single man should march from the post by *his* order.

"Then," exclaimed Lee, "I will order them myself."

"That makes a wide difference," rejoined Heath. "You are my senior, but I have received positive written instructions from him who is superior to us both, and I will not *myself* break those orders."

In proof of his words Heath produced the recent letter received from Washington, repeating his former orders that no troops should be removed from that post. Lee glanced over the letter.

"The commander-in-chief is now at a distance and does not know what is necessary here so well as I do."

He asked a sight of the return book of the division. It was brought by Major Huntington, the deputy adjutant-general. Lee ran his eye over it and chose two regiments.

"You will order them to march early to-morrow morning to join me," said he to the major.

Heath, ruffling with the pride of military law, turned to the major with an air of authority.

"Issue such orders at your peril!" exclaimed he. Then addressing Lee, "Sir," said he, "if you come to this post and mean to issue orders here which will break the positive ones I have received, I pray you to do it completely yourself and through your own deputy adjutant-general who is present, and not draw me or any of my family in as partners in the guilt."

"It is right," said Lee. "Colonel Scammel, do you issue the order."

It was done accordingly. But Heath's punctilious scruples were not yet satisfied.

"I have one more request to make, sir," said he to Lee, "and that is that you will be pleased to give me a certificate that you *exercise command* at this post and order from it these regiments."

Lee hesitated to comply, but George Clinton, who was present, told him he could not refuse a request so reasonable. He accordingly wrote, "For the satisfaction of General Heath and at his request, I do certify that I am commanding officer at this present writing in this post and that I have in that capacity ordered Prescott's and Wyllis' regiments to march."

Heath's military punctilio was satisfied and he smoothed his ruffled plumes. Early the next morning the regiments moved from their cantonments ready to embark, when Lee again rode up to his door. "Upon further consideration," said he, "I have concluded not to take the two regiments with me—you may order them to return to their former post."

"This conduct of General Lee," adds Heath in his memoirs, "appeared not a little extraordinary, and one is almost at a loss to account for it. He had been a soldier from his youth, had a perfect knowledge of service in all its branches, but was rather obstinate in his temper and could scarcely brook being crossed in anything in the line of his profession."[1]

It was not until the 4th of December that Lee crossed the Hudson and began a laggard march, though aware of the imminent peril of Washington and his army—how different from the celerity of his movements in his expedition to the South!

In the meantime Washington, who was at Trenton, had profited by a delay of the enemy at Brunswick and removed most of the stores and baggage of the army across the Delaware. And, being reinforced by fifteen hundred of the Pennsylvania militia procured by Mifflin, [he] prepared to face about and march back to Princeton with such of his troops as were fit for service, there to be governed by circumstances and the movements of General Lee. Accordingly, on the 5th of December he sent about twelve hundred men in the advance to reinforce Lord Stirling, and the next day set off himself with the residue.

"The general has gone forward to Princeton," writes Colonel Reed, "where there are about three thousand men, with which, I fear, he will not be able to make any stand."[2]

While on the march, Washington received a letter from Greene, who was at Princeton, informing him of a report that Lee was "at the heels of the enemy." "I should think," adds Greene, "he had better keep on the flanks than the rear, unless it were possible to concert an attack at the same instant of time in front and rear. . . . I think General Lee must be confined within the lines of some general plan or else his operations will be independent of yours. His own troops, General St. Clair's and the militia must form a respectable army."

Lee had no idea of conforming to a general plan. He had an independent plan of his own and was at that moment at Pompton,

[1] The above scene is given almost literally from General Heath's *Memoirs*.
[2] Reed to the President of Congress.

indulging speculations on military greatness and the lamentable want of it in his American contemporaries. In a letter from that place to Governor Cooke of Rhode Island, he imparts his notions on the subject. "Theory joined to practice, or a heaven-born genius, can alone constitute a general. As to the latter, God Almighty indulges the world very rarely with the spectacle, and I do not know, from what I have seen, that he has been more profuse of this ethereal spirit to the Americans than to other nations."

While Lee was thus loitering and speculating, Cornwallis, knowing how far he was in the rear and how weak was the situation of Washington's army, and being himself strongly reinforced, made a forced march from Brunswick and was within two miles of Princeton. Stirling, to avoid being surrounded, immediately set out with two brigades for Trenton. Washington, too, receiving intelligence by express of these movements, hastened back to that place and caused boats to be collected from all quarters, and the stores and troops transported across the Delaware. He himself crossed with the rear-guard on Sunday morning and took up his quarters about a mile from the river, causing the boats to be destroyed and troops to be posted opposite the fords. He was conscious, however, as he said, that with his small force he could make no great opposition should the enemy bring boats with them. Fortunately they did not come thus provided.

The rear-guard, says an American account, had barely crossed the river when Lord Cornwallis "came marching down with all the pomp of war, in great expectation of getting boats and immediately pursuing." Not one was to be had there or elsewhere, for Washington had caused the boats for an extent of seventy miles up and down the river to be secured on the right bank. His lordship was effectually brought to a stand. He made some moves with two columns, as if he would cross the Delaware above and below, either to push on to Philadelphia or to entrap Washington in the acute angle made by the bend of the river opposite Bordentown. An able disposition of American troops along the upper part of the river, and of a number of galleys below, discouraged any attempt of the kind. Cornwallis therefore gave up the pursuit, distributed the German troops in cantonments along the left bank of the river and stationed his main force at Brunswick, trusting to be able before long to cross the Delaware on the ice.

On the 8th, Washington wrote to the President of Congress:

"There is not a moment's time to be lost in assembling such a force as can be collected, as the object of the enemy cannot now be doubted in the smallest degree. Indeed, I shall be out in my conjecture, for it is only conjecture, if the late embarkation at New York is not for Delaware River to co-operate with the army under General Howe, who, I am informed from good authority, is with the British troops, and his whole force upon this route. I have no certain intelligence of General Lee, although I have sent expresses to him and lately a Colonel Humpton, to bring me some accurate accounts of his situation. I last night despatched another gentleman to him (Major Hoops), desiring he would hasten his march to the Delaware, on which I would provide boats near a place called Alexandria, for the transportation of his troops. I cannot account for the slowness of his march."

In further letters to Lee, Washington urged the peril of Philadelphia. "Do come on," writes he. "Your arrival may be fortunate and, if it can be effected without delay, it may be the means of preserving a city whose loss must prove of the most fatal consequence to the cause of America."

Putnam was now detached to take command of Philadelphia and put it in a state of defense, and General Mifflin to have charge of the munitions of war deposited there. By their advice Congress hastily adjourned on the 12th of December, to meet again on the 20th at Baltimore.

Washington's whole force at this time was about five thousand five hundred men, one thousand of them Jersey militia, fifteen hundred militia from Philadelphia, and a battalion of five hundred of the German yeomanry of Pennsylvania. Gates, however, he was informed, was coming on with seven regiments detached by Schuyler from the Northern department. Reinforced by these and the troops under Lee, he hoped to be able to attempt a stroke upon the enemy's forces, which lay a good deal scattered and, to all appearances, in a state of security. "A lucky blow in this quarter," writes he, "would be fatal to them and would most certainly raise the spirits of the people, which are quite sunk by our late misfortunes."[3]

While cheering himself with these hopes and trusting to speedy aid from Lee, that wayward commander, though nearly three

<hr>

[3] Washington to Gov. Trumbull, 14th Dec.

weeks had elapsed since he had received Washington's orders and entreaties to join him with all possible despatch, was no farther on his march than Morristown in the Jerseys, where, with militia recruits, his force was about four thousand men. In a letter written by him on the 8th of December to a committee of Congress, he says: "If I was not taught to think the army with General Washington had been considerably reinforced I should immediately join him, but as I am assured he is very strong I should imagine we can make a better impression by beating up and harassing their detached parties in their rear, for which purpose a good post at Chatham seems the best calculated. It is a happy distance from Newark, Elizabethtown, Woodbridge and Boundbrook. We shall, I expect, annoy, distract and consequently weaken them in a desultory war."[4]

On the same day he writes from Chatham in reply to Washington's letter by Major Hoops, just received: "I am extremely shocked to hear that your force is so inadequate to the necessity of your situation, as I had been taught to think you had been considerably reinforced. Your last letters proposing a plan of surprises and forced marches convinced me that there was no danger of your being obliged to pass the Delaware, in consequence of which proposals I have put myself in a position the most convenient to co-operate with you by attacking their rear. I cannot persuade myself that Philadelphia is their object at present. . . . It will be difficult, I am afraid, to join you, but cannot I do you more service by attacking their rear?"

This letter, sent by a light-horseman, received an instant reply from Washington. "Philadelphia, beyond all question, is the object of the enemy's movements, and nothing less than our utmost exertions will prevent General Howe from possessing it. The force I have is weak, and utterly incompetent to that end. I must therefore entreat you to push on with every possible succor you can bring."[5]

On the 9th, Lee, who was at Chatham, received information from Heath that three of the regiments detached under Gates from the Northern army had arrived from Albany at Pe. kskill. He instantly writes to him to forward them without loss of time to

[4] Am. Archives, 5th Series, iii., 1121.
[5] Am. Archives, 5th Series, iii., 1138.

Morristown. "I am in hopes," adds he, "to reconquer (if I may so express myself) the Jerseys. It was really in the hands of the enemy before my arrival."

On the 11th, Lee writes to Washington from Morristown, where he says his troops had been obliged to halt two days for want of shoes. He now talked of crossing the great Brunswick post-road and, by a forced night's march, making his way to the ferry above Burlington, where boats should be sent up from Philadelphia to receive him.

"I am much surprised," writes Washington in reply, "that you should be in any doubt respecting the route you should take, after the information you have received upon that head. A large number of boats was procured and is still retained at Tinicum under a strong guard to facilitate your passage across the Delaware. I have so frequently mentioned our situation and the necessity of your aid that it is painful for me to add a word on the subject. . . . Congress have directed Philadelphia to be defended to the last extremity. The fatal consequences that must attend its loss are but too obvious to every one. Your arrival may be the means of saving it."

In detailing the close of General Lee's march, so extraordinary for its tardiness, we shall avail ourselves of the memoir, already cited, of General Wilkinson, who was at that time a brigade major about twenty-two years of age and was accompanying General Gates, who had been detached by Schuyler with seven regiments to reinforce Washington. Three of these regiments had descended the Hudson to Peekskill and were ordered by Lee to Morristown. Gates had embarked with the remaining four, and landed with them at Esopus, whence he took a back route by the Delaware and the Minisink.

On the 11th of December he was detained by a heavy snow-storm in a sequestered valley near the Wallpeck in New Jersey. Being cut off from all information respecting the adverse armies, he detached Major Wilkinson to seek Washington's camp with a letter stating the force under his command and inquiring what route he should take. Wilkinson crossed the hills on horseback to Sussex court-house, took a guide and proceeded down the country. Washington, he soon learnt, had passed the Delaware several days before. The boats, he was told, had been removed from the ferries, so that he would find some difficulty in getting over, but Major-

General Lee was at Morristown. Finding such obstacles in his way to the commander-in-chief, he determined to seek the second in command and ask orders from him for General Gates. Lee had decamped from Morristown on the 12th of December but had marched no farther than Vealtown, barely eight miles distant. There he left General Sullivan with the troops while he took up his quarters three miles off, at a tavern at Baskingridge. As there was not a British cantonment within twenty miles, he took but a small guard for his protection, thinking himself perfectly secure.

About four o'clock in the morning, Wilkinson arrived at his quarters. He was presented to the general as he lay in bed, and delivered into his hands the letter of General Gates. Lee, observing it was addressed to Washington, declined opening it until apprised by Wilkinson of its contents and the motives of his visit. He then broke the seal and recommended Wilkinson to take repose. The latter lay down on his blanket before a comfortable fire among the officers of his suite, "for we were not encumbered in those days," says he, "with beds or baggage."

Lee, naturally indolent, lingered in bed until eight o'clock. He then came down in his usual slovenly style, half-dressed, in slippers and blanket coat, his collar open and his linen apparently of some days' wear. After some inquiries about the campaign in the North, he gave Wilkinson a brief account of the operations of the main army, which he condemned in strong terms and in his usual sarcastic way. He wasted the morning in altercation with some of the militia, particularly the Connecticut light horse, "several of whom," says Wilkinson, "appeared in large, full-bottomed perukes and were treated very irreverently. One wanted forage, another his horse shod, another his pay, a fourth provisions, etc., to which the general replied: 'Your wants are numerous but you have not mentioned the last—you want to go home and shall be indulged, for d—— you, you do no good here.'"

Colonel Scammel, the adjutant-general, called from General Sullivan for orders concerning the morning march. After musing a moment or two, Lee asked him if he had a manuscript map of the country. It was produced and spread upon a table. Wilkinson observed Lee trace with his finger the route from Vealtown to Pluckamin, thence to Somerset court-house, and on by Rocky Hill to Princeton. He then returned to Pluckamin and traced the route in the same manner by Boundbrook to Brunswick, and after a close inspection carelessly said to Scammel: "Tell General Sullivan to move down towards Pluckamin; that I will soon be with him."

This, observes Wilkinson, was off his route to Alexandria on the Delaware, where he had been ordered to cross, and directly on that towards Brunswick and Princeton. He was convinced therefore that Lee meditated an attack on the British post at the latter place.

From these various delays they did not sit down to breakfast before ten o'clock. After breakfast Lee sat writing a reply to General Gates, in which, as usual, he indulged in sarcastic comments on the commander-in-chief.

"The ingenious manœuvre of Fort Washington," writes he, "has completely unhinged the goodly fabric we had been building. There never was so d—d a stroke. *Entre nous*, a certain great man is most damnably deficient. He has thrown me into a situation where I have my choice of difficulties: if I stay in this province I risk myself and army, and if I do not stay the province is lost forever. . . . As to what relates to yourself, if you think you can be in time to aid the general, I would have you by all means go. You will at least save your army," etc.[6]

While Lee was writing, Wilkinson was looking out of a window down a lane about a hundred yards in length, leading from the house to the main road. Suddenly a party of British dragoons turned a corner of the avenue at full charge. "Here, sir, are the British cavalry!" exclaimed Wilkinson.

"Where?" replied Lee, who had just signed his letter.

"Around the house!"—for they had opened file and surrounded it.

"Where is the guard? D—— the guard, why don't they fire?" Then after a momentary pause—"Do, sir, see what has become of the guard."

The guards, alas, unwary as their general, and chilled by the air of a frosty morning, had stacked their arms and repaired to the south side of a house on the opposite side of the road to sun themselves, and were now chased by the dragoons in different directions. In fact, a tory who had visited the general the evening before to complain of the loss of a horse taken by the army, having found where Lee was to lodge and breakfast, had ridden eighteen miles in the night to Brunswick and given the information and had piloted back Colonel Harcourt with his dragoons.[7]

The women of the house would fain have concealed Lee in a bed, but he rejected the proposition with disdain. Wilkinson, according to his own account, posted himself in a place where only one person could approach at a time, and there took his stand, a pistol in each hand, resolved to shoot the first and second assailant and then appeal to his sword. While in this "unpleasant situation," as he terms it, he heard a voice declare, "If the general does not surrender in five minutes I will set fire to the house!" After a short pause the threat was repeated with a solemn oath. Within two minutes he heard it proclaimed: "Here is the general. He has surrendered."

There was a shout of triumph, but a great hurry to make sure of the prize before the army should arrive to the rescue. A trumpet sounded the recall to the dragoons, who were chasing the scattered guards. The general, bareheaded and in his slippers and blanket coat, was mounted on Wilkinson's horse, which stood at the door, and the troop clattered off with their prisoner to Brunswick. In three hours the booming of the cannon in that direction told the exultation of the enemy.[8] They boasted of having taken the American Palladium, for they considered Lee the most scientific and experienced of the rebel generals.

On the departure of the troops, Wilkinson, finding the coast clear, ventured from his stronghold, repaired to the stable, mounted the first horse he could find and rode full speed in quest of General Sullivan, whom he found under march toward Pluckamin. He handed him the letter to Gates, written by Lee the moment before his capture, and still open. Sullivan, having read it, returned it to Wilkinson and advised him to rejoin General Gates without delay. For his own part, being now in command, he changed his route and pressed forward to join the commander-in-chief.

The loss of Lee was a severe shock to the Americans, many of whom, as we have shown, looked to him as the man who was to rescue them from their critical and well-nigh desperate situation. With their regrets, however, were mingled painful doubts, caused

[7] Joseph Trumbull to Governor Trumbull. *Am. Archives*, 5th Series, iii., 1265.
[8] *Ibid.*

by his delay in obeying the repeated summons of his commander-in-chief when the latter was in peril, and by his exposing himself so unguardedly in the very neighborhood of the enemy. Some at first suspected that he had done so designedly and with collusion, but this was soon disapproved by the indignities attending his capture, and his rigorous treatment subsequently by the British, who affected to consider him a deserter from his having formerly served in their army.

Wilkinson, who was at that time conversant with the cabals of the camp and apparently in the confidence of some of the leaders, points out what he considers the true secret of Lee's conduct. His military reputation, originally very high, had been enhanced of late by its being generally known that he had been opposed to the occupation of Fort Washington; while the fall of that fortress and other misfortunes of the campaign, though beyond the control of the commander-in-chief, had quickened the discontent which, according to Wilkinson, had been generated against him at Cambridge, and raised a party against him in Congress.

"It was confidently asserted at the time," adds he, "but is not worthy of credit, that a motion had been made in that body tending to supersede him in the command of the army. In this temper of the times, if General Lee had anticipated General Washington in cutting the cordon of the enemy between New York and the Delaware, the commander-in-chief would probably have been superseded. In this case, Lee would have succeeded him."

What an unfortunate change would it have been for the country! Lee was undoubtedly a man of brilliant talents, shrewd sagacity and much knowledge and experience in the art of war, but he was wilful and uncertain in his temper, self-indulgent in his habits and an egoist in warfare, boldly dashing for a soldier's glory rather than warily acting for a country's good. He wanted those great moral qualities which, in addition to military capacity, inspired such universal confidence in the wisdom, rectitude and patriotism of Washington, enabling him to direct and control legislative bodies as well as armies; to harmonize the jarring passions and jealousies of a wide and imperfect confederacy; and to cope with the varied exigencies of the Revolution.

The very retreat which Washington had just effected through the Jerseys bore evidence to his generalship. Thomas Paine, who had accompanied the army "from Fort Lee to the edge of Pennsylvania," thus speaks in one of his writings published at the time: "With a handful of men we sustained an orderly retreat for nearly an hundred miles, brought off our ammunition, all our field-pieces, the greatest part of our stores, and had four rivers to pass. None can say that our retreat was precipitate, for we were three weeks in performing it, that the country might have time to come in. Twice we marched back to meet the enemy and remained out until dark. The sign of fear was not seen in our camp, and had not some of the cowardly and disaffected inhabitants spread false alarms through the country, the Jerseys had never been ravaged."

And this is his testimony to the moral qualities of the commander-in-chief, as evinced in this time of perils and hardships: "Voltaire has remarked that King William never appeared to full advantage but in difficulties and in action. The same remark may be made of General Washington, for the character fits him. There is a natural firmness in some minds which cannot be unlocked by trifles but which, when unlocked, discovers a cabinet of fortitude; and I reckon it among those kinds of public blessings which we do not immediately see, that God hath blessed him with uninterrupted health and given him a mind that can even flourish upon care."[9]

[9] *American Crisis*, No. 1.

Chapter 27

DEFEAT OF THE BRITISH AT TRENTON

"Before you receive this letter," writes Washington to his brother Augustine, "you will undoubtedly have heard of the captivity of General Lee. This is an additional misfortune and the more vexatious as it was by his own folly and imprudence and without a view to effect any good that he was taken. As he went to lodge three miles out of his own camp and within twenty miles of the enemy, a rascally tory rode in the night to give notice of it to the enemy, who sent a party of light horse that seized him and carried him off with every mark of triumph and indignity."

This is the severest comment that the magnanimous spirit of Washington permitted him to make on the conduct and fortunes of the man who would have supplanted him, and this is made in his private correspondence with his brother. No harsh strictures on them appear in his official letters to Congress or the Board of War; nothing but regret for his capture, as a loss to the service.

In the same letter he speaks of the critical state of affairs. "If every nerve is not strained to recruit the army with all possible expedition, I think the game is pretty nearly up. . . . You can form no idea of the perplexity of my situation. No man I believe ever had a greater choice of evils and less means to extricate himself from them. However, under a full persuasion of the justice of our cause, I cannot entertain an idea that it will finally sink, though it may remain for some time under a cloud."

Fortunately, Congress, prior to their adjournment, had resolved that "until they should otherwise order, General Washington should be possessed of all power to order and direct all things relative to the department and to the operations of war." Thus empowered, he proceeded immediately to recruit three battalions of artillery. To those whose terms were expiring, he promised an augmentation of twenty-five per cent upon their pay, and a bounty of ten dollars to the men for six weeks' service.

"It was no time," he said, "to stand upon expense, nor in matters of self-evident exigency to refer to Congress at the distance of a hundred and thirty or forty miles." "If any good officers will offer to raise men upon continental pay and establishment in this quarter, I shall encourage them to do so, and regiment them when they have done it. It may be thought that I am going a good deal out of the line of my duty to adopt these measures or to advise thus freely. A character to lose, an estate to forfeit, the inestimable blessings of liberty at stake and a life devoted must be my excuse."[1]

The promise of increased pay and bounties had kept together for a time the dissolving army. The local militia began to turn out freely. Colonel John Cadwalader, a gentleman of gallant spirit and cultivated mind and manners, brought a large volunteer detachment, well equipped, and composed principally of Philadelphia troops. Washington, who held Cadwalader in high esteem, assigned him an important station at Bristol, with Colonel Reed, who was his intimate friend, as an associate. They had it in charge to keep a watchful eye upon Count Donop's Hessians, who were cantoned along the opposite shore from Bordentown to the Black Horse.

On the 20th of December arrived General Sullivan in camp, with the troops recently commanded by the unlucky Lee. They were in a miserable plight, destitute of almost everything, many of them fit only for the hospital, and those whose terms were nearly out, thinking of nothing but their discharge. About four hundred of them, who were Rhode Islanders, were sent down under Colonel Hitchcock to reinforce Cadwalader, who was now styled brigadier-general by courtesy lest the continental troops might object to act under his command.

On the same day arrived General Gates with the remnants of four regiments from the Northern army. With him came Wilkinson, who now resumed his station as brigade-major in St. Clair's brigade, to which he belonged. To his memoirs we are indebted for notices of the commander-in-chief. "When the divisions of Sullivan and Gates joined General Washington," writes Wilkinson, "he found his numbers increased, yet his difficulties were not

[1] Letter to the President of Congress.

sensibly diminished. Ten days would disband his corps and leave him 1,400 men, miserably provided in all things. I saw him in that gloomy period, dined with him and attentively marked his aspect. Always grave and thoughtful, he appeared at that time pensive and solemn in the extreme."

There were vivid schemes forming under that solemn aspect. The time seemed now propitious for the *coup de main* which Washington had of late been meditating. Everything showed careless confidence on the part of the enemy. Howe was in winter quarters at New York. His troops were loosely cantoned about the Jerseys, from the Delaware to Brunswick, so that they could not readily be brought to act in concert on a sudden alarm. The Hessians were in the advance, stationed along the Delaware, facing the American lines, which were along the west bank. Cornwallis, thinking his work accomplished, had obtained leave of absence and was likewise at New York, preparing to embark for England. Washington had now between five and six thousand men fit for service. With these he meditated to cross the river at night at different points and make simultaneous attacks upon the Hessian advance posts.

He calculated upon the eager support of his troops, who were burning to revenge the outrages on their homes and families committed by these foreign mercenaries. They considered the Hessians mere hirelings, slaves to a petty despot, fighting for sordid pay and actuated by no sentiment of patriotism or honor. They had rendered themselves the horror of the Jerseys by rapine, brutality and heartlessness. At first, their military discipline had inspired awe, but of late they had become careless and unguarded, knowing the broken and dispirited state of the Americans, and considering them incapable of any offensive enterprise.

A brigade of three Hessian regiments, those of Rahl, Lossberg and Knyphausen, was stationed at Trenton. Colonel Rahl had the command of the post at his own solicitation and in consequence of the laurels he had gained at White Plains and Fort Washington. We have before us journals of two Hessian lieutenants and a corporal, which give graphic particulars of the colonel and his post. According to their representations, he, with all his bravery, was little fitted for such an important command. He lacked the necessary vigilance and forecast.

One of the lieutenants speaks of him in a sarcastic vein and evidently with some degree of prejudice. According to his account, there was more bustle than business at the post. The men were harassed with watches, detachments and pickets, without purpose and without end. The cannon must be drawn forth every day from their proper places and paraded about the town, seemingly only to make a stir and uproar.

The lieutenant was especially annoyed by the colonel's passion for music. Whether his men when off duty were well or ill clad, whether they kept their muskets clean and bright and their ammunition in good order was of little moment to the colonel, he never inquired about it. But the music! that was the thing! the hautboys —he never could have enough of them. The main guard was at no great distance from his quarters, and the music could not linger there long enough. There was a church close by, surrounded by palings. The officer on guard must march round and round it with his men and musicians, looking, says the lieutenant, like a Catholic procession, wanting only the cross and the banner and chanting choristers.

According to the same authority, Rahl was a boon companion, made merry until a late hour in the night and then lay in bed until nine o'clock in the morning. When the officers came to parade between ten and eleven o'clock and presented themselves at headquarters, he was often in his bath, and the guard must be kept waiting half an hour longer. On parade, too, when any other commander would take occasion to talk with his staff officers and others upon duty about the concerns of the garrison, the colonel attended to nothing but the music—he was wrapped up in it, to the great disgust of the testy lieutenant.

And then, according to the latter, he took no precautions against the possibility of being attacked. A veteran officer, Major von Dechow, proposed that some works should be thrown up, where the cannon might be placed, ready against any assault. "Works!—pooh—pooh." The colonel made merry with the very idea, using an unseemly jest which we forbear to quote. "An assault by the rebels! Let them come! We'll at them with the bayonet."

The veteran Dechow gravely persisted in his counsel. "Herr Colonel," said he respectfully, "it costs almost nothing. If it does not help, it does not harm." The pragmatical lieutenant too joined in the advice and offered to undertake the work. The jovial colonel only repeated his joke, went away laughing at them both, and no works were thrown up.

The lieutenant, sorely nettled, observes sneeringly: "He believed the name of Rahl more fearful and redoubtable than all the works of Vauban and Cohorn, and that no rebel would dare to encounter it. A fit man truly to command a corps! And still more to defend a place lying so near an enemy having a hundred times his advantages. Everything with him was done heedlessly and without forecast."[2]

Such is the account given of this brave but inconsiderate and light-hearted commander; given, however, by an officer not of his regiment. The honest corporal already mentioned, who was one of Rahl's own men, does him more justice. According to his journal, rumors that the Americans meditated an attack had aroused the vigilance of the colonel, and on the 21st of December he had reconnoitered the banks of the Delaware with a strong detachment quite to Frankfort to see if there were any movements of the Americans indicative of an intention to cross the river. He had returned without seeing any but had since caused pickets and alarm posts to be stationed every night outside the town.[3]

Such was the posture of affairs at Trenton at the time the *coup de main* was meditated.

Whatever was to be done, however, must be done quickly, before the river was frozen. An intercepted letter had convinced Washington of what he had before suspected, that Howe was only waiting for that event to resume active operations, cross the river on the ice and push triumphantly to Philadelphia.

He communicated his project to Gates and wished him to go to Bristol, take command there and co-operate from that quarter. Gates, however, pleaded ill health and requested leave to proceed to Philadelphia.[4]

The request may have surprised Washington, considering the spirited enterprise that was on foot. But Gates, as has before been observed, had a disinclination to serve immediately under the commander-in-chief. Like Lee, he had a disparaging opinion of him, or rather an impatience of his supremacy. He had moreover an ulterior object in view. Having been disappointed and

2 Tagebuch eines Hessischen Officiers.—MS.
3 Tagebuch des Corporals Johannes Reuber.—MS.
4 Washington to Gates. Gates's papers.

chagrined in finding himself subordinate to General Schuyler in the Northern campaign, he was now intent on making interest among the members of Congress for an independent command. Washington urged that on his way to Philadelphia he would at least stop for a day or two at Bristol to concert a plan of operations with Reed and Cadwalader and adjust any little questions of etiquette and command that might arise between the continental colonels who had gone thither with Lee's troops and the volunteer officers stationed there.

He does not appear to have complied even with this request. According to Wilkinson's account, he took quarters at Newtown and set out thence for Baltimore on the 24th of December, the very date before that of the intended *coup de main*. He prevailed on Wilkinson to accompany him as far as Philadelphia. On the road he appeared to be much depressed in spirits but he relieved himself, like Lee, by criticising the plans of the commander-in-chief. "He frequently," writes Wilkinson, "expressed the opinion that, while Washington was watching the enemy above Trenton, they would construct bateaux, pass the Delaware in his rear and take possession of Philadelphia before he was aware. And that instead of vainly attempting to stop Sir William Howe at the Delaware, General Washington ought to retire to the south of the Susquehanna and there form an army. He said it was his intention to propose this measure to Congress at Baltimore and urged me to accompany him to that place, but my duty forbade the thought."

Here we have somewhat of a counterpart to Lee's project of eclipsing the commander-in-chief. Evidently the two military veterans who had once been in conclave with him at Mount Vernon considered the truncheon of command falling from his grasp.

The projected attack upon the Hessian posts was to be threefold.

1st. Washington was to cross the Delaware with a considerable force at McKonkey's Ferry (now Taylorsville), about nine miles above Trenton, and march down upon that place, where Rahl's cantonment comprised a brigade of fifteen hundred Hessians, a troop of British light horse and a number of chasseurs.

2d. General Ewing, with a body of Pennsylvania militia, was to cross at a ferry about a mile below Trenton, secure the bridge over the Assunpink Creek, a stream flowing along the south side of the town, and cut off any retreat of the enemy in that direction.

3d. General Putnam, with the troops occupied in fortifying Philadelphia and those under General Cadwalader, was to cross below Burlington and attack the lower posts under Count Donop. The several divisions were to cross the Delaware at night so as to be ready for simultaneous action by five o'clock in the morning.

Seldom is a combined plan carried into full operation. Symptoms of an insurrection in Philadelphia obliged Putnam to remain with some force in that city, but he detached five or six hundred of the Pennsylvania militia under Colonel Griffin, his adjutant-general, who threw himself into the Jerseys to be at hand to co-operate with Cadwalader.

A letter from Washington to Colonel Reed, who was stationed with Cadwalader, shows the anxiety of his mind and his consciousness of the peril of the enterprise.

"Christmas day at night, one hour before day, is the time fixed upon for our attempt upon Trenton. For Heaven's sake keep this to yourself, as the discovery of it may prove fatal to us, our numbers, I am sorry to say, being less than I had any conception of. Yet nothing but necessity, dire necessity, will, nay must, justify an attack. Prepare, and in concert with Griffin, attack as many of their posts as you possibly can, with a prospect of success. The more we can attack at the same instant, the more confusion we shall spread and the greater good will result from it. . . . I have ordered our men to be provided with three days' provision ready cooked, with which, and their blankets, they are to march. For if we are successful, which Heaven grant, and the circumstances favor, we may push on. I shall direct every ferry and ford to be well guarded and not a soul suffered to pass without an officer's going down with the permit. Do the same with you."

It has been said that Christmas night was fixed upon for the enterprise because the Germans are prone to revel and carouse on that festival, and it was supposed a great part of the troops would be intoxicated and in a state of disorder and confusion, but in truth Washington would have chosen an earlier day had it been in his power. "We could not ripen matters for the attack before the time mentioned," said he in his letter to Reed, "so much out of sorts and so much in want of everything are the troops under Sullivan."

Early on the eventful evening (Dec. 25th), the troops destined for Washington's part of the attack, about two thousand four hundred strong, with a train of twenty small pieces, were paraded near McKonkey's Ferry, ready to pass as soon as it grew dark, in the hope of being all on the other side by twelve o'clock. Washington repaired to the ground accompanied by Generals Greene, Sullivan, Mercer, Stephen and Lord Stirling. Greene was full of ardor for the enterprise, eager no doubt to wipe out the recollection of Fort Washington. It was indeed an anxious moment for all.

We have here some circumstances furnished to us by the memoirs of Wilkinson. That officer had returned from Philadelphia and brought a letter from Gates to Washington. There was some snow on the ground and he had traced the march of the troops for the last few miles by the blood from the feet of those whose shoes were broken. Being directed to Washington's quarters, he found him, he says, alone, with his whip in his hand, prepared to mount his horse. "When I presented the letter of General Gates to him, before receiving it, he exclaimed with solemnity, 'What a time is this to hand me letters!' I answered that I had been charged with it by General Gates. 'By General Gates! Where is he?' 'I left him this morning in Philadelphia.' 'What was he doing there?' 'I understood him that he was on his way to Congress.' He earnestly repeated, 'On his way to Congress!' then broke the seal, and I made my bow and joined General St. Clair on the bank of the river."

Did Washington surmise the incipient intrigues and cabals that were already aiming to undermine him? Had Gates's eagerness to push on to Congress, instead of remaining with the army in a moment of daring enterprise, suggested any doubts as to his object? Perhaps not. Washington's nature was too noble to be suspicious, and yet he had received sufficient cause to be distrustful.

Boats being in readiness, the troops began to cross about sunset. The weather was intensely cold. The wind was high, the current strong, the river full of floating ice. Colonel Glover with his amphibious regiment of Marblehead fishermen was in advance; the same who had navigated the army across the Sound in its retreat from Brooklyn on Long Island to New York. They were men accustomed to battle with the elements, yet with all their skill and experience the crossing was difficult and perilous. Washington, who had crossed with the troops, stood anxiously yet patiently on the eastern bank, while one precious hour after another elapsed until the transportation of the artillery should be effected. The night was dark and tempestuous, the drifting ice drove the boats out of their course and threatened them with destruction. Colonel Knox, who attended to the crossing of the artillery, assisted with his labors but still more with his "stentorian lungs," giving orders and directions.

It was three o'clock before the artillery was landed, and nearly four before the troops took up their line of march. Trenton was nine miles distant and not to be reached before daylight. To surprise it, therefore, was out of the question. There was no making a retreat without being discovered and harassed in repassing the river. Besides, the troops from the other points might have crossed, and co-operation was essential to their safety. Washington resolved to push forward and trust to Providence.

He formed the troops into two columns. The first he led himself, accompanied by Greene, Stirling, Mercer and Stephen. It was to make a circuit by the upper or Pennington road to the north of Trenton. The other, led by Sullivan and including the brigade of St. Clair, was to take the lower river road, leading to the west end of the town. Sullivan's column was to halt a few moments at a cross-road leading to Howland's Ferry to give Washington's column time to effect its circuit, so that the attack might be simultaneous. On arriving at Trenton they were to force the outer guards and push directly into the town before the enemy had time to form.

The Hessian journals before us enable us to give the reader a glance into the opposite camp on this eventful night. The situation of Washington was more critical than he was aware. Notwithstanding the secrecy with which his plans had been conducted, Colonel Rahl had received a warning from General Grant at Princeton of the intended attack, and of the very time it was to be made, but stating that it was to be by a detachment under Lord Stirling. Rahl was accordingly on the alert.

It so happened that about dusk of this very evening, when Washington must have been preparing to cross the Delaware, there were alarm guns and firing at the Trenton outpost. The whole garrison was instantly drawn out under arms, and Colonel Rahl hastened to the outpost. It was found in confusion, and six men wounded. A body of men had emerged from the woods, fired upon the picket and immediately retired.[5] Colonel Rahl, with two companies and a field-piece, marched through the woods and made the rounds of the outposts, but seeing and hearing nothing and finding all quiet, returned. Supposing this to be the attack against which he had been warned, and that it was "a mere flash in the pan," he relapsed into his feeling of security, and, as the night was cold and stormy, permitted the troops to return to their quarters and lay aside their arms. Thus the garrison and its unwary commander slept in fancied security at the very time that Washington and his troops were making their toilsome way across the Delaware. How perilous would have been their situation had their enemy been more vigilant!

It began to hail and snow as the troops commenced their march, and increased in violence as they advanced, the storm driving the sleet in their faces. So bitter was the cold that two of the men were frozen to death that night. The day dawned by the time Sullivan halted at the cross-road. It was discovered that the storm had rendered many of the muskets wet and useless. "What is to be done?" inquired Sullivan of St. Clair. "You have nothing for it but to push on and use the bayonet," was the reply. While some of the soldiers were endeavoring to clear their muskets, and squibbing off priming, Sullivan despatched an officer to apprise the commander-in-chief of the condition of their arms. He came back half dismayed by an indignant burst of Washington, who ordered him to return instantly and tell General Sullivan to "advance and charge."

It was about eight o'clock when Washington's column arrived in the vicinity of the village. The storm, which had rendered the march intolerable, had kept every one within doors, and the snow had deadened the tread of the troops and the rumbling of the artillery. As they approached the village, Washington, who was in front, came to a man that was chopping wood by the roadside, and inquired, "Which way is the Hessian picket?" "I don't know," was the surly reply. "You may tell," said Captain Forest of the ar-

---

[5] Who it was that made this attack upon the outpost is not clearly ascertained. The Hessian lieutenant who commanded at the picket says it was a patrol sent out by Washington, under command of a captain, to reconnoiter, with strict orders not to engage, but if discovered, to retire instantly as silently as possible. Colonel Reed, in a memorandum, says it was an advance party returning from the Jerseys to Pennsylvania.—See *Life and Corresp.*, vol. i., p. 277.

tillery, "for that is General Washington." The aspect of the man changed in an instant. Raising his hands to heaven, "God bless and prosper you!" cried he. "The picket is in that house, and the sentry stands near that tree." [6]

The advance guard was led by a brave young officer, Captain William A. Washington, seconded by Lieutenant James Monroe (in after years President of the United States). They received orders to dislodge the picket. Here happened to be stationed the very lieutenant whose censures of the negligence of Colonel Rahl we have just quoted. By his own account, he was very near being entrapped in the guard-house. His sentries, he says, were not alert enough, and had he not stepped out of the picket house himself and discovered the enemy, they would have been upon him before his men could scramble to their arms. "Der feind! Der feind! Heraus! Heraus!" (The enemy! The enemy! Turn out! Turn out!) was now the cry. He at first, he says, made a stand, thinking he had a mere marauding party to deal with; but seeing heavy battalions at hand, gave way and fell back upon a company stationed to support the picket, but which appears to have been no better prepared against surprise.

By this time the American artillery was unlimbered. Washington kept beside it, and the column proceeded. The report of fire-arms told that Sullivan was at the lower end of the town. Colonel Stark led his advance guard and did it in gallant style. The attacks, as concerted, were simultaneous. The outposts were driven in. They retreated, firing from behind houses. The Hessian drums beat to arms. The trumpets of the light horse sounded the alarm. The whole place was in an uproar. Some of the enemy made a wild and undirected fire from the windows of their quarters. Others rushed forth in disorder and attempted to form in the main street, while dragoons hastily mounted, and, galloping about, added to the confusion. Washington advanced with his column to the head of King Street, riding beside Captain Forest of the artillery. When Forest's battery of six guns was opened the general kept on the left and advanced with it, giving directions to the fire. His position was an exposed one and he was repeatedly entreated to fall back, but all such entreaties were useless when once he became heated in action.

The enemy were training a couple of cannon in the main street

[6] Wilkinson's *Memoirs*, vol. i., p. 129.

1. WASHINGTON, BY WERTMÜLLER

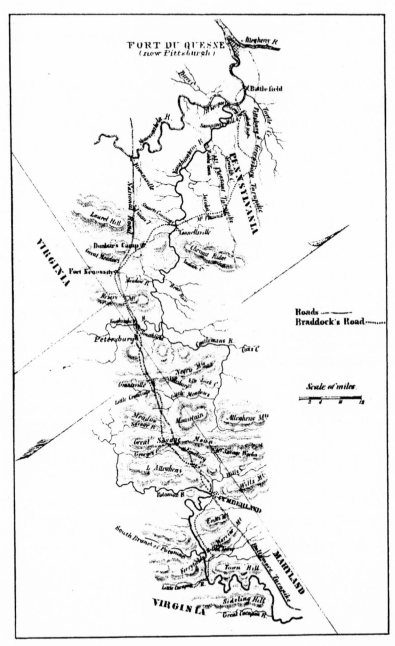

2. BRADDOCK'S ROUTE

3. WASHINGTON, BY PEALE

4. MARTHA WASHINGTON

to form a battery, which might have given the Americans a serious check, but Captain Washington and Lieutenant Monroe, with a part of the advanced guard, rushed forward, drove the artillerists from their guns and took the two pieces when on the point of being fired. Both of these officers were wounded, the captain in the wrist, the lieutenant in the shoulder.

While Washington advanced on the north of the town, Sullivan approached on the west and detached Stark to press on the lower or south end of the town. The British light horse and about five hundred Hessians and chasseurs had been quartered in the lower part of the town. Seeing Washington's column pressing in front and hearing Stark thundering in their rear, they took headlong flight by the bridge across the Assunpink, and so along the banks of the Delaware toward Count Donop's encampment at Bordentown. Had Washington's plan been carried into full effect, their retreat would have been cut off by General Ewing, but that officer had been prevented from crossing the river by the ice.

Colonel Rahl, according to the account of the lieutenant who had commanded the picket, completely lost his head in the confusion of the surprise. The latter, when driven in by the American advance, found the colonel on horseback, endeavoring to rally his panic-stricken and disordered men but himself sorely bewildered. He asked the lieutenant what was the force of the assailants. The latter answered that he had seen four or five battalions in the woods, three of them had fired upon him before he had retreated —"but," added he, "there are other troops to the right and left, and the town will soon be surrounded." The colonel rode in front of his troops. "Forward! March! Advance! Advance!" cried he. With some difficulty he succeeded in extricating his troops from the town and leading them into an adjacent orchard.

Now was the time, writes the lieutenant, for him to have pushed for another place, there to make a stand. At this critical moment he might have done so with credit and without loss. The colonel seems to have had such an intention. A rapid retreat by the Princeton road was apparently in his thoughts but he lacked decision. The idea of flying before the rebels was intolerable. Some one, too, exclaimed at the ruinous loss of leaving all their baggage to be plundered by the enemy.

Changing his mind, he made a rash resolve. "All who are my grenadiers, forward!" cried he and went back, writes his corporal, like a storm upon the town. "What madness was this!" writes the critical lieutenant. "A town that was of no use to us, that but ten or fifteen minutes before he had gladly left, that was now filled with three or four thousand enemies stationed in houses or behind walls and hedges, and a battery of six cannon planted on the main street. And he to think of retaking it with his six or seven hundred men and their bayonets!"

Still he led his grenadiers bravely but rashly on, when, in the midst of his career, he received a fatal wound from a musket ball and fell from his horse. His men, left without their chief, were struck with dismay. Heedless of the orders of the second in command, they retreated by the right up the banks of the Assunpink, intending to escape to Princeton. Washington saw the design and threw Colonel Hand's corps of Pennsylvania riflemen in their way, while a body of Virginia troops gained their left. Brought to a stand and perfectly bewildered, Washington thought they were forming in order of battle and ordered a discharge of canister shot.

"Sir, they have struck," exclaimed Forest.

"Struck!" echoed the general.

"Yes, sir, their colors are down."

"So they are!" replied Washington and spurred in that direction, followed by Forest and his whole command.

The men grounded their arms and surrendered at discretion. "But had not Colonel Rahl been severely wounded," remarks his loyal corporal, "we would never have been taken alive!"

The skirmishing had now ceased in every direction. Major Wilkinson, who was with the lower column, was sent to the commander-in-chief for orders. He rode up, he says, at the moment that Colonel Rahl, supported by a file of sergeants, was presenting his sword. "On my approach," continues he, "the commander-in-chief took me by the hand and observed, 'Major Wilkinson, this is a glorious day for our country!' his countenance beaming with complacency, whilst the unfortunate Rahl, who the day before would not have changed fortunes with him, now pale, bleeding and covered with blood, in broken accents seemed to implore those attentions which the victor was well disposed to bestow on him."

He was in fact conveyed with great care to his quarters, which were in the house of a kind and respectable Quaker family.

The number of prisoners taken in this affair was nearly one

thousand, of which thirty-two were officers. The veteran Major von Dechow, who had urged in vain the throwing up of breast-works, received a mortal wound, of which he died in Trenton. Washington's triumph, however, was impaired by the failure of the two simultaneous attacks. General Ewing, who was to have crossed before day at Trenton Ferry and taken possession of the bridge leading out of the town, over which the light horse and Hessians retreated, was prevented by the quantity of ice in the river. Cadwalader was hindered by the same obstacle. He got part of his troops over but found it impossible to embark his cannon and was obliged therefore to return to the Pennsylvania side of the river. Had he and Ewing crossed, Donop's quarters would have been beaten up and the fugitives from Trenton intercepted.

By the failure of this part of his plan, Washington had been ex-posed to the most imminent hazard. The force with which he had crossed, twenty-four hundred men, raw troops, was not enough to cope with the veteran garrison had it been properly on its guard. And then there were the troops under Donop at hand to co-operate with it. Nothing saved him but the utter panic of the enemy, their want of proper alarm places and their exaggerated idea of his forces: for one of the journals before us (the corporal's) states that he had with him 15,000 men, and another 6,000.[7] Even now that the place was in his possession he dared not linger in it. There was a superior force under Donop below him and a strong battalion of infantry at Princeton. His own troops were exhausted by the operations of the night and morning in cold, rain, snow and storm. They had to guard about a thousand prisoners taken in ac-tion or found concealed in houses. There was little prospect of suc-cor, owing to the season and the state of the river. Washington gave up therefore all idea of immediately pursuing the enemy or keeping possession of Trenton, and determined to recross the Del-aware with his prisoners and captured artillery. Understanding that the brave but unfortunate Rahl was in a dying state, he paid him a visit before leaving Trenton, accompanied by General Greene. They found him at his quarters in the house of a Quaker family. Their visit and the respectful consideration and unaffected sympathy manifested by them evidently soothed the feelings of

[7] The lieutenant gives the latter number on the authority of Lord Stirling, but his lordship meant the whole number intended for the three several at-tacks. The force that actually crossed with Washington was what we have stated.

the unfortunate soldier, now stripped of his late won laurels and resigned to die rather than outlive his honor.[8]

We have given a somewhat sarcastic portrait of the colonel drawn by one of his lieutenants. Another, Lieutenant Piel, paints with a soberer and more reliable pencil.

"For our whole ill luck," writes he, "we have to thank Colonel Rahl. It never occurred to him that the rebels might attack us, and therefore he had taken scarce any precautions against such an event. In truth I must confess we have universally thought too little of the rebels, who until now have never on any occasion been able to withstand us. Our brigadier (Rahl) was too proud to retire a step before such an enemy, although nothing remained for us but to retreat.

"General Howe had judged this man from a wrong point of view or he would hardly have intrusted such an important post as Trenton to him. He was formed for a soldier but not for a general. At the capture of Fort Washington he had gained much honor while under the command of a great general but he lost all his renown at Trenton where he himself was general. He had courage to dare the hardiest enterprise but he alone wanted the cool presence of mind necessary in a surprise like that at Trenton. His vivacity was too great. One thought crowded on another so that he could come to no decision. Considered as a private man, he was deserving of high regard. He was generous, open-handed, hospitable; never cringing to his superiors nor arrogant to his inferiors; but courteous to all. Even his domestics were treated more like friends than servants."

The loyal corporal, too, contributes his mite of praise to his dying commander. "In his last agony," writes the grateful soldier, "he yet thought of his grenadiers and entreated General Washington that nothing might be taken from them but their arms. A promise was given," adds the corporal, "and was kept."

The Hessian prisoners were conveyed across the Delaware by Johnson's Ferry into Pennsylvania. The private soldiers were marched off immediately to Newtown. The officers, twenty-three in number, remained in a small chamber in the Ferry House, where, according to their own account, they passed a dismal night, sore at heart that their recent triumphs at White Plains and Fort Washington should be so suddenly eclipsed.

[8] *Journal of Lieutenant Piel.*

On the following morning they were conducted to Newtown under the escort of Colonel Weedon. "His exterior," writes Lieutenant Piel, "spoke but little in his favor, yet he won all our hearts by his kind and friendly conduct."

At Newtown the officers were quartered in inns and private houses, the soldiers in the church and jail. The officers paid a visit to Lord Stirling, whom some of them had known from his being captured at Long Island. He received them with great kindness. "Your general, Van Heister," said he, "treated me like a brother when I was a prisoner, and so, gentlemen, will you be treated by me."

"We had scarce seated ourselves," continues Lieutenant Piel, "when a long, meagre, dark-looking man whom we took for the parson of the place stepped forth and held a discourse in German in which he endeavored to set forth the justice of the American side in this war. He told us he was a Hanoverian born; called the King of England nothing but the Elector of Hanover; and spoke of him so contemptuously that his garrulity became intolerable. We answered that we had not come to America to inquire which party was in the right but to fight for the king.

"Lord Stirling, seeing how little we were edified by the preacher, relieved us from him by proposing to take us with him to visit General Washington. The latter received us very courteously, though we understood very little of what he said, as he spoke nothing but English, a language in which none of us at that time were strong. In his aspect shines forth nothing of the great man that he is universally considered. His eyes have scarce any fire. There is, however, a smiling expression on his countenance when he speaks, that wins affection and respect. He invited four of our officers to dine with him. The rest dined with Lord Stirling." One of those who dined with the commander-in-chief was the satirical lieutenant whom we have so often quoted and who was stationed at the picket on the morning of the attack. However disparagingly he may have thought of his unfortunate commander, he evidently had a very good opinion of himself.

"General Washington," writes he in his journal, "did me the honor to converse a good deal with me concerning the unfortunate affair. I told him freely my opinion that even our dispositions had been bad, otherwise we should not have fallen into his hands. He asked me if I could have made better dispositions and in what manner? I told him yes, stated all the faults of our arrangements and showed him how I would have done, and would have managed to come out of the affair with honor."

We have no doubt, from the specimens furnished in the lieutenant's journal, that he went largely into his own merits and achievements, and the demerits and shortcomings of his luckless commander. Washington, he added, not only applauded his exposition of what he would have done but made him a eulogy thereupon, and upon his watchfulness and the defense he had made with his handful of men when his picket was attacked. Yet according to his own account, in his journal, with all his watchfulness, he came near being caught napping.

"General Washington," continues he, "is a courteous and polite man, but very cautious and reserved, talks little and has a crafty (listige) physiognomy." We surmise the lieutenant had the most of the talk on that occasion and that the crafty or sly expression in Washington's physiognomy may have been a lurking but suppressed smile provoked by the lieutenant's self-laudation and wordiness.

The Hessian prisoners were subsequently transferred from place to place until they reached Winchester in the interior of Virginia. Wherever they arrived, people thronged from far and near to see these terrible beings of whom they had received such formidable accounts, and were surprised and disappointed to find them looking like other men. At first they had to endure the hootings and revilings of the multitude for having hired themselves out to the trade of blood. And they especially speak of the scoldings they received from old women in the villages, who upbraided them for coming to rob them of their liberty.

"At length," writes the corporal in his journal, "General Washington had written notices put up in town and country that we were innocent of this war and had joined in it not of our free will but through compulsion. We should therefore be treated not as enemies but friends. From this time," adds he, "things went better with us. Every day came many out of the towns, old and young, rich and poor, and brought us provisions and treated us with kindness and humanity."[9]

[9] Tagebuch des Corporals Johannes Reuber.—MS.

Chapter 28

CORNWALLIS IN THE JERSEYS

Bent upon following up his blow [Washington, on the Pennsylvania side of the Delaware], had barely allowed his troops a day or two to recover from recent exposure and fatigue, that they might have strength and spirit to pursue the retreating enemy, beat up other of their quarters and entirely reverse affairs in the Jerseys. In this spirit he had written to Generals McDougall and Maxwell at Morristown to collect as large a body of militia as possible and harass the enemy in flank and rear. Heath, also, had been ordered to abandon the Highlands, which there was no need of guarding at this season of the year, and hasten down with the eastern militia as rapidly as possible by the way of Hackensack, continuing on until he should send him further orders. "A fair opportunity is offered," said he, "of driving the enemy entirely from the Jerseys or at least to the extremity of the province."

Men of influence also were despatched by him into different parts of the Jerseys to spirit up the militia to revenge the oppression, the ravage and insults they had experienced from the enemy, especially from the Hessians. "If what they have suffered," said he, "does not rouse their resentment they must not possess the feelings of humanity."

On the 29th his troops began to cross the river. It would be a slow and difficult operation, owing to the ice. Two parties of light troops, therefore, were detached in advance, whom Colonel Reed was to send in pursuit of the enemy. They marched into Trenton about two o'clock and were immediately put on the traces of Donop, to hang on his rear and harass him until other troops should come up. Cadwalader also detached a party of riflemen from Bordentown with like orders. Donop, in retreating, had divided his force, sending one part by a cross-road to Princeton and hurrying on with the remainder to Brunswick. Notwithstanding the severity of the weather and the wretchedness of the road, it was a service of animation and delight to the American troops to hunt back these Hessians through the country they had recently outraged and over ground which they themselves had trodden so painfully and despondingly in their retreat. In one instance the riflemen surprised and captured a party of refugees who lingered in the rear-guard, among whom were several newly-made officers. Never was there a more sudden reversal in the game of war than this retreat of the heavy German veterans harassed by light parties of a raw militia, which they so lately had driven like chaff before them.

While this was going on, Washington was effecting the passage of his main force to Trenton. He himself had crossed on the 29th of December but it took two days more to get the troops and artillery over the icy river, and that with great labor and difficulty. And now came a perplexity. With the year expired the term of several regiments which had seen most service and become inured to danger. Knowing how indispensable were such troops to lead on those which were raw and undisciplined, Washington had them paraded and invited to re-enlist. It was a difficult task to persuade them. They were haggard with fatigue and hardship and privation of every kind, and their hearts yearned for home. By the persuasions of their officers, however, and a bounty of ten dollars, the greater proportion of those from the eastward were induced to remain six weeks longer.

Hard money was necessary in this emergency. How was it to be furnished? The military chest was incompetent. On the 30th, Washington wrote by express to Robert Morris, the patriot financier at Philadelphia, whom he knew to be eager that the blow should be followed up. "If you could possibly collect a sum, if it were but one hundred, or one hundred and fifty pounds, it would be of service."

Morris received the letter in the evening. He was at his wit's end to raise the sum, for hard money was scarce. Fortunately a wealthy Quaker in this moment of exigency supplied "the sinews of war," and early the next morning the money was forwarded by the express.

At this critical moment, too, Washington received a letter from a committee of Congress transmitting him resolves of that body dated the 27th of December, investing him with military powers quite dictatorial. "Happy is it for this country," write the committee, "that the general of their forces can safely be intrusted with the most unlimited power, and neither personal security, liberty or property, be in the least degree endangered thereby."[1]

Washington's acknowledgment of this great mark of confidence was noble and characteristic. "I find Congress have done me the honor to intrust me with powers, in my military capacity, of the highest nature and almost unlimited extent. Instead of thinking myself freed from all *civil* obligations by this mark of their confidence, I shall constantly bear in mind that, as the sword was the last resort for the preservation of our liberties, so it ought to be the first thing laid aside when those liberties are firmly established."

General Howe was taking his ease in winter quarters at New York, waiting for the freezing of the Delaware to pursue his triumphant march to Philadelphia, when tidings were brought him of the surprise and capture of the Hessians at Trenton. "That three old established regiments of a people who made war their profession should lay down their arms to a ragged and undisciplined militia, and that with scarcely any loss on either side," was a matter of amazement. He instantly stopped Lord Cornwallis, who was on the point of embarking for England, and sent him back in all haste to resume the command in the Jerseys.

The ice in the Delaware impeded the crossing of the American troops and gave the British time to draw in their scattered cantonments and assemble their whole force at Princeton. While his troops were yet crossing, Washington sent out Colonel Reed to reconnoiter the position and movements of the enemy and obtain information. Six of the Philadelphia light horse, spirited young fellows but who had never seen service, volunteered to accompany Reed. They patrolled the country to the very vicinity of Princeton but could collect no information from the inhabitants, who were harassed, terrified and bewildered by the ravaging marches to and fro of friend and enemy.

Emerging from a wood almost within view of Princeton, they caught sight, from a rising ground, of two or three red-coats passing from time to time from a barn to a dwelling-house. Here must be an outpost. Keeping the barn in a line with the house so

[1] *Am. Archives*, 5th Series, iii., 1510.

as to cover their approach, they dashed up to the latter without
being discovered and surrounded it. Twelve British dragoons were
within, who, though well armed, were so panic-stricken that they
surrendered without making defense. A commissary also was
taken. The sergeant of the dragoons alone escaped. Colonel Reed
and his six cavaliers returned in triumph to headquarters. Important information was obtained from their prisoners. Lord Cornwallis had joined General Grant the day before at Princeton with
a reinforcement of chosen troops. They had now seven or eight
thousand men and were pressing wagons for a march upon Trenton.[2]

Cadwalader, stationed at Crosswicks, about seven miles distant
between Bordentown and Trenton, sent intelligence to the same
purport, received by him from a young gentleman who had escaped from Princeton.

Word too was brought from other quarters that General Howe
was on the march with a thousand light troops with which he had
landed at Amboy.

The situation of Washington was growing critical. The enemy
were beginning to advance their large pickets towards Trenton.
Everything indicated an approaching attack. The force with him
was small. To retreat across the river would destroy the dawn of
hope awakened in the bosoms of the Jersey militia by the late
exploit, but to make a stand without reinforcements was impossible. In this emergency he called to his aid General Cadwalader
from Crosswicks and General Mifflin from Bordentown, with their
collective forces, amounting to about three thousand six hundred
men. He did it with reluctance, for it seemed like involving them
in the common danger, but the exigency of the case admitted of
no alternative. They promptly answered to his call and, marching
in the night, joined him on the 1st of January.

Washington chose a position for his main body on the east side
of the Assunpink. There was a narrow stone bridge across it, where
the water was very deep—the same bridge over which part of
Rahl's brigade had escaped in the recent affair. He planted his artillery so as to command the bridge and the fords. His advance
guard was stationed about three miles off in a wood, having in
front a stream called Shabbakong Creek.

Early on the morning of the 2d came certain word that Corn-

2 *Life of Reed*, i., 282.

wallis was approaching with all his force. Strong parties were sent out under General Greene, who skirmished with the enemy and harassed them in their advance. By twelve o'clock they reached the Shabbakong and halted for a time on its northern bank. Then, crossing it and moving forward with rapidity, they drove the advance guard out of the woods and pushed on until they reached a high ground near the town. Here Hand's corps of several battalions was drawn up, and held them for a time in check. All the parties in advance ultimately retreated to the main body, on the east side of the Assunpink, and found some difficulty in crowding across the narrow bridge.

From all these checks and delays it was nearly sunset before Cornwallis with the head of his army entered Trenton. His rearguard under General Leslie rested at Maiden Head, about six miles distant and nearly half way between Trenton and Princeton. Forming his troops into columns, he now made repeated attempts to cross the Assunpink at the bridge and the fords but was as often repulsed by the artillery. For a part of the time Washington, mounted on a white horse, stationed himself at the south end of the bridge, issuing his orders. Each time the enemy was repulsed there was a shout along the American lines. At length they drew off, came to a halt and lighted their camp fires. The Americans did the same, using the neighboring fences for the purpose. Sir William Erskine, who was with Cornwallis, urged him, it is said, to attack Washington that evening in his camp but his lordship declined. He felt sure of the game which had so often escaped him. He had at length, he thought, got Washington into a situation from which he could not escape but where he might make a desperate stand, and he was willing to give his wearied troops a night's repose to prepare them for the closing struggle. He would be sure, he said, to "bag the fox in the morning."

A cannonade was kept up on both sides until dark but with little damage to the Americans. When night closed in, the two camps lay in sight of each other's fires, ruminating the bloody action of the following day. It was the most gloomy and anxious night that had yet closed in on the American army throughout its series of perils and disasters, for there was no concealing the impending danger. But what must have been the feelings of the commander-in-chief as he anxiously patrolled his camp and considered his desperate position? A small stream, fordable in several places, was all that separated his raw, inexperienced army from an enemy vastly superior in numbers and discipline, and stung to action by the mortification of a late defeat. A general action with them must be ruinous. But how was he to retreat? Behind him was the Delaware, impassable from floating ice. Granting even (a thing not to be hoped) that a retreat across it could be effected, the consequences would be equally fatal. The Jerseys would be left in possession of the enemy, endangering the immediate capture of Philadelphia and sinking the public mind into despondency.

In this darkest of moments a gleam of hope flashed upon his mind: a bold expedient suggested itself. Almost the whole of the enemy's force must by this time be drawn out of Princeton and advancing by detachments toward Trenton, while their baggage and principal stores must remain weakly guarded at Brunswick. Was it not possible by a rapid night-march along the Quaker road, a different road from that on which General Leslie with the rearguard was resting, to get past that force undiscovered, come by surprise upon those left at Princeton, capture or destroy what stores were left there and then push on to Brunswick? This would save the army from being cut off, would avoid the appearance of a defeat and might draw the enemy away from Trenton, while some fortunate stroke might give additional reputation to the American arms. Even should the enemy march on to Philadelphia, it could not in any case be prevented; while a counter-blow in the Jerseys would be a great consolation.

Such was the plan which Washington revolved in his mind on the gloomy banks of the Assunpink and which he laid before his officers in a council of war held after nightfall at the quarters of General Mercer. It was met with instant concurrence, being of that hardy, adventurous kind which seems congenial with the American character. One formidable difficulty presented itself. The weather was unusually mild. There was a thaw, by which the roads might be rendered deep and miry and almost impassable. Fortunately, or rather providentially, as Washington was prone to consider it, the wind veered to the north in the course of the evening. The weather became intensly cold, and in two hours the roads were once more hard and frost-bound. In the meantime the baggage of the army was silently removed to Burlington, and every other preparation was made for a rapid march. To deceive the enemy, men were employed to dig trenches near the bridge within hearing of the British sentries, with orders to continue noisily at work until daybreak. Others were to go the rounds, relieve guards at the bridge and fords, keep up the camp fires and maintain all the appearance of a regular encampment. At daybreak they were to hasten after the army.

In the dead of the night the army drew quietly out of the encampment and began its march. General Mercer, mounted on a favorite gray horse, was in the advance with the remnant of his flying camp, now but about three hundred and fifty men, principally relics of the brave Delaware and Maryland regiments, with some of the Pennsylvania militia. Among the latter were youths belonging to the best families in Philadelphia. The main body followed under Washington's immediate command.

The Quaker road was a complete roundabout, joining the main road about two miles from Princeton, where Washington expected to arrive before daybreak. The road, however, was new and rugged, cut through woods, where the stumps of trees broke the wheels of some of the baggage trains and retarded the march of the troops, so that it was near sunrise of a bright, frosty morning when Washington reached the bridge over Stony Brook, about three miles from Princeton. After crossing the bridge, he led his troops along the bank of the brook to the edge of a wood, where a by-road led off on the right through low grounds and was said by the guides to be a short cut to Princeton and less exposed to view. By this road Washington defiled with the main body, ordering Mercer to continue along the brook with his brigade until he should arrive at the main road, where he was to secure and if possible destroy a bridge over which it passes, so as to intercept any fugitives from Princeton and check any retrograde movements of the British troops which might have advanced towards Trenton.

Hitherto the movements of the Americans had been undiscovered by the enemy. Three regiments of the latter, the 17th, 40th and 55th, with three troops of dragoons, had been quartered all night in Princeton, under marching orders to join Lord Cornwallis in the morning. The 17th regiment under Colonel Mawhood was already on the march. The 55th regiment was preparing to follow. Mawhood had crossed the bridge by which the old or main road to Trenton passes over Stony Brook and was proceeding through a wood beyond when, as he attained the summit of a hill about sunrise, the glittering of arms betrayed to him the movement of Mercer's troops to the left, who were filing along the Quaker road to secure the bridge as they had been ordered.

The woods prevented him from seeing their number. He supposed them to be some broken portion of the American army flying before Lord Cornwallis. With this idea, he faced about and made a retrograde movement to intercept them or hold them in check while messengers spurred off at all speed to hasten forward the regiments still lingering at Princeton, so as completely to surround them.

The woods concealed him until he had recrossed the bridge of Stony Brook, when he came in full sight of the van of Mercer's brigade. Both parties pushed to get possession of a rising ground on the right near the house of a Mr. Clark of the peaceful Society of Friends. The Americans, being nearest, reached it first and formed behind a hedge fence which extended along a slope in front of the house, whence, being chiefly armed with rifles, they opened a destructive fire. It was returned with great spirit by the enemy. At the first discharge Mercer was dismounted, "his gallant gray" being crippled by a musket ball in the leg. One of his colonels, also, was mortally wounded and carried to the rear. Availing themselves of the confusion thus occasioned, the British charged with the bayonet. The American riflemen, having no weapon of the kind, were thrown into disorder and retreated. Mercer, who was on foot, endeavored to rally them, when a blow from the butt end of a musket felled him to the ground. He rose and defended himself with his sword but was surrounded, bayoneted repeatedly and left for dead.

Mawhood pursued the broken and retreating troops to the brow of the rising ground on which Clark's house was situated, when he beheld a large force emerging from a wood and advancing to the rescue. It was a body of Pennsylvania militia, which Washington, on hearing the firing, had detached to the support of Mercer. Mawhood instantly ceased pursuit, drew up his artillery and by a heavy discharge brought the militia to a stand.

At this moment Washington himself arrived at the scene of action, having galloped from the by-road in advance of his troops. From a rising ground he beheld Mercer's troops retreating in confusion, and the detachment of militia checked by Mawhood's artillery. Everything was at peril. Putting spurs to his horse, he dashed past the hesitating militia, waving his hat and cheering them on. His commanding figure and white horse made him a conspicuous object for the enemy's marksmen but he heeded it not. Galloping forward under the fire of Mawhood's battery, he called upon Mercer's broken brigade. The Pennsylvanians rallied at the sound of his voice and caught fire from his example. At the same time the 7th Virginia regiment emerged from the wood and moved forward with loud cheers while a fire of grapeshot was opened by Captain Moulder of the American artillery from the brow of a ridge to the south.

Colonel Mawhood, who a moment before had thought his triumph secure, found himself assailed on every side and separated from the other British regiments. He fought, however, with great bravery and for a short time the action was desperate. Washington was in the midst of it, equally endangered by the random fire of his own men and the artillery and musketry of the enemy. His aide-de-camp, Colonel Fitzgerald, a young and ardent Irishman, losing sight of him in the heat of the fight when enveloped in dust and smoke, dropped the bridle on the neck of his horse and drew his hat over his eyes, giving him up for lost. When he saw him, however, emerge from the cloud, waving his hat, and beheld the enemy giving way, he spurred up to his side. "Thank God," said he, "your Excellency is safe!" "Away, my dear colonel, and bring up the troops," was the reply, "the day is our own!" It was one of those occasions in which the latent fire of Washington's character blazed forth.

Mawhood by this time had forced his way at the point of the bayonet through gathering foes, though with heavy loss, back to the main road and was in full retreat towards Trenton to join Cornwallis. Washington detached Major Kelly with a party of Pennsylvania troops to destroy the bridge at Stony Brook, over which Mawhood had retreated, so as to impede the advance of General Leslie from Maiden Head.

In the meantime the 55th regiment, which had been on the left and nearer Princeton, had been encountered by the American advance guard under General St. Clair, and after some sharp fighting in a ravine had given way and was retreating across fields and along a by-road to Brunswick. The remaining regiment, the 40th, had not been able to come up in time for the action. A part of it fled toward Brunswick. The residue took refuge in the college at Princeton, recently occupied by them as barracks. Artillery was now brought to bear on the college, and a few shot compelled those within to surrender.

In this brief but brilliant action, about one hundred of the British were left dead on the field, and nearly three hundred taken prisoners, fourteen of whom were officers. Among the slain was Captain Leslie, son of the Earl of Leven. His death was greatly lamented by his captured companions.

The loss of the Americans was about twenty-five or thirty men and several officers. Among the latter was Colonel Haslet, who had distinguished himself throughout the campaign by being among the foremost in services of danger. He was indeed a gallant officer and gallantly seconded by his Delaware troops.

A greater loss was that of General Mercer. He was said to be either dead or dying in the house of Mr. Clark, whither he had been conveyed by his aide-de-camp, Major Armstrong, who found him, after the retreat of Mawhood's troops, lying on the field gashed with several wounds and insensible from cold and loss of blood. Washington would have ridden back from Princeton to visit him and have him conveyed to a place of greater security, but was assured that, if alive, he was too desperately wounded to bear removal. In the meantime he was in good hands, being faithfully attended to by his aide-de-camp, Major Armstrong, and treated with the utmost care and kindness by Mr. Clark's family."[3]

Under these circumstances Washington felt compelled to leave his old companion in arms to his fate. Indeed, he was called away by the exigencies of his command, having to pursue the routed regiments which were making a headlong retreat to Brunswick. In this pursuit he took the lead at the head of a detachment of cavalry. At Kingston, however, three miles to the northeast of Princeton, he pulled up, restrained his ardor, and held a council of war on horseback. Should he keep on to Brunswick or not? The capture of the British stores and baggage would make his triumph complete, but on the other hand his troops were excessively fatigued by their rapid march all night and hard fight in the morning. All of them had been one night without sleep and some of them two, and many were half-starved. They were without blankets, thinly clad, some of them barefooted, and this in freezing weather. Cornwallis would be upon them before they could reach Brunswick. His rear-guard, under General Leslie, had been

[3] See Washington to Colonel Reed, Jan. 15.

quartered but six miles from Princeton, and the retreating troops must have roused them. Under these considerations, it was determined to discontinue the pursuit and push for Morristown. There they would be in a mountainous country, heavily wooded, in an abundant neighborhood and on the flank of the enemy, with various defiles by which they might change their position according to his movements.

Filing off to the left, therefore, from Kingston and breaking down the bridges behind him, Washington took the narrow road by Rocky Hill to Pluckamin. His troops were so exhausted that many in the course of the march would lie down in the woods on the frozen ground and fall asleep, and were with difficulty roused and cheered forward. At Pluckamin he halted for a time to allow them a little repose and refreshment. While they are taking breath we will cast our eyes back to the camp of Cornwallis to see what was the effect upon him of this masterly movement of Washington. His lordship had retired to rest at Trenton with the sportsman's vaunt that he would "bag the fox in the morning." Nothing could surpass his surprise and chagrin when at daybreak the expiring watchfires and deserted camp of the Americans told him that the prize had once more evaded his grasp, that the general whose military skill he had decried had outgeneralled him.

For a time he could not learn whither the army, which had stolen away so silently, had directed its stealthy march. By sunrise, however, there was the booming of cannon, like the rumbling of distant thunder, in the direction of Princeton. The idea flashed upon him that Washington had not merely escaped but was about to make a dash at the British magazines at Brunswick. Alarmed for the safety of his military stores, his lordship forthwith broke up his camp and made a rapid march towards Princeton. As he arrived in sight of the bridge over Stony Brook, he beheld Major Kelly and his party busy in its destruction. A distant discharge of round shot from his field-pieces drove them away but the bridge was already broken. It would take time to repair it for the passage of the artillery, so Cornwallis in his impatience urged his troops breast-high through the turbulent and icy stream and again pushed forward. He was brought to a stand by the discharge of a thirty-two pounder from a distant breastwork. Supposing the Americans to be there in force and prepared to make resistance, he sent out some horsemen to reconnoiter, and advanced to storm the battery.

There was no one there. The thirty-two pounder had been left behind by the Americans, as too unwieldy, and a match had been applied to it by some lingerer of Washington's rear-guard.

Without further delay Cornwallis hurried forward, eager to save his magazines. Crossing the bridge at Kingston, he kept on along the Brunswick road, supposing Washington still before him. The latter had got far in the advance during the delays caused by the broken bridge at Stony Brook and the discharge of the thirty-two pounder, and the alteration of his course at Kingston had carried him completely out of the way of Cornwallis. His lordship reached Brunswick towards evening and endeavored to console himself, by the safety of the military stores, for being so completely foiled and out-manoeuvred.

Washington in the meantime was all on the alert. The lion part of his nature was aroused. And while his weary troops were in a manner panting upon the ground around him, he was despatching missives and calling out aid to enable him to follow up his successes.

Colonel Reed was ordered to send out rangers and bodies of militia to scour the country, waylay foraging parties, cut off supplies and keep the cantonments of the enemy in a state of siege. "I would not suffer a man to stir beyond their lines," writes Washington, "nor suffer them to have the least communication with the country."

Washington, having received reinforcements of militia, continued, with his scanty army, to carry on his system of annoyance. The situation of Cornwallis, who but a short time before traversed the Jerseys so triumphantly, became daily more and more irksome. Spies were in his camp to give notice of every movement, and foes without to take advantage of it, so that not a foraging party could sally forth without being waylaid. By degrees he drew in his troops which were posted about the country and collected them at New Brunswick and Amboy so as to have a communication by water with New York, whence he was now compelled to draw nearly all his supplies, "presenting," to use the words of Hamilton, "the extraordinary spectacle of a powerful army straitened within narrow limits by the phantom of a military force and never permitted to transgress those limits with impunity."

In fact, the recent operations in the Jerseys had suddenly changed the whole aspect of the war and given a triumphant close to what had been a disastrous campaign.

The troops which for months had been driven from post to post, apparently an undisciplined rabble, had all at once turned upon their pursuers and astounded them by brilliant stratagems and daring exploits. The commander whose cautious policy had been sneered at by enemies and regarded with impatience by misjudging friends, had all at once shown that he possessed enterprise as well as circumspection, energy as well as endurance, and that beneath his wary coldness lurked a fire to break forth at the proper moment. This year's campaign, the most critical one of the war, and especially the part of it which occurred in the Jerseys, was the ordeal that made his great qualities fully appreciated by his countrymen and gained for him from the statesmen and generals of Europe the appellation of the American Fabius.

Chapter 29

ENCAMPMENT AT MORRISTOWN

The British commanders had been outgeneralled, attacked and defeated. They had nearly been driven out of the Jerseys, and were now hemmed in and held in check by Washington and his handful of men castled among the heights of Morristown. So far from holding possession of the territory they had so recently overrun, they were fain to ask safe conduct across it for a convoy to their soldiers captured in battle. It must have been a severe trial to the pride of Cornwallis when he had to inquire by letter of Washington whether money and stores could be sent to the Hessians captured at Trenton, and a surgeon and medicines to the wounded at Princeton. And Washington's reply must have conveyed a reproof still more mortifying: No molestation, he assured his lordship, would be offered to the convoy by any part of the regular army under his command. But "he could not answer for the militia, who were resorting to arms in most parts of the State and were excessively exasperated at the treatment they had met with from both Hessian and British troops."

In fact, the conduct of the enemy had roused the whole country against them. The proclamations and printed protections of the British commanders, on the faith of which the inhabitants in general had stayed at home and forbore to take up arms, had proved of no avail. The Hessians could not or would not understand them, but plundered friend and foe alike.[1] The British soldiery often followed their example, and the plunderings of both were at times attended by those brutal outrages on the weaker sex which

[1] "These rascals plunder all indiscriminately. If they see anything they like, they say, 'Rebel good for Hesse-mans,' and seize upon it for their own use. They have no idea of the distinctions between whig and tory."—*Letter of Hazard the Postmaster.*

inflame the dullest spirits to revenge. The whole State was thus roused against its invaders. In Washington's retreat of more than a hundred miles through the Jerseys, he had never been joined by more than one hundred of its inhabitants. Now sufferers of both parties rose as one man to avenge their personal injuries. The late quiet yeomanry armed themselves and scoured the country in small parties to seize on stragglers, and the militia began to signalize themselves in voluntary skirmishes with regular troops.

In effect, Washington ordered a safe conduct to be given to the Hessian baggage as far as Philadelphia, and to the surgeon and medicines to Princeton, and permitted a Hessian sergeant and twelve men, unarmed, to attend the baggage until it was delivered to their countrymen.

Morristown, where the main army was encamped, had not been chosen by Washington as a permanent post but merely as a halting-place, where his troops might repose after their excessive fatigues and their sufferings from the inclement season. Further considerations persuaded him that it was well situated for the system of petty warfare which he meditated, and induced him to remain there. It was protected by forests and rugged heights. All approach from the seaboard was rendered difficult and dangerous to a hostile force by a chain of sharp hills, extending from Pluckamin, by Boundbrook and Springfield, to the vicinity of the Passaic River, while various defiles in the rear afforded safer retreats into a fertile and well-peopled region.[2] It was nearly equidistant from Amboy, Newark and Brunswick, the principal posts of the enemy, so that any movement made from them could be met by a counter movement on his part, while the forays and skirmishes by which he might harass them would school and season his own troops. He had three faithful generals with him: Greene, his reliance on all occasions; swarthy Sullivan, whose excitable temper and quick sensibilities he had sometimes to keep in check by friendly counsels and rebukes, but who was a good officer and loyally attached to him; and brave, genial, generous Knox, never so happy as when by his side. He had lately been advanced to the rank of brigadier at his recommendation, and commanded the artillery.

Washington's military family at this time was composed of his aides-de-camp, Colonels Meade and Tench Tilghman of Philadelphia, gentlemen of gallant spirit, amiable tempers and cultivated manners; and his secretary, Colonel Robert H. Harrison of

2 Wilkinson's *Memoirs*, vol. i., p. 149.

Maryland, the "old secretary," as he was familiarly called among his associates and by whom he was described as "one in whom every man had confidence and by whom no man was deceived."

Washington's headquarters at first were in what was called the Freemason's Tavern, on the north side of the village green. His troops were encamped about the vicinity of the village, at first in tents, until they could build log huts for shelter against the winter's cold. The main encampment was near Bottle Hill, in a sheltered valley which was thickly wooded and had abundant springs. It extended southeasterly from Morristown and was called the Lowantica Valley from the Indian name of a beautiful, limpid brook which ran through it and lost itself in a great swamp.[3]

To counteract the proclamation of the British commissioners, promising amnesty to all in rebellion who should, in a given time, return to their allegiance, Washington now issued a counter proclamation (Jan. 25th), commanding every person who had subscribed a declaration of fidelity to Great Britain or taken an oath of allegiance, to repair within thirty days to headquarters or the quarters to the nearest general officer of the continental army or of the militia and there take the oath of allegiance to the United States of America, and give up any protection, certificate or passport he might have received from the enemy; at the same time granting full liberty to all such as preferred the interest and protection of Great Britain to the freedom and happiness of their country, forthwith to withdraw themselves and families within the enemy's lines. All who should neglect or refuse to comply with this order were to be considered adherents to the crown and treated as common enemies.

This measure met with objections at the time, some of the timid or over-cautious thinking it inexpedient; others, jealous of the extraordinary powers vested in Washington, questioning whether he had not transcended these powers and exercised a degree of despotism.

The small-pox, which had been fatally prevalent in the preceding year, had again broken out, and Washington feared it might spread through the whole army. He took advantage of the interval of comparative quiet to have his troops inoculated. Houses were set apart in various places as hospitals for inoculation, and a church was appropriated for the use of those who had taken the malady in

[3] Notes of the Rev. Joseph F. Tuttle, MS.

the natural way. Among these the ravages were frightful. The traditions of the place and neighborhood give lamentable pictures of the distress caused by this loathsome disease in the camp and in the villages, wherever it had not been parried by inoculation.

"Washington," we are told, "was not an unmoved spectator of the griefs around him, and might be seen in Hanover and in Lowantica Valley, cheering the faith and inspiring the courage of his suffering men."[4] It was this paternal care and sympathy which attached his troops personally to him. They saw that he regarded them not with the eye of a general but of a patriot, whose heart yearned towards them as countrymen suffering in one common cause.

A striking contrast was offered throughout the winter and spring between the rival commanders, Howe at New York and Washington at Morristown. Howe was a soldier by profession. War with him was a career. The camp was, for the time, country and home. Easy and indolent by nature, of convivial and luxurious habits and somewhat addicted to gaming, he found himself in good quarters at New York and was in no hurry to leave them. The tories rallied around him. The British merchants residing there regarded him with profound devotion. His officers, too, many of them young men of rank and fortune, gave a gayety and brilliancy to the place. And the wealthy royalists forgot in a round of dinners, balls and assemblies the hysterical alarms they had once experienced under the military sway of Lee.

Washington, on the contrary, was a patriot soldier, grave, earnest, thoughtful, self-sacrificing. War to him was a painful remedy, hateful in itself but adopted for a great national good. To the prosecution of it all his pleasures, his comforts, his natural inclinations and private interests were sacrificed. And his chosen officers were earnest and anxious like himself, with their whole thoughts directed to the success of the magnanimous struggle in which they were engaged.

So, too, the armies were contrasted. The British troops, many of them perchance slightly metamorphosed from vagabonds into soldiers, all mere men of the sword, were well clad, well housed, and surrounded by all the conveniences of a thoroughly appointed army with a "rebel country" to forage. The American troops for the most part were mere yeomanry, taken from their rural homes; ill

[4] Notes of the Rev. Joseph F. Tuttle, MS.

sheltered, ill clad, ill fed and ill paid, with nothing to reconcile them to their hardships but love for the soil they were defending and the inspiring thought that it was *their country*. Washington, with paternal care, endeavored to protect them from the depraving influences of the camp. "Let vice and immorality of every kind be discouraged as much as possible in your brigade," writes he in a circular to his brigadier-generals, "and, as a chaplain is allowed to each regiment, see that the men regularly attend divine worship. Gaming of every kind is expressly forbidden, as being the foundation of evil and the cause of many a brave and gallant officer's ruin."

The fame of the American struggle for independence was bringing foreign officers as candidates for admission into the patriot army and causing great embarrassment to the commander-in-chief. "They seldom," writes Washington, "bring more than a commission and a passport, which we know may belong to a bad as well as a good officer. Their ignorance of our language and their inability to recruit men are insurmountable obstacles to their being engrafted in our continental battalions, for our officers, who have raised their men and have served through the war upon pay that has not hitherto borne their expenses, would be disgusted if foreigners were put over their heads. And I assure you, few or none of these gentlemen look lower than field officers' commissions. . . . Some general mode of disposing of them must be adopted, for it is ungenerous to keep them in suspense and a great charge to themselves, but I am at a loss to know how to point out this mode."

Congress determined that no foreign officers should receive commissions who were not well acquainted with the English language and did not bring strong testimonials of their abilities. Still there was embarrassment. Some came with brevet commissions from the French government and had been assured by Mr. Deane, American commissioner at Paris, that they would have the same rank in the American army. This would put them above American officers of merit and hard service, whose commissions were of more recent date. One Monsieur Ducoudray, on the strength of an agreement with Dr. Deane, expected to have the rank of major-general and to be put at the head of the artillery. Washington deprecated the idea of intrusting a department, on which the very salvation of the army might depend, to a foreigner who had no other tie to bind him to the interests of the country than honor.

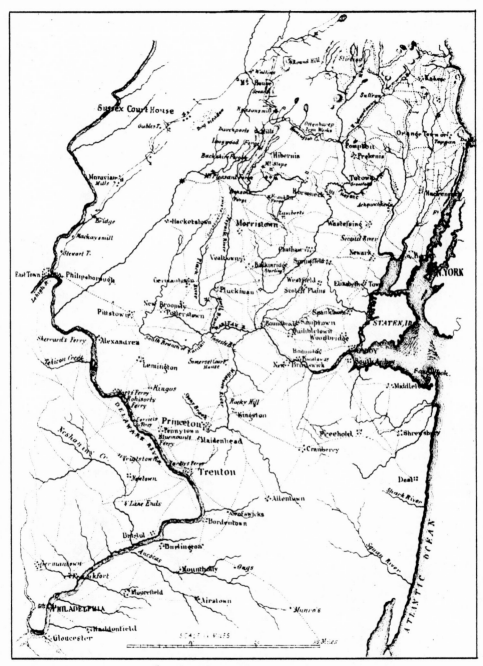

5. PART OF NEW JERSEY

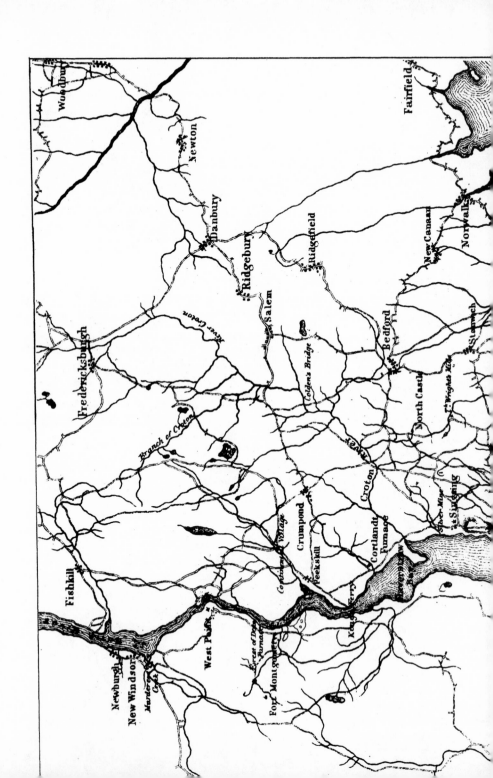

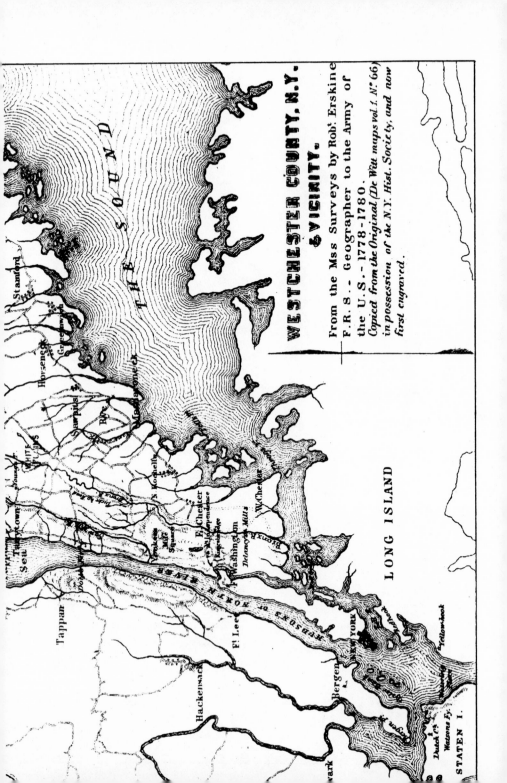

WESTCHESTER COUNTY, N.Y.
& VICINITY.

From the Mss Surveys by Rob.t Erskine
F.R.S.- Geographer to the Army of
the U.S.- 1778-1780.
*Copied from the Original (De Witt maps vol.1. N.o 66)
in possession of the N.Y. Hist. Society, and now
first engraved.*

THE SOUND

LONG ISLAND

STATEN I.

NEW YORK

Stamford

Greenwich

Horseneck

White Plains

Tappan

Hackensack

F.t Lee

F.t Washington

E. Chester

W. Chester

Brooklyn

Delancey's Mills

N. Rochelle

HUDSON or NORTH RIVER

Bergen

Tarrytown

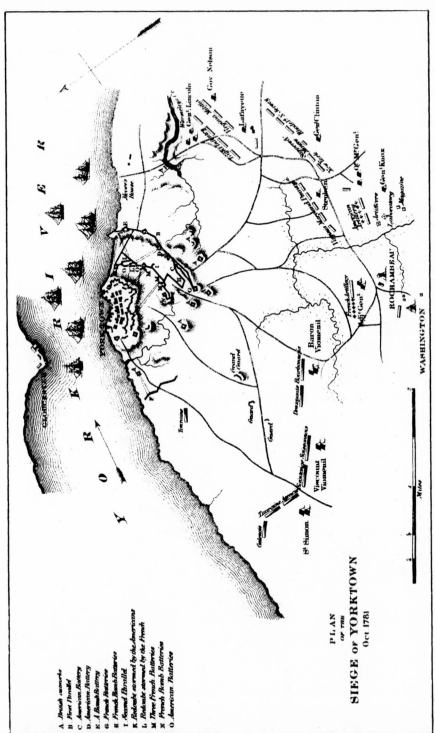

7. SIEGE OF YORKTOWN

Besides, he observed, it would endanger the loss to the service of General Knox, "a man of great military reading, sound judgment and clear perceptions. He has conducted the affairs of that department with honor to himself and advantage to the public and will resign if any one is put over him."

In fact, the report that Ducoudray was to be a major-general with a commission dated in the preceding year caused a commotion among the American officers of that rank but whose commissions were of later date. Congress eventually determined not to ratify the contract entered into between Mr. Deane and Monsieur Decoudray, and resolved that the commissions of foreign officers received into the service should bear date on the day of their being filled up by Washington.

Among the foreign candidates for appointments was one Colonel Conway, a native of Ireland but who, according to his own account, had been thirty years in the service of France, and claimed to be a chevalier of the order of St. Louis, of which he wore the decoration. Mr. Deane had recommended him to Washington as an officer of merit and had written to Congress that he considered him well qualified for the office of adjutant or brigadier-general, and that he had given him reason to hope for one or the other of these appointments. Colonel Conway pushed for that of brigadier-general. It had been conferred some time before by Congress on two French officers, De Fermois and Deborre, who, he had observed, had been inferior to him in the French service, and it would be mortifying now to hold rank below them.

"I cannot pretend," writes Washington to the president, "to speak of Colonel Conway's merits or abilities of my own knowledge. He appears to be a man of candor and, if he has been in service as long as he says, I should suppose him infinitely better qualified to serve us than many who have been promoted, as he speaks our language."

Conway accordingly received the rank of brigadier-general, of which he subsequently proved himself unworthy. He was boastful and presumptuous and became noted for his intrigues and for a despicable cabal against the commander-in-chief, which went by his name and of which we shall have to speak hereafter.

A candidate of a different stamp had presented himself in the preceding year, the gallant, generous-spirited Thaddeus Kosciuszko. He was a Pole of an ancient and noble family of

Lithuania and had been educated for the profession of arms at the military school at Warsaw, and subsequently in France. Disappointed in a love affair with a beautiful lady of rank with whom he had attempted to elope, he had emigrated to this country, and came provided with a letter of introduction from Dr. Franklin to Washington.

"What do you seek here?" inquired the commander-in-chief.

"To fight for American independence."

"What can you do?"

"Try me."

Washington was pleased with the curt yet comprehensive reply, and with his chivalrous air and spirit, and at once received him into his family as an aide-de-camp.[5] Congress shortly afterwards appointed him an engineer with the rank of colonel. He proved a valuable officer throughout the Revolution and won an honorable and lasting name in our country.

It had been Washington's earnest wish in the early part of the spring to take advantage of the inactivity of the enemy and attempt some "capital stroke" for the benefit of the next campaign, but the want of troops prevented him. He now planned a night expedition for Putnam, exactly suited to the humor of the old general. He was to descend the Hudson in boats, surprise Fort Independence at Spyt den Duivel Creek, capture the garrison and sweep the road between that post and the Highlands. Putnam was all on fire for the enterprise, when movements on the part of the enemy, seemingly indicative of a design upon Philadelphia, obliged Washington to abandon the project and exert all his vigilance in watching the hostile operations in the Jerseys.

Accordingly, towards the end of May he broke up his cantonments at Morristown and shifted his camp to Middlebrook, within ten miles of Brunswick. His whole force fit for duty was now about seven thousand three hundred men, all from the States south of the Hudson. There were forty-three regiments forming ten brigades, commanded by Brigadiers Muhlenberg, Weedon, Woodford, Scott, Smallwood, Deborre, Wayne, Dehaas, Conway and Maxwell. These were apportioned into five divisions of two brigades each, under Major-Generals Greene, Stephen, Sullivan, Lincoln and Stirling. The artillery was commanded by Knox. Sullivan, with his division, was stationed on the right at Princeton. With the rest of his force Washington fortified himself in a position naturally strong, among hills in the rear of the village of Middlebrook. His camp was on all sides difficult of approach, and he rendered it still more so by intrenchments. The high grounds about it commanded a wide view of the country around Brunswick, the road to Philadelphia and the course of the Raritan, so that the enemy could make no important movement on land without his perceiving it.

It was now the beautiful season of the year, and the troops from their height beheld a fertile and well cultivated country spread before them, "painted with meadows, green fields and orchards, studded with villages and affording abundant supplies and forage." A part of their duty was to guard it from the ravage of the enemy while they held themselves ready to counteract his movements in every direction.

On the 31st of May reports were brought to camp that a fleet of a hundred sail had left New York and stood out to sea. Whither bound and how freighted was unknown. If they carried troops, their destination might be Delaware Bay. Eighteen transports, also, had arrived at New York with troops in foreign uniforms. Were they those which had been in Canada, or others immediately from Germany? Those who had reconnoitered them with glasses could not tell. All was matter of anxious conjecture.

Lest the fleet which had put to sea should be bound farther south than Delaware Bay, Washington instantly wrote to Patrick Henry, at that time governor of Virginia, putting him on his guard. "Should this fleet arrive on your coast, and the enemy attempt to penetrate the country or make incursions, I would recommend that the earliest opposition be made by parties and detachments of militia without waiting to collect a large body. I am convinced that this would be attended with the most salutary consequences, and that greater advantages would be derived from it than by deferring the opposition till you assembled a number equal to that of the enemy."

The troops in foreign uniforms which had landed from the transports proved to be Anspachers and other German mercenaries. There were British reinforcements also and, what was particularly needed, a supply of tents and camp equipage. Sir William Howe had been waiting for the latter, and likewise until the ground should be covered with grass.[6]

The country was now in full verdure, affording "green forage" in

[6] Evidence of Major-General Gray before the House of Commons.

abundance, and all things seemed to Sir William propitious for the opening of the campaign. Early in June, therefore, he gave up ease and gayety and luxurious life at New York and, crossing into the Jerseys, set up his headquarters at Brunswick.

As soon as Washington ascertained that Sir William's attention was completely turned to this quarter, he determined to strengthen his position with all the force that could be spared from other parts, so as to be able, in case a favorable opportunity presented, to make an attack upon the enemy. In the meantime he would harass them with his light militia troops, aided by a few Continentals, so as to weaken their numbers by continual skirmishes. With this view, he ordered General Putnam to send down most of the continental troops from Peekskill, leaving only a number sufficient, in conjunction with the militia, to guard that post against surprise. They were to proceed in three divisions, under Generals Parsons, McDougall and Glover, at one day's march distant from each other.

[Benedict] Arnold in this critical juncture had been put in command of Philadelphia, a post which he had been induced to accept, although the question of rank had not been adjusted to his satisfaction. His command embraced the western bank of the Delaware with all its fords and passes, and he took up his station there with a strong body of militia, supported by a few Continentals, to oppose any attempt of the enemy to cross the river. He was instructed by Washington to give him notice by expresses, posted on the road, if any fleet should appear in Delaware Bay, and to endeavor to concert signals with the camp of Sullivan at Princeton by alarm fires upon the hills.

On the night of the 13th of June, General Howe sallied forth in great force from Brunswick, as if pushing directly for the Delaware, but his advanced guard halted at Somerset court-house, about eight or nine miles distant. Apprised of this movement, Washington at daybreak reconnoitered the enemy from the heights before the camp. He observed their front halting at the court-house but a few miles distant, while troops and artillery were grouped here and there along the road, and the rear-guard was still at Brunswick. It was a question with Washington and his generals, as they reconnoitered the enemy with their glasses, whether this was a real move toward Philadelphia or merely a lure to tempt them down from their strong position. In this uncertainty Washington drew out his army in battle array along the heights but kept quiet. In the present state of his forces it was his plan not to risk a general action, but should the enemy really march toward the Delaware, to hang heavily upon their rear. Their principal difficulty would be in crossing that river, and there, he trusted, they would meet with spirited opposition from the continental troops and militia stationed on the western side under Arnold and Mifflin.

The British took up a strong position, having Millstone Creek on their left, the Raritan all along their front, and their right resting on Brunswick, and proceeded to fortify themselves with bastions.

While thus anxiously situated, Washington on the 14th received a letter from Colonel Reed, his former secretary and confidential friend. A coolness had existed on the general's part ever since he had unwarily opened the satirical letter of General Lee, yet he had acted towards Reed with his habitual highmindedness, and had recently nominated him as general of cavalry. The latter had deeply deplored the interruption of their once unreserved intercourse. He had long, he said, desired to have one hour of private conversation with Washington on the subject of Lee's letter but had deferred it in the hope of obtaining his own letter to which that was an answer. In that he had been disappointed by Lee's captivity. On the present occasion Reed's heart was full, and he refers to former times in language that is really touching:

"I am sensible, my dear sir," writes he, "how difficult it is to regain lost friendship. But the consciousness of never having justly forfeited yours, and the hope that it may be in my power fully to convince you of it, are some consolation for an event which I never think of but with the greatest concern. In the meantime, my dear general, let me entreat you to judge of me by realities, not by appearances, and believe that I never entertained or expressed a sentiment incompatible with that regard I professed for your person and character and which, whether I shall be so happy as to possess your future good opinion or not, I shall carry to my grave with me.

"A late perusal of the letters you honored me with at Cambridge and New York last year afforded me a melancholy pleasure. I cannot help acknowledging myself deeply affected, in a comparison with those which I have since received. I should not, my dear sir, have trespassed on your time and patience at this juncture so long, but that a former letter upon this subject I fear has miscarried. And whatever may be my future destination and course of life, I could not support the reflection of being thought ungrateful and insincere to a friendship which was equally my pride and my pleasure. May God Almighty crown your virtue, my dear and much respected general, with deserved success, and make your life as happy and honorable to yourself as it has been useful to your country."

The heart of Washington was moved by this appeal, and though in the midst of military preparations, with a hostile army at hand, he detained Colonel Reed's messenger long enough to write a short letter in reply: "to thank you," said he, "as I do most sincerely, for the friendly and affectionate sentiments contained in yours towards me, and to assure you that I am perfectly convinced of the sincerity of them.

"True it is, I felt myself hurt by a certain letter which appeared at that time to be the echo of one from you. I was hurt—not because I thought my judgment wronged by the expressions contained in it but because the same sentiments were not communicated immediately to myself. The favorable manner in which your opinions upon all occasions had been received, the impressions they made and the unreserved manner in which I wished and required them to be given, entitled me, I thought, to your advice upon any point in which I appeared to be wanting. To meet with anything, then, that carried with it a complexion of withholding that advice from me, and censuring my conduct to another, was such an argument of disingenuity that I was not a little mortified at it. However, I am perfectly satisfied that matters were not as they appeared from the letter alluded to."

Washington was not of a distrustful spirit. From this moment, we are told, all estrangement disappeared and the ancient relations of friendly confidence between him and Colonel Reed were restored.[7] His whole conduct throughout the affair bears evidence of his candor and magnanimity.

[7] *Life of Reed*, by his grandson.

Chapter 30

INROADS FROM THE NORTH

The American and British armies, strongly posted, as we have shown, the former along the heights of Middlebrook, the other beyond the Raritan, remained four days grimly regarding each other, both waiting to be attacked. The Jersey militia, which now turned out with alacrity, repaired some to Washington's camp, others to that of Sullivan. The latter had fallen back from Princeton and taken a position behind the Sourland Hills.

Howe pushed out detachments and made several feints as if to pass by the American camp and march to the Delaware, but Washington was not to be deceived. "The enemy will not move that way," said he, "until they have given this army a severe blow. The risk would be too great to attempt to cross a river where they must expect to meet a formidable opposition in front and would have such a force as ours in their rear." He kept on the heights, therefore, and strengthened his intrenchments.

Baffled in these attempts to draw his cautious adversary into a general action, Howe on the 19th suddenly broke up his camp and pretended to return with some precipitation to Brunswick, burning as he went several valuable dwelling-houses. Washington's light troops hovered round the enemy as far as the Raritan and Millstone, which secured their flanks, would permit, but the main army kept to its stronghold on the heights.

On the next day came warlike news from the North. Amesbury, a British spy, had been seized and examined by Schuyler. Burgoyne was stated as being arrived at Quebec to command the forces in an invasion from Canada. While he advanced with his main force by Lake Champlain, a detachment of British troops, Canadians and Indians, led by Sir John Johnson, was to penetrate by Oswego to the Mohawk River and place itself between Fort Stanwix and Fort Edward.

If this information was correct, Ticonderoga would soon be attacked. The force there might be sufficient for its defense, but Schuyler would have no troops to oppose the inroad of Sir John Johnson, and he urged a reinforcment. Washington forthwith sent orders to Putnam to procure sloops and hold four Massachusetts regiments in readiness to go up the river at a moment's warning. Still, if the information of the spy was correct, he doubted the ability of the enemy to carry the reported plan into effect. It did not appear that Burgoyne had brought any reinforcements from Europe. If so, he could not move with a greater force than five thousand men. The garrison at Ticonderoga was sufficiently strong, according to former accounts, to hold it against an attack. Burgoyne certainly would never leave it in his rear, and if he invested it he would not have a sufficient number left to send one body to Oswego and another to cut off the communications between Fort Edward and Fort George. Such was Washington's reasoning in a reply to Schuyler. In the meantime he retained his mind unflurried by these new rumors, keeping from his heights a vigilant eye upon General Howe.

On the 22d Sir William again marched out of Brunswick, but this time proceeded towards Amboy, again burning several houses on the way, hoping perhaps that the sight of columns of smoke rising from a ravaged country would irritate the Americans and provoke an attack. Washington sent out three brigades under General Greene to fall upon the rear of the enemy while Morgan hung upon their skirts with his riflemen. At the same time the army remained paraded on the heights, ready to yield support if necessary.

Finding that Howe had actually sent his heavy baggage and part of his troops over to Staten Island by a bridge of boats which he had thrown across, Washington on the 24th left the heights and descended to Quibbletown (now New Market), six or seven miles on the road to Amboy, to be nearer at hand for the protection of his advanced parties, while Lord Stirling with his division and some light troops was at Matouchin church, closer to the enemy's lines to watch their motions and be ready to harass them while crossing to the island.

General Howe now thought he had gained his point. Recalling

those who had crossed, he formed his troops into two columns, the right led by Cornwallis, the left by himself, and marched back rapidly by different routes from Amboy. He had three objects in view: to cut off the principal advanced parties of the Americans; to come up with and bring the main body into an engagement near Quibbletown; or that Lord Cornwallis, making a considerable circuit to the right, should turn the left of Washington's position, get to the heights, take possession of the passes and oblige him to abandon that stronghold where he had hitherto been so secure.[1]

Washington, however, had timely notice of his movements and, penetrating his design, regained his fortified camp at Middlebrook and secured the passes of the mountains. He then detached a body of light troops under Brigadier-General Scott, together with Morgan's riflemen, to hang on the flank of the enemy and watch their motions.

Cornwallis in his circuitous march dispersed the light parties of the advance but fell in with Lord Stirling's division, strongly posted in a woody country and well covered by artillery judiciously disposed. A sharp skirmish ensued, when the Americans gave way and retreated to the hills with the loss of a few men and three field-pieces, while the British halted at Westfield, disappointed in the main objects of their enterprise. They remained at Westfield until the afternoon of the 27th, when they moved toward Spanktown (now Rahway), plundering all before them and, it is said, burning several houses, but pursued and harassed the whole way by the American light troops.[2]

Perceiving that every scheme of bringing the Americans to the general action, or at least of withdrawing them from their strongholds, was rendered abortive by the caution and prudence of Washington, and aware of the madness of attempting to march to the Delaware through a hostile country with such a force in his rear, Sir William Howe broke up his headquarters at Amboy on the last of June and crossed over to Staten Island on the floating bridge. His troops that were encamped opposite to Amboy struck their tents on the following day and marched off to the old camping ground on the bay of New York. The ships got under way and moved down round the island, and it was soon apparent that at length the enemy had really evacuated the Jerseys.

[1] *Civil War in America*, vol. i., p. 247.
[2] Letter to the President of Congress, 28th June, 1777.

The question now was, what would be their next move? A great stir among the shipping seemed to indicate an expedition by water. But whither? Circumstances occurred to perplex the question.

Scarce had the last tent been struck and the last transport disappeared from before Amboy, when intelligence arrived from General St. Clair announcing the appearance of a hostile fleet on Lake Champlain, and that General Burgoyne with the whole Canada army was approaching Ticonderoga. The judgment and circumspection of Washington were never more severely put to the proof. Was this merely a diversion with a small force of light troops and Indians, intended to occupy the attention of the American forces in that quarter while the main body of the army in Canada should come round by sea and form a junction with the army under Howe? But General Burgoyne, in Washington's opinion, was a man of too much spirit and enterprise to return from England merely to execute a plan from which no honor was to be derived. Did he really intend to break through by the way of Ticonderoga? In that case it must be Howe's plan to co-operate with him. Had all the recent manœuvres of the enemy in the Jerseys, which had appeared so enigmatical to Washington, been merely a stratagem to amuse him until they should receive intelligence of the movements of Burgoyne? If so, Sir William must soon throw off the mask. His next move, in such case, would be to ascend the Hudson, seize on the Highland passes before Washington could form a union with the troops stationed there, and thus open the way for the junction with Burgoyne. Should Washington, however, on such a presumption, hasten with his troops to Peekskill, leaving General Howe on Staten Island, what would prevent the latter from pushing to Philadelphia by South Amboy or any other route?

Such were the perplexities and difficulties presenting themselves under every aspect of the case, and discussed by Washington in his correspondence with his accustomed clearness. In this dilemma he sent Generals Parsons and Varnum with a couple of brigades in all haste to Peekskill, and wrote to Generals George Clinton and Putnam, the former to call out the New York militia from Orange and Ulster counties, the latter to summon the militia from Connecticut, and as soon as such reinforcements should be at hand, to despatch four of the strongest Massachusetts regiments to the aid of Ticonderoga. At the same time the expediency was suggested to General Schuyler of having all the cattle and vehicles removed from such parts of the country which he might think the enemy intended to penetrate.

General Sullivan, moreover, was ordered to advance with his division towards the Highlands as far as Pompton, while Washington moved his own camp back to Morristown to be ready either to push on to the Highlands or fall back upon his recent position at Middlebrook, according to the movements of the enemy. "If I can keep General Howe below the Highlands," said he, "I think their schemes will be entirely baffled."

Deserters from Staten Island and New York soon brought word to the camp that transports were being fitted up with berths for horses, and taking in three weeks' supply of water and provender. All this indicated some other destination than that of the Hudson. Lest an attempt on the Eastern States should be intended, Washington sent a circular to their governors to put them on their guard.

In the midst of his various cares, his yeoman soldiery, the Jersey militia, were not forgotten. It was their harvest time, and the State being evacuated, there was no immediate call for their services. He dismissed therefore almost the whole of them to their homes.

Captain Graydon, whose memoirs we have heretofore had occasion to quote, paid a visit to the camp at this juncture in company with Colonel Miles and Major West, all American prisoners on Long Island but who had been liberated on parole. Graydon remarks that to their great surprise they saw no military parade upon their journey, nor any indication of martial vigor on the part of the country. Here and there [was] a milita man with his contrasted colored cape and facings, doubtless someone who had received his furlough and was bound home to his farm. Captains, majors and colonels abounded in the land but were not to be found at the head of their men.

When he arrived at the camp he could see nothing which deserved the name of army. "I was told, indeed," remarks he, "that it was much weakened by detachments and I was glad to find there was some cause for the present paucity of soldiers. I could not doubt, however, that things were going on well. The commander-in-chief and all about him were in excellent spirits." The three officers waited on Washington at his marquee in the evening. In the course of conversation he asked them what they conceived to be the objects of General Howe. Colonel Miles replied, a co-operation with the Northern army by means of the Hudson. Washington acknowledged that indications and probabilities tended to that conclusion. Nevertheless, he had little doubt the object of Howe was Philadelphia.

Graydon and his companions dined the next day at headquarters. There was a large party, in which were several ladies. Colonel Alexander Hamilton, who, in the preceding month of April, had been received into Washington's family as aide-de-camp, presided at the head of the table and "acquitted himself," writes Graydon, "with an ease, propriety and vivacity which gave me the most favorable impression of his talents and accomplishments."

We may here observe that the energy, skill and intelligence displayed by Hamilton throughout the last year's campaign, whenever his limited command gave him opportunity of evincing them, had won his entrance to headquarters, where his quick discernment and precocious judgment were soon fully appreciated. Strangers were surprised to see a youth, scarce twenty years of age, received into the implicit confidence and admitted into the gravest counsels of a man like Washington. While his uncommon talents thus commanded respect rarely inspired by one of his years, his juvenile appearance and buoyant spirit made him a universal favorite. Harrison, the "old secretary," much his senior, looked upon him with an almost paternal eye and, regarding his diminutive size and towering spirit, used to call him "the little lion," while Washington would now and then speak of him by the cherishing appellation of "my boy."[8]

We will now turn to the North and lift the curtain for a moment to give the reader a glance at affairs in that quarter, about which there were such dubious rumors.

The armament advancing against Ticonderoga of which Gen-

[8] Communicated to the author by the late Mrs. Hamilton.

NOTE.—A veteran officer of the Revolution used to speak in his old days of the occasion on which he first saw Hamilton. It was during the memorable retreat through the Jerseys. "I noticed," said he, "a youth, a mere stripling, small, slender, almost delicate in frame, marching beside a piece of artillery with a cocked hat pulled down over his eyes, apparently lost in thought, with his hand resting on the cannon and every now and then patting it as he mused, as if it were a favorite horse or a pet plaything."

eral St. Clair had given intelligence was not a mere diversion but a regular invasion, the plan of which had been devised by the king, Lord George Germaine and General Burgoyne, the latter having returned to England from Canada in the preceding year. The junction of the two armies—that in Canada and that under General Howe in New York—was considered the speediest mode of quelling the rebellion, and as the security and good government of Canada required the presence of Governor Sir Guy Carleton, three thousand men were to remain there with him. The residue of the army was to be employed upon two expeditions, the one under General Burgoyne, who was to force his way to Albany, the other under Lieutenant-Colonel St. Leger, who was to make a diversion on the Mohawk River.

The invading army was composed of three thousand seven hundred and twenty-four British rank and file, three thousand and sixteen Germans, mostly Brunswickers, two hundred and fifty Canadians and four hundred Indians. Beside these there were four hundred and seventy-three artillery-men; in all nearly eight thousand men. The army was admirably appointed. Its brass train of artillery was extolled as perhaps the finest ever allotted to an army of the size. General Phillips, who commanded the artillery, had gained great reputation in the wars in Germany. Brigadier-Generals Fraser, Powel and Hamilton were also officers of distinguished merit. So was Major-General the Baron Riedesel, a Brunswicker who commanded the German troops.

While Burgoyne with the main force proceeded from St. John's, Colonel St. Leger with a detachment of regulars and Canadians about seven hundred strong was to land at Oswego and, guided by Sir John Johnson at the head of his loyalist volunteers, tory refugees from his former neighborhood and a body of Indians, was to enter the Mohawk country, draw the attention of General Schuyler in that direction, attack Fort Stanwix and, having ravaged the valley of the Mohawk, rejoin Burgoyne at Albany, where it was expected they would make a triumphant junction with the army of Sir William Howe.

General Burgoyne left St. John's on the 16th of June. Some idea may be formed of his buoyant anticipation of a triumphant progress through the country by the manifold and lumbering appurtenances of a European camp with which his army was encumbered. In this respect he had committed the same error in his campaign through a wilderness of lakes and forests that had once embarrassed the unfortunate Braddock in his march across the mountains of Virginia.

Schuyler was uncertain as to the plans and force of the enemy. If information gathered from scouts and a captured spy might be relied on, Ticonderoga would soon be attacked, but he trusted the garrison was sufficient to maintain it. This information he transmitted to Washington from Fort Edward on the 16th, the very day that Burgoyne embarked at St. John's.

On the following day Schuyler was at Ticonderoga. The works were not in such a state of forwardness as he had anticipated, owing to the tardy arrival of troops and the want of a sufficient number of artificers. The works in question related chiefly to Mount Independence, a high circular hill on the east side of the lake, immediately opposite to the old fort and considered the most defensible. A star fort with pickets crowned the summit of the hill, which was table land. Half way down the side of the hill was a battery, and at the foot were strongly intrenched works well mounted with cannon. Here the French General de Fermois, who had charge of this fort, was posted.

As this part of Lake Champlain is narrow, a connection was kept up between the two forts by a floating bridge supported on twenty-two sunken piers in caissons formed of very strong timber. Between the piers were separate floats fifty feet long and twelve feet wide, strongly connected by iron chains and rivets. On the north side of the bridge was a boom composed of large pieces of timber secured by riveted bolts, and beside this was a double iron chain with links an inch and a half square. The bridge, boom and chain were four hundred yards in length. This immense work, the labor of months, on which no expense had been spared, was intended, while it afforded a communication between the two forts, to protect the upper part of the lake, presenting under cover of their guns a barrier which it was presumed no hostile ship would be able to break through.

Having noted the state of affairs and the wants of the garrison, Schuyler hastened to Fort George, whence he sent on provisions for upwards of sixty days, and from the banks of the Hudson additional carpenters and working cattle. "Business will go in better train and I hope with much more spirit," writes he to Congress. "And I trust we shall still be able to put everything in such order as to give the enemy a good reception and, I hope, a repulse should they attempt a real attack, which I conjecture will not be soon, if at all; although I expect they will approach with their fleet to keep us in alarm and to draw our attention from other quarters where they may mean a real attack."

His idea was that while their fleet and a small body of troops might appear before Ticonderoga and keep up continual alarms, the main army might march from St. François and St. John's towards the Connecticut River and make an attempt on the Eastern States. "A manœuvre of this kind," observes he, "would be in General Burgoyne's way and, if successful, would be attended with much honor to him. . . . I am the more confirmed in this conjecture, as the enemy cannot be ignorant how very difficult if not impossible it will be for them to penetrate to Albany, unless in losing Ticonderoga we should lose not only all our cannon but most of the army designed for this department."

In the meantime Burgoyne with his amphibious and semi-barbarous armaments was advancing up the lake. On the 21st of June he encamped at the River Boquet several miles north of Crown Point.

The garrison of Ticonderoga meanwhile were anxiously on the lookout. Their fortress, built on a hill, commanded an extensive prospect over the bright and beautiful lake and its surrounding forests, but there were long points and promontories at a distance to intercept the view.

By the 24th, scouts began to bring in word of the approaching foe. Bark canoes had been seen filled with white men and savages, then three vessels under sail and one at anchor above Split Rock, and behind it the radeau *Thunderer*, noted in the last year's naval fight. Anon came word of encampments sufficient for a large body of troops, on both sides of Gilliland's Creek, with bateaux plying about its waters, and painted warriors gliding about in canoes, while a number of smokes rising out of the forest at a distance beyond gave signs of an Indian camp.

St. Clair wrote word of all this to Schuyler and that it was supposed the enemy were waiting the arrival of more force. He did not, however, think they intended to attack, but to harass for the purpose of giving confidence to the Indians.

Schuyler transmitted a copy of St. Clair's letter to Washington. He urged Washington for reinforcements as soon as possible. At the same time he wrote to St. Clair to keep scouts on the east side of the lake near the road leading from St. John's to New Hampshire, and on the west on the road leading to the north branch of the Hudson. This done, he hastened to Albany to forward reinforcements and bring up the militia.

While there he received word from St. Clair that the enemy's fleet and army were arrived at Crown Point and had sent off detachments, one up Otter Creek to cut off the communication by Skenesborough, and another on the west side of the lake to cut off Fort George. It was evident a real attack on Ticonderoga was intended. Claims for assistance came hurrying on from other quarters. A large force (St. Leger's) was said to be arrived at Oswego, and Sir John Johnson with his myrmidons on his way to attack Fort Schuyler, the garrison of which was weak and poorly supplied with cannon.

Schuyler bestirs himself with his usual zeal amid the thickening alarms. He writes urgent letters to the Committee of Safety of New York, to General Putnam at Peekskill, to the governor of Connecticut, to the president of Massachusetts, to the committee of Berkshire, and lastly to Washington, stating the impending dangers and imploring reinforcements. He exhorts General Herkimer to keep the militia of Tryon County in readiness to protect the western frontier and to check the inroad of Sir John Johnson, and he assures St. Clair that he will move to his aid with the militia of New York as soon as he can collect them.

Dangers accumulate at Ticonderoga according to advices from St. Clair (28th). Seven of the enemy's vessels are lying at Crown Point. The rest of their fleet is probably but a little lower down. Morning guns are heard distinctly at various places. Some troops have debarked and encamped at Chimney Point. There is no prospect, he says, of being able to defend Ticonderoga unless militia come in, and he has thought of calling in those from Berkshire.

The enemy came advancing up the lake on the 30th, their main body under Burgoyne on the west side, the German reserve under Baron Riedesel on the east, communication being maintained by frigates and gunboats which in a manner kept pace between them. It was a magnificent array of warlike means, and the sound of drum and trumpet along the shores and now and then the thundering of a cannon from the ships were singularly in contrast with the usual silence of a region little better than a wilderness.

On the first of July, Burgoyne encamped four miles north of Ticonderoga and began to intrench, and to throw a boom across the lake. His advanced guard under General Fraser took post at Three Mile Point, and the ships anchored just out of gunshot of the fort.

General St. Clair was a gallant Scotchman who had seen service in the old French war as well as in this, and beheld the force arrayed against him without dismay. It is true his garrison was not so numerous as it had been represented to Washington, not exceeding three thousand five hundred men, of whom nine hundred were militia. They were badly equipped, also, and few had bayonets, yet, as Major Livingston reported, they were in good heart. St. Clair confided, however, in the strength of his position and the works which had been constructed in connection with it, and trusted he should be able to resist any attempt to take it by storm.

Schuyler at this time was at Albany, sending up reinforcements of continental troops and militia and awaiting the arrival of further reinforcements, for which sloops had been sent down to Peekskill.

He was endeavoring also to provide for the security of the department in other quarters. The savages had been scalping in the neighborhood of Fort Schuyler. A set of renegade Indians were harassing the settlements on the Susquehanna, and the threatenings of Brant, the famous Indian chief, and the prospect of a British inroad by the way of Oswego, had spread terror through Tryon County, the inhabitants of which called upon him for support.

The enemy's manœuvre of intrenching themselves and throwing a boom across the lake, of which St. Clair informed him, made him doubt of their being in great force or intending a serious attack.

In the meantime he awaited the arrival of the troops from Peekskill with impatience. On the 5th they had not appeared. "The moment they do," writes he, "I shall move with them. If they do not arrive by to-morrow I go without them and will do the best I can with the militia." He actually did set out at 8 o'clock on the morning of the 7th.

Such was the state of affairs in the north, of which Washington from time to time had been informed. An attack on Ticonderoga appeared to be impending, but as the garrison was in good heart, the commander resolute and troops were on the way to reinforce him, a spirited and perhaps successful resistance was anticipated by Washington. His surprise may therefore be imagined, on receiving a letter from Schuyler dated July 7th [1777], conveying the astounding intelligence that Ticonderoga was evacuated!

Schuyler had just received the news at Stillwater on the Hudson when on his way with reinforcements for the fortress. The first account was so vague that Washington hoped it might prove incorrect. It was confirmed by another letter from Schuyler, dated on the 9th at Fort Edward. A part of the garrison had been pursued by a detachment of the enemy as far as Fort Anne in that neighborhood, where the latter had been repulsed. As to St. Clair himself and the main part of his forces, they had thrown themselves into the forest, and nothing was known what had become of them!

"I am here," writes Schuyler, "at the head of a handful of men, not above fifteen hundred, with little ammunition, not above five rounds to a man, having neither balls nor lead to make any. The country is in the deepest consternation; no carriages to remove the stores from Fort George, which I expect every moment to hear is attacked; and what adds to my distress is that a report prevails that I had given orders for the evacuation of Ticonderoga."

Washington was totally at a loss to account for St. Clair's movement. To abandon a fortress which he had recently pronounced so defensible, and to abandon it apparently without firing a gun! And then the strange uncertainty as to his subsequent fortunes, and the whereabouts of himself and the main body of his troops! "The affair," writes Washington, "is so mysterious that it baffles even conjecture."

His first attention was to supply the wants of General Schuyler. An express was sent to Springfield for musket cartridges, gunpowder, lead and cartridge papers. Ten pieces of artillery with harness and proper officers were to be forwarded from Peekskill, as well as intrenching tools. Of tents he had none to furnish, neither could heavy cannon be spared from the defense of the Highlands.

Six hundred recruits, on their march from Massachusetts to Peekskill, were ordered to repair to the reinforcement of Schuyler. This was all the force that Washington could venture at this moment to send to his aid. But this addition to his troops, supposing those under St. Clair should have come in and any number of militia have turned out, would probably form an army equal if not superior to that said to be under Burgoyne. Besides, it was Washington's idea that the latter would suspend his operations until General Howe should make a movement in concert. Supposing that movement would be an immediate attempt against the Highlands, he ordered Sullivan with his division to Peekskill to reinforce General Putnam. At the same time he advanced with his main army to Pompton and thence to the Clove, a rugged defile through the Highlands on the west side of the Hudson. Here he encamped within eighteen miles of the river to watch and be at hand to oppose the designs of Sir William Howe, whatever might be their direction.

On the morning of the 14th came another letter from Schuyler, dated Fort Edward, July 10th. He had that morning received the first tidings of St. Clair and his missing troops and of their being fifty miles east of him.

Washington hailed the intelligence with that hopeful spirit which improved every ray of light in the darkest moments.

"I am happy to hear," writes he, "that General St. Clair and his army are not in the hands of the enemy. I really feared they had become prisoners. The evacuation of Ticonderoga and Mount Independence is an event of chagrin and surprise not apprehended, nor within the compass of my reasoning. . . . This stroke is severe indeed and has distressed us much. But, notwithstanding things at present have a dark and gloomy aspect, I hope a spirited opposition will check the progress of General Burgoyne's army and that the confidence derived from his success will hurry him into measures that will in their consequences be favorable to us. We should never despair. Our situation before has been unpromising and has changed for the better, so I trust it will again. If new difficulties arise we must only put forth new exertions and proportion our efforts to the exigency of the times."

His spirit of candor and moderation is evinced in another letter.

"I will not condemn or even pass censure upon any officer unheard, but I think it a duty which General St. Clair owes to his own character to insist upon an opportunity of giving his reasons for his sudden evacuation of a post which, but a few days before, he by his own letters thought tenable, at least for a while. People at a distance are apt to form wrong conjectures, and if General St. Clair has good reasons for the step he has taken, I think the sooner he justifies himself the better. I have mentioned these matters because he may not know that his conduct is looked upon as very unaccountable by all ranks of people in this part of the country. If he is reprehensible the public have an undoubted right to call for that justice which is due from an officer who betrays or gives up his post in an unwarrantable manner."[4]

Having stated the various measures adopted by Washington for the aid of the Northern army at this critical juncture, we will leave him at his encampment in the Clove, anxiously watching the movements of the fleet and the lower army, while we turn to the north to explain the mysterious retreat of General St. Clair.

[4] Letter to Schuyler, 18th July, 1777.

Chapter 31

FALL OF TICONDEROGA

In the accounts given in the preceding chapter of the approach of Burgoyne to Ticonderoga, it was stated that he had encamped four miles north of the fortress and intrenched himself. On the 2d of July, Indian scouts made their appearance in the vicinity of a blockhouse and some outworks about the strait or channel leading to Lake George. As General St. Clair did not think the garrison sufficient to defend all the outposts, these works with some adjacent sawmills were set on fire and abandoned. The extreme left of Ticonderoga was weak and might easily be turned. A post had therefore been established in the preceding year, nearly half a mile in advance of the old French lines, on an eminence to the north of them. General St. Clair through singular remissness had neglected to secure it. Burgoyne soon discovered this neglect and hastened to detach Generals Phillips and Fraser with a body of infantry and light artillery to take possession of this post. They did so without opposition. Heavy guns were mounted upon it. Fraser's whole corps was stationed there. The post commanded the communication by land and water with Lake George so as to cut off all supplies from that quarter. In fact, such were the advantages expected from this post, thus neglected by St. Clair, that the British gave it the significant name of Mount Hope.

The enemy now proceeded gradually to invest Ticonderoga. A line of troops was drawn from the western part of Mount Hope round to Three Mile Point, where General Fraser was posted with the advance guard while General Riedesel encamped with the German reserve in a parallel line on the opposite side of Lake Champlain at the foot of Mount Independence. For two days the enemy occupied themselves in making their advances and securing these positions, regardless of a cannonade kept up by the American batteries.

St. Clair began to apprehend that a regular siege was intended, which would be more difficult to withstand than a direct assault. He kept up a resolute aspect, however, and went about among his troops, encouraging them with the hope of a successful resistance but enjoining incessant vigilance and punctual attendance at the alarm posts at morning and evening roll-call.

With all the pains and expense lavished by the Americans to render these works impregnable, they had strangely neglected the master key by which they were all commanded. This was Sugar Hill, a rugged height, the termination of a mountain ridge which separates Lake Champlain from Lake George. It stood to the south of Ticonderoga, beyond the narrow channel which connected the two lakes, and rose precipitously from the waters of Champlain to the height of six hundred feet. It had been pronounced by the Americans too distant to be dangerous. Colonel Trumbull, some time an aide-de-camp to Washington and subsequently an adjutant, had proved the contrary in the preceding year by throwing a shot from a six-pounder in the fort nearly to the summit. It was then pronounced inaccessible to an enemy. This Trumbull had likewise proved to be an error by clambering with Arnold and Wayne to the top, whence they perceived that a practicable road for artillery might easily and readily be made. Trumbull had insisted that this was the true point for the fort, commanding the neighboring heights, the narrow parts of both lakes and the communication between. A small but strong fort here, with twenty-five heavy guns and five hundred men, would be as efficient as one hundred guns and ten thousand men on the extensive works of Ticonderoga.[1] His suggestions were disregarded. Their wisdom was now to be proved.

The British General Phillips, on taking his position, had regarded the hill with a practised eye. He caused it to be reconnoitered by a skilful engineer. The report was that it overlooked and had the entire command of Fort Ticonderoga and Fort Independence, being about fourteen hundreds yards from the former and fifteen hundred from the latter; that the ground could be levelled for cannon and a road cut up the defiles of the mountain in four-and-twenty hours.

[1] Trumbull's *Autobiography*, p. 32.

Measures were instantly taken to plant a battery on that height. While the American garrisons were entirely engaged in a different direction, cannonading Mount Hope and the British lines without material effect and without provoking a reply, the British troops were busy throughout the day and night cutting a road through rocks and trees and up rugged defiles. Guns, ammunition and stores, all were carried up the hill in the night. The cannon were hauled up from tree to tree, and before morning the ground was levelled for the battery on which they were to be mounted. To this work, thus achieved by a *coup de main*, they gave the name of Fort Defiance.

On the 5th of July, to their astonishment and consternation, the garrison beheld a legion of red-coats on the summit of this hill, constructing works which must soon lay the fortress at their mercy.

In this sudden and appalling emergency General St. Clair called a council of war. What was to be done? The batteries from this new fort would probably be open the next day. By that time Ticonderoga might be completely invested and the whole garrison exposed to capture. They had not force sufficient for one half the works, and General Schuyler, supposed to be at Albany, could afford them no relief. The danger was imminent. Delay might prove fatal. It was unanimously determined to evacuate both Ticonderoga and Mount Independence that very night and retreat to Skenesborough (now Whitehall) at the upper part of the lake about thirty miles distant, where there was a stockaded fort. The main body of the army, led by General St. Clair, were to cross to Mount Independence and push for Skenesborough by land, taking a circuitous route through the woods on the east side of the lake by way of Castleton.

The cannon, stores and provisions, together with the wounded and the women, were to be embarked on board of two hundred bateaux and conducted to the upper extremity of the lake by Colonel Long with six hundred men, two hundred of whom in five armed galleys were to form a rear-guard.

It was now three o'clock in the afternoon, yet all the preparations were to be made for the coming night, and that with as little bustle and movement as possible, for they were overlooked by Fort Defiance and their intentions might be suspected. Everything therefore was done quietly but alertly. In the meantime, to amuse the enemy, a cannonade was kept up every half hour toward the new battery on the hill. As soon as the evening closed and their movements could not be discovered, they began in all haste to load the boats. Such of the cannon as could not be taken were ordered to be spiked. It would not do to knock off their trunnions, lest the noise should awaken suspicions. In the hurry several were left uninjured. The lights in the garrison being previously extinguished, their tents were struck and put on board of the boats, and the women and the sick embarked. Everything was conducted with such silence and address that although it was a moonlight night the flotilla departed undiscovered and was soon under the shadows of the mountains and overhanging forests.

The retreat by land was not conducted with equal discretion and mystery. General St. Clair had crossed over the bridge to the Vermont side of the lake by three o'clock in the morning and set forward with his advance through the woods toward Hubbardton. But before the rear-guard under Colonel Francis got in motion the house at Fort Independence, which had been occupied by the French General de Fermois, was set on fire—by his orders, it is said, though we are loth to charge him with such indiscretion, such gross and wanton violation of the plan of retreat. The consequences were disastrous. The British sentries at Mount Hope were astonished by a conflagration suddenly lighting up Mount Independence and revealing the American troops in full retreat, for the rear-guard, disconcerted by this sudden exposure, pressed forward for the woods in the utmost haste and confusion.

The drums beat to arms in the British camp. Alarm guns were fired from Mount Hope. General Fraser dashed into Ticonderoga with his pickets, giving orders for his brigade to arm in all haste and follow. By daybreak he had hoisted the British flag over the deserted fortress. Before sunrise he had passed the bridge and was in full pursuit of the American rear-guard. Burgoyne was roused from his morning slumbers on board of the frigate *Royal George* by the alarm guns from Fort Hope, and a message from General Fraser announcing the double retreat of the Americans by land and water. From the quarter-deck of the frigate he soon had confirmation of the news. The British colors were flying on Fort Ticonderoga, and Fraser's troops were glittering on the opposite shore.

Burgoyne's measures were prompt. General Riedesel was ordered to follow and support Fraser with a part of the German troops. Garrisons were thrown into Ticonderoga and Mount Independence. The main part of the army was embarked on board of the frigates and gunboats. The floating bridge with its boom and chain, which had cost months to construct, was broken through by nine o'clock when Burgoyne set out with his squadron in pursuit of the flotilla.

We left the latter making its retreat on the preceding evening towards Skenesborough. The lake above Ticonderoga becomes so narrow that in those times it was frequently called South River. Its beautiful waters wound among mountains covered with primeval forests. The bateaux, deeply laden, made their way slowly in a lengthened line, sometimes under the shadows of the mountains, sometimes in the gleam of moonlight. The rear-guard of armed galleys followed at wary distance. No immediate pursuit, however, was apprehended. The floating bridge was considered an effectual impediment to the enemy's fleet. Gayety therefore prevailed among the fugitives. They exulted in the secrecy and dexterity with which they had managed their retreat and amused themselves with the idea of what would be the astonishment of the enemy at daybreak. The officers regaled merrily on the stores saved from Ticonderoga and, knocking off the necks of bottles of wine, drank a pleasant *reveille* to General Burgoyne.

About three o'clock in the afternoon of the succeeding day the heavily laden bateaux arrived at Skenesborough. The disembarkation had scarcely commenced when the thundering of artillery was heard from below. Could the enemy be at hand? It was even so. The British gunboats, having pushed on in advance of the frigates, had overtaken and were firing upon the galleys. The latter defended themselves for a while but at length two struck and three were blown up. The fugitives from them brought word that the British ships not being able to come up, troops and Indians were landing from them and scrambling up the hills, intending to get in the rear of the fort and cut off all retreat.

All now was consternation and confusion. The bateaux, the storehouses, the fort, the mill were all set on fire, and a general flight took place toward Fort Anne, about twelve miles distant. Some made their way in boats up Wood Creek, a winding stream.

The main body, under Colonel Long, retreated by a narrow defile
cut through the woods, harassed all night by alarms that the Indians were close in pursuit. Both parties reached Fort Anne by
daybreak. It was a small picketed fort near the junction of Wood
Creek and East Creek, about sixteen miles from Fort Edward.
General Schuyler arrived at the latter place on the following day.
The number of troops with him was inconsiderable, but, hearing
of Colonel Long's situation, he immediately sent him a small reinforcement with provisions and ammunition and urged him to
maintain his post resolutely.

On the same day Colonel Long's scouts brought in word that
there were British red-coats approaching. They were in fact a regiment under Lieutenant-Colonel Hill, detached from Skenesborough by Burgoyne in pursuit of the fugitives. Long sallied forth
to meet them, posting himself at a rocky defile where there was a
narrow pathway along the border of Wood Creek. As the enemy
advanced he opened a heavy fire upon them in front, while a part
of his troops crossing and recrossing the creek and availing themselves of their knowledge of the ground, kept up a shifting attack
from the woods in flank and rear. Apprehensive of being surrounded, the British took post upon a high hill to their right,
where they were warmly besieged for nearly two hours and, according to their own account, would certainly have been forced, had
not some of their Indian allies arrived and set up the much-
dreaded war-whoop. It was answered with three cheers by the British upon the hill. This changed the fortune of the day. The Americans had nearly expended their ammunition and had not enough
left to cope with this new enemy. They retreated therefore to Fort
Anne, carrying with them a number of prisoners, among whom
were a captain and surgeon. Supposing the troops under Colonel
Hill an advance guard of Burgoyne's army, they set fire to the fort
and pushed on to Fort Edward, where they gave the alarm that
the main force of the enemy was close after them and that no one
knew what had become of General St. Clair and the troops who
had retreated with him. We shall now clear up the mystery of his
movements.

His retreat through the woods from Mount Independence continued the first day until night, when he arrived at Castleton,
thirty miles from Ticonderoga. His rear-guard halted about six

miles short, at Hubbardton, to await the arrival of stragglers. It was composed of three regiments under Colonels Seth Warner, Francis and Hale, in all about thirteen hundred men.

Early the next morning, a sultry morning of July, while they were taking their breakfast they were startled by the report of fire-arms. Their sentries had discharged their muskets and came running in with word that the enemy were at hand.

It was General Fraser with his advance of eight hundred and fifty men, who had pressed forward in the latter part of the night and now attacked the Americans with great spirit notwithstanding their superiority in numbers. In fact, he expected to be promptly reinforced by Riedesel and his Germans. The Americans met the British with great spirit, but at the very commencement of the action Colonel Hale, with a detachment placed under his command to protect the rear, gave way, leaving Warner and Francis with but seven hundred men to bear the brunt of the battle. These posted themselves behind logs and trees in "backwoods" style, whence they kept up a destructive fire and were evidently gaining the advantage when General Riedesel came pressing into the action with his German troops, drums beating and colors flying. There was now an impetuous charge with the bayonet. Colonel Francis was among the first who fell, gallantly fighting at the head of his men. The Americans, thinking the whole German force upon them, gave way and fled, leaving the ground covered with their dead and wounded. Many others who had been wounded perished in the woods where they had taken refuge. Their whole loss in killed, wounded and taken was upwards of three hundred; that of the enemy one hundred and eighty-three. Several officers were lost on both sides. Among those wounded of the British was Major Ackland of the grenadiers, of whose further fortunes in the war we shall have to speak hereafter.

The noise of the firing when the action commenced had reached General St. Clair at Castleton. He immediately sent orders to two militia regiments which were in his rear, and within two miles of the battle-ground, to hasten to the assistance of his rear-guard. They refused to obey and hurried forward to Castleton. At this juncture St. Clair received information of Burgoyne's arrival at Skenesborough and the destruction of the American works there. Fearing to be intercepted at Fort Anne, he immediately changed his route, struck into the woods on his left and directed his march to Rutland, leaving word for Warner to follow him. The latter overtook him two days afterwards with his shattered force reduced to ninety men. As to Colonel Hale, who had pressed towards Castleton at the beginning of the action, he and his men were overtaken the same day by the enemy, and the whole party captured without making any fight. It has been alleged in his excuse, with apparent justice, that he and a large portion of his men were in feeble health and unfit for action. For his own part, he died while yet a prisoner, and never had the opportunity, which he sought, to vindicate himself before a court-martial.

On the 12th St. Clair reached Fort Edward, his troops haggard and exhausted by their long retreat through the woods. Such is the story of the catastrophe at Fort Ticonderoga, which caused so much surprise and concern to Washington, and of the seven days' mysterious disappearance of St. Clair, which kept every one in the most painful suspense.

The loss of artillery, ammunition, provisions and stores in consequence of the evacuation of these northern posts was prodigious, but the worst effect was the consternation spread throughout the country. A panic prevailed at Albany, the people running about as if distracted, sending off their goods and furniture.[2] The great barriers of the North, it was said, were broken through and there was nothing to check the triumphant career of the enemy.

The invading army, both officers and men, according to a British writer of the time, "were highly elated with their fortune and deemed that and their prowess to be irresistible. They regarded their enemy with the greatest contempt and considered their own toils to be nearly at an end and Albany already in their hands."

In England too, according to the same author, the joy and exultation were extreme not only at court but with all those who hoped or wished the unqualified subjugation and unconditional submission of the colonies. "The loss in reputation was greater to the Americans," adds he, "and capable of more fatal consequences than that of ground, of posts, of artillery or of men. All the contemptuous and most degrading charges which had been made by their enemies, of their wanting the resolution and abilities of men, even in defense of what was dear to them, were now repeated and

2 MS. Letter of Richard Varick to Schuyler.

believed. . . . It was not difficult to diffuse an opinion that the war in effect was over and that any further resistance would render the terms of their submission worse. Such," he concludes, "were some of the immediate effects of the loss of those grand keys of North America: Ticonderoga and the lakes."[3]

[3] *Hist. Civil War in America*, vol. i., p. 283.

Chapter 32

WASHINGTON'S DOUBT AND PERPLEXITY

A spirited exploit to the eastward was performed during the prevalence of adverse news from the North. General Prescott had command of the British forces in Rhode Island. His harsh treatment of Colonel Ethan Allen and his haughty and arrogant conduct on various occasions had rendered him peculiarly odious to the Americans. Lieutenant-Colonel Barton, who was stationed with a force of Rhode Island militia on the mainland, received word that Prescott was quartered at a country house near the western shore of the island about four miles from Newport, totally unconscious of danger though in a very exposed situation. He determined if possible to surprise and capture him. Forty resolute men joined him in the enterprise. Embarking at night in two boats at Warwick Neck, they pulled quietly across the bay with muffled oars, undiscovered by the ships of war and guard-boats; landed in silence; eluded the vigilance of the guard stationed near the house; captured the sentry at the door and surprised the general in his bed. His aide-de-camp leaped from the window but was likewise taken. Colonel Barton returned with equal silence and address and arrived safe at Warwick with his prisoners. A sword was voted to him by Congress and he received a colonel's commission in the regular army.

Washington hailed the capture of Prescott as a peculiarly fortunate circumstance, furnishing him with an equivalent for General Lee. He accordingly wrote to Sir William Howe, proposing the exchange. "This proposition," writes he, "being agreeable to the letter and spirit of the agreement subsisting between us, will I hope have your approbation. I am the more induced to expect it as it will not only remove one ground of controversy between us but in its consequences effect the exchanges of Lieutenant-Colonel

Campbell and the Hessian officers for a like number of ours of equal rank in your possession."

No immediate reply was received to this letter, Sir William Howe being at sea. In the meantime Prescott remained in durance. "I would have him genteelly accommodated but strongly guarded," writes Washington. "I would not admit him to parole, as General Howe has not thought proper to grant General Lee that indulgence."[1]

Washington continued his anxious exertions to counteract the operations of the enemy, forwarding artillery and ammunition to Schuyler, with all the camp furniture that could be spared from his own encampment and from Peekskill. A part of Nixon's brigade was all the reinforcement he could afford in his present situation. "To weaken this army more than is prudent," writes he, "would perhaps bring destruction upon it, and I look upon the keeping it upon a respectable footing as the only means of preventing a junction of Howe's and Burgoyne's armies, which if effected may have the most fatal consequences."

Schuyler had earnestly desired the assistance of an active officer well acquainted with the country. Washington sent him Arnold. "I need not," writes he, "enlarge upon his well-known activity, conduct and bravery. The proofs he has given of all these have gained him the confidence of the public and of the army, the Eastern troops in particular."

The question of rank, about which Arnold was so tenacious, was yet unsettled and though, had his promotion been regular, he would have been superior in command to General St. Clair, he assured Washington that on the present occasion his claim should create no dispute.

Schuyler in the meantime, aided by Kosciuszko the Pole, who was engineer in his department, had selected two positions on Moses Creek, four miles below Fort Edward, where the troops which had retreated from Ticonderoga, and part of the militia, were throwing up works.

To impede the advance of the enemy, he had caused trees to be felled into Wood Creek so as to render it unnavigable, and the roads between Fort Edward and Fort Anne to be broken up, the cattle in that direction to be brought away and the forage de-

[1] Letter to Governor Trumbull. *Correspondence of the Revolution*, vol. i., Sparks.

stroyed. He had drawn off the garrison from Fort George, who left the buildings in flames. "Strengthened by that garrison, who are in good health," writes he, "and if the militia, who are here, or an equal number, can be prevailed on to stay and the enemy give me a few days more, which I think they will be obliged to do, I shall not be apprehensive that they will be able to force the posts I am about to occupy."

Washington cheered on his faithful coadjutor. His reply to Schuyler (July 22d) was full of that confident hope, founded on sagacious forecast, with which he was prone to animate his generals in times of doubt and difficulty.

"Though our affairs for some days past have worn a dark and gloomy aspect, I yet look forward to a fortunate and happy change. I trust General Burgoyne's army will meet sooner or later an effectual check and, as I suggested before, that the success he has had will precipitate his ruin. From your accounts, he appears to be pursuing that line of conduct which of all others is most favorable to us. I mean acting in detachment. This conduct will certainly give room for enterprise on our part and expose his parties to great hazard. Could we be so happy as to cut one of them off, supposing it should not exceed four, five or six hundred men, it would inspirit the people and do away much of their present anxiety. In such an event they would lose sight of past misfortunes and, urged at the same time by a regard to their own security, they would fly to arms and afford every aid in their power."

While he thus suggested bold enterprises he cautioned Schuyler not to repose too much confidence in the works he was projecting, so as to collect in them a large quantity of stores. "I begin to consider lines as a kind of trap," writes he, "and not to answer the valuable purposes expected from them unless they are in passes which cannot be avoided by the enemy."

In circulars addressed to the brigadier-generals of militia in the western parts of Massachusetts and Connecticut, he warned them that the evacuation of Ticonderoga had opened a door by which the enemy, unless vigorously opposed, might penetrate the northern part of the State of New York and the western parts of New Hampshire and Massachusetts and, forming a junction with General Howe, cut off the communication between the Eastern and Northern States.

"It cannot be supposed," adds he, "that the small number of

continental troops assembled at Fort Edward is alone sufficient to check the progress of the enemy. To the militia therefore must we look for support in this time of trial, and I trust that you will immediately upon receipt of this, if you have not done it already, march with at least one third of the militia under your command and rendezvous at Saratoga unless directed to some other place by General Schuyler or General Arnold."

Washington now ordered that all the vessels and river craft not required at Albany should be sent down to New Windsor and Fishkill and kept in readiness, for he knew not how soon the movements of General Howe might render it suddenly necessary to transport part of his forces up the Hudson.

Further letters from Schuyler urged the increasing exigencies of his situation. It was harvest time. The militia, impatient at being detained from their rural labors, were leaving him in great numbers. In a council of general officers it had been thought advisable to give leave of absence to half lest the whole should depart. He feared those who remained would do so but a few days. The enemy were steadily employed cutting a road toward him from Skenesborough. From the number of horse they were reported to have and to expect, they might intend to bring their provisions on horseback. If so, they would be able to move with expedition. In this position of affairs he urged to be reinforced as speedily as possible.

Washington in reply informed him that he had ordered a further reinforcement of General Glover's brigade, which was all he could possibly furnish in his own exigencies. He trusted affairs with Schuyler would soon wear a more smiling aspect, that the Eastern States, who were so deeply concerned in the matter, would exert themselves, by effectual succor, to enable him to check the progress of the enemy and repel a danger by which they were immediately threatened. From the information he had received, he supposed the force of the enemy to be little more than five thousand.

"They seem," said he, "to be unprovided with wagons to transport the immense quantity of baggage and warlike apparatus, without which they cannot pretend to penetrate the country. You mention their having a great number of horses, but they must nevertheless require a considerable number of wagons, as there are many things which cannot be transported on horses. They can never think of advancing without securing their rear, and the force with which they can act against you will be greatly reduced by detachments necessary for that purpose. And as they have to cut out their passage and to remove the impediments you have thrown in their way before they can proceed, this circumstance, with the encumbrance they must feel in their baggage, stores, etc., will inevitably retard their march and give you leisure and opportunity to prepare a good reception for them. . . . I have directed General Lincoln to repair to you as speedily as the state of his health, which is not very perfect, will permit. This gentleman has always supported the character of a judicious, brave, active officer, and he is exceedingly popular in the State of Massachusetts, to which he belongs. He will have a degree of influence over the militia which cannot fail of being highly advantageous. I have intended him more particularly for the command of the militia, and I promise myself it will have a powerful tendency to make them turn out with more cheerfulness and to inspire them with perseverance to remain in the field and with fortitude and spirit to do their duty while in it."[2]

Washington highly approved of a measure suggested by Schuyler, of stationing a body of troops somewhere about the Hampshire Grants (Vermont), so as to be in the rear or on the flank of Burgoyne should he advance. It would make the latter, he said, very circumspect in his advances if it did not entirely prevent them. It would keep him in continual anxiety for his rear and oblige him to leave the posts behind him much stronger than he would otherwise do. He advised that General Lincoln should have the command of the corps thus posted, "as no person could be more proper for it."

He recommended moreover that in case the enemy should make any formidable movement in the neighborhood of Fort Schuyler (Stanwix) on the Mohawk River, General Arnold or some other sensible, spirited officer should be sent to take charge of that post, keep up the spirits of the inhabitants and cultivate and improve the favorable disposition of the Indians.

The reader will find in the sequel what a propitious effect all these measures had upon the fortunes of the Northern campaign, and with what admirable foresight Washington calculated all its chances. Due credit must also be given to the sagacious counsels

[2] Schuyler's Letter Book.

and executive energy of Schuyler, who suggested some of the best moves in the campaign and carried them vigorously into action. Never was Washington more ably and loyally seconded by any of his generals.

But now the attention of the commander-in-chief is called to the seaboard. On the 23d of July, the fleet, so long the object of watchful solicitude, actually put to sea. The force embarked, according to subsequent accounts, consisted of thirty-six British and Hessian battalions, including the light infantry and grenadiers, with a powerful artillery; a New York corps of provincials, or royalists, called the Queen's Rangers, and a regiment of light horse; between fifteen and eighteen thousand men in all. The force left with General Sir Henry Clinton for the protection of New York consisted of seventeen battalions, a regiment of light horse and the remainder of the provincial corps.[3]

The destination of the fleet was still a matter of conjecture. Just after it had sailed, a young man presented himself at one of General Putnam's outposts. He had been a prisoner in New York, he said, but had received his liberty and a large reward on undertaking to be the bearer of a letter from General Howe to Burgoyne. This letter his feelings of patriotism prompted him to deliver up to General Putnam. The letter was immediately transmitted by the general to Washington. It was in the handwriting of Howe and bore his signature. In it he informed Burgoyne that instead of any designs up the Hudson, he was bound to the east against Boston. "If," said he, "according to my expectations, we may succeed in getting possession of it I shall without loss of time proceed to co-operate with you in the defeat of the rebel army opposed to you. Clinton is sufficiently strong to amuse Washington and Putnam. I am now making demonstrations to the southward, which I think will have the full effect in carrying our plan into execution."

Washington at once pronounced the letter a feint. "No stronger proof could be given," said he, "that Howe is not going to the eastward. The letter was evidently intended to fall into our hands. If there were not too great a risk of the dispersion of their fleet, I should think their putting to sea a mere manoeuvre to deceive, and the North River still their object. I am persuaded more than ever that Philadelphia is the place of destination."

[3] *Civil War in America*, vol. i., p. 250.

He now set out with his army for the Delaware, ordering
Sullivan and Stirling with their divisions to cross the Hudson from
Peekskill and proceed towards Philadelphia. Every movement and
order showed his doubt and perplexity and the circumspection
with which he had to proceed. On the 30th he writes from
Coryell's Ferry, about thirty miles from Philadelphia, to General
Gates, who was in that city: "As we are yet uncertain as to the
real destination of the enemy, though the Delaware seems the
most probable, I have thought it prudent to halt the army at this
place, Howell's Ferry and Trenton, at least till the fleet actually
enters the bay and puts the matter beyond a doubt. From hence
we can be on the proper ground to oppose them before they can
possibly make their arrangements and dispositions for an attack. . . . That the post in the Highlands may not be left too
much exposed, I have ordered General Sullivan's division to halt
at Morristown, whence it will march southward if there should be
occasion, or northward upon the first advice that the enemy
should be throwing any force up the North River. General Howe's
in a manner abandoning General Burgoyne, is so unaccountable a
matter that, till I am fully assured it is so, I cannot help casting
my eyes continually behind me. As I shall pay no regard to any
flying reports of the appearance of the fleet, I shall expect an account of it from you the moment you have ascertained it to your
satisfaction."

On the 31st he was informed that the enemy's fleet of two
hundred and twenty-eight sail had arrived the day previous at the
Capes of Delaware. He instantly wrote to Putnam to hurry on two
brigades which had crossed the river and to let Schuyler and the
commanders in the Eastern States know that they had nothing to
fear from Howe and might bend all their forces, continental and
militia, against Burgoyne. In the meantime he moved his camp to
Germantown, about six miles from Philadelphia, to be at hand for
the defense of that city.

The very next day came word by express that the fleet had again
sailed out of the Capes and apparently shaped its course eastward.
"This surprising event gives me the greatest anxiety," writes he to
Putnam (August 1), "and unless every possible exertion is made,
may be productive of the happiest consequences to the enemy and
the most injurious to us. . . . The importance of preventing Mr.
Howe's getting possession of the Highlands by a *coup de main* is

infinite to America and, in the present situation of things, every effort that can be thought of must be used. The probability of his going to the eastward is exceedingly small, and the ill effects that might attend such a step inconsiderable in comparison with those that would inevitably attend a successful stroke on the Highlands."

Under this impression Washington sent orders to Sullivan to hasten back with his division and the two brigades which had recently left Peekskill and to recross the Hudson to that post as speedily as possible, intending to forward the rest of the army with all the expedition in his power. He wrote also to General George Clinton to reinforce Putnam with as many of the New York militia as could be collected. Clinton, be it observed, had just been installed governor of the State of New York, the first person elevated to that office under the constitution. He still continued in actual command of the militia of the State, and it was with great satisfaction that Washington subsequently learnt he had determined to resume the command of Fort Montgomery in the Highlands. "There cannot be a more proper man," writes he, "on every account."

Washington moreover requested Putnam to send an express to Governor Trumbull, urging assistance from the militia of his State without a moment's loss of time. "Connecticut cannot be in more danger through any channel than this, and every motive of its own interest and the general good demands its utmost endeavors to give you effectual assistance. Governor Trumbull will, I trust, be sensible of this."

And here we take occasion to observe that there could be no surer reliance for aid in time of danger than the patriotism of Governor Trumbull, nor were there men more ready to obey a sudden appeal to arms than the yeomanry of Connecticut, however much their hearts might subsequently yearn toward the farms and firesides they had so promptly abandoned. No portion of the Union was more severely tasked throughout the Revolution for military services; and Washington avowed when the great struggle was over that, "if all the States had done their duty as well as the little State of Connecticut, the war would have been ended long ago.[4]

For several days Washington remained at Germantown in pain-

[4] Communicated by Professor B. Silliman.

ful uncertainty about the British fleet; whether gone to the south or to the east. The intense heat of the weather made him unwilling again to move his army, already excessively harassed by marchings and counter-marchings. Concluding at length that the fleet had actually gone to the east, he was once more on the way to recross the Delaware when an express overtook him on the 10th of August with tidings that three days before it had been seen off Sinepuxent Inlet about sixteen leagues south of the Capes of Delaware.

Again he came to a halt and waited for further intelligence. Danger suggested itself from a different quarter. Might it not be Howe's plan, by thus appearing with his ships at different places, to lure the army after him and thereby leave the country open for Sir Henry Clinton with the troops at New York to form a junction with Burgoyne? With this idea Washington wrote forthwith to the veteran Putnam to be on the alert, collect all the force he could to strengthen his post at Peekskill and send down spies to ascertain whether Sir Henry Clinton was actually at New York and what troops he had there. "If he has the number of men with him that is reported," observes Washington, "it is probably with the intention to attack you from below while Burgoyne comes down upon you from above."

The old general, whose boast it was that he never slept but with one eye, was already on the alert. A circumstance had given him proof positive that Sir Henry was in New York, and had roused his military ire. A spy, sent by that commander, had been detected furtively collecting information of the force and condition of the post at Peekskill and had undergone a military trial. A vessel of war came up the Hudson in all haste and landed a flag of truce at Verplanck's Point, by which a message was transmitted to Putnam from Sir Henry Clinton, claiming Edmund Palmer as a lieutenant in the British service.

The reply of the old general was brief but emphatic.

"HEADQUARTERS, 7th Aug., 1777.

"Edmund Palmer, an officer in the enemy's service, was taken as a spy lurking within our lines. He has been tried as a spy, condemned as a spy and shall be executed as a spy, and the flag is ordered to depart immediately.

"ISRAEL PUTNAM.

"P. S.—He has accordingly been executed."

Governor Clinton, the other guardian of the Highlands, and actually at his post at Fort Montgomery, was equally on the alert. He had faithfully followed Washington's directions in ordering out militia from different counties to reinforce his own garrison and the army under Schuyler. "I never knew the militia come out with greater alacrity," writes he, "but, as many of them have yet a great part of their harvests in the field, I fear it will be difficult to detain them long unless the enemy will make some movements that indicate a design of coming this way suddenly, and so obvious as to be believed by the militia."

At the same time, the worthy governor expressed his surprise that the Northern army had not been reinforced from the eastward. "The want of confidence in the general officers to the northward," adds he, "is the specious reason. To me it appears a very weak one. Common gratitude to a sister State, as well as duty to the continent at large, conspire in calling on our eastern neighbors to step forth on this occasion."

One measure more was taken by Washington, during this interval, in aid of the northern department. The Indians who accompanied Burgoyne were objects of great dread to the American troops, especially the militia. As a counterpoise to them, he now sent up Colonel Morgan with five hundred riflemen to fight them in their own way. "They are all chosen men," said he "selected from the army at large and well acquainted with the use of rifles and with that mode of fighting. I expect the most eminent services from them and I shall be mistaken if their presence does not go far towards producing a general desertion among the savages." It was indeed an arm of strength which he could but ill spare from his own army.

Putnam was directed to have sloops ready to transport them up the Hudson, and Gates was informed of their being on the way and about what time he might expect them, as well as two regiments from Peekskill under colonels Van Courtlandt and Livingston.

"With these reinforcements, besides the militia under General Lincoln," writes Washington to Gates, "I am in hopes you will find yourself at least equal to stop the progress of Mr. Burgoyne and, by cutting off his supplies of provisions, to render his situation very ineligible." Washington was thus in a manner carrying on two games at once, with Howe on the seaboard and with Burgoyne on the upper waters of the Hudson, and endeavoring by skilful movements to give check to both. It was an arduous and complicated task, especially with his scanty and fluctuating means and the wide extent of country and great distances over which he had to move his men.

His measures to throw a force in the rear of Burgoyne were now in a fair way of being carried into effect. Lincoln was at Bennington. Stark had joined him with a body of New Hampshire militia, and a corps of Massachusetts militia was arriving. "Such a force in his rear," observed Washington, "will oblige Burgoyne to leave such strong posts behind as must make his main body very weak and extremely capable of being repulsed by the force we have in front."

During his encampment in the neighborhood of Philadelphia, Washington was repeatedly at that city, making himself acquainted with the military capabilities of the place and its surrounding country and directing the construction of fortifications on the river. In one of these visits he became acquainted with the young Marquis de Lafayette, who had recently arrived from France, in company with a number of French, Polish and German officers, among whom was the Baron de Kalb. The marquis was not quite twenty years of age, yet had already been married nearly three years to a lady of rank and fortune. Full of the romance of liberty, he had torn himself from his youthful bride, turned his back upon the gayeties and splendors of a court, and in defiance of impediments and difficulties multiplied in his path had made his way to America to join its hazardous fortunes.

He sent in his letters of recommendation to Mr. Lovell, Chairman of the Committee of Foreign Affairs, and applied the next day at the door of Congress to know his success. Mr. Lovell came forth and gave him but little encouragement. Congress in fact was embarrassed by the number of foreign applications, many without merit. Lafayette immediately sent in the following note: "After my sacrifices I have the right to ask two favors. One is to serve at my own expense. The other to commence by serving as a volunteer."[5]

This simple appeal had its effect. It called attention to his peculiar case, and Congress resolved on the 31st of July that in consideration of his zeal, his illustrious family and connections, he

5 *Memoirs du Gen. Lafayette*, tom. i., p. 19.

should have the rank of major-general in the army of the United States.

It was at a public dinner where a number of members of Congress were present that Lafayette first saw Washington. He immediately knew him, he said, from the officers who surrounded him, by his commanding air and person. When the party was breaking up, Washington took him aside, complimented him in a gracious manner on his disinterested zeal and the generosity of his conduct, and invited him to make headquarters his home. "I cannot promise you the luxuries of a court," said he, "but as you have become an American soldier, you will doubtless accommodate yourself to the fare of an American army."

Many days had now elapsed without further tidings of the fleet. What had become of it? Had Howe gone against Charleston? If so, the distance was too great to think of following him. Before the army, debilitated and wasted by a long march under a summer sun in an unhealthy climate, could reach there, he might accomplish every purpose he had in view and re-embark his troops to turn his arms against Philadelphia or any other point without the army being at hand to oppose him.

What, under these uncertainties, was to be done? Remain inactive, in the remote probability of Howe's returning this way, or proceed to the Hudson with a view either to oppose Burgoyne or make an attempt upon New York? A successful stroke with respect to either might make up for any losses sustained in the South. The latter was unanimously determined in a council of war, in which the Marquis de Lafayette took part. As it was however a movement that might involve the most important consequences, Washington sent his aide-de-camp, Colonel Alexander Hamilton, with a letter to the President of Congress requesting the opinion of that body. Congress approved the decision of the council, and the army was about to be put in march, when all these tormenting uncertainties were brought to an end by intelligence that the fleet had actually entered the Chesapeake and anchored at Swan Point, at least two hundred miles within the capes. "By General Howe's coming so far up the Chesapeake," writes Washington, "he must mean to reach Philadelphia by that route, though to be sure it is a strange one."

The mystery of these various appearances and vanishings, which had caused so much wonder and perplexity, is easily explained.

Shortly before putting to sea with the ships of war, Howe had sent a number of transports, and a ship cut down as a floating battery, up the Hudson, which had induced Washington to despatch troops to the Highlands. After putting to sea, the fleet was a week in reaching the Capes of Delaware. When there, the commanders were deterred from entering the river by reports of measures taken to obstruct its navigation. It was then determined to make for Chesapeake Bay and approach in that way as near as possible to Philadelphia. Contrary winds, however, kept them for a long time from getting into the bay.

Lafayette, in his memoirs, describes a review of Washington's army which he witnessed about this time. "Eleven thousand men, but tolerably armed and still worse clad, presented," he said, "a singular spectacle. In this parti-colored and often naked state, the best dresses were hunting shirts of brown linen. Their tactics were equally irregular. They were arranged without regard to size, excepting that the smallest men were the front rank. With all this, there were good-looking soldiers conducted by zealous officers."

"We ought to feel embarrassed," said Washington to him, "in presenting ourselves before an officer just from the French army."

"It is to learn and not to instruct that I come here," was Lafayette's apt and modest reply, and it gained him immediate popularity.

The marquis, however, had misconceived the nature of his appointment. His commission was merely honorary, but he had supposed it given with a view to the command of a division of the army. This misconception on his part caused Washington some embarrassment. The marquis, with his characteristic vivacity and ardor, was eager for immediate employ. He admitted that he was young and inexperienced, but always accompanied the admission with the assurance that, so soon as Washington should think him fit for the command of a division, he would be ready to enter upon the duties of it and, in the meantime, offered his services for a smaller command. "What the designs of Congress respecting this gentleman are, and what line of conduct I am to pursue to comply with their design and his expectations," writes Washington, "I know not, and beg to be instructed."

"The numberless applications for employment by foreigners under their respective appointments," continues he, "add no small embarrassment to a command which, without it, is abundantly perplexed by the different tempers I have to do with, and the different modes which the respective States have pursued in nominating and arranging their officers. The combination of all is but too just a representation of a great chaos, from whence we are endeavoring, how successfully time only can show, to draw some regularity and order."[6]

How truly is here depicted one of the great difficulties of his command, continually tasking his equity and equanimity. In the present instance it was intimated to Washington that he was not bound by the tenor of Lafayette's commission to give him a command but was at liberty to follow his own judgment in the matter. This still left him in a delicate situation with respect to the marquis, whose prepossessing manners and self-sacrificing zeal inspired regard but whose extreme youth and inexperience necessitated caution. Lafayette, however, from the first attached himself to Washington with an affectionate reverence, the sincerity of which could not be mistaken, and soon won his way into a heart which, with all its apparent coldness, was naturally confiding and required sympathy and friendship. And it is a picture well worthy to be hung up in history, this cordial and enduring alliance of the calm, dignified, sedate Washington, mature in years and wisdom, and the young, buoyant, enthusiastic Lafayette.

The several divisions of the army had been summoned to the immediate neighborhood of Philadelphia, and the militia of Pennsylvania, Delaware and the northern parts of Virginia were called out. Many of the militia, with Colonel Proctor's corps of artillery, had been ordered to rendezvous at Chester on the Delaware, about twelve miles below Philadelphia, and, by Washington's orders, General Wayne left his brigade under the next in command and repaired to Chester to arrange the troops assembling there.

As there had been much disaffection to the cause evinced in Philadelphia, Washington, in order to encourage its friends and dishearten its enemies, marched with the whole army through the city down Front and up Chestnut Street. Great pains were taken to make the display as imposing as possible. All were charged to keep to their ranks, carry their arms well and step in time to the music of the drums and fifes, collected in the centre of each brigade. "Though indifferently dressed," says a spectator, "they

6 Washington to Benjamin Harrison. Sparks, v., 35.

held well-burnished arms and carried them like soldiers, and looked in short as if they might have faced an equal number with a reasonable prospect of success." To give them something of a uniform appearance, they had sprigs of green in their hats.

Washington rode at the head of the troops attended by his numerous staff, with the Marquis de Lafayette by his side. The long column of the army, broken into divisions and brigades, the pioneers with their axes, the squadrons of horse, the extended trains of artillery, the tramp of steed, the bray of trumpet and the spirit-stirring sound of drum and fife all had an imposing effect on a peaceful city unused to the sight of marshalled armies. The disaffected, who had been taught to believe the American forces much less than they were in reality, were astonished as they gazed on the lengthening procession of a host which to their unpractised eyes appeared innumerable; while the whigs, gaining fresh hope and animation from the sight, cheered the patriot squadrons as they passed.

Having marched through Philadelphia, the army continued on to Wilmington at the confluence of Christiana Creek and the Brandywine, where Washington set up his headquarters, his troops being encamped on the neighboring heights.

We will now revert to the other object of Washington's care and solicitude, the invading army of Burgoyne in the north, and will see how far his precautionary measures were effective.

[Burgoyne experienced serious reverses in his movement southward.]

Chapter 33

CORNWALLIS ENTERS PHILADELPHIA

On the 25th of August the British army under General Howe began to land from the fleet in Elk River at the bottom of Chesapeake Bay. The place where they landed was about six miles
below the Head of Elk (now Elkton), a small town, the capital of
Cecil County. This was seventy miles from Philadelphia, ten miles
farther from that city than they had been when encamped at
Brunswick. The intervening country, too, was less open than the
Jerseys and cut up by deep streams. Sir William had chosen this
circuitous route in the expectation of finding friends among the
people of Cecil County and of the lower counties of Pennsylvania,
many of whom were Quakers and noncombatants and many persons disaffected to the patriot cause.

Early in the evening, Washington received intelligence that the
enemy were landing. There was a quantity of public and private
stores at the Head of Elk which he feared would fall into their
hands if they moved quickly. Every attempt was to be made to
check them. The divisions of Generals Greene and Stephen were
within a few miles of Wilmington. Orders were sent for them to
march thither immediately. The two other divisions, which had
halted at Chester to refresh, were to hurry forward. Major-General
Armstrong, the same who had surprised the Indian village of Kit-
taning in the French war and who now commanded the Pennsylvania militia, was urged to send down in the cool of the night all
the men he could muster, properly armed. "The first attempt of
the enemy," writes Washington, "will be with light parties to seize
horses, carriages and cattle, and we must endeavor to check them
at the outset."

General Rodney, therefore, who commanded the Delaware militia, was ordered to throw out scouts and patrols toward the enemy

to watch their motions and to move near them with his troops as soon as he should be reinforced by the Maryland militia.

Light troops were sent out early in the morning to hover about and harass the invaders. Washington himself, accompanied by General Greene and the Marquis de Lafayette and their aides, rode forth to reconnoiter the country in the neighborhood of the enemy and determine how to dispose of his forces when they should be collected. The only eminences near Elk were Iron Hill and Gray's Hill, the latter within two miles of the enemy. It was difficult however to get a good view of their encampment and judge of the number that had landed. Hours were passed in riding from place to place reconnoitering and taking a military survey of the surrounding country. At length a severe storm drove the party to take shelter in a farm-house. Night came on dark and stormy. Washington showed no disposition to depart. His companions became alarmed for his safety. There was risk of his being surprised, being so near the enemy's camp. He was not to be moved either by advice or entreaties, but remained all night under the farmer's roof. When he left the house at daybreak, however, says Lafayette, he acknowledged his imprudence, and that the most insignificant traitor might have caused his ruin.

Indeed, he ran a similar risk to that which in the previous year had produced General Lee's catastrophe.

The country was in a great state of alarm. The inhabitants were hurrying off their most valuable effects, so that it was difficult to procure cattle and vehicles to remove the public stores. The want of horses and the annoyances given by the American light troops, however, kept Howe from advancing promptly and gave time for the greater part of the stores to be saved.

To allay the public alarm, Howe issued a proclamation on the 27th, promising the strictest regularity and order on the part of his army, with security of person and property to all who remained quietly at home, and pardon to those under arms who should promptly return to their obedience. The proclamation had a quieting effect, especially among the loyalists, who abounded in these parts.

The divisions of Generals Greene and Stephen were now stationed several miles in advance of Wilmington, behind White Clay Creek, about ten miles from the Head of Elk. General Smallwood and Colonel Gist had been directed by Congress to take command of the militia of Maryland, who were gathering on the western shore, and Washington sent them orders to co-operate with General Rodney and get in the rear of the enemy.

Washington now felt the want of Morgan and his riflemen, whom he had sent to assist the Northern army. To supply their place, he formed a corps of light troops by drafting a hundred men from each brigade. The command was given to Major-General Maxwell, who was to hover about the enemy and give them continual annoyance.

The army about this time was increased by the arrival of General Sullivan and his division of three thousand men. He had recently, while encamped at Hanover in Jersey, made a gallant attempt to surprise and capture a corps of one thousand provincials stationed on Staten Island at a distance from the fortified camp and opposite the Jersey shore. The attempt was partially successful. A number of the provincials were captured, but the regulars came to the rescue. Sullivan had not brought sufficient boats to secure a retreat. His rear-guard was captured while waiting for the return of the boats, yet not without a sharp resistance. There was loss on both sides, but the Americans suffered most. Congress had directed Washington to appoint a court of inquiry to investigate the matter. In the meantime Sullivan, whose gallantry remained undoubted, continued in command.

There were now in camp several of those officers and gentlemen from various parts of Europe who had recently pressed into the service, and the suitable employment of whom had been a source of much perplexity to Washington. General Deborre, the French veteran of thirty years' service, commanded a brigade in Sullivan's division. Brigadier-General Conway, the Gallicized Hibernian, was in the division of Lord Stirling. Beside these, there was Louis Fleury, a French gentleman of noble descent who had been educated as an engineer and had come out at the opening of the Revolution to offer his services. Washington had obtained for him a captain's commission. Another officer of distinguished merit was the Count Pulaski, a Pole recommended by Dr. Franklin as an officer famous throughout Europe for his bravery and conduct in defense of the liberties of his country against Russia, Austria and Prussia. In fact, he had been commander-in-chief of the forces of the insurgents. He served at present as a volunteer in the light horse, and as that department was still without a head and the cavalry was a main object of attention among the military of Poland, Washington suggested to Congress the expediency of giving him the command of it. "This gentleman, we are told," writes Washington, "has been like us engaged in defending the liberty and independence of his country, and has sacrificed his fortune to his zeal for those objects. He derives from hence a title to our respect, that ought to operate in his favor as far as the good of the service will permit."

At this time Henry Lee of Virginia, of military renown, makes his first appearance. He was in the twenty-second year of his age, and in the preceding year had commanded a company of Virginia volunteers. He had recently signalized himself in scouting parties, harassing the enemy's pickets. Washington, in a letter to the President of Congress (August 30th), writes: "This minute twenty-four British prisoners arrived, taken yesterday by Captain Lee of the light horse." His adventurous exploits soon won him notoriety and the popular appellation of "Light-horse Harry." He was favorably noticed by Washington throughout the war.

Several days were now passed by the commander-in-chief almost continually in the saddle, reconnoitering the roads and passes and making himself acquainted with the surrounding country, which was very much intersected by rivers and small streams running chiefly from northwest to southeast. He had now made up his mind to risk a battle in the open field. It is true his troops were inferior to those of the enemy in number, equipments and discipline. Hitherto, according to Lafayette, "they had fought combats but not battles." Still those combats had given them experience, and though many of them were militia, or raw recruits, yet the divisions of the army had acquired a facility at moving in large masses and were considerably improved in military tactics. At any rate, it would never do to let Philadelphia, at that time the capital of the States, fall without a blow. There was a carping spirit abroad, a disposition to cavil and find fault, which was prevalent in Philadelphia and creeping into Congress; something of the nature of what had been indulged respecting General Schuyler and the army of the North. Public impatience called for a battle. It was expected even by Europe. His own valiant spirit required it, though hitherto he had been held in check by superior considerations of expediency and by the controlling interference of Congress. Congress itself now spurred him on, and he gave way to the native ardor of his character.

The British army, having effected a landing, in which by the way it had experienced but little molestation, was formed into two divisions. One, under Sir William Howe, was stationed at Elkton, with its advanced guard at Gray's Hill, about two miles off. The other division, under General Knyphausen, was on the opposite side of the ferry, at Cecil Court House. On the third of September the enemy advanced in considerable force with three field-pieces, moving with great caution, as the country was difficult, woody and not well known to them. About three miles in front of White Clay Creek their vanguard was encountered by General Maxwell and his light troops and a severe skirmish took place. The fire of the American sharpshooters and riflemen as usual was very effective, but being inferior in number and having no artillery, Maxwell was compelled to retreat across White Clay Creek with the loss of about forty killed and wounded. The loss of the enemy was supposed to be much greater.

The main body of the American army was now encamped on the east side of Red Clay Creek on the road leading from Elkton to Philadelphia. The light infantry were in the advance at White Clay Creek. The armies were from eight to ten miles apart. In this position Washington determined to await the threatened attack.

On the 5th of September he made a stirring appeal to the army in his general orders, stating the object of the enemy, the capture of Philadelphia. They had tried it before, from the Jerseys, and had failed. He trusted they would be again disappointed. In their present attempt their all was at stake. The whole would be hazarded in a single battle. If defeated in that, they were totally undone and the war would be at an end. Now then was the time for the most strenuous exertions. One bold stroke would free the land from rapine, devastation and brutal outrage. "Two years," said he, "have we maintained the war and struggled with difficulties innumerable, but the prospect has brightened. Now is the time to reap the fruit of all our toils and dangers. If we behave like men this third campaign will be our last."

Washington's numerical force at this time was about fifteen thousand men, but from sickness and other causes the effective force, militia included, did not exceed eleven thousand, and most of these were indifferently armed and equipped. The strength of the British was computed at eighteen thousand men but, it is thought, not more than fifteen thousand were brought into action.

On the 8th the enemy advanced in two columns, one appeared

preparing to attack the Americans in front while the other extended its left up the west side of the creek, halting at Milltown, somewhat to the right of the American position. Washington now suspected an intention on the part of Sir William Howe to march by his right, suddenly pass the Brandywine, gain the heights north of that stream and cut him off from Philadelphia. He summoned a council of war, therefore, that evening, in which it was determined immediately to change their position, and move to the river in question. By two o'clock in the morning the army was under march and by the next evening was encamped on the high grounds in the rear of the Brandywine. The enemy on the same evening moved to Kennet Square, about seven miles from the American position.

The Brandywine Creek, as it is called, commences with two branches, called the East and West branches, which unite in one stream flowing from west to east about twenty-two miles and emptying itself into the Delaware about twenty-five miles below Philadelphia. It has several fords. One called Chadd's Ford was at that time the most practicable and in the direct route from the enemy's camp to Philadelphia. As the principal attack was expected here, Washington made it the centre of his position, where he stationed the main body of his army, composed of Wayne's, Weedon's and Muhlenberg's brigades, with the light infantry under Maxwell. An eminence immediately above the ford had been intrenched in the night and was occupied by Wayne and Proctor's artillery. Weedon's and Muhlenberg's brigades, which were Virginian troops and formed General Greene's division, were posted in the rear on the heights as a reserve to aid either wing of the army. With these Washington took his stand. Maxwell's light infantry were thrown in the advance south of the Brandywine and posted on high ground each side of the road leading to the ford.

The right wing of the army, commanded by Sullivan and composed of his division and those of Stephen and Stirling, extended up the Brandywine two miles beyond Washington's position. Its light troops and videttes were distributed quite up to the forks. A few detachments of ill-organized and undisciplined cavalry extended across the creek on the extreme right. The left wing, composed of the Pennsylvania militia under Major-General Armstrong, was stationed about a mile and a half below the main body to protect the lower fords, where the least danger was apprehended. The

Brandywine, which ran in front of the whole line, was now the only obstacle, if such it might be called, between the two armies.

Early on the morning of the 11th a great column of troops was descried advancing on the road leading to Chadd's Ford. A skirt of woods concealed its force but it was supposed to be the main body of the enemy. If so, a general conflict was at hand.

The Americans were immediately drawn out in order of battle. Washington rode along the front of the ranks and was everywhere received with acclamations. A sharp firing of small arms soon told that Maxwell's light infantry were engaged with the vanguard of the enemy. The skirmishing was kept up for some time with spirit, when Maxwell was driven across the Brandywine below the ford. The enemy, who had advanced but slowly, did not attempt to follow, but halted on commanding ground and appeared to reconnoiter the American position with a view to an attack. A heavy cannonading commenced on both sides about ten o'clock. The enemy made repeated dispositions to force the ford, which brought on as frequent skirmishes on both sides of the river, for detachments of the light troops occasionally crossed over. One of these skirmishes was more than usually severe, the British flank-guard was closely pressed, a captain and ten or fifteen men were killed and the guard was put to flight, but a large force came to their assistance and the Americans were again driven across the stream. All this while there was the noise and uproar of a battle but little of the reality. The enemy made a great thundering of cannon but no vigorous onset, and Colonel Harrison, Washington's "old secretary," seeing this cautious and dilatory conduct on their part, wrote a hurried note to Congress expressing his confident belief that the enemy would be repulsed.

Towards noon came an express from Sullivan with a note received from a scouting party reporting that General Howe, with a large body of troops and a park of artillery, was pushing up the Lancaster road, doubtless to cross at the upper fords and turn the right flank of the American position.

Startled by the information, Washington instantly sent off Colonel Theodoric Bland with a party of horse to reconnoiter above the forks and ascertain the truth of the report. In the meantime he resolved to cross the ford, attack the division in front of him with his whole force and rout it before the other could arrive. He gave orders for both wings to co-operate when, as Sullivan was preparing to cross, Major Spicer of the militia rode up, just from the forks, and assured him there was no enemy in that quarter. Sullivan instantly transmitted the intelligence to Washington, whereupon the movement was suspended until positive information could be obtained. After a time came a man of the neighborhood, Thomas Cheyney by name, spurring in all haste, the mare he rode in foam, and himself out of breath. Dashing up to the commander-in-chief, he informed him that he must instantly move or he would be surrounded. He had come upon the enemy unawares, had been pursued and fired upon, but the fleetness of his mare had saved him. The main body of the British was coming down on the east side of the stream and was near at hand. Washington replied, that from information just received, it could not be so. "You are mistaken, general," replied the other vehemently. "My life for it, you are mistaken." Then reiterating the fact with an oath and making a draft of the road in the sand, "put me under guard," added he, "until you find my story true."

Another despatch from Sullivan corroborated it. Colonel Bland, whom Washington had sent to reconnoiter above the forks, had seen the enemy two miles in the rear of Sullivan's right, marching down at a rapid rate while a cloud of dust showed that there were more troops behind them.

In fact, the old Long Island stratagem had been played over again. Knyphausen with a small division had engrossed the attention of the Americans by a feigned attack at Chadd's Ford, kept up with great noise and prolonged by skirmishes; while the main body of the army under Cornwallis, led by experienced guides, had made a circuit of seventeen miles, crossed the two forks of the Brandywine and arrived in the neighborhood of Birmingham meeting-house two miles to the right of Sullivan. It was a capital stratagem, secretly and successfully conducted.

Finding that Cornwallis had thus gained the rear of the army, Washington sent orders to Sullivan to oppose him with the whole right wing, each brigade attacking as soon as it arrived upon the ground. Wayne in the meantime was to keep Knyphausen at bay at the ford, and Greene, with the reserve, to hold himself ready to give aid wherever required.

Lafayette, as a volunteer, had hitherto accompanied the commander-in-chief, but now, seeing there was likely to be warm work with the right wing, he obtained permission to join Sullivan and spurred off with his aide-de-camp to the scene of action. From his narrative we gather some of the subsequent details.

Sullivan, on receiving Washington's orders, advanced with his own, Stephen's and Stirling's divisions and began to form a line in front of an open piece of wood. The time which had been expended in transmitting intelligence, receiving orders and marching, had enabled Cornwallis to choose his ground and prepare for action. Still more time was given him from the apprehension of the three generals, upon consultation, of being outflanked upon the right, and that the gap between Sullivan's and Stephen's divisions was too wide and should be closed up. Orders were accordingly given for the whole line to move to the right, and while in execution, Cornwallis advanced rapidly with his troops in the finest order and opened a brisk fire of musketry and artillery. The Americans made an obstinate resistance, but, being taken at a disadvantage, the right and left wings were broken and driven into the woods. The centre stood firm for a while but, being exposed to the whole fire of the enemy, gave way at length also. The British in following up their advantage got entangled in the wood. It was here that Lafayette received his wound. He had thrown himself from his horse and was endeavoring to rally the troops, when he was shot through the leg with a musket ball and had to be assisted into the saddle by his aide-de-camp.

The Americans rallied on a height to the north of Dilworth and made a still more spirited resistance than at first but were again dislodged and obliged to retreat with a heavy loss.

While this was occurring with the right wing, Knyphausen, as soon as he learnt from the heavy firing that Cornwallis was engaged, made a push to force his way across Chadd's Ford in earnest. He was vigorously opposed by Wayne with Proctor's artillery, aided by Maxwell and his infantry. Greene was preparing to second him with the reserve, when he was summoned by Washington to the support of the right wing, which the commander-in-chief had found in imminent peril.

Greene advanced to the relief with such celerity that it is said, on good authority, his division accomplished the march, or rather run, of five miles in less than fifty minutes. He arrived too late to save the battle but in time to protect the broken masses of the right wing, which he met in full flight. Opening his ranks from time to time for the fugitives and closing them the moment they had passed, he covered their retreat by a sharp and well-directed fire from his field-pieces. His grand stand was made at a place about a mile beyond Dilworth, which, in reconnoitering the neighborhood, Washington had pointed out to him as well calculated for a second position should the army be driven out of the first. And here he was overtaken by Colonel Pinckney, an aide-de-camp of the commander-in-chief, ordering him to occupy this position and protect the retreat of the army. The orders were implicitly obeyed. Weedon's brigade was drawn up in a narrow defile flanked on both sides by woods and perfectly commanding the road, while Greene, with Muhlenberg's brigade, passing to the right took his station on the road. The British came on impetuously, expecting but faint opposition. They met with a desperate resistance and were repeatedly driven back. It was the bloody conflict of the bayonet, deadly on either side and lasting for a considerable time. Weedon's brigade on the left maintained its stand also with great obstinacy, and the check given to the enemy by these two brigades allowed time for the broken troops to retreat. Weedon's was at length compelled by superior numbers to seek the protection of the other brigade, which he did in good order, and Greene gradually drew off the whole division in face of the enemy, who, checked by this vigorous resistance and seeing the day far spent, gave up all further pursuit.

The brave stand made by these brigades had, likewise, been a great protection to Wayne. He had for a long time withstood the attacks of the enemy at Chadd's Ford, until the approach, on the right, of some of the enemy's troops who had been entangled in the woods showed him that the right wing had been routed. He now gave up the defense of his post and retreated by the Chester Road. Knyphausen's troops were too fatigued to pursue him, and the others had been kept back, as we have shown, by Greene's division. So ended the varied conflict of the day.

Lafayette gives an animated picture of the general retreat in which he became entangled. He had endeavored to rejoin Washington but loss of blood compelled him to stop and have his wound bandaged. While thus engaged, he came near being captured. All around him was headlong terror and confusion. Chester road, the common retreat of the broken fragments of the army, from every quarter was crowded with fugitives, with cannon, with baggage cars, all hurrying forward pell-mell and obstructing each other while the thundering of cannon and volleying of musketry by the contending parties in the rear added to the confusion and panic of the flight.

The dust, the uproar and the growing darkness threw everything into chaos. There was nothing but a headlong struggle forward. At Chester, however, twelve miles from the field of battle, there was a deep stream with a bridge, over which the fugitives would have to pass. Here Lafayette set a guard to prevent their further flight. The commander-in-chief arriving soon after with Greene and his gallant division, some degree of order was restored and the whole army took its post behind Chester for the night.

The scene of this battle, which decided the fate of Philadelphia, was within six-and-twenty miles of that city, and each discharge of cannon could be heard there. The two parties of the inhabitants, whig and tory, were to be seen in groups in the squares and public places, waiting the event in anxious silence. At length a courier arrived. His tidings spread consternation among the friends of liberty. Many left their homes. Entire families abandoned everything in terror and despair and took refuge in the mountains. Congress the same evening determined to quit the city and repair to Lancaster, whence they subsequently removed to Yorktown. Before leaving Philadelphia, however, they summoned the militia of Pennsylvania and the adjoining States to join the main army without delay, and ordered down fifteen hundred continental troops from Putnam's command on the Hudson. They also clothed Washington with power to suspend officers for misbehavior; to fill up all vacancies under the rank of brigadiers; to take all provisions and other articles necessary for the use of the army, paying or giving certificates for the same; and to remove, or secure for the benefit of the owners, all goods and effects which might otherwise fall into the hands of the enemy and be serviceable to them. These extraordinary powers were limited to the circumference of seventy miles round headquarters and were to continue in force sixty days unless sooner revoked by Congress.

Notwithstanding the rout and precipitate retreat of the American army, Sir William Howe did not press the pursuit but passed the night on the field of battle and remained the two following days at Dilworth, sending out detachments to take post at Concord and Chester and seize on Wilmington, whither the sick and wounded were conveyed. "Had the enemy marched directly to Derby," observes Lafayette, "the American army would have been cut up and destroyed. They lost a precious night and it is perhaps the greatest fault in a war in which they have committed many."[1]

Washington as usual profited by the inactivity of Howe, quietly retreating through Derby (on the 12th) across the Schuylkill to Germantown, within a short distance of Philadelphia, where he gave his troops a day's repose. Finding them in good spirits and in nowise disheartened by the recent affair, which they seemed to consider a check rather than a defeat, he resolved to seek the enemy again and give him battle. As preliminary measures, he left some of the Pennsylvania militia in Philadelphia to guard the city. Others, under General Armstrong, were posted at the various passes of the Schuylkill with orders to throw up works. The floating bridge on the lower road was to be unmoored and the boats collected and taken across the river.

Having taken these precautions against any hostile movement by the lower road, Washington recrossed the Schuylkill on the 14th and advanced along the Lancaster road with the intention of turning the left flank of the enemy. Howe, apprised of his intention, made a similar disposition to outflank him. The two armies came in sight of each other near the Warren Tavern twenty-three miles from Philadelphia and were on the point of engaging but were prevented by a violent storm of rain, which lasted for four-and-twenty hours.

This inclement weather was particularly distressing to the Americans, who were scantily clothed, most of them destitute of blankets and separated from their tents and baggage. The rain penetrated their cartridge-boxes and the ill-fitted locks of their muskets, rendering the latter useless, being deficient in bayonets. In this plight Washington gave up for the present all thought of attacking the enemy, as their discipline in the use of the bayonet, with which they were universally furnished, would give them a great superiority in action.

"The hot-headed politicians," writes one of his officers, "will no doubt censure this part of his conduct, while the more judicious will approve it as not only expedient but, in such a case, highly commendable. It was without doubt chagrining to a person of his fine feelings to retreat before an enemy not more in number than

---

[1] *Memoirs*, tom. i., p. 26.

himself, yet with a true greatness of spirit he sacrificed them to the good of his country."[2] There was evidently a growing disposition again to criticise Washington's movements, yet how well did this officer judge of him.

The only aim at present was to get some dry and secure place where the army might repose and refit. All day and for a great part of the night they marched under a cold and pelting rain and through deep and miry roads to the Yellow Springs, thence to Warwick, on French Creek, a weary march in stormy weather for troops desitute of every comfort and nearly a thousand of them actually barefooted. At Warwick furnace, ammunition and a few muskets were obtained to aid in disputing the passage of the Schuylkill and the advance of the enemy on Philadelphia.

From French Creek, Wayne was detached with his division to get in the rear of the enemy, form a junction with General Smallwood and the Maryland militia and, keeping themselves concealed, watch for an opportunity to cut off Howe's baggage and hospital train. In the meantime Washington crossed the Schuylkill at Parker's Ford and took a position to defend that pass of the river.

Wayne set off in the night and, by a circuitous march, got within three miles of the left wing of the British encamped at Tredyffrin and, concealing himself in a wood, waited the arrival of Smallwood and his militia. At daybreak he reconnoitered the camp, where Howe, checked by the severity of the weather, had contented himself with uniting his columns and remained under shelter. All day Wayne hovered about the camp. There were no signs of marching. All kept quiet but lay too compact to be attacked with prudence. He sent repeated messages to Washington describing the situation of the enemy and urging him to come on and attack them in their camp. "Their supineness," said he, in one of his notes, "answers every purpose of giving you time to get up. If they attempt to move I shall attack them at all events. . . . There never was nor never will be a finer opportunity of giving the enemy a fatal blow than at present. For God's sake push on as fast as possible."

Again, at a later hour, he writes: "The enemy are very quiet, washing and cooking. I expect General Maxwell on the left flank every moment and, as I lay on the right, we only want you in their

[2] *Memoir of Major Samuel Shaw*, by Hon. Josiah Quincy.

rear to complete Mr. Howe's business. I believe he knows nothing of my situation, as I have taken every precaution to prevent any intelligence getting to him, at the same time keeping a watchful eye on his front, flanks and rear."

His motions, however, had not been so secret as he imagined. He was in a part of the country full of the disaffected, and Sir William had received accurate information of his force and where he was encamped. General Grey with a strong detachment was sent to surprise him at night in his lair. Late in the evening, when Wayne had set his pickets and sentinels and thrown out his patrols, a countryman brought him word of the meditated attack. He doubted the intelligence but strengthened his pickets and patrols and ordered his troops to sleep upon their arms.

At eleven o'clock the pickets were driven in at the point of the bayonet—the enemy were advancing in column. Wayne instantly took post on the right of his position to cover the retreat of the left, led by Colonel Humpton, the second in command. The latter was tardy, and incautiously paraded his troops in front of their fires so as to be in full relief. The enemy rushed on without firing a gun. All was the silent but deadly work of the bayonet and the cutlass. Nearly three hundred of Humpton's men were killed or wounded, and the rest put to flight. Wayne gave the enemy some well-directed volleys and then, retreating to a small distance, rallied his troops and prepared for further defense. The British, however, contented themselves with the blow they had given and retired with very little loss, taking with them between seventy and eighty prisoners, several of them officers, and eight baggage wagons heavily laden.

General Smallwood, who was to have co-operated with Wayne, was within a mile of him at the time of this attack, and would have hastened to his assistance with his well-known intrepidity; but he had not the corps under his command with which he had formerly distinguished himself, and his raw militia fled in a panic at the first sight of a return party of the enemy.

Wayne was deeply mortified by the result of this affair and, finding it severely criticised in the army, demanded a court-martial, which pronounced his conduct everything that was to be expected from an active, brave and vigilant officer. Whatever blame there was in the matter fell upon his second in command, who, by delay or misapprehension of orders and an unskilful position of his troops, had exposed them to be massacred.

On the 21st Sir William Howe made a rapid march high up the Schuylkill on the road leading to Reading, as if he intended either to capture the military stores deposited there or to turn the right of the American army. Washington kept pace with him on the opposite side of the river up to Pott's Grove about thirty miles from Philadelphia.

The movement on the part of Howe was a mere feint. No sooner had he drawn Washington so far up the river than, by a rapid countermarch on the night of the 22d, he got to the ford below, threw his troops across on the next morning and pushed forward for Philadelphia. By the time Washington was apprised of this counter-movement, Howe was too far on his way to be overtaken by harassed, barefooted troops worn out by constant marching. Feeling the necessity of immediate reinforcements, he wrote on the same day to Putnam at Peekskill: "The situation of our affairs in this quarter calls for every aid and for every effort. I therefore desire that, without a moment's loss of time, you will detach as many effective rank and file under proper generals and officers as will make the whole number, including those with General McDougall, amount to twenty-five hundred privates and noncommissioned fit for duty.

"I must urge you, by every motive, to send this detachment without the least possible delay. No considerations are to prevent it. It is our first object to defeat if possible the army now opposed to us here."

On the next day (24th) he wrote also to General Gates. "This army has not been able to oppose General Howe's with the success that was wished, and needs a reinforcement. I therefore request, if you have been so fortunate as to oblige General Burgoyne to retreat to Ticonderoga, or if you have not and circumstances will admit, that you will order Colonel Morgan to join me again with his corps. I sent him up when I thought you materially wanted him and, if his services can be dispensed with now, you will direct his immediate return."

Having called a council of officers and taken their opinions, which concurred with his own, Washington determined to remain some days at Pott's Grove to give repose to his troops and await the arrival of reinforcements.

Sir William Howe halted at Germantown, within a short distance of Philadelphia, and encamped the main body of his army in and about that village, detaching Lord Cornwallis with a large

force and a number of officers of distinction to take formal possession of the city. That general marched into Philadelphia on the
26th with a brilliant staff and escort and followed by splendid
legions of British and Hessian grenadiers, long trains of artillery
and squadrons of light dragoons, the finest troops in the army, all
in their best array, stepping to the swelling music of the band playing "God save the King," and presenting, with their scarlet uniforms, their glittering arms and flaunting feathers, a striking contrast to the poor patriot troops who had recently passed through
the same streets, weary and wayworn, and happy if they could
cover their raggedness with a brown linen hunting-frock and decor-
ate their caps with a sprig of evergreen.

In this way the British took possession of the city, so long the
object of their awkward attempts and regarded by them as a triumphant acquisition, having been the seat of the general government,
the capital of the confederacy. Washington maintained his characteristic equanimity. "This is an event," writes he to Governor
Trumbull, "which we have reason to wish had not happened and
which will be attended with several ill consequences, but I hope it
will not be so detrimental as many apprehend, and that a little
time and perseverance will give us some favorable opportunity of
recovering our loss and of putting our affairs in a more flourishing
condition."

[Burgoyne's reverses continued. However, the New York expedition of Sir Henry Clinton to win control of the Highlands succeeded. After burning Kingston, the seat of the state legislature,]
the enemy proceeded in their ravages, destroying the residences of
conspicuous patriots at Rhinebeck, Livingston Manor and elsewhere, and among others the mansion of the widow of the brave
General Montgomery; trusting to close their desolating career by a
triumphant junction with Burgoyne at Albany.

Chapter 34

DEFEAT OF BURGOYNE AT SARATOGA

While Sir Henry Clinton had been thundering in the Highlands, Burgoyne and his army had been wearing out hope within their intrenchments, vigilantly watched but unassailed by the Americans. They became impatient even of this impunity. "The enemy, though he can bring four times more soldiers against us, shows no desire to make an attack," writes a Hessian officer.[1]

Arnold too was chafing in the camp and longing for a chance as usual "to right himself" by his sword. In a letter to Gates he tries to goad him on. "I think it my duty (which nothing shall deter me from doing) to acquaint you the army are clamorous for action. The militia (who compose great part of the army) are already threatening to go home. One fortnight's inaction will, I make no doubt, lessen your army by sickness and desertion, at least four thousand men. In which time the enemy may be reinforced, and make good their retreat.

"I have reason to think, from intelligence since received, that had we improved the 20th of September it might have ruined the enemy. That is past. Let me entreat you to improve the present time."

Gates was not to be goaded into action. He saw the desperate situation of Burgoyne and bided his time. "Perhaps," writes he, "despair may dictate to him to risk all upon one throw. He is an old gamester and in his time has seen all chances. I will endeavor to be ready to prevent his good fortune and, if possible, secure my own."[2]

On the 7th of October, but four or five days remained of the time Burgoyne had pledged himself to await the co-operation of Sir Henry Clinton. He now determined to make a grand move-

[1] Schlözer's *Briefwechsel.*
[2] Letter to Gov. Clinton. Gates's *Papers.*

ment on the left of the American camp to discover whether he could force a passage, should it be necessary to advance, or dislodge it from its position should it have to retreat. Another object was to cover a forage of the army, which was suffering from the great scarcity.

For this purpose fifteen hundred of his best troops, with two twelve-pounders, two howitzers and six six-pounders, were to be led by himself, seconded by Major-Generals Phillips and Riedesel and Brigadier-General Fraser. "No equal number of men," say the British accounts, "were ever better commanded, and it would have been difficult indeed to have matched the men with an equal number."[8]

On leaving his camp, Burgoyne committed the guard of it on the high grounds to Brigadier-Generals Hamilton and Specht, and of the redoubts on the low grounds near the river to Brigadier-General Gall.

Forming his troops within three-quarters of a mile of the left of the Americans, though covered from their sight by the forest, he sent out a corps of rangers, provincials and Indians to skulk through the woods, get in their rear and give them an alarm at the time the attack took place in front.

The movement, though carried on behind the screen of forests, was discovered. In the afternoon the advanced guard of the American centre beat to arms. The alarm was repeated throughout the line. Gates ordered his officers to their alarm posts and sent forth Wilkinson, the adjutant-general, to inquire the cause. From a rising ground in an open place he descried the enemy in force, their foragers busy in a field of wheat, the officers reconnoitering the left wing of the camp with telescopes from the top of a cabin.

Returning to the camp, Wilkinson reported the position and movements of the enemy; that their front was open, their flanks rested on woods, under cover of which they might be attacked, and their right was skirted by a height; that they were reconnoitering the left, and he thought offered battle.

"Well, then," replied Gates, "order out Morgan to begin the game."

A plan of attack was soon arranged. Morgan with his riflemen and a body of infantry was sent to make a circuit through the woods and get possession of the heights on the right of the enemy,

[8] *Civil War in America*, i., 302.

while General Poor with his brigade of New York and New Hampshire troops and a part of Learned's brigade, were to advance against the enemy's left. Morgan was to make an attack on the heights as soon as he should hear the fire opened below.

Burgoyne now drew out his troops in battle array. The grenadiers under Major Ackland, with the artillery under Major Williams, formed the left and were stationed on a rising ground with a rivulet called Mill creek in front. Next to them were the Hessians under Riedesel, and British under Phillips, forming the centre. The light infantry, under Lord Balcarras, formed the extreme right; having in the advance a detachment of five hundred picked men under General Fraser, ready to flank the Americans as soon as they should be attacked in front.

He had scarce made these arrangements when he was astonished and confounded by a thundering of artillery on his left and a rattling fire of rifles on the woody heights on his right. The troops under Poor advanced steadily up the ascent where Ackland's grenadiers and Williams's artillery were stationed, received their fire and then rushed forward. Ackland's grenadiers received the first brunt but it extended along the line as detachment after detachment arrived, and was carried on with inconceivable fury. The Hessian artillerists spoke afterwards of the heedlessness with which the Americans rushed upon the cannon while they were discharging grapeshot. The artillery was repeatedly taken and retaken, and at length remained in possession of the Americans, who turned it upon its former owners. Major Ackland was wounded in both legs and taken prisoner. Major Williams of the artillery was also captured.

The headlong impetuosity of the attack confounded the regular tacticians. Much of this has been ascribed to the presence and example of [Benedict] Arnold. That daring officer, who had lingered in the camp in expectation of a fight, was exasperated at having no command assigned him. On hearing the din of battle, he could restrain no longer his warlike impulse, but threw himself on his horse and sallied forth. Gates saw him issuing from the camp. "He'll do some rash thing!" cried he and sent his aide-de-camp, Major Armstrong, to call him back. Arnold surmised his errand and evaded it. Putting spurs to his horse, he dashed into the scene of action and was received with acclamation. Being the superior officer in the field, his orders were obeyed of course. Putting himself at the head of the troops of Learned's brigade, he attacked the Hessians in the enemy's centre and broke them with repeated charges.

Indeed, for a time his actions seemed to partake of frenzy, riding hither and thither, brandishing his sword and cheering on the men to acts of desperation. In one of his paroxysms of excitement he struck and wounded an American officer on the head with his sword, without, as he afterwards declared, being conscious of the act. Wilkinson asserts that he was partly intoxicated, but Arnold needed only his own irritated pride and the smell of gunpowder to rouse him to acts of madness.

Morgan in the meantime was harassing the enemy's right wing with an incessant fire of small-arms and preventing it from sending any assistance to the centre. General Fraser with his chosen corps for some time rendered great protection to this wing. Mounted on an iron-gray charger, his uniform of a field-officer made him a conspicuous object for Morgan's sharpshooters. One bullet cut the crupper of his horse, another grazed. his mane. "You are singled out, general," said his aide-de-camp, "and had better shift your ground." "My duty forbids me to fly from danger," was the reply. A moment afterwards he was shot down by a marksman posted in a tree. Two grenadiers bore him to the camp. His fall was a death-blow to his corps.

The arrival on the field of a large reinforcement of New York troops under General Ten Broeck completed the confusion. Burgoyne saw that the field was lost and now only thought of saving his camp. The troops nearest to the lines were ordered to throw themselves within them while Generals Phillips and Riedesel covered the retreat of the main body, which was in danger of being cut off. The artillery was abandoned, all the horses, and most of the men who had so bravely defended it, having been killed. The troops though hard pressed retired in good order.

Scarcely had they entered the camp when it was stormed with great fury, the Americans, with Arnold at their head, rushing to the lines under a severe discharge of grape-shot and small-arms. Lord Balcarras defended the intrenchments bravely. The action was fierce and well sustained on either side. After an ineffectual attempt to make his way into the camp in this quarter at the point of the bayonet, Arnold spurred his horse toward the right flank of the camp occupied by the German reserve, where Lieutenant-

Colonel Brooks was making a general attack with a Massachusetts regiment. Here, with a part of a platoon, he forced his way into a sally-port, but a shot from the retreating Hessians killed his horse and wounded him in the same leg which had received a wound before Quebec. He was borne off from the field but not until the victory was complete, for the Germans retreated from the works, leaving on the field their brave defender, Lieutenant-Colonel Breyman, mortally wounded.

The night was now closing in. The victory of the Americans was decisive. They had routed the enemy, killed and wounded a great number, made many prisoners, taken their field-artillery and gained possession of a part of their works which laid open the right and the rear of their camp. They lay all night on their arms within half a mile of the scene of action, prepared to renew the assault upon the camp in the morning.

Burgoyne shifted his position during the night to heights about a mile to the north, close to the river and covered in front by a ravine. Early in the morning the Americans took possession of the camp which he had abandoned. A random fire of artillery and small-arms was kept up on both sides during the day. The British sharpshooters stationed in the ravine did some execution, and General Lincoln was wounded in the leg while reconnoitering. Gates, however, did not think it advisable to force a desperate enemy when in a strong position, at the expense of a prodigal waste of blood. He took all measures to cut off his retreat and insure a surrender. General Fellows, with 1,400 men, had already been sent to occupy the high ground east of the Hudson opposite Saratoga Ford. Other detachments were sent higher up the river in the direction of Lake George.

Burgoyne saw that nothing was left for him but a prompt and rapid retreat to Saratoga. It was a dismal retreat. The rain fell in torrents. The roads were deep and broken and the horses weak and half-starved from want of forage. At daybreak there was a halt to refresh the troops and give time for the bateaux laden with provisions to come abreast. In three hours the march was resumed, but before long there was another halt to guard against an American reconnoitering party which appeared in sight.

It rained terribly through the residue of the 9th, and in consequence of repeated halts [the retreating army] did not reach Saratoga until evening. A detachment of Americans had arrived there before them and were throwing up intrenchments on a commanding height at Fish Kill. They abandoned their work, forded the Hudson and joined a force under General Fellows posted on the hills east of the river. The bridge over the Fish Kill had been destroyed. The artillery could not cross until the ford was examined. Exhausted by fatigue, the men for the most part had not strength nor inclination to cut wood nor make fire, but threw themselves upon the wet ground in their wet clothes and slept under the continuing rain.

At daylight on the 10th the artillery and the last of the troops passed the fords of the Fish Kill and took a position upon the heights and in the redoubts formerly constructed there. To protect the troops from being attacked in passing the ford by the Americans who were approaching, Burgoyne ordered fire to be set to the farmhouses and other buildings on the south side of the Fish Kill. Amongst the rest, the noble mansion of General Schuyler, with storehouses, granaries, mills and the other appurtenances of a great rural establishment, was entirely consumed. Burgoyne himself estimated the value of property destroyed at ten thousand pounds sterling. The measure was condemned by friend as well as foe but he justified it on the principles of self-preservation.

The force under General Fellows posted on the opposite hills of the Hudson now opened a fire from a battery commanding the ford of that river. Thus prevented from crossing, Burgoyne thought to retreat along the west side as far as Fort George on the way to Canada, and sent out workmen under a strong escort to repair the bridges and open the road toward Fort Edward. The escort was soon recalled and the work abandoned, for the Americans under Gates appeared in great force on the heights south of the Fish Kill and seemed preparing to cross and bring on an engagement.

The opposite shores of the Hudson were now lined with detachments of Americans. Bateaux laden with provisions, which had attended the movements of the army, were fired upon, many taken, some retaken with loss of life. It was necessary to land the provisions from such as remained and bring them up the hill into the camp, which was done under a heavy fire from the American artillery.

Burgoyne called now a general council of war, in which it was resolved, since the bridges could not be repaired, to abandon the artillery and baggage, let the troops carry a supply of provisions upon their backs, push forward in the night and force their way across the fords at or near Fort Edward.

Before the plan could be put in execution scouts brought word that the Americans were intrenched opposite those fords and encamped in force with cannon on the high ground between Fort Edward and Fort George. In fact, by this time the American army, augmented by militia and volunteers from all quarters, had posted itself in strong positions on both sides of the Hudson so as to extend three-fourths of a circle round the enemy.

Giving up all further attempt at retreat, Burgoyne now fortified his camp on the heights to the north of Fish Kill, still hoping that succor might arrive from Sir Henry Clinton or that an attack upon his trenches might give him some chance of cutting his way through.

In this situation his troops lay continually on their arms. His camp was subjected to cannonading from Fellows's batteries on the opposite side of the Hudson, Gates's batteries on the south of Fish Kill and a galling fire from Morgan's riflemen stationed on heights in the rear.

Burgoyne was now reduced to despair. His forces were diminished by losses, by the desertion of Canadians and royalists and the total defection of the Indians. And on inspection it was found that the provisions on hand, even upon short allowance, would not suffice for more than three days. A council of war therefore was called of all the generals, field-officers and captains commanding troops. The deliberations were brief. All concurred in the necessity of opening a treaty with General Gates for a surrender on honorable terms. While they were yet deliberating, an eighteen-pound ball passed through the tent, sweeping across the table round which they were seated.

Negotiations were accordingly opened on the 13th under sanction of a flag. Lieutenant Kingston, Burgoyne's adjutant-general, was the bearer of a note proposing a cessation of hostilities until terms could be adjusted.

The first terms offered by Gates were that the enemy should lay down their arms within their intrenchments and surrender themselves prisoners of war. These were indignantly rejected, with an intimation that, if persisted in, hostilities must recommence.

Counter-proposals were then made by General Burgoyne and

finally accepted by General Gates. According to these, the British troops were to march out of the camp, with artillery and all the honors of war, to a fixed place where they were to pile their arms at a word of command from their own officers. They were to be allowed a free passage to Europe upon condition of not serving again in America during the present war. The army was not to be separated, especially the men from the officers. Roll-calling and other regular duties were to be permitted. The officers were to be on parole and to wear their sidearms. All private property to be sacred, no baggage to be searched or molested. All persons appertaining to or following the camp, whatever might be their country, were to be comprehended in these terms of capitulation.

Schuyler's late secretary, Colonel Varick, who was still in camp, writes to him on the 19th: "Burgoyne says he will send all his general officers at ten in the morning to finish and settle the business. This I trust will be accomplished before twelve and then I shall have the honor and happiness of congratulating you on the glorious success of our arms. I wish to God I could stay under your command.

"If you wish to see Burgoyne you will be necessitated to see him here."[4]

In the night of the 16th, before the articles of capitulation had been signed, a British officer from the army below made his way into the camp with despatches from Sir Henry Clinton, announcing that he had captured the forts in the Highlands and had pushed detachments farther up the Hudson. Burgoyne now submitted to the consideration of his officers "whether it was consistent with public faith, and if so, expedient, to suspend the execution of the treaty and trust to events." His own opinion inclined in the affirmative but the majority of the council determined that the public faith was fully plighted. The capitulation was accordingly signed by Burgoyne on the 17th of October.

The British army at the time of the surrender was reduced by capture, death and desertion from nine thousand to five thousand seven hundred and fifty-two men. That of Gates, regulars and militia, amounted to ten thousand five hundred and fifty-four men on duty, between two and three thousand being on the sick list or absent on furlough.

By this capitulation the Americans gained a fine train of ar-

4 Schuyler's *Papers.*

tillery, seven thousand stand of arms and a great quantity of clothing, tents and military stores of all kinds.

When the British troops marched forth to deposit their arms at the appointed place, Colonel Wilkinson, the adjutant-general, was the only American soldier to be seen. Gates had ordered his troops to keep rigidly within their lines, that they might not add by their presence to the humiliation of a brave enemy. In fact, throughout all his conduct during the campaign, British writers and Burgoyne himself give him credit for acting with great humanity and forbearance.

Wilkinson in his memoirs describes the first meeting of Gates and Burgoyne which took place at the head of the American camp. They were attended by their staffs and by other general officers. Burgoyne was in a rich royal uniform, Gates in a plain blue frock. When they had approached nearly within sword's length they reined up and halted. Burgoyne, raising his hat most gracefully, said: "The fortune of war, General Gates, has made me your prisoner," to which the other, returning his salute, replied, "I shall always be ready to testify that it has not been through any fault of your Excellency."

"We passed through the American camp," writes the already cited Hessian officer, "in which all the regiments were drawn out beside the artillery, and stood under arms. Not one of them was uniformly clad. Each had on the clothes which he wore in the fields, the church or the tavern. They stood however like soldiers, well arranged and with a military air in which there was but little to find fault with. All the muskets had bayonets and the sharpshooters had rifles. The men all stood so still that we were filled with wonder. Not one of them made a single motion as if he would speak with his neighbor. Nay more, all the lads that stood there in rank and file, kind nature had formed so trim, so slender, so nervous that it was a pleasure to look at them, and we all were surprised at the sight of such a handsome, well-formed race.[5] In all earnestness," adds he, "English America surpasses the most of Europe in the growth and looks of its male population. The whole nation has a natural turn and talent for war and a soldier's life."

He made himself somewhat merry, however, with the equipments of the officers. A few wore regimentals, and those fashioned to their own notions as to cut and color, being provided by them-

[5] *Briefe aus Neu England.* Schlözer's *Briefwechsel.*

selves. Brown coats with sea-green facings, white linings and silver trimmings, and gray coats in abundance, with buff facings and cuffs, and gilt buttons; in short, every variety of pattern.

The brigadiers and generals wore uniforms and belts which designated their rank, but most of the colonels and other officers were in their ordinary clothes, a musket and bayonet in hand and a cartridge-box or powder-horn over the shoulder. But what especially amused him was the variety of uncouth wigs worn by the officers, the lingerings of an uncouth fashion.

Most of the troops thus noticed were the hastily levied militia, the yeomanry of the country. "There were regular regiments also," he said, "which, for want of time and cloth, were not yet equipped in uniform. These had standards with various emblems and mottoes, some of which had for us a very satirical signification.

"But I must say, to the credit of the enemy's regiments," continues he, "that not a man was to be found therein who, as we marched by, made even a sign of taunting, insulting exultation, hatred or any other evil feeling. On the contrary, they seemed as though they would rather do us honor. As we marched by the great tent of General Gates, he invited in the brigadiers and commanders of regiments, and various refreshments were set before them. Gates is between fifty and sixty years of age; wears his own thin gray hair; is active and friendly and, on account of the weakness of his eyes, constantly wears spectacles. At headquarters we met many officers who treated us with all possible politeness."

The surrender of Burgoyne was soon followed by the evacuation of Ticonderoga and Fort Independence, the garrisons retiring to the Isle aux Noix and St. John's. As to the armament on the Hudson, the commanders whom Sir Henry Clinton had left in charge of it received in the midst of their desolating career the astounding intelligence of the capture of the army with which they had come to co-operate. Nothing remained for them therefore but to drop down the river and return to New York.

Chapter 35

BATTLE OF GERMANTOWN

Having given the catastrophe of the British invasion from the North, we will revert to that part of the year's campaign which was passing under the immediate eye of Washington. We left him encamped at Pott's Grove towards the end of September, giving his troops a few days' repose after their severe fatigues. Being rejoined by Wayne and Smallwood with their brigades, and other troops being arrived from the Jerseys, his force amounted to about eight thousand Continentals and three thousand militia. With these he advanced on the 30th of September to Skippack Creek, about fourteen miles from Germantown, where the main body of the British army lay encamped, a detachment under Cornwallis occupying Philadelphia.

Immediately after the battle of Brandywine, Admiral Lord Howe with great exertions had succeeded in getting his ships of war and transports round from the Chesapeake into the Delaware and had anchored them along the western shore from Reedy Island to Newcastle. They were prevented from approaching nearer by obstructions which the Americans had placed in the river. The lowest of these were at Billingsport (or Bylling's Point), where chevaux-de-frise in the channel of the river were protected by a strong redoubt on the Jersey shore. Higher up were Fort Mifflin on Mud (or Fort) Island, and Fort Mercer on the Jersey shore, with chevaux-de-frise between them. Washington had exerted himself to throw a garrison into Fort Mifflin and keep up the obstructions of the river.

"If these can be maintained," said he, "General Howe's situation will not be the most agreeable, for if his supplies can be stopped by water it may easily be done by land. To do both shall be my utmost endeavor, and I am not without hope that the acquisition of Philadelphia may, instead of his good fortune, prove his ruin."[1]

Sir William Howe was perfectly aware of this and had concerted operations with his brother by land and water to reduce the forts and clear away the obstructions of the river. With this view he detached a part of his force into the Jerseys to proceed in the first instance against the fortifications at Billingsport.

Washington had been for some days anxiously on the lookout for some opportunity to strike a blow of consequence, when two intercepted letters gave him intelligence of this movement. He immediately determined to make an attack upon the British camp at Germantown, while weakened by the absence of this detachment. To understand the plan of the attack, some description of the British place of encampment is necessary.

Germantown at that time was little more than one continued street extending two miles north and south. The houses were mostly of stone, low and substantial, with steep roofs and projecting eaves. They stood apart from each other, with fruit trees in front and small gardens. Beyond the village and about a hundred yards east of the road, stood a spacious stone edifice with ornamented grounds, statues, groves and shrubbery, the country-seat of Benjamin Chew, chief justice of Pennsylvania previous to the Revolution. We shall have more to say concerning this mansion presently.

Four roads approached the village from above, that is, from the north. The Skippack, which was the main road, led over Chestnut Hill and Mount Airy down to and through the village toward Philadelphia, forming the street of which we have just spoken. On its right and nearly parallel was the Monatawny or Ridge road, passing near the Schuylkill and entering the main road below the village.

On the left of the Skippack or main road was the Limekiln road, running nearly parallel to it for a time and then turning towards it, almost at right angles so as to enter the village at the market-place. Still farther to the left or east, and outside of all, was the Old York road, falling into the main road some distance below the village.

The main body of the British forces lay encamped across the lower part of the village, divided into almost equal parts by the main street or Skippack road. The right wing, commanded by

1 Letter to the President of Congress. Sparks, v., 71.

General Grant, was to the east of the road, the left wing to the west. Each wing was covered by strong detachments and guarded by cavalry. General Howe had his headquarters in the rear.

The advance of the army, composed of the 2d battalion of British light infantry with a train of artillery, was more than two miles from the main body, on the west of the road, with an outlying picket stationed with two six-pounders at Allen's house on Mount Airy. About three quarters of a mile in the rear of the light infantry lay encamped in a field opposite "Chew's House" the 40th regiment of infantry under Colonel Musgrave.

According to Washington's plan for the attack, Sullivan was to command the right wing, composed of his own division, principally Maryland troops, and the division of General Wayne. He was to be sustained by a *corps de reserve* under Lord Stirling composed of Nash's North Carolina and Maxwell's Virginia brigades, and to be flanked by the brigade of General Conway. He was to march down the Skippack road and attack the left wing. At the same time General Armstrong with the Pennsylvania militia was to pass down the Monatawny or Ridge road and get upon the enemy's left and rear.

Greene with the left wing, composed of his own division and the division of General Stephen and flanked by McDougall's brigade, was to march down the Limekiln road so as to enter the village at the market-house. The two divisions were to attack the enemy's right wing in front, McDougall with his brigade to attack it in flank, while Smallwood's division of Maryland militia and Forman's Jersey brigade, making a circuit by the Old York road, were to attack it in the rear. Two thirds of the forces were thus directed against the enemy's right wing under the idea that, if it could be forced, the whole army must be pushed into the Schuylkill or compelled to surrender. The attack was to begin on all quarters at daybreak.[2]

About dusk on the 3d of October the army left its encampment at Matuchen Hills by its different routes. Washington accompanied the right wing. It had fifteen miles of weary march to make over rough roads, so that it was after daybreak when the troops emerged from the woods on Chestnut Hill. The morning was dark with a heavy fog. A detachment advanced to attack the enemy's

[2] Letter of Washington to the President of Congress. Letter of Sullivan to the President of New Hampshire.

out-picket, stationed at Allen's house. The patrol was led by Captain Allen McLane, a brave Maryland officer, well acquainted with the ground and with the position of the enemy. He fell in with double sentries, whom he killed with the loss of one man. The alarm, however, was given. The distant roll of a drum and the call to arms resounded through the murky air. The picket guard, after discharging their two six-pounders, were routed, and retreated down the south side of Mount Airy to the battalion of light infantry who were forming in order of battle. As their pursuers descended into the valley, the sun rose but was soon obscured. Wayne led the attack upon the light infantry. "They broke at first," writes he, "without waiting to receive us, but soon formed again, when a heavy and well-directed fire took place on both sides."

They again gave way, but being supported by the grenadiers, returned to the charge. Sullivan's division and Conway's brigade formed on the west of the road and joined in the attack. The rest of the troops were too far to the north to render any assistance. The infantry, after fighting bravely for a time, broke and ran, leaving their artillery behind. They were hotly pursued by Wayne. His troops remembered the bloody 20th of September and the ruthless slaughter of their comrades. "They pushed on with the bayonet," says Wayne, "and took ample vengeance for that night's work." The officers endeavored to restrain their fury towards those who cried for mercy, but to little purpose. It was a terrible mêlée. The fog, together with the smoke of the cannonry and musketry, made it almost as dark as night. Our people, mistaking one another for the enemy, frequently exchanged shots before they discovered their error. The whole of the enemy's advance were driven from their camping ground, leaving their tents standing, with all their baggage. Colonel Musgrave, with six companies of the 40th regiment, threw himself into Chew's House, barricaded the doors and lower windows and took post above stairs. The main torrent of the retreat passed by, pursued by Wayne into the village.

As the residue of this division of the army came up to join in the pursuit, Musgrave and his men opened a fire of musketry upon them from the upper windows of his citadel. This brought them to a halt. Some of the officers were for pushing on, but General Knox stoutly objected, insisting on the old military maxim, never to leave a garrisoned castle in the rear.

His objection unluckily prevailed. A flag was sent with a summons to surrender. A young Virginian, Lieutenant Smith, volunteered to be the bearer. As he was advancing he was fired upon and received a mortal wound. This house was now cannonaded, but the artillery was too light to have the desired effect. An attempt was made to set fire to the basement. He who attempted it was shot dead from a grated cellar window. Half an hour was thus spent in vain. Scarce any of the defenders of the house were injured, though many of the assailants were slain. At length a regiment was left to keep guard upon the mansion and hold its garrison in check, and the rear division again pressed forward.

This half hour's delay, however, of one half of the army disconcerted the action. The divisions and brigades thus separated from each other by the skirmishing attack upon Chew's House could not be reunited. The fog and smoke rendered all objects indistinct at thirty yards' distance. The different parts of the army knew nothing of the position or movements of each other, and the commander-in-chief could take no view nor gain any information of the situation of the whole. The original plan of attack was only effectively carried into operation in the centre. The flanks and rear of the enemy were nearly unmolested. Still the action, though disconnected, irregular and partial, was animated in various quarters. Sullivan, being reinforced by Nash's North Carolina troops and Conway's brigade, pushed on a mile beyond Chew's House, where the left wing of the enemy gave way before him.

Greene and Stephen with their divisions, having had to make a circuit, were late in coming into action and became separated from each other, part of Stephen's division being arrested by a heavy fire from Chew's House and pausing to return it. Greene, however, with his division, comprising the brigades of Muhlenberg and Scott, pressed rapidly forward, drove an advance regiment of light infantry before him, took a number of prisoners and made his way quite to the market-house in the centre of the village, where he encountered the right wing of the British drawn up to receive him. The impetuosity of his attack had an evident effect upon the enemy, who began to waver. Forman and Smallwood, with the Jersey and Maryland militia, were just showing themselves on the right flank of the enemy, and our troops seemed on the point of carrying the whole encampment.

At this moment a singular panic seized our army. Various causes are assigned for it. Sullivan alleges that his troops had expended all their cartridges and were alarmed by seeing the enemy gathering on their left and by the cry of a light horseman that the enemy were getting round them. Wayne's division, which had pushed the enemy three miles, was alarmed by the approach of a large body of American troops on its left flank, which it mistook for foes, and fell back in defiance of every effort of its officers to rally it. In its retreat it came upon Stephen's division and threw it into a panic, being, in its turn, mistaken for the enemy. Thus all fell into confusion and our army fled from their own victory.

In the meantime the enemy, having recovered from the first effects of the surprise, advanced in their turn. General Grey brought up the left wing and pressed upon the American troops as they receded. Lord Cornwallis with a squadron of light horse from Philadelphia arrived just in time to join in the pursuit.

The retreat of the Americans was attended with less loss than might have been expected and they carried off all their cannon and wounded. This was partly owing to the good generalship of Greene in keeping up a retreating fight with the enemy for nearly five miles, and partly to a check given by Wayne, who turned his cannon upon the enemy from an eminence near White Marsh Church and brought them to a stand. The retreat continued through the day to Perkiomen Creek, a distance of twenty miles.

The loss of the enemy in this action is stated by them to be seventy-one killed, four hundred and fifteen wounded and fourteen missing. Among the killed was Brigadier-General Agnew. The American loss was one hundred and fifty killed, five hundred and twenty-one wounded and about four hundred taken prisoners. Among the killed was General Nash of North Carolina. Among the prisoners was Colonel Matthews of Virginia, who commanded a Virginia regiment in the left wing. Most of his officers and men were killed or wounded in fighting bravely near the market-house, and he himself received several bayonet wounds.

Speaking of Washington's conduct amidst the perplexities of this confused battle, General Sullivan writes, "I saw with great concern our brave commander-in-chief exposing himself to the hottest fire of the enemy in such a manner that regard for my country obliged me to ride to him and beg him to retire. He, to gratify me and some others, withdrew to a small distance, but his anxiety for the fate of the day soon brought him up again, where he remained till our troops had retreated."

The sudden retreat of the army gave him surprise, chagrin and mortification. "Every account," said he subsequently in a letter to the President of Congress, "confirms the opinion I at first entertained that our troops retreated at the instant when victory was declaring herself in our favor. The tumult, disorder and even despair which, it seems, had taken place in the British army, were scarcely to be paralleled, and, it is said so strongly did the ideas of a retreat prevail that Chester was fixed on for their rendezvous. I can discover no other cause for not improving this happy opportunity than the extreme haziness of the weather."

No one was more annoyed than Wayne. "Fortune smiled on us for full three hours," writes he, "the enemy were broke, dispersed and flying in all quarters. We were in possession of their whole encampment, together with their artillery park, etc., etc. A *wind-mill* attack was made upon a house into which six light companies had thrown themselves to avoid our bayonets. Our troops were deceived by this attack, thinking it something formidable. They fell back to assist—the enemy believing it to be a retreat, followed —confusion ensued, and we ran away from the arms of victory open to receive us."

In fact, as has justly been observed by an experienced officer, the plan of attack was too widely extended for strict concert and too complicated for precise co-operation, as it had to be conducted in the night and with a large proportion of undisciplined militia, and yet, a bewildering fog alone appears to have prevented its complete success.

But although the Americans were balked of the victory which seemed within their grasp, the impression made by the audacity of this attempt upon Germantown was greater, we are told, than that caused by any single incident of the war after Lexington and Bunker's Hill.[3]

A British military historian, a contemporary, observes: "In this action the Americans acted upon the offensive, and though repulsed with loss, showed themselves a formidable adversary, capable of charging with resolution and retreating with good order. The hope therefore entertained from the effect of any action with them as decisive and likely to put a speedy termination to the war, was exceedingly abated."[4]

The battle had its effect also in France. The Count De Ver-

[3] Reed's *Memoirs*, vol. i., p. 319.
[4] *Civil War in America*, i., 269.

gennes observed to the American commissioners in Paris on their first interview that nothing struck him so much as General Washington's attacking and giving battle to General Howe's army; that to bring an army raised within a year to this pass promised everything.

The effect on the army itself may be judged from letters written at the time by officers to their friends. "Though we gave away a complete victory," writes one, "we have learned this valuable truth, that we are able to beat them by vigorous exertion and that we are far superior in point of swiftness. We are in high spirits. Every action gives our troops fresh vigor and a greater opinion of their own strength. Another bout or two must make the situation of the enemy very disagreeable."[5]

Another writes to his father: "For my own part, I am so fully convinced of the justice of the cause in which we are contending, and that Providence in its own good time will succeed and bless it, that, were I to see twelve of the United States overrun by our cruel invaders, I should still believe the thirteenth would not only save itself but also work out the deliverance of the others."[6]

Washington remained a few days at Perkiomen Creek to give his army time to rest and recover from the disorder incident to a retreat. Having been reinforced by the arrival of twelve hundred Rhode Island troops from Peekskill under General Varnum, and nearly a thousand Virginia, Maryland and Pennsylvania troops, he gradually drew nearer to Philadelphia and took a strong position at White Marsh, within fourteen miles of that city. By a resolution of Congress, all persons taken within thirty miles of any place occupied by British troops in the act of conveying supplies to them were subjected to martial law. Acting under the resolution, Washington detached large bodies of militia to scour the roads above the city and between the Schuylkill and Chester to intercept all supplies going to the enemy.

On the forts and obstructions in the river, Washington mainly counted to complete the harassment of Philadelphia. These defenses had been materially impaired. The works at Billingsport had been attacked and destroyed and some of the enemy's ships had forced their way through the chevaux-de-frise placed there. The American frigate *Delaware*, stationed in the river between the

5 Capt. Heth to Col. Lamb.
6 Major Shaw. *Memoirs*, by Josiah Quincy, p. 41.

upper forts and Philadelphia, had run aground before a British battery and been captured.

It was now the great object of the Howes to reduce and destroy, and of Washington to defend and maintain, the remaining forts and obstructions. For Mifflin, which we have already mentioned, was erected on a low, green, reedy island in the Delaware, a few miles below Philadelphia and below the mouth of the Schuylkill. It consisted of a strong redoubt with extensive outworks and batteries. There was but a narrow channel between the island and the Pennsylvanian shore. The main channel, practicable for ships, was on the other side. In this were sunk strong chevaux-de-frise, difficult either to be weighed or cut through, and dangerous to any ships that might run against them, subjected as they would be to the batteries of Fort Mifflin on one side and on the other to those of Fort Mercer, a strong work at Red Bank on the Jersey shore.

Fort Mifflin was garrisoned by troops of the Maryland line under Lieutenant-Colonel Samuel Smith of Baltimore and had kept up a brave defense against batteries erected by the enemy on the Pennsylvania shore. A reinforcement of Virginia troops made the garrison between three and four hundred strong.

Floating batteries, galleys and fire-ships commanded by Commodore Hazelwood were stationed under the forts and about the river.

Fort Mercer had hitherto been garrisoned by militia, but Washington now replaced them by four hundred of General Varnum's Rhode Island Continentals. Colonel Christopher Greene was put in command, a brave officer who had accompanied Arnold in his rough expedition to Canada and fought valiantly under the walls of Quebec. "The post with which you are intrusted," writes Washington in his letter of instructions, "is of the utmost importance to America. The whole defense of the Delaware depends upon it, and consequently all the enemy's hopes of keeping Philadelphia, and finally succeeding in the present campaign."

Colonel Greene was accompanied by Captain Mauduit Duplessis, who was to have the direction of the artillery. He was a young French engineer of great merit who had volunteered in the American cause and received a commission from Congress. The chevaux-de-frise in the river had been constructed under his superintendence.

Greene, aided by Duplessis, made all haste to put Fort Mercer in a state of defense, but before the outworks were completed he was surprised (October 22d) by the appearance of a large force emerging from a wood within cannon-shot of the fort. Their uniforms showed them to be Hessians. They were in fact four battalions, twelve hundred strong, of grenadiers, picked men, beside light infantry and chasseurs, all commanded by Count Donop, who had figured in the last year's campaign.

Colonel Greene, in nowise dismayed by the superiority of the enemy forming in glistening array before the wood, prepared for a stout resistance. In a little while an officer was descried riding slowly up with a flag, accompanied by a drummer. Greene ordered his men to keep out of sight, that the fort might appear but slightly garrisoned.

When within proper distance, the drummer sounded a parley and the officer summoned the garrison to surrender, with a threat of no quarter in case of resistance.

Greene's reply was that the post would be defended to the last extremity.

The flag rode back and made report. Forthwith the Hessians were seen at work throwing up a battery within half a mile of the outworks. It was finished by four o'clock and opened a heavy cannonade, under cover of which the enemy were preparing to approach.

As the American outworks were but half finished and were too extensive to be manned by the garrison, it was determined by Greene and Duplessis that the troops should make but a short stand there; to gall the enemy in their approach and then retire within the redoubt, which was defended by a deep intrenchment boarded and fraised.

Donop led on his troops in gallant style under cover of a heavy fire from his battery. They advanced in two columns to attack the outworks in two places. As they advanced they were excessively galled by a flanking fire from the American galleys and batteries and by sharp volleys from the outworks. The latter, however, as had been concerted, were quickly abandoned by the garrison. The enemy entered at two places and, imagining the day their own, the two columns pushed on with shouts to storm different parts of the redoubt. As yet no troops were to be seen, but as one of the columns approached the redoubt on the north side, a tremendous discharge of grape-shot and musketry burst forth from the embrasures in front and a half-masked battery on the left. The slaughter was prodigious. The column was driven back in confusion. Count Donop, with the other column, in attempting the south side of the redoubt, had passed the abatis. Some of his men had traversed the fosse. Others had clambered over the pickets, when a similar tempest of artillery and musketry burst upon them. Some were killed on the spot, many were wounded and the rest were driven out. Donop himself was wounded and remained on the spot. Lieutenant-Colonel Mingerode, the second in command, was also dangerously wounded. Several other of the best officers were slain or disabled.

Lieutenant-Colonel Linsing, the oldest remaining officer, endeavored to draw off the troops in good order but in vain. They retreated in confusion, hotly pursued, and were again cut up in their retreat by the flanking fire from the galleys and floating batteries.

The loss of the enemy in killed and wounded in this brief but severe action was about four hundred men. That of the Americans eight killed and twenty-nine wounded.

As Captain Mauduit Duplessis was traversing the scene of slaughter after the repulse, he was accosted by a voice from among the slain: "Whoever you are, draw me hence." It was the unfortunate Count Donop. Duplessis had him conveyed to a house near the fort, where every attention was paid to his comfort. He languished for three days, during which Duplessis was continually at his bedside. "This is finishing a noble career early," said the count sadly, as he found his death approaching. Then, as if conscious of the degrading service in which he had fallen, hired out by his prince to aid a foreign power in quelling the brave struggle of a people for their liberty, and contrasting it with that in which the chivalrous youth by his bedside was engaged, "I die," added he bitterly, "the victim of my ambition and of the avarice of my sovereign."[7] He was but thirty-seven years of age at the time of his death.

According to the plan of the enemy, Fort Mifflin, opposite to Fort Mercer, was to have been attacked at the same time by water. The force employed was the *Augusta* of sixty-four guns, the *Roebuck* of forty-four, two frigates, the *Merlin* sloop of eighteen guns, and a galley. They forced their way through the lower line of chevaux-de-frise but the *Augusta* and *Merlin* ran aground below

[7] De Chastellux, vol. i., p. 266.

the second line, and every effort to get them off proved fruitless. To divert attention from their situation, the other vessels drew as near to Fort Mifflin as they could and opened a cannonade, but the obstructions in the river had so altered the channel that they could not get within very effective distance. They kept up a fire upon the fort throughout the evening and recommenced it early in the morning, as did likewise the British batteries on the Pennsylvania shore, hoping that under cover of it the ships might be got off. A strong adverse wind, however, kept the tide from rising sufficiently to float them.

The Americans discovered their situation and sent down four fire-ships to destroy them but without effect. A heavy fire was now opened upon them from the galleys and floating batteries. It was warmly returned. In the course of the action a red-hot shot set the *Augusta* on fire. It was impossible to check the flames. All haste was made with boats to save the crew, while the other ships drew off as fast as possible to get out of reach of the explosion. She blew up, however, while the second lieutenant, the chaplain, the gunner and several of the crew were yet on board, most of whom perished. The *Merlin* was now set on fire and abandoned. The *Roebuck* and the other vessels dropped down the river, and the attack on Fort Mifflin was given up.

These signal repulses of the enemy had an animating effect on the public mind and were promptly noticed by Congress. Colonel Greene, who commanded at Fort Mercer, Lieutenant-Colonel Smith of Maryland, who commanded at Fort Mifflin, and Commodore Hazelwood, who commanded the galleys, received the thanks of that body, and subsequently a sword was voted to each as a testimonial of distinguished merit.

Chapter 36

THE CONWAY CABAL

We have heretofore had occasion to advert to the annoyances and perplexities occasioned to Washington by the claims and pretensions of foreign officers who had entered into the service. Among the officers who came out with Lafayette was the Baron De Kalb, a German by birth but who had long been employed in the French service, and though a silver-haired veteran sixty years of age, was yet fresh and active and vigorous, which some attributed to his being a rigid water drinker. In the month of September, Congress had given him the commission of major-general, to date with that of Lafayette.

This instantly produced a remonstrance from Brigadier-General Conway, the Gallic Hibernian of whom we have occasionally made mention, who considered himself slighted and forgot, in their giving a superior rank to his own to a person who had not rendered the cause the least service and who had been his inferior in France. He claimed therefore for himself the rank of major-general, and was supported in his pretensions by persons both in and out of Congress, especially by Mifflin the quartermaster-general.

Washington had already been disgusted by the overweening presumption of Conway, and was surprised to hear that his application was likely to be successful. He wrote on the 17th of October to Richard Henry Lee, then in Congress, warning him that such an appointment would be as unfortunate a measure as ever was adopted, one that would give a fatal blow to the existence of the army.

"Upon so interesting a subject," observes he, "I must speak plainly. The duty I owe my country, the ardent desire I have to promote its true interests, and justice to individuals, require this of me. General Conway's merit as an officer and his importance in this army exist more in his own imagination than in reality. For it is a maxim with him to leave no service of his own untold, nor to want anything which is to be obtained by importunity. . . . I would ask why the youngest brigadier in the service should be put over the heads of the oldest and thereby take rank and command of gentlemen who but yesterday were his seniors, gentlemen who, as I will be bound to say in behalf of some of them at least, are of sound judgment and unquestionable bravery. . . . This truth I am well assured of, that they will not serve under him. I leave you to guess therefore at the situation this army would be in at so important a crisis if this event should take place."

This opposition to his presumptuous aspirations at once threw Conway into a faction forming under the auspices of General Mifflin. This gentleman had recently tendered his resignation of the commission of major-general and quartermaster-general on the plea of ill-health but was busily engaged in intrigues against the commander-in-chief, towards whom he had long cherished a secret hostility. Conway now joined with him heart and hand, and soon became so active and prominent a member of the faction that it acquired the name of *Conway's Cabal*. The object was to depreciate the military character of Washington in comparison with that of Gates, to whom was attributed the whole success of the Northern campaign. Gates was perfectly ready for such an elevation. He was intoxicated by his good fortune and seemed to forget that he had reaped where he had not sown, and that the defeat of Burgoyne had been insured by plans concerted and put in operation before his arrival in the Northern Department.

In fact, in the excitement of his vanity Gates appears to have forgotten that there was a commander-in-chief to whom he was accountable. He neglected to send him any despatch on the subject of the surrender of Burgoyne, contenting himself with sending one to Congress, then sitting at Yorktown. Washington was left to hear of the important event by casual rumor and was for several days in anxious uncertainty until he received a copy of the capitulation in a letter from General Putnam.

Gates was equally neglectful to inform him of the disposition he intended to make of the army under his command. He delayed even to forward Morgan's rifle corps, though their services were no longer needed in his camp and were so much required in the south. It was determined therefore in a council of war that one of Washington's staff should be sent to Gates to represent the critical state of affairs, and that a large reinforcement from the Northern army would in all probability reduce General Howe to the same situation with Burgoyne should he remain in Philadelphia without being able to remove the obstructions in the Delaware and open a free communication with his shipping.

Colonel Alexander Hamilton, his youthful but intelligent aide-de-camp, was charged with this mission. He bore a letter from Washington to Gates dated October 30th, of which the following is an extract:

"By this opportunity I do myself the pleasure to congratulate you on the signal success of the army under your command in compelling General Burgoyne and his whole force to surrender themselves prisoners of war, an event that does the highest honor to the American arms and which I hope will be attended with the most extensive and happy consequences. At the same time I cannot but regret that a matter of such magnitude and so interesting to our general operations should have reached me by report only, or through the channel of letters not bearing that authenticity which the importance of it required and which it would have received by a line under your signature stating the simple fact."

Such was the calm and dignified notice of an instance of official disrespect almost amounting to insubordination. It is doubtful whether Gates in his state of mental effervescence felt the noble severity of the rebuke.

The officer whom Gates had employed as bearer of his despatch to Congress was Wilkinson, his adjutant-general and devoted sycophant, a man at once pompous and servile. He was so long on the road that the articles of the treaty, according to his own account, reached the grand army before he did the Congress. Even after his arrival at Yorktown he required three days to arrange his papers, preparing to deliver them in style. At length, eighteen days after the surrender of Burgoyne had taken place, he formally laid the documents concerning it before Congress, preluding them with a message in the name of Gates but prepared the day before by himself, and following them up by comments, explanatory and eulogistic, of his own.

He evidently expected to produce a great effect by this rhetorical display and to be signally rewarded for his good tidings, but

Congress were as slow in expressing their sense of his services as he had been in rendering them. He swelled and chafed under this neglect but affected to despise it. In a letter to his patron, Gates, he observes: "I have not been honored with any mark of distinction from Congress. Indeed, should I receive no testimony of their approbation of my conduct I shall not be mortified. My hearty contempt of the world will shield me from such pitiful sensations."[1]

A proposal was at length made in Congress that a sword should be voted to him as the bearer of such auspicious tidings, upon which Dr. Witherspoon, a shrewd Scot, exclaimed, "I think ye'll better gie the lad a *pair of spurs*."[2]

A few days put an end to Wilkinson's suspense and probably reconciled him to the world. He was breveted a brigadier-general. A fortuitous circumstance, which we shall explain hereafter, apprised Washington about this time that a correspondence derogatory to his military character and conduct was going on between General Conway and General Gates. It was a parallel case with Lee's correspondence of the preceding year and Washington conducted himself in it with the same dignified forbearance, contenting himself with letting Conway know, by the following brief note dated November 9th, that his correspondence was detected.

"Sir, A letter which I received last night contained the following paragraph: 'In a letter from General Conway to General Gates, he says, "Heaven has determined to save your country, or a weak general and bad counsellors would have ruined it."'

"I am, sir, your humble servant,

"George Washington."

The brevity of this note rendered it the more astounding. It was a hand-grenade thrown into the midst of the cabal. The effect upon other members we shall show hereafter. It seems at first to have prostrated Conway. An epistle of his friend Mifflin to Gates intimates that Conway endeavored to palliate to Washington the censorious expressions in his letter by pleading the careless freedom of language indulged in familiar letter writing. No other record of such explanation remains, and that probably was not received as satisfactory. Certain it is, he immediately sent in his resignation. To some he alleged, as an excuse for resigning, the disparaging way in which he had been spoken of by some members

1 Gates's *Papers*, N. Y. Hist. Soc. Lib.
2 *Life of Lord Stirling*, by W. A. Duer, p. 182.

of Congress. To others he observed that the campaign was at an end, and there was a prospect of a French war. The real reason he kept to himself and Washington suffered it to remain a secret. His resignation, however, was not accepted by Congress. On the contrary, he was supported by the cabal and was advanced to further honors, which we shall specify hereafter.

In the meantime the cabal went on to make invidious comparisons between the achievements of the two armies, deeply derogatory to that under Washington. Publicly he took no notice of them but they drew from him the following apology for his army in a noble and characteristic letter to his friend, the celebrated Patrick Henry, then governor of Virginia.

"The design of this is only to inform you, and with great truth I can do it, strange as it may seem, that the army which I have had under my immediate command has not, at any one time since General Howe's landing at the Head of Elk, been equal in point of numbers to his. In ascertaining this I do not confine myself to continental troops but comprehend militia. The disaffected and lukewarm in this State, in whom unhappily it too much abounds, taking advantage of the distraction in the government, prevented those vigorous exertions which an invaded State ought to have yielded. . . . I was left to fight two battles in order if possible to save Philadelphia, with less numbers than composed the army of my antagonist, whilst the world has given us at least double. This impression, though mortifying in some points of view, I have been obliged to encourage because, next to being strong, it is best to be thought so by the enemy. And to this cause, principally, I think is to be attributed the slow movements of General Howe.

"How different the case in the Northern Department! There the States of New York and New England, resolving to crush Burgoyne, continued pouring in their troops till the surrender of that army, at which time not less than fourteen thousand militia, as I have been informed, were actually in General Gates's camp, and those composed for the most part of the best yeomanry in the country, well armed and in many instances supplied with provisions of their own carrying. Had the same spirit pervaded the people of this and the neighboring States, we might before this time have had General Howe nearly in the situation of General Burgoyne. . . .

"My own difficulties in the course of the campaign have been not a little increased by the extra aid of continental troops which the gloomy prospect of our affairs in the north immediately after the reduction of Ticonderoga induced me to spare from this army. But it is to be hoped that all will yet end well. If the cause is advanced, indifferent is it to me where or in what quarter it happens."

The non-arrival of reinforcements from the Northern army continued to embarrass Washington's operations. [Although Washington urged upon General Gates the importance of the latter's sending him reinforcements without delay, Gates was tardy in responding.]

Washington found it more necessary than usual, at this moment, to assert his superior command from the attempts which were being made to weaken his stand in the public estimation. Still he was not aware of the extent of the intrigues that were in progress around him, in which we believe honest Putnam had no share. There was evidently a similar game going on with that which had displaced the worthy Schuyler. The surrender of Burgoyne, though mainly the result of Washington's farseeing plans, had suddenly trumped up Gates into a quasi rival. A letter written to Gates at the time and still existing among his papers lays open the spirit of the cabal. It is without signature, but in the handwriting of James Lovell, member of Congress from Massachusetts, the same who had supported Gates in opposition to Schuyler. The following are extracts:

"You have saved our Northern Hemisphere, and in spite of consummate and repeated blundering you have changed the condition of the Southern campaign, on the part of the enemy, from offensive to defensive. . . . The campaign here must soon close. If our troops are obliged to retire to Lancaster, Reading, Bethlehem, etc., for winter-quarters, and the country below is laid open to the enemy's flying parties, great and very general will be the murmur —so great, so general, that nothing inferior to a commander-in-chief will be able to resist the mighty torrent of public clamor and public vengeance.

"We have had a noble army melted down by ill-judged marches, marches that disgrace the authors and directors and which have occasioned the severest and most just sarcasm and contempt of our enemies.

"How much are you to be envied, my dear general! How different your conduct and your fortune!

"A letter from Colonel Mifflin, received at the writing of the last paragraph, gives me the disagreeable intelligence of the loss of our fort on the Delaware. You must know the consequences—loss of the river, boats, galleys, ships of war, etc.; good winter-quarters to the enemy; and a general retreat, or ill-judged, blind attempt on our part to save a gone character.

"Conway, Spotswood, Connor, Ross and Mifflin resigned, and many other brave and good officers are preparing their letters to Congress on the same subject. In short, this army will be totally lost unless you come down and collect the virtuous band who wish to fight under your banner and with their aid save the Southern Hemisphere. Prepare yourself for a jaunt to this place—Congress must send for you."[8]

Under such baleful supervision, of which, as we have observed, he was partly conscious, Washington was obliged to carry on a losing game, in which the very elements seemed to conspire against him.

On the evening of the 24th of November [he] reconnoitered carefully and thoughtfully the lines and defenses about Philadelphia from the opposite side of the Schuylkill. His army was now considerably reinforced. The garrison was weakened by the absence of a large body of troops under Lord Cornwallis in the Jerseys. Some of the general officers thought this an advantageous moment for an attack upon the city. Such was the opinion of Lord Stirling and especially General Wayne, Mad Anthony as he was familiarly called, always eager for some daring enterprise. The recent victory at Saratoga had dazzled the public mind and produced a general impatience for something equally striking and effective in that quarter. Reed, Washington's former secretary, now a brigadier-general, shared largely in this feeling. He had written a letter to Gates congratulating him on having "reduced his proud and insolent enemy to the necessity of laying his arms at his feet," assuring him that it would "enroll his name with the happy few who shine in history not as conquerors but as distinguished generals. I have for some time," adds he, "volunteered with this army, which, notwithstanding the labors and efforts of its amiable chief, has yet gathered no laurels."[4]

Reed was actually at headquarters as a volunteer, again enjoying much of Washington's confidence and anxious that he should do something to meet the public wishes. Washington was aware of

[8] Gates's *Papers*, N. Y. Hist. Soc. Lib.
[4] Reed to Gates. Gates's *Papers*.

this prevalent feeling and that it was much wrought on by the intrigues of designing men and by the sarcasms of the press. He was now reconnoitering the enemy's works to judge of the policy of the proposed attack. "A vigorous exertion is under consideration," writes Reed. "God grant it may be successful!"[5]

Everything in the neighborhood of the enemy's lines bore traces of the desolating hand of war. Several houses, owned probably by noted patriots, had been demolished, others burnt. Villas stood roofless. Their doors and windows and all the woodwork had been carried off to make huts for the artillery. Nothing but bare walls remained. Gardens had been trampled down and destroyed. Not a fence nor fruit-tree was to be seen. The gathering gloom of a November evening heightened the sadness of this desolation.

With an anxious eye Washington scrutinized the enemy's works. They appeared to be exceedingly strong. A chain of redoubts extended along the most commanding ground from the Schuylkill to the Delaware. They were framed, planked and of great thickness, and were surrounded by a deep ditch inclosed and fraised. The intervals were filled with an abatis, in constructing which all the apple-trees of the neighborhood, besides forest trees, had been sacrificed.[6]

The idea of Lord Stirling and those in favor of an attack was that it should be at different points at daylight, the main body to attack the lines to the north of the city while Greene, embarking his men in boats at Dunk's Ferry and passing down the Delaware, and Potter, with a body of Continentals and militia moving down the west side of the Schuylkill, should attack the eastern and western fronts.

Washington saw that there was an opportunity for a brilliant blow that might satisfy the impatience of the public and silence the sarcasms of the press, but he saw that it must be struck at the expense of a fearful loss of life.

Returning to camp, he held a council of war of his principal officers, in which the matter was debated at great length and with some warmth but without coming to a decision. At breaking up, Washington requested that each member of the council would give his opinion the next morning in writing, and he sent off a messenger in the night for the written opinion of General Greene.

[5] Reed to President Wharton.
[6] *Life and Cor. of Reed*, vol. i., p. 341.

Only four members of the council, Stirling, Wayne, Scott and Woodford, were in favor of an attack, of which Lord Stirling drew up the plan. Eleven (including Greene) were against it, objecting, among other things, that the enemy's lines were too strong and too well supported, and their force too numerous, well disciplined and experienced to be assailed without great loss and the hazard of a failure.

Had Washington been actuated by mere personal ambition and a passion for military fame, or had he yielded to the goadings of faction and the press, he might have disregarded the loss and hazarded the failure. But his patriotism was superior to his ambition. He shrank from a glory that must be achieved at such a cost, and the idea of an attack was abandoned.

At this juncture (November 27th) a modification took place in the Board of War, indicative of the influence which was operating in Congress. It was increased from three to five members: General Mifflin, Joseph Trumbull, Richard Peters, Colonel Pickering, and last though certainly not least, General Gates. Mifflin's resignation of the commission of quartermaster-general had recently been accepted, but that of major-general was continued to him though without pay. General Gates was appointed president of the board, and the President of Congress was instructed to express to him, in communicating the intelligence, the high sense which that body entertained of his abilities and peculiar fitness to discharge the duties of that important office, upon the right execution of which the success of the American cause so eminently depended; and to inform him it was their intention to continue his rank as major-general, and that he might officiate at the board or in the field as occasion might require; furthermore, that he should repair to Congress with all convenient despatch to enter upon the duties of his appointment. It was evidently the idea of the cabal that Gates was henceforth to be the master-spirit of the war. His friend Lovell, chairman of the committee of foreign relations, writes to him on the same day to urge him on.

"We want you at different places but we want you most near Germantown. Good God! What a situation we are in! How different from what might have been justly expected! You will be astonished when you know accurately what numbers have at one time and another been collected near Philadelphia to wear out stockings, shoes and breeches. Depend upon it, for every ten soldiers placed under the command of our Fabius, five recruits will be wanted annually during the war. The brave fellows at Fort Mifflin and Red Bank have despaired of succor and been obliged to quit. The naval departments have fallen into circumstances of seeming disgrace. Come to the Board of War if only for a short season. . . . If it was not for the defeat of Burgoyne and the strong appearance of European war, our affairs are Fabiused into a very disagreeable posture."[7]

While busy faction was thus at work both in and out of Congress to undermine the fame and authority of Washington, General Howe, according to his own threat, was preparing to "drive him beyond the mountains."

At this time, one of the earliest measures recommended by the Board of War and adopted by Congress showed the increasing influence of the cabal. Two inspectors-general were to be appointed for the promotion of discipline and reformation of abuses in the army, and one of the persons chosen for this important office was Conway, with the rank, too, of major-general! This was tacitly in defiance of the opinion so fully expressed by Washington of the demerits of the man and the ruinous effects to be apprehended from his promotion over the heads of brigadiers of superior claims. Conway, however, was the secret colleague of Gates, and Gates was now the rising sun.

Winter had now set in with all its severity. The troops, worn down by long and hard service, had need of repose. Poorly clad, also, and almost destitute of blankets, they required a warmer shelter than mere tents against the inclemencies of the season. The nearest towns which would afford winter-quarters were Lancaster, York and Carlisle, but should the army retire to any one of these, a large and fertile district would be exposed to be foraged by the foe, and its inhabitants perhaps to be dragooned into submission.

Much anxiety was felt by the Pennsylvania Legislature on the subject, who were desirous that the army should remain in the field. General Reed, in a letter to the president of that body, writes: "A line of winter-quarters had been proposed and supported by some of his [Washington's] principal officers, but I believe I may assure you he will not come into it but take post as near the enemy and cover as much of the country as the nakedness and wretched condition of some part of the army will admit. To keep the field entirely is impracticable, and so you would think if you saw the plight we were in. You will soon know the plan, and as it has been adopted principally upon the opinions of the gentlemen of this State, I hope it will give satisfaction to you and the gentlemen around you. If it is not doing what we would, it is doing what we can, and I must say the general has shown a truly feeling and patriotic respect for us on this occasion, in which you would agree with me if you knew all the circumstances."

The plan adopted by Washington, after holding a council of war and weighing the discordant opinions of his officers, was to hut the army for the winter at Valley Forge in Chester County on the west side of the Schuylkill, about twenty miles from Philadelphia. Here he would be able to keep a vigilant eye on that city and at the same time protect a great extent of country.

Sad and dreary was the march to Valley Forge, uncheered by the recollection of any recent triumph as was the march to winter-quarters in the preceding year. Hungry and cold were the poor fellows who had so long been keeping the field, for provisions were scant, clothing worn out, and so badly off were they for shoes that the footsteps of many might be tracked in blood. Yet at this very time, we are told, "hogsheads of shoes, stockings and clothing were lying at different places on the roads and in the woods, perishing for want of teams or of money to pay the teamsters."[8]

Such were the consequences of the derangement of the commissariat.

Arrived at Valley Forge on the 17th, the troops had still to brave the wintry weather in their tents until they could cut down trees and construct huts for their accommodation. Those who were on the sick list had to seek temporary shelter wherever it could be found among the farmers of the neighborhood. According to the regulations in the orderly book, each hut was to be fourteen feet by sixteen, with walls of logs, filled in with clay, six feet and a half high. The fireplaces were of logs plastered, and logs split into rude planks or slabs furnished the roofing. A hut was allotted to twelve non-commissioned officers and soldiers. A general officer had a hut to himself. The same was allowed to the staff of each brigade and regiment and the field-officer of each regiment, and a hut to the commissioned officers of each company. The huts of

[8] Gordon's *Hist. Am. War*, vol. ii., p. 279.

the soldiery fronted on streets. Those of the officers formed a line in the rear, and the encampment gradually assumed the look of a rude military village.

Scarce had the troops been two days employed in these labors when, before daybreak on the 22d, word was brought that a body of the enemy had made a sortie toward Chester, apparently on a foraging expedition. Washington issued orders to Generals Huntington and Varnum to hold their troops in readiness to march against them. Their replies bespeak the forlorn state of the army.

"Fighting will be far preferable to starving," writes Huntington. "My brigade are out of provisions, nor can the commissary obtain any meat. I have used every argument my imagination can invent to make the soldiers easy but I despair of being able to do it much longer."

"It's a very pleasing circumstance to the division under my command," writes Varnum, "that there is a probability of their marching. Three days successively we have been destitute of bread. Two days we have been entirely without meat. The men must be supplied or they cannot be commanded."

In fact, a dangerous mutiny had broken out among the famishing troops in the preceding night, which their officers had had great difficulty in quelling.

Washington instantly wrote to the President of Congress on the subject.

"I do not know from what cause this alarming deficiency or rather total failure of supplies arises, but unless more vigorous exertions and better regulations take place in that line (the commissaries' department) immediately, the army must dissolve. I have done all in my power by remonstrating, by writing, by ordering the commissaries on this head, from time to time, but without any good effect, or obtaining more than a present scanty relief. Owing to this, the march of the army has been delayed on more than one interesting occasion in the course of the present campaign, and had a body of the enemy crossed the Schuylkill this morning, as I had reason to expect, the divisions which I ordered to be in readiness to march and meet them could not have moved."

Scarce had Washington despatched this letter, when he learnt that the Legislature of Pennsylvania had addressed a remonstrance to Congress against his going into winter-quarters instead of keeping in the open field. This letter, received in his forlorn situation, surrounded by an unhoused, scantily clad, half-starved army, shivering in the midst of December's snow and cold, put an end to his forbearance and drew from him another letter to the President of Congress, dated on the 23d, which we shall largely quote, not only for its manly and truthful eloquence but for the exposition it gives of the difficulties of his situation, mainly caused by unwise and intermeddling legislation.

And first as to the commissariat:

"Though I have been tender heretofore of giving any opinion or lodging complaints, as the change in that department took place contrary to my judgment and the consequences thereof were predicted; yet, finding that the inactivity of the army, whether for want of provisions, clothes or other essentials, is charged to my account not only by the common vulgar but by those in power, it is time to speak plain in exculpation of myself. With truth, then, I can declare that no man, in my opinion, ever had his measures more impeded than I have by every department of the army.

"Since the month of July we have had no assistance from the quartermaster-general, and to want of assistance from this department the commissary-general charges great part of his deficiency. To this I am to add that notwithstanding it is a standing order and often repeated, that the troops shall always have two days' provisions by them, that they might be ready at any sudden call, yet an opportunity has scarcely ever offered of taking an advantage of the enemy, that it has not been either totally obstructed or greatly impeded on this account. . . . As a proof of the little benefit received from a clothier-general, as a further proof of the inability of an army under the circumstances of this to perform the common duties of soldiers (besides a number of men confined to hospitals for want of shoes, and others in farmers' houses on the same account), we have, by a field return this day made, no less than two thousand eight hundred and ninety-eight men now in camp unfit for duty because they are barefoot and otherwise naked. By the same return it appears that our whole strength in continental troops, including the Eastern brigades which have joined us since the surrender of General Burgoyne, exclusive of the Maryland troops sent to Wilmington, amounts to no more than eight thousand two hundred in camp fit for duty; notwithstanding which, and that since the 4th instant, our numbers fit for duty, from the hardships and exposures they have undergone, particularly on account of blankets (numbers have been obliged, and still are, to sit up all night by fires instead of taking comfortable rest in a natural and common way), have decreased near two thousand men.

"We find gentlemen, without knowing whether the army was really going into winter-quarters or not (for I am sure no resolution of mine could warrant the remonstrance), reprobating the measure as much as if they thought the soldiers were made of stocks or stones and equally insensible of frost and snow, and moreover as if they conceived it easily practicable for an inferior army, under the disadvantages I described ours to be—which are by no means exaggerated—to confine a superior one, in all respects well appointed and provided for a winter's campaign, within the city of Philadelphia, and to cover from depredation and waste the States of Pennsylvania and Jersey. But what makes this matter still more extraordinary in my eye is that these very gentlemen, who are well apprised of the nakedness of the troops from ocular demonstration, who thought their own soldiers worse clad than others and who advised me near a month ago to postpone the execution of a plan I was about to adopt in consequence of a resolve in Congress for seizing clothes under strong assurances that an ample supply would be collected in ten days agreeably to a decree of the State (not one article of which, by the by, is yet come to hand), should think a winter's campaign, and the covering of those States from the invasion of an enemy, so easy and practicable a business. I can assure those gentlemen that it is a much easier and less distressing thing to draw remonstrances in a comfortable room by a good fireside than to occupy a cold, bleak hill and sleep under frost and snow without clothes or blankets. However, although they seem to have little feeling for the naked and distressed soldiers, I feel abundantly for them and from my soul I pity those miseries which it is neither in my power to relieve nor prevent.

"It is for these reasons therefore that I have dwelt upon the subject, and it adds not a little to my other difficulties and distress to find that much more is expected from me than is possible to be performed and that, upon the ground of safety and policy, I am obliged to conceal the true state of the army from public view and thereby expose myself to detraction and calumny."

In the present exigency, to save his camp from desolation and to relieve his starving soldiery, he was compelled to exercise the authority recently given him by Congress to forage the country round, seize supplies wherever he could find them and pay for them in money or in certificates redeemable by Congress. He exercised these powers with great reluctance. Rurally inclined himself, he had a strong sympathy with the cultivators of the soil and ever regarded the yeomanry with a paternal eye. He was apprehensive moreover of irritating the jealousy of military sway prevalent throughout the country, and of corrupting the morals of the army. "Such procedures," writes he to the President of Congress "may give a momentary relief but if repeated will prove of the most pernicious consequence. Beside spreading disaffection, jealousy and fear among the people, they never fail, even in the most veteran troops under the most rigid and exact discipline, to raise in the soldiery a disposition to licentiousness, to plunder and robbery, difficult to suppress afterward, and which has proved not only ruinous to the inhabitants but in many instances to armies themselves. I regret the occasion that compelled us to the measure the other day, and shall consider it the greatest of our misfortunes if we should be under the necessity of practising it again."

With these noble and high-spirited appeals to Congress, we close Washington's operations for 1777, one of the most arduous and eventful years of his military life and one of the most trying to his character and fortunes. He began it with an empty army chest and a force dwindled down to four thousand half-disciplined men. Throughout the year he had had to contend not merely with the enemy but with the parsimony and meddlesome interference of Congress. In his most critical times that body had left him without funds and without reinforcements. It had made some promotions contrary to his advice and contrary to military usage, thereby wronging and disgusting some of his bravest officers. It had changed the commissariat in the very midst of a campaign and thereby thrown the whole service into confusion.

Among so many cross-purposes and discouragements, it was a difficult task for Washington to "keep the life and soul of the army together." Yet he had done so. Marvellous indeed was the manner in which he had soothed the discontents of his aggrieved officers and reconciled them to an ill-requiting service. And still more marvellous [was] the manner in which he had breathed his own spirit of patience and perseverance in his yeoman soldiery during their sultry marchings and countermarchings through the Jerseys under all kinds of privations, with no visible object of pursuit to stimulate their ardor, hunting as it were the rumored apparitions of an unseen fleet.

All this time, too, while endeavoring to ascertain and counteract the operations of Lord Howe upon the ocean and his brother upon the land, he was directing and aiding military measures against Burgoyne in the North. Three games were in a manner going on under his supervision. The operations of the commander-in-chief are not always most obvious to the public eye. Victories may be planned in his tent, of which subordinate generals get the credit. And most of the moves which ended in giving a triumphant check to Burgoyne may be traced to Washington's shifting camp in the Jerseys.

It has been an irksome task in some of the preceding chapters to notice the under-current of intrigue and management by which some part of this year's campaign was disgraced, yet even-handed justice requires that such machinations should be exposed. [Washington] was painfully aware of them, yet in no part of the war did he more thoroughly evince that magnanimity which was his grand characteristic than in the last scenes of this campaign, where he rose above the tauntings of the press, the sneerings of the cabal, the murmurs of the public, the suggestions of some of his friends and the throbbing impulses of his own courageous heart, and adhered to that Fabian policy which he considered essential to the safety of the cause. To dare is often the impulse of selfish ambition or hare-brained valor. To forbear is at times the proof of real greatness.

Chapter 37

THE CABAL CONTINUED

While censure and detraction had thus dogged Washington throughout his harassing campaign and followed him to his forlorn encampment at Valley Forge, Gates was the constant theme of popular eulogium and was held up by the cabal as the only one capable of retrieving the desperate fortunes of the South. Letters from his friends in Congress urged him to hasten on, take his seat at the head of the Board of War, assume the management of military affairs and *save the country!*

Gates was not a strong-minded man. Is it a wonder, then, that his brain should be bewildered by the fumes of incense offered up on every side? In the midst of his triumph, however, while feasting on the sweets of adulation, came the withering handwriting on the wall! It is an epistle from his friend Mifflin.

"My dear General, an extract from Conway's letter to you has been procured and sent to headquarters. The extract was a collection of just sentiments, yet such as should not have been intrusted to any of your family. General Washington inclosed it to Conway without remarks. . . . My dear General, take care of your sincerity and frank disposition. They cannot injure yourself but may injure some of your best friends. Affectionately yours."

Nothing could surpass the trouble and confusion of mind of Gates on the perusal of this letter. Part of his correspondence with Conway had been sent to headquarters. But what part? What was the purport and extent of the alleged extracts? How had they been obtained? Who had sent them? Mifflin's letter specified nothing, and this silence as to particulars left an unbounded field for tormenting conjecture. In fact, Mifflin knew nothing in particular when he wrote, nor did any of the cabal. The laconic nature of Washington's note to Conway had thrown them all in confusion.

None knew the extent of the correspondence discovered, nor how far they might be individually compromised.

Gates in his perplexity suspected that his portfolio had been stealthily opened and his letters copied. But which of them?—and by whom? He wrote to Conway and Mifflin, anxiously inquiring what part of their correspondence had been thus surreptitiously obtained and "who was the villain that had played him this treacherous trick. There is scarcely a man living," says he, "who takes a greater care of his letters than I do. I never fail to lock them up, and keep the key in my pocket. . . . No punishment is too severe for the wretch who betrayed me, and I doubt not your friendship for me, as well as your zeal for our safety, will bring the name of this miscreant to light."[1]

Gates made rigid inquiries among the gentlemen of his staff. All disavowed any knowledge of the matter. In the confusion and perturbation of his mind, his suspicions glanced or were turned upon Colonel Hamilton as the channel of communication, he having had free access to headquarters during his late mission from the commander-in-chief. In this state of mental trepidation Gates wrote on the 8th of December the following letter to Washington:

"Sir, I shall not attempt to describe what, as a private gentleman, I cannot help feeling on representing to my mind the disagreeable situation in which confidential letters, when exposed to public inspection, may place an unsuspecting correspondent. But, as a public officer, I conjure your Excellency to give me all the assistance you can in tracing the author of the infidelity which put extracts from General Conway's letters to me into your hands. Those letters have been stealingly copied, but which of them, when and by whom, is to me as yet an unfathomable secret. . . . It is, I believe, in your Excellency's power to do me and the United States a very important service by detecting a wretch who may betray me and capitally injure the very operations under your immediate directions. . . . The crime being eventually so important, that the least loss of time may be attended with the worst consequences, and it being unknown to me whether the letter came to you from a member of Congress or from an officer, I shall have the honor of transmitting a copy of this to the president that the Congress may, in concert with your Excellency, obtain as soon

[1] Gates's *Papers*, N. Y. Hist. Soc. Lib.

as possible a discovery which so deeply affects the safety of the States. Crimes of that magnitude ought not to remain unpunished."

A copy of this letter was transmitted by Gates to the President of Congress.

Washington replied with characteristic dignity and candor.

"Your letter of the 8th ultimo," writes he (January 4th), "came to my hand a few days ago and, to my great surprise, informed me that a copy of it had been sent to Congress, for what reason I find myself unable to account. But as some end was doubtless intended to be answered by it, I am laid under the disagreeable necessity of returning my answer through the same channel lest any member of that honorable body should harbor an unfavorable suspicion of my having practised some indirect means to come at the contents of the confidential letters between you and General Conway.

"I am to inform you, then, that Colonel Wilkinson, on his way to Congress in the month of October last, fell in with Lord Stirling at Reading and, not in confidence that I ever understood, informed his aide-de-camp, Major McWilliams, that General Conway had written this to you: 'Heaven has been determined to save your country, or a weak general and bad counsellors would have ruined it.' Lord Stirling, from motives of friendship, transmitted the account with this remark, 'The inclosed was communicated by Colonel Wilkinson to Major McWilliams. Such wicked duplicity of conduct I shall always think it my duty to detect.'"

Washington adds that the letter written by him to Conway was merely to show that gentleman that he was not unapprised of his intriguing disposition.

"Neither this letter nor the information which occasioned it was ever directly or indirectly communicated by me to a single officer in this army out of my own family, excepting the Marquis de Lafayette, who, having been spoken to on the subject by General Conway, applied for and saw, under injunctions of secrecy, the letter which contained Wilkinson's information, so desirous was I of concealing every matter that could in its consequences give the smallest interruption to the tranquillity of this army or afford a gleam of hope to the enemy by dissensions therein. . . . Till Lord Stirling's letter came to my hands I never knew that General Conway, whom I viewed in the light of a stranger to you, was a correspondent of yours, much less did I suspect that I was the subject of your confidential letters. Pardon me then for adding, that so far from conceiving the safety of the States can be affected or in the smallest degree injured by a discovery of this kind, or that I should be called upon in such solemn terms to point out the author, I considered the information as coming from yourself and given to forewarn and consequently to forearm me against a secret enemy, or in other words a dangerous incendiary, in which character, sooner or later, this country will know General Conway. But in this, as in other matters of late, I have found myself mistaken."

This clear and ample answer explained the enigma of the laconic note to Conway and showed that the betrayal of the defamatory correspondence was due to the babbling of Wilkinson. Following the mode adopted by Gates, Washington transmitted his reply through the hands of the President of Congress, and thus this matter, which he had generously kept secret, became blazoned before Congress and the world.

A few days after writing the above letter Washington received the following warning from his old and faithful friend, Dr. Craik, dated from Maryland January 6th.

"Notwithstanding your unwearied diligence and the unparalleled sacrifice of domestic happiness and ease of mind which you have made for the good of your country, yet you are not wanting in secret enemies who would rob you of the great and truly deserved esteem your country has for you. Base and villainous men, through chagrin, envy or ambition, are endeavoring to lessen you in the minds of the people and taking underhand methods to traduce your character. The morning I left camp I was informed that a strong faction was forming against you in the new Board of War and in the Congress. . . . The method they are taking is by holding General Gates up to the people and making them believe that you have had a number three or four times greater than the enemy and have done nothing; that Philadelphia was given up by your management; and that you have had many opportunities of defeating the enemy. It is said they dare not appear openly as your enemies but that the new Board of War is composed of such leading men as will throw such obstacles and difficulties in your way as to force you to resign."[2]

An anonymous letter to Patrick Henry, dated from Yorktown January 12th, says among other things, "We have only passed the

2 Sparks, *Washington's Writings*, vol. v., p. 493.

Red Sea. A dreary wilderness is still before us, and unless a Moses or a Joshua are raised up in our behalf we must perish before we reach the promised land. . . . But is our case desperate? By no means. We have wisdom, virtue and strength enough to save us if they could be called into action. The northern army has shown us what Americans are capable of doing with a general at their head. The spirit of the southern army is no way inferior to the spirit of the northern. A Gates, a Lee or a Conway would in a few weeks render them an irresistible body of men.

"The last of the above officers has accepted of the new office of inspector-general of our army in order to reform abuses, but the remedy is only a palliative one. In one of his letters to a friend, he says, 'a great and good God hath decreed America to be free, or the [general] and weak counsellors would have ruined her long ago.' "[3]

Another anonymous paper, probably by the same hand, dated January 17th and sent to Congress under a cover directed to the president, Mr. Laurens, decried all the proceedings of the southern army, declaring that the proper method of attacking, beating and conquering the enemy had never as yet been adopted by the commander-in-chief; that the late success to the northward was owing to a change of the commanders; that the southern army would have been alike successful had a similar change taken place. After dwelling on the evils and derangements prevalent in every department, it draws the conclusion, "that the head cannot possibly be sound when the whole body is disordered; that the people of America have been guilty of idolatry by making a man their God, and the God of heaven and earth will convince them by woful experience that he is only a man; that no good may be expected from the standing army until Baal and his worshippers are banished from the camp."[4]

Instead of laying this mischievous paper before Congress, Mr. Laurens remitted it to Washington. He received the following reply:

"I cannot sufficiently express the obligations I feel to you for your friendship and politeness upon an occasion in which I am so deeply interested. I was not unapprised that a malignant faction had been for some time forming to my prejudice, which, conscious

[3] *Ibid.*
[4] *Ibid.*, p. 497.

as I am of having ever done all in my power to answer the important purposes of the trust reposed in me, could not but give me some pain on a personal account. But my chief concern arises from an apprehension of the dangerous consequences which intestine dissensions may produce to the common cause.

"My enemies take an ungenerous advantage of me. They know the delicacy of my situation, and that motives of policy deprive me of the defense I might otherwise make against their insidious attacks. They know I cannot combat their insinuations, however injurious, without disclosing secrets which it is of the utmost moment to conceal. But why should I expect to be exempt from censure, the unfailing lot of an elevated station? Merit and talent, with which I can have no pretensions of rivalship, have ever been subject to it. My heart tells me that it has ever been my unremitted aim to do the best that circumstances would permit, yet I may have been very often mistaken in my judgment of the means, and may in many instances deserve the imputation of error."

Gates was disposed to mark his advent to power by a striking operation. A notable project had been concerted by him and the Board of War for a winter irruption into Canada. An expedition was to proceed from Albany, cross Lake Champlain on the ice, burn the British shipping at St. John's and press forward to Montreal. Washington was not consulted in the matter. The project was submitted to Congress and sanctioned by them without his privity.

One object of the scheme was to detach the Marquis de Lafayette from Washington, to whom he was devotedly attached, and bring him into the interests of the cabal. For this purpose he was to have the command of the expedition, an appointment which it was thought would tempt his military ambition. Conway was to be second in command, and it was trusted that his address and superior intelligence would virtually make him the leader.

The first notice that Washington received of the project was in a letter from Gates inclosing one to Lafayette, informing the latter of his appointment and requiring his attendance at Yorktown to receive his instructions.

Gates in his letter to Washington asked his opinion and advice, evidently as a matter of form. The latter expressed himself obliged by the "polite request" but observed that, as he neither knew the extent of the objects in view nor the means to be employed to effect them, it was not in his power to pass any judgment upon the subject. He wished success to the enterprise, "both as it might advance the public good and confer personal honor on the Marquis de Lafayette, for whom he had a very particular esteem and regard."

The cabal, however, had overshot their mark. Lafayette, who was aware of their intrigues, was so disgusted by the want of deference and respect to the commander-in-chief evinced in the whole proceeding, that he would at once have declined the appointment had not Washington himself advised him strongly to accept it.

He accordingly proceeded to Yorktown, where Gates already had his little court of schemers and hangers on. Lafayette found him at table, presiding with great hilarity, for he was social in his habits and in the flush of recent success. The young marquis had a cordial welcome to his board, which in its buoyant conviviality contrasted with the sober decencies of that of the thoughtful commander-in-chief in his dreary encampment at Valley Forge. Gates in his excitement was profuse of promises. Everything was to be made smooth and easy for Lafayette. He was to have at least two thousand five hundred fighting men under him. Stark, the veteran Stark, was ready to co-operate with a body of Green Mountain Boys. "Indeed," cries Gates, chuckling, "General Stark will have burnt the fleet before your arrival!"

It was near the end of the repast. The wine had circulated freely and toasts had been given according to the custom of the day. The marquis thought it time to show his flag. One toast, he observed, had been omitted, which he would now propose. Glasses were accordingly filled and he gave, "The commander-in-chief of the American armies." The toast was received without cheering.

Lafayette was faithful to the flag he had unfurled. In accepting the command, he considered himself detached from the main army and under the immediate orders of the commander-in-chief. He had a favorable opinion of the military talents of Conway but he was aware of the game he was playing. He made a point therefore of having the Baron de Kalb appointed to the expedition, whose commission, being of older date than that of Conway, would give him the precedence of that officer and make him second in command. This was reluctantly ceded by the cabal, who found themselves baffled by the loyalty in friendship of the youthful soldier.

Lafayette set out for Albany without any very sanguine expectations. Writing to Washington from Flemington amid the difficulties of winter travel, he says: "I go on very slowly, sometimes drenched by rain, sometimes covered with snow, and not entertaining many handsome thoughts about the projected incursion into Canada. Lake Champlain is too cold for producing the least bit of laurel and, if I am not starved, I shall be as proud as if I had gained three battles.[5]

Washington's letter of the 4th of January on the subject of the Conway correspondence had not reached General Gates until the 22d of January, after his arrival at Yorktown. No sooner did Gates learn from its context that all Washington's knowledge of that correspondence was confined to a single paragraph of a letter, and that merely as quoted in conversation by Wilkinson, than the whole matter appeared easily to be explained or shuffled off. He accordingly took pen in hand and addressed Washington as follows on the 23d of January: "The letter which I had the honor to receive yesterday from your Excellency has relieved me from unspeakable uneasiness. I now anticipate the pleasure it will give you when you discover that what has been conveyed to you for an extract of General Conway's letter to me was not an information which friendly motives induced a man of honor to give, that injured virtue might be forearmed against secret enemies. The paragraph which your Excellency has condescended to transcribe is spurious. It was certainly fabricated to answer the most selfish and wicked purposes."

He then goes on to declare that the genuine letter of Conway was perfectly harmless, containing judicious remarks upon the want of discipline in the army but making no mention of weak generals or bad counsellors.

"Particular actions rather than persons were blamed, but with impartiality, and I am convinced he did not aim at lessening, in my opinion, the merit of any person. His letter was perfectly harmless. However, now that various reports have been circulated concerning its contents, they ought not to be submitted to the solemn inspection of those who stand most high in the public esteem.

"Anxiety and jealousy would arise in the breast of very respectable officers who, sensible of faults which inexperience and that

[5] Sparks's *Cor. Am. Rev.* vol. ii., p. 74.

alone may have led them into, would be unnecessarily disgusted if they perceived a probability of such errors being recorded.

"Honor forbids it, and patriotism demands that I should return the letter into the hands of the writer. I will do it; but at the same time I declare that the paragraph conveyed to your Excellency as a genuine part of it was, in words as well as in substance, a wicked forgery.

"About the beginning of December, I was informed that letter had occasioned an explanation between your Excellency and that gentleman. Not knowing whether the whole letter or a part of it had been stealingly copied, but fearing malice had altered its original texture, I own, sir, that a dread of the mischiefs which might attend the forgery I suspected would be made put me some time in a most painful situation. When I communicated to the officers in my family the intelligence which I had received, they all entreated me to rescue their characters from the suspicions they justly conceived themselves liable to until the guilty persons should be known. To facilitate the discovery I wrote to your Excellency but, unable to learn whether General Conway's letters had been transmitted to you by a member of Congress or a gentleman in the army, I was afraid much time would be lost in the course of the inquiry and that the States might receive some capital injury from the infidelity of the person who I thought had stolen a copy of the obnoxious letter. Was it not probable that the secrets of the army might be obtained and betrayed through the same means to the enemy? For this reason, sir, not doubting that Congress would most cheerfully concur with you in tracing out the criminal, I wrote to the president and inclosed to him a copy of my letter to your Excellency.

"About the time I was forwarding those letters, Brigadier-General Wilkinson returned to Albany. I informed him of the treachery which had been committed but I concealed from him the measures I was pursuing to unmask the author. Wilkinson answered he was assured it never would come to light and endeavored to fix my suspicions on Lieutenant-Colonel Troup,[6] who he said might have incautiously conversed on the substance of General Conway's letter with Colonel Hamilton, whom you had sent not long before to Albany. I did not listen to this insinuation against your aide-de-camp and mine."

[6] At that time an aide-de-camp of Gates.

In the original draft of this letter, which we have seen among the papers of General Gates, he adds, as a reason for not listening to the insinuation, that he considered it even as ungenerous. "But," pursues he, "the light your Excellency has just assisted me with, exhibiting the many qualifications which are necessarily blended together in the head and heart of General Wilkinson, I would not omit this fact. It will enable your Excellency to judge whether or not he would scruple to make such a forgery as that which he now stands charged with, and ought to be exemplarily punished."

This, with considerable more to the same purport, intended to make Wilkinson the scape-goat, stands cancelled in the draft and was omitted in the letter sent to Washington, but by some means, fair or foul, it came to the knowledge of Wilkinson, who has published it at length in his memoirs and who, it will be found, resented the imputation thus conveyed.

General Conway, also, in a letter to Washington (dated January 27th), informs him that the letter had been returned to him by Gates and that he found with great satisfaction that "the paragraph so much spoken of did not exist in the said letter, nor anything like it." He had intended, he adds, to publish the letter but had been dissuaded by President Laurens and two or three members of Congress to whom he had shown it, lest it should inform the enemy of a misunderstanding among the American generals. He therefore depended upon the justice, candor and generosity of General Washington to put a stop to the forgery.

On the 9th of February, Washington wrote Gates a long and searching reply to his letters of the 8th and 23d of January, analyzing them and showing how, in spirit and import, they contradicted each other and how sometimes the same letter contradicted itself. How in the first letter the reality of the extracts was by implication allowed, and the only solicitude shown was to find out the person who brought them to light, while, in the second letter the whole was pronounced "in word as well as in substance, a wicked forgery."

"It is not my intention," observes Washington, "to contradict this assertion but only to intimate some considerations which tend to induce a supposition that, though none of General Conway's letters to you contained the offensive passage mentioned, there might have been something in them too nearly related to it, that could give such an extraordinary alarm. If this were not the case, how easy in the first instance to have declared there was nothing exceptionable in them and to have produced the letters themselves in support of it? The propriety of the objections suggested against submitting them to inspection may very well be questioned. 'The various reports circulated concerning their contents,' were perhaps so many arguments for making them speak for themselves to place the matter upon the footing of certainty. Concealment in an affair which had made so much noise, though not by *my* means, will naturally lead men to conjecture the worst and it will be a subject of speculation even to candor itself. The anxiety and jealousy you apprehend from revealing the letter will be very apt to be increased by suppressing it."

We forbear to follow Washington through his stern analysis but we cannot omit the concluding paragraph of his strictures on the character of Conway.

"Notwithstanding the hopeful presages you are pleased to figure to yourself of General Conway's firm and constant friendship to America, I cannot persuade myself to retract the prediction concerning him, which you so emphatically wish had not been inserted in my last. A better acquaintance with him than I have reason to think you have had, from what you say, and a concurrence of circumstances oblige me to give him but little credit for the qualifications of his heart, of which, at least, I beg leave to assume the privilege of being a tolerable judge. Were it necessary, more instances than one might be adduced from his behavior and conversation to manifest that he is capable of all the malignity of detraction and all the meanness of intrigue to gratify the absurd resentment of disappointed vanity or to answer the purposes of personal aggrandizement and promote the interest of faction."

Gates evidently quailed beneath this letter. In his reply, February 19th, he earnestly hoped that no more of that time, so precious to the public, might be lost upon the subject of General Conway's letter.

"Whether that gentleman," says he, "does or does not deserve the suspicions you express would be entirely indifferent to me did he not possess an office of high rank in the army of the United States. As to the gentleman, I have no personal connection with him, nor had I any correspondence previous to his writing the letter which has given offense, nor have I since written to him save to certify what I know to be the contents of that letter. He therefore must be responsible, as I heartily dislike controversy, even upon my own account and much more in a matter wherein I was only accidentally concerned," etc., etc.

The following was the dignified but freezing note with which Washington closed this correspondence.

"Valley Forge, 24th Feb. 1778.

"Sir, I yesterday received your favor of the 19th instant. I am as averse to controversy as any man and, had I not been forced into it, you never would have had occasion to impute to me even the shadow of a disposition towards it. Your repeatedly and solemnly disclaiming any offensive views in those matters which have been the subject of our past correspondence makes me willing to close with the desire you express of burying them hereafter in silence and, as far as future events will permit, oblivion. My temper leads me to peace and harmony with all men, and it is peculiarly my wish to avoid any personal feuds or dissensions with those who are embarked in the same great national interests with myself, as every difference of this kind must, in its consequences, be very injurious. I am, sir," etc.

Among the various insidious artifices resorted to about this time to injure the character of Washington and destroy public confidence in his sincerity was the publication of a series of letters purporting to be from him to some members of his family and to his agent, Mr. Lund Washington, which, if genuine, would prove him to be hollow-hearted and faithless to the cause he was pretending to uphold. They had appeared in England in a pamphlet form as if printed from originals and drafts found in possession of a black servant of Washington, who had been left behind ill at Fort Lee when it was evacuated. They had recently been reprinted at New York in Rivington's *Royal Gazette*, the first letter making its appearance on the 14th of February. It had also been printed at New York in a handbill, and extracts published in a Philadelphia paper.

Washington took no notice of this publication at the time, but in private correspondence with his friends he observes: "These letters are written with a great deal of art. The intermixture of so many family circumstances (which, by the by, want foundation in truth) gives an air of plausibility which renders the villainy greater, as the whole is a contrivance to answer the most diabolical purposes. Who the author of them is I know not. From information or acquaintance he must have had some knowledge of the component parts of my family but he has most egregiously mistaken facts in several instances. The design of his labors is as clear as the sun in its meridian brightness."[7] And in another letter, he observes: "They were written to show that I was an enemy to independence, and with a view to create distrust and jealousy. It is no easy matter to decide whether the villainy or the artifice of these letters is greatest."[8]

The author of these letters was never discovered. He entirely failed in his object. The letters were known at once to be forgeries.

[7] Letter to Gen. Henry Lee, Virginia.—Sparks's *Writings of Washington*, vol. v., 378.
[8] Letter to Landon Carter. *Idem.*, p. 391.

Chapter 38

BRITISH EVACUATION OF PHILADELPHIA

The Conway letter was destined to be a further source of trouble to the cabal. Lord Stirling, in whose presence, at Reading, Wilkinson had cited the letter and who had sent information of it to Washington, was not told that Wilkinson, on being questioned by General Conway, had declared that no such words as those reported, nor any to the same effect, were in the letter.

His lordship immediately wrote to Wilkinson, reminding him of the conversation at Reading and telling him of what he had recently heard.

"I well know," writes his lordship, "that it is impossible you could have made any such declaration, but it will give great satisfaction to many of your friends to know whether Conway made such inquiry and what was your answer. They would also be glad to know what were the words of the letter, and I should be very much obliged to you for a copy of it."

Wilkinson found that his tongue had again brought him into difficulty but he trusted to his rhetoric rather than his logic to get him out of it. He wrote in reply that he perfectly remembered spending a social day with his lordship at Reading, in which the conversation became general, unreserved and copious, though the tenor of his lordship's discourse and the nature of their situation made it confidential.

"I cannot, therefore," adds he logically, "recapitulate particulars or charge my memory with the circumstances you mention. But, my lord, I disdain low craft, subtlety and evasion, and will acknowledge it is possible in the warmth of social intercourse, when the mind is relaxed and the heart is unguarded, that observations may have elapsed which have not since occurred to me. On my late arrival in camp, Brigadier-General Conway informed me that he had been charged by General Washington with writing a letter to Major-General Gates, which reflected on the general and the army. The particulars of this charge, which Brigadier-General Conway then repeated, I cannot now recollect. I had read the letter alluded to. I did not consider the information conveyed in his Excellency's letter, as expressed by Brigadier-General Conway, to be literal, and well remember replying to that effect in dubious terms. I had no inducement to stain my veracity, were I ever so prone to that infamous vice, as Brigadier Conway informed me he had justified the charge.

"I can scarce credit my senses when I read the paragraph in which you request an extract from a private letter which had fallen under my observation. I have been indiscreet, my lord, but be assured I will not be dishonorable."

This communication of Lord Stirling, Wilkinson gives as the first intimation he had received of his being implicated in the disclosure of Conway's letter. When he was subsequently on his way to Yorktown to enter upon his duties as secretary of the Board of War, he learnt at Lancaster that General Gates had denounced him as the betrayer of that letter and had spoken of him in the grossest language.

"I was shocked by this information," writes he. "I had sacrified my lineal rank at General Gates's request. I had served him with zeal and fidelity, of which he possessed the strongest evidence. Yet he had condemned me unheard for an act of which I was perfectly innocent and against which every feeling of my soul revolted with horror. . . . I worshipped honor as the jewel of my soul and did not pause for the course to be pursued, but I owed it to disparity of years and rank, to former connection and the affections of my own breast, to drain the cup of conciliation and seek an explanation."

The result of these and other misfortunes, expressed with that grandiloquence on which Wilkinson evidently prided himself, was a letter to Gates reminding him of the zeal and devotion with which he had uniformly asserted and maintained his cause. "But sir," adds he, "in spite of every consideration, you have wounded my honor and must make acknowledgment or satisfaction for the injury.

"In consideration of our past connection, I descend to that explanation with you which I should have denied any other man.

The inclosed letters unmask the villain and evince my innocence. My lord shall bleed for his conduct but it is proper I first see you."

The letters inclosed were those between him and Lord Stirling, the exposition of which he alleges ought to acquit him of sinister intention and stamp the report of his lordship to General Washington with palpable falsehood.

Gates writes briefly in reply. "Sir, The following extract of a letter from General Washington to me will show you how your honor has been called in question, which is all the explanation necessary upon this matter. Any other satisfaction you may command."

Then followed the extracts giving the information communicated by Wilkinson to Major McWilliams, Lord Stirling's aide-de-camp.

"After reading the whole of the above extract," adds Gates, "I am astonished, if you really gave Major McWilliams such information, how you could intimate to me that it was *possible* Colonel Troup *had conversed* with Colonel Hamilton upon the subject of General Conway's letter."

According to Wilkinson's story he now proceeded to Yorktown, purposely arriving in the twilight to escape observation. There he met with an old comrade, Captain Stoddart, recounted his wrongs and requested him to be the bearer of a message to General Gates. Stoddart refused and warned him that he was running headlong to destruction. "But ruin," observes Wilkinson, "had no terrors for an ardent young man who prized his honor a thousand fold more than his life and who was willing to hazard his eternal happiness in its defense."

He accidentally met with another military friend, Lieutenant-Colonel Ball of the Virginia line, "whose spirit was as independent as his fortune." He willingly became bearer of the following note from Wilkinson to General Gates:

"Sir, I have discharged my duty to you and to my conscience. Meet me to-morrow morning behind the English church and I will there stipulate the satisfaction which you have promised to grant," etc.

Colonel Ball was received with complaisance by the general. The meeting was fixed for eight o'clock in the morning, with pistols.

At the appointed time Wilkinson and his second, having put

their arms in order, were about to sally forth, when Captain Stoddart made his appearance and informed Wilkinson that Gates desired to speak with him. Where? In the street near the door. "The surprise robbed me of circumspection," continues Wilkinson. "I requested Colonel Ball to halt, and followed Captain Stoddart. I found General Gates unarmed and alone and was received with tenderness but manifest embarrassment. He asked me to walk, turned into a back street and we proceeded in silence till we passed the buildings, when he burst into tears, took me by the hand and asked me 'how I could think he wished to injure me?' I was too deeply affected to speak, and he relieved my embarrassment by continuing: 'I injure you! It is impossible. I should as soon think of injuring my own child.' This language," observes Wilkinson, "not only disarmed me but awakened all my confidence and all my tenderness. I was silent. And he added, 'Besides, there was no cause for injuring you, as Conway acknowledged his letter and has since said much harder things to Washington's face.'

"Such language left me nothing to require," continues Wilkinson. "It was satisfactory beyond expectation and rendered me more than content. I was flattered and pleased. And if a third person had doubted the sincerity of the explanation I would have insulted him."

A change soon came over the spirit of this maudlin scene. Wilkinson attended as secretary at the War Office. "My reception from the president, General Gates," writes he, "did not correspond with his recent professions. He was civil but barely so, and I was at a loss to account for his coldness, yet had no suspicion of his insincerity."

Wilkinson soon found his situation at the Board of War uncomfortable and after the lapse of a few days set out for Valley Forge. On his way thither he met Washington's old friend, Dr. Craik, and learnt from him that his promotion to the rank of brigadier-general by brevet had been remonstrated against to Congress by forty-seven colonels. He therefore sent in his resignation, not wishing, he said, to hold it unless he could wear it to the honor and advantage of his country. "And this conduct," adds he, "however repugnant to fashionable ambition, I find consistent with those principles in which I early drew my sword in the present contest."

At Lancaster, Wilkinson, recollecting his resolve that Lord Stirling "should bleed for his conduct," requested his friend, Colonel Moylan, to deliver a "peremptory message" to his lordship. The colonel considered the measure rather precipitate and suggested that a suitable acknowledgement from his lordship would be a more satisfactory reparation of the wrong than a sacrifice of the life of either of the parties. "There is not in the whole range of my friends, acquaintance and, I might add, in the universe," exclaims Wilkinson, "a man of more sublimated sentiment, or who combined with sound discretion a more punctilious sense of honor, than Colonel Moylan." Taking the colonel's advice, therefore, he moderated his peremptory message to the following note:

"My Lord, The propriety or impropriety of your communicating to his Excellency any circumstance which passed at your lordship's board at Reading I leave to be determined by your own feelings and the judgment of the public. But as the affair has eventually induced reflections on my integrity, the sacred duty I owe my honor obliges me to request from your lordship's hand that the conversation which you have published passed in a private company during a convivial hour."

His lordship accordingly gave it under his hand that the words passed under such circumstances but under no injunction of secrecy. Whereupon Wilkinson's irritable but easily pacified honor was appeased and his sword slept in its sheath.

At Valley Forge Wilkinson had an interview with Washington in which the subject of General Conway's letter was discussed and the whole correspondence between Gates and the commander-in-chief laid before him.

"This exposition," writes Wilkinson, "unfolded to me a scene of perfidy and duplicity of which I had no suspicion." It drew from him the following letter to Washington, dated March 28th: "I beg you to receive the grateful homage of a sensible mind for your condescension in exposing to me General Gates's letters which unmask his artifices and efforts to ruin me. The authenticity of the information received through Lord Stirling I cannot confirm, as I solemnly assure your Excellency I do not remember the conversation which passed on that occasion, nor can I recollect particular passages of that letter, as I had but a cursory view of it at a late hour. However I so well remember its general tenor that, although

General Gates has pledged his word it was a wicked and malicious forgery, I will stake my reputation, if the genuine letter is produced, that words to the same effect will appear."

A few days afterwards, Wilkinson addressed the following letter to the President of Congress:

"Sir, While I make my acknowledgments to Congress for the appointment of Secretary to the Board of War and Ordnance, I am sorry I should be constrained to resign that office; but, after the acts of *treachery* and *falsehood* in which I have detected Major-General Gates, the president of that board, it is impossible for me to reconcile it to my honor to serve with him."[1]

After recording this letter in his memoirs, Wilkinson adds: "I had previously resigned my brevet of brigadier-general on grounds of patriotism, but I still retained my commission of colonel, which was never to my knowledge revoked. Yet the dominant influence of General Gates, and the feuds and factions and intrigues which prevailed in Congress and in the army of that day, threw me out of employ."

There we shall leave him. It was a kind of retirement which we apprehend he had richly merited, and we doubt whether his country would have been the loser had he been left to enjoy it for the remainder of his days.

Throughout all the intrigues and manœuvres of the cabal, a part of which we have laid before the reader, Washington had conducted himself with calmness and self-command, speaking on the subject to no one but a very few of his friends, lest a knowledge of those internal dissensions should injure the service.

In a letter to Patrick Henry he gives his closing observations concerning them.

"I cannot precisely mark the extent of their views but it appeared in general that General Gates was to be exalted on the ruin of my reputation and influence. This I am authorized to say, from undeniable facts in my own possession, from publications, the evident scope of which could not be mistaken, and from private detractions industriously circulated. General Mifflin, it is commonly supposed, bore the second part in the cabal, and General Conway, I know, was a very active and malignant partisan, but I have good reason to believe that their machinations have recoiled most sensibly upon themselves."

[1] Wilkinson's *Memoirs*, vol. i., p. 409.

An able and truthful historian, to whose researches we are indebted for most of the documents concerning the cabal, gives it as his opinion that there is not sufficient evidence to prove any concerted plan of action or any fixed design among the leaders. A few aspiring men like Gates and Mifflin might have flattered themselves with indefinite hopes and looked forward to a change as promising the best means of aiding their ambitious views, but that it was not probable they had united in any clear or fixed purpose.[2]

These observations are made with that author's usual candor and judgment; yet, wanting as the intrigues of the cabal might be in plan or fixed design, they were fraught with mischief to the public service, inspiring doubts of its commanders and seeking to provoke them to desperate enterprises. They harassed Washington in the latter part of his campaign, contributed to the dark cloud that hung over his gloomy encampment at Valley Forge and might have effected his downfall had he been more irascible in his temper, more at the mercy of impulse and less firmly fixed in the affections of the people. As it was, they only tended to show wherein lay his surest strength. Jealous rivals he might have in the army, bitter enemies in Congress, but the soldiers loved him, and the large heart of the nation always beat true to him.

The following anecdote of the late Governor Jay, one of our purest and most illustrious statesmen, is furnished to us by his son Judge Jay:

"Shortly before the death of John Adams, I was sitting alone with my father, conversing about the American Revolution. Suddenly he remarked, 'Ah, William! The history of that Revolution will never be known. Nobody now alive knows it but John Adams and myself.' Surprised at such a declaration, I asked him to what he referred? He briefly replied, 'The proceedings of the old Congress.' Again I inquired, 'What proceedings?' He answered, 'Those against Washington. From first to last there was a most bitter party against him.'"

As the old Congress always sat with closed doors, the public knew no more of what passed within than what it was deemed expedient to disclose.

During the winter's encampment in Valley Forge the distresses of the army continued to increase. The surrounding country for a

---

[2] Sparks's *Writings of Washington*, vol. v., Appendix—where there is a series of documents respecting the Conway Cabal.

great distance was exhausted and had the appearance of having been pillaged. In some places where the inhabitants had provisions and cattle they denied it, intending to take them to Philadelphia, where they could obtain greater prices. The undisturbed communication with the city had corrupted the minds of the people in its vicinage. "This State is sick even unto the death," said Gouverneur Morris.

The parties sent out to forage too often returned empty-handed. "For some days past there has been little less than a famine in the camp," writes Washington on one occasion. "A part of the army has been a week without any kind of flesh, and the rest three or four days. Naked and starving as they are, we cannot enough admire the incomparable patience and fidelity of the soldiery, that they have not been, ere this, excited by their suffering to a general mutiny and desertion."

A British historian cites as a proof of the great ascendency of Washington over his "raw and undisciplined troops" that so many remained with him throughout the winter, in this wretched situation and still more wretched plight, almost naked, often on short allowance, with great sickness and mortality and a scarcity of medicines, their horses perishing by hundreds from hunger and the severity of the season.

He gives a striking picture of the indolence and luxury which reigned at the same time in the British army in Philadelphia. It is true the investment of the city by the Americans rendered provisions dear and fuel scanty but the consequent privations were felt by the inhabitants, not by invaders. The latter revelled as if in a conquered place. Private houses were occupied without rendering compensation. The officers were quartered on the principal inhabitants, many of whom were of the Society of "Friends." Some even transgressed so far against propriety as to introduce their mistresses into the quarters thus oppressively obtained. The quiet habits of the city were outraged by the dissolute habits of a camp. Gaming prevailed to a shameless degree. A foreign officer kept a faro bank at which he made a fortune, and some of the young officers ruined themselves.[3]

The spring opened without any material alteration in the dispositions of the armies. Washington at one time expected an attack upon his camp but Sir William was deficient in the neces-

[3] Stedman.

sary enterprise. He contented himself with sending out parties which foraged the surrounding country for many miles and scoured part of the Jerseys, bringing in considerable supplies. These forays were in some instances accompanied by wanton excesses and needless bloodshed, the more unjustifiable as they met with feeble resistance, especially in the Jerseys, where it was difficult to assemble militia in sufficient force to oppose them.

Another ravaging party ascended the Delaware in flat-bottomed boats and galleys, set fire to public storehouses in Bordentown containing provisions and munitions of war, burnt two frigates, several privateers and a number of vessels of various classes, some of them laden with military stores.

[The ascendancy of the Conway cabal ended. Gates was placed in command of the northern department, with limited powers and under Washington's orders, and Conway, in an impertinent letter to the President of Congress, threatened to resign his commission. To his surprise his resignation was accepted and his efforts to get reinstated failed. He left for France during the year.]

The capture of Burgoyne and his army was now operating with powerful effect on the cabinets of both England and France. With the former it was coupled with the apprehension that France was about to espouse the American cause. The consequence was Lord North's "Conciliatory Bills," as they were called, submitted by him to Parliament and passed with but slight opposition. One of these bills regulated taxation in the American colonies in a manner which, it was trusted, would obviate every objection. The other authorized the appointment of commissioners clothed with powers to negotiate with the existing governments, to proclaim a cessation of hostilities, to grant pardons and to adopt other measures of a conciliatory nature. [But the bills were rejected by Congress.]

The tidings of the capitulation of Burgoyne had been equally efficacious in quickening the action of the French cabinet. The negotiations, which had gone on so slowly as almost to reduce our commissioners to despair, were brought to a happy termination, and on the 2d of May, a messenger arrived express from France with two treaties, one of amity and commerce, the other of defensive alliance, signed in Paris on the 6th of February by M. Gérard on the part of France, and by Benjamin Franklin, Silas Deane and Arthur Lee on the part of the United States. This last treaty stipulated that should war ensue between France and England it should be made a common cause by the contracting parties, in which neither should make truce or peace with Great Britain without the consent of the other, nor either lay down their arms until the independence of the United States was established.

These treaties were unanimously ratified by Congress and their promulgation was celebrated by public rejoicings throughout the country. The 6th of May was set apart for a military fête at the camp at Valley Forge. The army was assembled in best array. There was solemn thanksgiving by the chaplains at the head of each brigade, after which [there were] a grand parade, a national discharge of thirteen guns, a general *feu de joie* and shouts of the whole army, "Long live the King of France—Long live the friendly European Powers—Huzza for the American States." A banquet succeeded, at which Washington dined in public with all the officers of his army, attended by a band of music. Patriotic toasts were given and heartily cheered.

"I never was present," writes a spectator, "where there was such unfeigned and perfect joy as was discovered in every countenance. Washington retired at five o'clock, on which there was universal huzzaing and clapping of hands—'Long live General Washington.' The non-commissioned officers and privates followed the example of their officers as he rode past their brigades. The shouts continued till he had proceeded a quarter of a mile, and a thousand hats were tossed in the air. Washington and his suite turned round several times and cheered in reply."

The military career of Sir William Howe in the United States was now drawing to a close. His conduct of the war had given much dissatisfaction in England. His enemies observed that everything gained by the troops was lost by the general; that he had suffered an enemy with less than four thousand men to reconquer a province which he had recently reduced, and lay a kind of siege to his army in their winter-quarters[4]; and that he had brought a sad reverse upon the British arms by failing to co-operate vigorously and efficiently with Burgoyne.

Sir William, on his part, had considered himself slighted by the ministry. His suggestions, he said, were disregarded, and the reinforcements withheld which he considered indispensable for the successful conduct of the war. He had therefore tendered his resig-

4 Stedman, vol. i., p. 84.

nation, which had been promptly accepted, and Sir Henry Clinton ordered to relieve him. Clinton arrived in Philadelphia on the 8th of May and took command of the army on the 11th.

The exchange of General Lee for General Prescott, so long delayed by various impediments, had recently been effected, and Lee was reinstated in his position of second in command. Colonel Ethan Allen, also, had been released from his long captivity in exchange for Colonel Campbell. Allen paid a visit to the camp at Valley Forge, where he had much to tell of his various vicissitudes and hardships. Washington, in a letter to the President of Congress suggesting that something should be done for Allen, observes: "His fortitude and firmness seem to have placed him out of the reach of misfortune. There is an original something about him that commands admiration, and his long captivity and sufferings have only served to increase, if possible, his enthusiastic zeal. He appears very desirous of rendering his services to the States and of being employed, and at the same time he does not discover any ambition for high rank."

In a few days a brevet commission of colonel arrived for Allen, but he had already left camp for his home in Vermont, where he appears to have hung up his sword, for we meet with no further achievements by him on record.

Indications continued to increase of the departure of troops from Philadelphia. The military quarters were in a stir and bustle, effects were packed up, many sold at auction, baggage and heavy cannon embarked, transports fitted up for the reception of horses, and hay taken on board. Was the whole army to leave the city, or only a part? The former was probable. A war between France and England appeared to be impending. In that event Philadelphia would be an ineligible position for the British army.

New York, it was concluded, would be the place of destination, either as a rendezvous, or a post whence to attempt the occupation of the Hudson. Would they proceed thither by land or water? Supposing the former, Washington would gladly have taken post in Jersey to oppose or harass them on their march through that State. His camp, however, was encumbered by upwards of three thousand sick and covered a great amount of military stores. He dared not weaken it by detaching a sufficient force, especially as it was said the enemy intended to attack him before their departure.

For three weeks affairs remained in this state. Washington held his army ready to march toward the Hudson at a moment's warning, and sent General Maxwell with a brigade of Jersey troops to co-operate with Major-General Dickinson and the militia of that State in breaking down the bridges and harassing the enemy, should they actually attempt to march through it. At the same time he wrote to General Gates, who was now at his post on the Hudson, urging him to call in as large a force of militia as he could find subsistence for, and to be on the alert for the protection of that river.

The delay of the British to evacuate Philadelphia tasked the sagacity of Washington. The force in the city in the meantime had been much reduced. Five thousand men had been detached to aid in a sudden descent on the French possessions in the West Indies; three thousand more to Florida. Most of the cavalry with other troops had been shipped with the provision train and heavy baggage to New York. The effective force remaining with Sir Henry was now about nine or ten thousand men. That under Washington was a little more than twelve thousand Continentals and about thirteen hundred militia.

[Sir Henry Clinton evacuated Philadelphia "with great secrecy and despatch," beginning early on the morning of June 18, and fought his way to the neighborhood of Sandy Hook by June 30.] He lost many men by desertion, Hessians especially, during his march through the Jerseys, which, with his losses by killed, wounded and captured, had diminished his army more than two thousand men. The storms of the preceding winter had cut off the peninsula of Sandy Hook from the main-land and formed a deep channel between them. Fortunately the squadron of Lord Howe had arrived the day before and was at anchor within the Hook. A bridge was immediately made across the channel with the boats of the ships, over which the army passed to the Hook on the 5th of July and thence was distributed.

It was now encamped in three divisions on Staten Island, Long Island and the Island of New York apparently without any immediate design of offensive operations. There was a vigorous press in New York to man the large ships and fit them for sea but this was in consequence of a report that a French fleet had arrived on the coast.

Relieved by this intelligence from all apprehensions of an expedition by the enemy up the Hudson, Washington relaxed the speed of his movements and halted for a few days at Paramus, sparing his troops as much as possible during the extreme summer heats.

[In the most prominent battle, that of Monmouth, consequent on Clinton's movement to the coast, General Lee was charged with retreating against Washington's orders. He now requested an immediate trial in an effort to prove his innocence.]

The following were the charges:

1st. Disobedience of orders in not attacking the enemy on the 28th June, agreeably to repeated instructions.

2d. Misbehavior before the enemy on the same day by making an unnecessary, disorderly and shameful retreat.

3d. Disrespect to the commander-in-chief in two letters, dated the 1st of July and the 28th of June.

A court-martial was accordingly formed on the 4th of July at Brunswick, the first halting place. It was composed of one major-general, four brigadiers and eight colonels, with Lord Stirling as president. It moved with the army and convened subsequently at Paramus, Peekskill and Northcastle, the trial lasting until the 12th of August. From the time it commenced, Washington never mentioned Lee's name when he could avoid it, and when he could not, he mentioned it without the smallest degree of acrimony or disrespect.

Lee, on the contrary, indulged his natural irritability of temper and sharpness of tongue. When put on his guard against any intemperate railings against Washington, as calculated to injure his cause, he spurned at the advice.

"No attack, it seems, can be made on General Washington but it must recoil on the assailant. I never entertained the most distant wish or intention of attacking General Washington. I have ever honored and respected him as a man and a citizen. But if the circle which surrounds him chooses to erect him into an infallible divinity, I shall certainly prove a heretic, and if, great as he is, he can attempt wounding everything I ought to hold dear, he must thank his priests if his deityship gets scratched in the scuffle."[5]

The result of the prolonged and tedious investigation was that he was found guilty of all the charges exhibited against him. The second charge, however, was softened by omitting the word *shameful*, and convicting him of making an "unnecessary and in some

[5] Letter to Joseph Reed. Sparks, *Biog. of Lee*, p. 174.

instances a disorderly retreat." He was sentenced to be suspended from all command for one year, the sentence to be approved or set aside by Congress.

[Congress approved the sentence. An insolent note from Lee to the President of Congress caused his dismissal from the service and he retired to his estate in Virginia.]

Chapter 39

OPERATIONS BY SEA AND LAND

While encamped at Paramus, Washington in the night of the
13th of July received a letter from Congress informing him of the
arrival of a French fleet on the coast, instructing him to concert
measures with the commander, the Count D'Estaing, for offensive
operations by sea and land, and empowering him to call on the
States from New Hampshire to New Jersey inclusive, to aid with
their militia.

The fleet in question was composed of twelve ships of the line
and six frigates, with a land force of four thousand men. On board
of it came M. Gérard, minister from France to the United States,
and the Hon. Silas Deane, one of the American ministers who
had effected the late treaty of alliance. The fleet had sailed from
Toulon on the 13th of April. After struggling against adverse
winds for eighty-seven or eighty-eight days, it had made its appearance off the northern extremity of the Virginia coast and anchored
at the mouth of the Delaware on the 8th of July.

The count was unfortunate in the length of his voyage. Had he
arrived in ordinary time he might have entrapped Lord Howe's
squadron in the river, co-operated with Washington in investing
the British army by sea and land and, by cutting off its retreat to
New York, compelled it to surrender.

Finding the enemy had evacuated both city and river, the count
sent up the French minister and Mr. Deane to Philadelphia in a
frigate and then, putting to sea, continued along the coast. A little
earlier and he might have intercepted the squadron of Lord Howe
on its way to New York. It had had but a very few days the advantage of him, and when he arrived with his fleet in the road outside
of Sandy Hook he descried the British ships quietly anchored inside of it.

A frank and cordial correspondence took place forthwith between the count and Washington, and a plan of action was concerted between them by the intervention of confidential officers, Washington's aides-de-camp, Laurens and Hamilton, boarding the fleet while off the Hook, and Major Chouin, a French officer of merit, repairing to the American headquarters.

The first idea of the count was to enter at Sandy Hook and capture or destroy the British fleet composed of six ships of the line, four fifty-gun ships and a number of frigates and smaller vessels. Should he succeed in this, which his greatly superior force rendered probable, he was to proceed against the city with the co-operation of the American forces. To be at hand for such purpose, Washington crossed the Hudson with his army at King's Ferry and encamped at White Plains about the 20th of July.

In the meantime New York was once more in a violent perturbation. "British seamen," says a writer of the times, "endured the mortification for the first time of seeing a British fleet blocked up and insulted in their own harbor, and the French flag flying triumphant without. And this was still more embittered and aggravated by beholding every day vessels under English colors captured under their very eyes by the enemy."[1] The army responded to their feelings. Many royalists of the city, too, hastened to offer their services as volunteers. There was, in short, a prodigious stir in every department, military and naval.

On the other hand, the French officers and crews were in the highest state of excitement and exultation. The long low point of Sandy Hook was all that intervened between them and a splendid triumph, and they anticipated the glory of "delivering America from the English colors which they saw waving on the other side of a simple barrier of sand, upon so great a crowd of masts."[2]

Several experienced American pilots and masters of vessels, however, who had accompanied Colonels Laurens and Hamilton on board of the fleet, declared that there was not sufficient depth of water on the bar to admit the safe passage of the largest ships, one of which carried 80 and another 90 guns. The attempt therefore was reluctantly abandoned and the ships anchored about four miles off, near Shrewsbury on the Jersey coast, taking in provisions and water.

[1] *Brit. Ann. Register*, for 1778, p. 229.
[2] Letter of the Count.

The enterprise which the American and French commanders deemed next worthy of a combined operation was the recapture of Rhode Island proper, that is to say, the island which gives its name to the State, and which the enemy had made one of their military depots and strongholds. In anticipation of such an enterprise Washington on the 17th of July wrote to General Sullivan, who commanded at Providence, ordering him to make the necessary preparations for a descent from the mainland upon the island, and authorizing him to call in reinforcements of New England militia. He subsequently sent to his aid the Marquis de Lafayette with two brigades (Varnum's and Glover's). Quartermaster-General Greene also was detached for the service, being a native of the island, well acquainted with its localities and having great influence among its inhabitants. Sullivan was instructed to form his whole force, Continental, State and militia, into two equal divisions, one to be commanded by Greene, the other by Lafayette.

On the 22d of July the French fleet, having finished taking in its supplies, appeared again in full force off the bar at Sandy Hook. The British, who supposed they had only been waiting on the Shrewsbury coast for the high tides of the latter part of July, now prepared for a desperate conflict. And, indeed, had the French fleet been enabled to enter, it is difficult to conceive a more terrible and destructive struggle than would have ensued between these gallant and deadly rivals, with their powerful armaments brought side to side and cramped up in so confined a field of action.

D'Estaing, however, had already determined his course. After a few demonstrations off the harbor he stood away to the eastward and on the 29th arrived off Point Judith, coming to anchor within five miles of Newport.

Rhode Island (proper), the object of this expedition, is about sixteen miles long, running deep into the great Narraganset Bay. Seaconnet Channel separates it on the east from the mainland, and on the west the main channel passes between it and Conanicut Island. The town of Newport is situated near the south end of the island, facing the west, with Conanicut Island in front of it. It was protected by batteries and a small naval force. Here General Sir Robert Pigott, who commanded in the island, had his headquarters. The force under him was about six thousand strong, variously posted about the island, some in works at the north end, but the greater part within strongly intrenched lines extending across the island about three miles from the town.

General Greene hastened from Providence on hearing of the arrival of the fleet of Count D'Estaing and went on board of it at the anchorage to concert a plan of operations. Some questions of etiquette and precedence rose between them in settling the mode in which the attack was to be conducted. It was at length agreed that the fleet should force its way into the harbor at the same time that the Americans approached by land, and that the landing of the troops from the ships on the west side of the island should take place at the same time that the Americans should cross Seaconnet Channel and land on the east side near the north end. This combined operation was to have been carried promptly into effect but was postponed until the 10th of August to give time for the reinforcements sent by Washington to arrive. The delay was fatal to the enterprise.

[Newport was relieved by the arrival of Lord Howe's fleet. The opposing fleets, battered by a storm, were unable to engage. The French fleet sailed for Boston to refit, and General Sullivan had to extricate his forces from the island.]

The failure of the combined enterprise against Rhode Island was a cause of universal chagrin and disappointment, but to none more so than to Washington, as is evident from the following passage of a letter to his brother, John Augustine:

"An unfortunate storm, and some measures taken in consequence of it by the French Admiral, blasted in one moment the fairest hopes that ever were conceived; and, from a moral certainty of success, rendered it a matter of rejoicing to get our own troops safe off the island. If the garrison of that place, consisting of nearly six thousand men, had been captured, as there was in appearance at least, a hundred to one in favor of it, it would have given the finishing blow to British pretensions of sovereignty over this country and would, I am persuaded, have hastened the departure of the troops in New York as fast as their canvas wings would carry them away."

But what gave Washington the greatest solicitude was the effect of this disappointment upon the public mind. The failure of the enterprise was generally attributed to the departure of the French fleet from Newport, and there was at one time such popular exasperation that it was feared the means of repairing the French ships at Boston would be withheld. Count D'Estaing and the other French officers, on their part, were irritated by the protests of the American officers and the expressions in Sullivan's general order derogatory to French loyalty. The count addressed a letter to Congress, explaining and vindicating his conduct subsequent to his arrival on the coast.

Washington regarded this mutual irritation which had so suddenly sprung up between the army and the fleet with the most poignant anxiety. He wrote to Sullivan and Greene on the subject, urging them to suppress the feuds and jealousies which had already arisen, to conceal as much as possible from the soldiery and public the misunderstandings which had occurred between the officers of the two nations, to discountenance all illiberal or unfriendly observations on the part of the army and to cultivate the utmost harmony and good-will.

Congress also endeavored to suppress the protest of the officers of Sullivan's army which had given so much offense and, in a public resolution, expressed their perfect approbation of the conduct of the count and their sense of his zeal and attachment.

Nothing perhaps tended more to soothe his wounded sensibilities than a letter from Washington, couched in the most delicate and considerate language.

"If the deepest regret, that the best concerted enterprise and bravest exertions should have been rendered fruitless by a disaster which human prudence was incapable of foreseeing or preventing, can alleviate disappointment, you may be assured that the whole continent sympathizes with you. It will be a consolation for you to reflect that the thinking part of mankind do not form their judgment from events, and that their equity will ever attach equal glory to those actions which deserve success and those which have been crowned with it. It is in the trying circumstances to which your Excellency has been exposed that the virtues of a great mind are displayed in their brightest lustre and that a general's character is better known than in the hour of victory. It was yours, by every title which can give it, and the adverse element, which robbed you of your prize, can never deprive you of the glory due to you."

About the beginning of December, Washington distributed his troops for the winter in a line of strong cantonments extending from Long Island Sound to the Delaware. General Putnam commanded at Danbury, General McDougall in the Highlands, while the headquarters of the commander-in-chief were near Middlebrook in the Jerseys. The objects of this arrangement were the protection of the country, the security of the important posts on the Hudson and the safety, discipline and easy subsistence of the army.

In the course of this winter he devised a plan of alarm signals which General Philemon Dickinson was employed to carry into effect. On Bottle Hill, which commanded a vast map of country, sentinels kept watch day and night. Should there be an irruption of the enemy, an eighteen-pounder, called the Old Sow, fired every half hour, gave the alarm in the daytime or in dark and stormy nights; an immense fire or beacon at other times. On the booming of that heavy gun, lights sprang up from hill to hill along the different ranges of heights, the country was aroused, and the yeomanry, hastily armed, hurried to their gathering places.

Washington was now doomed to experience great loss in the narrow circle of those about him on whose attachment and devotion he could place implicit reliance. The Marquis de Lafayette, seeing no immediate prospect of active employment in the United States and anticipating a war on the continent of Europe, was disposed to return to France to offer his services to his sovereign. Desirous, however, of preserving a relation with America, he merely solicited from Congress the liberty of going home for the next winter, engaging himself not to depart until certain that the campaign was over. Washington backed his application for a furlough, as an arrangement that would still link him with the service, expressing his reluctance to part with an officer who united "to all the military fire of youth an uncommon maturity of judgment." Congress in consequence granted the marquis an unlimited leave of absence, to return to America whenever he should find it convenient.

Much of the winter was passed by Washington in Philadelphia, occupied in devising and discussing plans for the campaign of 1779. It was an anxious moment with him. Circumstances which inspired others with confidence filled him with solicitude. The alliance with France had produced a baneful feeling of security, which, it appeared to him, was paralyzing the energies of the country. England, it was thought, would now be too much occupied in securing her position in Europe to increase her force or extend her operations in America. Many therefore considered the war as virtually at an end and were unwilling to make the sacrifices or supply the means necessary for important military undertakings.

Dissensions, too, and party feuds were breaking out in Congress owing to the relaxation of that external pressure of a common and imminent danger, which had heretofore produced a unity of sentiment and action. That august body had in fact greatly deteriorated since the commencement of the war. Many of those whose names had been as watchwords at the Declaration of Independence had withdrawn from the national councils, occupied either by their individual affairs or by the affairs of their individual States. Washington, whose comprehensive patriotism embraced the whole Union, deprecated and deplored the dawning of this sectional spirit. America, he declared, had never stood in more imminent need of the wise, patriotic and spirited exertions of her sons than at this period. The States, separately, were too much engaged in their local concerns and had withdrawn too many of their ablest men from the general council for the good of the common weal.

"Our political system," observed he, "is like the mechanism of a clock. It is useless to keep the smaller wheels in order if the greater one, the prime mover of the whole, is neglected." It was his wish therefore that each State should not only choose but absolutely compel its ablest men to attend Congress, instructed to investigate and reform public abuses.

Nothing can exceed his appeal to the patriotism of his native State, Virginia, in a letter to Colonel Harrison, the speaker of its House of Delegates, written on the 30th of December:

"Our affairs are in a more distressed, ruinous and deplorable condition than they have been since the commencement of the war. By a faithful laborer, then, in the cause; by a man who is daily injuring his private estate without the smallest earthly advantage, not common to all in case of a favorable issue to the dispute; by one who wishes the prosperity of America most devoutly but sees it, or thinks he sees it, on the brink of ruin; you are besought most earnestly, my dear Colonel Harrison, to exert yourself in endeavoring to rescue your country by sending your best and ablest men to Congress. These characters must not slumber nor sleep at home in such a time of pressing danger. They must not content themselves with the enjoyment of places of honor or profit in their own state while the common interests of America are mouldering and sinking into irretrievable ruin. . . . If I were to be called upon to draw a picture of the times and of men from what I have seen, heard and in part know, I should in one word say that idleness, dissipation and extravagance seem to have laid fast hold of most of them; that speculation, peculation and an insatiable thirst for riches seem to have got the better of every other consideration and almost of every order of men; that party disputes and personal quarrels are the great business of the day; while the momentous concerns of an empire, a great and accumulating debt, ruined finances, depreciated money and want of credit, which in its consequences is the want of everything, are but secondary considerations and postponed from day to day, from week to week, as if our affairs wore the most promising aspect. . . . In the present situation of things I cannot help asking where are Mason, Wythe, Jefferson, Nicholas, Pendleton, Nelson, and another I could name? And why, if you are sufficiently impressed with your danger, do you not, as New York has done in the case of Mr. Jay, send an extra member or two, for at least a limited time, till the great business of the nation is put upon a more respectable and happy establishment? . . . I confess to you I feel more real distress on account of the present appearance of things than I have done at any one time since the commencement of the dispute."

Nothing seems to have disgusted him more during his visit to Philadelphia than the manner in which the concerns of the patriot camp were forgotten amid the revelry of the capital.

"An assembly, a concert, a dinner, a supper, that will cost three or four hundred pounds will not only take off men from acting in this business but even from thinking of it, while a great part of the officers of our army, from absolute necessity, are quitting the service, and the more virtuous few, rather than do this, are sinking by sure degrees into beggary and want."

In discussing the policy to be observed in the next campaign Washington presumed the enemy would maintain their present posts and conduct the war as heretofore, in which case he was for remaining entirely on the defensive with the exception of such minor operations as might be necessary to check the ravages of the Indians. The country, he observed, was in a languid and exhausted state and had need of repose. The interruption to agricultural pursuits, and the many hands abstracted from husbandry by military service, had produced a scarcity of bread and forage and rendered it difficult to subsist large armies. Neither was it easy to recruit these armies. There was abundance of employment, wages were high, the value of money was low, consequently there was but little temptation to enlist. Plans had been adopted to remedy the deranged state of the currency but they would be slow in operation. Great economy must in the meantime be observed in the public expenditure.

The participation of France in the war, also, and the prospect that Spain would soon be embroiled with England must certainly divide the attention of the enemy and allow America a breathing time. These and similar considerations were urged by Washington in favor of a defensive policy. One single exception was made by him. The horrible ravages and massacres perpetrated by the Indians and their tory allies at Wyoming had been followed by similar atrocities at Cherry Valley in the State of New York and called for signal vengeance to prevent a repetition. Washington knew by experience that Indian warfare to be effective should never be merely defensive but must be carried into the enemy's country. The Six Nations, the most civilized of the savage tribes, had proved themselves the most formidable. His idea was to make war upon them in their own style, penetrate their country, lay waste their villages and settlements and at the same time destroy the British post at Niagara, that nestling place of tories and refugees.

The policy thus recommended was adopted by Congress. An expedition was set on foot to carry that part relative to the Indians into execution. But here a circumstance occurred which Washington declared gave him more pain than anything that had happened in the war. A Jersey brigade being ordered to march, the officers of the first regiment hesitated to obey. By the depreciation of paper money their pay was incompetent to their support. It was in fact merely nominal. The consequence was, as they alleged, that they were loaded with debt and their families at home were starving, yet the Legislature of their State turned a deaf ear to their complaints. Thus aggrieved, they addressed a remonstrance to the Legislature on the subject of their pay, intimating that should it not receive the immediate attention of that body they might, at the expiration of three days, be considered as having resigned and other officers might be appointed in their place.

Here was one of the many dilemmas which called for the judgment, moderation and great personal weight and influence of Washington. He was eminently the soldier's friend but he was no less thoroughly the patriot general. He knew and felt the privations and distresses of the army and the truth of the grievances complained of, but he saw also the evil consequences that might result from such a course as that which the officers had adopted. Acting therefore as a mediator, he corroborated the statements of the complainants on the one hand, urging on government the necessity of a more general and adequate provision for the officers of the army and the danger of subjecting them to too severe and continued privations. On the other hand, he represented to the officers the difficulties with which government itself had to contend from a deranged currency and exhausted resources, and the unavoidable delays that consequently impeded its moneyed operations. He called upon them therefore for a further exertion of that patience and perseverance which had hitherto done them the highest honor at home and abroad, had inspired him with unlimited confidence in their virtue and consoled him amidst every perplexity and reverse of fortune to which the national affairs had been exposed.

"Now that we have made so great a progress to the attainment of the end we have in view," observed he, "anything like a change of conduct would imply a very unhappy change of principle and a forgetfulness, as well of what we owe to ourselves as to our country. Did I suppose it possible this could be the case even in a single regiment of the army, I should be mortified and chagrined beyond expression. I should feel it as a wound given to my own honor, which I consider as embarked with that of the army at large.

"But the gentlemen," adds he, "cannot be in earnest. They cannot seriously intend anything that would be a stain on their former reputation. They have only reasoned wrong about the means of obtaining a good end, and on consideration, I hope and flatter myself, they will renounce what must appear to be improper. At the opening of a campaign, when under marching orders for an important service, their own honor, duty to the public and to themselves, and a regard to military propriety, will not suffer them to persist in a measure which would be a violation of them all. It will even wound their delicacy coolly to reflect that they have hazarded a step which has an air of dictating to their country by taking advantage of the necessity of the moment, for the declaration they have made to the State at so critical a time, that unless they obtain relief in the short period of three days they must be considered out of the service, has very much that aspect."

These and other observations of similar purport were contained in a letter to General Maxwell, their commander, to be laid before the officers. It produced a respectful reply but one which intimated no disposition to swerve from their determination. After reiterating their grievances, "We are sorry," added they, "that you should imagine we meant to disobey orders. It was and is still our determination to march with our regiment and to do the duty of officers until the Legislature shall have a reasonable time to appoint others, but no longer. We beg leave to assure your Excellency that we have the highest sense of your ability and virtues; that executing your orders has ever given us pleasure; that we love the service and love our country;—but when that country gets so lost to virtue and justice as to forget to support its servants, it then becomes their duty to retire from its service."

A commander of less magnanimity than Washington would have answered this letter by a stern exercise of military rule and driven the really aggrieved parties to extremity. He nobly contented himself with the following comment on it, forming a paragraph of a letter to General Maxwell. "I am sorry the gentlemen persist in the principles which dictated the step they have taken, as, the more the affair unfolds itself, the more reason I see to disapprove it. But in the present view they have of the matter, and with their present feelings, it is not probable any new argument that could be offered would have more influence than the former. While, therefore, the gentlemen continue in the execution of their duty, as they declare themselves heartily disposed to do, I shall only regret that they have taken a step of which they must hereafter see the impropriety."

The Legislature of New Jersey imitated the forbearance of Washington. Compounding with their pride, they let the officers know that on their withdrawing the memorial, the subject-matter of it would be promptly attended to. It was withdrawn. Resolutions were immediately passed granting pecuniary supplies to both officers and soldiers. The money was forthwith forwarded to camp and the brigade marched.

Such was the paternal spirit exercised by Washington in all the difficulties and discontents of the army. How clearly he understood the genius and circumstances of the people he was called upon to manage, and how truly was he their protector even more than their commander!

Chapter 40

SUFFERINGS OF THE ARMY AT MORRISTOWN

The situation of Sir Henry Clinton must have been mortifying in the extreme to an officer of lofty ambition and generous aims. His force, between sixteen and seventeen thousand strong, was superior in number, discipline and equipment to that of Washington, yet his instructions confined him to a predatory warfare carried on by attacks and marauds at distant points, harassing, it is true, yet irritating to the country intended to be conciliated and brutalizing to his own soldiery. Such was the nature of an expedition set on foot against the commerce of the Chesapeake, by which commerce the armies were supplied and the credit of the government sustained. On the 9th of May [1779] a squadron under Sir George Collier, convoying transports and galleys with twenty-five hundred men commanded by General Mathew, entered these waters, took possession of Portsmouth without opposition, sent out armed parties against Norfolk, Suffolk, Gosport, Kemp's Landing and other neighboring places, where were immense quantities of provisions, naval and military stores and merchandise of all kinds, with numerous vessels, some on the stocks, others richly laden. Wherever they went a scene of plunder, conflagration and destruction ensued. A few days sufficed to ravage the whole neighborhood.

While this was going on at the South, Washington received intelligence of movements at New York and in its vicinity which made him apprehend an expedition against the Highlands of the Hudson.

Since the loss of forts Montgomery and Clinton, the main defenses of the Highlands had been established at the sudden bend of the river where it winds between West Point and Constitution Island. Two opposite forts commanded this bend, and an iron chain which was stretched across it.

Washington had projected two works also just below the Highlands, at Stony Point and Verplanck's Point, to serve as outworks on the mountain passes and to protect King's Ferry, the most direct and convenient communication between the Northern and Middle States.

A small but strong fort had been erected on Verplanck's Point and was garrisoned by seventy men under Captain Armstrong. A more important work was in progress at Stony Point. When completed, these two forts on opposite promontories would form as it were the lower gates of the Highlands, miniature Pillars of Hercules, of which Stony Point was the Gibraltar.

To be at hand in case of any real attempt upon the Highlands, Washington drew up with his forces in that direction, moving by the way of Morristown.

An expedition up the Hudson was really the object of Sir Henry Clinton's movements, and for this he was strengthened by the return of Sir George Collier with his marauding ships and forces from Virginia. On the 30th of May, Sir Henry set out on his second grand cruise up the Hudson, with an armament of about seventy sail, great and small, and one hundred and fifty flat boats. Admiral Sir George Collier commanded the armament, and there was a land force of about five thousand men under General Vaughan.

The first aim of Sir Henry was to get possession of Stony and Verplanck's Points. His former expedition had acquainted him with the importance of this pass of the river. On the morning of the 31st the forces were landed in two divisions, the largest under General Vaughan on the east side of the river about seven or eight miles below Verplanck's Point. The other, commanded by Sir Henry in person, landed in Haverstraw Bay, about three miles below Stony Point. There were but about thirty men in the unfinished fort. They abandoned it on the approach of the enemy and retreated into the Highlands, having first set fire to the blockhouse. The British took quiet possession of the fort in the evening, dragged up a cannon and mortars in the night and at daybreak opened a furious fire upon Fort Lafayette. It was cannonaded at the same time by the armed vessels, and a demonstration was made on it by the division under General Vaughan. Thus surrounded, the little garrison of seventy men was forced to surrender with no other stipulation than safety to their persons and to the property they had in the fort. Major André was aide-de-camp to Sir Henry and signed the articles of capitulation.

Sir Henry Clinton stationed garrisons in both posts and set to work with great activity to complete the fortification of Stony Point. His troops remained for several days in two divisions on the opposite sides of the river. The fleet generally fell down a little below King's Ferry. Some of the square-rigged vessels, however, with others of a smaller size, and flat-bottomed boats having troops on board, dropped down Haverstraw Bay and finally disappeared behind the promontories which advance across the upper part of the Tappan Sea.

Some of the movements of the enemy perplexed Washington exceedingly. He presumed, however, that the main object of Sir Henry was to get possession of West Point, the guardian fortress of the river, and that the capture of Stony and Verplanck's Points were preparatory steps. He would fain have dislodged him from these posts, which cut off all communication by the way of King's Ferry, but they were too strong; he had not the force nor military apparatus necessary. Deferring any attempt on them for the present, he took measures for the protection of West Point. Leaving General Putnam and the main body of the army at Smith's Clove, a mountain pass in the rear of Haverstraw, he removed his headquarters to New Windsor to be near West Point in case of need and to press the completion of its works. General McDougall was transferred to the command of the Point. Three brigades were stationed at different places on the opposite side of the river, under General Heath, from which fatigue parties crossed daily to work on the fortifications.

This strong disposition of the American forces checked Sir Henry's designs against the Highlands. Contenting himself therefore for the present with the acquisition of Stony and Verplanck's Points, he returned to New York, where he soon set on foot a desolating expedition along the seaboard of Connecticut. That State, while it furnished the American armies with provisions and recruits and infested the sea with privateers, had hitherto experienced nothing of the horrors of war within its borders. Sir Henry, in compliance with his instructions from government, was now about to give it a scourging lesson, and he entertained the hope that in so doing he might draw down Washington from his mountain fastnesses and lay open the Hudson to a successful incursion.

[The British under General Tryon attacked New Haven, Fairfield and Norwalk, burning Fairfield to the ground and greatly damaging the other two towns.] These acts of devastation were accompanied by atrocities, inevitable where the brutal passions of the soldiery are aroused. They were unprovoked, too, by any unusual acts of hostility, the militia having no time to assemble, excepting in small parties for the defense of their homes and firesides.

As a kind of counter-check to Sir Henry, [Washington] had for some days been planning the recapture of Stony Point and Fort Lafayette. He had reconnoitered them in person. Spies had been thrown into them and information collected from deserters. Stony Point, having been recently strengthened by the British, was now the most important. It was a rocky promontory advancing far into the Hudson, which washed three sides of it. A deep morass, covered at high water, separated it from the mainland, but at low tide might be traversed by a narrow causeway and bridge. The promontory was crowned by strong works furnished with heavy ordnance commanding the morass and causeway. Lower down were two rows of abatis, and the shore at the foot of the hill could be swept by vessels of war anchored in the river. The garrison was about six hundred strong, commanded by Lieutenant-Colonel Johnson.

To attempt the surprisal of this isolated post, thus strongly fortified, was a perilous enterprise. General Wayne, Mad Anthony as he was called from his daring valor, was the officer to whom Washington proposed it, and he engaged in it with avidity. According to Washington's plan, it was to be attempted by light infantry only, at night and with the utmost secrecy, securing every person they met to prevent discovery. Between one and two hundred chosen men and officers were to make the surprise, preceded by a vanguard of prudent, determined men, well commanded, to remove obstructions, secure sentries and drive in the guards. The whole were to advance with fixed bayonets and unloaded muskets. All was to be done with the bayonet. These parties were to be followed by the main body at a small distance to support and reinforce them or to bring them off in case of failure. All were to wear white cockades or feathers and to have a watchword, so as to be distinguished from the enemy. "The usual time for exploits of this kind," observes Washington, "is a little before day, for which reason a vigilant officer is then more on the watch. I therefore recommend a midnight hour."

On getting possession of Stony Point, Wayne was to turn its guns upon Fort Lafayette and the shipping. A detachment was to march down from West Point by Peekskill to the vicinity of Fort Lafayette and hold itself ready to join in the attack upon it as soon as the cannonade began from Stony Point.

On the 15th of July, about mid-day, Wayne set out with his light infantry from Sandy Beach, fourteen miles distant from Stony Point. The roads were rugged, across mountains, morasses and narrow defiles, in the skirts of the Dunderberg, where frequently it was necessary to proceed in single file. About eight in the evening they arrived within a mile and a half of the forts without being discovered. Not a dog barked to give the alarm—all the dogs in the neighborhood had been privately destroyed beforehand. Bringing the men to a halt, Wayne and his principal officers went nearer and carefully reconnoitered the works and their environs so as to proceed understandingly and without confusion. Having made their observations, they returned to the troops. Midnight, it will be recollected, was the time recommended by Washington for the attack. About half-past eleven the whole moved forward, guided by a negro of the neighborhood who had frequently carried in fruit to the garrison and served the Americans as a spy. He led the way accompanied by two stout men disguised as farmers. The countersign was given to the first sentinel, posted on high ground west of the morass. While the negro talked with him, the men seized and gagged him. The sentinel posted at the head of the causeway was served in the same manner, so that hitherto no alarm was given. The causeway, however, was overflowed, and it was some time after twelve o'clock before the troops could cross, leaving three hundred men under General Muhlenberg on the western side of the morass as a reserve.

At the foot of the promontory the troops were divided into two columns for simultaneous attacks on opposite sides of the works. One hundred and fifty volunteers, led by Lieutenant-Colonel Fleury, seconded by Major Posey, formed the vanguard of the right column, one hundred volunteers under Major Stewart the vanguard of the left. In advance of each was a forlorn hope of twenty men, one led by Lieutenant Gibbon, the other by Lieutenant Knox. It was their desperate duty to remove the abatis. So well had the whole affair been conducted that the Americans were close upon the outworks before they were discovered. There was then severe skirmishing at the pickets. The Americans used the bayonet. The others discharged their muskets. The reports roused the garrison. Stony Point was instantly in an uproar. The drums beat to arms. Every one hurried to his alarm post. The works were hastily manned, and a tremendous fire of grape-shot and musketry opened upon the assailants.

The two columns forced their way with the bayonet at opposite points, surmounting every obstacle. Colonel Fleury was the first to enter the fort and strike the British flag. Major Posey sprang to the ramparts and shouted, "The fort is our own." Wayne, who led the right column, received at the inner abatis a contusion on the head from a musket ball and would have fallen to the ground but his two aides-de-camp supported him. Thinking it was a death wound, "Carry me into the fort," said he, "and let me die at the head of my column." He was borne in between his aides and soon recovered his self-possession. The two columns arrived nearly at the same time and met in the centre of the works. The garrison surrendered at discretion.

At daybreak, as Washington directed, the guns of the fort were turned on Fort Lafayette and the shipping. The latter cut their cables and dropped down the river. Through a series of blunders, the detachment from West Point which was to have co-operated did not arrive in time, and came unprovided with suitable ammunition for their battering artillery. This part of the enterprise therefore failed. Fort Lafayette held out.

The storming of Stony Point stands out in high relief as one of the most brilliant achievements of the war. The Americans had effected it without firing a musket. On their part it was the silent, deadly work of the bayonet. The fierce resistance they met at the outset may be judged by the havoc made in their forlorn hope. Out of twenty-two men, seventeen were either killed or wounded. The whole loss of the Americans was fifteen killed and eighty-three wounded. Of the garrison, sixty-three were slain, including two officers. Five hundred and fifty-three were taken prisoners, among whom were a lieutenant-colonel, four captains and twenty-three subaltern officers.

Wayne in his despatches writes: "The humanity of our brave soldiery, who scorned to take the lives of a vanquished foe when calling for mercy, reflects the highest honor on them and accounts for the few of the enemy killed on the occasion." His words reflect honor on himself.

A British historian confirms his eulogy. "The conduct of the Americans upon this occasion was highly meritorious," writes he, "for they would have been fully justified in putting the garrison to the sword, not one man of which was put to death but in fair combat."[1]

Tidings of the capture of Stony Point and the imminent danger of Fort Lafayette reached Sir Henry Clinton just after his conference with Sir George Collier at Throg's Neck. The expedition against New London was instantly given up, the transports and troops were recalled, a forced march was made to Dobbs Ferry on the Hudson, a detachment was sent up the river in transports to relieve Fort Lafayette, and Sir Henry followed with a greater force, hoping Washington might quit his fastnesses and risk a battle for the possession of Stony Point.

Again the Fabian policy of the American commander-in-chief disappointed the British general. Having well examined the post in company with an engineer and several general officers, he found that at least fifteen hundred men would be required to maintain it, a number not to be spared from the army at present.

The works, too, were only calculated for defense on the land side and were open towards the river, where the enemy depended upon protection from their ships. It would be necessary to construct them anew, with great labor. The army, also, would have to be in the vicinity, too distant from West Point to aid in completing or defending its fortifications, and exposed to the risk of a general action on unfavorable terms.

For these considerations, in which all his officers concurred, Washington evacuated the post on the 18th, removing the cannon and stores and destroying the works, after which he drew his forces together in the Highlands and established his quarters at West Point, not knowing but that Sir Henry might attempt a retaliatory stroke on that most important fortress. The latter retook possession of Stony Point and fortified and garrisoned it more strongly than ever, but was too wary to risk an attempt upon the strong-

[1] Stedman, vol. i., p. 145.

holds of the Highlands. Finding Washington was not to be tempted out of them, he ordered the transports to fall once more down the river and returned to his former encampment at Philipsburg.

Of [Washington's] singularly isolated situation with respect to public affairs, we have evidence in the following passage of a letter to Edmund Randolph, who had recently taken a seat in Congress:

"I shall be happy in such communications as your leisure and other considerations will permit you to transmit to me, for I am as totally unacquainted with the political state of things and what is going forward in the great national council as if I was an alien when a competent knowledge of the temper and designs of our allies from time to time and the frequent changes and complexion of affairs in Europe might, as they ought to do, have a considerable influence on the operations of our army and would in many cases determine the propriety of measures which under a cloud of darkness can only be groped at. I say this upon a presumption that Congress, either through their own ministers or that of France, must be acquainted in some degree with the plans of Great Britain and the designs of France and Spain. If I mistake in this conjecture, it is to be lamented that they have not better information. Or, if political motives render disclosures of this kind improper, I am content to remain in ignorance."

Of the style of living at headquarters we have a picture in the following letter to Doctor John Cochran, the surgeon-general and physician of the army. It is almost the only instance of sportive writing in all Washington's correspondence.

"Dear Doctor, I have asked Mrs. Cochran and Mrs. Livingston to dine with me tomorrow, but am I not in honor bound to apprise them of their fare? As I hate deception, even where the imagination only is concerned, I will. It is needless to premise that my table is large enough to hold the ladies. Of this they had ocular proof yesterday. To say how it is usually covered is more essential, and this shall be the purport of my letter.

"Since our arrival at this happy spot we have had a ham, sometimes a shoulder of bacon, to grace the head of the table. A piece of roast beef adorns the foot, and a dish of beans or greens, almost imperceptible, decorates the centre. When the cook has a mind to cut a figure, which I presume will be the case tomorrow, we have two beefsteak pies, or dishes of crabs, in addition, one on each side

of the centre dish, dividing the space and reducing the distance between dish and dish to about six feet, which, without them, would
be about twelve feet apart. Of late he has had the surprising
sagacity to discover that apples will make pies, and it is a question
if, in the violence of his efforts, we do not get one of apples instead
of having both of beefsteaks. If the ladies can put up with such en-
tertainment and will submit to partake of it on plates once tin but
now iron (not become so by the labor of scouring), I shall be
happy to see them."

The arrival of Admiral Arbuthnot with a fleet bringing three
thousand troops and a supply of provisions and stores
strengthened the hands of Sir Henry Clinton. Still he had not
sufficient force to warrant any further attempt up the Hudson,
Washington by his diligence in fortifying West Point having rendered that fastness of the Highlands apparently impregnable. Sir
Henry turned his thoughts therefore towards the South, hoping by
a successful expedition in that direction to counterbalance ill success in other quarters. As this would require large detachments, he
threw up additional works on New York Island and at Brooklyn to
render his position secure with the diminished force that would
remain with him.

At this juncture news was received of the arrival of the Count
D'Estaing with a formidable fleet on the coast of Georgia, having
made a successful cruise in the West Indies, in the course of which
he had taken St. Vincent's and Grenada. A combined attack upon
New York was again talked of. In anticipation of it, Washington
called upon several of the Middle States for supplies of all kinds
and reinforcements of militia. Sir Henry Clinton, also, changed his
plans, caused Rhode Island to be evacuated, the troops and stores
to be brought away, the garrisons brought off from Stony and
Verplanck's Points, and all his forces to be concentrated at New
York, which he endeavored to put in the strongest posture of
defense.

Intelligence recently received, too, that Spain had joined France
in hostilities against England, contributed to increase the solicitude
and perplexities of the enemy while it gave fresh confidence to the
Americans.

The Chevalier de la Luzerne, minister from France, with Mons.
Barbé Marbois, his secretary of legation, having recently landed at
Boston, paid Washington a visit at his mountain fortress, bringing
letters of introduction from Lafayette. The chevalier, not having

yet announced himself to Congress, did not choose to be received in his public character. "If he had," writes Washington, "except paying him military honors, it was not my intention to depart from that plain and simple manner of living which accords with the real interest and policy of men struggling under every difficulty for the attainment of the most inestimable blessing of life, *liberty*."

In conformity with his intention, he welcomed the chevalier to the mountains with the thunder of artillery and received him at his fortress with military ceremonial, but very probably surprised him with the stern simplicity of his table while he charmed him with the dignity and grace with which he presided at it. The ambassador evidently acquitted himself with true French suavity and diplomatic tact. "He was polite enough," writes Washington, "to approve my principle, and condescended to appear pleased with our Spartan living. In a word, he made us all exceedingly happy by his affability and good humor while he remained in camp."

Washington's anticipations of a combined operation with D'Estaing against New York were again disappointed. The French admiral, on arriving on the coast of Georgia, had been persuaded to co-operate with the Southern army under General Lincoln in an attempt to recover Savannah, which had fallen into the hands of the British during the preceding year. For three weeks a siege was carried on with great vigor by regular approaches on land, and cannonade and bombardment from the shipping. On the 9th of October, although the approaches were not complete and no sufficient breach had been effected, Lincoln and D'Estaing, at the head of their choicest troops, advanced before daybreak to storm the works. The assault was gallant but unsuccessful. Both Americans and French had planted their standards on the redoubts but were finally repulsed. After the repulse, both armies retired from before the place, the French having lost in killed and wounded upwards of six hundred men, the Americans about four hundred. D'Estaing himself was among the wounded and the gallant Count Pulaski among the slain. The loss of the enemy was trifling, being protected by their works.

The Americans recrossed the Savannah River into South Carolina. The militia returned to their homes, and the French re-embarked.

The tidings of this reverse, which reached Washington late in

November, put an end to all prospect of co-operation from the French fleet. A consequent change took place in all his plans. The militia of New York and Massachusetts, recently assembled, were disbanded and arrangements were made for the winter. The army was thrown into two divisions. One was to be stationed under General Heath in the Highlands for the protection of West Point and the neighboring posts. The other and principal division was to be hutted near Morristown, where Washington was to have his headquarters. The cavalry were to be sent to Connecticut.

Understanding that Sir Henry Clinton was making preparations at New York for a large embarkation of troops, and fearing they might be destined against Georgia and Carolina, he resolved to detach the greater part of his Southern troops for the protection of those States; a provident resolution in which he was confirmed by subsequent instructions from Congress. Accordingly, the North Carolina brigade took up its march for Charleston in November, and the whole of the Virginia line in December.

Notwithstanding the recent preparations at New York, the ships remained in port and the enemy held themselves in collected force there. Doubts began to be entertained of some furtive design nearer at hand, and measures were taken to protect the army against an attack when in winter quarters. Sir Henry, however, was regulating his movements by those the French fleet might make after the repulse at Savannah. Intelligence at length arrived that it had been dispersed by a violent storm. Count D'Estaing, with a part, had shaped his course for France. The rest had proceeded to the West Indies.

Sir Henry now lost no time in carrying his plans into operation. Leaving the garrison of New York under the command of Lieutenant-General Knyphausen, he embarked several thousand men on board of transports, to be convoyed by five ships of the line and several frigates under Admiral Arbuthnot, and set sail on the 26th of December, accompanied by Lord Cornwallis, on an expedition intended for the capture of Charleston and the reduction of South Carolina.

The dreary encampment at Valley Forge has become proverbial for its hardships, yet they were scarcely more severe than those suffered by Washington's army during the present winter while hutted among the heights of Morristown. The winter set in early and was uncommonly rigorous. The transportation of supplies was obstructed, the magazines were exhausted and the commissaries had neither money nor credit to enable them to replenish them. For weeks at a time the army was on half allowance, sometimes without meat, sometimes without bread, sometimes without both. There was a scarcity too of clothing and blankets, so that the poor soldiers were starving with cold as well as hunger.

Washington wrote to President Reed of Pennsylvania, entreating aid and supplies from that State to keep his army from disbanding. "We have never," said he, "experienced a like extremity at any period of the war."[2]

The year 1780 opened upon a famishing camp. "For a fortnight past," writes Washington on the 8th of January, "the troops, both officers and men, have been almost perishing with want. Yet," adds he feelingly, "they have borne their sufferings with a patience that merits the approbation and ought to excite the sympathies of their countrymen."

The severest trials of the Revolution in fact were not in the field, where there were shouts to excite and laurels to be won, but in the squalid wretchedness of ill-provided camps, where there was nothing to cheer and everything to be endured. To suffer was the lot of the revolutionary soldier.

A rigorous winter had much to do with the actual distresses of the army, but the root of the evil lay in the derangement of the currency. Congress had commenced the war without adequate funds and without the power of imposing direct taxes. To meet pressing emergencies, it had emitted paper money which, for a time, passed currently at par but sank in value as further emissions succeeded, and that already in circulation remained unredeemed. The several States added to the evil by emitting paper in their separate capacities. Thus the country gradually became flooded with a "Continental currency," as it was called, irredeemable and of no intrinsic value. The consequence was a general derangement of trade and finance. The Continental currency declined to such a degree that forty dollars in paper were equivalent to only one in specie.

Congress attempted to put a stop to this depreciation by making paper money a legal tender, at its nominal value, in the discharge of debts however contracted. This opened the door to knavery and added a new feature to the evil.

[2] *Life of Reed*, ii., 189.

The commissaries now found it difficult to purchase supplies for the immediate wants of the army and impossible to provide any stores in advance. They were left destitute of funds, and the public credit was prostrated by the accumulating debts suffered to remain uncancelled. The changes which had taken place in the commissary department added to this confusion. The commissary-general, instead of receiving, as heretofore, a commission on expenditures, was to have a fixed salary in paper currency, and his deputies were to be compensated in like manner without the usual allowance of rations and forage. No competent agents could be procured on such terms, and the derangement produced throughout the department compelled Colonel Wadsworth, the able and upright commissary-general, to resign.

In the present emergency Washington was reluctantly compelled by the distresses of the army to call upon the counties of the State for supplies of grain and cattle proportioned to their respective abilities. These supplies were to be brought into the camp within a certain time, the grain to be measured and the cattle estimated by any two of the magistrates of the county in conjunction with the commissary, and certificates to be given by the latter specifying the quantity of each and the terms of payment.

Wherever a compliance with this call was refused, the articles required were to be impressed. It was a painful alternative, yet nothing else could save the army from dissolution or starving. Washington charged his officers to act with as much tenderness as possible, graduating the exaction according to the stock of each individual, so that no family should be deprived of what was necessary to its subsistence.

"While your measures are adapted to the emergency," writes he to Colonel Matthias Ogden, "and you consult what you owe to the service, I am persuaded you will not forget that, as we are compelled by necessity to take the property of citizens for the support of an army on which their safety depends, we should be careful to manifest that we have a reverence for their rights and wish not to do anything which that necessity, and even their own good, do not absolutely require."

To the honor of the magistrates and the people of Jersey, Washington testifies that his requisitions were punctually complied with, and in many counties exceeded. Too much praise indeed cannot be given to the people of this State for the patience with which most of them bore these exactions, and the patriotism with which many of them administered to the wants of their countrymen in arms. Exhausted as the State was by repeated drainings, yet, at one time, when deep snows cut off all distant supplies, Washington's army was wholly subsisted by it. "Provisions came in with hearty good-will from the farmers in Medham, Chatham, Hanover and other rural places, together with stockings, shoes, coats, and blankets; while the women met together to knit and sew for the soldiery."[3]

As the winter advanced the cold increased in severity. It was the most intense ever remembered in the country. The great bay of New York was frozen over. No supplies could come to the city by water. Provisions grew scanty and there was such lack of fire-wood that old transports were broken up and uninhabited wooden houses pulled down for fuel. The safety of the city was endangered. The ships of war, immovably ice-bound in its harbor, no longer gave it protection. The insular security of the place was at an end. An army with its heaviest artillery and baggage might cross the Hudson on the ice. The veteran Knyphausen began to apprehend an invasion and took measures accordingly. The seamen of the ships and transports were landed and formed into companies, and the inhabitants of the city were embodied, officered and subjected to garrison duty.

Washington was aware of the opportunity which offered itself for a signal *coup de main* but was not in a condition to profit by it. His troops, hutted among the heights of Morristown, were half fed, half clothed and inferior in number to the garrison of New York. He was destitute of funds necessary to fit them for the enterprise, and the quartermaster could not furnish means of transportation.

[3] From manuscript notes by the Rev. Joseph Tuttle. This worthy clergyman gives many anecdotes illustrative of the active patriotism of the Jersey women. Anna Kitchel, wife of a farmer of Whippany, is repeatedly his theme of well-merited eulogium. Her potato bin, meal bag and granary, writes he, had always some comfort for the patriot soldiers. When unable to billet them in her house, a huge kettle filled with meat and vegetables was hung over the fire, that they might not go away hungry.

Chapter 41

END OF THE CAMPAIGN IN THE JERSEYS

The return of spring brought little alleviation to the sufferings of the army at Morristown. All means of supplying its wants or recruiting its ranks were paralyzed by the continued depreciation of the currency. The troops were paid in paper money at its nominal value. A memorial of the officers of the Jersey line to the legislature of their State represented the depreciation to be so great that four months' pay of a private soldier would not procure for his family a single bushel of wheat. The pay of a colonel would not purchase oats for his horse, and a common laborer or express rider could earn four times the pay in paper of an American officer.

Congress, too, in its exigencies, being destitute of the power of levying taxes, which vested in the State governments, devolved upon those governments, in their separate capacities, the business of supporting the army. This produced a great inequality in the condition of the troops, according to the means and the degree of liberality of their respective States. Some States furnished their troops amply, not only with clothing but with many comforts and conveniences. Others were more contracted in their supplies. While others left their troops almost destitute. Some of the States, too, undertook to make good to their troops the loss in their pay caused by the depreciation of the currency. As this was not general, it increased the inequality of condition. Those who fared worse than others were incensed not only against their own State but against the confederacy. They were disgusted with a service that made such injurious distinctions. Some of the officers resigned, finding it impossible under actual circumstances to maintain an appearance suitable to their rank. The men had not this resource. They murmured and showed a tendency to seditious combinations.

These and other defects in the military system were pressed by Washington upon the attention of Congress in a letter to the president. "It were devoutly to be wished that a plan could be devised by which everything relating to the army could be conducted on a general principle under the direction of Congress. This alone can give harmony and consistency to our military establishment, and I am persuaded it will be infinitely conducive to public economy."[1]

In consequence of this letter it was proposed in Congress to send a committee of three of its members to headquarters to consult with the commander-in-chief and, in conjunction with him, to effect such reforms and changes in the various departments of the army as might be deemed necessary. Warm debates ensued. It was objected that this would put too much power into a few hands and especially into those of the commander-in-chief: "that his influence was already too great; that even his virtues afforded motives for alarm; that the enthusiasm of the army, joined to the kind of dictatorship already confided to him, put Congress and the United States at his mercy; that it was not expedient to expose a man of highest virtues to such temptations."[2]

The foregoing passage from a despatch of the French minister to his government is strongly illustrative of the cautious jealousy still existing in Congress with regard to military power, even though wielded by Washington.

After a prolonged debate a committee of three was chosen by ballot. It consisted of General Schuyler and Messrs. John Matthews and Nathaniel Peabody. It was a great satisfaction to Washington to have his old friend and coadjutor, Schuyler, near him in this capacity, in which, he declared, no man could be more useful, "from his perfect knowledge of the resources of the country, the activity of his temper, his fruitfulness of expedients and his sound military sense."[3]

The committee on arriving at the camp found the disastrous state of affairs had not been exaggerated. For five months the army had been unpaid. Every department was destitute of money or credit. There were rarely provisions for six days in advance. On some occasions the troops had been for several successive days without meat. There was no forage. The medical department had neither tea, chocolate, wine, nor spirituous liquors of any kind.

[1] *Washington's Writings*, Sparks, vol. vii., p. ii.
[2] *Ibid.*, vii., p. 15.
[3] Washington to James Duane, Sparks, vii., 34.

"Yet the men," said Washington, "have borne their distress in general with a firmness and patience never exceeded, and every commendation is due to the officers for encouraging them to it by exhortation and example. They have suffered equally with the men and, their relative situations considered, rather more." Indeed, we have it from another authority that many officers for some time lived on bread and cheese rather than take any of the scanty allowance of meat from the men.[4]

To soothe the discontents of the army and counteract the alarming effects of the currency, Congress now adopted the measure already observed by some of the States and engaged to make good to the continental and the independent troops the difference in the value of their pay caused by this depreciation; and that all moneys or other articles heretofore received by them should be considered as advanced on account and comprehended at their just value in the final settlement.

At this gloomy crisis came a letter from the Marquis de Lafayette, dated April 12th, announcing his arrival at Boston. [Lafayette] arrived at headquarters on the 12th of May, where he made known the result of his visit to France. His generous efforts at court had been crowned with success and he brought the animating intelligence that a French fleet under the Chevalier de Ternay was to put to sea early in April, bring a body of troops under the Count de Rochambeau, and might soon be expected on the coast to co-operate with the American forces. This, however, he was at liberty to make known only to Washington and Congress.

Remaining but a single day at headquarters, he hastened on to the seat of government, where he met the reception which his generous enthusiasm in the cause of American Independence had so fully merited. Congress, in a resolution on the 16th of May, pronounced his return to America to resume his command a fresh proof of the disinterested zeal and persevering attachment which had secured him the public confidence and applause, and received with pleasure a "tender of the further services of so gallant and meritorious an officer."

Within three days after the departure of the marquis from Morristown, Washington, in a letter to him, gave his idea of the plan which it would be proper for the French fleet and army to pursue on their arrival upon the coast. The reduction of New York

[4] Gen. William Laine to Joseph Reed. Reed's *Memoirs*, vol. ii., p. 201.

he considered the first enterprise to be attempted by the co-operating forces. The whole effective land force of the enemy he estimated at about eight thousand regulars and four thousand refugees, with some militia on which no great dependence could be placed. Their naval force consisted of one seventy-four-gun ship and three or four small frigates. In this situation of affairs the French fleet might enter the harbor and gain possession of it without difficulty, cut off its communications and, with the co-operation of the American army, oblige the city to capitulate. He advised Lafayette therefore to write to the French commanders, urging them, on their arrival on the coast, to proceed with their land and naval forces with all expedition to Sandy Hook and there await further advices. Should they learn, however, that the expedition under Sir Henry Clinton had returned from the South to New York, they were to proceed to Rhode Island.

In the meantime the army with which Washington was to co-operate in the projected attack upon New York was so reduced by the departure of troops whose term had expired and the tardiness in furnishing recruits that it did not amount quite to four thousand rank and file fit for duty. Among these was a prevalent discontent. Their pay was five months in arrear. If now paid, it would be in Continental currency without allowance for depreciation, consequently almost worthless for present purposes.

A long interval of scarcity and several days of actual famine brought matters to a crisis. On the 15th of May, in the dusk of the evening, two regiments of the Connecticut line assembled on their parade by beat of drum and declared their intention to march home bag and baggage "or, at best, to gain subsistence at the point of the bayonet." Colonel Meigs, while endeavoring to suppress the mutiny, was struck by one of the soldiers. Some officers of the Pennsylvania line came to his assistance, parading their regiments. Every argument and expostulation was used with the mutineers. They were reminded of their past good conduct, of the noble objects for which they were contending and of the future indemnifications promised by Congress. Their answer was that their sufferings were too great to be allayed by promises in which they had little faith. They wanted present relief and some present substantial recompense for their services.

It was with difficulty they could be prevailed upon to return to their huts. Indeed, a few turned out a second time, with their packs, and were not to be pacified. These were arrested and confined.

This mutiny, Washington declared, had given him infinitely more concern than anything that had ever happened, especially as he had no means of paying the troops excepting in Continental money, which, said he, "is evidently impracticable from the immense quantity it would require to pay them as much as would make up the depreciation." His uneasiness was increased by finding that printed handbills were secretly disseminated in his camp by the enemy, containing addresses to the soldiery persuading them to desert.[5]

In this alarming state of destitution, Washington looked around anxiously for bread for his famishing troops. New York, Jersey, Pennsylvania and Maryland were what he termed his "flour country." Virginia was sufficiently tasked to supply the South. New York by legislative coercion had already given all that she could spare from the subsistence of her inhabitants. Jersey was exhausted by the long residence of the army. Maryland had made great exertions and might still do something more, and Delaware might contribute handsomely in proportion to her extent, but Pennsylvania was now the chief dependence, for that State was represented to be full of flour. Washington's letter of the 16th of December to President Reed had obtained temporary relief from that quarter. He now wrote to him a second time, and still more earnestly,

"Every idea you can form of our distresses will fall short of the reality. There is such a combination of circumstances to exhaust the patience of the soldiery that it begins at length to be worn out, and we see in every line of the army features of mutiny and sedition. All our departments, all our operations, are at a stand, and unless a system very different from that which has a long time prevailed be immediately adopted throughout the States, our affairs must soon become desperate beyond the possibility of recovery."

Nothing discouraged Washington more than the lethargy that seemed to deaden the public mind. He speaks of it with a degree of despondency scarcely ever before exhibited.

"I have almost ceased to hope. The country is in such a state of

[5] Letter to the President of Cong., May 27. Sparks, vii., 54.

insensibility and indifference to its interests that I dare not flatter myself with any change for the better."

And again, "The present juncture is so interesting that if it does not produce corresponding exertions it will be a proof that motives of honor, public good and even self-preservation have lost their influence on our minds. This is a decisive moment; one of the most, I will go further and say *the* most important America has seen. The court of France has made a glorious effort for our deliverance, and if we disappoint its intentions by our supineness, we must become contemptible in the eyes of all mankind, nor can we after that venture to confide that our allies will persist in an attempt to establish what, it will appear, we want inclination or ability to assist them in."

With these and similar observations he sought to rouse President Reed to extraordinary exertions.

"This is a time," writes he, "to hazard and to take a tone of energy and decision. All parties but the disaffected will acquiesce in the necessity and give it their support." He urges Reed to press upon the Legislature of Pennsylvania the policy of investing its executive with plenipotentiary powers. "I should then expect everything from your ability and zeal. This is no time for formality or ceremony. The crisis in every point of view is extraordinary, and extraordinary expedients are necessary. I am decided in this opinion."

His letter procured relief for the army from the legislature, and a resolve empowering the president and council during its recess to declare martial law should circumstances render it expedient. "This," observes Reed, "gives us a power of doing what may be necessary without attending to the ordinary course of law, and shall endeavor to exercise it with prudence and moderation."[6]

In like manner Washington endeavored to rouse the dormant fire of Congress and impart to it his own indomitable energy.

"Certain I am," writes he to a member of that body, "unless Congress speak in a more decisive tone, unless they are vested with powers by the several States competent to the purposes of war or assume them as matters of right, and they and the States respectively act with more energy than they have hitherto done, that our cause is lost. We can no longer drudge on in the old way. By ill-

6 Sparks, *Corr. of the Rev.*, vol. ii., p. 466.

timing the adoption of measures, by delays in the execution of them, or by unwarrantable jealousies, we incur enormous expenses and derive no benefit from them. One State will comply with a requisition of Congress. Another neglects to do it. A third executes it by halves. And all differ either in the manner, the matter or so much in point of time that we are always working up-hill. And while such a system as the present one, or rather want of one, prevails, we shall ever be unable to apply our strength or resources to any advantage. I see one head gradually changing into thirteen. I see one army branching into thirteen, which, instead of looking up to Congress as the supreme controlling power of the United States, are considering themselves dependent on their respective States. In a word, I see the powers of Congress declining too fast for the consideration and respect which are due to them as the great representative body of America, and I am fearful of the consequences."[7]

[Charleston fell before the forces of Sir Henry Clinton, and the Americans were also defeated in several lesser engagements.]

Sir Henry now persuaded himself that South Carolina was subdued, and proceeded to station garrisons in various parts to maintain it in subjection. In the fulness of his confidence he issued a proclamation on the 3d of June discharging all the military prisoners from their paroles after the 20th of the month excepting those captured in Fort Moultrie and Charleston. All thus released from their parole were reinstated in the rights and duties of British subjects but at the same time they were bound to take an active part in support of the government hitherto opposed by them. Thus the protection afforded them while prisoners was annulled by an arbitrary fiat—neutrality was at an end. All were to be ready to take up arms at a moment's notice. Those who had families were to form a militia for home defense. Those who had none were to serve with the royal forces. All who should neglect to return to their allegiance or should refuse to take up arms against the independence of their country were to be considered as rebels and treated accordingly.

Having struck a blow which, as he conceived, was to insure the subjugation of the South, Sir Henry embarked for New York on the 5th of June [1780] with a part of his forces, leaving the residue

[7] Letter to Joseph Jones. Sparks, vii., 67.

under the command of Lord Cornwallis, who was to carry the war into North Carolina and thence into Virginia.

A handbill published by the British authorities in New York reached Washington's camp on the 1st of June and made known the surrender of Charleston. A person from Amboy reported, moreover, that on the 30th of May he had seen one hundred sail of vessels enter Sandy Hook. These might bring Sir Henry Clinton with the whole or part of his force. In that case, flushed with his recent success, he might proceed immediately up the Hudson and make an attempt upon West Point in the present distressed condition of the garrison. So thinking, Washington wrote to General Howe, who commanded that important post, to put him on his guard, and took measures to have him furnished with supplies.

The report concerning the fleet proved to be erroneous, but on the 6th of June came a new alarm. The enemy, it was said, were actually landing in force at Elizabethtown Point to carry fire and sword into the Jerseys!

It was even so. Knyphausen, through spies and emissaries, had received exaggerated accounts of the recent outbreak in Washington's camp and of general discontent among the people of New Jersey and was persuaded that a sudden show of military protection, following up the news of the capture of Charleston, would produce a general desertion among Washington's troops and rally back the inhabitants of the Jerseys to their allegiance to the crown.

In this belief he projected a descent into the Jerseys with about five thousand men and some light artillery, who were to cross in divisions in the night of the 5th of June from Staten Island to Elizabethtown Point.

The first division, led by Brigadier-General Sterling, actually landed before dawn of the 6th and advanced as silently as possible. The heavy and measured tramp of the troops, however, caught the ear of an American sentinel stationed at a fork where the roads from the old and new point joined. He challenged the dimly descried mass as it approached and, receiving no answer, fired into it. That shot wounded General Sterling in the thigh and ultimately proved mortal. The wounded general was carried back, and Knyphausen took his place.

This delayed the march until sunrise and gave time for the troops of the Jersey line, under Colonel Elias Dayton, stationed in

Elizabethtown, to assemble. They were too weak in numbers, however, to withstand the enemy, but retreated in good order, skirmishing occasionally. The invading force passed through the village. In the advance [was] a squadron of dragoons of Simcoe's regiment of Queen's Rangers, with drawn swords and glittering helmets, followed by British and Hessian infantry.[8]

Signal guns and signal fires were rousing the country. The militia and yeomanry armed themselves with such weapons as were at hand and hastened to their alarm posts. The enemy took the old road, by what was called Galloping Hill, toward the village of Connecticut Farms, fired upon from behind walls and thickets by the hasty levies of the country.

At Connecticut Farms the retreating troops under Dayton fell in with the Jersey brigade under General Maxwell, and, a few militia joining them, the Americans were enabled to make some stand and even to hold the enemy in check. The latter, however, brought up several field-pieces and, being reinforced by a second division which had crossed from Staten Island some time after the first, compelled the Americans again to retreat. Some of the enemy, exasperated at the unexpected opposition they had met with throughout their march, and pretending that the inhabitants of this village had fired upon them from their windows, began to pillage and set fire to the houses.

It so happened that to this village the Rev. James Caldwell, "the rousing gospel preacher," had removed his family as to a place of safety, after his church at Elizabethtown had been burnt down by the British in January. On the present occasion he had retreated with the regiment to which he was chaplain. His wife, however, remained at the parsonage with her two youngest children, confiding in the protection of Providence and the humanity of the enemy.

When the sacking of the village took place she retired with her children into a back room of the house. Her infant of eight months was in the arms of an attendant. She herself was seated on the side of a bed holding a child of three years by the hand, and was engaged in prayer. All was terror and confusion in the village when suddenly a musket was discharged in at the window. Two balls struck her in the breast and she fell dead on the floor. The

[8] Passages in the History of Elizabethtown, Capt W. C. De Hart.

parsonage and church were set on fire and it was with difficulty her body was rescued from the flames.

In the meantime Knyphausen was pressing on with his main force towards Morristown. The booming of alarm guns had roused the country. Every valley was pouring out its yeomanry. Two thousand were said to be already in arms below the mountains.

Within half a mile of Springfield, Knyphausen halted to reconnoiter. That village, through which passes the road to Springfield, had been made the American rallying-point. It stands at the foot of what are called the Short Hills, on the west side of Rahway River, which runs in front of it. On the bank of the river, General Maxwell's Jersey brigade and the militia of the neighborhood were drawn up to dispute the passage. And on the Short Hills in the rear was Washington with the main body of his forces, not mutinous and in confusion but all in good order, strongly posted and ready for action.

Washington had arrived and taken his position that afternoon prepared to withstand an encounter though not to seek one. All night his camp fires lighted up the Short Hills, and he remained on the alert, expecting to be assailed in the morning. But in the morning no enemy was to be seen.

Knyphausen had experienced enough to convince him that he had been completely misinformed as to the disposition of the Jersey people and of the army. Disappointed as to the main objects of his enterprise, he had retreated under cover of the night to the place of his debarkation, intending to recross to Staten Island immediately.

In the camp at the Short Hills was the Reverend James Caldwell, whose home had been laid desolate. He was still ignorant of the event but had passed a night of great anxiety and, procuring the protection of a flag, hastened back in the morning to Connecticut Farms. He found the village in ashes and his wife a mangled corpse!

In the course of the day Washington received a letter from Colonel Alexander Hamilton, who was reconnoitering the neighborhood of Elizabethtown Point. "I have seen the enemy," writes he. "Those in view I calculate at about three thousand. There may be, and probably are, enough others out of sight. They have sent all their horses to the other side except about fifty or sixty. Their baggage has also been sent across, and their wounded. It is not ascertained that any of their infantry have passed on the other side. . . . The present movement may be calculated to draw us down and betray us into an action. They may have desisted from their intention of passing till night for fear of our falling upon their rear."

As Washington was ignorant of the misinformation which had beguiled Knyphausen into this enterprise, the movements of that general, his sudden advance and as sudden retreat were equally inexplicable. At one time he supposed his inroad to be a mere foraging incursion; then, as Hamilton had suggested, a device to draw him down from his stronghold into the plain, where the superiority of the British force would give them the advantage.

Knyphausen in fact had been impeded in crossing his troops to Staten Island by the low tide and deep muddy shore, which rendered it difficult to embark the cavalry, and by a destructive fire kept up by militia posted along the river banks and the adjacent woods. In the meanwhile he had time to reflect on the ridicule that would await him in New York should his expedition prove fruitless and end in what might appear a precipitate flight. This produced indecision of mind and induced him to recall the troops which had already crossed and which were necessary, he said, to protect his rear.

For several days he lingered with his troops at Elizabethtown and the Point beyond, obliging Washington to exercise unremitting vigilance for the safety of the Jerseys and of the Hudson. It was a great satisfaction to the latter to be joined by Major Henry Lee, who with his troop of horse had hastened on from the vicinity of Philadelphia, where he had recently been stationed.

In the meantime the tragical fate of Mrs. Caldwell produced almost as much excitement throughout the country as that which had been caused in a preceding year by the massacre of Miss McCrea. She was connected with some of the first people of New Jersey, was winning in person and character and universally beloved. Knyphausen was vehemently assailed in the American papers, as if responsible for this atrocious act. The enemy, however, attributed her death to a random shot discharged in a time of confusion, or to the vengeance of a menial who had a deadly pique against her husband. But the popular voice persisted in execrating it as the wilful and wanton act of a British soldier.

On the 17th of June the fleet from the South actually arrived in the bay of New York, and Sir Henry Clinton landed his troops on Staten Island but almost immediately re-embarked them, as if meditating an expedition up the river.

Fearing for the safety of West Point, Washington set off on the 21st of June with the main body of his troops towards Pompton, while General Greene, with Maxwell and Stark's brigades, Lee's dragoons and the militia of the neighborhood, remained encamped on the Short Hills to cover the country and protect the stores at Morristown.

Washington's movements were slow and wary. He was unwilling to be far from Greene until better informed of the designs of the enemy. At Rockaway Bridge, about eleven miles beyond Morristown, he received word on the 23d that the enemy were advancing from Elizabethtown against Springfield. Supposing the military depot at Morristown to be their ultimate object, he detached a brigade to the assistance of Greene and fell back five or six miles so as to be in supporting distance of him.

The re-embarkation of the troops at Staten Island had in fact been a stratagem of Sir Henry Clinton to divert the attention of Washington and enable Knyphausen to carry out the enterprise which had hitherto hung fire. No sooner did the latter ascertain that the American commander-in-chief had moved off with his main force towards the Highlands than he sallied from Elizabethtown five thousand strong, with a large body of cavalry and fifteen or twenty pieces of artillery, hoping not merely to destroy the public stores at Morristown but to get possession of those difficult hills and defiles, among which Washington's army had been so securely posted and which constituted the strength of that part of the country.

It was early on the morning of the 23d that Knyphausen pushed forward toward Springfield. Besides the main road which passes directly through the village toward Morristown, there is another, north of it, called the Vauxhall road, crossing several small streams, the confluence of which forms the Rahway. These two roads unite beyond the village in the principal pass of the Short Hills. The enemy's troops advanced rapidly in two compact columns, the right one by the Vauxhall road, the other by the main or direct road. General Greene was stationed among the Short

Hills about a mile above the town. His troops were distributed at various posts, for there were many passes to guard.

At five o'clock in the morning signal-guns gave notice of the approach of the enemy. The drums beat to arms throughout the camp. The troops were hastily called in from their posts among the mountain passes, and preparations were made to defend the village.

Major Lee, with his dragoons and a picket-guard, was posted on the Vauxhall road to check the right column of the enemy in its advance. Colonel Dayton with his regiment of New Jersey militia was to check the left column on the main road. Colonel Angel of Rhode Island, with about two hundred picked men and a piece of artillery, was to defend a bridge over the Rahway a little west of the town. Colonel Shreve, stationed with his regiment at a second bridge over a branch of the Rahway east of the town, was to cover if necessary the retreat of Colonel Angel. Those parts of Maxwell and Stark's brigades which were not thus detached were drawn up on high grounds in the rear of the town, having the militia on their flanks.

There was some sharp fighting at a bridge on the Vauxhall road, where Major Lee with his dragoons and a picket-guard held the right column at bay. A part of the column, however, forded the stream above the bridge, gained a commanding position and obliged Lee to retire.

The left column met with similar opposition from Dayton and his Jersey regiment. None showed more ardor in the fight than Caldwell the chaplain. The image of his murdered wife was before his eyes. Finding the men in want of wadding, he galloped to the Presbyterian church and brought thence a quantity of Watts' psalm and hymn books, which he distributed for the purpose among the soldiers. "Now," cried he, "put Watts into them, boys!"

The severest fighting of the day was at the bridge over the Rahway. For upwards of half an hour Colonel Angel defended it with his handful of men against a vastly superior force. One fourth of his men were either killed or disabled. The loss of the enemy was still more severe. Angel was at length compelled to retire. He did so in good order, carrying off his wounded and making his way through the village to the bridge beyond it. Here his retreat was bravely covered by Colonel Shreve, but he too was obliged to give way before the overwhelming force of the enemy and join the brigades of Maxwell and Stark upon the hill.

General Greene, finding his front too much extended for his small force, and that he was in danger of being outflanked on the left by the column pressing forward on the Vauxhall road, took post with his main body on the first range of hills, where the roads were brought near to a point, and passed between him and the height occupied by Stark and Maxwell. He then threw out a detachment which checked the farther advance of the right column of the enemy along the Vauxhall road and secured that pass through the Short Hills. Feeling himself now strongly posted, he awaited with confidence the expected attempt of the enemy to gain the height.

No such attempt was made. The resistance already experienced, especially at the bridge, and the sight of militia gathering from various points, dampened the ardor of the hostile commander. He saw that should he persist in pushing for Morristown he would have to fight his way through a country abounding with difficult passes, every one of which would be obstinately disputed, and that the enterprise, even if successful, might cost too much, besides taking him too far from New York at a time when a French armament might be expected.

Before the brigade detached by Washington arrived at the scene of action, therefore, the enemy had retreated. Previous to their retreat they wreaked upon Springfield the same vengeance they had inflicted on Connecticut Farms. The whole village, excepting four houses, was reduced to ashes. Their second retreat was equally ignoble with their first. They were pursued and harassed the whole way to Elizabethtown by light scouting parties and by the militia and yeomanry of the country, exasperated by the sight of the burning village. Lee, too, came upon their rear-guard with his dragoons, captured a quantity of stores abandoned by them in the hurry of retreat and made prisoners of several refugees.

It was sunset when the enemy reached Elizabethtown. During the night they passed over to Staten Island by their bridge of boats. By six o'clock in the morning all had crossed and the bridge had been removed—and the State of New Jersey, so long harassed by the campaignings of either army, was finally evacuated by the enemy.

It had proved a school of war to the American troops. The

incessant marchings and counter-marchings, the rude encampments, the exposures to all kinds of hardship and privation, the alarms, the stratagems, the rough encounters and adventurous enterprises of which this had been the theatre for the last three or four years, had rendered the patriot soldier hardy, adroit and long-suffering, had accustomed him to danger, inured him to discipline and brought him nearly on a level with the European mercenary in the habitudes and usages of arms, while he had the superior incitements of home, country and independence. The ravaging incursions of the enemy had exasperated the most peace-loving parts of the country, made soldiers of the husbandmen, acquainted them with their own powers and taught them that the foe was vulnerable.

The recent ineffectual attempts of a veteran general to penetrate the fastnesses of Morristown, though at the head of a veteran force, "which would once have been deemed capable of sweeping the whole continent before it," was a lasting theme of triumph to the inhabitants. And it is still the honest boast among the people of Morris County, that "the enemy never were able to get a footing among our hills." At the same time the conflagration of villages, by which they sought to cover or revenge their repeated failures, and their precipitate retreat, harassed and insulted by half-disciplined militia and a crude, rustic levy, formed an ignominious close to the British campaign in the Jerseys.

Chapter 42

BENEDICT ARNOLD'S TREASON

Apprehensive that the next move of the enemy would be up the Hudson, Washington resumed his measures for the security of West Point, moving towards the Highlands in the latter part of June. Circumstances soon convinced him that the enemy had no present intention of attacking that fortress but merely menaced him at various points to retard his operations and oblige him to call out the militia, thereby interrupting agriculture, distressing the country and rendering his cause unpopular. Having therefore caused the military stores in the Jerseys to be removed to more remote and secure places, he countermanded by letter the militia, which were marching to camp from Connecticut and Massachusetts.

It was not until the beginning of September that [he] received word of the disastrous reverse [of American forces under General Gates at Camden, South Carolina.] The shock was the greater, as previous reports from that quarter had represented the operations a few days preceding the action as much in our favor. It was evident to Washington that the course of war must ultimately tend to the Southern States, yet the situation of affairs in the North did not permit him to detach any sufficient force for their relief. All that he could do for the present was to endeavor to hold the enemy in check in that quarter.

[He] still cherished the idea of a combined attack upon New York as soon as a French naval force should arrive. The destruction of the enemy here would relieve this part of the Union from an internal war and enable its troops and resources to be united with those of France in vigorous efforts against the common enemy elsewhere. Hearing therefore that the Count de Guichen with his West India squadron was approaching the coast, Washington prepared to proceed to Hartford in Connecticut, there to hold a conference with the Count de Rochambeau and the Chevalier de Ternay and concert a plan for future operations, of which the attack on New York was to form the principal feature.

We have now to enter upon a sad episode of our revolutionary history—the treason of Arnold. Of the military skill, daring enterprise and indomitable courage of this man, ample evidence has been given in the foregoing pages. Of the implicit confidence reposed in his patriotism by Washington, sufficient proof is manifested in the command with which he was actually intrusted. But Arnold was false at heart and at the very time of seeking that command had been for many months in traitorous correspondence with the enemy.

The first idea of proving recreant to the cause he had vindicated so bravely appears to have entered his mind when the charges preferred against him by the council of Pennsylvania were referred by Congress to a court-martial. Before that time he had been incensed against Pennsylvania. But now his wrath was excited against his country, which appeared so insensible to his services. Disappointment in regard to the settlement of his accounts added to his irritation, and mingled sordid motives with his resentment, and he began to think how, while he wreaked his vengeance on his country, he might do it with advantage to his fortunes.

With this view he commenced a correspondence with Sir Henry Clinton in a disguised handwriting and, under the signature of Gustavus, representing himself as a person of importance in the American service, who, being dissatisfied with the late proceedings of Congress, particularly the alliance with France, was desirous of joining the cause of Great Britain could he be certain of personal security and indemnification for whatever loss of property he might sustain. His letters occasionally communicated articles of intelligence of some moment, which proved to be true and induced Sir Henry to keep up the correspondence, which was conducted on his part by his aide-de-camp, Major John André, likewise in a disguised hand and under the signature of John Anderson.

Months elapsed before Sir Henry discovered who was his secret correspondent. Even after discovering it he did not see fit to hold out any very strong inducements to Arnold for desertion. The latter was out of command and had nothing to offer but his services, which in his actual situation were scarcely worth buying.

In the meantime the circumstances of Arnold were daily becoming more desperate. Debts were accumulating and creditors becoming more and more importunate as his means to satisfy them decreased. The public reprimand he had received was rankling in his mind and filling his heart with bitterness. Still he hesitated on the brink of absolute infamy and attempted a halfway leap. Such was his proposition to M. de Luzerne to make himself subservient to the policy of the French government on condition of receiving a loan equal to the amount of his debts. This he might have reconciled to his conscience by the idea that France was an ally and its policy likely to be friendly. It was his last card before resorting to utter treachery. Failing in it, his desperate alternative was to get some important command, the betrayal of which to the enemy might obtain for him a munificent reward.

He may possibly have had such an idea in his mind some time previously when he sought the command of a naval and military expedition which failed to be carried into effect; but such certainly was the secret of his eagerness to obtain the command of West Point, the great object of British and American solicitude on the possession of which were supposed by many to hinge the fortunes of the war.

He took command of the post and its dependencies about the beginning of August [1780] fixing his headquarters at Beverley, a country seat a little below West Point, on the opposite or eastern side of the river. It stood in a lonely part of the Highlands high up from the river, yet at the foot of a mountain covered with woods. It was commonly called the Robinson House, having formerly belonged to Washington's early friend, Colonel Beverley Robinson, who had obtained a large part of the Phillipse estate in this neighborhood by marrying one of the heiresses. Colonel Robinson was a royalist, had entered into the British service and was now residing in New York, and Beverley with its surrounding lands had been confiscated.

From this place Arnold carried on a secret correspondence with Major André. Their letters, still in disguised hands and under the names of Gustavus and John Anderson, purported to treat merely of commercial operations, but the real matter in negotiation was the betrayal of West Point and the Highlands to Sir Henry Clinton. This stupendous piece of treachery was to be consummated at the time when Washington with the main body of his army would be drawn down towards King's Bridge and the French troops landed on Long Island in the projected co-operation against New York. At such time a flotilla under Rodney, having on board a large land force, was to ascend the Hudson to the Highlands, which would be surrendered by Arnold almost without opposition under pretext of insufficient force to make resistance. The immediate result of his surrender, it was anticipated, would be the defeat of the combined attempt upon New York, and its ultimate effect might be the dismemberment of the Union and the dislocation of the whole American scheme of warfare.

[Major André was captured while carrying incriminating papers, and Arnold's treachery was exposed.]

Notwithstanding Washington's apparent tranquillity and real self-possession, it was a time of appalling distrust. How far the treason had extended, who else might be implicated in it, was unknown. Arnold had escaped, and was actually on board of the *Vulture*. He knew everything about the condition of the posts. Might he not persuade the enemy, in the present weak state of the garrisons, to attempt a *coup de main*? Washington instantly therefore despatched a letter to Colonel Wade, who was in temporary command at West Point.

"General Arnold is gone to the enemy," writes he. "I have just now received a line from him inclosing one to Mrs. Arnold, dated on board the *Vulture*. I request that you will be as vigilant as possible, and as the enemy may have it in contemplation to attempt some enterprise, *even to-night*, against these posts, I wish you to make, immediately after the receipt of this, the best disposition you can of your force so as to have a proportion of men in each work on the west side of the river."

A regiment stationed in the Highlands was ordered to the same duty, as well as a body of the Massachusetts militia from Fishkill. At half-past seven in the evening, Washington wrote to General Greene, who in his absence commanded the army at Tappan, urging him to put the left division in motion as soon as possible, with orders to proceed to King's Ferry, where, or before they should arrive there, they would be met with further orders. "The division," writes he, "will come on light, leaving their heavy baggage to follow. You will also hold all the troops in readiness to move on the shortest notice. Transactions of a most interesting nature and such as will astonish you have been just discovered."

His next thought was about André. He was not acquainted with him personally, and the intrigues in which he had been engaged and the errand on which he had come made him consider him an artful and resolute person. He had possessed himself of dangerous information, and in a like manner had been arrested with the key of the citadel in his pocket. On the same evening, therefore, Washington wrote to Colonel Jameson, charging that every precaution should be taken to prevent Major André from making his escape.

"He will no doubt effect it, if possible. And in order that he may not have it in his power, you will send him under the care of such a party and so many officers as to preclude him from the least opportunity of doing it. That he may be less liable to be recaptured by the enemy, who will no doubt make every effort to regain him, he had better be conducted to this place by some upper road rather than by the route of Crompond. I would not wish Mr. André to be treated with insult, but he does not appear to stand upon the footing of a common prisoner of war, and therefore he is not entitled to the usual indulgences which they receive and is to be most closely and narrowly watched."

In the meantime, Mrs. Arnold remained in her room in a state bordering on frenzy. Arnold might well confide in the humanity and delicacy of Washington in respect to her. He regarded her with the sincerest commiseration, acquitting her of all previous knowledge of her husband's guilt. On remitting to her, by one of his aides-de-camp, the letter of her husband written from on board of the *Vulture*, he informed her that he had done all that depended upon himself to have him arrested, but not having succeeded, he experienced a pleasure in assuring her of his safety.[1]

A letter of Hamilton's written at the time, with all the sympathies of a young man, gives a touching picture of Washington's first interview with her. "She for a time entirely lost herself. The general went up to see her and she upraided him with being in a plot to murder her child. One moment she raved, another she melted into tears, sometimes she pressed her infant to her bosom and lamented its fate occasioned by the imprudence of its father in a manner that would have pierced insensibility itself. All the sweetness of beauty, all the loveliness of innocence, all the tenderness of a wife and all the fondness of a mother showed themselves in her appearance and conduct."

[1] *Memoirs of Lafayette*, vol. i., p. 264.

During the brief time she remained at the Robinson House she was treated with the utmost deference and delicacy, but soon set off, under a passport of Washington, for her father's house in Philadelphia.

[Major André was hanged as a spy.]

Arnold was now made brigadier-general in the British service and put on an official level with honorable men who scorned to associate with the traitor. What golden reward he was to have received had his treason been successful is not known, but six thousand three hundred and fifteen pounds sterling were paid to him as a compensation for losses which he pretended to have suffered in going over to the enemies of his country.

The vilest culprit, however, shrinks from sustaining the obloquy of his crimes. Shortly after his arrival in New York, Arnold published an address to the inhabitants of America, in which he endeavored to vindicate his conduct. He alleged that he had originally taken up arms merely to aid in obtaining a redress of grievances. He had considered the Declaration of Independence precipitate, and the reasons for it obviated by the subsequent proffers of the British government, and he inveighed against Congress for rejecting those offers without submitting them to the people.

Finally, the treaty with France, a proud, ancient and crafty foe, the enemy of the Protestant faith and of real liberty, had completed, he said, the measure of his indignation and determined him to abandon a cause sustained by iniquity and controlled by usurpers.

Besides this address, he issued a proclamation inviting the officers and soldiers of the American army, who had the real interest of their country at heart and who were determined to be no longer the tools and dupes of Congress and of France, to rally under the royal standard and fight for true American liberty, holding out promises of large bounties and liberal subsistence, with compensation for all the implements and accoutrements of war they might bring with them.

Speaking of this address, "I am at a loss," said Washington, "which to admire most, the confidence of Arnold in publishing it, or the folly of the enemy in supposing that a production signed by so infamous a character will have any weight with the people of these States, or any influence upon our officers abroad." He was right. Both the address and the proclamation were regarded by

Americans with the contempt they merited. None rallied to the standard of the renegade but a few deserters and refugees who were already within the British lines and prepared for any desperate or despicable service.

We have here to note the altered fortunes of the once prosperous General Gates. His late defeat at Camden had withered the laurels snatched at Saratoga. As in the one instance he had received exaggerated praise, so in the other he suffered undue censure. The sudden annihilation of an army from which so much had been expected, and the retreat of the general before the field was absolutely lost, appeared to demand a strict investigation. Congress therefore passed a resolution (October 5th) requiring Washington to order a court of inquiry into the conduct of Gates as commander of the Southern army and to appoint some other officer to the command until the inquiry should be made. Washington at once selected Greene for the important trust, the well-tried officer whom he would originally have chosen, had his opinion been consulted, when Congress so unadvisedly gave the command to Gates. In the present instance his choice was in concurrence with the expressed wishes of the delegates of the three Southern States, conveyed to him by one of their number.

With regard to the court of inquiry, it was to be conducted in the quarter in which Gates had acted, where all the witnesses were and where alone the requisite information could be obtained. Baron Steuben, who was to accompany Greene to the South, was to preside, and the members of the court were to be such general and field-officers of the continental troops as were not present at the battle of Camden, or, having been present, were not wanted as witnesses, or were persons to whom General Gates had no objection. The affair was to be conducted with the greatest impartiality and with as much despatch as circumstances would permit.

[Congress was to rescind its resolution regarding an inquiry, the basis being insufficient evidence and Gates's difficulty in defending himself as a result of the death of his son. Gates was exonerated in the opinion of his fellow-officers. He was to retire to his Virginia farm.]

The state of the army was growing more and more a subject of solicitude to the commander-in-chief. He felt weary of struggling on with such scanty means and such vast responsibility. The campaign which at its commencement had seemed pregnant with favorable events, had proved sterile and inactive and was drawing to a close. The short terms for which most of the troops were enlisted must soon expire and then the present army would be reduced to a mere shadow.

[But we] will here add that the repeated and elaborate reasonings of Washington, backed by dear-bought experience, slowly brought Congress to adopt a system suggested by him for the organization and support of the army, according to which troops were to be enlisted to serve throughout the war, and all officers who continued in service until the return of peace were to receive half pay during life.

Chapter 43

MUTINY IN THE ARMY

[Around this time the Marquis de Chastellux arrived in Washington's camp.] He was on a tour of curiosity while the French troops at Rhode Island were in winter quarters, and came on the invitation of his relative, the Marquis de Lafayette, who was to present him to Washington. In after years he published an account of his tour, in which we have graphic sketches of the camp and the commanders. He arrived with his aides-de-camp on the afternoon of November 23d and sought the headquarters of the commander-in-chief. They were in a large farm-house. There was a spacious tent in the yard before it for the general, and several smaller tents in an adjacent field for his guards. Baggage wagons were arranged about for the transportation of the general's effects, and a number of grooms were attending to very fine horses belonging to general officers and their aides-de-camp. Everything was in perfect order.

As De Chastellux rode up he observed Lafayette in front of the house, conversing with an officer, tall of stature, with a mild and noble countenance. It was Washington. De Chastellux alighted and was presented by Lafayette. His reception was frank and cordial. Washington conducted him into the house. Dinner was over but Generals Knox, Wayne and Howe, and Colonels Hamilton, Tilghman and other officers were still seated round the board. Washington introduced De Chastellux to them and ordered a repast for the former and his aides-de-camp. All remained at table, and a few glasses of claret and Madeira promoted sociability. The marquis soon found himself at his ease with Washington. "The goodness and benevolence which characterize him," observes he, "are felt by all around him. But the confidence he inspires is never familiar. It springs from a profound esteem for his virtues and a great opinion of his talents."

In the evening, after the guests had retired, Washington conducted the marquis to a chamber prepared for him and his aides-de-camp, apologizing with frank and simple politeness that his scanty quarters did not afford more spacious accommodation.

The next morning, horses were led up after breakfast; they were to review the troops and visit Lafayette's encampment, seven miles distant. The horses which De Chastellux and Washington rode had been presented to the latter by the State of Virginia. There were fine blood horses also for the aides-de-camp. "Washington's horses," writes De Chastellux, "are as good as they are beautiful, and all perfectly trained. He trains them all himself. He is a very good and a very hardy cavalier, leaping the highest barriers and riding very fast without rising in the stirrups, bearing on the bridle or suffering his horse to run as if wild."

In the camp of artillery where General Knox received them, the marquis found everything in perfect order and conducted in the European style. Washington apologized for no salute being fired. Detachments were in movement at a distance, in the plan of operations, and the booming of guns might give an alarm or be mistaken for signals.

Incessant and increasing rain obliged Washington to make but a short visit to Lafayette's camp, whence, putting spurs to his horse, he conducted his French visitors back to headquarters on as fast a gallop as bad roads would permit.

There were twenty guests at table that day at headquarters. The dinner was in the English style: large dishes of butcher's meat and poultry, with different kinds of vegetables, followed by pies and puddings and a dessert of hickory nuts. Washington's fondness for the latter was noticed by the marquis and indeed was often a subject of remark. He would sit picking them by the hour after dinner as he sipped his wine and conversed.

One of the general's aides-de-camp sat by him at the end of the table, according to custom, to carve the dishes and circulate the wine. Healths were drunk and toasts were given. The latter were sometimes given by the general through his aide-de-camp. The conversation was tranquil and pleasant. Washington willingly entered into some details about the principal operations of the war, "but always" says the marquis, "with a modesty and conciseness which proved sufficiently that it was out of pure complaisance that he consented to talk about himself."

Wayne was pronounced agreeable and animated in conversation, and possessed of wit, but Knox, with his genial aspect and cordial manners, seems to have won De Chastellux's heart. "He is thirty-five years of age," writes he, "very stout but very active, a man of talent and intelligence, amiable, gay, sincere and loyal. It is impossible to know him without esteeming him, and to see him without loving him."

It was about half-past seven when the company rose from the table, shortly after which those who were not of the household departed. There was a light supper of three or four dishes, with fruit and abundance of hickory nuts. The cloth was soon removed. Bordeaux and Madeira wine were placed upon the table and conversation went on. Colonel Hamilton was the aide-de-camp who officiated, and announced the toasts as they occurred. "It is customary," writes the marquis, "towards the end of the supper to call upon each one for a *sentiment,* that is to say, the name of some lady to whom he is attached by some sentiment either of love, friendship or simple preference."

It is evident there was extra gayety at the table of the commander-in-chief during this visit, in compliment to his French guests. But we are told that gay conversation often prevailed at the dinners at headquarters among the aides-de-camp and young officers, in which Washington took little part, though a quiet smile would show that he enjoyed it.

We have been tempted to quote freely the remarks of De Chastellux, as they are those of a cultivated man of society, whose position and experience made him a competent judge, and who had an opportunity of observing Washington in a familiar point of view.

Speaking of his personal appearance, he writes: "His form is noble and elevated, well-shaped and exactly proportioned, his physiognomy mild and agreeable, but such that one does not speak in particular of any one of his traits. In quitting him there remains simply the recollection of a fine countenance. His air is neither grave nor familiar. One sees sometimes on his forehead the marks of thought but never of inquietude. While inspiring respect, he inspires confidence, and his smile is always that of benevolence.

"Above all it is interesting," continues the marquis, "to see him in the midst of the general officers of his army. General in a republic, he has not the imposing state of a marshal of France who gives the *order*. Hero in a republic, he excites a different sort of respect, which seems to originate in this sole idea, that the welfare of each individual is attached to his person."

He sums up his character in these words. "Brave without temerity; laborious without ambition; generous without prodigality; noble without pride; virtuous without severity; he seems always to stop short of that limit where the virtues, assuming colors more vivid but more changeable and dubious, might be taken for defects."

At the end of November the army went into winter quarters: the Pennsylvania line in the neighborhood of Morristown, the Jersey line about Pompton, the New England troops at West Point and the other posts of the Highlands, and the New York line was stationed at Albany to guard against any invasion from Canada.

The French army remained stationed at Newport, excepting the Duke of Lauzun's legion, which was cantoned at Lebanon in Connecticut. Washington's headquarters were established at New Windsor on the Hudson.

Washington apprehended a design on the part of the enemy to carry the stress of war into the Southern States. Conscious that he was the man to whom all looked in time of emergency, and who was in a manner responsible for the general course of military affairs, he deeply felt the actual impotency of his position.

In a letter to Franklin, who was minister plenipotentiary at the court of Versailles, he strongly expresses his chagrin.

"Disappointed of the second division of French troops but more especially in the expected naval superiority, which was the pivot upon which everything turned, we have been compelled to spend an inactive campaign after a flattering prospect at the opening of it and vigorous struggles to make it a decisive one on our part. Latterly we have been obliged to become spectators of a succession of detachments from the army at New York in aid of Lord Cornwallis, while our naval weakness and the political dissolution of a great part of our army put it out of our power to counteract them at the southward or to take advantage of them here."

The last of these detachments to the South took place on the 20th of December but was not destined, as Washington had supposed, for Carolina. Sir Henry Clinton had received information that the troops already mentioned as being under General Leslie in the Chesapeake had by orders from Cornwallis sailed for

Charleston to reinforce his lordship, and this detachment was to take their place in Virginia. It was composed of British, German and refugee troops, about seventeen hundred strong, and was commanded by Benedict Arnold, now a brigadier-general in His Majesty's service. Sir Henry Clinton, who distrusted the fidelity of the man he had corrupted, sent with him Colonels Dundas and Simcoe, experienced officers by whose advice he was to be guided in every important measure. He was to make an incursion into Virginia, destroy the public magazines, assemble and arm the loyalists and hold himself ready to co-operate with Lord Cornwallis. He embarked his troops in a fleet of small vessels and departed on his enterprise animated by the rancorous spirit of a renegade, and prepared, as he vaunted, to give the Americans a blow "that would make the whole continent shake." We shall speak of his expedition hereafter.

As Washington beheld one hostile armament after another winging its way to the South and received applications from that quarter for assistance which he had not the means to furnish, it became painfully apparent to him that the efforts to carry on the war had exceeded the natural capabilities of the country. Its widely diffused population and the composition and temper of some of its people rendered it difficult to draw together its resources. Commerce was almost extinct. There was not sufficient natural wealth on which to found a revenue. Paper currency had depreciated through want of funds for its redemption, until it was nearly worthless. The mode of supplying the army by assessing a proportion of the productions of the earth had proved ineffectual, oppressive and productive of an alarming opposition. Domestic loans yielded but trifling assistance. The patience of the army was nearly exhausted. The people were dissatisfied with the mode of supporting the war, and there was reason to apprehend that under the pressure of impositions of a new and odious kind, they might imagine they had only exchanged one kind of tyranny for another.

We give but a few of many considerations which Washington was continually urging upon the attention of Congress in his full and perspicuous manner, the end of which was to enforce his opinion that a foreign loan was indispensably necessary to a continuance of the war.

His earnest counsels and entreaties were at length successful in determining Congress to seek aid both in men and money from abroad. Accordingly, on the 28th of December they commissioned Lieutenant-Colonel John Laurens, special minister at the court of Versailles, to apply for such aid. The situation he had held as aide-de-camp to the commander-in-chief had given him an opportunity of observing the course of affairs and acquainting himself with the wants and resources of the country, and he was instructed to confer with Washington, previous to his departure, as to the objects of his mission. Not content with impressing him verbally with his policy, Washington gave him a letter of instructions for his government, to be used as occasion might require. In this he advised him to solicit a loan sufficiently large to be a foundation for substantial arrangements of finance, to revive public credit and give vigor to future operations. Next to a loan of money, a naval force was to be desired, sufficient to maintain a constant superiority on the American coast; also additional succor in troops. In a word, a means of co-operation by sea and land with purse and sword, competent by a decided effort to attain once for all the great objects of the alliance, the liberty and independence of the United States.

He was to show at the same time the ample means possessed by the nation to repay the loan, from its comparative freedom from debt and its vast and valuable tracts of unsettled lands, the variety and fertility of its climates and soils, and its advantages of every kind for a lucrative commerce and rapid increase of population and prosperity.

Scarce had Colonel Laurens been appointed to this mission when a painful occurrence proved the urgent necessity of the required aid.

In the arrangement for winter quarters, the Pennsylvania line, consisting of six regiments, was hutted near Morristown. These troops had experienced the hardships and privations common to the whole army. General Wayne, who commanded them, had a soldier's sympathy in the sufferings of his men, and speaks of them in feeling language:

"Poorly clothed, badly fed and worse paid," writes he, "some of them not having received a paper dollar for near twelve months; exposed to winter's piercing cold, to drifting snows and chilling blasts, with no protection but old worn-out coats, tattered linen overalls and but one blanket between three men. In this situation the enemy begin to work upon their passions, and have found means to circulate some proclamations among them. . . . The officers in general, as well as myself, find it necessary to stand for hours every day exposed to wind and weather among the poor naked fellows while they are working at their huts and redoubts, often assisting with our own hands in order to produce a conviction to their minds that we share, and more than share, every vicissitude in common with them; sometimes asking to participate their bread and water. The good effect of this conduct is very conspicuous and prevents their murmuring in public, but the delicate mind and eye of humanity are hurt, very much hurt, at their visible distress and private complainings."

How strongly are here depicted the trials to which the soldiers of the Revolution were continually subjected. But the Pennsylvania line had an additional grievance peculiar to themselves. Many of them had enlisted to serve "for three years, or during war," that is to say, for less than three years should the war cease in less time. When, however, having served for three years, they sought their discharge, the officers, loth to lose such experienced soldiers, interpreted the terms of enlistment to mean three years or to the end of the war, should it continue for a longer time.

This chicanery naturally produced great exasperation. It was heightened by the conduct of a deputation from Pennsylvania which, while it left veteran troops unpaid, distributed gold by handfuls among raw six-month levies, whose time was expiring, as bounties on their re-enlisting for the war.

The first day of the new year arrived. The men were excited by an extra allowance of ardent spirits. In the evening, at a preconcerted signal, a great part of the Pennsylvania line, non-commissioned officers included, turned out under arms, declaring their intention to march to Philadelphia and demand redress from Congress. Wayne endeavored to pacify them. They were no longer to be pacified by words. He cocked his pistol. In an instant their bayonets were at his breast. "We love, we respect you," cried they, "but you are a dead man if you fire. Do not mistake us. We are not going to the enemy. Were they now to come out, you would see us fight under your orders with as much resolution and alacrity as ever."[1]

Their threat was not an idle one. In an attempt to suppress the mutiny there was a bloody affray in which numbers were wounded

[1] Quincy's *Memoir of Major Shaw*, p. 85.

on both sides, among whom were several officers. One captain was killed.

Three regiments which had taken no part in the mutiny were paraded under their officers. The mutineers compelled them to join their ranks. Their number being increased to about thirteen hundred, they seized upon six field-pieces and set out in the night for Philadelphia under command of their sergeants.

Fearing the enemy might take advantage of this outbreak, Wayne detached a Jersey brigade to Chatham and ordered the militia to be called out there. Alarm fires were kindled upon the hills. Alarm guns boomed from post to post. The country was soon on the alert.

Wayne was not "Mad Anthony" on the present occasion. All his measures were taken with judgment and forecast. He sent provisions after the mutineers, lest they should supply their wants from the country people by force. Two officers of rank spurred to Philadelphia to apprise Congress of the approach of the insurgents and put it upon its guard. Wayne sent a despatch with news of the outbreak to Washington. He then mounted his horse, and accompanied by Colonels Butler and Stewart, two officers popular with the troops, set off after the mutineers, either to bring them to a halt or to keep with them and seek every occasion to exert a favorable influence over them.

Washington received Wayne's letter at his headquarters at New Windsor on the 3d of January. His first impulse was to set out at once for the insurgent camp. Second thoughts showed the impolicy of such a move. Before he could overtake the mutineers they would either have returned to their duty or their affair would be in the hands of Congress. How far, too, could his own troops be left with safety, distressed as they were for clothing and provisions? Beside, the navigation of the Hudson was still open. Should any disaffection appear in the neighboring garrison of West Point, the British might send up an expedition from New York to take advantage of it. Under these circumstances he determined to continue at New Windsor.

He wrote to Wayne, however, approving of his intention to keep with the troops and improve every favorable interval of passion. His letter breathes that paternal spirit with which he watched over the army and that admirable moderation mingled with discipline with which he managed and moulded their way-ward moods.

"Opposition," said he, "as it did not succeed in the first in-stance, cannot be effectual while the men remain together, but will keep alive resentment and may tempt them to turn about and go in a body to the enemy, who, by their emissaries, will use every argument and means in their power to persuade them that it is their only asylum; which, if they find their passage stopped at the Delaware and hear that the Jersey militia are collecting in their rear, they may think but too probable. I would therefore recom-mend it to you to cross the Delaware with them, draw from them what they conceive to be their principal grievances, and promise faithfully to represent to Congress and to the State the substance of them, and endeavor to obtain a redress. If they could be stopped at Bristol or Germantown, the better. I look upon it, that if you can bring them to a negotiation, matters may be afterwards accommodated, but that an attempt to reduce them by force will either drive them to the enemy or dissipate them in such a manner that they will never be recovered."

How clearly one reads in this letter that temperate and mag-nanimous spirit which moved over the troubled waters of the Rev-olution, allayed the fury of the storms and controlled everything into place.

Having visited the Highland posts of the Hudson and satisfied himself of the fidelity of the garrisons, Washington ordered a de-tachment of eleven hundred men to be ready to march at a moment's warning. General Knox, also, was despatched by him to the Eastern States to represent to their governments the alarming crisis produced by a long neglect of the subsistence of the army and to urge them to send on immediately money, clothing and other supplies for their respective lines.

In the meantime, as Washington had apprehended, Sir Henry Clinton received intelligence at New York of the mutiny and has-tened to profit by it. Emissaries were despatched to the camp of the mutineers holding out offers of pardon, protection and ample pay if they would return to their allegiance to the crown. On the 4th of January, although the rain poured in torrents, troops and cannon were hurried on board of vessels of every description and transported to Staten Island, Sir Henry accompanying them.

There they were to be held in readiness, either to land at Amboy in the Jerseys, should the revolters be drawn in that direction, or to make a dash at West Point should the departure of Washington leave that post assailable.

General Wayne and his companions, Colonels Butler and Stewart, had overtaken the insurgent troops on the 3d of January at Middlebrook. They were proceeding in military form under the control of a self-constituted board of sergeants whose orders were implicitly obeyed. A sergeant-major, who had formerly deserted from the British army, had the general command.

Conferences were held by Wayne with sergeants delegated from each regiment. They appeared to be satisfied with the mode and promises of redress held out to them, but the main body of the mutineers persisted in revolt and proceeded on the next day to Princeton. Wayne hoped they might continue further on and would gladly have seen them across the Delaware beyond the influence of the enemy, but their leaders clung to Princeton lest in further movements they might not be able to keep their followers together. Their proceedings continued to be orderly, military forms were still observed, they obeyed their leaders, behaved well to the people of the country and committed no excesses.

General Wayne and Colonels Butler and Stewart remained with them in an equivocal position, popular but without authority, and almost in durance. The insurgents professed themselves still ready to march under them against the enemy but would permit none other of their former officers to come among them. The Marquis de Lafayette, General St. Clair and Colonel Laurens, the newly-appointed minister to France, arrived at the camp and were admitted, but afterwards were ordered away at a short notice.

The news of the revolt caused great consternation in Philadelphia. A committee of Congress set off to meet the insurgents, accompanied by Reed, the president of Pennsylvania, and one or two other officers, and escorted by a city troop of horse. The committee halted at Trenton, whence President Reed wrote to Wayne requesting a personal interview at four o'clock in the afternoon at four miles' distance from Princeton. Wayne was moreover told to inform the troops that he (Reed) would be there to receive any propositions from them and redress any injuries they might have sustained, but that after the indignities they had offered to the marquis and General St. Clair he could not venture to put himself in their power.

Wayne, knowing that the letter was intended for his troops more than for himself, read it publicly on the parade. It had a good effect upon the sergeants and many of the men. The idea that the president of their State should have to leave the seat of government and stoop to treat with them touched their sectional pride and their home feelings. They gathered round the horseman who had brought the letter, and inquired anxiously whether President Reed was unkindly disposed towards them, intimating privately their dislike to the business in which they were engaged.

Still, it was not thought prudent for President Reed to trust himself within their camp. Wayne promised to meet him on the following day (7th), though it seemed uncertain whether he was master of himself or whether he was not a kind of prisoner. Tidings had just been received of the movements of Sir Henry Clinton and of tempting overtures he intended to make, and it was feared the men might listen to them. Three of the light horse were sent in the direction of Amboy to keep a lookout for any landing of the enemy.

At this critical juncture two of Sir Henry's emissaries arrived in the camp and delivered to the leaders of the malcontents a paper containing his seductive proposals and promises. The mutineers, though openly arrayed in arms against their government, spurned at the idea of turning "Arnolds," as they termed it. The emissaries were seized and conducted to General Wayne, who placed them in confinement, promising that they should be liberated should the pending negotiation fail.

This incident had a great effect in inspiring hope of the ultimate loyalty of the troops, and the favorable representations of the temper of the men, made by General Wayne in a personal interview, determined President Reed to venture among them. The consequences of their desertion to the enemy were too alarming to be risked. "I have but one life to lose," said he, "and my country has the first claim to it."[2]

As he approached Princeton with his suite he found guards regularly posted, who turned out and saluted him in military style. The whole line was drawn out under arms near the college, and

[2] Letter to the Executive Council.

the artillery on the point of firing a salute. He prevented it, lest it should alarm the country. It was a hard task for him to ride along the line as if reviewing troops regularly organized, but the crisis required some sacrifice of the kind. The sergeants were all in the places of their respective officers and saluted the president as he passed. Never were mutineers more orderly and decorous.

The propositions now offered to the troops were: To discharge all those who had enlisted indefinitely for three years or during the war; the fact to be inquired into by three commissioners appointed by the executive—where the original enlistment could not be produced in evidence, the oath of the soldier to suffice.

To give immediate certificates for the deficit in their pay caused by the depreciation of the currency, and the arrearages to be settled as soon as circumstances would permit.

To furnish them immediately with certain specified articles of clothing which were most wanted.

These propositions proving satisfactory, the troops set out for Trenton, where the negotiation was concluded.

Most of the artillerists and many of the infantry obtained their discharges, some on their oaths, others on account of the vague terms under which they had been enlisted. Forty days' furlough was given to the rest, and thus for a time the whole insurgent force was dissolved.

The two spies who had tampered with the fidelity of the troops were tried by a courtmartial, found guilty and hanged at the crossroads near Trenton. A reward of fifty guineas each was offered to two sergeants who had arrested and delivered them up. They declined accepting it, saying they had merely acted by order of the board of sergeants. The hundred guineas were then offered to the board. Their reply is worthy of record.

"It was not," said they, "for the sake or through any expectation of reward, but for the love of our country that we sent the spies immediately to General Wayne. We therefore do not consider ourselves entitled to any other reward but the love of our country and do jointly agree to accept of no other."

The accommodation entered into with the mutineers of the Pennsylvania line appeared to Washington of doubtful policy and likely to have a pernicious effect on the whole army. His apprehensions were soon justified by events. On the night of the 20th of January a part of the Jersey troops stationed at Pompton rose in arms, claiming the same terms just yielded to the Pennsylvanians. For a time it was feared the revolt would spread throughout the line.

Sir Henry Clinton was again on the alert. Troops were sent to Staten Island to be ready to cross into the Jerseys, and an emissary was despatched to tempt the mutineers with seductive offers.

In this instance Washington adopted a more rigorous course than in the other. The present insurgents were not so formidable in point of numbers as the Pennsylvanians. The greater part of them, also, were foreigners, for whom he felt less sympathy than for native troops. He was convinced, too, of the fidelity of the troops under his immediate command, who were from the Eastern States. A detachment from the Massachusetts line was sent under Major-General Howe, who was instructed to compel the mutineers to unconditional submission, to grant them no terms while in arms or in a state of resistance; and on their surrender, instantly to execute a few of the most active and incendiary leaders. "You will also try," added he, "to avail yourself of the services of the militia, representing to them how dangerous to civil liberty is the precedent of armed soldiers dictating to their country."

His orders were punctually obeyed and were crowned with complete success. Howe had the good fortune, after a tedious night march, to surprise the mutineers napping in their huts just at daybreak. Five minutes only were allowed them to parade without their arms and give up the ringleaders. This was instantly complied with, and two of them were executed on the spot. Thus the mutiny was quelled, the officers resumed their command and all things were restored to order.[3]

Thus terminated an insurrection which for a time had spread alarm among the friends of American liberty and excited the highest hopes of its foes. The circumstances connected with it had ultimately a beneficial effect in strengthening the confidence of those friends by proving that, however the Americans might quarrel with their own government, nothing could again rally them under the royal standard.

A great cause of satisfaction to Washington was the ratification of the articles of confederation between the States, which took place not long after this agitating juncture. A set of articles had been submitted to Congress by Dr. Franklin as far back as 1775. A

[3] Quincy's *Memoir of Major Shaw*, p. 89.

form had been prepared and digested by a committee in 1776 and agreed upon with some modifications in 1777, but had ever since remained in abeyance in consequence of objections made by individual States. The confederation was now complete, and Washington, in a letter to the president of Congress, congratulated him and the body over which he presided on an event long wished for and which he hoped would have the happiest effects upon the politics of this country and be of essential service to our cause in Europe.

It was, after all, an instrument far less efficacious than its advocates had anticipated, but it served an important purpose in binding the States together as a nation and keeping them from falling asunder into individual powers after the pressure of external danger should cease to operate.

Chapter 44

ARNOLD'S MARAUDINGS

The armament with which Arnold boasted he was "to shake the continent" met with that boisterous weather which often rages along our coast in the winter. His ships were tempest-tost and scattered and half of his cavalry horses and several of his guns had to be thrown overboard. It was the close of the year when he anchored in the Chesapeake.

Virginia at the time was almost in a defenseless state. Baron Steuben, who had the general command there, had recently detached such of his regular troops, as were clothed and equipped, to the south to reinforce General Greene. The remainder, five or six hundred in number, deficient in clothing, blankets and tents, were scarcely fit to take the field, and the volunteers and militia lately encamped before Portsmouth had been disbanded. Governor Jefferson, on hearing of the arrival of the fleet, called out the militia from the neighboring counties but few could be collected on the spur of the moment, for the whole country was terror-stricken and in confusion.

Having land and sea forces at his command, Arnold opened the new year with a buccaneering ravage. Ascending James River with some small vessels which he had captured, he landed on the 4th of January with nine hundred men at Westover, about twenty-five miles below Richmond, and pushed for the latter place, at that time little more than a village though the metropolis of Virginia. Halting for the night within twelve miles of it, he advanced on the following day with as much military parade as possible so as to strike terror into a militia patrol, which fled back to Richmond, reporting that a British force, fifteen hundred strong, was at hand.

It was Arnold's hope to capture the governor, but the latter, after providing for the security of as much as possible of the public stores, had left Richmond the evening before on horseback to join his family at Tuckahoe, whence on the following day he conveyed them to a place of safety. Governor Jefferson got back by noon to Manchester on the opposite side of James River in time to see Arnold's marauders march into the town. Many of the inhabitants had fled to the country. Some stood terrified spectators on the hills. Not more than two hundred men were in arms for the defense of the place. These, after firing a few volleys, retreated to Richmond and Shockoe Hills, whence they were driven by the cavalry, and Arnold had possession of the capital. He sent some of the citizens to the governor, offering to spare the town, provided his ships might come up James River to be laden with tobacco from the warehouses. His offer was indignantly rejected, whereupon fire was set to the public edifices, stores and workshops, private houses were pillaged and a great quantity of tobacco consumed.

While this was going on, Colonel Simcoe had been detached to Westham, six miles up the river, where he destroyed a cannon foundry and sacked a public magazine, broke off the trunnions of the cannon and threw into the river the powder which he could not carry away; and, after effecting a complete devastation, rejoined Arnold at Richmond, which during the ensuing night resounded with the drunken orgies of the soldiery.

Having completed his ravage at Richmond, Arnold re-embarked at Westover and fell slowly down the river, landing occasionally to burn, plunder and destroy, pursued by Steuben with a few continental troops and all the militia that he could muster. General Nelson, also, with similar levies opposed him. Lower down the river some skirmishing took place, a few of Arnold's troops were killed and a number wounded, but he made his way to Portsmouth, opposite Norfolk, where he took post on the 20th of January and proceeded to fortify.

Steuben would have attempted to drive him from this position but his means were totally inadequate. Collecting from various parts of the country all the force that could be mustered, he so disposed it at different points as to hem the traitor in, prevent his making further incursions and drive him back to his intrenchments should he attempt any.

Governor Jefferson returned to Richmond after the enemy had left it, and wrote thence to the commander-in-chief an account of this ravaging incursion of "the parricide Arnold." It was mortifying to Washington to see so inconsiderable a party committing such extensive depredations with impunity, but it was his opinion that their principal object was to make a diversion in favor of Cornwallis. And as the evils to be apprehended from Arnold's predatory incursions were not to be compared with the injury to the common cause and the danger to Virginia in particular which would result from the conquest of the State to the southward, he adjured Jefferson not to permit attention to immediate safety so to engross his thoughts as to divert him from measures for reinforcing the Southern army.

About this time an important resolution was adopted in Congress. Washington had repeatedly in his communications to that body attributed much of the distresses and disasters of the war to the congressional mode of conducting business through committees and "boards," thus causing irregularity and delay, preventing secrecy and augmenting expense. He was greatly rejoiced therefore when Congress decided to appoint heads of departments, secretaries of foreign affairs, of war and of marine, and a superintendent of finance. "I am happy, thrice happy, on private as well as public account," writes he, "to find that these are in train. For it will ease my shoulders of an immense burthen which the deranged and perplexed situation of our affairs and the distresses of every department of the army had placed upon them."

General Sullivan, to whom this was written and who was in Congress, was a warm friend of Washington's aide-de-camp, Colonel Hamilton, and he sounded the commander-in-chief as to the qualifications of the colonel to take charge of the department of finance. "I am unable to answer," replied Washington, "because I never entered upon a discussion with him, but this I can venture to advance, from a thorough knowledge of him, that there are few men to be found of his age who have more general knowledge than he possesses, and none whose soul is more firmly engaged in the cause or who exceeds him in probity and sterling virtue."

This was a warm eulogium for one of Washington's circumspect character but it was sincere. Hamilton had been four years in his military family and always treated by him with marked attention and regard. Indeed, it had surprised many to see so young a man admitted like a veteran into his counsels. It was but a few days after Washington had penned the eulogium just quoted, when a scene took place between him and the man he had praised so liberally, that caused him deep chagrin. We give it as related by Hamilton himself in a letter to General Schuyler, one of whose daughters he had recently married.

"An unexpected change has taken place in my situation," writes Hamilton (February 18th). "I am no longer a member of the general's family. This information will surprise you, and the manner of the change will surprise you more. Two days ago the general and I passed each other on the stairs. He told me he wanted to speak to me. I answered that I would wait on him immediately. I went below and delivered Mr. Tilghman a letter to be sent to the commissary, containing an order of a pressing and interesting nature.

"Returning to the general, I was stopped on the way by the Marquis de Lafayette, and we conversed together about a minute on a matter of business. He can testify how impatient I was to get back and that I left him in a manner which, but for our intimacy, would have been more than abrupt. Instead of finding the general, as is usual, in his room, I met him at the head of the stairs, where, accosting me in an angry tone, 'Colonel Hamilton (said he), you have kept me waiting at the head of the stairs these ten minutes. I must tell you, sir, you treat me with disrespect.' I replied without petulancy but with decision, 'I am not conscious of it, sir, but since you have thought it necessary to tell me so, we part.' 'Very well, sir (said he), if it be your choice,' or something to this effect, and we separated. I sincerely believe my absence which gave so much umbrage did not last two minutes.

"In less than an hour after, Tilghman came to me in the general's name, assuring me of his great confidence in my abilities, integrity, usefulness, etc., and of his desire, in a candid conversation, to heal a difference which could not have happened but in a moment of passion. I requested Mr. Tilghman to tell him—1st. That I had taken my resolution in a manner not to be revoked. 2d. That a conversation could serve no other purpose than to produce explanations, mutually disagreeable, though I certainly would not refuse an interview if he desired it, yet I would be happy if he would permit me to decline it. 3d. That though determined to leave the family, the same principles which had kept me so long in it would continue to direct my conduct towards him when out of it. 4th. That, however, I did not wish to distress him or the public business by quitting him before he could derive other assistance by the return of some of the gentlemen who were absent. 5th. And that, in the meantime, it depended on him to let our behavior to each other be the same as if nothing had happened. He consented to decline the conversation and thanked me for my offer of continuing my aid in the manner I had mentioned.

"I have given you so particular a detail of our difference, from the desire I have to justify myself in your opinion. Perhaps you may think I was precipitate in rejecting the overture made by the general to an accommodation. I assure you, my dear sir, it was not the effect of resentment. It was the deliberate result of maxims I had long formed for the government of my own conduct."

In considering this occurrence, as stated by Hamilton himself, we think he was in the wrong. His hurrying past the general on the stairs without pausing, although the latter expressed a wish to speak with him; his giving no reason for his haste, which, however "pressing" the letter he had to deliver, he could have spared at least a moment to do; his tarrying below to talk with the Marquis de Lafayette, the general all this time remaining at the head of the stairs, had certainly an air of great disrespect, and we do not wonder that the commander-in-chief was deeply offended at being so treated by his youthful aide-de-camp. His expression of displeasure was measured and dignified however irritated he may have been, and such an explanation, at least, was due to him as Hamilton subsequently rendered to General Schuyler through a desire to justify himself in that gentleman's opinion. The reply of Hamilton, on the contrary, savored very much of petulance, however devoid he may have considered it of that quality, and his avowed determination "to part" simply because taxed by the general with want of respect was singularly curt and abrupt.

Washington's subsequent overture, intended to soothe the wounded sensitiveness of Hamilton and soften the recent rebuke by assurances of unaltered confidence and esteem, strikes us as in the highest degree noble and gracious and furnishes another instance of that magnanimity which governed his whole conduct. We trust that General Schuyler, in reply to Hamilton's appeal, intimated that he had indeed been precipitate in rejecting such an overture.

The following passage in Hamilton's letter to Schuyler gives the real key to his conduct on this occasion:

"I always disliked the office of an aide-de-camp, as having in it a kind of personal dependence. I refused to serve in this capacity with two major-generals at an early period of the war. Infected however with the enthusiasm of the times, an idea of the general's character overcame my scruples and induced me to accept his invitation to enter into his family. . . . It has been often with great difficulty that I have prevailed on myself not to renounce it; but while, from motives of public utility, I was doing violence to my feelings, I was always determined, if there should ever happen a breach between us, never to consent to an accommodation. I was persuaded that when once that nice barrier which marked the boundaries of what we owed to each other should be thrown down, it might be propped again but could never be restored."

Hamilton in fact had long been ambitious of an independent position and of some opportunity, as he said, "to raise his character above mediocrity." When an expedition by Lafayette against Staten Island had been meditated in the autumn of 1780, he had applied to the commander-in-chief, through the marquis, for the command of a battalion which was without a field officer. Washington had declined on the ground that giving him a whole battalion might be a subject of dissatisfaction, and that, should any accident happen to him in the actual state of affairs at headquarters, the commander-in-chief would be embarrassed for want of his assistance.

He had next been desirous of the post of adjutant-general, which Colonel Alexander Scammel was about to resign, and was recommended for that office by Lafayette and Greene, but, before their recommendations reached Washington, he had already sent in to Congress the name of Brigadier-General Hand, who received the nomination.

These disappointments may have rendered Hamilton doubtful of his being properly appreciated by the commander-in-chief, impaired his devotion to him and determined him, as he says, "if there should ever happen a breach between them, never to consent to an accommodation." It almost looks as if, in his highstrung and sensitive mood, he had been on the watch for an offense and had grasped at the shadow of one.

Some short time after the rupture had taken place, Washington received a letter from Lafayette, then absent in Virginia, in which the marquis observes: "Considering the footing I am upon with your Excellency, it would perhaps appear strange to you that I never mentioned a circumstance which lately happened in your family. I was the first who knew of it, and from that moment exerted every means in my power to prevent a separation which I knew was not agreeable to your Excellency. To this measure I was prompted by affection to you but I thought it was improper to mention anything about it until you were pleased to impart it to me."

The following was Washington's reply: "The event which you seem to speak of with regret, my friendship for you would most assuredly have induced me to impart to you the moment it happened, had it not been for the request of Hamilton, who desired that no mention should be made of it. Why this injunction on me, while he was communicating it himself, is a little extraordinary. But I complied, and religiously fulfilled it."

We are happy to add that though a temporary coolness took place between the commander-in-chief and his late favorite aide-de-camp, it was but temporary. The friendship between these illustrious men was destined to survive the Revolution and to signalize itself through many eventful years, and stands recorded in the correspondence of Washington almost at the last moment of his life.[1]

In a former chapter we left Benedict Arnold fortifying himself at Portsmouth after his ravaging incursion. At the solicitation of Governor Jefferson, backed by Congress, the Chevalier de la Luzerne had requested the French commander at the eastward to send a ship of the line and some frigates to Chesapeake Bay to oppose the traitor. Fortunately, at this juncture a severe snow-storm (Jan. 22d) scattered Arbuthnot's blockading squadron, wrecking one ship of the line and dismasting others, and enabled the French fleet at Newport to look abroad, and Rochambeau wrote to Washington that the Chevalier Destouches, who commanded the fleet, proposed to send three or four ships to the Chesapeake.

Washington feared the position of Arnold and his well-known address might enable him to withstand a mere attack by sea. Anxious to insure his capture, he advised that Destouches should send his whole fleet and that De Rochambeau should embark about a thousand men on board of it, with artillery and apparatus for a siege, engaging, on his own part to send off immediately a detachment of twelve hundred men to co-operate.

---

[1] His last letter to Hamilton, in which he assures him of "his very great esteem and regard," was written by Washington but two days before his death.—Sparks, xi., 469.

"The destruction of the corps under the command of Arnold," writes he, "is of such immense importance to the welfare of the southern States that I have resolved to attempt it with the detachment I now send in conjunction with the militia, even if it should not be convenient for your Excellency to detach a part of your force, provided M. Destouches is able to protect our operations by such a disposition of his fleet as will give us the command of the bay and prevent succors from being sent from New York."

Before the receipt of this letter, the French commanders, acting on their first impulse, had about the 9th of February detached M. de Tilly with a sixty-gun ship and two frigates to make a dash into the Chesapeake. Washington was apprised of their sailing just as he was preparing to send off the twelve hundred men spoken of in his letter to De Rochambeau. He gave the command of this detachment to Lafayette, instructing him to act, in conjunction with the militia and the ships sent by Destouches, against the enemy's corps actually in Virginia. As the case was urgent, he was to suffer no delay, when on the march, for want either of provisions, forage or wagons, but where ordinary means did not suffice he was to resort to military impress. "You are to do no act whatever with Arnold," said the letter of instruction, "that directly or by implication may screen him from the punishment due to his treason and desertion, which, if he should fall into your hands, you will execute in the most summary manner."

Washington wrote at the same time to the Baron Steuben, informing him of the arrangements and requesting him to be on the alert. "If the fleet should have arrived before this gets to hand," said he, "secrecy will be out of the question. If not, you will conceal your expectations and only seem to be preparing for defense. Arnold, on the appearance of the fleet, may endeavor to retreat through North Carolina. If you take any measure to obviate this, the precaution will be advisable. Should you be able to capture this detachment with its chief, it will be an event as pleasing as it will be useful."

Lafayette set out on his march on the 22d of February, and Washington was indulging the hope that, scanty as was the naval force sent to the Chesapeake, the combined enterprise might be successful, when on the 27th he received a letter from the Count de Rochambeau announcing its failure. De Tilly had made his dash into Cheasapeake Bay but Arnold had been apprised by the

British Admiral Arbuthnot of his approach and had drawn his ships high up Elizabeth River. The water was too shallow for the largest French ships to get within four leagues of him. One of De Tilly's frigates ran aground and was got off with difficulty, and that commander, seeing that Arnold was out of his reach and fearing to be himself blockaded should he linger, put to sea and returned to Newport, having captured during his cruise a British frigate of forty-four guns, and two privateers with their prizes.

The French commanders now determined to follow the plan suggested by Washington and operate in the Chesapeake with their whole fleet and a detachment of land troops, being, as they said, disposed to risk everything to hinder Arnold from establishing himself at Portsmouth.

Washington set out for Newport to concert operations with the French commanders. Before his departure he wrote to Lafayette on the 1st of March, giving him intelligence of these intentions, and desiring him to transmit it to the Baron Steuben.

"I have received a letter," adds he, "from General Greene, by which it appears that Cornwallis with twenty-five hundred men was penetrating the country with great rapidity and Greene with a much inferior force retiring before him, having determined to pass the Roanoke. This intelligence and an apprehension that Arnold may make his escape before the fleet can arrive in the bay, induces me to give you greater latitude than you had in your original instructions. You are at liberty to concert a plan with the French general and naval commander for a descent into North Carolina to cut off the detachment of the enemy which had ascended Cape Fear River, intercept if possible Cornwallis and relieve General Greene and the Southern States. This, however, ought to be a secondary object, attempted in case of Arnold's retreat to New York or in case his reduction should be attended with too much delay. There should be strong reasons to induce a change of our first plan against Arnold if he is still in Virginia."

Washington arrived at Newport on the 6th of March and found the French fleet ready for sea, the troops, eleven hundred strong, commanded by General the Baron de Viomenil, being already embarked.

Washington went immediately on board of the admiral's ship, where he had an interview with the Count de Rochambeau and arranged the plan of the campaign. Returning on shore, he was received by the inhabitants with enthusiastic demonstrations of affection and was gratified to perceive the harmony and good-will between them and the French army and fleet. Much of this he attributed to the wisdom of the commanders and the discipline of the troops, but more to magnanimity on the one part and gratitude on the other, and he hailed it as a happy presage of lasting friendship between the two nations.

On the 8th of March [1781] at ten o'clock at night, he writes to Lafayette: "I have the pleasure to inform you that the whole fleet went out with a fair wind this evening about sunset. We have not heard of any move of the British in Gardiner's Bay. Should we luckily meet with no interruption from them, and Arnold should continue in Virginia until the arrival of M. Destouches, I flatter myself you will meet with that success which I most ardently wish, not only on the public, but your own account."

The British fleet made sail in pursuit on the morning of the 10th. As the French had so much the start, it was hoped they would reach Chesapeake Bay before them. Washington felt the present to be a most important moment. "The success of the expedition now in agitation," said he, "seems to depend upon a naval superiority, and the force of the two fleets is so equal that we must rather hope for than entertain an assurance of victory. The attempt, however, made by our allies to dislodge the enemy in Virginia is a bold one, and should it fail will nevertheless entitle them to the thanks of the public."

On returning to his headquarters at New Windsor, Washington on the 20th of March found letters from General Greene informing him that he had saved all his baggage, artillery and stores notwithstanding the hot pursuit of the enemy, and was now in his turn following them but that he was greatly in need of reinforcements.

"My regard for the public good and my inclination to promote your success," writes Washington in reply, "will prompt me to give every assistance and to make every diversion in your favor. But what can I do if I am not furnished with the means? From what I saw and learned while at the eastward, I am convinced the levies will be late in the field, and I fear far short of the requisition. I most anxiously wait the event of the present operation in Virginia. If attended with success, it may have the happiest influence on our Southern affairs by leaving the forces of Virginia free to act. For while there is an enemy in the heart of a country you can expect neither men nor supplies from it in that full and regular manner in which they ought to be given."

In the meantime Lafayette with his detachment was pressing forward by forced marches for Virginia. Arriving at the Head of Elk on the 3d of March, he halted until he should receive tidings respecting the French fleet. A letter from the Baron Steuben spoke of the preparations he was making, and the facility of taking the fortifications at Portsmouth, "sword in hand." The youthful marquis was not so sanguine as the veteran baron. "Arnold," said he, "has had so much time to prepare and plays so deep a game, nature has made the position so respectable, and some of the troops under his orders have been in so many actions that I do not flatter myself to succeed so easily." On the 7th he received Washington's letter of the 1st, apprising him of the approaching departure of the whole fleet with land forces.

Lafayette now conducted his troops by water to Annapolis, and concluding, from the time the ships were to sail and the winds which had since prevailed, the French fleet must be already in the Chesapeake, he crossed the bay in an open boat to Virginia and pushed on to confer with the American and French commanders, get a convoy for his troops and concert matters for a vigorous cooperation. Arriving at York on the 14th, he found the Baron Steuben in the bustle of military preparations and confident of having five thousand militia ready to co-operate. These, with Lafayette's detachment, would be sufficient for the attack by land. Nothing was wanting but a co-operation by sea, and the French fleet had not yet appeared though double the time necessary for the voyage had elapsed. The marquis repaired to General Muhlenburg's camp near Suffolk and reconnoitered with him the enemy's works at Portsmouth. This brought on a trifling skirmish but everything appeared satisfactory, everything promised complete success.

On the 20th, word was brought that a fleet had come to anchor within the capes. It was supposed of course to be the French and now the capture of the traitor was certain. He himself, from certain signs, appeared to be in great confusion. None of his ships ventured down the bay. An officer of the French navy bore down to visit the fleet but returned with the astounding intelligence that it was British!

Admiral Arbuthnot had in fact overtaken Destouches on the 16th of March off the capes of Virginia. Their forces were nearly equal, eight ships of the line and four frigates on each side, the French having more men, the English more guns. An engagement took place which lasted about an hour. The British van at first took the brunt of the action and was severely handled. The centre came up to its relief. The French line was broken and gave way, but rallied and formed again at some distance. The crippled state of some of his ships prevented the British admiral from bringing on a second encounter. Nor did the French seek one, but shaped their course the next day back to Newport. Both sides claimed a victory. The British certainly effected the main objects they had in view; the French were cut off from the Chesapeake. The combined enterprise against Portsmouth was disconcerted and Arnold was saved. Great must have been the apprehensions of the traitor while that enterprise threatened to entrap him. He knew the peculiar peril impending over him. It had been announced in the sturdy reply of an American prisoner to his inquiry what his countrymen would do to him if he were captured. "They would cut off the leg wounded in the service of your country and bury it with the honors of war. The rest of you they would hang!"

The feelings of Washington on hearing of the result of the enterprise may be judged from the following passage of a letter to Colonel John Laurens, then minister at Paris. "The failure of this expedition, which was most flattering in the commencement, is much to be regretted, because a successful blow in that quarter would in all probability have given a decisive turn to our affairs in all the Southern States, because it has been attended with considerable expense on our part and much inconvenience to the State of Virginia by the assembling of our militia, because the world is disappointed at not seeing Arnold in gibbets, and above all because we stood in need of something to keep us afloat till the result of your mission is known. For be assured, my dear Laurens, day does not follow night more certainly than it brings with it some additional proof of the impracticability of carrying on the war without the aids you were directed to solicit. As an honest and candid man, as a man whose all depends on the final and happy termination of the present contest, I assert this while I give it decisively as my opinion, that without a foreign loan our present force, which is but the remnant of an army, cannot be kept together this campaign, much less will it be increased and in readiness for another. . . . If France delays a timely and powerful aid in the critical posture of our affairs it will avail us nothing should she attempt it hereafter. We are at this hour suspended in the balance not from choice but from hard and absolute necessity, and you may rely on it as a fact that we cannot transport the provisions from the States in which they are assessed, to the army, because we cannot pay the teamsters, who will no longer work for certificates. . . . In a word, we are at the end of our tether, and now or never our deliverance must come. . . . How easy would it be to retort the enemy's own game upon them, if it could be made to comport with the general plan of war, to keep a superior fleet always in these seas, and France would put us in condition to be active by advancing us money. The ruin of the enemy's schemes would then be certain. The bold game they are now playing would be the means of effecting it, for they would be reduced to the necessity of concentrating their force at capital points, thereby giving up all the advantages they have gained in the Southern States, or be vulnerable everywhere."

Washington's anxiety was now awakened for the safety of General Greene. Two thousand troops had sailed from New York under General Phillips, probably to join with the force under Arnold and proceed to reinforce Cornwallis. Should they form a junction, Greene would be unable to withstand them. With these considerations Washington wrote to Lafayette, urging him, since he was already three hundred miles, which was half the distance, on the way, to push on with all possible speed to join the Southern army, sending expresses ahead to inform Greene of his approach.

The letter found Lafayette on the 8th of April at the Head of Elk, preparing to march back with his troops to the banks of the Hudson. On his return through Virginia, he had gone out of his way and travelled all night for the purpose of seeing Washington's mother at Fredericksburg, and paying a visit to Mount Vernon. He now stood ready to obey Washington's orders and march to reinforce General Greene, but his troops, who were chiefly from the Eastern States, murmured at the prospect of a campaign in a southern climate, and desertions began to occur. Upon this he announced in general orders that he was about to enter on an enterprise of great difficulty and danger, in which he trusted his soldiers would not abandon him. Any, however, who were unwilling, should receive permits to return home.

As he had anticipated, their pride was roused by this appeal. All engaged to continue forward. So great was the fear of appearing a laggard or a craven, that a sergeant, too lame to march, hired a place in a cart to keep up with the army. In the zeal of the moment Lafayette borrowed money on his own credit from the Baltimore merchants to purchase summer clothing for his troops, in which he was aided too by the ladies of the city, with whom he was deservedly popular.

The detachment from New York under General Phillips arrived at Portsmouth on the 26th of March. That officer immediately took command, greatly to the satisfaction of the British officers, who had been acting under Arnold. The force now collected there amounted to three thousand five hundred men. The garrison of New York had been greatly weakened in furnishing this detachment, but Cornwallis had urged the policy of transferring the seat of war to Virginia even at the expense of abandoning New York, declaring that until that State was subdued, the British hold upon the Carolinas must be difficult if not precarious.

The disparity in force was now so great that the Baron Steuben had to withdraw his troops and remove the military stores into the interior. Many of the militia, too, their term of three months being expired, stacked their arms and set off for their homes, and most of the residue had to be discharged.

General Phillips had hitherto remained quiet in Portsmouth, completing the fortifications but evidently making preparations for an expedition. On the 16th of April he left one thousand men in garrison and, embarking the rest in small vessels of light draught, proceeded up James River, destroying armed vessels, public magazines and a ship-yard belonging to the State.

Landing at City Point, he advanced against Petersburg, a place of deposit of military stores and tobacco. He was met about a mile below the town by about one thousand militia under General Muhlenburg, who, after disputing the ground inch by inch for nearly two hours with considerable loss on both sides, retreated across the Appomattox, breaking down the bridge behind them.

Phillips entered the town, set fire to the tobacco warehouses and destroyed all the vessels lying in the river. Repairing and crossing the bridge over the Appomattox, he proceeded to Chesterfield Court-house, where he destroyed barracks and public stores, while Arnold, with a detachment, laid waste the magazines of tobacco in the direction of Warwick. A fire was opened by the latter from a few field-pieces on the river bank upon a squadron of small vessels which had been intended to co-operate with the French fleet against Portsmouth. The crews scuttled or set fire to them and escaped to the north side of the river.

This destructive course was pursued until they arrived at Manchester, a small place opposite Richmond, where the tobacco warehouses were immediately in a blaze. Richmond was a leading object of this desolating enterprise, for there a great part of the military stores of the State had been collected. Fortunately, Lafayette with his detachment of two thousand men had arrived there by forced marches the evening before, and being joined by about two thousand militia and sixty dragoons (the latter principally young Virginians of family), had posted himself strongly on the high banks on the north side of the river.

There being no bridge across the river at that time, General Phillips did not think it prudent to attempt a passage in face of such a force so posted, but was extremely irritated at being thus foiled by the celerity of his youthful opponent, who now assumed the chief command of the American forces in Virginia.

Returning down the south bank of the river to the place where his vessels awaited him, General Phillips re-embarked on the 2d of May and dropped slowly down the river below the confluence of the Chickahominy. He was followed cautiously, and his movements watched by Lafayette, who posted himself behind the last-named river.

Despatches from Cornwallis now informed Phillips that his lordship was advancing with all speed from the South to effect a junction with him. The general immediately made a rapid move to regain possession of Petersburg where the junction was to take place. Lafayette attempted by forced marches to get there before him but was too late. Falling back therefore, he recrossed James River and stationed himself some miles below Richmond to be at hand for the protection of the public stores collected there.

During this main expedition of Phillips some of his smaller vessels had carried on the plunder and devastation in other of the rivers emptying into the Chesapeake Bay, setting fire to the houses where they met with resistance. One had ascended the Potomac and menaced Mount Vernon. Lund Washington, who had charge of the estate, met the flag which the enemy sent on shore, and saved the property from ravage by furnishing the vessel with provisions. Lafayette, who heard of the circumstance, and was sensitive for the honor of Washington, immediately wrote to him on the subject. "This conduct of the person who represents you on your estate," writes he, "must certainly produce a bad effect and contrast with the courageous replies of some of your neighbors, whose houses in consequence have been burnt. You will do what you think proper, my dear general, but friendship makes it my duty to give you confidentially the facts."

Washington, however, had previously received a letter from Lund himself, stating all the circumstances of the case, and had immediately written him a reply. He had no doubt that Lund had acted from his best judgment and with a view to preserve the property and buildings from impending danger, but he was stung to the quick by the idea that his agent should go on board of the enemy's vessel, carry them refreshments and "commune with a parcel of plundering scoundrels," as he termed them.

"It would have been a less painful circumstance to me to have heard," writes he, "that in consequence of your noncompliance with their request they had burnt my house and laid my plantation in ruins. You ought to have considered yourself as my representative and should have reflected on the bad example of communicating with the enemy and making a voluntary offer of refreshments to them with a view to prevent a conflagration."

In concluding his letter, he expresses his opinion that it was the intention of the enemy to prosecute the plundering plan they had begun, and that it would end in the destruction of his property, but adds that he is "prepared for the event." He advises his agent to deposit the valuable and least bulky articles in a place of safety. "Such and so many things as are necessary for common and present use must be retained and must run their chance through the fiery trial of this summer."

Such were the steadfast purposes of Washington's mind when war was brought home to his door and threatening his earthly paradise of Mount Vernon.

In the meantime the desolating career of General Phillips was brought to a close. He had been ill for some days previous to his arrival at Petersburg, and by the time he reached there was no longer capable of giving orders. He died four days afterwards, honored and deeply regretted by his brothers in arms as a meritorious and well-tried soldier. What made his death to be more sensibly felt by them at this moment was that it put the traitor Arnold once more in the general command.

He held it, however, but for a short time, as Lord Cornwallis arrived at Petersburg on the 20th of May after nearly a month's weary marching from Wilmington. His lordship, on taking command, found his force augmented by a considerable detachment of Royal Artillery, two battalions of light infantry, the 76th and 80th British regiments, a Hessian regiment, Lieutenant-Colonel Simcoe's corps of Queen's rangers, cavalry and infantry, one hundred yagers, Arnold's legion of royalists, and the garrison of Portsmouth. He was cheered also by intelligence that Lord Rawdon had obtained an advantage over General Greene before Camden, and that three British regiments had sailed from Cork for Charleston. His mind, we are told, was now set at ease with regard to Southern affairs. His spirits, so long jaded by his harassing tramps about the Carolinas, were again lifted up by his augmented strength, and Tarleton assures us that his lordship indulged in "brilliant hopes of a glorious campaign in those parts of America where he commanded."[2] How far these hopes were realized we shall show in a future page.

2 Tarleton, *History of the Campaign*, p. 291.

Chapter 45

CORNWALLIS AT YORKTOWN

After the grand reconnaissance of the posts on New York Island related in a former page, the confederate armies remained encamped about Dobbs Ferry and the Greenburg hills, awaiting an augmentation of force for their meditated attack. To Washington's great disappointment, his army was but tardily and scantily recruited, while the garrison of New York was augmented by the arrival of three thousand Hessian troops from Europe. In this predicament he despatched a circular letter to the governments of the Eastern States, representing his delicate and embarrassed situation.

"Unable to advance with prudence beyond my present position while perhaps in the general opinion my force is equal to the commencement of operations against New York, my conduct must appear, if not blamable, highly mysterious at least. Our allies, who were made to expect a very considerable augmentation of force by this time, instead of seeing a prospect of advancing must conjecture upon good grounds that the campaign will waste fruitlessly away. It will be no small degree of triumph to our enemies, and will have a pernicious influence upon our friends in Europe, should they find such a failure of resource or such a want of energy to draw it out that our boasted and extensive preparations end only in idle parade. . . . The fulfilment of my engagement must depend upon the degree of vigor with which the executives of the several States exercise the powers with which they have been vested, and enforce the laws lately passed for filling up and supplying the army. In full confidence that the means which have been voted will be obtained, I shall continue my operations."

Until we study Washington's full, perspicuous letters, we know little of the difficulties he had to struggle with in conducting his campaigns. How often the sounding resolves of legislative bodies disappointed him. How often he had to maintain a bold front when his country failed to back him. How often, as in the siege of Boston, he had to carry on the war without powder!

In a few days came letters from Lafayette, dated 26th and 30th of July, speaking of the embarkation of the greatest part of Cornwallis's army at Portsmouth. "There are in Hampton Roads thirty transport ships full of troops, most of them red coats, and eight or ten brigs with cavalry on board." He supposed their destination to be New York, yet though wind and weather were favorable, they did not sail. "Should a French fleet now come into Hampton Roads," adds the sanguine marquis, "the British army would, I think, be ours."

At this juncture arrived the French frigate Concorde at Newport, bringing despatches from Admiral the Count de Grasse. He was to leave St. Domingo on the 3d of August with between twenty-five and thirty ships of the line and a considerable body of land forces and to steer immediately for the Chesapeake.

This changed the face of affairs and called for a change in the game. All attempt upon New York was postponed. The whole of the French army and as large a part of the Americans as could be spared were to move to Virginia and co-operate with the Count de Grasse for the redemption of the Southern States. Washington apprised the count by letter of this intention. He wrote also to Lafayette on the 15th of August: "By the time this reaches you, the Count de Grasse will either be in the Chesapeake or may be looked for every moment. Under these circumstances, whether the enemy remain in full force or whether they have only a detachment left, you will immediately take such a position as will best enable you to prevent their sudden retreat through North Carolina, which I presume they will attempt the instant they perceive so formidable an armament."

Should General Wayne, with the troops destined for South Carolina, still remain in the neighborhood of James River and the enemy have made no detachment to the southward, the marquis was to detain those troops until he heard again from Washington, and was to inform General Greene of the cause of their detention.

"You shall hear further from me," concludes the letter, "as soon as I have concerted plans and formed dispositions for sending a reinforcement from hence. In the meantime I have only to recommend a continuance of that prudence and good conduct which you have manifested through the whole of your campaign. You will be particularly careful to conceal the unexpected arrival of the count, because if the enemy are not apprised of it, they will stay on board their transports in the bay, which will be the luckiest circumstance in the world."

Washington's "soul was now in arms." At length, after being baffled and disappointed so often by the incompetency of his means, and above all thwarted by the enemy's naval potency, he had the possibility of coping with them both on land and sea. The contemplated expedition was likely to consummate his plans and wind up the fortunes of the war, and he determined to lead it in person. He would take with him something more than two thousand of the American army. The rest, chiefly Northern troops, were to remain with General Heath, who was to hold command of West Point and the other posts of the Hudson.

Perfect secrecy was maintained as to this change of plan. Preparations were still carried on as if for an attack upon New York. An extensive encampment was marked out in the Jerseys and ovens erected and fuel provided for the baking of bread, as if a part of the besieging force was to be stationed there, thence to make a descent upon the enemy's garrison on Staten Island in aid of the operations against the city. The American troops themselves were kept in ignorance of their destination. "General Washington," observes one of the shrewdest of them, "matures his great plans and designs under an impenetrable veil of secrecy, and while we repose the fullest confidence in our chief, our opinions (as to his intentions) must be founded only on doubtful conjecture."[1]

Previous to his decampment, Washington sent forward a party of pioneers to clear the roads towards King's Bridge, as if the posts recently reconnoitered were about to be attempted. On the 19th of August his troops were paraded with their faces in that direction. When all were ready, however, they were ordered to face about and were marched up along the Hudson River towards King's Ferry.

De Rochambeau, in like manner, broke up his encampment and took the road by White Plains, North Castle, Pine's Bridge and Crompond towards the same point. All Westchester County

[1] See Thacher's *Military Journal*, p. 322.

was again alive with the tramp of troops, the gleam of arms and the lumbering of artillery and baggage wagons along its roads.

On the 20th, Washington arrived at King's Ferry, and his troops began to cross the Hudson with their baggage, stores and cannon, and encamp at Haverstraw. He himself crossed in the evening and took up his quarters at Colonel Hay's at the White House. Thence he wrote confidentially to Lafayette, on the 21st, now first apprising him of his being on the march with the expedition, and repeating his injunctions that the land and naval forces already at the scene of action should so combine their operations that the English, on the arrival of the French fleet, might not be able to escape. He wrote also to the Count de Grasse (presuming that the letter would find him in the Chesapeake), urging him to send up all his frigates and transports to the Head of Elk by the 8th of September for the transportation of the combined army, which would be there by that time. He informed him also that the Count de Barras had resolved to join him in the Chesapeake with his squadron. One is reminded of the tissue of movements planned from a distance which ended in the capture of Burgoyne.

On the 22d, the French troops arrived by their circuitous route and began to cross to Stony Point with their artillery, baggage and stores. The operation occupied between two and three days, during which time Washington took the Count de Rochambeau on a visit to West Point to show him the citadel of the Highlands, an object of intense interest in consequence of having been the scene of Arnold's treason.

The two armies, having safely crossed the Hudson, commenced on the 25th their several lines of march towards the Jerseys; the Americans for Springfield on the Rahway, the French for Whippany towards Trenton. Both armies were still kept in the dark as to the ultimate object of their movement. An intelligent observer, already quoted, who accompanied the army, writes: "Our situation reminds me of some theatrical exhibition where the interest and expectations of the spectators are continually increasing and where curiosity is wrought to the highest point. Our destination has been for some time matter of perplexing doubt and uncertainty. Bets have run high on one side that we were to occupy the ground marked out on the Jersey shore to aid in the siege of New York. And on the other that we are stealing a march on the enemy and are actually destined to Virginia in pursuit of the army under Cornwallis. . . . A number of bateaux mounted on carriages have followed in our train, supposed for the purpose of conveying the troops over to Staten Island."[2]

The mystery was at length solved. "We have now passed all the enemy's posts," continues the foregoing writer, "and are pursuing our route with increased rapidity toward Philadelphia. Wagons have been prepared to carry the soldiers' packs, that they may press forward with greater facility. Our destination can no longer be a secret. Cornwallis is unquestionably the object of our present expedition. . . . His Excellency, General Washington, having succeeded in a masterly piece of generalship, has now the satisfaction of leaving his adversary to ruminate on his own mortifying situation and to anticipate the perilous fate which awaits his friend, Lord Cornwallis, in a different quarter."[3]

Washington had in fact reached the Delaware with his troops before Sir Henry Clinton was aware of their destination. It was too late to oppose their march, even had his forces been adequate. As a kind of counterplot, therefore, and in the hope of distracting the attention of the American commander and drawing off a part of his troops, he hurried off an expedition to the eastward to insult the State of Connecticut and attack her seaport of New London.

The command of this expedition, which was to be one of ravage and destruction, was given to Arnold, as if it was necessary to complete the measure of his infamy that he should carry fire and sword into his native State and desecrate the very cradle of his infancy.

On the 6th of September [1781] he appeared off the harbor of New London with a fleet of ships and transports and a force of two thousand infantry and three hundred cavalry, partly British troops, but a great part made up of American royalists and refugees and Hessian yagers.

New London stands on the west bank of the river Thames. The

---

[2] Thacher's *Military Journal*, p. 323.

[3] Washington several years afterwards, speaking of this important march in a letter to Noah Webster, writes: "That much trouble was taken and finesse used to misguide and bewilder Sir Henry Clinton in regard to the real object, by fictitious communications as well as by making a deceptive provision of ovens, forage and boats in his neighborhood, is certain. Nor were less pains taken to deceive our own army, for I had always conceived where the imposition does not completely take place at home it would never sufficiently succeed abroad."—Sparks, ix., 404.

approach to it was defended by two forts on opposite sides of the river, and about a mile below the town, Fort Trumbull on the west and Fort Griswold on the east side, on a height called Groton Hill. The troops landed in two divisions of about eight hundred men each, one under Lieutenant-Colonel Eyre on the east side, the other under Arnold on the west, on the same side with New London and about three miles below it. Arnold met with but little opposition. The few militia which manned an advance battery and Fort Trumbull abandoned their posts and crossed the river to Fort Griswold. He pushed on and took possession of the town.

Colonel Eyre had a harder task. The militia, about one hundred and fifty-seven strong, had collected in Fort Griswold, hastily and imperfectly armed it is true, some of them merely with spears, but they were brave men and had a brave commander, Colonel William Ledyard, brother of the celebrated traveller. The fort was square and regularly built. Arnold, unaware of its strength, had ordered Colonel Eyre to take it by a coup-de-main. He discovered his mistake and sent counter-orders but too late.

Colonel Eyre forced the pickets, made his way into the fosse and attacked the fort on three sides. It was bravely defended. The enemy were repeatedly repulsed. They returned to the assault, scrambled up on each other's shoulders, effected a lodgment on the fraise and made their way with fixed bayonets through the embrasures. Colonel Eyre received a mortal wound near the works. Major Montgomery took his place. A negro thrust him through with a spear as he mounted the parapet. Major Bromfield succeeded to the command and carried the fort at the point of the bayonet.

In fact, after the enemy were within the walls the fighting was at an end and the slaughter commenced. Colonel Ledyard had ordered his men to lay down their arms, but the enemy, exasperated by the resistance they had experienced and by the death of their officers, continued the deadly work of the musket and the bayonet. Colonel Ledyard, it is said, was thrust through with his own sword after yielding it up to Major Bromfield. Seventy of the garrison were slain and thirty-five desperately wounded, and most of them after the fort had been taken. The massacre was chiefly perpetrated by the tories, refugees and Hessians. Major Bromfield himself was a New Jersey loyalist. The rancor of such men against their patriot countrymen was always deadly. The loss of the enemy was two officers and forty-six soldiers killed and eight officers and one hundred and thirty-five soldiers wounded.

Arnold in the meantime had carried on the work of destruction at New London. Some of the American shipping had effected their escape up the river but a number were burnt. Fire, too, was set to the public stores. It communicated to the dwelling-houses and in a little while the whole place was wrapped in flames. The destruction was immense, not only of public but private property. Many families once living in affluence were ruined and rendered homeless.

Having completed his ravage, Arnold retreated to his boats, leaving the town still burning. Alarm guns had roused the country. The traitor was pursued by the exasperated yeomanry. He escaped their well-merited vengeance but several of his men were killed and wounded.

So ended his career of infamy in his native land, a land which had once delighted to honor him but in which his name was never thenceforth to be pronounced without a malediction.

The expedition, while it added one more hateful and disgraceful incident to this unnatural war, failed of its main object. It had not diverted Washington from the grand object on which he had fixed his mind. On the 30th of August he with his suite had arrived at Philadelphia about noon and alighted at the city tavern amidst enthusiastic crowds, who welcomed him with acclamations but wondered at the object of his vist.

During his sojourn in the city he was hospitably entertained at the house of Mr. Morris, the patriotic financier. The greatest difficulty with which he had to contend in his present enterprise was the want of funds, part of his troops not having received any pay for a long time and having occasionally given evidence of great discontent. The service upon which they were going was disagreeable to the Northern regiments, and the *douceur* of a little hard money would have an effect, Washington thought, to put them into a proper temper. In this emergency he was accommodated by the Count de Rochambeau with a loan of twenty thousand hard dollars, which Mr. Robert Morris engaged to repay by the 1st of October. This pecuniary pressure was relieved by the arrival in Boston on the 25th of August of Colonel John Laurens from his mission to France, bringing with him two and a half millions of livres in cash, being part of a subsidy of six millions of livres granted by the French king.

On the 2d of September the American troops passed through Philadelphia. Their line of march, including appendages and attendants, extended nearly two miles. The general officers and their staffs were well dressed and well mounted, and followed by servants and baggage. In the rear of every brigade were several field-pieces with ammunition wagons. The soldiers kept step to the sound of the drum and fife. In the rear followed a great number of wagons laden with tents, provisions and baggage, beside a few soldiers' wives and children. The weather was warm and dry. The troops as they marched raised a cloud of dust "like a smothering snow-storm," which almost blinded them. The begriming effect was especially mortifying to the campaigner whom we quote, "as ladies were viewing them from the windows of every house as they passed." Notwithstanding the dusty and somewhat ragged plight of the soldiery, however, they were cheered with enthusiasm by the populace, who hailed them as the war-worn defenders of the country.

The French troops entered on the following day but in different style. Halting within a mile of the city, they arranged their arms and accoutrements, brushed the dust off of their gay white uniforms faced with green, and then marched in with buoyant step and brilliant array to the swelling music of a military band. The streets were again thronged by the shouting populace.

At Philadelphia Washington received despatches from Lafayette, dated the 21st and 24th of August, from his camp at the Forks of York River in Virginia. The embarkation at Portsmouth which the marquis had supposed might be intended for New York was merely for Yorktown, where Cornwallis had determined to establish the permanent post ordered in his instructions.

Yorktown was a small place situated on a projecting bank on the south side of York River, opposite a promontory called Gloucester Point. The river between was not more than a mile wide, but deep enough to admit ships of a large size and burthen. Here concentrating his forces, he had proceeded to fortify the opposite points, calculating to have the works finished by the beginning of October, at which time Sir Henry Clinton intended to recommence operations on the Chesapeake. Believing that he had no present enemy but Lafayette to guard against, Cornwallis felt so secure in his position that he wrote to Sir Henry on the 22d of August, offering to detach a thousand or twelve hundred men to strengthen New York against the apprehended attack of the combined armies.

While Cornwallis, undervaluing his youthful adversary, felt thus secure, Lafayette, in conformity to the instructions of Washington, was taking measures to cut off any retreat by land which his lordship might attempt on the arrival of De Grasse. With this view he called upon General Thomas Nelson, the Governor of Virginia, for six hundred of the militia to be collected upon Blackwater, detached troops to the south of James River under pretext of a design to dislodge the British from Portsmouth, and requested General Wayne to move southward to be ready to cross James River at Westover.

As to himself, Lafayette was prepared, as soon as he should hear of the arrival of De Grasse, to march at once to Williamsburg and form a junction with the troops which were to be landed from the fleet. Thus a net was quietly drawn round Cornwallis by the youthful general while the veteran himself felt so secure that he was talking of detaching troops to New York.

Lafayette, at the time of writing his despatches, was ignorant that Washington had taken command of the expedition coming to his aid, and expressed an affectionate solicitude on the subject. "In the present state of affairs, my dear general," writes he, "I hope you will come yourself to Virginia and that, if the French army moves this way, I will have at least the satisfaction of beholding you, myself, at the head of the combined armies." In concluding his letter, he writes: "Adieu, my dear general. I heartily thank you for having ordered me to remain in Virginia, and to your goodness to me I am owing the most beautiful prospect I may ever behold."

The letter of Lafayette gave no account of the Count de Grasse, and Washington expressed himself distressed beyond measure to know what had become of that commander. He had heard of an English fleet at sea steering for the Chesapeake and feared it might arrive and frustrate all the flattering prospects in that quarter. Still, as usual, he looked to the bright side. "Of many contingencies," writes he, "we will hope for the most propitious events. Should the retreat of Lord Cornwallis by water be cut off by the arrival of either of the French fleets, I am persuaded you will do all in your power to prevent his escape by land. May that great felicity be reserved for you."

Washington left Philadelphia on the 5th of September on his way to the Head of Elk. About three miles below Chester he was met by an express bearing tidings of the arrival of the Count de Grasse in the Chesapeake with twenty-eight ships of the line. Washington instantly rode back to Chester to rejoice with the Count de Rochambeau, who was coming down to that place from Philadelphia by water. They had a joyous dinner together, after which Washington proceeded in the evening on his destination.

The express meantime reached Philadelphia most opportunely. There had been a grand review of the French troops, at which the president of Congress and all the fashion of the city were present. It was followed by a banquet given to the officers by the French Minister, the Chevalier de Luzerne. Scarce were the company seated at table when despatches came announcing the arrival of De Grasse and the landing of three thousand troops under the Marquis St. Simon, who, it was added, had opened a communication with Lafayette.

All now was mutual gratulation at the banquet. The news soon went forth and spread throughout the city. Acclamations were to be heard on all sides, and crowds assembling before the house of the French Minister rent the air with hearty huzzas for Louis the Sixteenth.

Washington reached the Head of Elk on the 6th. The troops and a great part of the stores were already arrived and beginning to embark. Thence he wrote to the Count de Grasse, felicitating him on his arrival and informing him that the van of the two armies were about to embark and fall down the Chesapeake, form a junction with the troops under the Count de St. Simon and the Marquis de Lafayette, and co-operate in blocking up Cornwallis in York River so as to prevent his retreat by land or his getting any supplies from the country.

"As it will be of the greatest importance," writes he, "to prevent the escape of his lordship from his present position, I am persuaded that every measure which prudence can dictate will be adopted for that purpose until the arrival of our complete force, when I hope his lordship will be compelled to yield his ground to the superior power of our combined forces."

Everything had thus far gone on well, but there were not vessels enough at the Head of Elk for the immediate transportation of all the troops, ordnance and stores. A part of the troops would have to proceed to Baltimore by land. Leaving General Heath to bring on the American forces, and the Baron de Viomenil the French, Washington, accompanied by De Rochambeau, crossed the Susquehanna early on the 8th and pushed forward for Baltimore. He was met by a deputation of the citizens, who made him a public address to which he replied, and his arrival was celebrated in the evening with illuminations.

On the 9th he left Baltimore a little after daybreak, accompanied only by Colonel Humphreys. The rest of his suite were to follow at their ease. For himself, he was determined to reach Mount Vernon that evening. Six years had elapsed since last he was under its roof, six wearing years of toil, of danger and of constant anxiety. During all that time and amid all his military cares he had kept up a regular weekly correspondence with his steward or agent, regulating all the affairs of his rural establishment with as much exactness as he did those of the army.

It was a late hour when he arrived at Mount Vernon, where he was joined by his suite at dinner-time on the following day and by the Count de Rochambeau in the evening. General Chastellux and his aides-de-camp arrived there on the 11th, and Mount Vernon was now crowded with guests, who were all entertained in the ample style of old Virginian hospitality. On the 12th, tearing himself away once more from the home of his heart, Washington with his military associates continued onward to join Lafayette at Williamsburg.

Chapter 46

SIEGE AND SURRENDER OF YORKTOWN

Lord Cornwallis had been completely roused from his dream of security by the appearance, on the 28th of August, of the fleet of Count de Grasse within the capes of the Delaware. Three French ships of the line and a frigate soon anchored at the mouth of York River. The boats of the fleet were immediately busy conveying three thousand three hundred land forces, under the Marquis de St. Simon, up James River to form the preconcerted junction with those under Lafayette.

Awakened to his danger, Cornwallis, as Washington had foreseen, meditated a retreat to the Carolinas. It was too late. York River was blocked up by French ships. James River was filled with armed vessels covering the transportation of the troops. His lordship reconnoitered Williamsburg. It was too strong to be forced, and Wayne had crossed James River to join his troops to those under the marquis. Seeing his retreat cut off in every direction, Cornwallis proceeded to strengthen his works, sending off repeated expresses to apprise Sir Henry Clinton of his perilous situation.

The Count de Grasse, eager to return to the West Indies, urged Lafayette to make an immediate attack upon the British army with the American and French troops under his command, without waiting for the combined force under Washington and Rochambeau, offering to aid him with marines and sailors from the ships. The admiral was seconded by the Marquis de St. Simon. They represented that the works at Yorktown were yet incomplete and that that place and Gloucester, immediately opposite, might be carried by storm by their superior force. It was a brilliant achievement which they held out to tempt the youthful commander but he remained undazzled. He would not, for the sake of personal distinction, lavish the lives of the brave men confided to him, but would await the arrival of the combined forces, when success might be attained with little loss and would leave to Washington the *coup de grace*, in all probability the closing triumph of the war.

The Count de Grasse had been but a few days anchored within the Chesapeake, and fifteen hundred of his seamen were absent, conveying the troops up James River, when Admiral Graves, who then commanded the British naval force on the American coast, appeared with twenty sail off the capes of Virginia. De Grasse, anxious to protect the squadron of the Count de Barras which was expected from Rhode Island and which it was the object of Graves to intercept, immediately slipped his cables and put to sea with twenty-four ships, leaving the rest to blockade York and James Rivers.

Washington received information of the sailing of the fleet from the capes shortly after his departure from Mount Vernon, and instantly despatched missives ordering the troops who were embarked at the Head of Elk to stop until the receipt of further intelligence, fearing that the navigation in Chesapeake Bay might not be secure. For two days he remained in anxious uncertainty, until, at Bowling Green, he was relieved by favorable rumors concerning the fleet, which were confirmed on his arriving at Williamsburg on the evening of the 14th.

Admiral Graves, it appeared, on the sallying forth of the French fleet, immediately prepared for action although he had five ships less than De Grasse. The latter, however, was not disposed to accept the challenge, his force being weakened by the absence of so many of his seamen, employed in transporting troops. His plan was to occupy the enemy by partial actions and skilful manœuvres so to retain his possession of the Chesapeake and cover the arrival of De Barras.

The vans of the two fleets, and some ships of the centre, engaged about four o'clock in the afternoon of the 7th of September. The conflict soon became animated. Several ships were damaged and many men killed and wounded on both sides.

De Grasse, who had the advantage of the wind, drew off after sunset satisfied with the damage done and sustained, and not disposed for a general action. Nor was the British admiral inclined to push the engagement so near night and on a hostile coast.

Among his ships that had suffered, one had been so severely handled that she was no longer seaworthy and had to be burnt. For four days the fleets remained in sight of each other, repairing damages and manœuvring, but the French, having still the advantage of the wind, maintained their prudent policy of avoiding a general engagement. At length De Grasse, learning that De Barras was arrived within the capes, formed a junction with him, and returned with him to his former anchoring ground with two English frigates which he had captured. Admiral Graves, disappointed in his hope of intercepting De Barras, and finding the Chesapeake guarded by a superior force with which he could not prudently contend; having, moreover, to encounter the autumnal gales in the battered state of several of his ships, left the coast and bore away for New York.

Under convoy of the squadron of De Barras came a fleet of transports conveying land forces under M. de Choisy, with siege artillery and military stores. It should be mentioned to the credit of De Barras that in his orders from the French minister of marine to come to America, he was left at liberty to make a cruise on the banks of Newfoundland so as not to be obliged to serve under De Grasse, who was his inferior in rank but whom the minister wished to continue in the command. "But De Barras," writes Lafayette, "nobly took the part of conducting, himself, the artillery from Rhode Island and of coming with all his vessels and placing himself under the orders of an admiral his junior in service."[1]

From Williamsburg, Washington sent forward Count Fersen, one of the aides-de-camp of De Rochambeau, to hurry on the French troops with all possible despatch. He wrote to the same purport to General Lincoln: "Every day we now lose is comparatively an age. As soon as it is in our power with safety, we ought to take our position near the enemy. Hurry on, then, my dear sir, with your troops on the wings of speed. The want of our men and stores is now all that retards our immediate operations. Lord Cornwallis is improving every moment to the best advantage, and every day that is given him to make his preparations may cost us many lives to encounter them."

It was with great satisfaction Washington learned that Admiral de Barras had anticipated his wishes in sending transports and prize vessels up the bay to assist in bringing on the French troops.

[1] *Memoirs of Lafayette*, tom. i., p. 467.

In the meantime he with Count de Rochambeau was desirous of having an interview with the admiral on board of his ship, provided he could send some fast-sailing cutter to receive them. A small ship, the *Queen Charlotte*, was furnished by the admiral for the purpose. It had been captured on its voyage from Charleston to New York, having Lord Rawdon on board, and had been ,, commodiously fitted up for his lordship's reception.

On board of this vessel Washington and De Rochambeau, with the Chevalier de Chastellux and Generals Knox and Duportail, embarked on the 18th and, proceeding down James River, came the next morning in sight of the French fleet riding at anchor in Lynn Haven Bay, just under the point of Cape Henry. About noon they got alongside of the admiral's ship, the *Ville de Paris*, and were received on board with great ceremony and naval and military parade. Admiral de Grasse was a tall, fine-looking man, plain in his address and prompt in the discharge of business. A plan of co-operation was soon arranged, to be carried into effect on the arrival of the American and French armies from the North, which were actually on their way down the Chesapeake from the Head of Elk. Business being despatched, dinner was served, after which they were conducted throughout the ship and received the visits of the officers of the fleet, almost all of whom came on board.

About sunset Washington and his companions took their leave of the admiral and returned on board of their own little ship, when the yards of all the ships of the fleet were manned and a parting salute was thundered from the *Ville de Paris*. Owing to storms and contrary winds and other adverse circumstances the party did not reach Williamsburg until the 22d, when intelligence was received that threatened to disconcert all the plans formed in the recent council on board ship.

Admiral Digby, it appeared, had arrived in New York with six ships of the line and a reinforcement of troops. This intelligence Washington instantly transmitted to the Count de Grasse by one of the Count de Rochambeau's aides-de-camp. De Grasse in reply expressed great concern, observing that the position of affairs was changed by the arrival of Digby. "The enemy," writes he, "is now nearly equal to us in strength and it would be imprudent in me to place myself in a situation that would prevent my attacking them should they attempt to afford succor." He proposed therefore to leave two vessels at the mouth of York River, and the corvettes and frigates in James River, which, with the French troops on shore, would be sufficient assistance, and to put to sea with the rest, either to intercept the enemy and fight them where there was good sea-room or to blockade them in New York should they not have sailed.

On reading this letter, Washington dreaded that the present plan of co-operation might likewise fall through, and the fruits of all his schemes and combinations be lost when within his reach. With the assistance of the fleet the reduction of Yorktown was demonstrably certain and the surrender of the garrison must go far to terminate the war, whereas the departure of the ships, by leaving an opening for succor to the enemy, might frustrate these brilliant prospects and involve the whole enterprise in ruin and disgrace. Even a momentary absence of the French fleet might enable Cornwallis to evacuate Yorktown and effect a retreat, with the loss merely of his baggage and artillery and perhaps a few soldiers. These and other considerations were urged in a letter to the count, remonstrating against his putting to sea. Lafayette was the bearer of the letter and seconded it with so many particulars respecting the situation of the armies, and argued the case so earnestly and eloquently, that the count consented to remain. It was, furthermore, determined in a council of war of his officers that a large part of the fleet should anchor in York River, four or five vessels be stationed so as to pass up and down James River, and a battery for cannon and mortars be erected with the aid of the allied troops on Point Comfort.

By the 25th the American and French troops were mostly arrived and encamped near Williamsburg, and preparations were made for the decisive blow.

Yorktown, as has already been noted, is situated on the south side of York River, immediately opposite Gloucester Point. Cornwallis had fortified the town with seven redoubts and six batteries on the land side connected by intrenchments, and there was a line of batteries along the river. The town was flanked on each side by deep ravines and creeks emptying into York River, their heads in front of the town being not more than half a mile apart. The enemy had availed themselves of these natural defenses in the arrangement of extensive outworks, with redoubts strengthened by abatis, field works mounted with cannon, and trees cut down and left with the branches pointed outward.

Gloucester Point had likewise been fortified, its batteries, with those of Yorktown, commanding the intervening river. Ships of war were likewise stationed on it, protected by the guns of the forts, and the channel was obstructed by sunken vessels.

The defense of Gloucester Point was confided to Lieutenant-Colonel Dundas with six or seven hundred men. The enemy's main army was encamped about Yorktown within the range of the outer redoubts and field works.

Washington and his staff bivouacked that night on the ground in the open air. He slept under a mulberry tree, the root serving for his pillow. On the following morning the two armies drew out on each side of Beaver Dam Creek. The Americans, forming the right wing, took station on the east side of the creek; the French, forming the left wing, on the west.

That evening Cornwallis received despatches from Sir Henry Clinton informing him of the arrival of Admiral Digby and that a fleet of twenty-three ships of the line, with about five thousand troops, would sail to his assistance probably on the 5th of October. A heavy firing would be made by them on arriving at the entrance of the Chesapeake. On hearing it, if all went on well at Yorktown, his lordship was to make three separate columns of smoke, and four should he still possess the post at Gloucester Point.

Cornwallis immediately wrote in reply: "I have ventured these last two days to look General Washington's whole force in the face in the position on the outside of my works, and have the pleasure to assure your Excellency that there is but one wish throughout the army, which is that the enemy would advance. . . . I shall retire this night within the works, and have no doubt, if relief arrives in any reasonable time, York and Gloucester will be both in the possession of His Majesty's troops. I believe your Excellency must depend more on the sound of our cannon than the signal of smokes for information. However, I will attempt it on the Gloucester side."[2]

That night his lordship accordingly abandoned his outworks and drew his troops within the town, a measure strongly censured by Tarleton in his Commentaries as premature, as cooping up the troops in narrow quarters and giving up a means of disputing inch by inch the approaches of the besiegers and thus gaining time to complete the fortifications of the town.

[2] *Correspondence relative to Defense of York*, p. 199.

The outworks thus abandoned were seized upon the next morning by detachments of American light infantry and French troops, and served to cover the troops employed in throwing up breastworks. Colonel Alexander Scammel, officer of the day, while reconnoitering the ground abandoned by the enemy, was set upon by a party of Hessian troopers. He attempted to escape but was wounded, captured and carried off to Yorktown. Washington, to whom he had formerly acted as aide-de-camp, interested himself in his favor, and at his request Cornwallis permitted him to be removed to Williamsburg, where he died in the course of a few days. He was an officer of much merit and his death was deeply regretted by Washington and the army.

The combined French and American forces were now twelve thousand strong exclusive of the Virginia militia which Governor Nelson had brought into the field. An instance of patriotic self-devotion on the part of this functionary is worthy of special record. The treasury of Virginia was empty. The governor, fearful that the militia would disband for want of pay, had endeavored to procure a loan from a wealthy individual on the credit of the State. In the precarious situation of affairs the guarantee was not deemed sufficient. The governor pledged his own property and obtained the loan at his individual risk.

On the morning of the 28th of September, the combined armies marched from Williamsburg toward Yorktown, about twelve miles distant, and encamped at night within two miles of it, driving in the pickets and some patrols of cavalry. General de Choisy was sent across York River with Lauzun's legion and General Weedon's brigade of militia to watch the enemy on the side of Gloucester Point.

By the 1st of October the line of the besiegers, nearly two miles from the works, formed a semicircle, each end resting on the river, so that the investment by land was complete; while the Count de Grasse, with the main fleet, remained in Lynn Haven Bay to keep off assistance by sea.

About this time the Americans threw up two redoubts in the night, which, on being discovered in the morning, were severely cannonaded. Three of the men were killed and several severely wounded. While Washington was superintending the works, a shot struck the ground close by him, throwing up a cloud of dust. The Rev. Mr. Evans, chaplain in the army, who was standing by him, was greatly agitated. Taking off his hat and showing it covered with sand, "See here, General," exclaimed he. "Mr. Evans," said Washington with grave pleasantry, "you had better carry that home and show it to your wife and children."[3]

The besieged army began now to be greatly distressed for want of forage, and had to kill many of their horses, the carcasses of which were continually floating down the river. In the evening of the 2d of October, Tarleton with his legion and the mounted infantry were passed over the river to Gloucester Point to assist in foraging. At daybreak Lieutenant-Colonel Dundas led out part of his garrison to forage the neighboring country. About ten o'clock the wagons and bat horses laden with Indian corn were returning, covered by a party of infantry, with Tarleton and his dragoons as a rear-guard. The wagons and infantry had nearly reached York River when word was brought that the enemy was advancing in force. The report was confirmed by a cloud of dust, from which emerged Lauzun and the French hussars and lancers.

Tarleton, with part of his legion, advanced to meet them. The rest, with Simcoe's dragoons, remained as a rear-guard in a skirt of woods. A skirmish ensued, gallantly sustained on each side, but the superiority of Tarleton's horses gave him the advantage. General Choisy hastened up with a corps of cavalry and infantry to support the hussars. In the medley fight, a dragoon's horse, wounded by a lance, plunged, and overthrew both Tarleton and his steed. The rear-guard rushed from their covert to rescue their commander. They came galloping up in such disorder that they were roughly received by Lauzun's hussars, who were drawn up on the plain. In the meantime Tarleton scrambled out of the mêlée, mounted another horse and ordered a retreat to enable his men to recover from their confusion. Dismounting forty infantry, he placed them in a thicket. Their fire checked the hussars in their pursuit. The British dragoons rallied and were about to charge, when the hussars retired behind their infantry, and a fire was opened upon the British by some militia from behind a fence. Tarleton again ordered a retreat to be sounded, and the conflict came to an end. The loss of the British in killed and wounded was one officer and eleven men, that of the French two officers and fourteen hussars. This was the last affair of Tarleton and his legion in the Revolutionary War.

[3] Thacher's *Military Journal*, p. 336.

The next day General Choisy, being reinforced by a detachment of marines from the fleet of De Grasse, cut off all communication by land between Gloucester and the country.

General Lincoln had the honor, on the night of the 6th of October 1781, of opening the first parallel before Yorktown. It was within six hundred yards of the enemy, nearly two miles in extent, and the foundations were laid for two redoubts. He had under him a large detachment of French and American troops, and the work was conducted with such silence and secrecy in a night of extreme darkness that the enemy were not aware of it until daylight. A severe cannonade was then opened from the fortifications, but the men were under cover and continued working—the greatest emulation and good-will prevailing between the officers and soldiers of the allied armies thus engaged.

By the afternoon of the 9th the parallel was completed and two or three batteries were ready to fire upon the town.

"General Washington put the match to the first gun," says an observer who was present. "A furious discharge of cannon and mortars immediately followed and Earl Cornwallis received his first salutation."[4]

Governor Nelson, who had so nobly pledged his own property to raise funds for the public service, gave another proof of his self-sacrificing patriotism on this occasion. He was asked which part of the town could be most effectively cannonaded. He pointed to a large handsome house on a rising ground as the probable headquarters of the enemy. It proved to be his own.[5]

The governor had an uncle in the town, very old, and afflicted with the gout. He had been for thirty years secretary under the royal colonial government and was still called Mr. Secretary Nelson. He had taken no part in the Revolution, unfitted perhaps for the struggle by his advanced age and his infirmities, and had remained in Yorktown when taken possession of by the English, not having any personal enmity to apprehend from them. He had two sons in Washington's army, who now were in the utmost alarm for his safety. At their request Washington sent in a flag, desiring that their father might be permitted to leave the place. "I was a witness," writes the Count de Chastellux in his memoirs, "of the cruel anxiety of one of those young men as he kept his eyes

---

[4] Thacher's *Military Journal.*
[5] Given on the authority of Lafayette. Sparks, viii., 201.

fixed upon the gate of the town by which the flag would come out. It seemed as if he were awaiting his own sentence in the reply that was to be received. Lord Cornwallis had not the inhumanity to refuse so just a request."

The appearance of the venerable secretary, his stately person, noble countenance and gray hairs, commanded respect and veneration. "I can never recall without emotion," writes the susceptible count, "his arrival at the headquarters of General Washington. He was seated, his attack of the gout still continuing, and while we stood around him he related with a serene visage what had been the effect of our batteries."[6]

His house had received some of the first shots. One of his negroes had been killed, and the headquarters of Lord Cornwallis had been so battered that he had been driven out of them.

The cannonade was kept up almost incessantly for three or four days from the batteries above mentioned and from three others managed by the French. "Being in the trenches every other night and day," writes an observer already quoted,[7] "I have a fine opportunity of witnessing the sublime and stupendous scene which is continually exhibiting. The bombshells from the besiegers and the besieged are incessantly crossing each other's path in the air. They are clearly visible in the form of a black ball in the day, but in the night they appear like a fiery meteor with a blazing tail, most beautifully brilliant, ascending majestically from the mortar to a certain altitude, and gradually descending to the spot where they are destined to execute their work of destruction. When a shell falls, it whirls round, burrows and excavates the earth to a considerable extent and, bursting, makes dreadful havoc around. . . . Some of our shells, over-reaching the town, are seen to fall into the river and, bursting, throw up columns of water like the spouting monsters of the deep."

The half-finished works of the enemy suffered severely, the guns were dismounted or silenced and many men killed. The red-hot shot from the French batteries northwest of the town reached the English shipping. The *Charon*, a forty-four gunship, and three large transports, were set on fire by them. The flames ran up the rigging to the tops of the masts. The conflagration, seen in the darkness of the night with the accompanying flash and thundering

[6] Chastellux, vol. ii., pp. 19–83.
[7] Thacher.

of cannon and soaring and bursting of shells, and the tremendous explosions of the ships, all presented a scene of mingled magnificence and horror.

On the night of the 11th the second parallel was opened by the Baron Steuben's division within three hundred yards of the works. The British now made new embrasures, and for two or three days kept up a galling fire upon those at work. The latter were still more annoyed by the flanking fire of two redoubts three hundred yards in front of the British works. As they enfiladed the entrenchments and were supposed also to command the communication between Yorktown and Gloucester, it was resolved to storm them both on the night of the 14th, the one nearest the river by a detachment of Americans commanded by Lafayette, the other by a French detachment led by the Baron de Viomenil.

In the arrangement for the American assault, Lafayette had given the honor of leading the advance to his own aide-de-camp, Lieutenant-Colonel Gimat. This instantly touched the military pride of Hamilton, who exclaimed against it as an unjust preference, it being his tour of duty. The marquis excused himself by alleging the arrangement had been sanctioned by the commander-in-chief and could not be changed by him. Hamilton forthwith made a spirited appeal by letter to Washington. The latter, who was ignorant of the circumstances of the case, sent for the marquis, and finding that it really was Hamilton's tour of duty, directed that he should be reinstated in it, which was done.[8] It was therefore arranged that Colonel Gimat's battalion should lead the van and be followed by that of Hamilton and that the latter should command the whole advanced corps.[9]

About eight o'clock in the evening rockets were sent up as signals for the simultaneous attack. Hamilton, to his great joy, led the advance of the Americans. The men, without waiting for the sappers to demolish the abatis in regular style, pushed them aside or pulled them down with their hands and scrambled over like rough bush-fighters. Hamilton was the first to mount the parapet, placing one foot on the shoulder of a soldier, who knelt on one knee for the purpose.[10] The men mounted after him. Not a musket was fired. The redoubt was carried at the point of the bay-

---

[8] Lee's *Memoirs of the War*, ii., 342.
[9] Lafayette to Washington. *Correspondence of the Rev.*, iii., 426.
[10] Leake's *Life of John Lamb*, p. 259.

onet. The loss of the Americans was one sergeant and eight privates killed, seven officers and twenty-five non-commissioned officers and privates wounded. The loss of the enemy was eight killed and seventeen taken prisoners. Among the latter was Major Campbell, who had commanded the redoubt. A New Hampshire captain of artillery would have taken his life in revenge of the death of his favorite Colonel Scammel, but Colonel Hamilton prevented him. Not a man was killed after he ceased to resist.[11]

The French stormed the other redoubt, which was more strongly garrisoned, with equal gallantry but less precipitation. They proceeded according to rule. The soldiers paused while the sappers removed the abatis, during which time they were exposed to a destructive fire and lost more men than did the Americans in their headlong attack. The abatis being removed, the troops rushed to the assault. The Chevalier de Lameth, Lafayette's adjutant-general, was the first to mount the parapet of the redoubt, and received a volley at arms' length from the Hessians who manned it. Shot through both knees, he fell back into the ditch and was conveyed away under care of his friend, the Count de Dumas. The Count de Deuxponts, leading on the royal grenadiers of the same name, was likewise wounded.

Washington was an intensely excited spectator of these assaults, on the result of which so much depended. He had dismounted, given his horse to a servant and taken his stand in the grand battery with Generals Knox and Lincoln and their staffs. The risk he ran of a chance shot while watching the attack through an embrasure made those about him uneasy. One of his aides-de-camp ventured to observe that the situation was very much exposed. "If you think so," replied he gravely, "you are at liberty to step back."

Shortly afterwards a musket ball struck the cannon in the embrasure, rolled along it, and fell at his feet. General Knox grasped his arm. "My dear general," exclaimed he, "we can't spare you yet." "It is a spent ball," replied Washington quietly. "No harm is done."

When all was over and the redoubts were taken, he drew a long breath and, turning to Knox, observed, "The work is done, *and well done!*" Then called to his servant, "William, bring me my horse."

[11] Thacher, p. 341.

In his despatches he declared that in these assaults nothing could exceed the firmness and bravery of the troops. Lafayette also testified to the conduct of Colonel Hamilton, "whose well-known talents and gallantry," writes he, "were on this occasion most conspicuous and serviceable."[12]

The redoubts thus taken were included the same night in the second parallel, and howitzers were mounted upon them the following day. The capture of them reduced Lord Cornwallis almost to despair. Writing that same day to Sir Henry Clinton, he observes: "My situation now becomes very critical. We dare not show a gun to their old batteries, and I expect that their new ones will open to-morrow morning. . . . The safety of the place is therefore so precarious that I cannot recommend that the fleet and army should run great risk in endeavoring to save us"—a generous abnegation of self on the part of the beleaguered commander. Had the fleet and army sailed, as he had been given to expect, about the 5th of October, they might have arrived in time to save his lordship, but at the date of the above letter they were still lingering in port. Delay of naval succor was fatal to British operations in this war.

The second parallel was now nearly ready to open. Cornwallis dreaded the effect of its batteries on his almost dismantled works. To retard the danger as much as possible, he ordered an attack on two of the batteries that were in the greatest state of forwardness, their guns to be spiked. It was made a little before daybreak of the 16th by about three hundred and fifty men under the direction of Lieutenant-Colonel Abercrombie. He divided his forces. A detachment of guards and a company of grenadiers attacked one battery, and a corps of light infantry the other.

The redoubts which covered the batteries were forced in gallant style and several pieces of artillery spiked. By this time the supporting troops from the trenches came up, and the enemy were obliged to retreat, leaving behind them seven or eight dead and six prisoners. The French, who had guard of this part of the trenches, had four officers and twelve privates killed or wounded, and the Americans lost one sergeant. The mischief had been done too hastily. The spikes were easily extracted, and before evening all the batteries and the parallel were nearly complete.

At this time the garrison could not show a gun on the side of

[12] Lafayette to Washington. *Cor. of the Rev.*, iii., 426.

the works exposed to attack, and the shells were nearly expended. The place was no longer tenable. Rather than surrender, Cornwallis determined to attempt an escape. His plan was to leave his sick and wounded and his baggage behind, cross over in the night to Gloucester Point, attack Choisy's camp before daybreak, mount his infantry on the captured cavalry horses and on such other as could be collected on the road, push for the upper country by rapid marches until opposite the fords of the great rivers, then turn suddenly northward, force his way through Maryland, Pennsylvania and the Jerseys, and join Sir Henry Clinton in New York.

It was a wild and daring scheme but his situation was desperate and the idea of surrender intolerable.

In pursuance of this design, sixteen large boats were secretly prepared. A detachment was appointed to remain and capitulate for the town's people, the sick and the wounded. A large part of the troops were transported to the Gloucester side of the river before midnight. And the second division had actually embarked, when a violent storm of wind and rain scattered the boats and drove them a considerable distance down the river. They were collected with difficulty. It was now too late to effect the passage of the second division before daybreak, and an effort was made to get back the division which had already crossed. It was not done until the morning was far advanced, and the troops in recrossing were exposed to the fire of the American batteries.

The hopes of Lord Cornwallis were now at an end. His works were tumbling in ruins about him under an incessant cannonade. His garrison was reduced in number by sickness and death, and exhausted by constant watching and severe duty. Unwilling to expose the residue of the brave troops, which had stood by him so faithfully, to the dangers and horrors of an assault which could not fail to be successful, he ordered a parley to be beaten about ten o'clock on the morning of the 17th and despatched a flag with a letter to Washington proposing a cessation of hostilities for twenty-four hours, and that two officers might be appointed by each side to meet and settle terms for the surrender of the posts of Yorktown and Gloucester.

Washington felt unwilling to grant such delay when reinforcements might be on the way for Cornwallis from New York. In reply therefore he requested that, previous to the meeting of commissioners, his lordship's proposals might be sent in writing to the American lines, for which purpose a suspension of hostilities during two hours from the delivery of the letter would be granted. This was complied with, but as the proposals offered by Cornwallis were not all admissible, Washington drew up a schedule of such terms as he would grant and transmitted it to his lordship.

The armistice was prolonged. Commissioners met, the Viscount de Noailles and Lieutenant-Colonel Laurens on the part of the allies, Colonel Dundas and Major Ross on the part of the British. After much discussion a rough draft was made of the terms of capitulation to be submitted to the British general. These Washington caused to be promptly transcribed and sent to Lord Cornwallis early in the morning of the 19th, with a note expressing his expectation that they would be signed by eleven o'clock, and that the garrison would be ready to march out by two o'clock in the afternoon. Lord Cornwallis was fain to comply and, accordingly, on the same day, the posts of Yorktown and Gloucester were surrendered to General Washington as commander-in-chief of the combined army, and the ships of war, transports and other vessels to the Count de Grasse as commander of the French fleet. The garrison of Yorktown and Gloucester, including the officers of the navy and seamen of every denomination, were to surrender as prisoners of war to the combined army, the land force to remain prisoners to the United States, the seamen to the King of France.

The garrison was to be allowed the same honors granted to the garrison of Charleston when it surrendered to Sir Henry Clinton. The officers were to retain their side arms, both officers and soldiers their private property, and no part of their baggage or papers was to be subject to search or inspection. The soldiers were to be kept in Virginia, Maryland or Pennsylvania, as much by regiments as possible and supplied with the same rations of provisions as the American soldiers. The officers were to be permitted to proceed upon parole to Europe or to any maritime port on the continent of America in possession of British troops. The *Bonetta* sloop-of-war was to be at the disposal of Lord Cornwallis to convey an aide-de-camp with despatches to Sir Henry Clinton with such soldiers as he might think proper to send to New York, and was to sail without examination.

It was arranged in the allied camp that General Lincoln should receive the submission of the royal army, precisely in the manner in which the submission of his own army had been received on the surrender of Charleston. An eye-witness has given us a graphic description of the ceremony.[18]

"At about twelve o'clock the combined army was drawn up in two lines more than a mile in length, the Americans on the right side of the road, the French on their left. Washington, mounted on a noble steed and attended by his staff, was in front of the former, the Count de Rochambeau and his suite, of the latter. The French troops, in complete uniform and well equipped, made a brilliant appearance, and had marched to the ground with a band of music playing, which was a novelty in the American service. The American troops, but part in uniform, and all in garments much the worse for wear, yet had a spirited, soldier-like air and were not the worse in the eyes of their countrymen for bearing the marks of hard service and great privations. The concourse of spectators from the country seemed equal in number to the military, yet silence and order prevailed.

"About two o'clock the garrison sallied forth and passed through with shouldered arms, slow and solemn steps, colors cased and drums beating a British march. They were all well clad, having been furnished with new suits prior to the capitulation. They were led by General O'Hara on horseback, who, on riding up to General Washington, took off his hat and apologized for the nonappearance of Lord Cornwallis on account of indisposition. Washington received him with dignified courtesy but pointed to Major-General Lincoln as the officer who was to receive the submission of the garrison. By him they were conducted into a field where they were to ground their arms. In passing through the line formed by the allied army, their march was careless and irregular and their aspect sullen, the order to 'ground arms' was given by their platoon officer with a tone of deep chagrin, and many of the soldiers threw down their muskets with a violence sufficient to break them. This irregularity was checked by General Lincoln, yet it was excusable in brave men in their unfortunate predicament. This ceremony over, they were conducted back to Yorktown to

[18] The number of prisoners made by the above capitulation amounted to 7,073, of whom 5,950 were rank and file. Six commissioned and twenty-eight non-commissioned officers and privates had previously been captured in the two redoubts or in the sortie of the garrison. The loss sustained by the garrison during the siege, in killed, wounded and missing, amounted to 552. That of the combined army in killed was about 300. The combined army to which Cornwallis surrendered was estimated at 16,000, of whom 7,000 were French, 5,500 Continentals and 3,500 militia.—*Holmes's Annals*, vol. ii., p. 333.

remain under guard until removed to their places of destination."[14]

On the following morning Washington in general orders congratulated the allied armies on the recent victory, awarding high praise to the officers and troops, both French and American, for their conduct during the siege, and specifying by name several of the generals and other officers who had especially distinguished themselves. All those of his army who were under arrest were pardoned and set at liberty. "Divine service," it was added, "is to be performed to-morrow in the several brigades and divisions. The commander-in-chief earnestly recommends that the troops not on duty should universally attend, with that seriousness of deportment and gratitude of heart which the recognition of such reiterated and astonishing interpositions of Providence demand of us."

Cornwallis felt deeply the humiliation of this close to all his wide and wild campaigning, and was made more sensitive on the subject by circumstances of which he soon became apprised. On the very day that he had been compelled to lay down his arms before Yorktown, the lingering armament intended for his relief sailed from New York. It consisted of twenty-five ships of the line, two fifty-gun ships and eight frigates, with Sir Henry Clinton and seven thousand of his best troops. Sir Henry arrived off the Capes of Virginia on the 24th and gathered information which led him to apprehend that Lord Cornwallis had capitulated. He hovered off the mouth of the Chesapeake until the 29th, when, having fully ascertained that he had come too late, he turned his tardy prows toward New York.

Cornwallis, in a letter written subsequently, renders the following testimony to the conduct of his captors: "The treatment in general that we have received from the enemy since our surrender has been perfectly good and proper, but the kindness and attention that has been shown to us by the French officers in particular, their delicate sensibility of our situation, their generous and pressing offer of money, both public and private, to any amount, has really gone beyond what I can possibly describe, and will, I hope, make an impression in the breast of every officer whenever the fortune of war shall put any of them into our power."

In the meantime the rejoicings which Washington had com-

14 Thacher, p. 346.

menced with appropriate solemnities in the victorious camp had spread throughout the Union. "Cornwallis is taken!" was the universal acclaim. It was considered a death-blow to the war.

Congress gave way to transports of joy. Thanks were voted to the commander-in-chief, to the Counts de Rochambeau and De Grasse, to the officers of the allied armies generally and to the corps of artillery and engineers especially. Two stands of colors, trophies of the capitulation, were voted to Washington, two pieces of field ordnance to De Rochambeau and De Grasse, and it was decreed that a marble column, commemorative of the alliance between France and the United States and of the victory achieved by their associated arms, should be erected in Yorktown. Finally, Congress issued a proclamation appointing a day for general thanksgiving and prayer in acknowledgment of this signal interposition of Divine Providence.

Far different was the feeling of the British ministry when news of the event reached the other side of the Atlantic. Lord George Germaine was the first to announce it to Lord North at his office in Downing Street. "And how did he take it?" was the inquiry. "As he would have taken a ball in the breast," replied Lord George, "for he opened his arms, exclaiming wildly as he paced up and down the apartment, 'O God! It is all over!' "[15]

15 Wraxall's *Historical Memoirs*, vol. ii., p. 99.

Chapter 47

DISCONTENT IN THE ARMY

Washington would have followed up the reduction of Yorktown by a combined operation against Charleston, and addressed a letter to the Count de Grasse on the subject, but the count alleged in reply that the orders of his court, ulterior projects and his engagements with the Spaniards rendered it impossible to remain the necessary time for the operation.

The prosecution of the Southern war, therefore, upon the broad scale which Washington had contemplated had to be relinquished, for without shipping and a convoy the troops and everything necessary for a siege would have to be transported by land with immense trouble, expense and delay, while the enemy by means of their fleets could reinforce or withdraw the garrison at pleasure.

Under these circumstances Washington had to content himself for the present with detaching two thousand Pennsylvania, Maryland and Virginia continental troops under General St. Clair for the support of General Greene, trusting that with this aid he would be able to command the interior of South Carolina and confine the enemy to the town of Charleston.

A dissolution of the combined forces now took place. The Marquis St. Simon embarked his troops on the last of October, and the Count de Grasse made sail on the 4th of November, taking with him two beautiful horses which Washington had presented to him in token of cordial regard.

Lafayette, seeing there was no probability of further active service in the present year, resolved to return to France on a visit to his family, and, with Washington's approbation, set out for Philadelphia to obtain leave of absence from Congress.

The British prisoners were marched to Winchester in Virginia and Fredrickstown in Maryland, and Lord Cornwallis and his principal officers sailed for New York on parole.

The main part of the American army embarked for the Head of Elk and returned northward under the command of General Lincoln, to be cantoned for the winter in the Jerseys and on the Hudson, so as to be ready for operations against New York or elsewhere in the next year's campaign.

The French army were to remain for the winter in Virginia, and the Count de Rochambeau established his headquarters at Williamsburg.

Having attended in person to the distribution of ordnance and stores, the departure of prisoners and the embarkation of the troops under Lincoln, Washington left Yorktown on the 5th of November and arrived the same day at Eltham, the seat of his friend Colonel Bassett. He arrived just in time to receive the last breath of John Parke Custis, the son of Mrs. Washington, as he had, several years previously, rendered tender and pious offices at the death-bed of his sister, Miss Custis. The deceased had been an object of Washington's care from childhood and been cherished by him with paternal affection. Formed under his guidance and instructions, he had been fitted to take a part in the public concerns of his country and had acquitted himself with credit as a member of the Virginia Legislature. He was but twenty-eight years old at the time of his death and left a widow and four young children. It was an unexpected event, and the dying scene was rendered peculiarly affecting from the presence of the mother and wife of the deceased. Washington remained several days at Eltham to comfort them in their afflictions. As a consolation to Mrs. Washington in her bereavement, he adopted the two youngest children of the deceased, a boy and girl, who thenceforth formed a part of his immediate family.

From Eltham, Washington proceeded to Mount Vernon, but public cares gave him little leisure to attend to his private concerns. We have seen how repeatedly his steady mind had been exercised, in the darkest times of the revolutionary struggle, in buoying up the public heart when sinking into despondency. He had now an opposite task to perform, to guard against an overweening confidence inspired by the recent triumph.

In a letter to General Greene he writes: "I shall remain but a few days here and shall proceed to Philadelphia, when I shall attempt to stimulate Congress to the best improvement of our late success by taking the most vigorous and effectual measures to be ready for an early and decisive campaign the next year. My greatest fear is that Congress, viewing this stroke in too important a point of light, may think our work too nearly closed and will fall into a state of languor and relaxation. To prevent this error, I shall employ every means in my power and if unhappily we sink into that fatal mistake, no part of the blame shall be mine."

Towards the end of November, Washington was in Philadelphia, where Congress received him with distinguished honors. His views were met by the military committee of Congress, with which he was in frequent consultation, and by the secretaries of war, finance and public affairs, who attended their conferences. Under his impulse and personal supervision, the military arrangements for 1782 were made with unusual despatch. On the 10th of December resolutions were passed in Congress for requisitions of men and money from the several States, and Washington backed those requisitions by letters to the respective governors, urging prompt compliance. Strenuous exertions too were made by Dr. Franklin, then minister in France, to secure a continuance of efficient aid from that power. And a loan of six millions had been promised by the king after hearing of the capitulation of Yorktown.

The persuasion that peace was at hand was, however, too prevalent for the public to be roused to new sacrifices and toils to maintain what was considered the mere shadow of a war. The States were slow in furnishing a small part of their respective quotas of troops and still slower in answering to the requisitions for money.

After remaining four months in Philadelphia, Washington set out in March [1782] to rejoin the army at Newburgh on the Hudson. The solicitude felt by him on account of the universal relaxation of the sinews of war was not allayed by reports of pacific speeches, and motions made in the British Parliament, which might be delusive.

"Even if the nation and parliament," said he, "are really in earnest to obtain peace with America, it will undoubtedly be wisdom in us to meet them with great caution and circumspection, and by all means to keep our arms firm in our hands, and instead of relaxing one iota in our exertions, rather to spring forward with redoubled vigor that we may take the advantage of every favorable opportunity until our wishes are fully obtained. No nation ever yet suffered in treaty by preparing, even in the moment of negotiation, most vigorously for the field."

Sir Guy Carleton arrived in New York early in May to take the place of Sir Henry Clinton, who had solicited his recall. In a letter dated May 7th, Sir Guy informed Washington of his being joined with Admiral Digby in the commission of peace. He transmitted at the same time printed copies of the proceedings in the House of Commons on the 4th of March respecting an address to the king in favor of peace, and of a bill reported in consequence thereof, authorizing the king to conclude a peace or truce with the revolted provinces of North America. As this bill, however, had not passed into a law when Sir Guy left England, it presented no basis for a negotiation, and was only cited by him to show the pacific disposition of the British nation, with which he professed the most zealous concurrence. Still, though multiplied circumstances gradually persuaded Washington of a real disposition on the part of Great Britain to terminate the war, he did not think fit to relax his preparations for hostilities.

Great discontents prevailed at this time in the army, both among officers and men. The neglect of the States to furnish their proportions of the sum voted by Congress for the prosecution of the war had left the army almost destitute. There was scarce money sufficient to feed the troops from day to day. Indeed there were days when they were absolutely in want of provisions. The pay of the officers, too, was greatly in arrear. Many of them doubted whether they would ever receive the half pay decreed to them by Congress for a term of years after the conclusion of the war, and fears began to be expressed that in the event of peace they would all be disbanded with their claims unliquidated, and themselves cast upon the community penniless, and unfitted, by long military habitudes, for the gainful pursuits of peace.

At this juncture Washington received an extraordinary letter from Colonel Lewis Nicola, a veteran officer, once commandant of Fort Mifflin, who had been in habits of intimacy with him and had warmly interceded in behalf of the suffering army. In this letter he attributed all the ills experienced and anticipated by the army and the public at large to the existing form of government. He condemned a republican form as incompatible with national prosperity and advised a mixed government like that of England, which he had no doubt, on its benefits being properly pointed out, would be readily adopted.

"In that case," he adds, "it will, I believe, be uncontroverted that the same abilities which have led us through difficulties, apparently insurmountable by human power, to victory and glory, those qualities that have merited and obtained the universal esteem and veneration of an army would be most likely to conduct and direct us in the smoother paths of peace. Some people have so connected the idea of tyranny and monarchy as to find it very difficult to separate them. It may therefore be requisite to give the head of such a constitution as I propose some title apparently more moderate; but, if all other things were once adjusted, I believe strong arguments might be produced for admitting the title of King, which, I conceive, would be attended with some material advantages."

Washington saw at once that Nicola was but the organ of a military faction disposed to make the army the basis of an energetic government and to place him at the head. The suggestion, backed by the opportunity, might have tempted a man of meaner ambition. From him it drew the following indignant letter:

"With a mixture of great surprise and astonishment I have read with attention the sentiments you have submitted to my perusal. Be assured, sir, no occurrence in the course of the war has given me more painful sensations than your information of there being such ideas existing in the army as you have expressed, and I must view with abhorrence and reprehend with severity. For the present, the communication of them will rest in my own bosom unless some further agitation of the matter shall make a disclosure necessary.

"I am much at a loss to conceive what part of my conduct could have given encouragement to an address which to me seems big with the greatest mischiefs that can befall my country. If I am not deceived in the knowledge of myself, you could not have found a person to whom your schemes are more disagreeable. At the same time, in justice to my own feelings, I must add that no man possesses a more sincere wish to see ample justice done to the army than I do. And as far as my powers and influence, in a constitutional way, extend, they shall be employed to the utmost of my abilities to effect it, should there be any occasion. Let me conjure you, then, if you have any regard for your country, concern for yourself or posterity, or respect for me, to banish these thoughts from your mind and never communicate, as from yourself or any one else, a sentiment of the like nature."

On the 2d of August, Sir Guy Carleton and Admiral Digby wrote a joint letter to Washington, informing him that they were acquainted, by authority, that negotiations for a general peace had already been commenced at Paris and that the independence of the United States would be proposed in the first instance by the British commissioner, instead of being made a condition of a general treaty.

Even yet, Washington was wary. "From the former infatuation, duplicity and perverse system of British policy," said he, "I confess I am induced to doubt everything, to suspect everything. . . . Whatever the real intention of the enemy may be, I think the strictest attention and exertion, which have ever been exercised on our part, instead of being diminished ought to be increased. Jealousy and precaution at least can do no harm. Too much confidence and supineness may be pernicious in the extreme."

What gave force to this policy was, that as yet no offers had been made on the part of Great Britain for a general cessation of hostilities, and, although the British commanders were in a manner tied down by the resolves of the House of Commons to a defensive war only, in the United States, they might be at liberty to transport part of their force to the West Indies to act against the French possessions in that quarter. With these considerations he wrote to the Count de Rochambeau, then at Baltimore, advising him, for the good of the common cause, to march his troops to the banks of the Hudson and form a junction with the American army.

The junction took place about the middle of September. The French army crossed the Hudson at King's Ferry to Verplanck's Point, where the American forces were paraded under arms to welcome them. The clothing and arms recently received from France or captured at Yorktown enabled them to make an unusually respectable appearance. Two lines were formed from the landing-place to headquarters, between which Count Rochambeau passed, escorted by a troop of cavalry, after which he took his station beside General Washington. The music struck up a French march, and the whole army passed in review before them.

The French army encamped on the left of the American, near Crompond, about ten miles from Verplanck's Point. The greatest good-will continued to prevail between the allied forces, though the Americans had but little means of showing hospitality to their gay Gallic friends. "Only conceive the mortification they must suffer, even the general officers," says Washington in a letter to the secretary of war, "when they cannot invite a French officer, a visiting friend or a travelling acquaintance to a better repast than whiskey hot from the still, and not always that, and a bit of beef without vegetables will afford them."

Speaking of a contemplated reduction of the army to take place on the 1st of January:

"While I premise that no one I have seen or heard of appears opposed to the principle of reducing the army as circumstances may require, yet I cannot help fearing the result of the measure in contemplation under present circumstances when I see such a number of men, goaded by a thousand stings of reflection on the past and of anticipation on the future, about to be turned into the world, soured by penury and what they call ingratitude of the public, involved in debts, without one farthing of money to carry them home after having spent the flower of their days, and many of them their patrimonies, in establishing the freedom and independence of their country, and suffered everything that human nature is capable of enduring on this side of death—I repeat it, that when I consider these irritating circumstances, without one thing to soothe their feelings or dispel the gloomy prospects, I cannot avoid apprehending that a train of evils will follow of a very serious and distressing nature. . . .

"I wish not to heighten the shades of the picture so far as the reality would justify me in doing it. I could give anecdotes of patriotism and distress which have scarcely ever been paralleled, never surpassed, in the history of mankind. But you may rely upon it, the patience and long-suffering of this army are almost exhausted, and that there was never so great a spirit of discontent as at this instant. While in the field, I think it may be kept from breaking out into acts of outrage, but when we retire into winter quarters, unless the storm is previously dissipated I cannot be at ease respecting the consequences. It is high time for a peace."

The anxious fears of Washington in regard to what might take place on the approaching reduction of the army were in some degree realized. After the meeting with the French army at Verplanck's Point, he had drawn up his forces to his former encampment at Newburgh, where he established his headquarters for the winter. In the leisure and idleness of a winter camp, the discontents of the army had time to ferment. The arrearages of pay became a topic of angry and constant comment, as well as the question whether the resolution of Congress granting half pay to officers who should serve to the end of the war would be carried into effect. Whence were the funds to arise for such half pay? The national treasury was empty. The States were slow to tax themselves. The resource of foreign loans was nearly exhausted. The articles of confederation required the concurrence of nine States to any act appropriating public money. There had never been nine States in favor of the half pay establishment. Was it probable that as many would concur in applying any scanty funds that might accrue, and which would be imperiously demanded for many other purposes, to the payment of claims known to be unpopular, and to the support of men who, the necessity for their services being at an end, might be regarded as drones in the community?

The result of these boding conferences was a memorial to Congress in December from the officers in camp on behalf of the army, representing the hardships of the case and proposing that a specific sum should be granted them for the money actually due and as a commutation for half pay. Three officers were deputed to present the memorial to Congress and watch over and promote its success.

The memorial gave rise to animated and long discussions in Congress. Some members were for admitting the claims as founded on engagements entered into by the nation. Others were for referring them to the respective States of the claimants. The winter passed away without any definite measures on the subject.

On the 10th of March 1783 an anonymous paper was circulated through the camp, calling a meeting at eleven o'clock the next day of the general and field officers, of an officer from each company and a delegate from the medical staff, to consider a letter just received from their representatives in Philadelphia, and what measures if any should be adopted to obtain that redress of grievances which they seemed to have solicited in vain.

On the following morning an anonymous address to the officers of the army was privately put into circulation. It professed to be from a fellow-soldier who had shared in their toils and mingled in their dangers and who till very lately had believed in the justice of his country.

"After a pursuit of seven long years," observed he, "the object for which we set out is at length brought within our reach. Yes, my friends, that suffering courage of yours was active once. It has conducted the United States of America through a doubtful and bloody war. It has placed her in the chair of independency, and peace returns to bless—whom? A country willing to redress your wrongs, cherish your worth and reward your services? A country courting your return to private life with tears of gratitude and smiles of admiration, longing to divide with you that independency which your gallantry has given and those riches which your wounds have preserved? Is this the case? Or is it rather a country that tramples upon your rights, disdains your cries and insults your distresses? Have you not more than once suggested your wishes and made known your wants to Congress—wants and wishes which gratitude and policy should have anticipated rather than evaded? And have you not lately, in the meek language of entreating memorials, begged from their justice what you could no longer expect from their favor? How have you been answered? Let the letter, which you are called to consider to-morrow, make reply!

"If this then be your treatment while the swords you wear are necessary for the defense of America, what have you to expect from peace when your voice shall sink and your strength dissipate by division; when those very swords, the instruments and companions of your glory, shall be taken from your sides and no remaining mark of military distinction left but your wants, infirmities and scars? Can you then consent to be the only sufferers by this Revolution and, retiring from the field, grow old in poverty, wretchedness and contempt? Can you consent to wade through the vile mire of dependency and owe the miserable remnant of that life to charity which has hitherto been spent in honor? If you can, go, and carry with you the jest of tories and the scorn of whigs; the ridicule and, what is worse, the pity of the world! Go, starve and be forgotten! But if your spirits should revolt at this; if you have sense enough to discover and spirit sufficient to oppose tyranny, under whatever garb it may assume, whether it be the plain coat of republicanism or the splendid robe of royalty; if you have yet learned to discriminate between a people and a cause, between men and principles; awake, attend to your situation and redress yourselves! If the present moment be lost, every future effort is in vain, and your threats then will be as empty as your entreaties now.

"I would advise you therefore to come to some final opinion upon what you can bear and what you will suffer. If your determination be in any proportion to your wrongs, carry your appeal from the justice to the fears of government. Change the milk-and-water style of your last memorial. Assume a bolder tone, decent but lively, spirited and determined, and suspect the man who would advise to more moderation and longer forbearance. Let two or three men who can feel as well as write be appointed to draw up your *last remonstrance*, for I would no longer give it the suing, soft, unsuccessful epithet of *memorial*. Let it represent in language that will neither dishonor you by its rudeness nor betray you by its fears what has been promised by Congress and what has been performed; how long and how patiently you have suffered; how little you have asked and how much of that little has been denied. Tell them that though you were the first, and would wish to be the last, to encounter danger, though despair itself can never drive you into dishonor, it may drive you from the field; that the wound, often irritated and never healed, may at length become incurable; and that the slightest mark of indignity from Congress now must operate like the grave and part you forever; that, in any political event, the army has its alternative. If peace, that nothing shall separate you from your arms but death; if war, that courting the auspices and inviting the direction of your illustrious leader you will retire to some unsettled country, smile in your turn and 'mock when their fear cometh on.' But let it represent also that should they comply with the request of your late memorial, it would make you more happy and them more respectable; that, while war should continue, you would follow their standard into the field; and when it came to an end, you would withdraw into the shade of private life and give the world another subject of wonder and applause—an army victorious over its enemies, victorious over itself."

This bold and eloquent but dangerous appeal, founded as it was upon the wrongs and sufferings of a gallant army and the shameful want of sympathy in tardy legislators, called for the full exercise of Washington's characteristic firmness, caution and discrimination.

In general orders he noticed the anonymous paper but expressed his confidence that the good sense of officers would prevent them from paying attention to such an irregular invitation, which he reprobated as disorderly. With a view to counteract its effects, he requested a like meeting of officers on the 15th instant to hear the report of the committee deputed to Congress. "After mature deliberation," added he, "they will devise what further measures ought to be adopted as most rational and best calculated to obtain the just and important object in view."

On the following day another anonymous address was circulated, written in a more moderate tone but to the same purport with the first and affecting to construe the general orders into an approbation of the object sought, only changing the day appointed for the meeting.

"Till now," it observes, "the commander-in-chief has regarded the steps you have taken for redress with good wishes alone. His ostensible silence has authorized your meetings and his private opinion sanctified your claims. Had he disliked the object in view, would not the same sense of duty which forbade you from meeting on the third day of the week have forbidden you from meeting on the seventh? Is not the same subject held up to your view? And has it not passed the seal of office and taken all the solemnity of an order? This will give system to your proceedings and stability to your resolves," etc., etc.

On Saturday the 15th of March the meeting took place. Washington had previously sent for the officers one by one in private, and enlarged on the loss of character to the whole army that would result from intemperate resolutions. At the meeting, General Gates was called to the chair. Washington rose and apologized for appearing there, which he had not intended to do when he issued the order directing the assemblage. The diligence, however, which had been used in circulating anonymous writings rendered it necessary he should give his sentiments to the army on the nature and tendency of them. He had taken this opportunity to do so and had committed his thoughts to writing, which, with the indulgence of his brother officers, he would take the liberty of reading to them.

He then proceeded to read a forcible and feeling address, pointing out the irregularity and impropriety of the recent anonymous summons and the dangerous nature of the anonymous address, a production, as he observed, addressed more to the feelings and passions than to the judgment; drawn with great art, calculated to inspire the mind with an idea of premeditated injustice in the sovereign power of the United States and to rouse all those resentments which must unavoidably flow from such a belief.

On these principles he had opposed the irregular and hasty meeting appointed in the anonymous summons, not from a disinclination to afford officers every opportunity, consistent with their own honor and the dignity of the army, to make known their grievances.

"If my conduct heretofore," said he, "has not evinced to you that I have been a faithful friend to the army, my declaration of it at this time would be equally unavailing and improper. But as I was among the first who embarked in the cause of our common country; as I have never left your side one moment but when called from you on public duty; as I have been the constant companion and witness of your distresses, and not among the last to feel and acknowledge your merits; as I have ever considered my own military reputation as inseparably connected with that of the army; as my heart has ever expanded with joy when I have heard its praises and my indignation has arisen when the mouth of detraction has been opened against it; it can scarcely be supposed at this last stage of the war that I am indifferent to its interests. . . .

"For myself," observes he in another part of his address, "a recollection of the cheerful assistance and prompt obedience I have experienced from you under every vicissitude of fortune, and the sincere affection I feel for an army I have so long had the honor to command, will oblige me to declare in this public and solemn manner, that for the attainment of complete justice for all your toils and dangers and the gratification of every wish, so far as may be done consistently with the great duty I owe my country and those powers we are bound to respect, you may fully command my services to the utmost extent of my abilities.

"While I give you these assurances and pledge myself in the most unequivocal manner to exert whatever abilities I am possessed of in your favor, let me entreat you, gentlemen, on your part not to take any measures which, viewed in the calm light of reason, will lessen the dignity and sully the glory you have hitherto maintained. Let me request you to rely on the plighted faith of your country and place a full confidence in the purity of the intentions of Congress; that, previous to your dissolution as an army, they will cause all your accounts to be fairly liquidated, as directed in the resolutions which were published to you two days ago; and that they will adopt the most effectual measures in their power to render ample justice to you for your faithful and meritorious services. And let me conjure you, in the name of our common country, as you value your own sacred honor, as you respect the rights of humanity and as you regard the military and national character of America, to express your utmost horror and detestation of the man who wishes, under any specious pretenses, to overturn the liberties of our country and who wickedly attempts to open the floodgates of civil discord and deluge our rising empire in blood. By thus determining and thus acting, you will pursue the plain and direct road to the attainment of your wishes. You will defeat the insidious designs of our enemies, who are compelled to resort from open force to secret artifice. You will give one more distinguished proof of unexampled patriotism and patient virtue rising superior to the pressure of the most complicated sufferings. And you will, by the dignity of your conduct, afford occasion for posterity to say, when speaking of the glorious example you have exhibited to mankind: 'Had this day been wanting, the world had never seen the last stage of perfection to which human nature is capable of attaining.' "

After he had concluded the address, he observed that as a corroborating testimony of the good disposition in Congress toward the army, he would communicate to them a letter received from a worthy member of that body, who on all occasions had approved himself their fast friend. He produced an able letter from the Hon. Joseph Jones, which, while it pointed out the difficulties and embarrassments of Congress, held up very forcibly the idea that the army would at all events be generously dealt with.

Major Shaw, who was present and from whose memoir we note this scene, relates that Washington, after reading the first paragraph of the letter, made a short pause, took out his spectacles and begged the indulgence of his audience while he put them on, observing at the same time that he had grown gray in their service and now found himself growing blind.

"There was something," adds Shaw, "so natural, so unaffected in this appeal, as rendered it superior to the most studied oratory. It forced its way to the heart, and you might see sensibility moisten every eye."

"Happy for America," continues Major Shaw, "that she has a patriot army, and equally so that Washington is its leader. I rejoice in the opportunity I have had of seeing this great man in a variety of situations—calm and intrepid when the battle raged, patient and persevering under the pressure of misfortune, moderate and possessing himself in the full career of victory. Great as these qualifications deservedly render him, he never appeared to me more truly so than at the assembly we have been speaking of. On other occasions he has been supported by the exertions of an army and the countenance of his friends, but on this he stood single and alone. There was no saying where the passions of an army which were not a little inflamed might lead, but it was generally allowed that further forbearance was dangerous and moderation had ceased to be a virtue. Under these circumstances he appeared not at the head of his troops but, as it were, in opposition to them, and for a dreadful moment the interests of the army and its general seemed to be in competition! He spoke—every doubt was dispelled and the tide of patriotism rolled again in its wonted course. Illustrious man! What he says of the army may with equal justice be applied to his own character: 'Had this day been wanting, the world had never seen the last stage of perfection to which human nature is capable of attaining.' "[1]

The moment Washington retired from the assemblage, a resolution was moved by the warm-hearted Knox, seconded by General Putnam and passed unanimously, assuring him that the officers reciprocated his affectionate expressions with the greatest sincerity of which the human heart is capable. Then followed resolutions declaring that no circumstances of distress or danger should induce a conduct calculated to sully the reputation and glory acquired at the price of their blood and eight years' faithful services; that they continued to have an unshaken confidence in the justice of Congress and their country; and that the commander-in-chief should be requested to write to the President of Congress, earnestly entreating a speedy decision on the late address forwarded by a committee of the army.

A letter was accordingly written by Washington, breathing that

[1] Quincy's *Memoir of Major Shaw*, p. 104.

generous yet well-tempered spirit with which he ever pleaded the cause of the army.

"The result of the proceedings of the grand convention of officers, which I have the honor of inclosing to your Excellency for the inspection of Congress, will, I flatter myself, be considered as the last glorious proof of patriotism which could have been given by men who aspired to the distinction of a patriot army, and will not only confirm their claim to the justice but will increase their title to the gratitude of their country.

"Having seen the proceedings on the part of the army terminate with perfect unanimity and in a manner entirely consonant to my wishes; being impressed with the liveliest sentiments of affection for those who have so long, so patiently and so cheerfully suffered and fought under my immediate direction; having, from motives of justice, duty and gratitude, spontaneously offered myself as an advocate for their rights; and having been requested to write to your Excellency, earnestly entreating the most speedy decision of Congress upon the subjects of the late address from the army to that honorable body; it only remains for me to perform the task I have assumed and to intercede on their behalf, as I now do, that the sovereign power will be pleased to verify the predictions I have pronounced and the confidence the army have reposed in the justice of their country."

After referring to further representations made by him to Congress on the subject of a half pay to be granted to officers for life, he adds: "If, besides the simple payment of their wages, a further compensation is not due to the sufferings and sacrifices of the officers, then have I been mistaken indeed. If the whole army had not merited whatever a grateful people can bestow, then I have been beguiled by prejudice and built opinion on the basis of error. If this country should not, in the event, perform everything which has been requested in the last memorial to Congress, then will my belief become vain, and the hope that has been excited, void of foundation. And if, as has been suggested for the purpose of inflaming their passions, the officers of the army are to be the only sufferers by the Revolution; if, retiring from the field, they are to grow old in poverty, wretchedness and contempt; if they are to wade through the vile mire of dependency and owe the miserable remnant of that life to charity which has hitherto been spent in honor; then shall I have learned what ingratitude is, then shall I have realized a tale which will embitter every moment of my future life. But I am under no such apprehensions. A country, rescued by their arms from impending ruin, will never leave unpaid the debt of gratitude."

This letter to the President was accompanied by other letters to members of Congress, all making similar direct and eloquent appeals. The subject was again taken up in Congress, nine States concurred in a resolution commuting the half pay into a sum equal to five years' whole pay, and the whole matter, at one moment so fraught with danger to the public, through the temperate wisdom of Washington was happily adjusted.

The anonymous addresses to the army, which were considered at the time so insidious and inflammatory and which certainly were ill-judged and dangerous, have since been avowed by General John Armstrong, a man who has sustained with great credit to himself various eminent posts under our government. At the time of writing them he was a young man, aide-de-camp to General Gates, and he did it at the request of a number of his fellow-officers, indignant at the neglect of their just claims by Congress and in the belief that the tardy movements of that body required the spur and the lash. Washington, in a letter dated 23d January 1797, says: "I have since had sufficient reason for believing that the object of the author was just, honorable and friendly to the country, though the means suggested by him were certainly liable to much misunderstanding and abuse."

Chapter 48

END OF HOSTILITIES

At length arrived the wished-for news of peace. A general treaty had been signed at Paris on the 20th of January. An armed vessel, the *Triumph*, belonging to the Count d'Estaing's squadron, arrived at Philadelphia from Cadiz on the 23d of March, bringing a letter from the Marquis de Lafayette to the President of Congress, communicating the intelligence. In a few days Sir Guy Carleton informed Washington by letter that he was ordered to proclaim a cessation of hostilities by sea and land.

A similar proclamation, issued by Congress, was received by Washington on the 17th of April. Being unaccompanied by any instructions respecting the discharge of the part of the army with him should the measure be deemed necessary, he found himself in a perplexing situation.

The accounts of peace received at different times had raised an expectation in the minds of those of his troops that had engaged "for the war" that a speedy discharge must be the consequence of the proclamation. Most of them could not distinguish between a proclamation of a cessation of hostilities and a definitive declaration of peace, and might consider any further claim on their military services an act of injustice. It was becoming difficult to enforce the discipline necessary to the coherence of an army. Washington represented these circumstances in a letter to the President and earnestly entreated a prompt determination on the part of Congress as to what was to be the period of the services of these men and how he was to act respecting their discharge.

One suggestion of his letter is expressive of his strong sympathy with the patriot soldier and his knowledge of what formed a matter of pride with the poor fellows who had served and suffered under him. He urged that, in discharging those who had been engaged "for the war," the non-commissioned officers and soldiers should be allowed to take with them, as their own property and as a gratuity, their arms and accoutrements.

"This act," observes he, "would raise pleasing sensations in the minds of these worthy and faithful men, who, from their early engaging in the war at moderate bounties, and from their patient continuance under innumerable distresses, have not only deserved nobly of this country but have obtained an honorable distinction over those who, with shorter terms, have gained large pecuniary rewards. This, at a comparatively small expense, would be deemed an honorable testimonial from Congress of the regard they bear to these distinguished worthies and the sense they have of their suffering virtues and services. . . .

"These constant companions of their toils, preserved with sacred attention, would be handed down from the present possessors to their children as honorary badges of bravery and military merit, and would probably be brought forth on some future occasion with pride and exultation, to be improved with the same military ardor and emulation in the hands of posterity as they have been used by their forefathers in the present establishment and foundation of our national independence and glory."

This letter despatched, he notified in general orders that the cessation of hostilities should be proclaimed at noon on the following day and read in the evening at the head of every regiment and corps of the army, "after which," adds he, "the chaplains with the several brigades will render thanks to Almighty God for all his mercies, particularly for his overruling the wrath of man to his own glory, and causing the rage of war to cease among the nations."

Having noticed that this auspicious day, the 19th of April, completed the eighth year of the war and was the anniversary of the eventful conflict at Lexington, he went on in general orders to impress upon the army a proper idea of the dignified part they were called upon to act.

"The generous task for which we first flew to arms being accomplished; the liberties of our country being fully acknowledged and firmly secured, and the characters of those who have persevered through every extremity of hardship, suffering, and danger being immortalized by the appellation of *the patriot army*, nothing now remains but for the actors of this mighty scene to preserve a perfect, unvarying consistency of character through the very last act, to close the drama with applause and to retire from the military theatre with the same approbation of angels and men which has crowned all their former virtuous actions."

The letter which he had written to the President produced a resolution in Congress that the service of the men engaged in the war did not expire until the ratification of the definitive articles of peace, but that the commander-in-chief might grant furloughs to such as he thought proper, and that they should be allowed to take their arms with them.

Washington availed himself freely of this permission. Furloughs were granted without stint. The men set out singly or in small parties for their rustic homes, and the danger and inconvenience were avoided of disbanding large masses, at a time, of unpaid soldiery. Now and then were to be seen three or four in a group, bound probably to the same neighborhood, beguiling the way with camp jokes and camp stories. The war-worn soldier was always kindly received at the farm-houses along the road, where he might shoulder his gun and fight over his battles. The men thus dismissed on furlough were never called upon to rejoin the army. Once at home, they sank into domestic life. Their weapons were hung up over their fireplaces, military trophies of the Revolution to be prized by future generations.

In the meantime Sir Guy Carleton was making preparations for the evacuation of the city of New York. The moment he had received the royal order for the cessation of hostilities, he had written for all the shipping that could be procured from Europe and the West Indies. As early as the 27th of April a fleet had sailed for different parts of Nova Scotia, carrying off about seven thousand persons with all their effects. A great part of these were troops but many were royalists and refugees, exiled by the laws of the United States. They looked forward with a dreary eye to their voyage, "bound," as one of them said, "to a country where there were nine months of winter and three months of cold weather every year."

On the 6th of May a personal conference took place between Washington and Sir Guy at Orangetown about the transfer of posts in the United States held by the British troops, and the delivery of all property stipulated by the treaty to be given up to the Americans. On the 8th of May, Egbert Benson, William S. Smith and Daniel Parker were commissioned by Congress to inspect and superintend at New York the embarkation of persons and property in fulfilment of the seventh article of the provisional treaty.

On the 8th of June, Washington addressed a letter to the governors of the several States on the subject of the dissolution of the army. The opening of it breathes that aspiration after the serene quiet of private life which had been his dream of happiness throughout the storms and trials of his anxious career, but the full fruition of which he was never to realize.

"The great object," said he, "for which I had the honor to hold an appointment in the service of my country being accomplished, I am now preparing to return to that domestic retirement which, it is well known, I left with the greatest reluctance; a retirement for which I never ceased to sigh through a long and painful absence, and in which (remote from the noise and trouble of the world) I meditate to pass the remainder of life in a state of undisturbed repose."

His letter then described the enviable condition of the citizens of America.

"Sole lords and proprietors of a vast tract of continent comprehending all the various soils and climates of the world and abounding with all the necessaries and conveniences of life; and acknowledged possessors of 'absolute freedom and independency.' This is the time of their political probation. This is the moment when the eyes of the whole world are turned upon them. This is the moment to establish or ruin their national character forever. This is the favorable moment to give such a tone to the federal government as will enable it to answer the ends of its institution. Or this may be the moment for relaxing the powers of the Union, annihilating the cement of the confederation and exposing us to become the sport of European politics which may play one State against another to prevent their growing importance and to serve their own interested purposes.

"With this conviction of the importance of the present crisis, silence in me would be a crime. I will therefore speak the language of freedom and sincerity without disguise.

"I am aware, however, that those who differ from me in political sentiment may perhaps remark that I am stepping out of the proper line of my duty and may possibly ascribe to arrogance or ostentation what I know is the result of the purest intention. But the rectitude of my own heart, which disdains such unworthy motives; the part I have hitherto acted in life; the determination I have formed of not taking any share in public business hereafter; the ardent desire I feel and shall continue to manifest of quietly enjoying, in private life, after all the toils of war, the benefits of a wise and liberal government will, I flatter myself, sooner or later convince my countrymen that I could have no sinister views in delivering with so little reserve the opinions contained in this address."

He then proceeded ably and eloquently to discuss what he considered the four things essential to the well-being and even the existence of the United States as an independent power.

First. An indissoluble union of the States under one federal head, and a perfect acquiescence of the several States in the full exercise of the prerogative vested in such a head by the Constitution.

Second. A sacred regard to public justice in discharging debts and fulfilling contracts made by Congress for the purpose of carrying on the war.

Third. The adoption of a proper peace establishment, in which care should be taken to place the militia throughout the Union on a regular, uniform and efficient footing. "The militia of this country must be considered as the palladium of our security and the first effectual resort in case of hostility. It is essential therefore that the same system should pervade the whole, that the formation and discipline of the militia of the continent should be absolutely uniform, and that the same species of arms, accoutrements and military apparatus should be introduced in every part of the United States."

And Fourth. A disposition among the people of the United States to forget local prejudices and policies, to make mutual concessions and to sacrifice individual advantages to the interests of the community.

These four things Washington pronounced the pillars on which the glorious character must be supported. "Liberty is the basis. And whosoever would dare to sap the foundation or overturn the structure, under whatever specious pretext he may attempt it, will merit the bitterest execration and the severest punishment which can be inflicted by his injured country."

Washington now found his situation at headquarters irksome.

There was little to do, and he was liable to be incessantly teased with applications and demands which he had neither the means nor power to satisfy. He resolved therefore to while away part of the time that must intervene before the arrival of the definitive treaty by making a tour to the northern and western parts of the State and visiting the places which had been the theatre of important military transactions. He had another object in view. He desired to facilitate as far as in his power the operations which would be necessary for occupying, as soon as evacuated by British troops, the posts ceded by the treaty of peace.

Governor Clinton accompanied him on the expedition. They set out by water from Newburgh, ascended the Hudson to Albany, visited Saratoga and the scene of Burgoyne's surrender, embarked on Lake George, where light boats had been provided for them, traversed that beautiful lake so full of historic interest, proceeded to Ticonderoga and Crown Point, and, after reconnoitering those eventful posts, returned to Schenectady, whence they proceeded up the valley of the Mohawk River, "to have a view," writes Washington, "of that tract of country which is so much celebrated for the fertility of its soil and the beauty of its situation." Having reached Fort Schuyler, formerly Fort Stanwix, they crossed over to Wood Creek, which empties into Oneida Lake and affords the water communication with Ontario. They then traversed the country to the head of the eastern branch of the Susquehanna and viewed Lake Otsego and the portage between that lake and the Mohawk River.

Washington returned to headquarters at Newburgh on the 5th of August after a tour of at least seven hundred and fifty miles, performed in nineteen days and for the most part on horseback.

In a letter to the Chevalier de Chastellux, written two or three months afterwards and giving a sketch of his tour through what was as yet an unstudied wilderness, he writes: "Prompted by these actual observations, I could not help taking a more extensive view of the vast inland navigation of these United States from maps and the information of others, and could not but be struck with the immense extent and importance of it and with the goodness of that Providence which has dealt its favors to us with so profuse a hand. Would to God we may have wisdom enough to improve them. I shall not rest contented till I have explored the western country and traversed those lines, or a great part of them, which have given bounds to a new empire."

The vast advantages of internal communication between the Hudson and the great lakes, which dawned upon Washington's mind in the course of this tour, have since been realized in that grand artery of national wealth, the Erie Canal.

By a proclamation of Congress, dated 18th of October, all officers and soldiers absent on furlough were discharged from further service, and all others who had engaged to serve during the war were to be discharged from and after the 3d of November. A small force only, composed of those who had enlisted for a definite time, were to be retained in service until the peace establishment should be organized.

In general orders of November 2d, Washington, after adverting to this proclamation, adds: "It only remains for the commander-in-chief to address himself once more, and that for the last time, to the armies of the United States, however widely dispersed the individuals who compose them may be, and to bid them an affectionate and a long farewell."

He then goes on to make them one of those paternal addresses which so eminently characterize his relationship with his army, so different from that of any other commander. He takes a brief view of the glorious struggle from which they had just emerged; the unpromising circumstances under which they had undertaken it, and the signal interposition of Providence in behalf of their feeble condition; the unparalleled perseverance of the American armies for eight long years through almost every possible suffering and discouragement, a perseverance which he justly pronounces to be little short of a standing miracle.

Adverting then to the enlarged prospects of happiness opened by the confirmation of national independence and sovereignty and the ample and profitable employments held out in a Republic so happily circumstanced, he exhorts them to maintain the strongest attachment to the union, and to carry with them into civil society the most conciliatory dispositions, proving themselves not less virtuous and useful as citizens than they had been victorious as soldiers, feeling assured that the private virtues of economy, prudence and industry would not be less amiable in civil life than the more splendid qualities of valor, perseverance and enterprise were in the field.

After a warm expression of thanks to the officers and men for the assistance he had received from every class and in every instance, he adds:

"To the various branches of the army the general takes this last and solemn opportunity of professing his invariable attachment and friendship. He wishes more than bare professions were in his power; that he was really able to be useful to them all in future life. He flatters himself, however, they will do him the justice to believe that whatever could with propriety be attempted by him has been done.

"And being now to conclude these his last public orders, to take his ultimate leave in a short time of the military character, and to bid a final adieu to the armies he has so long had the honor to command, he can only offer in their behalf his recommendations to their grateful country and his prayers to the God of armies. May ample justice be done them here and may the choicest of Heaven's favors, both here and hereafter, attend those who, under the Divine auspices, have secured innumerable blessings for others. With these wishes and this benediction, the commander-in-chief is about to retire from service. The curtain of separation will soon be drawn, and the military scene to him will be closed forever."

There was a straightforward simplicity in Washington's addresses to his army. They were so void of tumid phrases or rhetorical embellishments, the counsels given in them were so sound and practicable, the feelings expressed in them so kind and benevolent and so perfectly in accordance with his character and conduct that they always had an irresistible effect on the rudest and roughest hearts.

A person who was present at the breaking up of the army and whom we have had frequent occasion to cite, observes, on the conduct of the troops: "The advice of their beloved commander-in-chief, and the resolves of Congress to pay and compensate them in such manner as the ability of the United States would permit, operated to keep them quiet and prevent tumult, but no description would be adequate to the painful circumstances of the parting scene. Both officers and soldiers, long unaccustomed to the affairs of private life, turned loose on the world to starve and to become the prey to vulture speculators. Never can that melancholy day be forgotten when friends, companions for seven long years in joy and in sorrow, were torn asunder without the hope of ever meeting again, and with prospects of a miserable subsistence in future."[1]

[1] Thacher, p. 421.

Notwithstanding every exertion had been made for the evacuation of New York, such was the number of persons and the quantity of effects of all kinds to be conveyed away that the month of November was far advanced before it could be completed. Sir Guy Carleton had given notice to Washington of the time he supposed the different posts would be vacated, that the Americans might be prepared to take possession of them. In consequence of this notice, General George Clinton, at that time Governor of New York, had summoned the members of the State council to convene at East Chester on the 21st of November for the purpose of establishing civil government in the districts hitherto occupied by the British, and a detachment of troops was marched from West Point to be ready to take possession of the posts as they were vacated.

On the 21st the British troops were drawn in from the oft-disputed post of King's Bridge and from M'Gowan's Pass, also from the various posts on the eastern part of Long Island. Paulus Hook was relinquished on the following day, and the afternoon of the 25th of November was appointed by Sir Guy for the evacuation of the city and the opposite village of Brooklyn.

Washington in the meantime had taken his station at Harlem, accompanied by Governor Clinton, who in virtue of his office was to take charge of the city. They found there General Knox with the detachment from West Point. Sir Guy Carleton had intimated a wish that Washington would be at hand to take immediate possession of the city and prevent all outrage, as he had been informed of a plot to plunder the place whenever the king's troops should be withdrawn. He had engaged, also, that the guards of the redoubts on the East River, covering the upper part of the town, should be the first to be withdrawn and that an officer should be sent to give Washington's advanced guard information of their retiring.

Although Washington doubted the existence of any such plot as that which had been reported to the British commander, yet he took precautions accordingly. On the morning of the 25th the American troops, composed of dragoons, light infantry and artillery, moved from Harlem to the Bowery at the upper part of the city. There they remained until the troops in that quarter were withdrawn, when they marched into the city and took possession, the British embarking from the lower parts.

A formal entry then took place of the military and civil authorities. General Washington and Governor Clinton, with their suites, on horseback, led the procession, escorted by a troop of Westchester cavalry. Then came the lieutenant-governor and members of the council, General Knox and the officers of the army, the speaker of the Assembly, and a large number of citizens on horseback and on foot.

The city was now a scene of public festivity and rejoicing. The governor gave banquets to the French ambassador, the commander-in-chief, the military and civil officers and a large number of the most eminent citizens, and at night the public were entertained by splendid fireworks.

In the course of a few days Washington prepared to depart for Annapolis, where Congress was assembling, with the intention of asking leave to resign his command. A barge was in waiting about noon on the 4th of December [1783] at Whitehall Ferry to convey him across the Hudson to Paulus Hook. The principal officers of the army assembled at Fraunces's Tavern in the neighborhood of the ferry to take a final leave of him.

On entering the room and finding himself surrounded by his old companions in arms, who had shared with him so many scenes of hardship, difficulty and danger, his agitated feelings overcame his usual self-command. Filling a glass of wine and turning upon them his benignant but saddened countenance, "With a heart full of love and gratitude," said he, "I now take leave of you, most devoutly wishing that your latter days may be as prosperous and happy as your former ones have been glorious and honorable."

Having drunk this farewell benediction, he added with emotion, "I cannot come to each of you to take my leave, but shall be obliged if each of you will come and take me by the hand."

General Knox, who was nearest, was the first to advance. Washington, affected even to tears, grasped his hand and gave him a brother's embrace. In the same affectionate manner he took leave severally of the rest. Not a word was spoken. The deep feeling and manly tenderness of these veterans in the parting moment could find no utterance in words. Silent and solemn they followed their loved commander as he left the room, passed through a corps of light infantry and proceeded on foot to Whitehall Ferry. Having entered the barge, he turned to them, took off his hat and waved a silent adieu. They replied in the same manner, and having watched the barge until the intervening point of the battery shut it from sight, returned, still solemn and silent, to the place where they had assembled.[2]

On his way to Annapolis, Washington stopped for a few days at Philadelphia, where, with his usual exactness in matters of business, he adjusted with the Comptroller of the Treasury his accounts from the commencement of the war down to the 13th of the actual month of December. These were all in his own handwriting, and kept in the cleanest and most accurate manner, each entry being accompanied by a statement of the occasion and object of the charge.

The gross amount was about fourteen thousand five hundred pounds sterling, in which were included moneys expended for secret intelligence and service and in various incidental charges. All this, it must be noted, was an account of money actually expended in the progress of the war, not for arrearage of pay, for it will be recollected Washington accepted no pay. Indeed, on the final adjustment of his accounts he found himself a considerable loser, having frequently, in the hurry of business, neglected to credit himself with sums drawn from his private purse in moments of exigency.

The schedule of his public account furnishes not the least among the many noble and impressive lessons taught by his character and example. It stands a touchstone of honesty in office and a lasting rebuke on that lavish expenditure of the public money too often heedlessly, if not willfully, indulged by military commanders.

In passing through New Jersey, Pennsylvania and Maryland, the scenes of his anxious and precarious campaigns, Washington was everywhere hailed with enthusiasm by the people and greeted with addresses by legislative assemblies and learned and religious institutions. He accepted them all with that modesty inherent in his nature, little thinking that this present popularity was but the early outbreaking of a fame that was to go on widening and deepening from generation to generation and extending over the whole civilized world.

Being arrived at Annapolis, he addressed a letter to the President of Congress on the 20th of December, requesting to know in

2 Marshall's *Life of Washington*.

what manner it would be most proper to offer his resignation, whether in writing or at an audience. The latter mode was adopted, and the Hall of Congress appointed for the ceremonial.

A letter from Washington to the Baron Steuben, written on the 23d, concludes as follows: "This is the last letter I shall write while I continue in the service of my country. The hour of my resignation is fixed at twelve to-day, after which I shall become a private citizen on the banks of the Potomac."

At twelve o'clock the gallery, and a great part of the floor of the Hall of Congress, were filled with ladies, with public functionaries of the state and with general officers. The members of Congress were seated and covered, as representatives of the sovereignty of the union. The gentlemen present as spectators were standing and uncovered.

Washington entered, conducted by the Secretary of Congress, and took his seat in a chair appointed for him. After a brief pause the president (General Mifflin) informed him that "the United States, Congress assembled, were prepared to receive his communication."

Washington then rose, and in a dignified and impressive manner delivered a short address.

"The great events on which my resignation depended having at length taken place, I now have the honor of offering my sincere congratulations to Congress, and of presenting myself before them to surrender into their hands the trust committed to me, and to claim the indulgence of retiring from the service of my country."

After expressing his obligations to the army in general and acknowledging the peculiar services and distinguished merits of the confidential officers who had been attached to his person and composed his family during the war and whom he especially recommended to the favor of Congress, he continued:

"I consider it an indispensable duty to close this last solemn act of my official life by commending the interests of our dearest country to the protection of Almighty God; and those who have the superintendence of them, to his holy keeping.

"Having now finished the work assigned me, I retire from the great theatre of action and, bidding an affectionate farewell to this august body, under whose orders I have long acted, I here offer my commission and take my leave of all the employments of public life."

The next morning [he] left Annapolis and hastened to Mount Vernon, where he arrived the same day, on Christmas-eve, in a frame of mind suited to enjoy the sacred and genial festival.

"The scene is at last closed," said he in a letter to Governor Clinton. "I feel myself eased of a load of public care. I hope to spend the remainder of my days in cultivating the affections of good men and in the practice of the domestic virtues."

Chapter 49

WASHINGTON AT MOUNT VERNON

For some time after his return to Mount Vernon, Washington was in a manner locked up by the ice and snow of an uncommonly rigorous winter, so that social intercourse was interrupted and he could not even pay a visit of duty and affection to his aged mother at Fredericksburg. But it was enough for him at present that he was at length at home at Mount Vernon. Yet the habitudes of the camp still haunted him. He could hardly realize that he was free from military duties. On waking in the morning he almost expected to hear the drum going its stirring rounds and beating the reveillé.

During the winter storms, he anticipates the time when the return of the sun will enable him to welcome his friends and companions in arms to partake of his hospitality, and lays down his unpretending plan of receiving the curious visitors who are likely to throng in upon him.

"My manner of living," writes he to a friend, "is plain, and I do not mean to be put out of it. A glass of wine and a bit of mutton are always ready, and such as will be content to partake of them are always welcome. Those who expect more will be disappointed."

Some degree of economy was necessary, for his financial concerns had suffered during the war, and the products of his estate had fallen off during his long absence.

In the meantime the supreme council of Pennsylvania, properly appreciating the disinterestedness of his conduct and aware that popular love and popular curiosity would attract crowds of visitors to Mount Vernon and subject him to extraordinary expenses, had instructed their delegates in Congress to call the attention of that body to these circumstances with a view to produce some national reward for his eminent services. Before acting upon these instructions, the delegates were directed to send a copy of them to Washington for his approbation.

He received the document while buried in accounts and calculations and when, had he been of mercenary disposition, the offered intervention in his favor would have seemed most seasonable, but he at once most gratefully and respectfully declined it, jealously maintaining the satisfaction of having served his country at the sacrifice of his private interests.

Applications began to be made to him, by persons desirous of writing the history of the Revolution, for access to the public papers in his possession. He excused himself from submitting to their inspection those relative to the occurrences and transactions of his late command until Congress should see fit to open their archives to the historian.

His old friend, Dr. Craik, made a similar application to Washington in behalf of a person who purposed to write his memoirs. He replied that any memoir of his life distinct and unconnected with the general history of the war would rather hurt his feelings than flatter his pride, while he could not furnish the papers and information connected with it without subjecting himself to the imputation of vanity, adding: "I had rather leave it to posterity to think and say what they please of me than by any act of mine to have vanity or ostentation imputed to me."

As spring advanced, Mount Vernon, as had been anticipated, began to attract numerous visitors. They were received in the frank, unpretending style Washington had determined upon. It was truly edifying to behold how easily and contentedly he subsided from the authoritative commander-in-chief of armies into the quiet country gentleman. There was nothing awkward or violent in the transition. He seemed to be in his natural element. Mrs. Washington, too, who had presided with quiet dignity at headquarters and cheered the wintry gloom of Valley Forge with her presence, presided with equal amenity and grace at the simple board of Mount Vernon. She had a cheerful good sense that always made her an agreeable companion, and was an excellent manager. She has been remarked for an inveterate habit of knitting. It had been acquired, or at least fostered, in the wintry encampments of the Revolution, where she used to set an example to her lady visitors by diligently plying her needles, knitting stockings for the poor destitute soldiery.

In entering upon the out-door management of his estate, Washington was but doing in person what he had long been doing through others. He had never virtually ceased to be the agriculturist. Throughout all his campaigns he had kept himself informed of the course of rural affairs at Mount Vernon. By means of maps on which every field was laid down and numbered, he was enabled to give directions for their several cultivation and receive accounts of their several crops. No hurry of affairs prevented a correspondence with his overseer or agent, and he exacted weekly reports. Thus his rural were interwoven with his military cares, the agriculturist was mingled with the soldier and those strong sympathies with the honest cultivators of the soil and that paternal care of their interests to be noted throughout his military career, may be ascribed in a great measure to the sweetening influences of Mount Vernon. Yet as spring returned and he resumed his rides about the beautiful neighborhood of this haven of his hopes, he must have been mournfully sensible, now and then, of the changes which time and events had effected there.

The Fairfaxes, the kind friends of his boyhood and social companions of his riper years, were no longer at hand to share his pleasures and lighten his cares. There were no more hunting dinners at Belvoir. He paid a sad visit to that happy resort of his youth and contemplated with a mournful eye its charred ruins and the desolation of its once ornamented grounds. George William Fairfax, its former possessor, was in England. His political principles had detained him there during the war and part of his property had been sequestered. Still, though an exile, he continued in heart a friend to America, his hand had been open to relieve the distresses of Americans in England, and he kept up a cordial correspondence with Washington.

On the 17th of August [Washington] was gladdened by having the Marquis de Lafayette under his roof, who had recently arrived from France. The marquis passed a fortnight with him, a loved and cherished guest, at the end of which he departed for a time to be present at the ceremony of a treaty with the Indians.

Washington now prepared for a tour to the west of the Appalachian Mountains to visit his lands on the Ohio and Kanawha rivers. Dr. Craik, the companion of his various campaigns and who had accompanied him in 1770 on a similar tour, was to be his fellow-traveller. The way they were to travel may be gathered from Washington's directions to the doctor: "You will have occasion to take nothing from home but a servant to look after your horses, and such bedding as you may think proper to make use of. I will carry a marquee, some camp utensils, and a few stores. A boat, or some other kind of vessel, will be provided for the voyage down the river, either at my place on the Youghiogheny or Fort Pitt, measures for this purpose having already been taken. A few medicines and hooks and lines you may probably want."

This soldier-like tour, made in hardy military style, with tent, pack-horses and frugal supplies, took him once more among the scenes of his youthful expeditions when a land surveyor in the employ of Lord Fairfax, a leader of Virginia militia or an aide-de-camp of the unfortunate Braddock. A veteran now in years, and a general renowned in arms, he soberly permitted his steed to pick his way across the mountains by the old military route, still called Braddock's Road, over which he had spurred in the days of youthful ardor. His original intention had been to survey and inspect his lands on the Monongahela River, then to descend the Ohio to the Great Kanawha, where also he had large tracts of wild land. On arriving on the Monongahela, however, he heard such accounts of discontent and irritation among the Indian tribes that he did not consider it prudent to venture among them. Some of his land on the Monongahela was settled, the rest was in the wilderness and of little value in the present unquiet state of the country.

He abridged his tour, therefore; proceeded no farther west than the Monongahela; ascended that river and then struck southward through the wild, unsettled regions of the Alleghenies until he came out into the Shenandoah Valley near Staunton.

He returned to Mount Vernon on the 4th of October, having, since the 1st of September, travelled on horseback six hundred and eighty miles, for a great part of the time in wild, mountainous country where he was obliged to encamp at night. This, like his tour to the northern forts with Governor Clinton, gave proof of his unfailing vigor and activity.

During all this tour he had carefully observed the course and character of the streams flowing from the west into the Ohio, and the distance of their navigable parts from the head navigation of the rivers east of the mountains, with the nearest and best portage between them. For many years he had been convinced of the practicability of an easy and short communication between the Potomac and James rivers and the waters of the Ohio, and thence on to the great chain of lakes, and of the vast advantages that would result therefrom to the States of Virginia and Maryland. He had even attempted to set a company on foot to undertake at their own expense the opening of such a communication, but the breaking out of the Revolution had put a stop to the enterprise. One object of his recent tour was to make observations and collect information on the subject, and all that he had seen and heard quickened his solicitude to carry the scheme into effect.

Political as well as commercial interests, he conceived, were involved in the enterprise. He had noticed that the flanks and rear of the United States were possessed by foreign and formidable powers who might lure the Western people into a trade and alliance with them. The Western States, he observes, stood as it were upon a pivot, so that the touch of a feather might turn them any way. They had looked down the Mississippi and been tempted in that direction by the facilities of sending everything down the stream; whereas they had no means of coming to us but by long land transportations and rugged roads. The jealous and untoward disposition of the Spaniards, it was true, almost barred the use of the Mississippi, but they might change their policy and invite trade in that direction. The retention by the British government, also, of the posts of Detroit, Niagara and Oswego, though contrary to the spirit of the treaty, shut up the channel of trade in that quarter. These posts, however, would eventually be given up, and then, he was persuaded, the people of New York would lose no time in removing every obstacle in the way of a water communication.

At the opening of the year (1785) the entries in his diary show him diligently employed in preparations to improve his groves and shrubbery. On the 10th of January he notes that the white thorn is full in berry. On the 20th he begins to clear the pine-groves of undergrowth.

In February he transplants ivy under the walls of the garden to which it still clings. In March he is planting hemlock-trees, that most beautiful species of American evergreen, numbers of which had been brought hither from Occoquan. In April he is sowing holly berries in drills, some adjoining a green-brier hedge on the north side of the garden-gate, others in a semicircle on the lawn. Many of the holly bushes thus produced are still flourishing about the place in full vigor. He had learnt the policy, not sufficiently adopted in our country, of clothing his ornamented grounds as much as possible with evergreens, which resist the rigors of our winter and keep up a cheering verdure throughout the year. Of the trees fitted for shade in pasture-land he notes the locust, maple, black mulberry, black walnut, black gum, dogwood and sassafras, none of which, he observes, materially injure the grass beneath them.

Is then for once a soldier's dream realized? Is he in perfect enjoyment of that seclusion from the world and its distractions which he had so often pictured to himself amid the hardships and turmoils of the camp? Alas, no! The "post," that "herald of a noisy world," invades his quiet and loads his table with letters until correspondence becomes an intolerable burden.

He looks in despair at the daily accumulating mass of unanswered letters. "Many mistakenly think," writes he, "that I am retired to ease, and to that kind of tranquillity which would grow tiresome for want of employment. But at no period of my life, not in the eight years I served the public, have I been obliged to write so much myself as I have done since my retirement."[1] Again, "It is not the letters from my friends which give me trouble, or add aught to my perplexity. It is references to old matters with which I have nothing to do; applications which often cannot be complied with; inquiries which would require the pen of a historian to satisfy; letters of compliment as unmeaning perhaps as they are troublesome but which must be attended to; and the commonplace business which employs my pen and my time often disagreeably. These, with company, deprive me of exercise, and unless I can obtain relief, must be productive of disagreeable consequences."

From much of this drudgery of the pen he was subsequently relieved by Mr. Tobias Lear, a young gentleman of New Hampshire, a graduate of Harvard College, who acted as his private secretary and at the same time took charge of the instruction of the two children of the late Mr. Parke Custis, whom Washington had adopted.

There was another tax imposed by his celebrity upon his time and patience. Applications were continually made to him to sit for his likeness. The following is his sportive reply to Mr. Francis Hopkinson, who applied in behalf of Mr. Pine:

[1] Letter to Richard Henry Lee.

"'In for a penny in for a pound,' is an old adage. I am so hackneyed to the touches of the painters' pencil that I am altogether at their beck and sit 'like Patience on a monument' whilst they are delineating the lines of my face. It is a proof, among many others, of what habit and custom can accomplish. At first I was impatient at the request and as restive under the operation as a colt is under the saddle. The next time I submitted very reluctantly but with less flouncing. Now no dray-horse moves more readily to his thill than I to the painter's chair. It may easily be conceived, therefore, that I yield a ready obedience to your request and to the views of Mr. Pine."

It was not long after this that M. Houdon, an artist of great merit, chosen by Mr. Jefferson and Dr. Franklin, arrived from Paris to make a study of Washington for a statue for the Legislature of Virginia. He remained a fortnight at Mount Vernon, and having formed his model, took it with him to Paris, where he produced that excellent statue and likeness to be seen in the State House in Richmond, Virginia.

Being now in some measure relieved from the labors of the pen, Washington had more time to devote to his plan for ornamental cultivation of the grounds about his dwelling.

We find in his diary noted down with curious exactness each day's labor and the share he took in it; his frequent rides to the Mill Swamp; the Dogue Creek; the "Plantation of the Neck," and the other places along the Potomac in quest of young elms, ash-trees, white thorn, crab-apples, maples, mulberries, willows and lilacs; the winding walks which he lays out, and the trees and shrubs which he plants along them. Now he sows acorns and buck-eye nuts brought by himself from the Monongahela, now he opens vistas through the Pine Grove, commanding distant views through the woodlands, and now he twines round his columns scarlet honeysuckles which his gardener tells him will blow all the summer.

His care-worn spirit freshens up in these employments. With him Mount Vernon is a kind of idyl. The transient glow of poetical feeling which once visited his bosom, when in boyhood he rhymed beneath its groves, seems about to return once more, and we please ourselves with noting among the trees set out by him a group of young horse-chestnuts from Westmoreland, his native county, the haunt of his schoolboy days, which had been sent to him by Colonel Lee (Light-Horse Harry), the son of his "lowland beauty."

A diagram of the plan in which he had laid out his grounds still remains among his papers at Mount Vernon. The places are marked on it for particular trees and shrubs. Some of those trees and shrubs are still to be found in the places thus assigned to them. In the present neglected state of Mount Vernon its walks are overgrown and vegetation runs wild, but it is deeply interesting still to find traces of these toils in which Washington delighted, and to know that many of the trees which gave it its present umbrageous beauty were planted by his hand.

The ornamental cultivation of which we have spoken was confined to the grounds appertaining to what was called the mansion-house farm. All but his estate included four other farms lying contiguous and containing three thousand two hundred and sixty acres, each farm having its bailiff or overseer, with a house for his accommodation, barns and outhouses for the produce, and cabins for the negroes. On a general map of the estate, drawn out by Washington himself, these farms were all laid down accurately and their several fields numbered. He knew the soil and local qualities of each and regulated the culture of them accordingly.

In addition to these five farms there were several hundred acres of fine woodland, so that the estate presented a beautiful diversity of land and water. In the stables near the mansion-house were the carriage and saddle horses, of which he was very choice. On the four farms there were 54 draft horses, 12 mules, 317 head of black cattle, 360 sheep and a great number of swine, which last ran at large in the woods.

He now read much on husbandry and gardening and copied out treatises on those subjects. He corresponded also with the celebrated Arthur Young, from whom he obtained seeds of all kinds, improved ploughs, plans for laying out farm-yards, and advice on various parts of rural economy.

"Agriculture," writes he to him, "has ever been among the most favored of my amusements, though I have never possessed much skill in the art, and nine years' total inattention to it has added nothing to a knowledge which is best understood from practice. But with the means you have been so obliging as to furnish me, I shall return to it, though rather late in the day, with more alacrity than ever."

In the management of his estate he was remarkably exact. No negligence on the part of the overseers or those under them was passed unnoticed. He seldom used many words on the subject of his plans, rarely asked advice, but when once determined, carried them directly and silently into execution and was not easily dissuaded from a project when once commenced.

We have shown in a former chapter his mode of appointing time at Mount Vernon prior to the Revolution. The same system was in a great measure resumed. His active day began some time before the dawn. Much of his correspondence was despatched before breakfast, which took place at half-past seven. After breakfast he mounted his horse which stood ready at the door, and rode out to different parts of his estate, as he used to do to various parts of the camp, to see that all was right at the outposts and every one at his duty. At half-past two he dined.

If there was no company he would write until dark, or, if pressed by business, until nine o'clock in the evening. Otherwise he read in the evening or amused himself with a game of whist.

His secretary, Mr. Lear, after two years' residence in the family on the most confidential footing, says: "General Washington is, I believe, the only man of an exalted character who does not lose some part of his respectability by an intimate acquaintance. I have never found a single thing that could lessen my respect for him. A complete knowledge of his honesty, uprightness and candor in all his private transactions has sometimes led me to think him more than a man."

The children of Parke Custis formed a lively part of his household. He was fond of children and apt to unbend with them. Miss Custis, recalling in after life the scenes of her childhood, writes: "I have sometimes made him laugh most heartily from sympathy with my joyous and extravagant spirits." She observes, however, that "He was a silent, thoughtful man. He spoke little generally, never of himself. I never heard him relate a single act of his life during the war. I have often seen him perfectly abstracted, his lips moving, but no sound was perceptible."

An observant traveller, Mr. Elkanah Watson, who visited Mount Vernon in the winter of 1785, bearer of a letter of introduction from General Greene and Colonel Fitzgerald, gives a home picture of Washington in his retirement. Though sure that his credentials would secure him a respectful reception, he says: "I trembled with awe as I came into the presence of this great man. I found him at table with Mrs. Washington and his private family and was received in the native dignity and with that urbanity so peculiarly combined in the character of a soldier and an eminent private gentleman. He soon put me at my ease by unbending in a free and affable conversation.

"The cautious reserve which wisdom and policy dictated whilst engaged in rearing the glorious fabric of our independence was evidently the result of consummate prudence and not characteristic of his nature. I observed a peculiarity in his smile which seemed to illuminate his eye. His whole countenance beamed with intelligence, while it commanded confidence and respect.

"I found him kind and benignant in the domestic circle; revered and beloved by all around him; agreeably social, without ostentation; delighting in anecdote and adventures; without assumption; his domestic arrangements harmonious and systematic. His servants seemed to watch his eye and anticipate his every wish. Hence a look was equivalent to a command. His servant Billy, the faithful companion of his military career, was always at his side. Smiling content animated and beamed on every countenance in his presence."

In the evening Mr. Watson sat conversing for a full hour with Washington after all the family had retired, expecting perhaps to hear him fight over some of his battles, but if so, he was disappointed, for he observes: "He modestly waived all allusions to the events in which he had acted so glorious and conspicuous a part. Much of his conversation had reference to the interior country and to the opening of the navigation of the Potomac by canals and locks, at the Seneca, the Great and Little Falls. His mind appeared to be deeply absorbed by that object, then in earnest contemplation."

Mr. Watson had taken a severe cold, in the course of a harsh winter journey, and coughed excessively. Washington pressed him to take some remedies but he declined. After retiring for the night his coughing increased.

"When some time had elapsed," writes he, "the door of my room was gently opened and, on drawing my bed curtains, I beheld Washington himself, standing at my bedside with a bowl of hot tea in his hand. I was mortified and distressed beyond expression. This little incident, occurring in common life with an ordinary man, would not have been noticed, but as a trait of the benevolence and private virtue of Washington, deserves to be recorded."

The late Bishop White, in subsequent years, speaking of Washington's unassuming manners, observes: "I know no man who so carefully guarded against the discoursing of himself or of his acts or of anything that pertained to him, and it has occasionally occurred to me when in his company that, if a stranger to his person were present, he would never have known from anything said by him that he was conscious of having distinguished himself in the eye of the world."

An anecdote is told of Washington's conduct while commander-in-chief, illustrative of his benignant attention to others and his freedom from all assumption. While the army was encamped at Morristown, he one day attended a religious meeting where divine service was to be celebrated in the open air. A chair had been set out for his use. Just before the service commenced, a woman bearing a child in her arms approached. All the seats were occupied. Washington immediately rose, placed her in the chair which had been assigned to him, and remained standing during the whole service.[2]

The reverential awe which his deeds and elevated position threw around him was often a source of annoyance to him in private life, especially when he perceived its effect upon the young and gay. We have been told of a case in point, when he made his appearance at a private ball where all were enjoying themselves with the utmost glee. The moment he entered the room the buoyant mirth was checked, the dance lost its animation, every face was grave, every tongue was silent. He remained for a time, endeavoring to engage in conversation with some of the young people and to break the spell. Finding it in vain, he retired sadly to the company of the elders in an adjoining room, expressing his regret that his presence should operate as such a damper. After a little while light laughter and happy voices again resounded from the ballroom, upon which he rose cautiously, approached on tiptoe the door, which was ajar, and there stood for some time a delighted spectator of the youthful revelry.

Washington in fact, though habitually grave and thoughtful, was of a social disposition and loved cheerful society. He was fond of the dance, and it was the boast of many ancient dames in our day, who had been belles in the time of the Revolution, that they

[2] MS. notes of the Rev. Joseph F. Tuttle.

had danced minutes with him or had him for a partner in contra-dances. There were balls in camp in some of the dark times of the Revolution. "We had a little dance at my quarters," writes General Greene from Middlebrook in March 1779. "His Excellency and Mrs. Greene danced upwards of three hours without once sitting down. Upon the whole, we had a pretty little frisk."[3]

A letter of Colonel Tench Tilghman, one of Washington's aides-de-camp, gives an instance of the general's festive gayety when in the above year the army was cantoned near Morristown. A large company, of which the general and Mrs. Washington, General and Mrs. Greene, and Mr. and Mrs. Olney were part, dined with Colonel and Mrs. Biddle. Some little time after the ladies had retired from the table, Mr. Olney followed them into the next room. A clamor was raised against him as a deserter, and it was resolved that a party should be sent to demand him, and that if the ladies refused to give him up, he should be brought by force. Washington humored the joke and offered to head the party. He led it with great formality to the door of the drawing-room and sent in a summons. The ladies refused to give up the deserter. An attempt was made to capture him. The ladies came to the rescue. There was a mêlée, in the course of which his Excellency seems to have had a passage at arms with Mrs. Olney. The ladies were victorious, as they always ought to be, says the gallant Tilghman.

More than one instance is told of Washington's being surprised into hearty fits of laughter, even during the war. We have recorded one produced by the sudden appearance of old General Putnam on horseback, with a female prisoner en croupe. The following is another which occurred at the camp at Morristown. Washington had purchased a young horse of great spirit and power. A braggadocio of the army, vain of his horsemanship, asked the privilege of breaking it. Washington gave his consent, and with some of his officers attended to see the horse receive his first lesson. After much preparation, the pretender to equitation mounted into the saddle and was making a great display of his science, when the horse suddenly planted his forefeet, threw up his heels and gave the unlucky Gambado a somerset over his head. Washington, a thorough horseman and quick to perceive the ludicrous in these

8 Greene to Col. Wadsworth. MS.

matters, was so convulsed with laughter that, we are told, the tears ran down his cheeks.[4]

Still another instance is given, which occurred at the return of peace, when he was sailing in a boat on the Hudson and was so overcome by the drollery of a story told by Major Fairlie of New York, of facetious memory, that he fell back in the boat in a paroxysm of laughter. In that fit of laughter it was sagely presumed that he threw off the burden of care which had been weighing down his spirits throughout the war. He certainly relaxed much of his thoughtful gravity of demeanor when he had no longer the anxieties of a general command to harass him. The late Judge Brooke, who had served as an officer in the legion of Light-Horse Harry, used to tell of having frequently met Washington on his visits to Fredericksburg after the Revolutionary War, and how "hilarious" the general was on those occasions with "Jack Willis and other friends of his young days," laughing heartily at the comic songs which were sung at table.

Colonel Henry Lee, too, who used to be a favored guest at Mount Vernon, does not seem to have been much under the influence of that "reverential awe" which Washington is said to have inspired, if we may judge from the following anecdote. Washington one day at table mentioned his being in want of carriage horses and asked Lee if he knew where he could get a pair.

"I have a fine pair, general," replied Lee, "but you cannot get them."

"Why not?"

"Because you will never pay more than half price for anything, and I must have full price for my horses."

The bantering reply set Mrs. Washington laughing, and her parrot, perched beside her, joined in the laugh.[5] The general took this

[4] Notes of the Rev. Mr. Tuttle. MS.

[5] Another instance is on record of one of Washington's fits of laughter, which occurred in subsequent years. Judge Marshall and Judge Washington, a relative of the general, were on their way on horseback to visit Mount Vernon, attended by a black servant who had charge of a large portmanteau containing their clothes. As they passed through a wood on the skirts of the Mount Vernon grounds they were tempted to make a hasty toilet beneath its shade, being covered with dust from the state of the roads. Dismounting, they threw off their dusty garments while the servant took down the portmanteau. As he opened it, out flew cakes of windsor soap and fancy articles of all kinds. The man by mistake had changed their portmanteau at the last stopping place for one which resembled it, belonging to a Scotch pedlar. The consternation of the negro, and their own dismantled state, struck them so ludi-

familiar assault upon his dignity in great good part. "Ah, Lee, you are a funny fellow," said he. "See, that bird is laughing at you."[6]

Hearty laughter, however, was rare with Washington. The sudden explosions we hear of were the result of some sudden and ludicrous surprise. His general habit was a calm seriousness, easily softening into a benevolent smile.

In some few of his familiar letters, yet preserved and not relating to business, there is occasionally a vein of pleasantry and even of humor, but almost invariably they treat of matters of too grave import to admit of anything of the kind. It is to be deeply regretted that most of his family letters have been purposely destroyed.

The passion for hunting had revived with Washington on returning to his old hunting grounds, but he had no hounds. His kennel had been broken up when he went to the wars, and the dogs given away and it was not easy to replace them. After a time he received several hounds from France, sent out by Lafayette and other of the French officers, and once more sallied forth to renew his ancient sport. The French hounds, however, proved indifferent. He was out with them repeatedly, putting other hounds with them borrowed from gentlemen of the neighborhood. They improved after a while but were never stanch, and caused him frequent disappointments. Probably he was not as stanch himself as formerly. An interval of several years may have blunted his keenness, if we may judge from the following entry in his diary:

"Out after breakfast with my hounds, found a fox and ran him sometimes hard, and sometimes at cold hunting from 11 till near 2—when I came home and left the huntsmen with them, who followed in the same manner two hours or more, and then took the dogs off without killing."

While Washington was thus calmly enjoying himself, came a letter from Henry Lee, who was now in Congress, conveying a mournful piece of intelligence: "Your friend and second, the patriot and noble Greene, is no more. Universal grief reigns here." Greene died on the 18th of June [1786] at his estate of Mulberry

crously as to produce loud and repeated bursts of laughter. Washington, who happened to be out upon his grounds, was attracted by the noise, and so overcome by the strange plight of his friends and the whimsicality of the whole scene, that he is said to have actually rolled on the grass with laughter. —See *Life of Judge J. Smith.*

[6] Communicated to us in a letter from a son of Colonel Lee.

Grove on Savannah River, presented to him by the State of Georgia. His last illness was brief, caused by a stroke of the sun. He was but forty-four years of age.

The news of his death struck heavily on Washington's heart, to whom in the most arduous trials of the Revolution he had been a second self.

Chapter 50

THE NEW CONSTITUTION

From his quiet retreat at Mount Vernon, Washington, though ostensibly withdrawn from public affairs, was watching with intense solicitude the working together of the several parts in the great political confederacy, anxious to know whether the thirteen distinct States, under the present organization, could form a sufficiently efficient general government. He was daily becoming more and more doubtful of the solidity of the fabric he had assisted to raise. The form of confederation which had bound the States together and met the public exigencies during the Revolution, when there was a pressure of external danger, was daily proving more and more incompetent to the purposes of a national government. Congress had devised a system of credit to provide for the national expenditure and the extinction of the national debts, which amounted to something more than forty millions of dollars. The system experienced neglect from some States and opposition from others, each consulting its local interests and prejudices instead of the interests and obligations of the whole. In like manner treaty stipulations, which bound the good faith of the whole, were slighted if not violated by individual States, apparently unconscious that they must each share in the discredit thus brought upon the national name.

In a letter to James Warren, who had formerly been president of the Massachusetts Provincial Congress, Washington writes: "The confederation appears to me to be little more than a shadow without the substance, and Congress a nugatory body, their ordinances being little attended to. To me it is a solecism in politics, indeed it is one of the most extraordinary things in nature, that we should confederate as a nation and yet be afraid to give the rulers of that nation (who are creatures of our own making, appointed for a limited and short duration, and who are amenable for every action and may be recalled at any moment and are subject to all the evils which they may be instrumental in producing) sufficient powers to order and direct the affairs of the same. By such policy as this the wheels of government are clogged, and our brightest prospects and that high expectation which was entertained of us by the wondering world are turned into astonishment, and from the high ground on which we stood we are descending into the vale of confusion and darkness."[1]

Not long previous to the writing of this letter, Washington had been visited at Mount Vernon by commissioners who had been appointed by the legislatures of Virginia and Maryland to form a compact relative to the navigation of the rivers Potomac and Pocomoke and of part of the Chesapeake Bay and who had met at Alexandria for the purpose. During their visit at Mount Vernon, the policy of maintaining a naval force on the Chesapeake and of establishing a tariff of duties on imports to which the laws of both States should conform was discussed, and it was agreed that the commissioners should propose to the governments of their respective States the appointment of other commissioners, with powers to make conjoint arrangements for the above purposes, to which the assent of Congress was to be solicited.

The idea of conjoint arrangements between States, thus suggested in the quiet councils of Mount Vernon, was a step in the right direction and will be found to lead to important results.

From a letter written two or three months subsequently, we gather some of the ideas on national policy which were occupying Washington's mind.

"I have ever been a friend to adequate powers in Congress, without which, it is evident to me, we never shall establish a national character or be considered as on a respectable footing by the powers of Europe. We are either a united people under one head and for federal purposes, or we are thirteen independent sovereignties eternally counteracting each other. If the former, whatever such a majority of the States as the constitution points out conceives to be for the benefit of the whole, should in my humble opinion be submitted to by the minority. I can foresee no evil greater than disunion, than those *unreasonable* jealousies (I say unreasonable because I would have a *proper* jealousy always

[1] Sparks, ix., 139.

awake, and the United States on the watch to prevent individual
States from infracting the constitution with impunity) which are
continually poisoning our minds and filling them with imaginary
evils for the prevention of real ones."[2]

An earnest correspondence took place some months subsequently
between Washington and the illustrious patriot, John Jay, at
that time Secretary of Foreign Affairs, wherein the signs of the
times were feelingly discussed.

"Our affairs," writes Jay, "seem to lead to some crisis, something
that I cannot foresee or conjecture. I am uneasy and apprehensive,
more so than during the war. Then we had a fixed object, and
though the means and time of obtaining it were problematical, yet
I did firmly believe that we should ultimately succeed, because I
did firmly believe that justice was with us. The case is now altered.
We are going and doing wrong, and therefore I look forward to
evils and calamities, but without being able to guess at the instrument, nature or measure of them. . . . What I most fear is
that the better kind of people, by which I mean the people who
are orderly and industrious, who are content with their situations
and not uneasy in their circumstances, will be led by the insecurity
of property, the loss of public faith and rectitude, to consider the
charms of liberty as imaginary and delusive. A state of uncertainty
and fluctuation must disgust and alarm."

Washington, in reply, coincided in opinion that public affairs
were drawing rapidly to a crisis, and he acknowledged the event to
be equally beyond his foresight.

"We have errors," said he, "to correct. We have probably had
too good an opinion of human nature in forming our confederation. Experience has taught us that men will not adopt and
carry into execution measures the best calculated for their own
good without the intervention of coercive power. I do not conceive
we can exist long as a nation without lodging somewhere a power
which will pervade the whole Union in as energetic a manner as
the authority of the State governments extends over the several
States. To be fearful of investing Congress, constituted as that
body is, with ample authorities for national purposes appears to
me the very climax of popular absurdity and madness. Could
Congress exert them for the detriment of the people without injuring themselves in an equal or greater proportion? Are not their in-

[2] See Letter to James McHenry. Sparks, ix., 121.

terests inseparably connected with those of their constituents? By the rotation of appointments must they not mingle frequently with the mass of the citizens? Is it not rather to be apprehended, if they were not possessed of the powers before described, that the individual members would be induced to use them on many occasions very timidly and inefficaciously for fear of losing their popularity and future election? We must take human nature as we find it. Perfection falls not to the share of mortals.

"What then is to be done? Things cannot go on in the same strain forever. It is much to be feared, as you observe, that the better kind of people, being disgusted with these circumstances, will have their minds prepared for any revolution whatever. We are apt to run from one extreme to another. . . . I am told that even respectable characters speak of a monarchical form of government without horror. From thinking proceeds speaking, thence acting is often but a single step. But how irrevocable and tremendous! What a triumph for our enemies to verify their predictions! What a triumph for the advocates of despotism to find that we are incapable of governing ourselves, and that systems founded on the basis of equal liberty are merely ideal and fallacious! Would to God that wise measures may be taken in time to avert the consequences we have but too much reason to apprehend.

"Retired as I am from the world, I frankly acknowledge I cannot feel myself an unconcerned spectator. Yet, having happily assisted in bringing the ship into port and having been fairly discharged, it is not my business to embark again on the sea of troubles.

"Nor could it be expected that my sentiments and opinions would have much weight in the minds of my countrymen. They have been neglected, though given as a last legacy in a most solemn manner. I then perhaps had some claims to public attention. I consider myself as having none at present."

His anxiety on this subject was quickened by accounts of discontents and commotions in the Eastern States produced by the pressure of the times, the public and private indebtedness and the imposition of heavy taxes at a moment of financial embarrassment.

General Knox, now Secretary at War, who had been sent by Congress to Massachusetts to inquire into these troubles, thus writes about the insurgents: "Their creed is that the property of the United States has been protected from the confiscation of Britain by the joint exertions of *all*, and therefore ought to be *the common property of all*, and he that attempts opposition to this creed is an enemy to equity and justice and ought to be swept from off the face of the earth." Again, "They are determined to annihilate all debts public and private, and have agrarian laws, which are easily effected by the means of unfunded paper, which shall be a tender in all cases whatever."

In reply to Colonel Henry Lee in Congress, who had addressed several letters to him on the subject, Washington writes:

"You talk, my good sir, of employing influence to appease the present tumults in Massachusetts. I know not where that influence is to be found or, if attainable, that it would be a proper remedy for the disorders. *Influence* is not *government*. Let us have a government by which our lives, liberties and properties will be secured, or let us know the worst at once. There is a call for decision. Know precisely what the insurgents aim at. If they have *real* grievances, redress them if possible, or acknowledge the justice of them and your inability to do it at the moment. If they have not, employ the force of government against them at once. If this is inadequate, *all* will be convinced that the superstructure is bad and wants support. To delay one or other of these expedients is to exasperate on the one hand or to give confidence on the other. . . . Let the reins of government, then, be braced and held with a steady hand, and every violation of the constitution be reprehended. If defective, let it be amended, but not suffered to be trampled upon whilst it has an existence."

A letter to him from his former aide-de-camp, Colonel Humphreys, dated New Haven, November 1st, says: "The troubles in Massachusetts still continue. Government is prostrated in the dust, and it is much to be feared that there is not energy enough in that State to re-establish the civil powers. The leaders of the mob, whose fortunes and measures are desperate, are strengthening themselves daily, and it is expected that they will soon take possession of the continental magazine at Springfield, in which there are from ten to fifteen thousand stand of arms in excellent order.

"A general want of compliance with the requisitions of Congress for money seems to prognosticate that we are rapidly advancing to a crisis. Congress, I am told, are seriously alarmed and hardly know which way to turn or what to expect. Indeed, my dear

General, nothing but a good Providence can extricate us from the present convulsion.

"In case of civil discord, I have already told you it was seriously my opinion that you could not remain neuter and that you would be obliged, in self-defense, to take one part or the other, or withdraw from the continent. Your friends are of the same opinion."

Close upon the receipt of this letter came intelligence that the insurgents of Massachusetts, far from being satisfied with the redress which had been offered by their General Court, were still acting in open violation of law and government; and that the chief magistrate had been obliged to call upon the militia of the State to support the constitution.

"What, gracious God! is man," writes Washington, "that there should be such inconsistency and perfidiousness in his conduct. It was but the other day that we were shedding our blood to obtain the constitutions under which we now live; constitutions of our own choice and making; and now we are unsheathing the sword to overturn them. The thing is so unaccountable that I hardly know how to realize it, or to persuade myself that I am not under the illusion of a dream."

His letters to Knox show the trouble of his mind.

"I feel, my dear General Knox, infinitely more than I can express to you, for the disorders which have arisen in these States. Good God! Who, besides a tory could have foreseen, or a Briton predicted, them? I do assure you that even at this moment, when I reflect upon the present prospect of our affairs it seems to me to be like the vision of a dream. . . . After what I have seen, or rather what I have heard, I shall be surprised at nothing, for, if three years since, any person had told me that there would have been such a formidable rebellion as exists at this day against the laws and constitution of our own making, I should have thought him a bedlamite, a fit subject for a mad-house. . . . In regretting, which I have often done with the keenest sorrow, the death of our much lamented friend, General Greene, I have accompanied it of late with a query whether he would not have preferred such an exit to the scenes which, it is more than probable, many of his compatriots may live to bemoan."

To James Madison, also, he writes in the same strain.

"How melancholy is the reflection that in so short a time we should have made such large strides towards fulfilling the predictions of our transatlantic foes. 'Leave them to themselves and their government will soon dissolve.' Will not the wise and good strive hard to avert this evil? Or will their supineness suffer ignorance and the fine arts of self-interested and designing, disaffected and desperate characters to involve this great country in wretchedness and contempt? What stronger evidence can be given of the want of energy in our government than these disorders? If there is not power in it to check them, what security has a man for life, liberty or property? To you, I am sure I need not add aught on the subject. The consequences of a lax or inefficient government are too obvious to be dwelt upon. Thirteen sovereignties pulling against each other, and all tugging at the federal head, will soon bring ruin on the whole, whereas a liberal and energetic constitution, well checked and well watched to prevent encroachments, might restore us to that degree of respectability and consequence to which we had the fairest prospect of attaining."

Thus Washington, even though in retirement, was almost unconsciously exercising a powerful influence on national affairs. No longer the soldier, he was now becoming the statesman. The opinions and counsels given in his letters were widely effective. The leading expedient for federate organization, mooted in his conferences with the commissioners of Maryland and Virginia during their visit to Mount Vernon in the previous year, had been extended and ripened in legislative assemblies and ended in a plan of a convention composed of delegates from all the States, to meet in Philadelphia for the sole and express purpose of revising the federal system and correcting its defect, the proceedings of the convention to be subsequently reported to Congress and the several legislatures for approval and confirmation.

Washington was unanimously put at the head of the Virginia delegation, but for some time objected to accept the nomination. He feared to be charged with inconsistency in again appearing in a public situation after his declared resolution to the contrary. "It will have, also," said he, "a tendency to sweep me back into the tide of public affairs when retirement and ease are so much desired by me and so essentially necessary."[3]

These considerations were strenuously combated, for the weight and influence of his name and counsel were felt to be all-impor-

[3] Letter to Edmund Randolph, governor of Virginia.

tant in giving dignity to the delegation. Two things contributed to bring him to a favorable decision: First, an insinuation that the opponents of the convention were monarchists who wished the distractions of the country should continue until a monarchical government might be resorted to as an ark of safety. The other was the insurrection in Massachusetts.

Having made up his mind to serve as a delegate to the convention, he went into a course of preparatory reading on the history and principles of ancient and modern confederacies. An abstract of the general principles of each, with notes of their vices or defects, exists in his own handwriting among his papers, though it is doubted by a judicious commentator[4] whether it was originally drawn up by him, as several works are cited which are written in languages that he did not understand.

Before the time arrived for the meeting of the convention, which was the second Monday in May, his mind was relieved from one source of poignant solicitude by learning that the insurrection in Massachusetts had been suppressed with but little bloodshed and that the principals had fled to Canada. He doubted, however, the policy of the legislature of that State in disfranchising a large number of its citizens for their rebellious conduct, thinking more lenient measures might have produced as good an effect without entirely alienating the affections of the people from the government, beside depriving some of them of the means of gaining a livelihood.

On the 9th of May [1787] Washington set out in his carriage from Mount Vernon to attend the convention. At Chester, where he arrived on the 13th, he was met by General Mifflin, now speaker of the Pennsylvania Assembly, Generals Knox and Varnum, Colonel Humphreys, and other personages of note. At Gray's Ferry the city light horse were in attendance, by whom he was escorted into Philadelphia.

It was not until the 25th of May that a sufficient number of delegates were assembled to form a quorum, when they proceeded to organize the body, and by a unanimous vote Washington was called up to the chair as president.

The following anecdote is recorded by Mr. Leigh Pierce, who was a delegate from Georgia. When the convention first opened,

---

[4] Mr. Sparks. For this interesting document see *Writings of Washington*, vol. ix., Appendix, No. iv.

there were a number of propositions brought forward as great leading principles of the new government to be established. A copy of them was given to each member with an injunction of profound secrecy. One morning a member, by accident, dropped his copy of the propositions. It was luckily picked up by General Mifflin and handed to General Washington, who put it in his pocket. After the debates of the day were over and the question for adjournment was called for, Washington rose and, previous to putting the question, addressed the committee as follows: "Gentlemen, I am sorry to find that some one member of this body has been so neglectful of the secrets of the convention as to drop in the State House a copy of their proceedings, which, by accident, was picked up and delivered to me this morning. I must entreat gentlemen to be more careful lest our transactions get into the newspapers and disturb the public repose by premature speculations. I know not whose paper it is but there it is (throwing it down on the table). Let him who owns it take it."

At the same time he bowed, took his hat and left the room with a dignity so severe that every person seemed alarmed. "For my part, I was extremely so," adds Mr. Pierce, "for, putting my hand in my pocket, I missed my copy of the same paper, but, advancing to the table, my fears soon dissipated. I found it to be in the handwriting of another person."

Mr. Pierce found his copy at his lodgings in the pocket of a coat which he had changed that morning. No person ever ventured to claim the anonymous paper.

We forbear to go into the voluminous proceedings of this memorable convention, which occupied from four to seven hours each day for four months, and in which every point was the subject of able and scrupulous discussion by the best talent and noblest spirits of the country. Washington felt restrained, by his situation as president, from taking a part in the debates, but his well-known opinions influenced the whole. The result was the formation of the Constitution of the United States, which (with some amendments made in after years) still exists.

As the members on the last day of the session were signing the engrossed constitution, Dr. Franklin, looking towards the president's chair, at the back of which a sun was painted, observed to those persons next to him, "I have often and often, in the course of the session and the vicissitudes of my hopes and fears as to its issue, looked at that sun behind the president without being able to tell whether it was rising or setting. At length I have the happiness to know it is a rising and not a setting sun."[5]

"The business being closed," says Washington in his diary (Sept. 17th), "the members adjourned to the city tavern, dined together and took a cordial leave of each other. After which I returned to my lodgings, did some business with and received the papers from the secretary of the convention, and retired to meditate on the momentous work which had been executed."

"It appears to me little short of a miracle," writes he to Lafayette, "that the delegates from so many States, different from each other, as you know, in their manners, circumstances and prejudices, should unite in forming a system of national government so little liable to well-founded objections. Nor am I such an enthusiastic, partial or undiscriminating admirer of it, as not to perceive it is tinctured with some real though not radical defects. With regard to the two great points, the pivots upon which the whole machine must move, my creed is simply, First, that the general government is not invested with more powers than are indispensably necessary to perform the functions of a good government, and consequently, that no objection ought to be made against the quantity of power delegated to it.

"Secondly, that these powers, as the appointment of all rulers will for ever arise from and at short, stated intervals recur to the free suffrages of the people, are so distributed among the legislative, executive and judicial branches into which the general government is arranged, that it can never be in danger of degenerating into a monarchy, an oligarchy, an aristocracy or any other despotic or oppressive form so long as there shall remain any virtue in the body of the people.

"It will at least be a recommendation to the proposed constitution that it is provided with more checks and barriers against the introduction of tyranny, and those of a nature less liable to be surmounted, than any government hitherto instituted among mortals.

"We are not to expect perfection in this world, but mankind in modern times have apparently made some progress in the science of government. Should that which is now offered to the people of

[5] *The Madison Papers*, iii., 1624.

America be found on experiment less perfect than it can be made, a constitutional door is left open for its amelioration."

The constitution thus formed was forwarded to Congress and thence transmitted to the State legislatures, each of which submitted it to a State convention composed of delegates chosen for that express purpose by the people. The ratification of the instrument by nine States was necessary to carry it into effect, and as the several State conventions would assemble at different times, nearly a year must elapse before the decisions of the requisite number could be obtained.

During this time Washington resumed his retired life at Mount Vernon, seldom riding, as he says, beyond the limits of his own farms but kept informed by his numerous correspondents, such as James Madison, John Jay and Generals Knox, Lincoln and Armstrong, of the progress of the constitution through its various ordeals and of the strenuous opposition which it met with in different quarters, both in debate and through the press. A diversity of opinions and inclinations on the subject had been expected by him. "The various passions and motives by which men are influenced," said he, "are concomitants of fallibility and ingrafted into our nature." Still he never had a doubt that it would ultimately be adopted and, in fact, the national decision in its favor was more fully and strongly pronounced than even he had anticipated.

His feelings on learning the result were expressed with that solemn and religious faith in the protection of Heaven manifested by him in all the trials and vicissitudes through which his country had passed. "We may," said he, "with a kind of pious and grateful exultation, trace the finger of Providence through those dark and mysterious events which first induced the States to appoint a general convention and then led them, one after another, by such steps as were best calculated to effect the object, into an adoption of the system recommended by the General Convention, thereby, in all human probability, laying a lasting foundation for tranquillity and happiness when we had but too much reason to fear that confusion and misery were coming rapidly upon us."[6]

The testimonials of ratification having been received by Congress from a sufficient number of States, an act was passed by

[6] Letter to Jonathan Trumbull, 20th July, 1788.

that body on the 13th of September, appointing the first Wednesday in January 1789 for the people of the United States to choose electors of a president according to the constitution, and the first Wednesday in the month of February following for the electors to meet and make a choice. The meeting of the government was to be on the first Wednesday in March, and in the city of New York.

Chapter 51

WASHINGTON ELECTED PRESIDENT

The adoption of the Federal Constitution was another epoch in the life of Washington. Before the official forms of an election could be carried into operation, a unanimous sentiment throughout the Union pronounced him the nation's choice to fill the presidential chair. He looked forward to the possibility of his election with characteristic modesty and unfeigned reluctance, as his letters to his confidential friends bear witness.

The election took place at the appointed time and it was soon ascertained that Washington was chosen President for the term of four years from the 4th of March. By this time the arguments and entreaties of his friends and his own convictions of public expediency had determined him to accept, and he made preparations to depart for the seat of government as soon as he should receive official notice of his election. Among other duties, he paid a visit to his mother at Fredericksburg. It was a painful because likely to be a final one, for she was afflicted with a malady which, it was evident, must soon terminate her life. Their parting was affectionate but solemn. She had always been reserved and moderate in expressing herself in regard to the successes of her son, but it must have been a serene satisfaction at the close of her life to see him elevated by his virtues to the highest honor of his country.

From a delay in forming a quorum of Congress, the votes of the electoral college were not counted until early in April, when they were found to be unanimous in favor of Washington. At length, on the 14th of April, he received a letter from the president of Congress, duly notifying him of his election, and he prepared to set out immediately for New York, the seat of government. An entry in his diary, dated the 16th, says: "About ten o'clock I bade adieu to Mount Vernon, to private life and to domestic felicity, and with a mind oppressed with more anxious and painful sensations than I have words to express set out for New York with the best disposition to render service to my country in obedience to its call but with less hope of answering its expectations."

Would the reader know the effect upon Washington's mind of [his] triumphant entry into New York? It was to depress rather than to excite him. Modestly diffident of his abilities to cope with the new duties on which he was entering, he was overwhelmed by what he regarded as proofs of public expectation. Noting in his diary the events of the day, he writes: "The display of boats which attended and joined us on this occasion, some with vocal and some with instrumental music on board; the decorations of the ships, the roar of cannon and the loud acclamations of the people which rent the skies as I passed along the wharves, filled my mind with sensations as painful (considering the reverse of this scene, which may be the case after all my labors to do good) as they are pleasing."

The inauguration was delayed for several days, in which a question arose as to the form or title by which the President elect was to be addressed, and a committee in both Houses was appointed to report upon the subject. The question was stated without Washington's privity and contrary to his desire, as he feared that any title might awaken the sensitive jealousy of republicans at a moment when it was all-important to conciliate public good-will to the new form of government. It was a relief to him therefore when it was finally resolved that the address should be simply "the President of the United States," without any addition of title, a judicious form, which has remained to the present day.

The inauguration took place on the 30th of April. At nine o'clock in the morning there were religious services in all the churches, and prayers put up for the blessing of Heaven on the new government. At twelve o'clock the city troops paraded before Washington's door, and soon after the committees of Congress and heads of departments came in their carriages. At half-past twelve the procession moved forward, preceded by the troops. Next came the committees and heads of departments in their carriages, then Washington in a coach of state, his aide-de-camp, Colonel Humphreys, and his secretary, Mr. Lear, in his own carriage. The foreign ministers and a long train of citizens brought up the rear.

About two hundred yards before reaching the hall, Washington and his suite alighted from their carriages and passed through the troops, who were drawn up on each side, into the hall and senate chamber, where the Vice-President, the Senate and House of Representatives were assembled. The Vice-President, John Adams, recently inaugurated, advanced and conducted Washington to a chair of state at the upper end of the room. A solemn silence prevailed, when the Vice-President rose and informed him that all things were prepared for him to take the oath of office required by the Constitution.

The oath was to be administered by the Chancellor of the State of New York in a balcony in front of the senate chamber and in full view of an immense multitude occupying the street, the windows and even roofs of the adjacent houses. The balcony formed a kind of open recess, with lofty columns supporting the roof. In the centre was a table with a covering of crimson velvet, upon which lay a superbly bound Bible on a crimson velvet cushion. This was all the paraphernalia for the august scene.

All eyes were fixed upon the balcony when, at the appointed hour, Washington made his appearance, accompanied by various public functionaries and members of the Senate and House of Representatives. He was clad in a full suit of dark brown cloth, of American manufacture, with a steel-hilted dress sword, white silk stockings and silver shoe buckles. His hair was dressed and powdered in the fashion of the day and worn in a bag and solitaire.

His entrance on the balcony was hailed by universal shouts. He was evidently moved by this demonstration of public affection. Advancing to the front of the balcony, he laid his hand upon his heart, bowed several times and then retreated to an armchair near the table.

The populace appeared to understand that the scene had overcome him and were hushed at once into profound silence.

After a few moments Washington rose and again came forward. John Adams, the Vice-President, stood on his right; on his left the chancellor of the State, Robert R. Livingston; somewhat in the rear were Roger Sherman, Alexander Hamilton, Generals Knox and St. Clair, the Baron Steuben and others.

The chancellor advanced to administer the oath prescribed by the Constitution, and Mr. Otis, the secretary of the Senate, held up the Bible on its crimson cushion. The oath was read slowly and distinctly, Washington at the same time laying his hand on the open Bible. When it was concluded, he replied solemnly, "I swear —so help me God!" Mr. Otis would have raised the Bible to his lips but he bowed down reverently and kissed it.

The chancellor now stepped forward, waved his hand and exclaimed, "Long live George Washington, President of the United States!" At this moment a flag was displayed on the cupola of the hall, on which signal there was a general discharge of artillery on the Battery. All the bells of the city rang out a joyful peal and the multitude rent the air with acclamations.

Washington again bowed to the people and returned into the senate chamber, where he delivered to both houses of Congress his inaugural address, characterized by his usual modesty, moderation and good sense but uttered with a voice deep, slightly tremulous, and so low as to demand close attention in the listeners. After this he proceeded with the whole assemblage on foot to St. Paul's church, where prayers suited to the occasion were read by Dr. Prevost, Bishop of the Protestant Episcopal Church in New York, who had been appointed by the Senate one of the chaplains of Congress. So closed the ceremonies of the inauguration.

The whole day was one of sincere rejoicing, and in the evening there were brilliant illuminations and fireworks.

The eyes of the world were upon Washington at the commencement of his administration. He had won laurels in the field. Would they continue to flourish in the cabinet? His position was surrounded with difficulties. Inexperienced in the duties of civil administration, he was to inaugurate a new and untried system of government composed of States and people, as yet a mere experiment, to which some looked forward with buoyant confidence, many with doubt and apprehension.

He had moreover a high-spirited people to manage, in whom a jealous passion for freedom and independence had been strengthened by war and who might bear with impatience even the restraints of self-imposed government. The Constitution which he was to inaugurate had met with vehement opposition when under discussion in the general and State governments. Only three states, New Jersey, Delaware and Georgia, had accepted it unanimously. Several of the most important States had adopted it by a mere majority, five of them under an expressed expectation of specified amendments or modifications, while two States, Rhode Island and North Carolina, still stood aloof.

It is true the irritation produced by the conflict of opinions in the general and State conventions had in a great measure subsided, but circumstances might occur to inflame it anew. A diversity of opinions still existed concerning the new government. Some feared that it would have too little control over the individual States, that the political connection would prove too weak to preserve order and prevent civil strife; others, that it would be too strong for their separate independence and would tend toward consolidation and despotism.

The very extent of the country he was called upon to govern, ten times larger than that of any previous republic, must have pressed with weight upon Washington's mind. It presented to the Atlantic a front of fifteen hundred miles divided into individual States differing in the forms of their local governments, differing from each other in interests, in territorial magnitudes, in amount of population, in manners, soils, climates and productions, and the characteristics of their several peoples.

Beyond the Alleghenies extended regions almost boundless, as yet for the most part wild and uncultivated, the asylum of roving Indians and restless, discontented white men. Vast tracts, however, were rapidly being peopled and would soon be portioned into sections requiring local government. The great natural outlet for the exportation of the products of this region of inexhaustible fertility was the Mississippi, but Spain opposed a barrier to the free navigation of this river. Here was peculiar cause of solicitude. Before leaving Mount Vernon, Washington had heard that the hardy yeomanry of the far West were becoming impatient of this barrier and indignant at the apparent indifference of Congress to their prayers for its removal. He had heard, moreover, that British emissaries were fostering these discontents, sowing the seeds of disaffection and offering assistance to the Western people to seize on the city of New Orleans and fortify the mouth of the Mississippi; while, on the other hand, the Spanish authorities at New Orleans were represented as intriguing to effect a separation of the Western territory from the Union with a view or hope of attaching it to the dominion of Spain.

Great Britain, too, was giving grounds for territorial solicitude in these distant quarters by retaining possession of the Western posts, the surrender of which had been stipulated by treaty. Her plea was that debts due to British subjects, for which by the same treaty the United States were bound, remained unpaid. This the Americans alleged was a mere pretext, the real object of their retention being the monopoly of the fur trade; and to the mischievous influence exercised by these posts over the Indian tribes was attributed much of the hostile disposition manifested by the latter along the Western frontier.

While these brooding causes of anxiety existed at home, the foreign commerce of the Union was on a most unsatisfactory footing and required prompt and thorough attention. It was subject to maraud, even by the corsairs of Algiers, Tunis and Tripoli, who captured American merchant vessels and carried their crews into slavery, no treaty having yet been made with any of the Barbary powers excepting Morocco.

To complete the perplexities which beset the new government, the finances of the country were in a lamentable state. There was no money in the treasury. The efforts of the former government to pay or fund its debts had failed. There was a universal state of indebtedness, foreign and domestic, and public credit was prostrate.

In regard to the deportment of Washington at this juncture, we have been informed by one who had opportunities of seeing him that he still retained a military air of command which had become habitual to him. At levees and drawing-rooms he sometimes appeared cold and distant, but this was attributed by those who best knew him to the novelty of his position and his innate diffidence, which seemed to increase with the light which his renown shed about him. Though reserved at times, his reserve had nothing repulsive in it, and in social intercourse, where he was no longer under the eye of critical supervision, soon gave way to soldier-like frankness and cordiality. At all times his courtesy was genuine and benignant and totally free from that stately condescension sometimes mistaken for politeness. Nothing, we are told, could surpass the noble grace with which he presided at a ceremonial dinner, kindly attentive to all his guests but particularly attentive to put those at their ease in a favorable light who appeared to be most diffident.

As to Mrs. Washington, those who really knew her at the time speak of her as free from pretension or affectation, undazzled by her position and discharging its duties with the truthful simplicity and real good-breeding of one accustomed to preside over a hospitable mansion in the "Ancient Dominion." She had her husband's predilection for private life.

Congress reassembled on the 4th of January (1790), but a quorum of the two Houses was not present until the 8th, when the session was opened by Washington in form, with an address delivered before them in the Senate chamber.

Among the most important objects suggested in the address for the deliberation of Congress were provisions for national defense, provisions for facilitating intercourse with foreign nations and defraying the expenses of diplomatic agents, laws for the naturalization of foreigners, uniformity in the currency, weights and measures of the United States, facilities for the advancement of commerce, agriculture and manufactures, attention to the postoffice and post-roads, measures for the promotion of science and literature and for the support of public credit.

This last object was the one which Washington had more immediately at heart. The government was now organized apparently to the satisfaction of all parties but its efficiency would essentially depend on the success of a measure which Washington had pledged himself to institute and which was yet to be tried: namely, a system of finance adapted to revive the national credit and place the public debt in a condition to be paid off. The credit of the country was at a low ebb. The confederacy by its articles had the power of contracting debts for a national object, but no control over the means of payment. Thirteen independent legislatures could grant or withhold the means. The government was then a government under governments—the States had more power than Congress. At the close of the war the debt amounted to forty-two millions of dollars, but so little had the country been able to fulfil its engagements owing to the want of a sovereign legislature having the sole and exclusive power of laying duties upon imports and thus providing adequate resources, that the debt had swollen through arrears of interest to upwards of fifty-four millions.

Of this amount nearly eight millions were due to France, between three and four millions to private lenders in Holland, and about two hundred and fifty thousand in Spain, making, altogether, nearly twelve millions due abroad. The debt contracted at home amounted to upwards of forty-two millions, and was due, originally, to officers and soldiers of the Revolutionary War who had risked their lives for the cause; farmers who had furnished supplies for the public service or whose property had been assumed for it; capitalists who in critical periods of the war had adventured their fortunes in support of their country's independ ence. The domestic debt, therefore, could not have had a more sacred and patriotic origin, but in the long delay of national justice the paper which represented these outstanding claims had sunk to less than a sixth of its nominal value, and the larger portion of it had been parted with at that depreciated rate, either in the course of trade or to speculative purchasers, who were willing to take the risk of eventual payment, however little their confidence seemed to be warranted at the time by the pecuniary condition and prospects of the country.

The debt, when thus transferred, lost its commanding appeal to patriotic sympathy but remained as obligatory in the eye of justice. In the public newspapers, however, and in private circles, the propriety of a discrimination between the assignees and the original holders of the public securities was freely discussed. Beside the foreign and domestic debt of the Federal government, the States individually were involved in liabilities contracted for the common cause to an aggregate amount of about twenty-five millions of dollars, of which more than one half was due from three of them, Massachusetts and South Carolina each owing more than five millions and Virginia more than three and a half. The reputation and the well-being of the government were therefore at stake upon the issue of some plan to retrieve the national credit and establish it upon a firm and secure foundation.

The Secretary of the Treasury (Mr. Hamilton) had been directed by Congress to prepare such a plan during its recess. In the one thus prepared, he asserted what none were disposed to question, the propriety of paying the foreign debt according to its terms. He asserted also the equal validity of the original claims of the American creditors of the government, whether those creditors were the original holders of its certificates or subsequent purchasers of them at a depreciated value. The idea of any distinction between them, which some were inclined to advance, he repudiated as alike unjust, impolitic and impracticable. He urged moreover the assumption by the general government of the separate debts of the States contracted for the common cause, and that a like provision should be made for their payment as for the payment of those of the Union. They were all contracted in the struggle for national independence, not for the independence of any particular part. No more money would be required for their discharge as Federal than as State debts. Money could be raised more readily by the Federal government than by the States, and all clashing and jealousy between State and Federal debtors would thus be prevented.

A reason also which no doubt had great weight with him though he did not bring it under consideration in his report for fear, probably, of offending the jealousy of State sovereignty, dormant but not extinct, was that it would tend to unite the States financially as they were united politically, and strengthen the central government by rallying capitalists around it, subjecting them to its influence and rendering them agents of its will. He recommended therefore that the entire mass of debt be funded, the Union made responsible for it and taxes imposed for its liquidation. He suggested moreover the expediency, for the greater security of the debt and punctuality in the payment of interest, that the domestic creditors submit to an abatement of accruing interest.

The plan was reported to the House by Mr. Hamilton the 14th of January but did not undergo consideration until the 8th of February, when it was opposed with great earnestness, especially the point of assuming the State debts, as tending to consolidation, as giving an undue influence to the general government and as being of doubtful constitutionality. This financial union of the States was reprobated not only on the floor of Congress but in different parts of the Union as fraught with political evil. The Northern and Eastern States generally favored the plan, as did also South Carolina, but Virginia manifested a determined opposition. The measure, however, passed in Committee of the Whole on the 9th of March by a vote of thirty-one to twenty-six.

The funding of the State debts was supposed to benefit materially the Northern States, in which was the entire capital of the country, yet South Carolina voted for the assumption. The fact is, opinions were honestly divided on the subject. The great majority were aiming to do their duty, to do what was right, but their disagreement was the result of real difficulties incident to the intricate and complicated problem with which they had to deal.

A letter from Washington's monitory friend, Dr. Stuart of Virginia (dated March 15th), spoke with alarm of the jealous belief growing up in that quarter that the Northern and Eastern States were combining to pursue their own exclusive interests. Many, he observed, who had heretofore been warm supporters of the government were changing their sentiments from a conviction of the impracticability of union with States whose interests were so dissimilar. Washington had little sympathy with these sectional jealousies.

At this juncture (March 21st), when Virginia discontents were daily gaining strength, Mr. [Thomas] Jefferson arrived in New York to undertake the duties of the Department of State. [He had strong antipathies] to everything of a monarchical or aristocratical tendency. He had just been in Virginia, where the forms and ceremonials adopted at the seat of our government were subjects of cavil and sneer, where it was reported that Washington affected a monarchical style in his official intercourse, that he held court-like levees and Mrs. Washington queenly drawing-rooms at which none but the aristocracy were admitted, that the manners of both were haughty and their personal habits reserved and exclusive.

The impressions thus made on Jefferson's mind received a deeper stamp on his arrival in New York, from conversations with his friend Madison, in the course of which the latter observed that "the satellites and sycophants which surrounded Washington had wound up the ceremonials of the government to a pitch of stateliness which nothing but his personal character could have supported and which no character after him could ever maintain."

Thus prepossessed and premonished, Jefferson looked round him with an apprehensive eye and appears to have seen something to startle him at every turn. We give, from his private correspondence, his own account of his impressions.

"Being fresh from the French revolution while in its first and pure stage and, consequently, somewhat whetted up in my own republican principles, I found a state of things in the general society of the place which I could not have supposed possible. The revolution I had left, and that we had just gone through in the recent change of our own government, being the common topics of conversation, I was astonished to find the general prevalence of monarchical sentiments, insomuch that in maintaining those of republicanism I had always the whole company on my hands, never scarcely finding among them a single co-advocate in that argument unless some old member of Congress happened to be present. The furthest that any one would go in support of the republican features of our new government would be to say, 'The present Constitution is well as a beginning, and may be allowed a fair trial, but it is in fact only a stepping-stone to something better.' "

This picture, given under excitement and with preconceived notions, is probably overcharged; but, allowing it to be true, we can hardly wonder at it, viewed in connection with the place and times. New York during the session of Congress was the gathering place of politicians of every party. The revolution of France had made the forms of government once more the universal topics of conversation and revived the conflict of opinions on the subject. As yet, the history of the world had furnished no favorable examples of popular government. Speculative writers in England had contended that no government more popular than their own was consistent with either internal tranquillity, the supremacy of the laws or a great extent of empire. Our republic was ten times larger than any that had yet existed. Jay, one of the calmest thinkers of the Union, expressed himself dubiously on the subject.

"Whether any people could long govern themselves in an equal, uniform and orderly manner was a question of vital importance to the cause of liberty, but a question which, like others, whose solution depends on facts, could only be determined by experience—now, as yet, there had been very few opportunities of making the experiment."

Alexander Hamilton, though pledged and sincerely disposed to support the republican form with regard to our country, preferred *theoretically* a monarchical form, and being frank of speech and, as Gouverneur Morris writes, "prone to mount his hobby," may have spoken openly in favor of that form as suitable to France. And as his admirers took their creed from him, opinions of the kind may have been uttered pretty freely at dinner-tables. These, however, which so much surprised and shocked Mr. Jefferson, were probably merely speculative opinions broached in unguarded hours with no sinister design by men who had no thought of paving the way for a monarchy. They made, however, a deep impression on his apprehensive mind, which sank deeper and deeper until it became a fixed opinion with him that there was the desire and aim of a large party, of which Hamilton was the leader, to give regal form to the government.

Chapter 52

TWO POLITICAL PARTIES

The question of the assumption of the State debts was resumed in Congress on the 29th of March on a motion to commit, which was carried by a majority of two, the five members from North Carolina (now a State of the Union) who were strongly opposed to assumption having taken their seats and reversed the position of parties on the question. An angry and intemperate discussion was revived much to the chagrin of Washington, who was concerned for the dignity of Congress and who considered the assumption of the State debts, under proper restrictions and scrutiny into accounts, to be just and reasonable.[1] On the 12th of April, when the question to commit was taken, there was a majority of two against the assumption.

On the 26th the House was discharged, for the present, from proceeding on so much of the report as related to the assumption. Jefferson, who had arrived in New York in the midst of what he terms "this bitter and angry contest," had taken no concern in it, being, as he says, "a stranger to the ground, a stranger to the actors in it, so long absent as to have lost all familiarity with the subject and to be unaware of its object." We give his own account of an earnest effort made by Hamilton, who, he says, was "in despair" to resuscitate, through his influence, his almost hopeless project.

"As I was going to the President's one day, I met him [Hamilton] in the street. He walked me backwards and forwards before the President's door for half an hour. He painted pathetically the temper into which the legislature had been wrought, the disgust of those who were called the creditor States, the danger of the *secession* of their members and the separation of the States. He observed that the members of the administration ought to act in con-

[1] See letter to David Stuart, *Writings*, x., 98.

cert, that though this question was not in my department, yet a common duty should make it a common concern; that the President was the centre on which all administrative questions ultimately rested and that all of us should rally around him and support with joint efforts measures approved by him; and that the question having been lost by a small majority only, it was probable that an appeal from me to the judgment and discretion of some of my friends might effect a change in the vote, and the machine of government, now suspended, might be again set in motion.

"I told him that I was really a stranger to the whole subject; that not having yet informed myself of the system of finance adopted, I knew not how far this was a necessary sequence; that undoubtedly, if its rejection endangered a dissolution of our Union at this incipient stage, I should deem that the most unfortunate of all consequences, to avert which all partial and temporary evils should be yielded. I proposed to him, however, to dine with me the next day, and I would invite another friend or two, bring them into conference together, and I thought it impossible that reasonable men, consulting together coolly, could fail, by some mutual sacrifices of opinion, to form a compromise which was to save the Union.

"The discussion took place. I could take no part in it but an exhortatory one because I was a stranger to the circumstances which should govern it. But it was finally agreed that whatever importance had been attached to the rejection of this proposition, the preservation of the Union and of concord among the States was more important and that therefore it would be better that the vote of rejection should be rescinded, to effect which some members should change their votes. But it was observed that this pill would be peculiarly bitter to the Southern States and that some concomitant measure should be adopted to sweeten it a little to them. There had before been projects to fix the seat of government either at Philadelphia or at Georgetown on the Potomac, and it was thought that by giving it to Philadelphia for ten years and to Georgetown permanently afterwards, this might, as an anodyne, calm in some degree the ferment which might be excited by the other measure alone.

"Some two of the Potomac members (White and Lee, but White with a revulsion of stomach almost convulsive) agreed to change their votes, and Hamilton undertook to carry the other point. In doing this, the influence he had established over the Eastern members, with the agency of Robert Morris with those of the Middle States, effected his side of the engagement."[2]

The decision of Congress was ultimately in favor of assumption, though the form in which it finally passed differed somewhat from the proposition of Hamilton. A specific sum was assumed ($21,500,000), and this was distributed among the States in specific portions. Thus modified, it passed the Senate July 22d by the close vote of fourteen to twelve; and the House July 24th by thirty-four to twenty-eight, "after having," says Washington, "been agitated with a warmth and intemperance, with prolixity and threats which, it is to be feared, have lessened the dignity of Congress and decreased the respect once entertained for it."

The question about the permanent seat of government, which, from the variety of contending interests, had been equally a subject of violent contest, was now compromised. It was agreed that Congress should continue for ten years to hold its sessions at Philadelphia, during which time the public buildings should be erected at some place on the Potomac to which the government should remove at the expiration of the above term. A territory ten miles square, selected for the purpose on the confines of Maryland and Virginia, was ceded by those States to the United States and subsequently designated as the District of Columbia.

Congress adjourned on the 12th of August. Jefferson, commenting on the discord that had prevailed for a time among the members, observes that in the latter part of the session they had reacquired the harmony which had always distinguished their proceedings before the introduction of the two disagreeable subjects of the Assumption and the Residence. "These," said he, "really threatened, at one time, a separation of the legislature *sine die*."

"It is not foreseen," adds he sanguinely, "that anything so generative of dissension can arise again, and therefore the friends of government hope that that difficulty surmounted in the States, everything will work well."[3]

Washington, too, however grieved and disappointed he may have been by the dissensions which had prevailed in Congress, consoled himself by the fancied harmony of his cabinet. Singularly free himself from all jealousy of the talents and popularity of

[2] Jefferson's *Works*, ix., 293, *The Annas*.
[3] *Ibid.*, iii., 184.

others, and solely actuated by zeal for the public good, he had sought the ablest men to assist him in his arduous task, and supposed them influenced by the same unselfish spirit.

Yet, at this very moment a lurking spirit of rivalry between Jefferson and Hamilton was already existing and daily gaining strength. Jefferson, who, as we have intimated, already considered Hamilton a monarchist in his principles, regarded all his financial schemes with suspicion, as intended to strengthen the influence of the treasury and make its chief the master of every vote in the legislature, "which might give to the government the direction suited to his political views."

Under these impressions, Jefferson looked back with an angry and resentful eye to the manner in which Hamilton had procured his aid in effecting the measure of assumption. He now regarded it as a finesse by which he had been entrapped, and stigmatized the measure itself as a "fiscal manœuvre, to which he had most ignorantly and innocently been made to hold the candle."[4]

Congress reassembled according to adjournment on the first Monday in December at Philadelphia, which was now for a time the seat of government. A house belonging to Mr. Robert Morris, the financier, had been hired by Washington for his residence, and at his request had undergone additions and alterations "in a plain and neat and not by any means in an extravagant style."

His secretary, Mr. Lear, had made every preparation for his arrival and accommodation and, among other things, had spoken of the rich and elegant style in which the state carriage was fitted up. "I had rather have heard," replied Washington, "that my repaired coach was plain and elegant than rich and elegant."

Congress at its opening was chiefly occupied in financial arrangements intended to establish the public credit and provide for the expenses of government. According to the statement of the Secretary of the Treasury, an additional annual revenue of eight hundred and twenty-six thousand dollars would be required, principally to meet the additional charges arising from the assumption of the State debts. He proposed to raise it by an increase of the impost on foreign distilled spirits and a tax by way of excise on spirits distilled at home. An Impost and Excise bill was accordingly introduced into Congress and met with violent opposition.

4 *Ibid.*, ix., 92.

An attempt was made to strike out the excise but failed, and the whole bill was finally carried through the House.

Mr. Hamilton, in his former Treasury report, had recommended the establishment of a National Bank. He now in a special report urged the policy of the measure. A bill introduced in conformity with his views was passed in the Senate but vehemently opposed in the House, partly on considerations of policy but chiefly on the ground of constitutionality. On one side it was denied that the Constitution had given to Congress the power of incorporation, on the other side it was insisted that such power was incident to the power vested in Congress for raising money.

The question was argued at length and with great ardor, and after passing the House of Representatives by a majority of nineteen votes, came before the Executive for his approval. Washington was fully alive to the magnitude of the question and the interest felt in it by the opposing parties. The cabinet was divided on it. Jefferson and Randolph denied its constitutionality, Hamilton and Knox maintained it. Washington required of each minister the reasons of his opinion in writing and, after maturely weighing them, gave his sanction to the act and the bill was carried into effect.

The objection of Jefferson to a bank was not merely on constitutional grounds. In his subsequent writings he avows himself opposed to banks as introducing a paper instead of a cash system—raising up a moneyed aristocracy and abandoning the public to the discretion of avarice and swindlers. Paper money might have some advantages but its abuses were inevitable, and by breaking up the measure of value it made a lottery of all private property. These objections he maintained to his dying day, but he had others, which may have been more cogent with him in the present instance. He considered the bank as a powerful engine intended by Hamilton to complete the machinery by which the whole action of the legislature was to be placed under the direction of the Treasury, and shaped to further a monarchical system of government. Washington, he affirmed, was not aware of the drift or effect of Hamilton's schemes. "Unversed in financial projects and calculations and budgets, his approbation of them was bottomed on his confidence in the man."

Washington, however, was not prone to be swayed in his judgments by blind partiality. When he distrusted his own knowledge in regard to any important measure, he asked the written opinions of those of his council who he thought were better informed, and examined and weighed them and put them to the test of his almost unfailing sagacity. This was the way he had acted as a general in his military councils, and he found the same plan efficacious in his cabinet. His confidence in Hamilton's talents, information and integrity had led him to seek his counsels, but his approbation of those counsels was bottomed on a careful investigation of them. It was the same in regard to the counsels of Jefferson. They were received with great deference but always deliberately and scrupulously weighed.

The opposite policy of these rival statesmen brought them into incessant collision. "Hamilton and myself," writes Jefferson, "were daily pitted in the cabinet like two cocks." The warm-hearted Knox always sided with his old companion in arms, whose talents he revered. He is often noticed with a disparaging sneer by Jefferson in consequence. Randolph commonly adhered to the latter. Washington's calm and massive intellect overruled any occasional discord. His policy with regard to his constitutional advisers has been happily estimated by a modern statesman: "He sought no unit cabinet, according to the set phrase of succeeding times. He asked no suppression of sentiment, no concealment of opinion. He exhibited no mean jealousy of high talent in others. He gathered around him the greatest public men of that day, and some of them to be ranked with the greatest of any day. He did not leave Jefferson and Hamilton without the cabinet, to shake perhaps the whole fabric of government in their fierce wars and rivalries, but he took them within, where he himself might arbitrate their disputes as they arose, and turn to the best account for the country their suggestions as they were made."[5]

In the meantime two political parties were forming throughout the Union, under the adverse standards of these statesmen. Both had the good of the country at heart but differed as to the policy by which it was to be secured. The Federalists, who looked up to Hamilton as their model, were in favor of strengthening the general government so as to give it weight and dignity abroad and efficiency at home; to guard it against the encroachments of the individual States and a general tendency to anarchy. The other

[5] Speech of R. M. T. Hunter, of Virginia.

party, known as Republicans or Democrats and taking Mr. Jefferson's view of affairs, saw in all the measures advocated by the Federalists an intention to convert the Federal into a great central or consolidated government preparatory to a change from a republic to a monarchy.

In the month of March 1791 Washington set out on a tour through the Southern States, travelling with one set of horses and making occasional halts. The route projected and of which he had marked off the halting places, was by Fredericksburg, Richmond, Wilmington (N.C.) and Charleston, to Savannah; thence to Augusta, Columbia and the interior towns of North Carolina and Virginia, comprising a journey of eighteen hundred and eighty-seven miles, all which he accomplished without any interruption from sickness, bad weather or any untoward accident.

He returned to Philadelphia on the 6th of July, much pleased with his tour. It had enabled him, he said, to see with his own eyes the situation of the country and to learn more accurately the disposition of the people than he could have done from any verbal information.

A few weeks of autumn were passed by Washington at Mount Vernon with his family in rural enjoyment, and in instructing a new agent, Mr. Robert Lewis, in the management of his estate, his nephew, Major George A. Washington, who ordinarily attended to his landed concerns, being absent among the mountains in quest of health.

The second Congress assembled at Philadelphia on the 24th of October, and on the 25th Washington delivered his opening speech. After remarking upon the prosperous situation of the country, and the success which had attended its financial measures, he adverted to the offensive operations against the Indians, which government had been compelled to adopt for the protection of the Western frontier. Some of these operations, he observed, had been successful, others were still depending.

[An expedition under General St. Clair met with a disastrous defeat.]

Poor St. Clair's defeat has been paralleled with that of Braddock. No doubt when he realized the terrible havoc that had been made, he thought sadly of Washington's parting words, "Beware of a surprise!"

We have a graphic account of the manner in which the intelligence of the disaster was received by Washington at Philadelphia. Towards the close of a winter's day in December, an officer in uniform dismounted in front of the President's house and, giving the bridle to his servant, knocked at the door. He was informed by the porter that the President was at dinner and had company. The officer was not to be denied. He was on public business, he brought despatches for the President. A servant was sent to the dining-room to communicate the matter to Mr. Lear. The latter left the table and went into the hall, where the officer repeated what he had said to the porter. Mr. Lear, as secretary of the President, offered to take charge of the despatches and deliver them at the proper time. The officer replied that he was just arrived from the Western army. His orders were to deliver the despatches promptly to the President in person, but that he would wait his directions. Mr. Lear returned, and, in a whisper, communicated to the President what had passed. Washington rose from the table and went into the hall, whence he returned in a short time and resumed his seat, apologizing for his absence but without alluding to the cause of it. One of the company, however, overheard him, as he took his seat, mutter to himself with an ejaculation of extreme impatience, "I knew it would be so!"

Mrs. Washington held her drawing-room that evening. The gentlemen repaired thither from the table. Washington appeared there with his usual serenity, speaking courteously to every lady, as was his custom. By ten o'clock all the company had gone. Mrs. Washington retired soon after, and Washington and his secretary alone remained.

The general walked slowly backward and forward for some minutes in silence. As yet there had been no change in his manner. Taking a seat on the sofa by the fire, he told Mr. Lear to sit down. The latter had scarce time to notice that he was extremely agitated when he broke out suddenly: "It's all over!—St. Clair's defeated!—routed; the officers nearly all killed, the men by the wholesale; the rout complete; too shocking to think of; and a surprise into the bargain!" All this was uttered with great vehemence. Then pausing and rising from the sofa, he walked up and down the room in silence, violently agitated but saying nothing. When near the door he stopped short, stood still for a few moments, when there was another terrible explosion of wrath.

"Yes," exclaimed he, "HERE on this very spot, I took leave of him. I wished him success and honor. 'You have your instructions from the Secretary of War,' said I. 'I had a strict eye to them, and will add but one word, BEWARE OF A SURPRISE! You know how the Indians fight us. I repeat it, BEWARE OF A SURPRISE.' He went off with that, my last warning, thrown into his ears. And yet! To suffer that army to be cut to pieces, hacked, butchered, tomahawked by a surprise—the very thing I guarded him against —O God! O God!" exclaimed he, throwing up his hands and while his very frame shook with emotion, "he's worse than a murderer! How can he answer to his country! The blood of the slain is upon him—the curse of widows and orphans—the curse of heaven!"

Mr. Lear remained speechless, awed into breathless silence by the appalling tones in which this torrent of invective was poured forth. The paroxysm passed by. Washington again sat down on the sofa—he was silent—apparently uncomfortable, as if conscious of the ungovernable burst of passion which had overcome him.

"This must not go beyond this room," said he at length in a subdued and altered tone—there was another and a longer pause; then, in a tone quite low: "General St. Clair shall have justice," said he. "I looked hastily through the despatches, saw the whole disaster but not all the particulars. I will receive him without displeasure. I will hear him without prejudice. He shall have full justice."[6]

Washington had recovered his equanimity. "The storm," we are told, "was over, and no sign of it was afterwards seen in his conduct or heard in his conversation."

[6] Rush's *Washington in Domestic Life.*

Chapter 53

DISSENSION IN THE CABINET

Great heat and asperity were manifested in the discussions of Congress throughout the present session. Washington had observed with pain the political divisions which were growing up in the country and was deeply concerned at finding that they were pervading the halls of legislation. The press too was contributing its powerful aid to keep up and increase the irritation. Two rival papers existed at the seat of government. One was Fenno's *Gazette of the United States*, in which John Adams had published his *Discourses on Davila*. The other was the *National Gazette*, edited by Philip Freneau. Freneau had been editor of the *New York Daily Advertiser* but had come to Philadelphia in the autumn of 1791 to occupy the post of translating clerk in Mr. Jefferson's office, and had almost immediately (October 31) published the first number of his *Gazette*. Notwithstanding his situation in the office of the Secretary of State, Freneau became and continued to be throughout the session a virulent assailant of most of the measures of government excepting such as originated with Mr. Jefferson or were approved by him.

Heart-weary by the political strifes and disagreements which were disturbing the country and marring the harmony of his cabinet, the charge of government was becoming intolerably irksome to Washington and he longed to be released from it and to be once more master of himself, free to indulge those rural and agricultural tastes which were to give verdure and freshness to his future existence. He had some time before this expressed a determination to retire from public life at the end of his presidential term. But one more year of that term remained to be endured. He was congratulating himself with the thought, when Mr. Jefferson intimated that it was his intention to retire from office at the same time with himself.

Washington was exceedingly discomposed by this determination. Jefferson, in his *Annas*, assures us that the President remonstrated with him against it, "in an affectionate tone." For his own part, he observed, many motives compelled him to retire. It was only after much pressing that he had consented to take a part in the new government and get it under way. Were he to continue in it longer, it might give room to say that, having tasted the sweets of office, he could not do without them.

He observed, moreover, to Jefferson, that he really felt himself growing old; that his bodily health was less firm and his memory, always bad, was becoming worse. The other faculties of his mind, perhaps, might be evincing to others a decay of which he himself might be insensible. This apprehension, he said, particularly oppressed him.

His activity, too, had declined. Business was consequently more irksome, and the longing for tranquillity and retirement had become an irresistible passion. For these reasons he felt himself obliged, he said, to retire, yet he should consider it unfortunate if in so doing he should bring on the retirement of the great officers of government, which might produce a shock on the public mind of a dangerous consequence.

Jefferson in reply stated the reluctance with which he himself had entered upon public employment, and the resolution he had formed on accepting his station in the cabinet to make the resignation of the President the epoch of his own retirement from labors of which he was heartily tired. He did not believe, however, that any of his brethren in the administration had any idea of retiring. On the contrary, he had perceived at a late meeting of the trustees of the sinking fund that the Secretary of the Treasury had developed the plan he intended to pursue and that it embraced years in its view.

Washington rejoined that he considered the Treasury Department a limited one, going only to the single object of revenue, while that of the Secretary of State, embracing nearly all the objects of administration, was much more important, and the retirement of the officer therefore would be more noticed; that though the government had set out with a pretty general good-will, yet that symptoms of dissatisfaction had lately shown themselves far beyond what he could have expected; and to what height these might arise, in case of too great a change in the administration, could not be foreseen.

Subsequent to Washington's remonstrance with Mr. Jefferson, he had confidential conversations with Mr. Madison on the subject of his intended retirement from office at the end of the presidential term, and asked him to think what would be the proper time and mode of announcing his intention to the public, and intimating a wish that Mr. Madison would prepare for him the announcement.

Mr. Madison remonstrated in the most earnest manner against such a resolution, setting forth in urgent language the importance to the country of his continuing in the presidency. Washington listened to his reasoning with profound attention but still clung to his resolution.

In regard to St. Clair, we will here add that a committee of the House of Representatives ultimately inquired into the cause of the failure of his expedition and rendered a report in which he was explicitly exculpated. His adjutant-general also (Winthrop Sargent), in his private diary, testifies to St. Clair's coolness and bravery though debilitated by illness. Public sentiment, however, remained for a long time adverse to him, but Washington, satisfied with the explanations which had been given, continued to honor him with his confidence and friendship.

Congress adjourned on the 8th of May, and soon afterward Washington set off on a short visit to Mount Vernon. The season was in all its beauty, and never had this rallying place of his affections appeared to him more attractive. How could he give up the prospect of a speedy return to its genial pursuits and pleasures from the harassing cares and janglings of public life? On the 20th of May he wrote to Mr. Madison on the subject of their late conversation. "I have not been unmindful," says he, "of the sentiments expressed by you. On the contrary, I have again and again revolved them with thoughtful anxiety but without being able to dispose my mind to a longer continuation in the office I have now the honor to hold. I therefore still look forward with the fondest and most ardent wishes to spend the remainder of my days, which I cannot expect to be long, in ease and tranquillity."

He now renewed the request he had made Mr. Madison for advice as to the proper time and mode for announcing his intention of retiring, and for assistance in preparing the announcement. He then went on to suggest a number of the topics and ideas which the address was to contain, all to be expressed in "plain and modest terms." But in the main he left it to Mr. Madison to determine whether, in the first place, such an address would be proper; if so, what matters it ought to contain and when it ought to appear; whether at the same time with his [Washington's] declaration of his intention to retire, or at the close of his career.

Madison in reply approved of the measure and advised that the notification and address should appear together and be promulgated through the press in time to pervade every part of the Union by the beginning of November. With the letter he sent a draft of the address. Before concluding his letter, Madison expressed a hope that Washington would reconsider his idea of retiring from office, and that the country might not, at so important a juncture, be deprived of the inestimable advantage of having him at the head of its councils.

On the 23d of May, Jefferson also addressed a long letter to Washington on the same subject, [and] launched out against the public debt and all the evils which he apprehended from the funding system, the ultimate object of all which was, said he, "to prepare the way for a change from the present republican form of government to that of a monarchy, of which the English constitution is to be the model." He concluded by pronouncing the continuance of Washington at the head of affairs to be of the last importance.

"The confidence of the whole Union," writes he, "is centered in you. Your being at the helm will be more than an answer to every argument which can be used to alarm and lead the people in any quarter into violence or secession. North and South will hang together if they have you to hang on. And if the first corrective of a numerous representation should fail in its effect, your presence will give time for trying others not inconsistent with the union and peace of the States.

"I am perfectly aware of the oppression under which your present office lays your mind, and of the ardor with which you pant for retirement to domestic life. But there is sometimes an eminence of character on which society have such peculiar claims as to control the predilections of the individual for a particular walk of happiness and restrain him to that alone arising from the present and future benediction of mankind. This seems to be your condition, and the law imposed on you by Providence in forming your character and fashioning the events on which it was to operate; and it is to motives like these, and not to personal anxieties of mine or others, who have no right to call on you for sacrifices, that I appeal from your former determination and urge a revisal of it on the ground of change in the aspect of things. Should an honest majority result from the new and enlarged representation, should those acquiesce whose principles or interests they may control, your wishes for retirement would be gratified with less danger as soon as that shall be manifest, without awaiting the completion of the second period of four years. One or two sessions will determine the crisis, and I cannot but hope that you can resolve to add one or two more to the many years you have already sacrificed to the good of mankind."[1]

The letter of Jefferson was not received by Washington until after his return to Philadelphia, and the purport of it was so painful to him that he deferred from day to day having any conversation with that statesman on the subject. On the 10th of July, Washington had a conversation with Jefferson and endeavored with his usual supervising and moderating assiduity to allay the jealousies and suspicions which were disturbing the mind of that ardent politician. These, he intimated, had been carried a great deal too far. There might be *desires*, he said, among a few in the higher walks of life, particularly in the great cities, to change the form of government into a monarchy, but he did not believe there were any *designs*, and he believed the main body of the people in the Eastern States were as steadily for republicanism as in the Southern.

He now spoke with earnestness about articles in the public papers, especially in the *Gazette* edited by Freneau, the object of which seemed to be to excite opposition to the government, and which had actually excited it in Pennsylvania in regard to the excise law. "These articles," said he, feelingly, "tend to produce a separation of the Union, the most dreadful of calamities, and whatever tends to produce anarchy tends of course to produce a resort to monarchical government."

The articles in question had, it is true, been chiefly levelled at the Treasury Department, but Washington accepted no immunity from attacks pointed at any department of his government, assuming that they were aimed directly at himself. "In condemning the

[1] Writings, x., 508.

administration of the government, they condemned me," said he, "for, if they thought these were measures pursued contrary to my sentiments, they must conceive me too careless to attend to them or too stupid to understand them."

He acknowledged, indeed, that he had signed many acts of which he did not approve in all their parts, but never had he put his hand to one which he did not think eligible on the whole.

As to the bank which had been so much complained of, he observed that, until there was some infallible criterion of reason, a difference of opinion must be tolerated. He did not believe the discontents extended far from the seat of government. He had seen and spoken with many people in Maryland and Virginia in his late journey and had found them contented and happy.

Hamilton was equally strenuous with Jefferson in urging upon Washington the policy of a re-election as it regarded the public good, and wrote to him fully on the subject.

Not the cabinet, merely, divided as it was in its political opinions, but all parties, however discordant in other points, concurred in a desire that Washington should continue in office—so truly was he regarded as the choice of the nation.

But though the cabinet was united in feeling on this one subject, in other respects its dissensions were increasing in virulence. Hamilton, aggrieved by the attacks made in Freneau's paper upon his funding and banking system, his duty on home-made spirits and other points of his financial policy, and upon himself by holding him up as a monarchist at heart, and considering these attacks as originating in the hostility of Freneau's patron, Mr. Jefferson, addressed a note signed T.L. to the editor of the *Gazette of the United States*, in which he observes that the editor of the *National Gazette* received a salary from government, adding the significant query—whether this salary was paid him for translations or publications the design of which was to vilify those to whom the voice of the people had committed the administration of our public affairs, to oppose the measures of government, and, by false insinuations, to disturb the public peace? "In common life it is thought ungrateful for a man to bite the hand that puts bread in his mouth. But if the man is hired to do it, the case is altered."

In another article, dated August 4th, Mr. Hamilton, under the signature of "An American," gave some particulars of the negotiations which ended in the establishment of the *National Gazette,* devoted to the interests of a certain party of which Mr. Jefferson was the head. "An experiment," said he, "somewhat new in the history of political manœuvres in this country; a newspaper instituted by a public officer, and the editor of it regularly pensioned with the public money in the disposal of that officer. . . . But, it may be asked, is it possible that Mr. Jefferson, the head of a principal department of the government, can be the patron of a paper the evident object of which is to decry the government and its measures? If he disapproves of the government itself and thinks it deserving of his opposition, can he reconcile it to his own personal dignity and the principles of probity to hold an office under it and employ the means of official influence in that opposition? If he disapproves of the leading measures which have been adopted in the course of his administration, can he reconcile it with the principles of delicacy and propriety to hold a place in that administration and at the same time to be instrumental in vilifying measures which have been adopted by majorities of both branches of the legislature and sanctioned by the chief magistrate of the Union?"

This attack brought out an affidavit from Mr. Freneau, in which he declared that his coming to Philadelphia was his own voluntary act; that, as an editor of a newspaper, he had never been urged, advised or influenced by Mr. Jefferson, and that not a single line of his *Gazette* was ever directly or indirectly written, dictated or composed for it by the Secretary of State.

Washington had noticed this growing feud with excessive pain, and at length found it necessary to interfere and attempt a reconciliation between the warring parties.

Washington's solicitude for harmony in his cabinet had been rendered more anxious by public disturbances in some parts of the country. The excise law on ardent spirits distilled within the United States had, from the time of its enactment by Congress in 1791, met with opposition from the inhabitants of the western counties of Pennsylvania. It had been modified and rendered less offensive within the present year but the hostility to it had continued. Combinations were formed to defeat the execution of it, and the revenue officers were riotously opposed in the execution of their duties.

Determined to exert all the legal powers with which he was invested to check so daring and unwarrantable a spirit, Washington on the 15th of September issued a proclamation warning all persons to desist from such unlawful combinations and proceedings and requiring all courts, magistrates and officers to bring the infractors of the law to justice, copies of which proclamation were sent to the governors of Pennsylvania and of North and South Carolina.

On the 18th of October Washington made one more effort to allay the discord in his cabinet. Finding it impossible for the rival secretaries to concur in any system of politics, he urged them to accommodate their differences by mutual yieldings.

"A measure of this sort," observed he, "would produce harmony and consequent good in our public councils, and the contrary will inevitably produce confusion and serious mischiefs. And all for what? Because mankind cannot think alike, but would adopt different means to attain the same end. For I will frankly and solemnly declare that I believe the views of both to be pure and well meant, and that experience only will decide with respect to the salutariness of the measures which are the subjects of this dispute."

"Why, then, when some of the best citizens of the United States—men of discernment—uniform and tried patriots—who have no sinister views to promote but are chaste in their ways of thinking and acting, are to be found some on one side and some on the other of the questions which have caused these agitations— why should either of you be so tenacious of your opinions as to make no allowance for those of the other?

"I have a great, a sincere esteem and regard for you both, and ardently wish that some line could be marked out by which both of you could walk."

Chapter 54

WASHINGTON RE-ELECTED

It was after a long and painful conflict of feelings that Washington consented to be a candidate for a re-election. There was no opposition on the part of the public, and the vote for him in the Electoral College was unanimous. In a letter to a friend, he declared himself gratefully impressed by so distinguished and honorable a testimony of public approbation and confidence. In truth he had been apprehensive of being elected by but a meagre majority, which he acknowledged would have been a matter of chagrin. But though gratified to find that the hearts of his countrymen were still with him, it was with no emotion of pleasure that [he] looked forward to another term of public duty and a prolonged absence from the quiet retirement of Mount Vernon.

The session of Congress which was to close his present term, opened on the 5th of November. The continuance of the Indian war formed a painful topic in the President's address. Efforts at pacification had as yet been unsuccessful. Two brave officers, Colonel Hardin and Major Trueman, who had been sent to negotiate with the savages, had been severally murdered. Vigorous preparations were therefore making for an active prosecution of hostilities, in which Wayne was to take the field. Washington, with benevolent earnestness, dwelt upon the humane system of civilizing the tribes by inculcating agricultural tastes and habits.

The factious and turbulent opposition which had been made in some parts of the country to the collection of duties on spirituous liquors distilled in the United States was likewise adverted to by the President, and a determination expressed to assert and maintain the just authority of the laws trusting in the "full co-operation of the other departments of government and the zealous support of all good citizens." In a part of the speech addressed to the

House of Representatives, he expressed a strong hope that the state of the national finances was now sufficiently matured to admit of an arrangement for the redemption and discharge of the public debt.

The address was well received by both houses, and a disposition expressed to concur with the President's views and wishes. The discussion of the subjects to which he had called their attention soon produced vehement conflicts of opinion in the House, marking the growing virulence of parties. The Secretary of the Treasury, in reporting, at the request of the House, a plan for the annual reduction of so much of the national debt as the United States had a right to redeem, spoke of the expenses of the Indian war and the necessity of additional internal taxes. The consideration of the report was parried or evaded, and a motion made to reduce the military establishment. This gave an opportunity for sternly criticising the mode in which the Indian war had been conducted, for discussing the comparative merits and cost of regular and militia forces and for inveighing against standing armies, as dangerous to liberty. These discussions, while they elicited much heat, led to no present result and gave way to an inquiry into the conduct of the Secretary of the Treasury in regard to certain loans, which the President, in conformity to acts of Congress, had authorized him to make, but concerning the management of which he had not furnished detailed reports to the legislature.

The subject was opened by Mr. Giles of Virginia, who moved in the House of Representatives a series of resolutions seeking information in the matter, and who followed his resolutions by a speech charging the Secretary of the Treasury with official misconduct, and intimating that a large balance of public money had not been accounted for.

A report of the Secretary gave all the information desired, but the charges against him continued to be urged with great acrimony to the close of the session, when they were signally rejected, not more than sixteen members voting for any one of them.

The veneration inspired by the character of Washington, and the persuasion that he would never permit himself to be considered the head of a party, had hitherto shielded him from attack. A little circumstance, however, showed that the rancor of party was beginning to glance at him.

On his birthday (February 22d) many of the members of Congress were desirous of waiting on him in testimony of respect as chief magistrate of the Union, and a motion was made to adjourn for half an hour for the purpose. It met with serious opposition as a species of homage—it was setting up an idol dangerous to liberty—it had a bias towards monarchy.

Washington, though he never courted popularity, was attentive to the signs of public opinion and disposed to be guided by them when right. The time for entering upon his second term of Presidency was at hand. There had been much cavilling at the parade attending his first installation. Jefferson especially had pronounced it "not at all in character with the simplicity of republican government, and looking, as if wishfully, to those of European Courts."

To guide him on the coming occasion, Washington called the heads of departments together and desired they would consult with one another and agree on any changes they might consider for the better, assuring them he would willingly conform to whatever they should advise.

They held such consultation, and ultimately gave their individual opinions in writing with regard to the time, manner and place of the President's taking the oath of office. As they were divided in opinion and gave no positive advice as to any change, no change was made. On the 4th of March the oath was publicly administered to Washington by Mr. Justice Cushing in the Senate chamber in presence of the heads of departments, foreign ministers, such members of the House of Representatives as were in town, and as many other spectators as could be accommodated.

It was under gloomy auspices, a divided cabinet, an increasing exasperation of parties, a suspicion of monarchical tendencies, and a threatened abatement of popularity that Washington entered upon his second term of presidency. It was a portentous period in the history of the world, for in a little while came news of that tragical event, the beheading of Louis XVI. It was an event deplored by many of the truest advocates of liberty in America, who, like Washington, remembered that unfortunate monarch as the friend of their country in her revolutionary struggle. But others, zealots in the cause of political reform, considered it with complacency as sealing the downfall of the French monarchy and the establishment of a republic.

An event followed hard upon it to shake the quiet of the world.

Early in April intelligence was received that France had declared war against England. Popular excitement was now wound up to the highest pitch. What, it was asked, were the Americans to do in such a juncture? Could they remain unconcerned spectators of a conflict between their ancient enemy and republican France? Should they fold their arms and look coldly on a war, begun, it is true, by France, but threatening the subversion of the republic and the re-establishment of a monarchical government?

Many, in the wild enthusiasm of the moment, would at once have precipitated the country into a war. Fortunately this belligerent impulse was not general and was checked by the calm, controlling wisdom of Washington. He was at Mount Vernon when he received news of the war, and understood that American vessels were already designated and some fitting out to serve in it as privateers. He forthwith despatched a letter to Jefferson on the subject. "War having actually commenced between France and Great Britain," writes he, "it behooves the government of this country to use every means in its power to prevent the citizens thereof from embroiling us with either of those powers, by endeavoring to maintain a strict neutrality."

Hastening back to Philadelphia, he held a cabinet council on the 19th of April to deliberate on the measures proper to be observed by the United States in the present crisis and to determine upon a general plan of conduct for the Executive.

In this council it was unanimously determined that a proclamation should be issued by the President, "forbidding the citizens of the United States to take part in any hostilities on the seas and warning them against carrying to the belligerents any articles deemed contraband according to the modern usages of nations, and forbidding all acts and proceedings inconsistent with the duties of a friendly nation towards those at war."

It was unanimously agreed also that should the republic of France send a minister to the United States, he should be received.

No one at the present day questions the wisdom of Washington's proclamation of neutrality. It was our true policy to keep aloof from European war, in which our power would be inefficient, our loss certain. The measure, however, was at variance with the enthusiastic feelings and excited passions of a large portion of the citizens. They treated it for a time with some forbearance out of long-cherished reverence for Washington's name, but his popularity, hitherto unlimited, was no proof against the inflamed state of public feeling. The proclamation was stigmatized as a royal edict, a daring assumption of power, an open manifestation of partiality for England and hostility to France.

Washington saw that a deadly blow was aimed at his influence and his administration and that both were at hazard but he was convinced that neutrality was the true national policy, and he resolved to maintain it whatever might be his immediate loss of popular favor.

Washington had hitherto been annoyed and perplexed by having to manage a divided cabinet. He was now threatened with that cabinet's dissolution. Mr. Hamilton had informed him by letter that private as well as public reasons had determined him to retire from office towards the close of the next session, probably with a view to give Congress an opportunity to examine into his conduct. Now came a letter from Mr. Jefferson, dated July 31st, in which he recalled the circumstances which had induced him to postpone for a while his original intention of retiring from office at the close of the first four years of the republic. These circumstances, he observed, had now ceased to such a degree as to leave him free to think again of a day on which to withdraw. "At the close, therefore, of the ensuing month of September I shall beg leave to retire to scenes of greater tranquillity from those for which I am every day more and more convinced that neither my talents, tone of mind nor time of life fit me."

Washington was both grieved and embarrassed by this notification. Full of concern, he called upon Jefferson at his country residence near Philadelphia, pictured his deep distress at finding himself, in the present perplexing juncture of affairs about to be deserted by those of his cabinet on whose counsel he had counted and whose places he knew not where to find persons competent to supply; and, in his chagrin, again expressed his repentance that he himself had not resigned as he had once meditated.

The public mind, he went on to observe, was in an alarming state of ferment. Political combinations of various kinds were forming. Where all this would end he knew not. A new Congress was to assemble, more numerous than the last, perhaps of a different spirit. The first expressions of its sentiments would be important, and it would relieve him considerably if Jefferson would remain in office if it were only until the end of the session.

Jefferson, in reply, pleaded an excessive repugnance to public life and, what seems to have influenced him more sensibly, the actual uneasiness of his position. He was obliged, he said, to move in exactly the circle which he knew to bear him peculiar hatred, "the wealthy aristocrats, the merchants connected closely with England, the newly-created paper fortunes." Thus surrounded, his words were caught, multiplied, misconstrued and even fabricated, and spread abroad to his injury.

Mr. Jefferson pleaded moreover that the opposition of views between Mr. Hamilton and himself was peculiarly unpleasant, and destructive of the necessary harmony. With regard to the republican party he was sure it had not a view which went to the frame of the government. He believed the next Congress would attempt nothing material but to render their own body independent.

Washington replied that he believed the views of the republican party to be perfectly pure. "But when men put a machine into motion," said he, "it is impossible for them to stop it exactly where they would choose, or to say where it will stop. The Constitution we have is an excellent one if we can keep it where it is."

He again adverted to Jefferson's constant suspicion that there was a party disposed to change the Constitution into a monarchical form, declaring that there was not a man in the United States who would set his face more decidedly against such a change than himself.

"No rational man in the United States suspects you of any other disposition," cried Jefferson, "but there does not pass a week in which we cannot prove declarations dropping from the monarchical party that our government is good for nothing, is a milk-and-water thing which cannot support itself, that we must knock it down and set up something with more energy."

"If that is the case," rejoined Washington, "it is a proof of their insanity, for the republican spirit of the Union is so manifest and so solid that it is astonishing how any one can expect to move it."

We have only Jefferson's account of this and other interesting interviews of a confidential nature which he had with the President, and we give them generally almost in his own words, through which, partial as they may have been, we discern Washington's constant efforts to moderate the growing antipathies between the eminent men whom he had sought to assist him in conducting the government. He continued to have the highest opinion of Jefferson's abilities, his knowledge of foreign affairs, his thorough patriotism, and it was his earnest desire to retain him in his cabinet through the whole of the ensuing session of Congress, before the close of which he trusted the affairs of the country relating to foreign powers, Indian disturbances and internal policy would have taken a more decisive and, it was to be hoped, agreeable form than they then had. A compromise was eventually made, according to which Jefferson was to be allowed a temporary absence in the autumn, and on his return was to continue in office till January.

While the neutrality of the United States, so jealously guarded by Washington, was endangered by the intrigues of the French minister [Genêt], it was put to imminent hazard by ill-advised measures of the British cabinet.

There was such a scarcity in France in consequence of the failure of the crops that a famine was apprehended. England, availing herself of her naval ascendency, determined to increase the distress of her rival by cutting off all her supplies from abroad. In June 1793, therefore, her cruisers were instructed to detain all vessels bound to France with cargoes of corn, flour or meal, take them into port, unload them, purchase the cargoes, make a proper allowance for the freight and then release the vessels or to allow the masters of them, on a stipulated security, to dispose of their cargoes in a port in amity with England. This measure gave umbrage to all parties in the United States and brought out an earnest remonstrance from the government as being a violation of the law of neutrals and indefensible on any proper construction of the law of nations.

Another grievance which helped to swell the tide of resentment against Great Britain was the frequent impressment of American seamen, a wrong to which they were particularly exposed from national similarity.

To these may be added the persistence of Great Britain in holding the posts to the south of the lakes, which, according to treaty stipulations, ought to have been given up. Washington did not feel himself in a position to press our rights under the treaty with the vigorous hand that some would urge, questions having risen in some of the State courts to obstruct the fulfilment of our part of it, which regarded the payment of British debts contracted before the war.

The violent partisans of France thought nothing of these short-comings on our own part and would have had the forts seized at once, but Washington considered a scrupulous discharge of our own obligations the necessary preliminary, should so violent a measure be deemed advisable. His prudent and conscientious conduct in this particular, so in unison with the impartial justice which governed all his actions, was cited by partisan writers as indicative of his preference of England to "our ancient ally."

[Jefferson resigned as Secretary of State.] We subjoin his comprehensive character of Washington, the result of long observation and cabinet experience and written in after years, when there was no temptation to insincere eulogy:

"His integrity was most pure, his justice the most inflexible I have ever known, no motives of interest or consanguinity, of friendship or hatred, being able to bias his decision. He was indeed, in every sense of the word, a wise, a good and a great man."

Public affairs were becoming more and more complicated, and events in Europe were full of gloomy portent. "The news of this evening," writes John Adams to his wife on the 9th of January, "is that the queen of France is no more. When will savages be satisfied with blood? No prospect of peace in Europe, therefore none of internal harmony in America. We cannot well be in a more disagreeable situation than we are with all Europe, with all Indians and with all Barbary rovers. Nearly one half of the continent is in constant opposition to the other, and the President's situation, which is highly responsible, is very distressing."

Adams speaks of having had two hours' conversation with Washington alone in his cabinet but intimates that he could not reveal the purport of it, even by a hint. It had satisfied him, however, of Washington's earnest desire to do right, his close application to discover it, and his deliberate and comprehensive view of our affairs with all the world. "The anti-federalists and the Frenchified zealots," adds Adams, "have nothing now to do that I can conceive of but to ruin his character, destroy his peace and injure his health. He supports all their attacks with firmness, and his health appears to be very good."[1]

The report of Mr. Jefferson on commercial intercourse was soon taken up in the House in a committee of the whole. A series of res-

[1] *Life of John Adams*, vol. i., p. 461.

olutions based on it and relating to the privileges and restrictions of the commerce of the United States were introduced by Mr. Madison and became the subject of a warm and acrimonious debate. The report upheld the policy of turning the course of trade from England to France by discriminations in favor of the latter, and the resolutions were to the same purport. The idea was to oppose commercial resistance to commercial injury; to enforce a perfect commercial equality by retaliating impositions, assuming that the commercial system of Great Britain was hostile to the United States, a position strongly denied by some of the debaters.

Though the subject was, or might seem to be, of a purely commercial nature, it was inevitably mixed up with political considerations, according as a favorable inclination to England or France was apprehended. The debate waxed warm as it proceeded, with a strong infusion of bitterness. Fisher Ames stigmatized the resolutions as having *French* stamped upon the very face of them. Whereupon Colonel Parker of Virginia wished that there was a stamp on the forehead of every one to designate whether he were for France or England. For himself, he would not be silent and hear that nation abused to whom America was indebted for her rank as a nation. There was a burst of applause in the gallery but the indecorum was rebuked by the galleries being cleared.

The debate, which had commenced on the 13th of January (1794), was protracted to the 3d of February, when the question being taken on the first resolution it was carried by a majority of only five, so nearly were parties divided. The further consideration of the remaining resolutions was postponed to March, when it was resumed, but, in consequence of the new complexion of affairs, was suspended without a decision.

The next legislative movement was also productive of a warm debate, though connected with a subject which appealed to the sympathies of the whole nation. Algerine corsairs had captured eleven American merchant vessels and upwards of one hundred prisoners, and the regency manifested a disposition for further outrages. A bill was introduced into Congress proposing a force of six frigates to protect the commerce of the United States against the cruisers of this piratical power. The bill met with strenuous opposition. The force would require time to prepare it and would then be insufficient. It might be laying the foundation of a large permanent navy and a great public debt. It would be cheaper to purchase the friendship of Algiers with money, as was done by other nations of superior maritime force, or to purchase the protection of those nations. It seems hardly credible at the present day that such policy could have been urged before an American Congress without provoking a burst of scorn and indignation, yet it was heard without any emotion of the kind; and though the bill was eventually passed by both Houses, it was but by a small majority. It received the hearty assent of the President.

In the course of this session fresh instances had come before the government of the mischievous activity and audacity of Genêt, showing that, not content with compromising the neutrality of the United States at sea, he was attempting to endanger it by land. From documents received, it appeared that in November he had sent emissaries to Kentucky to enroll American citizens in an expedition against New Orleans and the Spanish possessions, furnishing them with blank commissions for the purpose.[2] It was an enterprise in which the adventurous people of that State were ready enough to embark through enthusiasm for the French nation and impatience at the delay of Spain to open the navigation of the Mississippi. Another expedition was to proceed against the Floridas, men for the purpose to be enlisted at the South to rendezvous in Georgia and to be aided by a body of Indians and by a French fleet, should one arrive on the coast.

A proclamation from Governor Moultrie checked all such enlistments in South Carolina but brought forth a letter from Genêt to Mr. Jefferson, denying that he had endeavored to raise an armed force in that State for the service of the republic.

"At the same time," adds he, "I am too frank to conceal from you that, authorized by the French nation to deliver brevets to such of your fellow-citizens who feel animated by a desire to serve the fairest of causes, I have accorded them to several brave republicans of South Carolina, whose intention appeared to me to be, in expatriating themselves, to go among the tribes of independent Indians, ancient friends and allies of France, to inflict if they could, in concert with them, the harm to Spaniards and Englishmen which the governments of those two nations had the baseness to do for a long time to your fellow-citizens under the name of these savages, the same as they have done recently under that of the Algerines."

[2] *American State Papers*, ii., 36.

Documents relating to these transactions were communicated to Congress by Washington early in January. But, though the expedition set on foot in South Carolina had been checked, it was subsequently reported that the one in Kentucky against Louisiana was still in progress and about to descend the Ohio.

These schemes showed such determined purpose on the part of Genêt to undermine the peace of the United States that Washington, without waiting a reply to the demand for his recall, resolved to keep no further terms with that headlong diplomat. The dignity, possibly the safety, of the United States depended upon immediate measures.

In a cabinet council it was determined to supersede Genêt's diplomatic functions, deprive him of the consequent privileges and arrest his person. A message to Congress avowing such determination was prepared, but at this critical juncture came despatches from Gouverneur Morris, announcing Genêt's recall.

The French minister of foreign affairs had, in fact, reprobated the conduct of Genêt as unauthorized by his instructions and deserving of punishment, and Mr. Fauchet, secretary of the executive council, was appointed to succeed him. Mr. Fauchet arrived in the United States in February.

About this time vigilance was required to guard against wrong from an opposite quarter. We have noticed the orders issued by Great Britain to her cruisers in June 1793, and the resentment thereby excited in the United States. On the 6th of the following month of November she had given them additional instructions to detain all vessels laden with the produce of any colony belonging to France or carrying supplies to any such colony, and to bring them with their cargoes to British ports for adjudication in the British courts of admiralty.

Captures of American vessels were taking place in consequence of these orders, and heightening public irritation. They were considered indicative of determined hostility on the part of Great Britain, and they produced measures in Congress preparatory to an apprehended state of war. An embargo was laid, prohibiting all trade from the United States to any foreign place for the space of thirty days, and vigorous preparations for defense were adopted with but little opposition.

On the 27th of March, resolutions were moved that all debts due to British subjects be sequestered and paid into the treasury as a fund to indemnify citizens of the United States for depredations sustained from British cruisers, and that all intercourse with Great Britain be interdicted until she had made compensation for these injuries and until she should make surrender of the Western posts.

The popular excitement was intense. Meetings were held on the subject of British spoliations. "Peace or war" was the absorbing question. The partisans of France were now in the ascendant. It was scouted as pusillanimous any longer to hold terms with England. "No doubt," said they, "she despises the proclamation of neutrality as an evidence of timidity. Every motive of self-respect calls on the people of the United States to show a proper spirit."

It was suggested that those who were in favor of resisting British aggressions should mount the tri-colored cockade, and forthwith it was mounted by many, while a democratic society was formed to correspond with the one at Philadelphia and aid in giving effect to these popular sentiments.

While the public mind was in this inflammable state, Washington received advices from Mr. Pinckney, the American minister in London, informing him that the British ministry had issued instructions to the commanders of armed vessels, revoking those of the 6th of November 1793. Lord Grenville also, in conversation with Mr. Pinckney, had explained the real motives for that order, showing that, however oppressive in its execution, it had not been intended for the special vexation of American commerce.

Washington laid Pinckney's letter before Congress on the 4th of April. It had its effect on both parties. Federalists saw in it a chance of accommodating difficulties, and therefore opposed all measures calculated to irritate. The other party did not press their belligerent propositions to any immediate decision, but showed no solicitude to avoid a rupture.

Jefferson, though reputed to be the head of the French party, avowed in a letter to Madison his hope that war would not result, but that justice would be obtained in a peaceable way,[3] and he repeats the hope in a subsequent letter. "My countrymen," writes he, "are groaning under the insults of Great Britain. I hope some means will turn up of reconciling our faith and honor with peace. I confess to you, I have seen enough of one war never to wish to see another."[4]

[3] Jefferson's Works, vol. iv., p. 102.
[4] Ibid., vol. iv., p. 104. Letter to John Adams.

" 'T is as great an error," writes Hamilton, at the same time, "for a nation to overrate as to underrate itself. Presumption is as great a fault as timidity. 'T is our error to overrate ourselves and to underrate Great Britain. We forget how little we can annoy, how much we may be annoyed."[5]

The war cry, however, is too obvious a means of popular excitement to be readily given up. Busy partisans saw that the feeling of the populace was belligerent, and every means were taken by the press and the democratic societies to exasperate this feeling. According to them the crisis called not for moderation but for decision, for energy. Still, to adhere to a neutral position would argue tameness—cowardice! Washington, however, was too morally brave to be clamored out of his wise moderation by such taunts. He resolved to prevent a war, if possible, by an appeal to British justice, to be made through a special envoy who should represent to the British government the injuries we had sustained from it in various ways, and should urge indemnification.

The French government, having so promptly complied with the wishes of the American government in recalling Citizen Genêt, requested, as an act of reciprocity, the recall of Gouverneur Morris, whose political sympathies were considered highly aristocratical. The request was granted accordingly, but Washington, in a letter to Morris notifying him of his being superseded, assured him of his own undiminished confidence and friendship.

James Monroe, who was appointed in his place, arrived at Paris in a moment of great reaction. Robespierre had terminated his bloody career on the scaffold and the reign of terror was at an end. The new minister from the United States was received in public by the Convention. The sentiments expressed by Monroe on delivering his credentials were so completely in unison with the feelings of the moment that the President of the Convention embraced him with emotion, and it was decreed that the American and French flags should be entwined and hung up in the hall of the Convention in sign of the union and friendship of the two republics.

Chiming in with the popular impulse, Monroe presented the American flag to the convention on the part of his country. It was received with enthusiasm, and a decree was passed, that the na-

5 Hamilton's Works, iv., 520.

tional flag of France should be transmitted in return to the government of the United States.

Washington in the meantime was becoming painfully aware that censorious eyes at home were keeping a watch upon his administration, and censorious tongues and pens were ready to cavil at every measure. "The affairs of this country cannot go wrong," writes he ironically to Gouverneur Morris. "There are so many watchful guardians of them and such infallible guides that no one is at a loss for a director at every turn."

This is almost the only instance of irony to be found in his usually plain, direct correspondence, and to us is mournfully suggestive of that soreness and weariness of heart with which he saw his conscientious policy misunderstood or misrepresented, and himself becoming an object of party hostility.

[Hamilton resigned as Secretary of the Treasury and Knox as Secretary of War.]

Chapter 55

DIFFICULTIES WITH CONGRESS

Washington had watched the progress of the mission of Mr. Jay to England with an anxious eye. He was aware that he had exposed his popularity to imminent hazard by making an advance toward a negotiation with that power. But what was of still greater moment with him, he was aware that the peace and happiness of his country were at stake on the result of that mission. It was moreover a mission of great delicacy, from the many intricate and difficult points to be discussed and the various and mutual grounds of complaint to be adjusted.

Mr. Jay, in a letter dated August 5, 1794, had informed him confidentially that the ministry were prepared to settle the matters in dispute upon just and liberal terms. Still, what those terms, which they conceived to be just and liberal, might prove when they came to be closely discussed, no one could prognosticate.

Washington hardly permitted himself to hope for the complete success of the mission. To "give and take" he presumed would be the result. In the meantime there were so many hot heads and impetuous spirits at home to be managed and restrained that he was anxious the negotiation might assume a decisive form and be brought to a speedy close. He was perplexed too, by what, under existing circumstances, appeared piratical conduct on the part of Bermudian privateers persisting in capturing American vessels.

At length, on the 7th of March 1795, four days after the close of the session of Congress, a treaty arrived which had been negotiated by Mr. Jay and signed by the ministers of the two nations on the 19th of November, and was sent out for ratification.

In a letter to Washington which accompanied the treaty, Mr. Jay wrote: "To do more was impossible. I ought not to conceal from you that the confidence reposed in your personal character was visible and useful throughout the negotiation."

Washington immediately made the treaty a close study. Some of the provisions were perfectly satisfactory. Of others he did not approve. On the whole he considered it a matter, to use his own expression, of "give and take," and believing the advantages to outweigh the objections, and that, as Mr. Jay alleged, it was the best treaty attainable, he made up his mind to ratify it should it be approved by the Senate.

As a system of predetermined hostility to the treaty, however, was already manifested, and efforts were made to awaken popular jealousy concerning it, Washington kept its provisions secret, that the public mind might not be preoccupied on the subject. In the course of a few days, however, enough leaked out to be seized upon by the opposition press to excite public distrust, though not enough to convey a distinct idea of the merits of the instrument. In fact, the people were predisposed to condemn, because vexed that any overtures had been made towards a negotiation, such overtures having been stigmatized as cowardly and degrading. If it had been necessary to send a minister to England, said they, it should have been to make a downright demand of reparation for wrongs inflicted on our commerce, and the immediate surrender of the Western posts.

In the meantime Jay arrived on the 28th of May and found that during his absence in Europe he had been elected governor of the State of New York, an honorable election, the result of no effort nor intrigue, but of the public sense entertained by his native State of his pure and exalted merit. He in consequence resigned the office of Chief Justice of the United States.

In the course of this month arrived Mr. Adet, who had been appointed by the French government to succeed Mr. Fauchet as minister to the United States. He brought with him the colors of France, which the convention had instructed him to present as a testimonial of friendship in return for the American flag which had been presented by Mr. Monroe. The presentation of the colors was postponed by him for the present.

The Senate was convened by Washington on the 8th of June, and the treaty of Mr. Jay was laid before it with its accompanying documents. The session was with closed doors, discussions were long and arduous and the treaty underwent a scrutinizing examination. The twelfth article met with special objections.

This article provided for a direct trade between the United

States and the British West India Islands, in American vessels not exceeding seventy tons burden, conveying the produce of the States or of the Islands. But it prohibited the exportation of molasses, sugar, coffee, cocoa or cotton in American vessels, either from the United States or the Islands, to any part of the world. Under this article it was a restricted intercourse but Mr. Jay considered the admission even of smaller vessels to the trade of these Islands an important advantage to the commerce of the United States. He had not sufficiently adverted to the fact that, among the prohibited articles, cotton was also a product of the Southern States. Its cultivation had been recently introduced there, so that when he sailed for Europe hardly sufficient had been raised for domestic consumption, and at the time of signing the treaty, very little if any had been exported. Still, it was now becoming an important staple of the South, and hence the objection of the Senate to this article of the treaty. On the 24th of June two thirds of the Senate, the constitutional majority, voted for the ratification of the treaty, stipulating, however, that an article be added suspending so much of the twelfth article as respected the West India trade, and that the President be requested to open without delay further negotiation on this head.

Here was a novel case to be determined. Could the Senate be considered to have ratified the treaty before the insertion of this new article? Was the act complete and final, so as to render it unnecessary to refer it back to that body? Could the President put his final seal upon an act before it was complete? After much reflection, Washington was satisfied of the propriety of ratifying the treaty with the qualification imposed by the Senate.

In the meantime the popular discontent which had been excited concerning the treaty was daily increasing. The secrecy which had been maintained with regard to its provisions was wrested into a cause of offense. Republics should have no secrets. The Senate should not have deliberated on the treaty with closed doors.

Such was the irritable condition of the public mind when on the 29th of June a Senator of the United States (Mr. Mason of Virginia) sent an abstract of the treaty to be published in a leading opposition paper in Philadelphia.

The whole country was immediately in a blaze. Beside the opposition party, a portion of the cabinet was against the ratification.

Of course it received but a faltering support while the attack upon it was vehement and sustained. The assailants seemed determined to carry their point by storm. Meetings to oppose the ratification were held in Boston, New York, Philadelphia, Baltimore and Charleston. The smaller towns throughout the Union followed their example. In New York a copy of the treaty was burnt before the governor's house. In Philadelphia it was suspended on a pole, carried about the streets and finally burnt in front of the British minister's house amid the shoutings of the populace. The whole country seemed determined, by prompt and clamorous manifestations of dissatisfaction, to make Washington give way.

He saw their purpose. He was aware of the odious points of view on which the treaty might justly be placed. His own opinion was not particularly favorable to it. But he was convinced that it was better to ratify it, in the manner the Senate had advised and with the reservation already mentioned, than to suffer matters to remain in their present unsettled and precarious state.

Before he could act upon this conviction a new difficulty arose to suspend his resolution. News came that the order of the British government of the 8th of June 1793 for the seizure of provisions in vessels going to French ports was renewed. Washington instantly directed that a strong memorial should be drawn up against this order, as it seemed to favor a construction of the treaty which he was determined to resist. While this memorial was in course of preparation he was called off to Mount Vernon. On his way thither, though little was said to him on the subject of the treaty, he found, he says, from indirect discourses that endeavors were making to place it in all the odious points of view of which it was susceptible, and in some which it would not admit.

The proceedings and resolves of town meetings, also, savoring as he thought of party prejudice, were forwarded to him by express and added to his disquiet. "Party disputes are now carried to such a length," writes he, "and truth is so enveloped in mist and false representation that it is extremely difficult to know through what channel to seek it. This difficulty, to one who is of no party and whose sole wish is to pursue with undeviating steps a path which would lead this country to respectability, wealth and happiness, is exceedingly to be lamented. But such, for wise purposes it is presumed, is the turbulence of human passions in party disputes, when victory more than *truth* is the palm contended for, that 'the post of honor is a *private station.*'"[1]

The opposition made to the treaty from meetings in different parts of the Union gave him the most serious uneasiness, from the effect it might have on the relations with France and England. His reply (July 28th) to an address from the selectmen of Boston, contains the spirit of his replies to other addresses of the kind and shows the principles which influenced him in regard to the treaty:

"In every act of my administration I have sought the happiness of my fellow-citizens. My system for the attainment of this object has uniformly been to overlook all personal, local and partial considerations, to contemplate the United States as one great whole, to confide that sudden impressions, when erroneous, would yield to candid reflection, and to consult only the substantial and permanent interests of our country.

"Nor have I departed from this line of conduct on the occasion which has produced the resolutions contained in your letter.

"Without a predilection for my own judgment, I have weighed with attention every argument which has at any time been brought into view. But the Constitution is the guide which I never can abandon. It has assigned to the President the power of making treaties with the advice and consent of the Senate. It was doubtless supposed that these two branches of government would combine, without passion and with the best means of information, those facts and principles upon which the success of our foreign relations will always depend; that they ought not to substitute, for their own conviction, the opinions of others or to seek truth through any channel but that of a temperate and well-informed investigation.

"Under this persuasion, I have resolved on the manner of executing the duty before me. To the high responsibility of it I freely submit, and you gentlemen, are at liberty to make these sentiments known as the grounds of my procedure. While I feel the most lively gratitude for the many instances of approbation from my country, I can no otherwise deserve it than by obeying the dictates of my conscience."[2]

The violence of the opposition increased. Washington perceived

[1] Sparks, *Writings*, xi., 40.
[2] *Ibid.*, xi., 2.

that the prejudices against the treaty were more extensive than was generally imagined.

"How should it be otherwise," said he, "when no stone has been left unturned that could impress on the minds of the people the most arrant misrepresentation of facts, that their rights have not only been *neglected* but absolutely *sold*, that there are no reciprocal advantages in the treaty, that the benefits are all on the side of Great Britain and, what seems to have had more weight with them than all the rest and to have been most pressed, that the treaty is made with the design to oppress the French in open violation of our treaty with that nation and contrary, too, to every principle of gratitude and sound policy."

Never during his administration had he seen a crisis, in his judgment, so pregnant with interesting events nor one from which, whether viewed on one side or on the other, more was to be apprehended.

If the treaty were ratified, the partisans of the French, "or rather," said he, "of war and confusion" would excite them to hostility; if not ratified, there was no foreseeing the consequences as it respected Great Britain. It was a crisis, he said, that most eminently called upon the administration to be wise and temperate as well as firm. The public clamor continued, and induced a reiterated examination of the subject but did not shake his purpose. "There is but one straight course," said he, "and that is to seek truth and pursue it steadily."[3]

The difficult and intricate questions pressing upon the attention of government left Washington little mood to enjoy the retirement of Mount Vernon, being constantly in doubt whether his presence in Philadelphia were not necessary. In his letters to Randolph he requested to be kept continually advised on this head. "While I am in office I shall never suffer private convenience to interfere with what I conceive to be my official duty." "I do not require more than a day's notice to repair to the seat of government."

His promptness was soon put to the test. Early in August came a mysterious letter, dated July 31, from Mr. Pickering, the Secretary of War.

"On the subject of the treaty," writes Pickering, "I confess I feel

[3] See Letters to Edmund Randolph. *Writings*, xi., pp. 45–51.

extreme solicitude and for a *special reason,* which can be communicated to you only in person. I entreat therefore that you will return with all convenient speed to the seat of government. In the meanwhile, for the reason above referred to, I pray you to decide on no important political measure, in whatever form it may be presented to you. Mr. Wolcott and I (Mr. Bradford concurring) waited on Mr. Randolph and urged his writing to request your return. He wrote in our presence, but we concluded a letter from one of us also expedient. With the utmost sincerity I subscribe myself yours and my country's friend. This letter is for your own eye alone."

The receipt of this enigmatical letter induced Washington to cut short his sojourn at Mount Vernon and hasten to Philadelphia. He arrived there on the 11th of August, and on the same day received a solution of the mystery. A despatch written by Fauchet, the French minister, to his government in the preceding month of November, was placed in Washington's hands with a translation of it made by Mr. Pickering. The despatch had been found on board of a French privateer, captured by a British frigate, and had been transmitted to the ministry. Lord Grenville, finding it contained passages relating to the intercourse of Mr. Randolph, the American Secretary of State, with Mr. Fauchet, had sent it to Mr. Hammond, the British minister in Philadelphia. He had put it into the hands of Mr. Wolcott, the Secretary of the Treasury, who had shown it to the Secretary of War and the Attorney-General; and the contents had been considered so extraordinary as to call forth the mysterious letter entreating the prompt return of Washington.

The following passages in Fauchet's intercepted despatch related to the Western insurrection and the proclamation of Washington:

"Two or three days before the proclamation was published, and of course before the cabinet had resolved on its measures, the Secretary of State came to my house. All his countenance was grief. He requested of me a private conversation. It was all over, he said to me; a civil war is about to ravage our unhappy country. Four men, by their talents, their influence and their energy, may save it. But, debtors of English merchants, they will be deprived of their liberty if they take the smallest step. Could you lend them instantaneously funds to shelter them from English prosecution? This inquiry astonished me much. It was impossible for me to make a satisfactory answer. You know my want of power and deficiency in pecuniary means. . . . Thus, with some thousands of dollars, the Republic could have decided on civil war or peace. Thus the consciences of the pretended patriots of America have already their price. What will be the old age of this government if it is thus already decrepit?"

The perusal of the letter gave Washington deep perplexity and concern. He revolved the matter in his mind in silence. The predominant object of his thoughts recently had been to put a stop to the public agitation on the subject of the treaty, and he postponed any new quesion of difficulty until decided measures had laid the other at rest. On the next day, therefore (12th), he brought before the cabinet the question of immediate ratification. All the members were in favor of it excepting Mr. Randolph. He had favored it before the news of the British provision order but now pronounced it unadvisable until that order were revoked, and there should be an end of the war between France and England. This led to further discussion and it was finally agreed to ratify the treaty immediately but to accompany the ratification with a strong memorial against the provision order. The ratification was signed by Washington on the 18th of August.

His conduct towards Randolph in the interim had been as usual, but now that the despatch of public business no longer demanded the entire attention of the cabinet, he proceeded to clear up the doubts occasioned by the intercepted despatch. Accordingly, on the following day, as Randolph entered the cabinet, Washington, who was conversing with Pickering and Wolcott, rose and handed to him the letter of Fauchet, asking an explanation of the questionable parts.

Randolph appears to have been less agitated by the production of the letter than hurt that the inquiry concerning it had not first been made of him in private. He postponed making any specific reply until he should have time to examine the letter at his leisure, and observed on retiring, that after the treatment he had experienced he could not think of remaining in office a moment longer.

In a letter to the President the same day he writes: "Your confidence in me, sir, has been unlimited and I can truly affirm unabused. My sensations, then, cannot be concealed when I find that confidence so suddenly withdrawn without a word or distant hint being previously dropped to me. This, sir, as I mentioned in your room, is a situation in which I cannot hold my present office, and therefore I hereby resign it.

"It will not, however, be concluded from hence that I mean to relinquish the inquiry. No, sir; very far from it. I will also meet any inquiry, and to prepare for it, if I learn there is a chance of overtaking Mr. Fauchet before he sails, I will go to him immediately.

"I have to beg the favor of you to permit me to be furnished with a copy of the letter, and I will prepare an answer to it, which I perceive that I cannot do as I wish, merely upon the few hasty memoranda which I took with my pencil.

"I am satisfied, sir, that you will acknowledge one piece of justice to be due on the occasion, which is, that, until an inquiry can be made, the affair shall continue in secrecy under your injunction. For, after pledging myself for a more specific investigation of all the suggestions, I here most solemnly deny that any overture came from me, which was to produce money to me or any others for me; and that in any manner, directly or indirectly, was a shilling ever received by me; nor was it ever contemplated by me that one shilling should be applied by Mr. Fauchet to any purpose relative to the insurrection."

Washington, in a reply on the following day, in which he accepted his resignation, observes: "Whilst you are in pursuit of means to remove the strong suspicions arising from this letter, no disclosure of its contents will be made by me; and I will enjoin the same on the public officers who are acquainted with the purport of it unless something will appear to render an explanation necessary on the part of the government, and of which I will be the judge."

And on a subsequent occasion he writes: "No man would rejoice more than I to find that the suspicions which have resulted from the intercepted letter were unequivocally and honorably removed."

Mr. Fauchet, in the meantime, having learnt previous to embarkation that his despatch had been intercepted, wrote a declaration denying that Mr. Randolph had ever indicated a willingness to receive money for personal objects, and affirming that he had had no intention to say anything in his letter to his government to the disadvantage of Mr. Randolph's character.[4]

4 Sparks's *Writings of Washington*, xi., 90.

Mr. Randolph now set to work to prepare a pamphlet in explanation of his conduct, intimating to his friends that in the course of his vindication he would bring things to view which would affect Washington more than anything which had yet appeared.[5]

While thus occupied he addressed several notes to Washington, requiring information on various points, and received concise answers to all his queries.

On one occasion, where he had required a particular paper, he published in the *Gazette* an extract from his note to Washington, as if fearing the request might be denied lest the paper in question should lay open many confidential and delicate matters.

In reply, Washington writes: "That you may have no cause to complain of the withholding of any paper, however private and confidential, which you shall think necessary in a case of so serious a nature, I have directed that you should have the inspection of my letter of the 22d of July, agreeably to your request, and you are at full liberty to publish, without reserve, *any* and *every* private and confidential letter I ever wrote to you; nay, more, every word I ever uttered to you or in your hearing, from whence you can derive any advantage in your vindication. I grant this permission inasmuch as the extract alluded to manifestly tends to impress on the public an opinion that something was passed between us which you should disclose with reluctance from motives of delicacy with respect to me. . . . That public will judge, when it comes to see your vindication, how far and how proper it has been for you to publish private and confidential communications which oftentimes have been written in a hurry, and sometimes without even copies being taken; and it will, I hope, appreciate my motives, even if it should condemn my prudence, in allowing you the unlimited allowance herein contained."

The merit of this unlimited license will be properly understood when it is known that at this time Washington was becoming more and more the object of the malignant attacks of the press. The ratification of the treaty had opened the vials of party wrath against him. "His military and political character," we are told, "was attacked with equal violence, and it was averred that he was totally destitute of merit either as a soldier or a statesman. He was charged with having violated the Constitution in negotiating a treaty without the previous advice of the Senate, and that he had

[5] *Ibid.*, xi., 89.

embraced within that treaty subjects belonging exclusively to the legislature, for which an impeachment was publicly suggested. Nay more, it was asserted that he had drawn from the treasury, for his private use, more than the salary annexed to his office."[6]

This last charge, so incompatible with the whole character and conduct of Washington, was fully refuted by the late Secretary of the Treasury, who explained that the President never himself touched any part of the compensation attached to his office, but that the whole was received and disbursed by the gentleman who superintended the expenses of his household, that the expenses at some times exceeded and at other times fell short of the quarter's allowance but that the aggregate fell within the allowance for the year.

The vindication which Mr. Randolph had been preparing appeared in December. In this he gave a narrative of the principal events relating to the case, his correspondence with the President, and the whole of the French minister's letter. He endeavored to explain those parts of the letter which had brought the purity of his conduct in question; but, as has been observed, "he had a difficult task to perform, as he was obliged to prove a negative, and to explain vague expressions and insinuations connected with his name in Fauchet's letter."[7]

Fauchet himself furnished the best vindication in his certificate above mentioned, but it is difficult to reconcile his certificate with the language of his official letter to his government. We are rather inclined to attribute to misconceptions and hasty inferences of the French minister the construction put by him in his letter on the conversation he had held with Mr. Randolph.

The latter injured his cause by the embittered feelings manifested in his vindication, and the asperity with which he spoke of Washington there and elsewhere. He deeply regretted it in after life, and in a letter to the Hon. Bushrod Washington, written in 1810, he says: "I do not retain the smallest degree of that feeling which roused me fifteen years ago against some individuals. . . . If I could now present myself before your venerated uncle it would be my pride to confess my contrition, that I suffered my irritation, let the cause be what it might, to use some of those expressions respecting him, which, at this moment of

---

[6] See Marshall's *Washington*, vol. ii., p. 370.
[7] Note of Mr. Sparks. *Washington's Writings*, xi., 90.

indifference to the ideas of the world, I wish to recall as being inconsistent with my subsequent conviction. My life will, I hope, be sufficiently extended for the recording of my sincere opinion of his virtues and merit, in a style which is not the result of a mind merely debilitated by misfortune, but that of Christian philosophy on which alone I depend for inward tranquillity."[8]

The feelings and position of Washington with regard to England at this juncture may be judged from a letter dated December 22d to Gouverneur Morris, then in London, and who was in occasional communication with Lord Grenville. Washington gives a detail of the various causes of complaint against the British government which were rankling in the minds of the American people, and which Morris was to mention unofficially, should he converse with Lord Grenville on the subject.

"I give you these details," writes he, "as evidences of the impolitic conduct of the British government towards these United States, that it may be seen how difficult it has been for the Executive, under such an accumulation of irritating circumstances, to maintain the ground of neutrality which had been taken, and at a time when the remembrance of the aid we had received from France in the Revolution was fresh in every mind, and while the partisans of that country were continually contrasting the affections of that people with the unfriendly disposition of the British government. And that, too, while their own sufferings during the war with the latter had not been forgotten.

"It is well known that peace has been (to borrow a modern phrase) the order of the day with me since the disturbances in Europe first commenced. My policy has been and will continue to be, while I have the honor to remain in the administration, to maintain friendly terms with but be independent of all the nations of the earth; to share in the broils of none; to fulfil our own engagements; to supply the wants and be carriers for them all. . . . Nothing short of self-respect and that justice which is essential to a national character ought to involve us in war. . . .

"By a firm adherence to these principles, and to the neutral policy which has been adopted, I have brought on myself a torrent of abuse in the factious papers of this country, and from the enmity of the discontented of all descriptions. But having no sinister objects in view, I shall not be diverted from my course by these, nor

[8] Marshall's *Life of Washington*, 2d edition, vol. ii., note xx.

any attempts which are or shall be made to withdraw the
confidence of my constituents from me. I have nothing to ask;
and, discharging my duty, I have nothing to fear from invective.
The acts of my administration will appear when I am no more,
and the intelligent and candid part of mankind will not condemn
my conduct without recurring to them."

In February the treaty with Great Britain, as modified by the
advice of the Senate, came back ratified by the King of Great Britain, and on the last of the month a proclamation was issued by
the President declaring it to be the supreme law of the land.

The opposition in the House of Representatives were offended
that Washington should issue this proclamation before the sense
of that body had been taken on the subject, and denied the power
of the President and Senate to complete a treaty without its sanction. They were bent on defeating it by refusing to pass the laws
necessary to carry it into effect and, as a preliminary, passed a resolution requesting the President to lay before the House the instruction to Mr. Jay and the correspondence and other documents
relative to the treaty.

Washington, believing that these papers could not be constitutionally demanded, resolved, he said, from the first moment and
from the fullest conviction of his mind, to resist the principle
which was evidently intended to be established by the House. He
only deliberated on the manner in which this could be done with
the least bad consequences.

After mature deliberation and with the assistance of the heads
of departments and the Attorney-General, he prepared and sent in
to the House an answer to their request. In this he dwelt upon the
necessity of caution and secrecy in foreign negotiations as one
cogent reason for vesting the power of making treaties in the President, with the advice and consent of the Senate, the principle on
which that body was formed confining it to a small number of
members.

To admit a right in the House of Representatives to demand
and have all papers respecting a foreign negotiation would, he observed, be to establish dangerous precedent.

"It does not occur to me," he added, "that the inspection of the
papers called for can be relative to any purpose under the cognizance of the House of Representatives except that of an impeachment, which the resolution has not expressed. I have no

disposition to withhold any information which the duty of my station would permit or the public good should require to be disclosed. And, in fact, all the papers affecting the negotiation with Great Britain had been laid before the Senate when the treaty itself had been communicated for their consideration and advice."

After various further remarks, he concludes: "As, therefore, it is perfectly clear to my understanding that the assent of the House of Representatives is not necessary to the validity of a treaty; as the treaty with Great Britain exhibits itself in all the objects requiring legislative provision; and on these, the papers called for can throw no light; and as it is essential to the due administration of the government that the boundaries fixed by the Constitution between the different departments should be observed, a just regard to the Constitution and to the duty of my office under all the circumstances of this case forbid a compliance with your request."

A resolution to make provision for carrying the treaty into effect gave rise to an animated and protracted debate. Meanwhile, the whole country became agitated on the subject. Meetings were held throughout the United States, and it soon became apparent that the popular feeling was with the minority in the House of Representatives, who favored the making of the necessary appropriations. The public will prevailed and, on the last day of April, the resolution was passed, though by a close vote of fifty-one to forty-eight. On the 1st of June this session of Congress terminated.

On the 12th of that month Washington, in a letter to Colonel Humphreys, then in Portugal, speaks of the recent political campaign: "The gazettes will give you a pretty good idea of the state of politics and parties in this country and will show you, at the same time, if Bache's *Aurora* is among them, in what manner I am attacked for persevering steadily in measures which, to me, appear necessary to preserve us, during the conflicts of belligerent powers, in a state of tranquillity. But these attacks, unjust and unpleasant as they are, will occasion no change in my conduct, nor will they produce any other effect in my mind than to increase the solicitude which long since has taken fast hold of my heart, to enjoy in the shades of retirement the consolation of believing that I have rendered to my country every service to which my abilities were competent—not from pecuniary or ambitious motives, nor from a desire to provide for any men further than their intrinsic merit entitled them, and surely not with a view of bringing my own relations into office. Malignity, therefore, may dart its shafts, but no earthly power can deprive me of the satisfaction of knowing that I have not, in the whole course of my administration, committed an intentional error."

The period for the presidential election was drawing near, and great anxiety began to be felt [regarding whether] Washington would consent to stand for a third term. No one, it was agreed, had greater claim to the enjoyment of retirement in consideration of public services rendered, but it was thought the affairs of the country would be in a very precarious condition should he retire before the wars of Europe were brought to a close. Washington, however, had made up his mind irrevocably on the subject, and resolved to announce, in a farewell address, his intention of retiring.

The publication of the address [in September in a Philadelphia paper, the *Daily Advertiser*,] produced a great sensation. Several of the State legislatures ordered it to be put on their journals. The address acted as a notice to hush the acrimonious abuse of him which the opposition was pouring forth under the idea that he would be a candidate for a renomination.

Congress formed a quorum on the fifth day of December, the first day of the session which succeeded the publication of the Farewell Address. On the 7th, Washington met the two Houses of Congress for the last time. In his speech he recommended an institution for the improvement of agriculture, a military academy, a national university and a gradual increase of the navy. In concluding his address he observes:

"The situation in which I now stand for the last time in the midst of the representatives of the people of the United States naturally recalls the period when the administration of the present form of government commenced, and I cannot omit the occasion to congratulate you and my country on the success of the experiment, nor to repeat my fervent supplications to the Supreme Ruler of the universe and Sovereign Arbiter of nations that his providential care may be still extended to the United States, that the virtue and happiness of the people may be preserved and that the government which they have instituted for the protection of their liberties may be perpetual."

The reverence and affection expressed for him in both Houses of Congress, and their regret at his intended retirement, were in unison with testimonials from various State legislatures and other public bodies, which were continually arriving since the publication of his Farewell Address.

Washington now began to count the days and hours that intervened between him and his retirement. [On March third, the last day of his official career,] he gave a kind of farewell dinner to the foreign ministers and their wives, Mr. and Mrs. Adams, Mr. Jefferson and other conspicuous personages of both sexes. "During the dinner much hilarity prevailed," says Bishop White, who was present. When the cloth was removed, Washington filled his glass: "Ladies and gentlemen," said he, "this is the last time I shall drink your health as a public man. I do it with sincerity, wishing you all possible happiness."

The gayety of the company was checked in an instant. All felt the importance of this leave-taking. Mrs. Liston, the wife of the British minister, was so much affected that tears streamed down her cheeks.

On the 4th of March an immense crowd had gathered about Congress Hall. At eleven o'clock Mr. Jefferson took the oath as Vice-President in the presence of the Senate, and proceeded with that body to the chamber of the House of Representatives, which was densely crowded, many ladies occupying chairs ceded to them by members.

After a time Washington entered amidst enthusiastic cheers and acclamations and the waving of handkerchiefs. Mr. Adams soon followed and was likewise well received but not with like enthusiasm. Having taken the oath of office, Mr. Adams, in his inaugural address, spoke of his predecessor as one "who, by a long course of great actions, regulated by prudence, justice, temperance and fortitude, had merited the gratitude of his fellow-citizens, commanded the highest praises of foreign nations, and secured immortal glory with posterity."

At the close of the ceremony, as Washington moved toward the door to retire, there was a rush from the gallery to the corridor that threatened the loss of life or limb, so eager were the throng to catch a last look of one who had so long been the object of public veneration. When Washington was in the street he waved his hat in return for the cheers of the multitude, his countenance radiant with benignity, his gray hairs streaming in the wind. The crowd followed him to his door. There, turning round, his countenance assumed a grave and almost melancholy expression, his eyes were bathed in tears, his emotions were too great for utterance, and only by gestures could he indicate his thanks and convey his farewell blessing.[9]

In the evening a splendid banquet was given to him by the principal inhabitants of Philadelphia in the Amphitheatre, which was decorated with emblematical paintings. All the heads of departments, the foreign ministers, several officers of the late army, and various persons of note were present. Among the paintings, one represented the home of his heart, the home to which he was about to hasten—Mount Vernon.

[9] From personal recollections of William A. Duer, late President of Columbia College.

Chapter 56

RETIREMENT AND DEATH

[Washington had spent but a few months at Mount Vernon when the relations between the United States and France reached a crisis as a consequence of the capture of American vessels by French cruisers and the rude treatment of American envoys by the French government. President Adams convened a special session of Congress and war seemed inevitable.]

The crisis was at once brought to Washington's own door. "You ought to be aware," writes Hamilton to him, May 19th, "that in the event of an open rupture with France, the public voice will again call you to command the armies of your country, and though all who are attached to you will, from attachment as well as public considerations, deplore an occasion which should once more tear you from that repose to which you have so good a right, yet it is the opinion of all those with whom I converse, that you will be compelled to make the sacrifice. All your past labors may demand, to give them efficacy, this further, this very great sacrifice."

The government was resolved upon vigorous measures. Congress on the 28th of May authorized Mr. Adams to enlist ten thousand men as a provisional army, to be called by him into actual service in case of hostilities.

Adams was perplexed by the belligerent duties thus suddenly devolved upon him. How should he proceed in forming an army? Should he call on all the old generals who had figured in the Revolution, or appoint a young set? Military tactics were changed and a new kind of enemy was to be met. "If the French come here," said he, "we will have to march with a quick step and attack, for in that way only they are said to be vulnerable."

These and other questions he propounded to Washington by letter on the 22d of June. "I must tax you sometimes for advice," writes he. "We must have your name if you will in any case permit us to use it. There will be more efficacy in it than in many an army."

And McHenry, the Secretary of War, writes about the same time: "You see how the storm thickens and that our vessel will soon require its ancient pilot. Will you—may we flatter ourselves that in a crisis so awful and important you will—accept the command of all our armies? I hope you will, because you alone can unite all hearts and all hands, if it is possible that they can be united."

In a reply to the President's letter, Washington writes, on the 4th of July: "At the epoch of my retirement an invasion of these States by any European power, or even the probability of such an event happening in my days, was so far from being contemplated by me that I had no conception that that or any other occurrence would arise in so short a period which could turn my eyes from the shade of Mount Vernon. . . . In case of *actual invasion* by a formidable force, I certainly should not intrench myself under the cover of age and retirement if my services should be required by my country to assist in repelling it."

And in his reply of the same date to the Secretary of War he writes: "I see as you do that clouds are gathering, and that a storm may ensue, and I find, too, from a variety of hints that my quiet, under the circumstances, does not promise to be of long continuance. . . .

"As my whole life has been dedicated to my country in one shape or another, for the poor remains of it it is not an object to contend for ease and quiet when all that is valuable is at stake, further than to be satisfied that the sacrifice I should make of these, is acceptable and desired by my country."

Before these letters were despatched he had already been nominated to the Senate (July 3d) commander-in-chief of all the armies raised or to be raised. His nomination was unanimously confirmed on the following day.

Early in November (1798) Washington left his retirement and repaired to Philadelphia at the earnest request of the Secretary of War to meet that public functionary and Major-Generals Hamilton and Pinckney, and make arrangements respecting the forces about to be raised. The Secretary had prepared a series of questions for their consideration, and others were suggested by Washington, all bearing upon the organization of the provisional army. Upon these Washington and the two major-generals were closely engaged for nearly five weeks, at great inconvenience and in a most inclement season. The result of their deliberations was reduced to form and communicated to the Secretary in two letters drafted by Hamilton, and signed by the commander-in-chief. Not the least irksome of Washington's task in his present position was to wade through volumes of applications and recommendations for military appointments, a task which he performed with extreme assiduity, anxious to avoid the influence of favor or prejudice, and sensitively alive to the evil of improper selections.

As it was part of the plan on which he had accepted the command of the army to decline the occupations of the office until circumstances should require his presence in the field, and as the season and weather rendered him impatient to leave Philadelphia, he gave the Secretary of War his views and plans for the charge and direction of military affairs and then set out once more for Mount Vernon.

As the year opened [he] continued to correspond with the Secretary of War and General Hamilton on the affairs of the provisional army. The recruiting business went on slowly, with interruptions, and there was delay in furnishing commissions to the officers who had been appointed. Washington, who was not in the secrets of the cabinet, was at a loss to account for this apparent torpor. The fact was that the military measures taken in America had really produced an effect on French policy. Efforts had been made by M. Talleyrand through unofficial persons to induce an amicable overture on the part of the United States.

Throughout succeeding months, Washington continued to superintend from a distance the concerns of the army, as his ample and minute correspondence manifests, and he was at the same time earnestly endeavoring to bring the affairs of his rural domain into order. A sixteen years' absence from home, with short intervals, had, he said, deranged them considerably, so that it required all the time he could spare from the usual avocations of life to bring them into tune again. It was a period of incessant activity and toil, therefore, both mental and bodily. He was for hours in his study occupied with his pen, and for hours on horseback riding the rounds of his extensive estate, visiting the various farms and superintending and directing the works in operation. All this he did with unfailing vigor, though now in his sixty-seventh year.

Winter had now set in, with occasional wind and rain and frost, yet Washington still kept up his active round of in-door and out-door avocations, as his diary records. He was in full health and vigor, dined out occasionally and had frequent guests at Mount Vernon and, as usual, was part of every day in the saddle, going the rounds of his estates and, in his military phraseology, "visiting the outposts."

He had recently walked with his favorite nephew about the grounds, showing the improvements he intended to make, and had especially pointed out the spot where he purposed building a new family vault, the old one being damaged by the roots of trees which had over-grown it and caused it to leak.

"This change," said he, "I shall make the first of all, for I may require it before the rest."

"When I parted from him," adds the nephew, "he stood on the steps of the front door, where he took leave of myself and another. . . . It was a bright frosty morning. He had taken his usual ride, and the clear healthy flush on his cheek, and his sprightly manner, brought the remark from both of us that we had never seen the general look so well. I have sometimes thought him decidedly the handsomest man I ever saw and, when in a lively mood, so full of pleasantry, so agreeable to all with whom he associated, that I could hardly realize he was the same Washington whose dignity awed all who approached him."[1]

For some time past Washington had been occupied in digesting a complete system on which his estate was to be managed for several succeeding years, specifying the cultivation of the several farms, with tables designating the rotations of the crops. It occupied thirty folio pages and was executed with that clearness and method which characterized all his business papers. This was finished on the 10th of December and was accompanied by a letter of that date to his manager or steward. It is a valuable document, showing the soundness and vigor of his intellect at this advanced stage of his existence, and the love of order that reigned throughout his affairs.

"My greatest anxiety," said he on a previous occasion, "is to have all these concerns in such a clear and distinct form that no reproach may attach itself to me when I have taken my departure for the land of spirits."[2]

It was evident, however, that, full of health and vigor, he looked

[1] Paulding's *Life of Washington*, vol. ii., p. 196.
[2] Letter to James McHenry. *Writings*, xi., 407.

forward to his long cherished hope, the enjoyment of a serene old age in this home of his heart.

According to his diary, the morning on which these voluminous instructions to his steward were dated was clear and calm, but the afternoon was lowering. The next day (11th), he notes that there was wind and rain, and "at night a large circle round the moon."

The morning of the 12th was overcast. About ten o'clock he mounted his horse and rode out as usual to make the rounds of his estate. The ominous ring round the moon which he had observed on the preceding night proved a fatal portent. "About one o'clock," he notes, "it began to snow, soon after to hail, and then turned to a settled cold rain." Having on an overcoat, he continued his ride without regarding the weather and did not return to the house until after three.

His secretary approached him with letters to be franked, that they might be taken to the post-office in the evening. Washington franked the letters but observed that the weather was too bad to send a servant out with them. Mr. Lear perceived that snow was hanging from his hair and expressed fears that he had got wet, but he replied, "No, his great-coat had kept him dry." As dinner had been waiting for him he sat down without changing his dress. "In the evening," writes his secretary, "he appeared as well as usual."

On the following morning the snow was three inches deep and still falling, which prevented him from taking his usual ride. He complained of a sore throat, and had evidently taken cold the day before. In the afternoon the weather cleared up and he went out on the grounds between the house and the river to mark some trees which were to be cut down. A hoarseness which had hung about him through the day grew worse towards night but he made light of it.

He was very cheerful in the evening as he sat in the parlor with Mrs. Washington and Mr. Lear, amusing himself with the papers which had been brought from the post-office. When he met with anything interesting or entertaining, he would read it aloud as well as his hoarseness would permit, or he listened and made occasional comments while Mr. Lear read the debates of the Virginia Assembly.

On retiring to bed, Mr. Lear suggested that he should take something to relieve the cold.

"No," replied he, "you know I never take anything for a cold. Let it go as it came."

In the night he was taken extremely ill with ague and difficulty of breathing. Between two and three o'clock in the morning he awoke Mrs. Washington, who would have risen to call a servant, but he would not permit her, lest she should take cold. At daybreak, when the servant woman entered to make a fire she was sent to call Mr. Lear. He found the general breathing with difficulty and hardly able to utter a word intelligibly. Washington desired that Dr. Craik, who lived in Alexandria, should be sent for and that in the meantime Rawlins, one of the overseers, should be summoned to bleed him before the doctor could arrive.

A gargle was prepared for his throat, but whenever he attempted to swallow any of it he was convulsed and almost suffocated. Rawlins made his appearance soon after sunrise but, when the general's arm was ready for the operation, became agitated.

"Don't be afraid," said the general, as well as he could speak.

Rawlins made an incision.

"The orifice is not large enough," said Washington.

The blood, however, ran pretty freely and Mrs. Washington, uncertain whether the treatment was proper and fearful that too much blood might be taken, begged Mr. Lear to stop it.

When he was about to untie the string the general put up his hand to prevent him, and as soon as he could speak, murmured, "More—more."

But Mrs. Washington's doubts prevailed, and the bleeding was stopped after about half a pint of blood had been taken. External applications were now made to the throat and his feet were bathed in warm water, but without affording any relief.

His old friend, Dr. Craik, arrived between eight and nine, and two other physicians, Drs. Dick and Brown, were called in. Various remedies were tried and additional bleeding, but all of no avail.

"About half-past four o'clock," writes Mr. Lear, "he desired me to call Mrs. Washington to his bedside, when he requested her to go down into his room and take from his desk his two wills which she would find there, and bring them to him, which she did. Upon looking at them, he gave her one, which he observed was useless as being superseded by the other, and desired her to burn it, which she did, and took the other and put it into her closet. After this was done, I returned to his bedside and took his hand. He said to me: 'I find I am going, my breath cannot last long. I believed from the first that the disorder would prove fatal. Do you arrange and record all my late military letters and papers. Arrange my accounts and settle my books, as you know more about them than any one else, and let Mr. Rawlins finish recording my other letters which he has begun.' I told him this should be done. He then asked if I recollected anything which it was essential for him to do, as he had but a very short time to continue with us. I told him that I could recollect nothing, but I hoped he was not so near his end. He observed, smiling, that he certainly was and that, as it was the debt which we all must pay, he looked to the event with perfect resignation."

In the course of the afternoon he appeared to be in great pain and distress from the difficulty of breathing, and frequently changed his posture in the bed. Mr. Lear endeavored to raise him and turn him with as much ease as possible.

"I am afraid I fatigue you too much," the general would say. Upon being assured to the contrary, "Well," observed he gratefully, "it is a debt we must pay to each other, and I hope when you want aid of this kind you will find it."

His servant Christopher had been in the room during the day, and almost the whole time on his feet. The general noticed it in the afternoon and kindly told him to sit down.

About five o'clock Dr. Craik came again into the room, and approached the bedside.

"Doctor," said the general, "I die hard but I am not afraid to go. I believed, from my first attack, that I should not survive it—my breath cannot last long."

The doctor pressed his hand in silence, retired from the bedside and sat by the fire absorbed in grief.

Between five and six the other physicians came in, and [Washington] was assisted to sit up in his bed.

"I feel I am going," said he. "I thank you for your attentions but I pray you will take no more trouble about me. Let me go off quietly. I cannot last long."

He lay down again. All retired excepting Dr. Craik. The general continued uneasy and restless but without complaining, frequently asking what hour it was.

Further remedies were tried without avail in the evening. He took whatever was offered him, did as he was desired by the physicians and never uttered sigh or complaint.

"About ten o'clock," writes Mr. Lear, "he made several attempts to speak to me before he could effect it. At length he said, 'I am just going. Have me decently buried, and do not let my body be put into the vault in less than three days after I am dead.' I bowed assent, for I could not speak. He then looked at me again and said, 'Do you understand me?' I replied, 'Yes.' ' 'Tis well,' said he.

"About ten minutes before he expired (which was between ten and eleven o'clock) his breathing became easier. He lay quietly. He withdrew his hand from mine and felt his own pulse. I saw his countenance change. I spoke to Dr. Craik, who sat by the fire. He came to the bedside. The general's hand fell from his wrist. I took it in mine and pressed it to my bosom. Dr. Craik put his hands over his eyes and he expired without a struggle or a sigh.

"While we were fixed in silent grief, Mrs. Washington, who was seated at the foot of the bed, asked with a firm and collected voice, 'Is he gone?' I could not speak, but held up my hand as a signal that he was no more. ' 'Tis well,' said she in the same voice. 'All is over now. I shall soon follow him. I have no more trials to pass through.' "

We add from Mr. Lear's account a few particulars concerning the funeral. The old family vault on the estate had been opened, the rubbish cleared away and a door made to close the entrance, which before had been closed with brick. The funeral took place on the 18th of December. About eleven o'clock the people of the neighborhood began to assemble. The corporation of Alexandria, with the militia and Free-masons of the place and eleven pieces of cannon, arrived at a later hour. A schooner was stationed off Mount Vernon to fire minute guns.

About three o'clock the procession began to move, passing out through the gate at the left wing of the house, proceeding round in front of the lawn and down to the vault, on the right wing of the house, minute-guns being fired at the time. The troops, horse and foot formed the escort, then came four of the clergy. Then the general's horse, with his saddle, holsters and pistols, led by two grooms in black. The body was borne by the Free-masons and officers. Several members of the family and old friends, among the number Dr. Craik and some of the Fairfaxes, followed as chief mourners. The corporation of Alexandria and numerous private persons closed the procession. The Rev. Mr. Davis read the funeral service at the vault and pronounced a short address, after which the Masons performed their ceremonies and the body was deposited in the vault.

Such were the obsequies of Washington, simple and modest, according to his own wishes, all confined to the grounds of Mount Vernon, which, after forming the poetical dream of his life, had now become his final resting-place.

On the opening of the will which he had handed to Mrs. Washington shortly before death, it was found to have been carefully drawn up by himself in the preceding July; and by an act in conformity with his whole career, one of its first provisions directed the emancipation of his slaves on the decease of his wife. It had long been his earnest wish that the slaves held by him in his own right should receive their freedom during his life, but he had found that it would be attended with insuperable difficulties on account of their intermixture by marriage with the "dower negroes," whom it was not in his power to manumit under the tenure by which they were held.

With provident benignity he also made provision in his will for such as were to receive their freedom under this devise but who, from age, bodily infirmities or infancy, might be unable to support themselves, and he expressly forbade, under any pretense whatsoever, the sale or transportation out of Virginia of any slave of whom he might die possessed. Though born and educated a slaveholder, this was all in consonance with feelings, sentiments and principles which he had long entertained.

In a letter to Mr. John F. Mercer in September 1786 he writes: "I never mean, unless some particular circumstances should compel me to it, to possess another slave by purchase, it being among my first wishes to see some plan adopted by which slavery in this country may be abolished by law." And eleven years afterwards, in August 1797, he writes to his nephew, Lawrence Lewis, in a letter which we have had in our hands, "I wish from my soul that the legislature of this State could see the policy of a gradual abolition of slavery. It might prevent much future mischief."

A deep sorrow spread over the nation when it was heard that Washington was no more. Congress, which was in session, immediately adjourned for the day. The next morning it was resolved that the Speaker's chair be shrouded with black, that the members and officers of the House wear black during the session and that a joint committee of both Houses be appointed to consider on the most suitable manner of doing honor to the memory of the man, "first in war, first in peace and first in the hearts of his fellow-citizens."

Public testimonials of grief and reverence were displayed in every part of the Union. Nor were these sentiments confined to the United States. When the news of Washington's death reached England, Lord Bridport, who had command of a British fleet of nearly sixty sail-of-the-line lying at Torbay, lowered his flag at half-mast, every ship following the example; and Bonaparte, First Consul of France, on announcing his death to the army, ordered that black crape should be suspended from all the standards and flags throughout the public service for ten days.

The character of Washington may want some of those poetical elements which dazzle and delight the multitude, but it possessed fewer inequalities and a rarer union of virtues than perhaps ever fell to the lot of one man: prudence, firmness, sagacity, moderation, an overruling judgment, an immovable justice, courage that never faltered, patience that never wearied, truth that disdained all artifice, magnanimity without alloy.

It seems as if Providence had endowed him in a preëminent degree with the qualities requisite to fit him for the high destiny he was called upon to fulfil—to conduct a momentous revolution which was to form an era in the history of the world and to inaugurate a new and untried government which, to use his own words, was to lay the foundation "for the enjoyment of much purer civil liberty and greater public happiness than have hitherto been the portion of mankind."

The fame of Washington stands apart from every other in history, shining with a truer lustre and a more benignant glory. With us his memory remains a national property, where all sympathies throughout our widely-extended and diversified empire meet in unison. Under all dissensions and amid all the storms of party, his precepts and example speak to us from the grave with a paternal appeal, and his name, by all revered, forms a universal tie of brotherhood, a watchword of our Union.